Louis I. Kahn:
In the Realm of Architecture

LouisI

Contents

It is with great pleasure that Ford Motor Company supports the first comprehensive retrospective of the work of Louis I. Kahn. As master architect, theorist, and teacher, Kahn exemplified the premise that original expression in design is fundamental to our lives. We at Ford share this belief, as well as the dedication to quality, innovation, and excellence that characterized Louis Kahn's life and work.

Acclaimed as one of the twentieth century's greatest architects—and perhaps the most important of his generation—Kahn was blessed with unmatched talent and fervent ideals. He embodied an independent and highly personal vision, which, evolving over time, set in motion a redirection of American architecture and influenced international trends.

We are pleased that the exhibition and this book will make the lasting legacy of Louis I. Kahn more accessible to audiences throughout the world.

Harold A. Poling
Chairman
Ford Motor Company

Foreword and Acknowledgments

Richard Koshalek, Director
Sherri Geldin, Associate Director
Elizabeth A. T. Smith, Curator

Organized by The Museum of Contemporary Art, Los Angeles, "Louis I. Kahn: In the Realm of Architecture" is the first comprehensive retrospective of this extraordinary architect's work. It occurs at a highly appropriate time in the evolution of late twentieth-century architecture and underscores MOCA's continued commitment to the investigation of the pivotal ideas and practices that have constituted the field of architecture since the mid-century. For contemporary architects searching for original expression in their work while seeking to connect it to larger cultural and societal forces, a study of the intensely focused career of Louis I. Kahn holds renewed value and relevance. For historians and critics grappling with the continuing evolution of architectural movements and directions, insights may be gained from contemplation of a body of work that defies simple categorization. For the general audience striving for a greater understanding of the world of architecture, the exhibition and the publication present a portrait of a great innovator, thinker, and teacher who believed passionately in architecture as one of the noblest, most spiritual, and most fundamental of human pursuits.

Closely examining all phases of Kahn's work, MOCA's exhibition and publication are organized into six major sections that interweave chronology, typology, and Kahn's personal philosophy of architecture. The exhibition explores the entire body of Kahn's work through a diverse selection of documents—drawings, sketches, paintings, scale models, archival and newly commissioned photographs, and artifacts. The exhibition and publication not only highlight the most significant and best-known architectural works by Kahn, but also examine and illuminate aspects of his career that have until now received only minimal attention.

The first section of the exhibition, titled "Adventures of Unexplored Places," chronicles Kahn's formative years—his Beaux-Arts training at the University of Pennsylvania, his early travels in Europe, his years of work in the offices of other architects, and his early independent designs for houses—through numerous drawings and artifacts that have never before been exhibited or published. Also presented here is a substantial subsection devoted to the crucial and innovative Philadelphia urban designs and City Tower series, spanning from the mid-1940s to the mid-1960s. The second section of the exhibition, titled "The Mind Opens to Realizations," marks the true beginning of Kahn's mature phase. With such works as the Yale University Art Gallery (1951–53), the Jewish Community Center, near Trenton, New Jersey (1954–59), and the Alfred Newton Richards Medical Research Building in Philadelphia (1957–65),

Kahn began to firmly establish his national and international reputation.

"Assembly . . . a Place of Transcendence," the third section of the exhibition, takes as its theme Kahn's contribution to the design of religious and governmental institutional structures, notably Sher-e-Bangla Nagar, the Capital of Bangladesh in Dhaka (1962–83), and the unexecuted Hurva Synagogue, Jerusalem (1967–74). The exhibition's fourth section, titled "The Houses of the Inspirations," includes Kahn's designs for centers of learning and research such as his Salk Institute for Biological Studies in La Jolla, California (1959–65), and the Indian Institute of Management in Ahmedabad (1962–74).

"The Forum of the Availabilities," the fifth section, traces Kahn's ideas at work in such projects as the Fine Arts Center, School, and Performing Arts Theater in Fort Wayne, Indiana (1959–73), and his late designs for public spaces including the Baltimore Inner Harbor (1969–73) and the Philadelphia Bicentennial Exposition (1971–73). Finally, in "Light, the Giver of All Presences," Kahn's reverence for light as the ultimate formgiver is shown through an examination of such works as the Kimbell Art Museum in Fort Worth, Texas (1966–72), the Yale Center for British Art (1969–74), and the unrealized Memorial to the Six Million Jewish Martyrs, designed for New York's Battery Park (1966–72).

Representing the culmination of almost a decade's work, the exhibition and the publication seek to examine Kahn's career anew and to redefine his significance for our own time. They have been realized through the intense and long-term commitment of numerous individuals. Early in the planning phase, MOCA drew together a unique group of collaborators whose expertise has greatly enriched all aspects of the project. The exhibition's organizing team, in addition to ourselves, has included guest co-curators and principal authors David B. Brownlee, Associate Professor of the History of Art, and David G. De Long, Professor of Architecture, both at the University of Pennsylvania, and Julia Moore Converse, Director of The Architectural Archives at the University of Pennsylvania. Having devoted years of rigorous scholarship to the subject of Louis I. Kahn, Drs. Brownlee and De Long have contributed immeasurable expertise to the content and structure of the exhibition and the publication. This project has also benefited greatly from the close collaboration of Ms. Converse, whose assiduous organization of the Kahn archives over the past decade has allowed for clear access to the voluminous documentation on

Kahn, which she highlights in her essay for this publication. In addition, she has been instrumental at every phase of this endeavor as our liaison to the East Coast members of the organizing team. We are also grateful for the crucial assistance provided by the project's research director, Peter S. Reed, G. Holmes Perkins Postgraduate Fellow and Lecturer in the History of Art at the University of Pennsylvania.

Working closely with the organizing team have been other creative collaborators, all of whom have been essential to the outcome of this effort. We extend deep thanks to architect Arata Isozaki for his evocative design of the exhibition. Mr. Isozaki and his project staff, headed by Nazila Shabestari, gave considerable thought to the exhibition over many years and their efforts have resulted in a sensitive and poetic presentation. Their installation design was inspired by the Mikveh Israel Synagogue, Philadelphia (1961–72), a pivotal, unbuilt project by Kahn. The modular exhibition walls they have designed are intended to suggest, in "ruinlike" fashion, the plan of this project. Grant Mudford has contributed stunning new photographs of Kahn's major American buildings, adding a unique dimension to both the exhibition and the publication. Serving as advisor to the modelmaking and project consultant to the exhibition and organizing team was the architect Marshall D. Meyers, a former associate of Kahn's. William Christensen, Linda Brenner, and Laura M. Kass crafted the handsome new scale models. Peter Kirby produced the exhibition's audiovisual component with great care and sensitivity. Massimo Vignelli, with Abigail Sturges, developed a refined and sensitive design for this publication, beautifully complementing the very content of the book. From the inception of this project James E. N. Huntley, former program officer of Ford Motor Company, lent tremendous support and encouragement, for which we are thankful. His profound appreciation of Kahn's legacy and his keen sensitivity to the exhibition's objectives have made him an invaluable advocate and colleague.

Vincent Scully, Sterling Professor of the History of Art at Yale University, whose incomparable scholarship and keen intuition have transformed the field of architectural history over the past several decades, has been a guiding spirit throughout this endeavor. We are grateful for his magnificent inspiration. For this publication he has also provided an introduction that offers profound observations on the work and ideas of Louis I. Kahn.

Also adding immensely to our understanding of Kahn's work are individual building essays that have been contributed by

Daniel S. Friedman, Kathleen James, Peter Kohane, Michael J. Lewis, Patricia Cummings Loud, Alex Soojung-Kim Pang with Preston Thayer, Peter S. Reed, Susan G. Solomon, Michelle Taillon Taylor, Elise Vider, Marc Philippe Vincent, Robin B. Williams, and Carla Yanni. We appreciate their focused attention to the project and their enrichment of the scholarship on Kahn.

Special thanks are due to Rizzoli International Publications for their generous collaboration on this publication, particularly Gianfranco Monacelli, President; David Morton, Senior Editor; and Lois Brown, Managing Editor. Their individual and collaborative contributions to this venture have been exceptional. For her thorough and diligent editing of the texts for this publication, we would like to extend our deep appreciation to Kate Norment.

We are also extremely grateful to the many photographers who have supplied us with the documentation critical to this endeavor. In particular, the work of John Ebstel and George Pohl, who spent many years working with Kahn, greatly enriches the project. Additionally, the Aga Kahn Award for Architecture, Shahidul Alam, Farooq Ameen, Kazi Ashraf, and Balkrishna V. Doshi assisted us in locating and obtaining many of the photographs of projects in India and Bangladesh reproduced herein.

During the course of the project several readers and scholars, including Denise Scott Brown, Elizabeth Grossman, William Jordy, John E. MacAllister, Jonas Salk, Charles Sawyer, Carles Vallhonrat, Robert Venturi, and Thomas Vreeland offered invaluable guidance to the exhibition's organizing team. The dedicated efforts of the research assistants and staff of The Architectural Archives at the University of Pennsylvania have also been critical to the outcome of this project. In this regard we thank Joan Brierton, Kevin D. Chun, Paul Clark, Omar Fawzy, Marcia F. Feuerstein, Joshua K. Gould, Stephen Harrison, Elizabeth Hitchcock, Suzan El Kholy, Durham Kraut, Mark Luellen, Paula Lupkin, David Roxburgh, David Tidey, Rebecca Williamson, and the late Elizabeth Greene Wiley. We would also like to thank Shilpa Mehta for her efforts in compiling the bibliography of Kahn's writings, Will Brown for his photography, and Suzanne Wheeling, Jeffrey Kwait, and John Taylor for their assistance with the drawings.

Special recognition must be given to members of the Kahn family for the enthusiasm, cooperation, and commitment they have shown toward this project from its inception. The encouragement and generosity of spirit extended by Kahn's wife Esther have been of inestimable value. Equally important have been the exceptional efforts of Kahn's daughter Sue Ann, to whom we are most grateful. Essential support and advice have also been provided by Anne Griswold Tyng and Alexandra Tyng, and by Harriet Pattison and Nathaniel Kahn.

The definitive character and scope of the exhibition would not have been possible without the cooperation of numerous individuals and institutions who lent generously to the lengthy traveling exhibition. The foremost lender of material has been The Architectural Archives of the University of Pennsylvania, whose Louis I. Kahn Collection is on permanent loan from the Pennsylvania Historical and Museum Commission. Without their participation, and the support of PHMC Executive Director Dr. Brent D. Glass, this exhibition and publication would not have been possible. Other institutions to whom we are most grateful are The Art Institute of Chicago; the British Architectural Library, London; the Canadian Centre for Architecture, Montreal; the First Unitarian Church, Rochester, New York; the Kimbell Art Museum, Fort Worth, Texas; The Museum of Modern Art, New York; the Philadelphia Museum of Art; the Franklin and Eleanor Roosevelt Institute, Hyde Park, New York; the Roosevelt Island Operating Corporation, New York; Saint Andrew's Priory, Valyermo, California; and the Salk Institute for Biological Studies, La Jolla, California. Individuals who graciously allowed us to borrow works from their personal collections include Arnold Garfinkel, Esther Kahn, Nathaniel Kahn, Sue Ann Kahn, Alexandra Tyng, Theodore T. Newbold and Helen Cunningham, Morton L. Paterson, and Anne Griswold Tyng.

Taking a somewhat nontraditional approach, MOCA has chosen to open the exhibition in Philadelphia—as a tribute to Kahn and a recognition of his lifelong connection to the city where so much of his most renowned work was done. Reflecting the global interest in Kahn's architecture, the exhibition will enjoy an extensive international tour, traveling from Philadelphia to Paris; New York; Gunma, Japan; Los Angeles; Fort Worth, Texas; and Columbus, Ohio. For their enthusiastic cooperation we would like to extend our sincere appreciation to our associates at each exhibition venue: Anne d'Harnoncourt, Director, and Suzanne Wells, Coordinator of Exhibitions, the Philadelphia Museum of Art; Dominique Bozo, Director, François Burkhardt, former Director, and Alain Guiheux, Exhibition Director, Architecture Committee, Centre Georges Pompidou, Centre de Création Industrielle, Paris;

Richard E. Oldenburg, Director, and Stuart Wrede, Director of the Department of Architecture, The Museum of Modern Art, New York; Kimio Nakayama, Director, the Museum of Modern Art, Gunma; Edmund Pillsbury, Director, and Patricia Cummings Loud, Slide Librarian, the Kimbell Art Museum, Fort Worth; and Robert Stearns, Director, and Sarah Rogers-Lafferty, Curator, the Wexner Center for the Arts, The Ohio State University, Columbus.

Important to the outcome of the project was the research conducted at various institutions in addition to the Louis I. Kahn Collection at The Architectural Archives of the University of Pennsylvania. For their assistance with our research efforts we gratefully acknowledge the staffs of the Bryn Mawr College Archives, Pennsylvania; the Architectural Drawings Collection, Avery Library, Columbia University, New York; the Phillips Exeter Academy Library, Exeter, New Hampshire; the Free Library of Philadelphia; The Athenaeum of Philadelphia; the Center for Advanced Study in the Visual Arts, National Gallery of Art, Washington, D.C.; the Canadian Centre for Architecture, Montreal; the Pennsylvania Academy of the Fine Arts, Philadelphia; The Museum of Modern Art, New York; the School of Architecture, Tulane University, New Orleans; Manuscripts and Archives, Sterling Memorial Library, Yale University; the American Heritage Center, University of Wyoming, Laramie; and the Fine Arts Library and the Van Pelt Library, the University of Pennsylvania.

Thanks are also extended to Louis I. Kahn's former associates and office staff: Kathleen Condé, Balkrishna V. Doshi, Gönül Aslanoğlu Evyapan, David Karp, Fred Langford, Gus Langford, Reyhan Tansal Larimer, Alan Levy, Santo Lipari, John E. MacAllister, Marshall Meyers, Harriet Pattison, David Polk, Anant Raje, Luis Vincent Rivera, Galen Schlosser, Anne Griswold Tyng, Carles Vallhonrat, Roy Vollmer, Henry Wilcots, David Wisdom, and Cengiz Yetken.

Among the many individuals who have assisted the organizing team in the research and administration of the project are Dr. Shahidul Alam, Diana Carroll-Wirth, Dr. and Mrs. Norman Fisher, George Forman, Dr. and Mrs. Robert Gallagher, Marcy Goodwin, Dr. Perween Hasan, Colleen Hurst, Mazharul Islam, Ms. Marlyn Ivory, Mr. and Mrs. Steven Korman, the late David Lloyd Kreeger, Mr. and Mrs. Michael Marder, Professor William Porter, Dr. Jonas Salk, the Sarabhai family, Dr. and Mrs. Bernard Shapiro, Robert Swanekamp, Ms. Jacquelyn H. Thomas, and Mr. and Mrs. Morton Weiss.

At the University of Pennsylvania, Lee G. Copeland, Edwin Deegan, Marco Frascari, Michael Meister, Alan Morrison, and G. Holmes Perkins have offered continuing support of this endeavor. The university's provision of research leaves to Drs. Brownlee and De Long further evidences their appreciation of the project's significance. In addition, Dr. Brownlee's work was greatly facilitated by a fellowship provided by the Center for Advanced Study in the Visual Arts, National Gallery of Art, Washington, D.C.

Numerous members of the MOCA staff have contributed immeasurably to the successful realization of this exhibition and publication. Catherine Gudis, Editor, and Sherri Schottlaender, Editorial Assistant, oversaw all aspects of the compilation, editing, and production of the publication, a complex and exceedingly demanding task that they dispatched with both grace and expertise. Erica Clark, Director of Development, was instrumental in raising the necessary funds and support for this ambitious project. We also wish to especially thank John Bowsher, Exhibition Production Manager, and his capable staff of preparators for deftly handling the myriad complexities of the exhibition's design and installation. Alma Ruiz, Exhibitions Coordinator, managed the international circulation of the exhibition with consummate diplomacy, while Mo Shannon, Registrar, and Robert Hollister, Assistant Registrar, diligently oversaw all matters pertaining to the shipping of the works on their global tour. The comprehensive educational program that accompanies the exhibition was led by Vas Prabhu, Director of Education, and members of her staff. Other staff members who have been integral to the organization of the exhibition and to whom we would like to extend thanks include Jack Wiant, Controller, Paul Schimmel, Chief Curator, Cynthia Anderson, Director of Communications, and Anna Graham, Public Information Officer. Colette Dartnall, Curatorial Secretary, assisted with the complex, multifaceted organizational tasks associated with the show with unfailing good cheer and professionalism, as did Julie Abrams, Administrative Assistant, and Nancy Rogers, former Administrative Coordinator. Additional support was provided by Robin Hanson, former Government Relations and Grants Manager, Sylvia Hohri, Marketing and Graphics Manager, Bonnie Born, Executive Assistant, and Elaine Cohen, Director's Secretary.

As always with an undertaking of this magnitude, we are deeply grateful to the museum's Board of Trustees for their unflagging encouragement and support. In particular, we would like to acknowledge Frederick M. Nicholas, Chairman, Douglas S. Cramer, President, Daisy Belin, Vice Chairman and Chairman of the Program Committee, and David R. Carpenter, John C. Cushman III, and Joel Wachs, Vice Chairmen.

Finally, we extend the utmost appreciation to our sponsors, who have made it possible for us to realize an unprecedented exhibition and publication on the architecture of Louis I. Kahn. This exhibition is made possible by Ford Motor Company. Under the leadership of Leo J. Brennan, Jr., Executive Director, Frank V. J. Darin, Vice President, and Mabel H. Brandon, Director of Corporate Programming, they bestowed an early and remarkably generous grant to MOCA enabling this project to assume an appropriately ambitious scale from the start. Significant support was also provided by Leslie H. Wexner, and by The Pew Charitable Trusts, under the aegis of Dr. Thomas W. Langfitt, President, Rebecca W. Rimel, Executive Director, and Ella King Torrey, Program Officer. For their additional assistance we would also like to thank Carter H. Manny, Jr., of the Graham Foundation for Advanced Studies in the Fine Arts, Robert F. Maguire and James Thomas of Maguire Thomas Partners, and the National Endowment for the Arts, a federal agency.

It is profoundly gratifying to have had the opportunity over many years to absorb the unique lessons of Louis I. Kahn and to now be able to convey to a broad public the greatness of his legacy. It is our hope that through this exhibition and publication Kahn's power to teach and to inspire will be perpetuated well into the twenty-first century.

Introduction

Vincent Scully

This exhibition, like any work dedicated to Kahn, has been profoundly worth doing. Kahn was a supremely great architect. That fact is becoming more apparent with every passing year. His work has a presence, an aura, unmatched by that of any other architect of the present day. Far beyond the works even of Frank Lloyd Wright, Mies van der Rohe, and Le Corbusier, it is brooding, remote, mysterious. Wright's buildings richly resolve the play of wonderful rhythms; those of Mies reduce space and matter to ultimate essentials, while Le Corbusier's do something of everything, embodying the twentieth-century human gesture most of all, at first light and urbane, at the end heavy, primitive, violent. Kahn's buildings, the very distillation of the twentieth century's later years, are primitive too, but they are wholly devoid of gesture, as if beyond that, or of a different breed. Their violence is latent, potential, precisely because they do not gesture or seem to strike any attitude at all. They are above all *built*. Their elements—always elemental, heavy—are assembled in solemn, load-bearing masses. Their joints are serious affairs, like the knees of *kouroi*, but have the articulation of beings not in human form. Their body is Platonic, abstractly geometric in the essential shapes of circle, square, and triangle translated into matter, as if literally frozen into mute musical chords. They shape spaces heavy with light like the first light ever loosed on the world, daggers of light, blossoms of light, suns and moons. They are silent. We feel their silence as a potent thing; some sound, a roll of drums, an organ peal, resonates in them just beyond the range of our hearing. They thrum with silence, as with the presence of God.

We try to think what other works of modern art have this curious high seriousness in the same degree: this determined link to the Ideal, this wholly specific physicality. Perhaps only some Russian novels come to mind, the works of Tolstoy most of all, perhaps those of Dostoyevski. I am reminded of the remark of a Russian student in Leningrad in 1965. It was at an exhibition of American architecture. Kahn and I were present. I ran a little seminar for especially interested students. Robert Venturi's house for Vanna Venturi came under discussion. One student, mindful perhaps of the Soviet Union's massive needs in housing and so on, asked, "Who needs it?" But another student instantly replied, "Everybody needs everything." And I thought, there it is, the real stuff, the generous, excessive Russian soul. We tend to forget that Kahn was Russian, after all. Those blue Tartar eyes didn't come from nowhere. Here we have to thank David Brownlee and David De Long for finding a photograph of Kahn's father in his uniform. Poor, Jewish, Estonian, only a paymaster, and noncommissioned, he nevertheless comes across as an Imperial Russian officer to the life, a veritable Vronski, played by Fredric March. He looks much like his son, jaunty and proud, while Lou Kahn himself, at his graduation from the University of Pennsylvania, glares ferociously at the camera like the young Gorky or the student Tolstoy. And like them Kahn wanted "everything," wanted to make everything true, right, deep, ideal, and whole if he could. I suppose he wanted all that more passionately than any other architect of our era has ever done. That is surely why, despite their obvious deficiencies in many fundamental aspects of architecture—contextuality, to name a contemporary interest, for one—Kahn's works convince us that their own intrinsic being is enough. They are thus the single wholly satisfactory achievement of the late modernist aim in architecture: to reinvent reality, to make all new.

They are more than that, though. They begin something. They effectively bring the International Style to a close and open the way to a much solider modernism, one in which the revival of the vernacular and classical traditions of architecture, and the corollary mass movement for historic preservation, would eventually come to play a central role. Kahn's greatest early associate, Robert Venturi, was to initiate these revivals of the urban tradition and to direct architecture toward a gentle contextuality unsympathetic to Kahn. Aldo Rossi in Italy was to move in a similar direction, creating a haunting poetry of urban types out of a vision of Italian vernacular and classical traditions not so different from that Kahn revealed in his pastels of Italian squares in 1950–51 and in some of his greatest buildings thereafter. Indeed, Kahn changed architecture for the better in every way, to some considerable degree changed the built environment as a whole and, beyond his knowledge or intention, made us value the fabric of the traditional city once more.

It is worth asking how this came about for Kahn. Here we should be as specific as Kahn himself. It came about because, after a lifetime of worrying about such things, Kahn discovered late in life how to transform the ruins of ancient Rome into modern buildings. This relationship, improbable enough on the face of it, is copiously demonstrated by the scores of photographs of Roman ruins that can be directly paired with views of almost all of Kahn's buildings from the Salk Institute onward. Before this Kahn had already spent some years trying to find his way back to history. Cut off from his modern-classical education at Pennsylvania, and thus from history, by the rise of the iconoclastic International Style in the 1930s, Kahn was

ready to look sympathetically at history once again at least from the time he began to teach at Yale in 1947. In 1950–51 he was reintroduced to Rome during his term as a fellow at the American Academy, where he studied Roman archaeological sites on his own and in the company of the great classicist Frank E. Brown, and traveled in Greece and Egypt as well. Soon he was making use of the Pyramids at Gizeh and of the Temple of Ammon at Karnak in various ways that I have discussed elsewhere.[1] It was only after he had adopted his early watercolors of San Gimignano for the towers of the Richards Medical Research Building, with attendant problems having to do largely with the reception of light, that the more purely Roman forms began to appear. They did so in a manner that suggests conversations with Robert Venturi, who had also spent a year in Rome, and most strikingly at the Salk Institute, especially in the project for the community center. "Ruins wrapped around buildings," Kahn called the resultant glass-free, keyhole-arched, thermal-windowed Roman forms.

Coincidentally enough, those ruins, open to the air, proved exactly suited to the climate and the simple brick technology of the subcontinent of India. They shaped Ahmedabad and Dhaka, where the crypto-portici can be compared with the Thermopolium at Ostia, while the main rooms at Ahmedabad closely echo the brick and concrete basilica of Hadrian's market, and the National Assembly Building at Dhaka combines the Temple of Jupiter above Ostia's forum with forms derived from plans of English castles and, as Brownlee and De Long suggest, with heaven knows what else. Most of all, Kahn's "brick order" at Ahmedabad and Dhaka derives from Roman brick and concrete construction heavily filtered through Piranesi's etchings of braced brick circles,[2] while a similar configuration in the portico of the outpatients' clinic at Dhaka closely resembles Ledoux's drawing of the architect's all-seeing eye.[3] Here the main historical point emerges clearly: Kahn was a Romantic-Classic architect, exactly as Piranesi and Ledoux had been. Like Piranesi he desired sublime effects (I have already tried to describe them), and like Ledoux he wanted them embodied in perfect, hard, geometric forms. Like those architects, and their many colleagues at the dawn of the modern age, Kahn wanted to begin architecture anew by concentrating upon the ruins of the ancient world and starting afresh from them. This is, I think, precisely why Kahn was indeed able to reinvigorate architecture toward the end of the late phase of the International Style. He was beginning modern architecture again as it had begun in the eighteenth century: with heavy, solid forms derived from structure rather than from the pictorial composition through which modern architects of the twentieth century had later attempted to rival the freedom of abstract painting. So Kahn's work, despite his travel sketches, is itself never pictorial. It is primitively architectural, thus pre-pictorial. That is why Kahn was, like Cézanne in painting, a true primitive in the way he had chosen, always saying that he liked "beginnings" and that a "good question was better than the best answer." It is no wonder that his buildings are full of ancient power. And, though he opened the way to the full classical revival of the present, he persistently refused to use classical details himself, confining himself always, in his own kind of modernist way, to the abstraction of the stripped ruin. Just so, in the last great years of his career, he would hardly use glass. This is true at Exeter, where he simply jammed the glass he did not need in India into the frame of a ruin and would not permit the four walls to join together as a completed building. At the Kimbell he employed only Romanoid arches, directly reflecting a specific set of ruins, and that was all, inside and out. Neither scheme could have been more purely Romantic-Classic.

This renders Kahn's achievement at the Yale Center for British Art all the more surprising. Because there, in his last building, Kahn made what amounted to a great step forward in time and in the development of modern architecture itself. He stepped, in fact, from the eighteenth-century Romantic-Classicism of Piranesi and Ledoux to the nineteenth-century Realism of Labrouste. When, in the Bibliothèque Sainte-Geneviève, of 1843–50, Labrouste asked himself how the ruins of Greece and Rome could be truly rationalized into modern buildings on modern streets, he worked out a system of base, block, column frame, and infilling panels of solid and glass which became the classic modern solution to the problem of the urban building all the way on through Richardson and Sullivan to Mies van der Rohe and the present time. It is this system that Kahn adopted at Yale and in which, for the first time and with miraculous reflection, glass came to life in his design.

He therefore seems to have been at the beginning of some new integration in his work when he died. What he would have made of his followers, who have themselves remade the profession of architecture and begun to heal the wounds that the modern age has inflicted on our cities, is perhaps not hard to tell. He would not have liked any of their work very much. He was always the lone hero, after all, pursuing a lonely quest. And while it is true that the journey to Canaan was largely initiated by him, he never completed it himself, shaping his own kingdom outside the promised land.

This exhibition and its catalogue represent the first extensive scholarship devoted to Louis I. Kahn's life and work since his drawings and office files became readily available for study. One is grateful to David Brownlee and David De Long, and to their students, for the good use to which they have put this material and for their painstaking documentation of all of Kahn's most important buildings and projects.

Notes

1. As in my introduction to the exhibition of Kahn's work at the Pennsylvania Academy of the Fine Arts in 1978 (*The Travel Sketches of Louis I. Kahn* [Philadelphia: Pennsylvania Academy of the Fine Arts, 1978]), to the Garland edition of Kahn's drawings (*The Louis I. Kahn Archive: Personal Drawings*, 7 vols. [New York: Garland Publishing, 1987]), and to Jan Hochstim, *The Paintings and Sketches of Louis I. Kahn* (New York: Rizzoli, 1991). These articles touch on the Roman relationships as well.
2. As in his *Antichità Romane*, vol. 4, in H. Volkmann, *G. B. Piranesi* (Berlin, 1965), pl. 37.
3. Reproduced at about the same time, along with Piranesi's *Carceri* and a number of nineteenth- and twentieth-century derivatives, in my *Modern Architecture* (New York: George Braziller, 1961), figs. 3–14.

Prologue

Louis I. Kahn: Compositions in a Fundamental Timbre

Sherri Geldin

To make a thing deliberately beautiful is a dastardly act; it's an act of mesmerism which beclouds the entire issue. I do not believe that beauty can be created overnight. It must start with the archaic first. The archaic begins like Paestum. Paestum is beautiful to me because it is less beautiful than the Parthenon. It is because from it the Parthenon came. Paestum is dumpy, it has unsure, scared proportions. But it is infinitely more beautiful to me because to me it represents the beginning of architecture. It is a time when the walls parted and the columns became and when music entered architecture. It was a beautiful time and we are still living on it.[1]

I feel fusion of the senses. To hear a sound is to see its space. Space has tonality, and I imagine myself composing a space lofty, vaulted, or under a dome, attributing to it a sound character alternating with the tones of the space, narrow and high, with graduating silver, light to darkness. The spaces of architecture in their light make me want to compose a kind of music, imagining a truth from the sense of a fusion of the disciplines and their orders.[2]

Louis I. Kahn

The notion of architectural and musical fusion in the universal precincts of artistic expression gained resonance with the death of the eminent composer Aaron Copland just as this essay on Louis Kahn was being conceived. Apart from sharing certain formative experiences—both Kahn and Copland were born at the dawn of the twentieth century, both were the sons of Russian Jewish immigrants, and both were taught at critical junctures by formidable European masters—they also shared a profoundly humanist ethos. Their lives spanned an epoch in which the once resolute belief in progress as the divine right and driving rhythm of life would gradually erode, yet both manifested an unshakable optimism as to the greater destiny of man. One built a towering sense of place through music; the other composed exquisite harmonies of space through design.

They found inspiration in diverse places. Copland laced scores with vivid threads of the American West, Appalachia, and Latin America while boldly experimenting with the colors and cadences of European modernism, American folk, and that irrepressible newcomer, jazz. Kahn turned instinctively toward Europe and its "archaic" sources: Tuscan hill towns, Scottish castles, medieval French citadels, and imperial Roman baths, all of which nurtured his lifelong fascination with the origins of architectural traditions. Neither approached his prototypes as mere copyist or pilferer; both sought wellsprings rather than models.

If Copland could be credited by the redoubtable Leonard Bernstein as the "composer who would lead American music out of the wilderness,"[3] so too could Kahn be praised for rescuing American architecture from its mid-century decline toward increasingly hollow modernist parodies, particularly of the International Style persuasion. Both were authentic pioneers; both embodied the necessary fortitude to prevail, even through inauspicious seasons. And each composed elegies to the human spirit.

Copland's rousing "Fanfare for the Common Man," though now somewhat hackneyed by indiscriminate use, intones the promise of dignity and grandeur for "everyman." Evoking an aura of nobility not conferred by wealth or title but rather achieved through egalitarian opportunity, it celebrates the triumph of the individual when allowed to realize his innate potential. In short, it is a symphonic rendition of the American dream reaching toward apotheosis in the twentieth century.

As Copland set the dream to music, Kahn committed it to architecture. He began with a deep and abiding respect for mankind's institutions and a confidence in the architect's ability to give them physical and emotional presence. He attached almost mythic significance to the "meeting place," to any setting where communal interaction occurs. It is hardly surprising, then, that Kahn's primary legacy (contrary to Wright's, for example) lies in his public buildings and projects. Together they constitute a stunning tribute to man's most civilizing ideals. His scientific centers, even when not functionally flawless, set an unprecedented standard for programmatic ambition and intent, boldly affirming the place of lively human exchange alongside that of solitary rigor in the process of scientific research. In fact, in its classical self-containment, protective compositional embrace, and commanding sweep, Kahn's Salk Institute recalls nothing so much as Jefferson's magnificent University of Virginia—two beacons of logic, clarity, and creative inspiration. Kahn's academic buildings, too, celebrate the quest for knowledge as the supreme human endeavor, encouraging the pursuit of enlightenment as its own incomparable reward. If the first classroom, in Kahn's view, consisted of "a man under a tree who did not know he was a teacher discussing his realization with a few who did not know they were students,"[4] then modern educational institutions, despite their far greater complexity, must somehow preserve both the intimacy and the openness of that spontaneous encounter. Kahn's governmental buildings also bespeak a remarkable faith in the power of informed and rational interchange. They are monuments to the virtue of collective discussion, debate, and self-determination, to the democratic ideal itself. His religious buildings and

projects seek to provide a pure, uncompromised shelter for contemplation of things spiritual. They aspire to evoke a state of grace that is without dogma or sectarian distinction, underscoring instead that which is universal and transcendent. And, finally, the cultural commissions, perhaps the most glorious of all Kahn's buildings, are paeans to the muse of the senses, temples in which to venerate beauty itself. Surprisingly self-effacing upon approach, they are nothing short of resplendent once inside.

It may be initially perplexing to note the absence of commercial buildings from this litany of praise, but on further reflection it seems fitting, though unfortunate all the same. Whether due to an unaccommodating architect, uncomprehending clients, or a mutual wariness that became self-perpetuating, this is one domain upon which Kahn left no mark. Yet one fully imagines that, under proper circumstances, he would have managed to imbue even that most banal bastion of commerce, the corporate office building, with just the right measure of humility and heroism.

As a thinker and a builder, Kahn was indisputably *sui generis*. His life's work is the manifestation of a fully deliberated and finely honed philosophy which, when put into words by the master himself, can be maddeningly circumlocutory and enigmatic. In brief, Kahn maintained that the form of a building, contrary to customary definition, has nothing to do with its shape or dimension but rather emanates from an amorphous yet distinct determination of the building's "will." Hence his oft-quoted query "What does the building want to be?" At this stage, one might almost conjure a primordial architectural soup, churning and bubbling until there evolves a sense of order and purpose uniquely suited to the life of the building at hand. The ensuing process of design is the act of giving tangible reality to this inherent will, deftly coaxing from it the physical attributes that give utmost expression to the primal form. A (very) loose musical analogy might lie in the nature of tone quality or timbre. "Fundamental" is the word used to describe any absolutely pure tone; it is the deepest tone which underlies the numerous overtones that make up a given sound. It is at that fundamental and irreducible point of origin, Kahn's "Volume Zero," that he attempted to engage his projects.

No wonder, then, that he never bowed at the altar of any particular design "style," for to do so would nullify his theory of primal form and its willful self-determination through design. That is not to suggest that Kahn was oblivious or impervious to historic and contemporary referents; rather, his mining of these resources was judiciously filtered and never seduced by mere surface sparkle. His foremost aim was to create buildings of unimpeachable integrity that candidly reveal their structure and uses while simultaneously creating safe harbor for body, mind, and soul. They are structures so comprehensive and economical in design that "each part serves to a maximum degree simultaneously as construction, spatial definition and its own sculptural embellishment."[5] If in the process he revitalized musty Beaux-Arts precepts or humanized the machinelike rigors of the International Style, these would seem more inadvertent—though happy—consequences than motivating impulses.

These are buildings composed with a subtle and provocative play of mass and volume, buildings where solid surfaces can virtually dissolve into luminous space, only to materialize anew, in Kahn's words, as "spent light." In these buildings there is a contrapuntal rhythm of solid and void that has poetically been likened to the "stark drama of being and nothingness."[6] And, most importantly, there is light, that magical source of energy that for Kahn is the defining element of space itself. In his view, "the choice of a structure is synonymous with the light which gives image to that space. . . . A plan of a building should read like a harmony of spaces in light."[7] His are buildings where light assumes palpable presence, a silvery incandescence summoned from nature, minutely calibrated by the architect yet rarely betraying human intervention.

These are buildings of exceptional dynamic range, astonishing in their protean feats. Despite formidable dimensions, they are consummately human in scale; despite largely "proletarian" materials, they exude richness and elegance; despite well-grounded heft and girth, they invariably manage to soar. They are shot through with amazing polarities, at once monumental and intimate, imposing but unintimidating, powerful yet humble. These are buildings that elicit response at all levels. They are compelling in their subtle ingenuity, moving in their modest splendor, and breathtaking in their silent luminosity.

By what strokes of imagination did Kahn arrive at his unique potion of architectural alchemy? This exhibition and its accompanying publication are attempts to address this question and to explore and illuminate the nature of his genius. It is a daunting but exhilarating challenge: How to convey the extraordinary experience of the buildings themselves when we are limited to the use of drawings, models, photographs, and text. How to encourage full comprehension—visual, visceral, intellectual, psychological, and emotional. How to probe a complex organic structure without dissecting it into a gaggle of identifiable but independently lifeless anatomical parts. And, finally, how to capture the fundamental life-force of Kahn's oeuvre and transmute it intact, undiluted and undiminished.

To start, we assembled the most promising team possible: scholars who have long immersed themselves in the study of Kahn; an architect whose abiding respect and affinity for Kahn is stunningly evident; a photographer whose keen sensibility is matched only by his dedication to the task; a graphic designer so attuned to Kahn's ethic that his opening query was "What does the book want to be?" We summon the artistry of these individual masters and hope in so doing that mastery is served.

We hope too that through this exhibition and publication, Kahn's lifelong commitment to teaching will be broadened and perpetuated. Learning from him—not simply citing his influence or invoking his name, but understanding his lessons and applying them with perspicacity and wisdom— may in fact be the greatest homage we could pay.

Can there be any doubt as to the timeliness of this endeavor? As we embark on the final decade of the twentieth century, we are everywhere confronted by lapses in confidence and reduced expectations, not just nationally, but on a global scale. The once unassailable notion of progress hovers in jeopardy; forward momentum seems episodic at best, shackled by ominous forces that progress itself so unwittingly spawned. What better moment to turn to those like Copland and Kahn, who sustained an unwavering belief in the dignity of the human condition and the power of creative expression to give it form and voice. They were among civilization's explorers, beckoned by a frontier spirit that had nothing to do with imperious conquest or personal glory and everything to do with genuine discovery and collective enrichment.

In Louis I. Kahn's philosophical construct, buildings emerge from the immeasurable origin of form and evolve through the measurable process of design, only to metamorphose upon completion back to the realm of the immeasurable. Until we personally experience his buildings, this seems an ambiguous theoretical conceit at best. But once we have penetrated such wondrous spaces and basked in such uncommon light, his meaning is revealed. For how, ultimately, does one measure the sublime?

Notes
1. Jan C. Rowan, "Wanting to Be: The Philadelphia School," *Progressive Architecture* 42 (April 1961): 161.
2. Louis I. Kahn, "Space and the Inspirations," *L'architecture d'aujourd'hui* 40 (February–March 1969): 15.
3. "Aaron Copland Dies: Music Found the American Mood," *Los Angeles Times*, December 3, 1990, A27 (citing *High Fidelity Magazine*, 1970).
4. Rowan, "Wanting to Be," 133.
5. William H. Jordy, "Medical Research Building for Pennsylvania University, Philadelphia," *Architectural Review* 79 (February 1961): 103.
6. Ibid., 100.
7. Rowan, "Wanting to Be," 132.

Louis I. Kahn lived for fifty years and worked as an architect for more than a quarter century before fame found him. His first five decades do not, however, contradict what he did later; neither do they explain it. He was, during that time, a successful architect within the boundaries imposed by youth, the Great Depression, and the Second World War. He learned, he built, he taught, and he devoted himself to the central preoccupations of his generation in architecture: the search for a modern language and the challenge of housing a needy society. He succeeded. But in later life he reformulated those concerns, subsuming them within a new understanding of the nature of architecture, and in doing so he established more rigorous criteria for success. And by those standards he succeeded again.

An Architect in the Making

Louis Kahn was born in 1901 on the Baltic fringe of imperial Russia, on the island of Ösel (now Saaremaa) in Estonia. His father, Leopold, was an Estonian, and his mother, Bertha Mendelsohn, was from Riga, Latvia, where she had met her husband while he was on leave from the paymaster corps of the Russian army (figs. 1, 2). After his military discharge, they settled on Saaremaa. Both were Jews, raised in the multilingual culture that flourished in the cosmopolitan borderland between Russian- and German-speaking Europe. They were poor, and in 1904 Leopold Kahn emigrated to America. He found work in Philadelphia, and in 1906 Bertha brought Louis, then five years old, and his younger sister and brother, Sarah and Oscar, to join him.

Philadelphia was then in the final decades of its peak industrial era. Preeminent in the manufacturing of clothing, the city had welcomed a vast population of new immigrants to work in its factories. The Kahns settled in the Northern Liberties, a poor immigrant district that lay on the edge of Center City, moving often during their first years in the country.[1] Leopold possessed substantial talents as a designer and glass painter, but he found little skilled employment, and a back injury caused him to give up the work he could find as a laborer. Although he kept a shop for a while, the family was supported principally by Bertha's work, making samples of knitted woolen clothing for local manufacturers. In a poor and sometimes disorderly household, Bertha Kahn preserved some of the cultural trappings of their European background. While this included German and Yiddish language, music, and literature, the family did not keep up the observances of their faith.

Louis had scarred his face in infancy when the bright colors of a coal fire attracted his too-close attention, and soon after arriving in Philadelphia he was stricken with scarlet fever. This raised the pitch of his voice and kept him from entering school on schedule. The combination of these blemishes and his late start made him shy around other students, but he soon found favor with his teachers because of his aptitude in drawing, and Philadelphia's old-fashioned but benevolent art community offered abundant encouragement.

While in grammar school, Kahn began to take courses in drawing, painting, and sculpture, walking several blocks across Philadelphia's gridded plan to the Public Industrial Art School, where talented students from the regular schools were given supplemental training. There he was befriended by the director, J. Liberty Tadd (1854–1917), an important educational theorist who emphasized large-scale drawing on blackboards and hands-on engagement with the media of sculpture.[2] When Kahn was admitted to the flagship of Philadelphia's school system, the selective Central High School, he continued his art with free Saturday classes at the Graphic Sketch Club, later renamed the Samuel S. Fleisher Art Memorial in honor of its great patron. His drawings won a series of citywide prizes. At the same time, he displayed an instinctive talent for music, piggybacking piano lessons on those paid for by a neighbor for her daughter, and so impressing one acquaintance that he was given an old piano. The large instrument filled much of the available space at home, and he often claimed that he had had to sleep on the piano because it displaced his bed.[3] Kahn was offered a music scholarship, but, on Tadd's advice, he turned it down to concentrate on the visual arts. He did make use of his musical talent, however, helping to support his family by playing the organ at movie theaters while a teenager.

In his senior year at Central High School (1919–20), Kahn took a course on architectural history taught by William F. Gray. It combined lectures and drawing assignments, with which Kahn sometimes helped his less talented classmates. The new subject fascinated him—"architecture struck me between the eye and the eyeball," he once told an interviewer—and he decided to give up his plans to study painting at the Pennsylvania Academy of the Fine Arts after graduation.[4] Instead, he would go to the University of Pennsylvania for training in architecture. Philadelphia had treated the young immigrant generously, and he always remembered its early kindness. "The city," he liked to say, "is a place where a small boy, as he walks through it, may see something that will tell him what he wants to do his whole life."[5]

Chapter 1

Adventures of Unexplored Places

Defining a Philosophy, 1901–51

1   *2*

Kahn's life in architecture began at the University of Pennsylvania, which then had the strongest architectural program in the country, one infused with the confident rigor of the École des Beaux-Arts of Paris. Like many American institutions, the university had imported a French-trained architect to head the design program, and in Paul Philippe Cret (1876–1945) they were unusually fortunate in their choice. Cret loved his adopted city and country, and they returned his affection. As a teacher he was reserved, but he and his staff (many of whom, by Kahn's time, were Cret's former students) did not fail to convey the seriousness of architecture and its central cultural position. The methods of the École, where Cret had been schooled on the rational, progressive side under the guidance of his atelier patron, Jean-Louis Pascal, and the professor of theory, Julien Guadet, were explained as something like a scientific system. Despite his unshaken belief in the primacy of classicism, to Cret architecture was not a matter of historical styles but a problem-solving art in which the creative architect translated the demands of the client's program into substance. New kinds of programs necessarily produced new architecture, and Cret taught that modern democracy would consequently achieve its own architectural expression. Without affectation he could proclaim to a gathering of Philadelphia architects in 1923, "Our architecture is modern and cannot be anything else."[6]

Kahn spent four years at the University of Pennsylvania, earning his bachelor's degree in architecture. His first-year studio critic was John Harbeson (1888–1986), a former Cret student and then a senior member of Cret's office. Harbeson was the author of *The Study of Architectural Design* (New York, 1926), an elegant guide to the Beaux-Arts teaching system as it had been reconstituted in America by the national Beaux-Arts Institute of Design, created by former students of the École. The institute set the programs for a ladder of competitions open to students in architecture schools and independent ateliers, leading to the Paris Prize and the chance to study at the fountainhead, the École itself. Many of Harbeson's illustrations were chosen from among the prize-winning work of Penn students, who in Kahn's time outpaced those from all other schools in their share of national awards.[7]

Kahn did well in this environment.[8] He excelled in the watercolor and freehand drawing required of architecture students and in courses devoted to the history of architecture, painting, and sculpture. His marks in the design studio were not as high, but in his senior year, with Cret as his critic, he won two second medals in Class A

projects set by the Beaux-Arts Institute of Design (and several mentions as well) and advanced to the second preliminary stage of the Paris Prize competition, finishing sixth and thereby just missing a place in the finals.[9]

Under the influence of his teachers, Kahn in his student work showed a preference for the austere vocabulary of what is sometimes called "stripped classicism," occasionally decorated with a species of free ornament akin to the Art Deco with which Paul Cret himself dabbled in the twenties and thirties. But it was planning, not the decoration of elevations, that stood at the center of Beaux-Arts teaching. In this, Kahn's schooling did not contradict the contemporary thinking of those Europeans who were formulating the philosophy of modern architecture. Proclamations like Le Corbusier's "The plan is the generator" would not have seemed alien. Indeed, at a meeting of Philadelphia's T-Square Club in 1927, Cret gave a generally favorable review of Le Corbusier's *Towards a New Architecture*, which had just been translated into English.[10]

Kahn's own planning in his student years steered away from the unremitting axial symmetry that was and is still often incorrectly judged to be the hallmark of the Beaux-Arts method. Indeed, Beaux-Arts design depended on the regular breaking and disguising of axes in order to preserve the freshness of their organizing effect, and Harbeson devoted an encouraging chapter in *The Study of Architectural Design* to asymmetrical plans. Kahn's last premiated student work, an army post he designed in the spring of his senior year, displayed his verve for just that type of organization (fig. 3). Around one end of a great parade ground he deployed the barracks for three battalions, but the other end of the composition was defined by an administration building (notably blocking the main entrance axis into the post) and two very unequal buildings for the post hospital and its operational headquarters. Dynamic balance rather than symmetry was evidently Kahn's objective, although it was imperfectly attained. This experience with nonaxial planning provided the foundation on which he would build his experiments with modernist composition in the thirties and forties, while the concern for planning in general would persist throughout his career.

When questioned by historians and critics, Kahn never failed to acknowledge the lessons he had learned from Cret and the Beaux-Arts at Penn. Even near the end of his life, when his architecture had moved from the Beaux-Arts, traversed the International Style, and reconstituted itself as

1. Bertha Kahn, ca. 1900.
2. Leopold Kahn in Russian army uniform, ca. 1900.
3. Plan of an army post, Class A project, Beaux-Arts Institute of Design, Spring 1924.

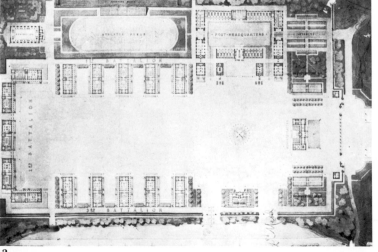

a vocabulary of its own, Kahn would trace the roots of this mature style back to his schooling. His emphasis on what he had come to call "form," the inherent essence that an architect had to discern in an architectural program before it was contaminated by practical considerations, was related to the Beaux-Arts emphasis on the preliminary, instinctive *esquisse*. As he said:

For beginning design problems Beaux-Arts training typically presented the student with a written program without comment from the instructor. He would study the problem, be given a period of a few hours in a cubicle (*en loge*) during which he would make a quick sketch [*esquisse*] of his solution without consultation. This sketch was filed as the basis for the elaboration of the problem which followed. Final drawings could not violate the essence of the initial *esquisse*. . . . This particular aspect of Beaux-Arts training was probably the most controversial because there was no exchange between the advocates of the programme and those who interpreted it, the architect. So the sketch depended on our intuitive powers. But the intuitive power is probably our most accurate sense. The sketch depended on our intuitive sense of appropriateness. I teach appropriateness. I don't teach anything else.[11]

Kahn also attributed the germ of his highly developed notion of a hierarchy between "served" and "servant" spaces, the latter often inserted in hollowed structural systems, to the *poché* or "pocketing" of spaces within masonry that was typical of the Beaux-Arts. And he claimed that his fascination with lighting as the maker of architectural environment had begun with the lessons about shade and shadow that Beaux-Arts rendering had taught him.[12]

Upon graduation in June 1924 (fig. 6), Kahn found a place in the office of the City Architect of Philadelphia, John Molitor (1872–1928), who had trained briefly in Paris and had made good connections in the city's architectural and political establishments. Kahn worked for a year as a draftsman, detailing drawings, and he was then seconded as chief of design to a special office set up by Molitor to design the major buildings for the Sesquicentennial International Exposition, which opened in Philadelphia in June 1926. In comparison to other international fairs, Philadelphia's celebration of the 150th anniversary of the Declaration of Independence was modest, and its public success was diminished by a dismal, rainy summer, but for a young architect it must have been exhilarating to design and build six huge buildings, constructed of wood and stucco over steel skeletons and totaling more than 1.5 million square feet. It was all done in less than a year.[13]

Although Molitor had two assistant architects assigned to the project, William S. Covell (1872–1956) and John Horace Frank (1873–1957), Kahn always claimed to have led the design work. It was surely he who made the dramatic drawings with which the buildings were introduced to the public in the fall of 1925, just in time to reassure the organizing committee, which had begun to worry about the ability of Molitor's office to carry off the huge undertaking (fig. 5).[14] Kahn's perspectives were full of chiaroscuro pyrotechnics, rendered with the slashing diagonal line that was to energize his drawings for the rest of his life. The buildings themselves were great sheds covered with pastel-tinted stucco (Molitor hoped that the fair would be called the "Rainbow City," just as the Columbian Exposition of 1893 had been dubbed the "White City"), and they afforded the young designer some chance to realize work on the scale of the visionary projects of the eighteenth-century architects Étienne-Louis Boullée and Claude-Nicolas Ledoux, with which he had probably become acquainted in college. As in some of his student work, the detailing, limited as it was, applied the waves and zigzags of Art Deco over a body of simplified modern classicism. The Exposition des Arts Décoratifs in Paris the previous summer (whence Art Deco took its name) had brought these motifs to the attention of many young architects.

Almost as soon as it had begun, the sesquicentennial was over, the site cleared and returned to a park, and Kahn was back in the ordinary routine of the City Architect's office, working chiefly on firehouses and playground buildings. After a few more months there he moved to the office of William H. Lee (1884–1971), then designing a number of buildings for Temple University. Kahn lived with his parents during this time, and after a year with Lee he had saved enough money for a long European trip of the kind that architects with his training were expected to make. He landed in Plymouth, England, on May 3, 1928, spent two weeks sketching in England—working in a dry, elegant illustrator's style—before moving on across the Low Countries and northern Germany.[15] He reached Denmark on June 29 and, after ten days, passed quickly through Sweden, Finland, and Estonia on his way to Riga, Latvia, where he had some relatives. It was also the jumping-off point for a visit to his birthplace on Saaremaa. He spent nearly a month of long Baltic summer evenings in those dimly remembered places, sleeping on the floor in his maternal grandmother's one-room house.[16] In mid-August Kahn left for Berlin, where he inspected the new housing projects (*Siedlungen*).[17] This was probably his first taste of the modern movement. After nearly two weeks in Germany,

4. *Sketch of the cathedral at Assisi, Winter 1928–29.*
5. *Palace of Liberal Arts, Sesquicentennial Exposition, Philadelphia, Pa., 1925–26. Perspective of portico, Fall 1925.*
6. *Left to right: Hyman Cunin, Louis Kahn, and Norman Rice on the steps of Hayden Hall, University of Pennsylvania, on graduation day, June 1924.*
7. *Louis and Esther Kahn on their honeymoon, Atlantic City, N.J., August 1930.*

4

5

6

7

he headed south, pausing for most of September in Austria and Hungary, where he started drawing again, intrigued by the Danube landscape. Its energetic forms were new to the city-bred architect.

On October 4, 1928, Kahn entered Italy, the traditional mecca for Beaux-Arts architects, where he was to spend five winter months.[18] Here he traveled slowly, drawing and making watercolors in Milan, Florence, San Gimignano, Assisi, and Rome, and he apparently spent a very long time sketching vernacular architecture on the Sorrento peninsula—in Positano, Amalfi, Ravello, and on the island of Capri. He visited the archaic Greek temples at Paestum, but no sketches have been found from there, nor any sketches of Roman antiquities. In Italy he encountered old friends from school and made new ones, notably the architects Louis Skidmore and Edward Durell Stone, with whom he traveled for a while.

It was in Europe that Kahn developed a new drawing style, based in part on a familiarity with contemporary currents in American art. For landscape, he began to rely on a sweeping hand that would lay out strong contours as it moved from side to side across the paper. When rendered in watercolor, the effect could be close to that achieved by American Scene painters or, if he reined in the chromatic range and applied the paint in flat panels, to the work of Charles Demuth and Georgia O'Keeffe (see fig. 242). For architecture, Kahn adopted a similarly broad handling of media, painting planes of color or using a carpenter's pencil whose wide, chisel-shaped lead laid organizing strata across the face of medieval and early Renaissance buildings (fig. 4). Full of the lively energy of nature and the tectonic strength of architecture, his Italian drawings bespoke confidence and independence. As he explained in an article about drawing published soon after his return, "I try in all my sketching not to be entirely subservient to my subject, but I have respect for it, and regard it as something tangible—alive—from which to extract my feelings. I have learned to regard it as no physical impossibility to move mountains and trees, or change cupolas and towers to suit my taste."[19]

Early in March, Kahn followed spring northward to Paris, where he spent about a month visiting with his Penn classmate Norman Rice (fig. 6), whom he had known since they had taken courses together at the Industrial Art School as ten-year-olds. Kahn had also recruited him to work on the sesquicentennial. Rice was then in the office of Le Corbusier, but Kahn did not make an effort to see the modernist's work.[20] More impressive to him was the vital energy of the Parisian metropolis—what he later called its "will to live"—and the integrity and completeness of its classical architecture and city planning. "For pure form (city form)," he said, "you can't beat that city."[21]

In April 1929 Kahn sailed for home. He found work immediately in the office of his revered teacher, Paul Cret, and his proposal of marriage was accepted by Esther Israeli (b. 1905), a beautiful research assistant in the Department of Neurosurgery at the University of Pennsylvania. He had met Esther at a party before sailing to Europe, intrigued her with talk about a newly acquired book on Rodin, and given her the book as a gift; they rapidly fell in love.[22] But Kahn did not write her from abroad, and she became engaged to someone else during his travels. Upon his return they argued, but reconciliation came after they saw each other in the audience at the Academy of Music, listening to the Philadelphia Orchestra. Kahn proposed to her during a visit to the Rodin Museum (designed by Cret), and they were married on August 14, 1930 (fig. 7).

Kahn's position with Cret was junior, and he was overshadowed by the senior members of the office, John Harbeson, William Hough, William Livingston, and Roy Larson. He worked on most of their major commissions during that period, which ranged in style from Cret's increasingly simple classicism—like the uncolumned Folger Library in Washington—to the jazzy modernity of his design for the General Exhibits Building at the Century of Progress Exhibition in Chicago. It must have been very provocative work for Kahn, who found himself, like most intelligent young architects of the time, torn between the lessons of the past and the enticements of the present. Here he could see his own teacher dealing intelligently with the same dilemma.

The romantic and artistic sweetness of those first months back in America diminished as the Depression settled over the country in the wake of the crash of 1929. Kahn and his fiancée put off plans to travel to Europe after their wedding, he to learn more about Walter Gropius and she to study with Freud, and within a year even Cret's office was starved for work. Kahn left before being asked to leave. Cret managed to arrange a place for him in the office of his friend Clarence Zantzinger, whose firm, Zantzinger, Borie, and Medary, had landed one of the first big Depression-era public works projects, the Treasury Building in Washington. A chameleon-like design with staid facades on the major thoroughfares and exuberant, Art Deco detail elsewhere, the Treasury Building was another work of transition. Kahn

labored on it until February 1932, when, at the very nadir of the Depression, he found himself out of work again.

Depression Modern
Kahn was unemployed for most of the next four years, supported by his wife and living with her parents, as they had since their marriage. But along with financial hardship came an unusual kind of architectural opportunity: the chance to pause and come to a new understanding of the role of his art at a time of great social demand and new technical and aesthetic potential. Philadelphia was an advantageous place in which to take that kind of holiday. In the bright shadow of George Howe and William Lescaze's Philadelphia Savings Fund Society Building (1929–32)—America's most visible contribution to international modernism—the Quaker city hosted a vigorous but gentlemanly debate about the future of architecture. The forum for much of that discussion was the *T-Square Club Journal of Philadelphia*, a new magazine, funded by Howe, which began publication in December 1930 and lasted for not quite two years.[23] In that short time, opinion was exchanged among many of the major forces in modern architecture. There was first of all George Howe himself, who, before his mid-life turn to modernism, had been trained in Paris and successfully established himself as one of the premier designers of Philadelphia's distinctive stone suburban houses—by turns inspired by low-slung Cotswold cottages and high-roofed French farms. There were also progressive Beaux-Arts architects, drawn from Penn's faculty and Cret's partnership—Harry Sternfeld, William Hough, Roy Larson, and John Harbeson—and Cret himself, all of whom contributed to or were profiled in *T-Square*. And there were essays by the leading Art Deco protagonists—the New York skyscraper builders Ralph Walker, Ely Jacques Kahn, and Raymond Hood and Philadelphia's Howell Lewis Shay. Finally, one could find the opinions of the more extreme modernists of every stripe: Frank Lloyd Wright, Richard Neutra, Rudolph Schindler, Norman Bel Geddes, Le Corbusier, Philip Johnson, and Buckminster Fuller (who took over the magazine and renamed it *Shelter* for its last three issues). No other magazine in America offered anything like this range of advanced opinion.

Kahn's classmate Norman Rice, having returned from his stint with Le Corbusier, was among the contributors, and his article "This New Architecture" (March 1931) offered one of the first careful expositions by an American of what, in the wake of the exhibition that opened at the Museum of Modern Art on February 10, 1932, would be christened the "International Style." (That show came to the Philadelphia

8. Cover design for T-Square Journal, *January 1932.*
9. Louis Kahn, ca. 1934.
10. Oscar Stonorov and Alfred Kastner. Carl Mackley Houses, Philadelphia, Pa., 1932–35.
11. Project for Northeast Philadelphia Housing Corporation, 1933. Bird's-eye perspective of windmill-plan house.

8

9

Museum of Art in April.) Kahn himself published "The Value and Aim in Sketching" in *T-Square* in May 1931, illustrated with some of his Italian drawings, and he prepared an unused cover design for the January 1932 issue of the magazine (fig. 8).

Kahn organized another center for the discussion of modern architecture in Philadelphia, the Architectural Research Group (ARG). In 1931, while still working in the Zantzinger office, he and Dominique Berninger, an unemployed French architect, assembled a group of about thirty young designers, most of whom were also out of work. They rented cheap rooms, borrowed drawing tools from the school board, and set to work. When he lost his job, Kahn devoted all his energies to the group, which once a week indulged in lunch at Ethel's Restaurant, a favored daily eating place among architects who were lucky enough to have jobs. David P. Wisdom, who was later to work for Kahn for many years, remembered seeing him for the first time in that setting: "this little guy who held forth" at the center of a group of admirers (fig. 9).[24]

Kahn now became a modernist. He studied intensely what was going on abroad, paging through the publications of Le Corbusier's work for the first time, and over the next two decades his architecture echoed many of the major themes of the International Style.[25] Most important to him were the new compositional strategies that it introduced, including open planning, and its emphasis on the social responsibility of the architect. He also participated in the widespread modernist experimentation with new building technologies.

It was social responsibility, and in particular the problems of mass housing, that was the chief concern of Kahn's Architectural Research Group. This issue was well established at the center of the discussion of modern architecture in Europe, but it still had a small following in the United States. Awareness grew, however, as slum conditions worsened because of the Depression. Philadelphia was the site of the first modernist *Siedlung* to be built in America, the Carl Mackley Houses, designed for the Full Fashioned Hosiery Workers Union by a pair of young émigré architects, Oscar Stonorov (1905–1970) and Alfred Kastner (1900–1975),[26] who had taken second place in the 1931 competition for the Palace of the Soviets in Moscow (fig. 10). The Mackley Houses were initially funded by a loan from Hoover's Reconstruction Finance Corporation, and they were taken over in the summer of 1933 as the first project in the much more ambitious program of Roosevelt's Public Works Administration.

Exhibited in a preliminary form during the Philadelphia stopover of the Museum of Modern Art's modern architecture show in 1932, the four long, tile-faced buildings were redesigned in 1933 and under construction in 1934. With their high standard of design and construction and such generous amenities as garages and a swimming pool, the Mackley Houses attracted nationwide attention.

Within a few years Kahn would work with both Stonorov and Kastner, but in the meantime his research group did its best to stay busy and attract local attention. In April 1933 they placed a model in the Better Homes Exhibition that showed their proposed rebuilding of a typical tract of South Philadelphia slum. Like the Mackley Houses, it consisted of four long buildings (their kin in Germany were called *Seilenbauten*) placed within a parklike setting.[27] The ARG scheme had been Americanized, again like the Stonorov and Kastner design, with garages and generous recreation facilities.

The ARG also put forward a proposal later in 1933 when the PWA launched its housing subsidy program.[28] Submitted on behalf of the Northeast Philadelphia Housing Corporation, their plan placed a variety of buildings within a network of gently curved, limited-traffic roads on a substantial, fifty-four-acre tract. The buildings included long apartment blocks, like those planned for South Philadelphia, and also row-house strips and four-unit, windmill-plan clusters designed by Kahn (fig. 11). With their corner windows and floating roof slabs, the windmill houses demonstrated the architect's familiarity with some of the signature details of modernism. But the rather conservative and placid facade composition was more like contemporary English work than the livelier avant-garde architecture on the Continent, and Kahn's unsureness can also be seen in the overt artifice of the unusual plan, with its cramped, enclosed stairhall. With the exception of the Mackley Houses, the PWA denied funding to all twelve of the schemes submitted by Philadelphians in 1933, and the members of the Architectural Research Group went their separate ways in May 1934.

In part, the breakup of the ARG had to do with the advent of the New Deal's work projects for architects. Kahn himself took a position as the head of a research "squad" under the coordination of Philadelphia's weak City Planning Commission. Partnered with the established firm of Henry Magaziner and Victor Eberhard (which had also sponsored the Architectural Research Group), he authored a proposal for building on another site in Northeast Philadelphia,

adjacent to the main Pennsylvania Railroad right-of-way.[29] Called St. Katherine's Village, it made use of the same mixture of building types that had been devised for the Northeast Philadelphia Housing Corporation.

At the same time, Kahn began to build, albeit very modestly, with clients coming from the socially and artistically progressive Jewish community in which he and his wife had many friends. Harry ("Mish") Buten, who owned a paint company, had Kahn modernize his store in Germantown in 1934. The work was carried out in partnership with Hyman Cunin, a Penn classmate who had also worked for Cret and been a member of the ARG (see fig. 6). Cunin had apparently secured the architectural registration that Kahn still lacked. In 1935, when Kahn had obtained his own credentials, the congregation of Ahavath Israel came to him for a new building to be inserted in a row of two-story houses close to the northern boundary of the city. For them he produced a plain, brick-faced box, pierced by factory-style steel windows and with a main sanctuary of notable and (at the time) refreshing austerity.

The generally slow pace of Depression-era work for Kahn was interrupted by more than a year of intense activity as an architect for the Division of Subsistence Homesteads. He was called to Washington in December 1935 by Alfred Kastner, a Hamburg-trained architect and one of the Mackley Houses designers, who had himself been recruited from Philadelphia to rescue a program called Jersey Homesteads. This was a scheme to relocate the families of 200 Jewish garment workers from New York to a site near Hightstown, New Jersey.[30] Benjamin Brown, a Ukrainian-born proponent of cooperative industry and a leader of the Jewish back-to-the-land movement, spearheaded the project, which was to include a cooperative clothing factory and a cooperative farm. Brown believed that the combination of these two seasonal enterprises would make the community self-sustaining; in addition, each house was to stand on enough ground to permit large-scale gardening. Supported by the International Ladies Garment Workers Union (ILGWU) and endorsed by Albert Einstein (who had taken up residence in nearby Princeton), the project advanced quickly during the first years of Roosevelt's administration. A design with Cape Cod–style cottages was worked out during the first half of 1935 and the pouring of foundation slabs begun, all under Brown's supervision.[31] But the Division of Subsistence Homesteads was moved into the Resettlement Administration in May 1935, and there the project came under sharp scrutiny. It was noted that Brown had not yet reached an agreement on the details for

12. Jersey Homesteads, Roosevelt, N.J., 1935–37. Houses under construction, July 1936.
13. Jersey Homesteads, Roosevelt, N.J., 1935–37. Perspective and plan of school, Fall 1936.
14. Illustration for Tax Exemption of Public Housing, 1939.

operating the factory with ILGWU president David Dubinsky, and it appeared that the houses would be very expensive. Rexford Tugwell, the "brain truster" whom Roosevelt had appointed to head the Resettlement Administration, decided to place the project more directly under federal supervision, and Kastner and Kahn (who carried the titles principal and assistant principal architect) were given the job.

In December 1935 the two young architects moved into offices in one of the World War I "temporary" buildings on the Mall. Their orders were to push the project ahead, and they were encouraged to utilize prefabricated construction. They used these demands to convert Jersey Homesteads into an ambitious experiment with adapting new technology and the modernist idiom of Europe to the needs of the American suburb. Robert W. Noble, who worked in their office, later observed, "Little cinder block houses held down by concrete slabs were never more completely studied."[32]

Kahn served as the head of the drafting room, submitting weekly reports and playing a role that he always called "co-designer."[33] Indeed, although junior architects in the office were given credit for four of the twelve house types worked out during the first months of 1936, it is evident that a single coordinating intelligence lay behind their variety of forms (fig. 12).[34] The numerous, predominantly one-story house plans were contrived to allow the pairing of units in an almost endless number of combinations. Economical construction with concrete slab roofs and floors and cinder-block walls (adopted after experiments with precast concrete wall sections ran into construction and licensing problems) allowed for a surprising number of luxuries. These included wood-block floors laid on top of the concrete, as well as carports. The plans were also generous, with many three- and even four-bedroom units designed for large families. Rooms were flung outward to create irregular plan perimeters that were more like the picturesque tradition of the American suburban house than modern, European-style workers' housing. It was a highly ambitious project, and when the house designs were displayed in the "Architecture in Government Housing" show at the Museum of Modern Art in June and July 1936, Lewis Mumford singled them out as "the most adventurous, the most stimulating" on display.[35] Others, however, were less infatuated with what the Philadelphia Inquirer called a "commune" headed by "a Russian-born little Stalin" (i.e., Benjamin Brown).[36]

Despite initial construction delays, the first houses at Jersey Homesteads were occupied in the early summer of 1936, only

about six months after Kastner and Kahn had begun work. When the clothing factory opened in August, however, there was not yet enough housing for the work force, although most of the houses were ready by January 1937.

In the fall of 1936 the architects began to plan the school, which was also to serve as a community center. Kahn studied several possible *partis*. These designs reflected his increasingly confident use of the Le Corbusian vocabulary, replete with slabs supported on slender *pilotis* and curvilinear walls that exploited the possibilities for free planning within such a structural system (fig. 13).[37] The school was still under study when Kahn was furloughed early in 1937, and Kastner decided its final design in May, settling on a composition that was much less extroverted than those sketched by Kahn.[38] The painter Ben Shahn received his first major commission for a large mural in the school lobby, depicting immigration and labor history, and he moved to Jersey Homesteads in 1938.

After Kahn returned to Philadelphia, he again found himself without steady employment, although he was now supervising the construction of Ahavath Israel. Together with Henry Klumb, a former assistant of Frank Lloyd Wright's whom he had met while working in Washington, he used his free time to study the possibilities of prefabricated steel housing.[39] Their work was supported by Samuel S. Fels, the soap maker and philanthropist, and in part they collaborated with Louis Magaziner, who provided Kahn with a mailing address and a drafting table in his office at 1701 Walnut Street. The steel construction system severely limited the architects' freedom, and some of the designs were very conservative, with pitched roofs. But Kahn wrung more out of the problem than most could have done, notably in a series of designs for small row houses that used a mid-roof monitor to light the upper halls and bathrooms.

The architectural doldrums of 1937 were interrupted in September when Congress passed the Wagner-Steagall Act, ending a two-year battle over public housing. The act put housing—and, with it, modern architecture—on a new, higher footing within the New Deal and promised increased opportunities for architects. Partly in response to a negative evaluation of the PWA program (which had built only one additional project in Philadelphia after the Mackley Houses), the act created the more powerful United States Housing Authority.[40] A parallel local movement gave birth to the Philadelphia Housing Authority in August 1937, also designed to build more vigorously.[41] Kahn, who had become a recognized authority on housing matters, found

employment with both the USHA and the PHA.

It was the Philadelphia Housing Authority that offered the first opportunities, conducting a competition in 1938 to select architects.[42] A team assembled by George Howe, with Kahn and Kenneth Day (1901?–1958) as its designers, won the right to design a project to eradicate the densely inhabited alleyways in the Southwark section of South Philadelphia, adjacent to historic Gloria Dei ("Old Swedes'") Church. Day claimed to have been responsible for the plan of the 950-unit project, which placed smaller apartments in towers and larger apartments in low rises, with a view to maintaining the high density of the site.[43] Kahn by himself designed another 1,500-unit PHA project, begun in 1939 for vacant land in West Philadelphia owned by the Pennsylvania Hospital for Mental and Nervous Diseases (called "Kirkbride's" after its founder, Dr. Thomas Kirkbride). In this time of matter-of-fact segregation, Old Swedes' was to be a project for whites and Kirkbride's was to be for blacks.

Federal funds were approved for both designs ($5,551,000 for Old Swedes'; $7,881,000 for Kirkbride's), but intense opposition came from members of the close-knit Italian community of Southwark, who did not want to be displaced from their small but generally well-maintained homes, and from the builders and real estate men who did not want the government to become more deeply involved in the housing market.[44] In a conference with federal and city housing officials on May 30, 1940, Mayor Robert E. Lamberton announced his own opposition to the plans. Calling public housing an untested social experiment, he opined, "Slum areas exist because some people are so utterly shiftless that any place where they live becomes a slum, and others are so poor that they cannot afford to live anywhere else."[45] The City Council declined to take the matter further.

This setback contributed to Kahn's politicization. He had come to recognize that housing was more than a matter of architectural design, and for the next decade he was an activist. Kahn had already spent five months in 1939 working with Catherine Bauer and Frederick Gutheim on a public education campaign launched by the United States Housing Authority to counter exactly the kind of concerns that had been raised in Philadelphia. He had first prepared the illustrations for some of the small pamphlets issued by the USHA to explain its mission and the character of public housing in general (fig. 14), and he then worked on the USHA's "Houses and Housing" exhibition, mounted at the Museum of Modern Art in New York. The show was designed

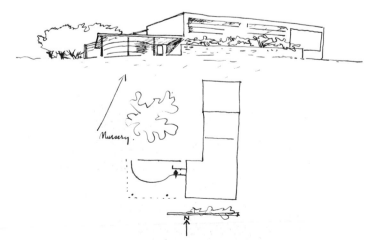

in part to make up for the absence of public housing in any of the several future-oriented dioramas at the New York World's Fair that summer. Kahn's contribution was a large panel entitled "Housing in the Rational City Plan," which analyzed the problems of Philadelphia and proposed remedies at every scale, ranging from the demolition of large parts of Center City and their replacement with clusters of towers (like those in Le Corbusier's most extreme proposals for Paris) to the efficient, zoned organization of the ordinary house plan.[46]

With this training, Kahn joined wholeheartedly in the campaign to reverse Philadelphia's official opposition to federally funded housing. But he and all those who had fought for decades for the establishment of the Philadelphia Housing Authority found their position complicated by the war clouds that began to sweep in from across the seas during that dark summer of 1940. On the one hand, Philadelphia's swelling population of war industry workers and servicemen had already begun to overtax the supply of housing, and Congress passed the Lanham Act in October, aimed at meeting this shortage. On the other hand, the legislation did not endorse projects like Kirkbride's and Old Swedes', planned by the PHA for funding by the USHA. Most Lanham Act money was allocated for wartime, emergency shelter only, and it was administered through the Federal Works Agency, the USHA being rightly suspected of seeking a permanent government presence in the housing market.

In an effort to steer wartime funding toward projects of lasting social value, Kahn allied himself with the Philadelphia Housing Guild, and with support from the Philadelphia Housing Association, the American Institute of Architects, the Tenants' League, and labor unions, he helped to organize a citywide protest meeting on December 10, 1940.[47] Kahn chaired the publicity committee, which made posters and educational exhibits for the meeting, and Edmund Bacon, having recently arrived in Philadelphia on the first step toward his long and celebrated tenure as executive director of the Planning Commission, headed the program committee. Their efforts, and efforts like theirs, helped to redirect some of the first Lanham Act money toward the construction of real communities.

Architecture at War
Kahn was himself soon working for the war effort. He spent most of 1941 and 1942 designing seven workers' communities, five of which, totaling more than 2,200 units, were built.[48] The projects were caught in a constant

15

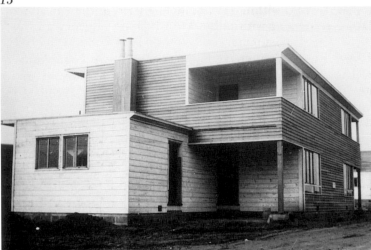

16

17

15. Pennypack Woods, Philadelphia, Pa., 1941–43. Family seated in front of row houses, ca. 1942.
16. Pennypack Woods, Philadelphia, Pa., 1941–43. Four-unit apartment building, January 1942.
17. Carver Court, Caln Township, Pa., 1941–43. Ground-freed and one-story buildings, ca. 1942.

crossfire between those, like Kahn, who wanted a national housing program and critics who could tolerate government involvement in the housing market only because of the wartime emergency and who sought to keep that involvement at a minimum. Despite this sniping, the projects afforded Kahn a rich opportunity to test solutions to basic problems in something like a laboratory environment. It may have been in the course of this testing that he began to have doubts about the functionalist course of modern architecture.

As the threat of war loomed, George Howe, who had assembled the team for Old Swedes', approached Kahn with the suggestion that they form a partnership and go after government work.[49] With his impeccable architectural credentials and social connections, Howe was an ideal partner, and he and Kahn had obtained the first of their wartime commissions, for Pine Ford Acres in Middletown, Pennsylvania, within days of the creation of the Division of Defense Housing within the Federal Works Agency on April 5, 1941. By midsummer 500 units at Pine Ford Acres and 1,000 units at Pennypack Woods, close to the St. Katherine's Village site in Northeast Philadelphia, were under construction, and Pine Ford Acres was occupied by fall. The firm sometimes employed as many as two dozen designers and draftsmen, and although there was no official hierarchy among them, Frederick Savage, Joseph N. Lacy, Charles Abbe, and David Wisdom served successively as informal "head draftsman" during the war years, a position Wisdom also held during all the years of Kahn's independent practice. They occupied George Howe's offices on the top floor of the old *Evening Bulletin* building, whose public spaces and ground floor facade had been sleekly modernized by Howe in 1936.

Within stringent financial limits (the average unit cost for these first projects was below $3,000), Howe and Kahn set out to build model communities that might set the standard for postwar planning. Like virtually all the wartime projects, theirs were built on open land rather than slum clearance sites, and despite the lack of single-family houses, they offered an appealing evocation of a suburban future. However, the most progressive feature of their work—the placement of housing within the greenery of superblocks, served by limited access roads—was lost on those who built postwar America.

Architecturally, the challenge thrown up by wartime housing was to introduce external variety without the kind of energetic (and expensive) planning that Kastner and Kahn

had utilized at Jersey Homesteads. Wartime houses were necessarily more compact, and the profiles of buildings blockier. With their means thus limited, Howe and Kahn experimented chiefly with variations on two building types: two-story row houses with two and three bedrooms, arranged in flat-roofed strips that resembled *Seilenbauten*, and single-bedroom apartments stacked in four-unit buildings. At Pine Ford and Pennypack, the row houses adopted the shallow plan that Kahn had used for his prefabricated houses in the 1930s, designed to allow good cross ventilation (fig. 15). The buildings with one-bedroom apartments differed slightly in the two projects, offering variations on a common theme. In order to place two apartments on each floor while offering all four families a ground-floor utility and storage room, Howe and Kahn designed these buildings with substantial first-floor "ears" that could accommodate the extra area needed at that level (fig. 16). The architects introduced varied coloring and used two widths of wooden siding in order to animate the facades; at Pine Ford the skylines were broken by peaked roofs— added to satisfy conservative critics.

While work was progressing on these first projects, Howe began to do an increasing amount of consulting work on housing in Washington, and he and Kahn added Oscar Stonorov to their partnership to help take up the load.[50] Stonorov had been one of the editors of the first volume of Le Corbusier's *Oeuvre complète*, and he had been paired with Kastner in the design of the Mackley Houses for the Full Fashioned Hosiery Workers. He had continued to strengthen his connections with organized labor during the thirties, attaching himself particularly to labor leaders who were interested in housing, like John Edelman of the Hosiery Workers, and he had advised Edelman in setting up Philadelphia's Labor Housing Conference in 1934.[51] This became one of the most effective groups in pushing for passage of the Wagner Act and the creation of the USHA, and it was Stonorov who suggested that Catherine Bauer, an eloquent propagandist of the housing movement, be brought to Philadelphia as its director. He made room for her and the fledgling organization in his office. Stonorov is not remembered as playing a key role in the design end of his partnership with Howe and Kahn, although he did handle a number of jobs himself on the side for friends and old clients.[52] But his activism and union connections transformed the shape of the practice.

The firm continued to explore the variations possible within the established housing types, and by the end of 1941, in time for Pearl Harbor, they had adopted a strong new arrangement for the multibedroom, row-house building. This was first seen in their designs for Carver Court, a 100-unit project for black steelworkers just outside Coatesville, Pennsylvania (fig. 17). They realized that by lifting all of the living quarters to the second floor, they could free the ground floor to provide ample storage and a carport that might easily be converted into one or more extra rooms. This "essential space," as they called it, was what made working-class homeowners put up with the other deficiencies of speculator-built, "dickey-front houses," and it was what was missing in government-built housing.[53] They did not claim authorship for the "ground-freed" house, which had clear antecedents in the *piloti*-lofted designs of Le Corbusier and many predecessors in American practice as well. But Carver Court was well publicized. With its cleanly detailed units gathered happily around a loop road at the foot of a wooded hillside, it was a special favorite of the organizers of the show "Built in USA, 1932–1944" at the Museum of Modern Art. It was with this design that Kahn first began to gain widespread attention. The ground-freed formula was immediately adopted by him for the Stanton Road Dwellings—300 units in Washington, D.C.—and for a second, 150-unit Coatesville project for white workers called Lincoln Highway, for which designs were prepared in late spring 1942.

But artistic merit did not guarantee that these works would be built, and an almost equal amount of energy had to be devoted to the political fight for public housing. Here, the old battlelines were still being contested, with conservatives loath to have the government build anything out of permanent materials or with lasting social value. At both Pine Ford and Pennypack, opposition forces delayed the construction of community buildings and stores—amenities that were sorely needed by the inhabitants of the relatively isolated settlements. Both Coatesville projects were fought in their entirety by local interests, who were especially opposed to the black housing. In combating this, Stonorov proved to be an effective lobbyist, convincing, for instance, his labor friends to "raise plain hell" over the Coatesville developments.[54]

In the end, the contested housing and community buildings were completed, and the latter showed what Kahn and his colleagues could accomplish when they faced fewer constraints (figs. 18, 19). In the community buildings the picturesque tradition of the American suburb was infused with an angular new geometry. The plans were frequently terminated or divided by oblique walls, and even the rectangular-plan units slid by each other on nonorthogonal trajectories that were, in turn, reflected in staggered,

sloping rooflines. The dynamism of these buildings seemed to express the feelings of an architect who was freed, at least for a moment, from the stringent requirements of wartime housing.

By the time these projects were complete, George Howe was no longer in Philadelphia, having left the partnership in February 1942 to accept an appointment as supervising architect of the Public Buildings Administration, the highest architectural post in the federal government. At the same time, Kahn and Stonorov's division of labor between design work and political work seems to have become increasingly clear. It was Stonorov, for instance, who led them into the most dramatic political battle to be fought over war housing, the great clash over the construction of a "Bomber City" for the workers at Henry Ford's Willow Run airplane factory, near Ypsilanti, Michigan.

The battleground had been chosen by Ford, who early in 1941 undertook to build a factory just outside Detroit's Wayne County in Washtenaw County, where he apparently reckoned that conservative rural politicians would help him fight the United Auto Workers.[55] The UAW's Walter Reuther was a friend of Stonorov's, and together they immediately hatched a plan to outflank Ford: they would get the government to build a large workers' city near the new plant, putting union members on the poll lists in Washtenaw County and creating a model for postwar planning at the same time.[56] President Roosevelt gave his blessing to the plan in November, and by December, Howe, Stonorov, and Kahn had built a model of such a community of 20,000 residences.[57] Stonorov had also begun to draw up a list of architects who might be asked to collaborate on the design, working in consultation with the architect Eero Saarinen, whose practice was located in nearby Bloomfield Hills, Michigan.[58] After powerful lobbying in Washington by the UAW, a site was selected, and in late May 1942 five architectural teams—including Stonorov and Kahn—were chosen to design five housing neighborhoods (now reduced to a total of 6,000 units). Saarinen and Swanson were put in charge of the community center. In June, Henry Ford announced that he would use every legal means to block the plan; great confusion was sown by Ford about the number of workers at the plant and the number of permanent, postwar jobs that it would provide. The federal government accordingly reduced the project in August to three 1,200-unit neighborhoods, and Stonorov and Kahn were told that only 900 of theirs would be built in the first phase.[59]

In the meantime Kahn had overseen the design of eight

19

20

21

18. *Pennypack Woods, Philadelphia, Pa., 1941–43. Bird's-eye perspective of preliminary design for community building. Inscribed Louis I. Kahn '42.*
19. *Pine Ford Acres, Middletown, Pa., 1941–43. Community building, ca. 1943.*

20. *Willow Run, Washtenaw County, Mich., 1942–43. Perspective of ground-freed building. Inscribed Louis I. Kahn 43.*
21. *Lily Ponds Houses, Washington, D.C., 1942–43. Houses, ca. 1943.*

building types for Willow Run, including a ground-freed model, adjusting the design as needed to allow for the growing shortage of timber (fig. 20).[60] He and Stonorov had to defend these designs against the fierce and essentially antimodernist criticism of Otis Winn, an architect who was originally retained to design one of the housing neighborhoods and was kept on as an advisor to the government after his neighborhood was cut. Winn apparently bore a grudge against Stonorov, and he shrewdly presented his criticism to the housing committee of the UAW, where underlying sentiments favored traditional, single-family houses. Stonorov argued back that Willow Run "should be a symbol of things to come and a prophetic statement in terms of housing and not an imitation, and a bad one at that, of what the operative builders are selling to the workers now."[61] But his defense was in vain, and, despite his friendship with Reuther, the UAW dismissed him from the advisory position that he had held with the union.[62] In October 1942 the entire project was canceled—replaced by temporary dormitories designed by Saarinen and Swanson. The collapse can be blamed on the diminution of union support.

As Willow Run was being killed, work was just beginning on the 475 units of the Lily Ponds Houses in Washington, D.C., identified from the start as a "demountable" project. It was composed entirely of clever one-story buildings with four small apartments whose bathrooms were backed up against each other beneath a gull-wing monitor (fig. 21). The exteriors were partly faced in rough tile, and the bare wood of the interior walls and ceilings was left unfinished. The rustic materials and reverse-pitch roof were evidence of Kahn's growing familiarity with the range of Le Corbusier's recent work, including his simple, quasi-primitive houses like the Sextant Villa, a summer cottage built for the Peyron family in La Palmyre-Les Mathes in 1935. It had been well illustrated in the third volume of Le Corbusier's *Oeuvre complète* (1939).

Kahn undertook one further wartime housing commission in 1944–45, a thorough redesign of the still unbuilt Stanton Road Dwellings. The concrete needed for ground-freed units was now unavailable, and so he had to devise a large number of other types, including relatively conventional brick row houses and three-story apartment buildings—rare in wartime. He took special pains over the site plan, which created many small, semiprivate courtyards between the buildings. George Howe, who had retained an interest in this long-developing project during his service in Washington, reviewed Kahn's design and praised it. But he also expressed reservations, in words that could probably have been echoed by any of the talented architects who labored on wartime housing:

I must say . . . that as I get further and further away from the engrossing work of solving a series of practically unsolvable problems, the more [the] unsatisfactory nature of housing project programs in general impresses me. The basis of city requirements for street widths, set backs, etc., is so rigid, extravagant and oppressive as to doom all solutions to comparative negation. This is all part of the general planning problem which faces us and which if we do not approach with imagination and freedom from restriction, we can make little progress in architectural design in general.

He added, "Do look me up. I miss you constantly."[63]

Plans For 194X
Stanton Road remained unbuilt, a victim of the impending peace. But the prospect of peacetime work also began to offer some of the freedoms that Howe missed. As the quantity of war work declined sharply in 1943–45, Stonorov and Kahn found themselves increasingly engaged in a series of imaginative projects, designed to shape the character of postwar architecture.[64] With the sponsorship of magazines and manufacturers of building materials, they designed houses, hotels, stores, office buildings, and entire neighborhood redevelopment projects. This farsighted work continued for several years after the war, and it brought with it a substantial involvement in social activism: in housing, city planning, trade unionism, and architectural politics. It also brought them some real commissions.

The most complex and widely recognized of Stonorov and Kahn's postwar-oriented projects was a pair of booklets on urban neighborhood planning that they prepared as part of an advertising campaign for Revere Copper and Brass. Written just as the Philadelphia City Planning Commission was being reincarnated with greater powers in 1943, the pamphlets used Philadelphia neighborhoods as examples of possible action. Stonorov was in charge of most of this work, but Kahn certainly did not dissent from the message the booklets conveyed, and his hand can be seen in some of the illustrations.

The work began in April 1943, when Stonorov was introduced to Revere's advertising representatives by Howard Myers, publisher of *Architectural Forum*. Revere was sponsoring a series of booklets on postwar architecture that they hoped would promote the use of their materials, although the advertising message in Stonorov and Kahn's

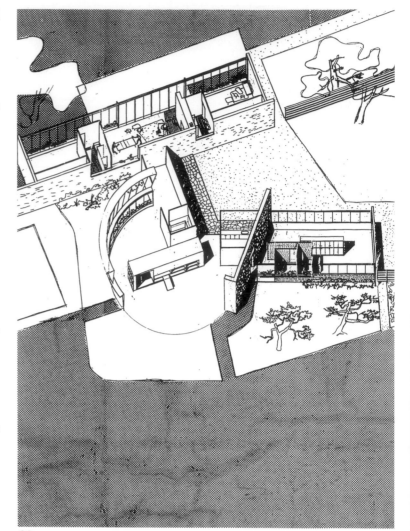

22

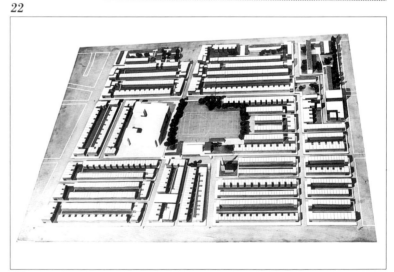

23

22. *Axonometric of teen and nursery building, for* Why City Planning is Your Responsibility, *April–May 1943.*
23. *Model Neighborhood Rehabilitation Project, Philadelphia, Pa., 1943. Educational model showing improvements.*

24. *A neighborhood organizational meeting, illustration for* You and Your Neighborhood: A Primer for Neighborhood Planning, *1944.*
25. *Illustration for* You and Your Neighborhood: A Primer for Neighborhood Planning, *1944.*

GIVE EVERYBODY A
CHANCE TO SPEAK UP—
RESOLVED:
TO FORM
A NEIGHBORHOOD
PLANNING COUNCIL

24

work was very restrained. Also in the series were Lawrence Kocher's *Homes to Enrich Our National Standard of Living* and Serge Chermayeff's *A Children's Center or Nursery School.* Stonorov and Kahn were commissioned to make a plan that would "integrate four existing city blocks into a community by providing it with a neighborhood nursery and playground, including a store."[65] A section of South Philadelphia was chosen for this exercise, and the partners rapidly designed the new facilities, including a small component of public housing. The nursery, combined with an activities center for teenagers, was to be a building of explosive constructivist geometry (fig. 22). It was probably Stonorov's work, as he claimed for the whole commission.[66] But the underlying premise of the project, that old neighborhoods ought to be preserved and strengthened rather than demolished and rebuilt, seemed to reflect Kahn's experience with Old Swedes', where he had discovered to his surprise that residents did not want to leave their old houses. The booklet argued for "*conservation and not outright destruction*" and described new schools, shopping centers, and open spaces as the "protective armor" with which to preserve "worthwhile older residential neighborhoods."[67] Most importantly, it called for grass-roots citizen participation in the planning process, with powerful neighborhood civic organizations to guide the professionals. The booklet was called *Why City Planning Is Your Responsibility.*

Announced on July 3, 1943, with a full-page advertisement in the *Saturday Evening Post* that invited readers to request copies, the booklet was an enormous success. It satisfied an evident hunger for information about postwar planning, and within a month Revere had distributed 110,000 copies.[68] This achievement seems to have whetted the architects' appetite for such work, and in the fall they joined a team of other Philadelphians in developing a cognate project, designing an educational model that could be used to show how another sample South Philadelphia neighborhood might supply itself with their "protective armor." Edmund Bacon spearheaded this effort, and the model was built by the Architects' Workshop, set up by the local chapter of the American Institute of Architects in cooperation with a host of other Philadelphia groups (fig. 23). By means of replaceable parts, the model showed the effects of the kind of work described in the Revere booklet. Kahn and Stonorov demonstrated it before the planning commission, the Philadelphia AIA, the League of Women Voters, and many city and neighborhood civic organizations during 1944. Photographs of it were also included in that year's "Look at Your Neighborhood" show at the Museum of Modern Art.

The model, in turn, formed the basis of Stonorov's proposal to Revere Copper for a second, more ambitious pamphlet. This was under discussion in the fall of 1943, and in February 1944 Revere Copper agreed to pay $5,000 for a community planning "primer."[69] The new booklet, which appeared in October, was vastly more sophisticated than their first effort, with many more illustrations (most by Stonorov) and a lively scenario. *You and Your Neighborhood: A Primer for Neighborhood Planning* followed the story of a neighborhood improvement campaign from its beginnings in a single family's dinner-table conversation. It told of the creation of a "neighborhood planning council" and the development of a plan (embodied in the model), and it explained how such a plan could be presented to the city planning commission (fig. 24). It went on to discuss how an entire city might be planned with concern for each of its neighborhoods, and it very elegantly explained how, in the accommodation of different activities and in the separation of incompatible uses, "the plan of a city is like the plan of a house" (fig. 25). This notion of the indissoluble bond between architecture and city planning was to be a hallmark of Kahn's mature work.[70]

The second booklet was also hugely successful, with distribution continuing for years. Its engaging narrative structure seemed to suggest itself for dramatic presentation, and, indeed, Stonorov campaigned for it to be made into a film.[71] Kahn sketched out an elaborate outline for the script, entitled "Can Neighborhoods Exist?" but, while the Museum of Modern Art and Revere expressed interest, the project came to nothing.[72]

The commitment to an alliance between architecture and community activism that underlay the Revere project was more Stonorov's than Kahn's, but, like Stonorov's engagement in union affairs, it was a commitment that Kahn appreciated and participated in insofar as he was able. Indeed, Kahn himself was active during the immediate postwar period in a number of political and social service organizations, including the Independent Citizens Committee of the Arts, Sciences, and Professions, a group dedicated to a liberal agenda on atomic energy, race relations, full employment, and a national health and welfare program.[73] Kahn faithfully served as a member of the board for the Philadelphia division of the committee, to which he was elected in 1946, although stories later abounded about his unwillingness to do political work. In 1946 he was also named to the Building Bureau of the National Jewish Welfare Board, which was charged with overseeing the architectural component of Jewish social

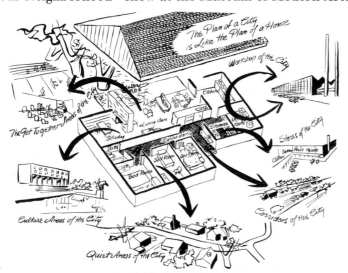

services, and throughout the late forties and fifties he was a member of the Welfare Board's executive committee.[74]

In matters closer to real architecture, Kahn brought out of the war years an even greater commitment to involvement. In April 1945 the Federal Public Housing Agency (successor to the USHA) established the Architectural Advisory Committee, with eight regional sub-units. Kahn was made a member of the committee and elected chairman of region two, which reached from New York to Washington. Here again he was conscientious, organizing a survey of existing housing projects with a view to improving standards for future construction.[75] Kahn continued to serve on the successor committee that advised the Public Housing Agency in the early fifties, and he joined the mass resignation from that committee in November 1951 to protest the deficiencies of the federal program.[76] In a related project, he chaired a committee of the Philadelphia AIA that prepared a report on housing in 1947, aimed at stimulating larger government involvement.[77]

Kahn's greatest political energy was devoted to the American Society of Planners and Architects.[78] He attended its preliminary meetings in 1944 at the Museum of Modern Art in New York and at Harvard, and he was also in attendance at the first general meeting on January 27, 1945, when George Howe gave the keynote address.[79] Modeled on CIAM (the Congrès Internationaux d'Architecture Moderne), the ASPA was set up to provide American modernists with an activist alternative to the AIA and to build stronger ties between city planning and architecture. The membership list brought together the radical forces in American architecture, from German émigrés to the homegrown ranks of housing advocates, and included Howe, Walter Gropius, and G. Holmes Perkins—modernists who were or would soon be in charge of the architecture programs at Yale, Harvard, and the University of Pennsylvania. Kahn was elected vice president for 1946 (Joseph Hudnut, the Harvard dean, was president), and in 1947 he served as president. Perkins was secretary/treasurer in both years. Kahn's involvement in the ASPA focused on the great debate over the selection of the site and the design of the headquarters building for the United Nations.[80] Jointly with the American branch of CIAM, the ASPA fought for an open and systematic planning process, but the possibility of this was forever lost in the turmoil that followed John D. Rockefeller's gift of the adopted site on the East River. Kahn, who had also participated in the campaign to bring the UN to Philadelphia, must have felt doubly thwarted by this turn of events.

On September 20, 1947, during Kahn's presidency, the ASPA annual meeting was held in Philadelphia; the highlight of the event was a reception at Stonorov's house in the country. The organization virtually ceased to exist after that date, perhaps a sign that modern architecture in America no longer needed a special advocate.

The tangible, architectural corollary of these years of quite intense social and political involvement was a group of modest commissions, largely undertaken after the frenzy of war housing had diminished. Many were for labor unions, for which Stonorov's responsibility was great, although the first such work predated Stonorov's partnership: a modest row house remodeled as the headquarters of the Battery Workers Union in 1940. Other union projects included the interior renovation of a health clinic for the International Ladies Garment Workers Union (1943–45), the remodeling of the headquarters of the shipyard workers union in Camden, New Jersey (1943–45, largely by Stonorov), an unbuilt headquarters building for the Moving Picture Operators' Union (1944), a rustic lodge for the Philadelphia members of the ILGWU at a camp in the Pocono Mountains (1945–47, fig. 26), two dormitories at a union-sponsored children's camp in Bucks County, Pennysylvania (1945–47), and another clinic renovation, for the American Federation of Labor at St. Luke's Hospital (1950–51). The client liaison for many of these commissions was garment workers leader Isidor Melamed, who would later hire Kahn to build his first prominent building in Philadelphia, the AFL Medical Services Building on Vine Street (1954–57).

Another small group of postwar commissions sprang from Kahn's involvement with Jewish social service activities. These included the Jewish Community Center of New Haven (discussed in 1948 and designed in 1950) and a place on the team that went to Palestine in 1949 to advise on emergency housing. The trip to Israel gave Kahn a chance to revisit Paris, and it also enabled him to return to the problems of prefabrication, an area of concern that he had ceded to Stonorov since their partnership. For Israel he proposed houses assembled from parabolic concrete sections, and, with the overconfidence that was to characterize many of his large, later projects, he exhorted the new settlers to "Turn the Building Emergency into a Major Industry" and make their homeland "the center of Building Fabrication of the Near East" (fig. 28).[81]

Of all these idealistic projects, the one that perhaps best captures the hopeful spirit of the time was the playground Kahn designed and built in 1946–47 for the Western Home

26. *Philadelphia Building at Unity House, Forest Park, Pa., 1945–47. End elevation.*
27. *Memorial Playground, Western Home for Children, Philadelphia, Pa., 1946–47. Axonometric. Inscribed Louis I. Kahn '46.*
28. *Jewish Agency for Palestine Emergency Housing, Israel, 1949. Perspective (detail of sheet). Inscribed Lou K.*
29. *Model furniture store for Pittsburgh Plate Glass, 1944. Perspective. Inscribed Lou K '44.*

for Children, an orphanage (fig. 27). It was located just
around the corner from the Graphic Sketch Club, where he
had spent so many boyhood Saturdays. His design possessed
all the happy clichés of the era: its play yard perimeter was
defined by jaunty angles and surrounded by a curving
walkway, there was an outdoor hearth sheltered by a
horizontal roof slab, and in the rear corner stood a
biomorphic concrete "fun sculpture" whose shapes were
echoed in a mural on the wall of an adjacent building. It
must have seemed perfectly complete when the pleased
sponsor told Kahn that he had seen "little Brownie Scouts
hopping gleefully around your fireplace."[82] In those years
Kahn was himself the new father of a daughter, Sue Ann.

In addition to doing community and socially oriented work
during the mid-forties, like many American architects
Stonorov and Kahn joined in the discussion of the future of
more mundane architectural forms—the miscellany of useful
buildings that would shape postwar America. They
produced imaginary designs for a number of these pragmatic
types, many of which were sponsored by the architectural
magazines, hungry to fill pages during the war and, like
everyone, eager to look beyond its privations.

Architectural Forum, which had followed Kahn's housing
work closely, invited him to submit a design for their "New
House 194X" feature, to appear in September 1942. With its
announced emphasis on prefabrication, this project
interested both Stonorov and Kahn, but work on Willow
Run kept them from meeting the deadline.[83] They were
luckier in making their submission for another "194X"
project, sponsored by *Forum* in 1943, when they were
among those invited to design an array of buildings for a
medium-size postwar city. Their assignment was a 200-room
hotel, for which they proposed a 13-story slab with
aluminum sunshades, marble cladding, and "plastic exterior
veneer" on all other surfaces.[84] Inside, everything was also
up-to-date: the public spaces were full of curved and
diagonal walls, placed with studied casualness, and the guest
rooms were equipped with molded plywood furniture and
smoothly curved, prefabricated bathroom units. This was
also the sleek vocabulary for the model glass-fronted
furniture and shoe stores they designed in 1944 for a
Pittsburgh Plate Glass publication (fig. 29).[85]

The largest concentration of this kind of speculative
architecture was in the design of houses—the postwar home
of the GI—for which the need was reckoned to be enormous.
Stonorov and Kahn applied themselves assiduously to the
"Design for Post-war Living" competition, sponsored by

27

28

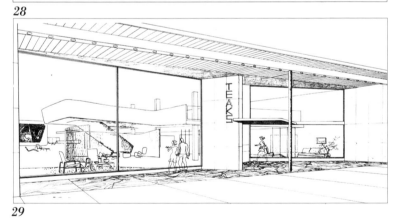

29

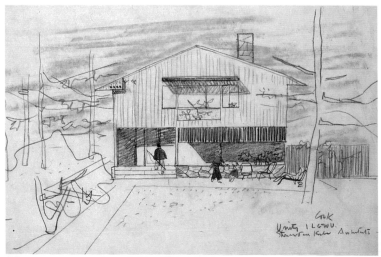

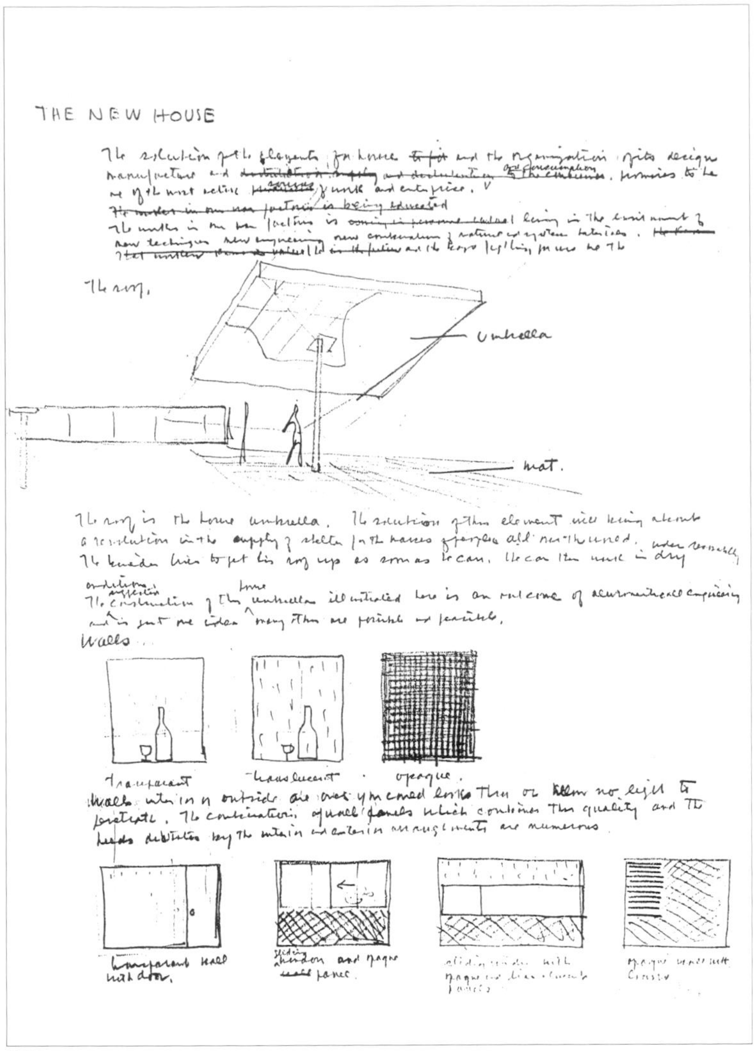
THE NEW HOUSE
umbrella
mat.
Walls
transparent
translucent
opaque
30

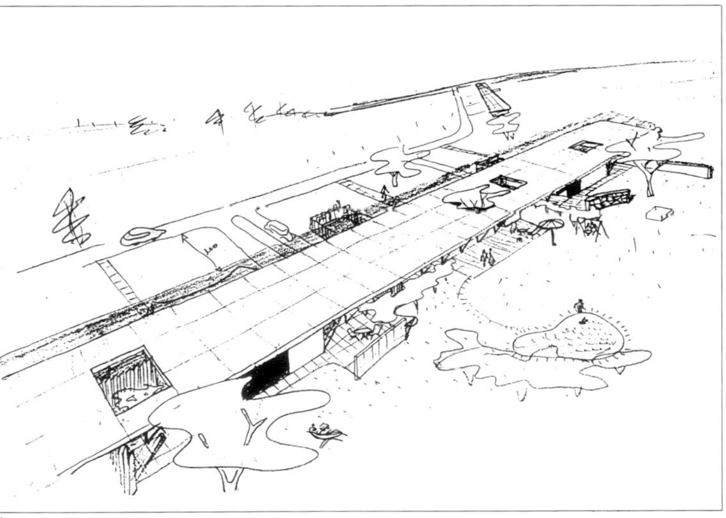
31

California Arts and Architecture in the spring of 1943. Their unsuccessful entry was a single-family version of the ground-freed house, developed directly out of their war housing work.[86]

Much more ambitious was the Parasol House system they devised in 1944 at the request of Hans Knoll, the furniture manufacturer. He invited them and six other architectural firms to join a "planning unit," set up to study the needs of contemporary households and devise new "equipment for living"—essentially furniture and appliances—for his clients to manufacture.[87] These were then to be placed within an ideal architectural environment. Kahn and Stonorov submitted drawings for molded plywood cabinets, a prefabricated stair, and bathroom and kitchen units—including the Thermostore refrigerator they had already mocked up for Gimbels department store in 1942–43.[88] But they put most of their effort into the architecture. Their proposed houses were defined by a roofing system that consisted of square slabs (apparently of steel construction) held aloft on slender columns (fig. 30). These parasol-like units were then stacked to make two-story houses or assembled to form the sheltering canopy for great strips of one-story row houses (fig. 31). Beneath this covering, with its insistent rational gridding, non-load-bearing walls were placed with the contrasting, somewhat cranky angularity that Kahn seems to have adopted as a badge of his freedom from the limitations of war housing (fig. 32). While many precedents for this form of free planning existed, including Le Corbusier's Dom-ino-type buildings and Mies van der Rohe's courtyard houses, and while the umbrella roof was predated by Wright's lily-pad columns for the Johnson Wax Administration Building, the synthesis of these elements was fresh and unencumbered by any obvious sense of quotation. Unfortunately, the architects' ambitions outpaced Knoll's, and they were not asked to develop any of their ideas further.

The last of these postwar-oriented house projects was commissioned in August 1945, ten days after VJ Day, when Stonorov was informed by Libbey-Owens-Ford Glass Company that he had been selected by a jury to design the Pennsylvania house in their forty-eight-state solar house program.[89] The design work was carried out by Kahn, assisted by Anne Griswold Tyng (b. 1920), a recent graduate of Gropius's Harvard program who had just joined the office.[90] Most of the other designers produced conventional houses with increased glazing toward the south, but Kahn and Tyng took the solar heating issue more seriously. During the spring of 1946 they created a trapezoidal house plan that

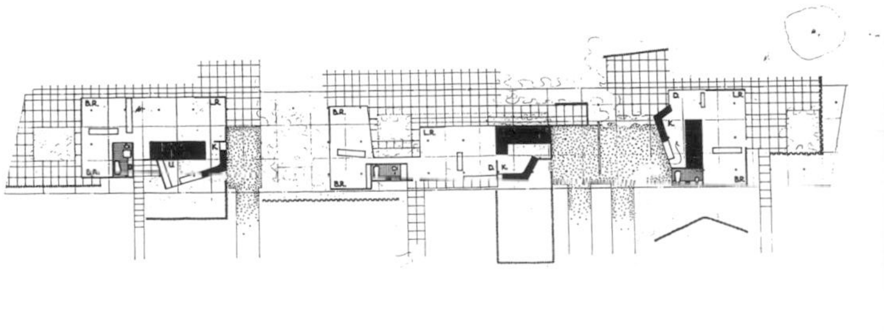

33

34

35

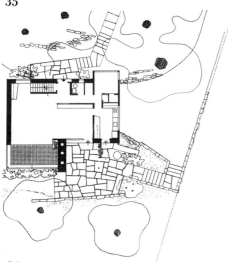

36

carefully oriented three of its facades to face the sun in its arcing passage across the sky (fig. 33).

More significant probably than the solar house design itself was the destructive effect it had on the partnership of Stonorov and Kahn. Libbey-Owens-Ford had commissioned the house for use in a book, and in January 1947, with publication approaching, they telegrammed Stonorov to inquire how the design should be credited. His reply, requesting that the byline "carry both our names," seems to have roused Kahn to anger. But while the answer that Kahn rushed off began "I do not agree with the general tone of Mr. Stonorov's telegram," he concluded by apparently asking for the same thing: shared credit.[91] In the end, the Pennsylvania solar house was published as the work of "Oscar Stonorov and Louis I. Kahn Architects," but the nasty tone of this now obscure argument reflected the rift that had opened between two contrary personalities.[92] With little housing work being done, the teaming of Stonorov's political acumen with Kahn's increasingly independent design sense had less to recommend it. They agreed to split amicably, dividing up the small number of commissions then under way, and on March 4, 1947, the movers transported Stonorov's papers to the Broad Street Station Building while Kahn moved to 1728 Spruce Street, a town house where George Howe also kept a small office.[93] Kahn, just turned forty-six, was now on his own.

The House
For the next few years the backbone of Kahn's work was single-family houses, which in some ways fulfilled the promise of the "194X" projects. They also reestablished the trajectory he had set for his practice on the eve of the war, when he had built a small house for his longtime friend Jesse Oser and his wife, Ruth (figs. 35, 36).[94] While the Oser house was one of Kahn's first independent commissions, it was a confident design, reflecting the extensive experience he had amassed since graduating from architecture school in 1924. It is also clear that in 1940, when the Oser house was designed, Kahn had come under the powerful influence of George Howe, whom he was about to join in a partnership to build wartime public housing. Although the Osers had limited funds, Kahn worked wonders to imitate for them the effect of Howe's great house of 1932–34 for William Stix Wasserman, which had been given the evocative modernist name Square Shadows (fig. 34). Kahn's homage to Howe can be seen in the modern steel casements—tugged to the corners of the facades—the projecting horizontal roof slabs, the staggering of exterior wall planes (achieved despite the compact plan required by the budget), and the carefully

30. Parasol House, 1944. Page mock-up.
31. Parasol House, 1944. Bird's-eye perspective.
32. Parasol House, 1944. Plan.
33. Pennsylvania Solar House, 1945–47. Perspective from southwest. Inscribed Louis Kahn '46.

34. George Howe. Wasserman house (Square Shadows), Whitemarsh Township, Pa., 1932–34.
35. Oser house, Elkins Park, Pa., 1940–42. Front facade, 1990.
36. Oser house, Elkins Park, Pa., 1940–42. First- and second-floor plans.

contrived juxtaposition of these avant-garde details with the traditional building stone of the region. Inside, beige woodwork of tough gum wood joined sleek built-in furniture in a modernist composition around the hearth, but the fireplace itself was faced with irregular Mercer tiles that bespoke contrasting, Arts and Crafts ideals. This complexity of meaning was characteristic of Howe and much of the best American architecture in this transitional period.

The Oser house was already under construction at the time of Pearl Harbor, and it was completed in 1942 despite wartime shortages. Not so lucky were Louis Broudo and his wife, friends of Esther Kahn's parents, for whom Kahn designed a similar small house for a lot close to the Osers'. Contract drawings and specifications for their house, with its more conservative peaked roof, were just being finished in December 1941 at the time of the Japanese surprise attack, and the project had to be abandoned.[95]

Aside from some renovations, which Kahn disliked cordially, and the imaginary projects sponsored by magazines and manufacturers, there was no more single-family house work for the duration of the war, and wartime, multi-unit housing did not offer the artistic opportunities of even the modest Oser house. But after VJ Day business slowly began to pick up as predicted. First to reach the office, in 1945–46, were several ambitious additions to suburban houses. Stonorov and Kahn added a two-story wing—based on the ground-freed model—to B. A. Bernard's handsome house overlooking French Creek in Kimberton, Bucks County. (This job probably came to them through Stonorov, whose own house was nearby.) They also designed a new, one-story wing for the Ardmore house owned by Lea and Arthur Finkelstein, both radiologists, whom Esther had met fifteen years earlier in her work at the University of Pennsylvania. The Finkelsteins had become close family friends, and, along with Jacob and "Kit" Sherman, the Finkelsteins and Kahns had vacationed together for many summers, including sojourns to Nova Scotia and more sedentary holidays in the house rented by the Finkelsteins at Lake Placid. Kahn could rarely take more than two weeks away from the office, but Esther usually spent a month with the two other couples. The Finkelstein project was the subject of long discussion, including a major redesign in 1948, but nothing was built. The same fate befell the largest of these first postwar house jobs, an enormous one-story wing containing a new dining room, playroom, guest suite, garage, and horse stall that Kahn designed in 1946 for the Baltimore house of Mr. and Mrs. Arthur Hooper (fig. 37). Kahn arranged the new rooms to shelter the backyard within

an architectural ell, a formula that Frank Lloyd Wright had established in his house for Herbert Jacobs (Westmoreland, Wisconsin, 1937) and that Richard Neutra also adopted in his postwar work.

This somewhat desultory rate of work accelerated rapidly after Stonorov and Kahn ended their partnership early in 1947. Over the next eighteen months, Kahn was engaged in the design of five substantial houses, three of which were built. His office staff during this period was very small, with David Wisdom and Anne Tyng being his principal assistants, and the work was shaped by Kahn's close artistic and growing romantic ties with Tyng.

The first of these houses to reach the design phase was a commission from Harry and Emily Ehle. It was brought to Kahn by Abel Sörensen, who had worked in the office during the Kahn-Stonorov partnership and joined the headquarters planning staff of the United Nations on Long Island after the war. In May 1947 Sörensen sketched the plan of an ell-shaped house, wrapped around a large patio, for the Ehles' site in suburban Haverford. This he sent to Kahn, who studied the elevations and imparted more energy to the rather conventional scheme during June, raising a butterfly-roof clerestory over the living room and establishing a vigorous interplay between masonry and wood-framed wall elements.[96] The result was too expensive for the Ehles, and during the first months of 1948 the Kahn office eliminated the garage and maid's quarters and reduced the size of the living room (fig. 40). But this, too, exceeded the budget of the client.

In early 1948, just as the second version of the Ehle house was being worked out, Kahn and Tyng were launching two other house projects. Carried through to quick completion, these departed decisively from the rather lackluster Ehle design, and they were full of the evidence of the two architects' sometimes diverging ideas. The first was a house for Dr. and Mrs. Philip Roche on a site just beyond the northwest boundary of Philadelphia in Conshohocken.[97] The Roche plan pulled all of the living quarters together into a compact rectangle, zoned for sleeping at one end and daytime functions at the other (fig. 41). Tyng was devoted to the planning discipline that she had seen at Harvard, and she seems to have contributed the defining 3'9" modularity of the design, while Kahn's diagonalism reemerged in the broken-backed mountain of chimney that erupted obliquely through the living room wall.[98]

The balance of ideas shifted more decisively toward Tyng in

37. Hooper house addition, Baltimore, Md., 1946. Rear perspective. Inscribed Louis I. Kahn, '46.
38. Weiss house, East Norriton Township, Pa., 1947–50. Front facade, ca. 1950.
39. Weiss house, East Norriton Township, Pa., 1947–50. Plan, ca. 1948.
40. Ehle house, Haverford, Pa., 1947–48. First-floor plan, redrawn 1990.
41. Roche house, Conshohocken, Pa., 1947–49. First-floor plan, redrawn 1990.

38

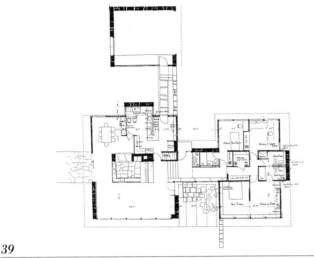

39

40

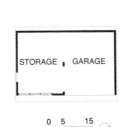

41

the almost exactly contemporary Weiss house, located further west of Philadelphia near Norristown.[99] Its more sharply bifurcated plan, worked out during the first half of 1948, bore the unmistakable impress of the "binuclear" division between daytime and nighttime activity that was associated with the work of Marcel Breuer, one of the leading members of the Harvard faculty during Tyng's study there (fig. 39). The sweeping reverse-pitch roof was also Breueresque, although Kahn had been experimenting with this form throughout the decade (fig. 38). Distinctively Kahn's own was the ingenious system of double-hung windows and shutters, which could be slid up and down to vary the lighting, privacy, and view. He had already sketched a related system of wall panels of varied opacity for the Parasol House, but now it was worked out in the complex detail needed to make it weatherproof and buildable. These designs marked the beginning of his decades-long experiment with the manipulation of natural light.

Kahn insisted that the Weiss house, with its bold use of local stonework and untinted wood, was "contemporary but does not break with tradition."[100] Citing the example of Pennsylvania barns in support of this position, he argued that "the continuity between what was valid yesterday and what is valid today is considered by every thinking architect." Many of his contemporaries did cast an admiring glance toward the past, but for Kahn this was to become an increasingly serious endeavor. When he and Tyng returned to the Weiss house some years after it was completed to paint a mural next to the craggy stone fireplace, they borrowed many of their motifs from the simple architecture of the Pennsylvania countryside. But also evident in the mural were the profiles of the Egyptian pyramids Kahn had visited early in 1951. He had begun to see that great architecture had to be of its own time and imbedded in the deeper historical stratigraphy of human achievement as well.

Kahn designed two other houses in the late forties, beginning both early in the summer of 1948, just after the plan of the Weiss house had been finalized. These houses showed a stronger assertion of Kahn's exuberance. The unbuilt project for Dr. and Mrs. Winslow Tompkins pushed its living room and dining room to the very brink of a precipitous, wooded slope that descended to Wissahickon Creek in Philadelphia (fig. 42). The dining room was cradled in a massive serpentine masonry wall, and the sleeping quarters, conceived as one block in the first plans of June, were split into two staggered units when a final set of finished drawings was made in September.[101]

42

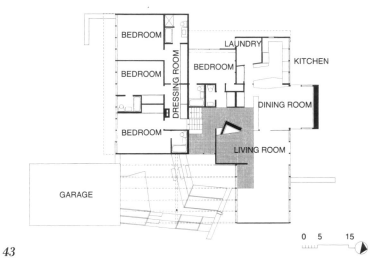

43

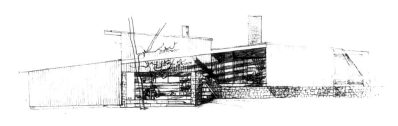

44

42. *Tompkins house,*
Philadelphia, Pa., 1947–49.
First-floor plan, redrawn 1990.
43. *Genel house, Wynnewood,*
Pa., 1948–51. Plan, redrawn
1990.
44. *Genel house, Wynnewood,*
Pa., 1948–51. East elevation,
early 1949. Inscribed Lou K.
45. *Genel house, Wynnewood,*
Pa., 1948–51. Entrance hall
with back of fireplace, ca.
1951.

46. *New wing, Philadelphia*
Psychiatric Hospital,
Philadelphia, Pa., 1944–46.
Perspective. Inscribed
Louis I. Kahn '46.
47. *New wing, Philadelphia*
Psychiatric Hospital,
Philadelphia, Pa., 1944–46.
Second-floor plan.

At the same time, Kahn and Tyng were at work on a house in suburban Wynnewood for Samuel Genel, who had once dated Esther Kahn and whose sister was Esther's classmate and a member of her sorority at the University of Pennsylvania.[102] The first plan in the summer of 1948 was a squat tee, with its stem pointed down a gentle hill that allowed the split-level placement of the garage underneath the bedrooms.[103] As developed during the first months of 1949, the plan grew into a lopsided binuclear arrangement, with the garage relocated downhill in a structure of its own and replaced on the ground floor of the main house by a playroom (fig. 43). An energetic interplay of ramping roof surfaces was introduced at this point, amplifying the effect of the terrain (fig. 44). The most striking component of the plan was the ell of masonry that rose between the living room and the front hall, framing the fireplace. This piece of elemental composition could also be read in elevation, where the marble-clad chimneystack rose in calculated juxtaposition to the brick and wood of the house (fig. 45). Even the exterior masonry was now executed in roughly squared stone, answering to a new sense of order. Kahn's interest in such abstraction can be attributed in part to Anne Tyng's influence and also to the studio work he had seen at Yale, where he had begun teaching in 1947.

The jostling of Kahn's freer planning against Tyng's sense of geometrical order continued in the two buildings he designed and built for the Philadelphia Psychiatric Hospital in 1948–52.[104] This was a project with a long prehistory. In 1937–38 he had studied the possibility of altering several buildings on a site in West Philadelphia for the hospital. In 1939 he had designed an entirely new building for a different site, only to have the client reject his work because of its cost and turn to another architect, with whom the project went ahead.[105] And in 1944–46 he and Stonorov had designed a large addition to that small building.

This third design, initiated during the final year of the war and the first year of peace, paved the way for the work done in 1948–52, but it got off to a slow start. The client was not sure of the program, and Kahn and Stonorov were beginning to be busy with small residential jobs, all of which was very frustrating to Isadore Rosenfield, the hospital design consultant teamed with them for this and the final project. Kahn tried to make light of their harried state in a letter to Rosenfield: "We are going crazy in our own little architectural hospital, doctoring up old buildings, handling our own psychiatric clients, appeasing our erratic and temperamental personnel. It all adds up to fine experience which can be applied to the hospital, so really no time is

45

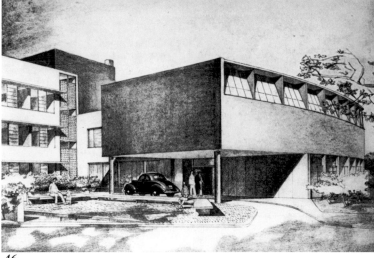

46

lost."[106] Rosenfield was unamused, and throughout their relationship he continued to criticize what he called their "strange and unprofessional conduct."[107]

The design that was worked out during the spring of 1946 provided a vast new ward block, a semidetached convalescent pavilion, and a hammerhead-shaped entrance pavilion with state-of-the-art insulin and electric-shock treatment rooms on its top floor (figs. 46, 47). In the oblique placement of building units across the site, the hospital recalled Kahn's wartime community centers, and it also seemed to reflect the calculated casualness with which the slabs of Alvar Aalto's famous tuberculosis sanatorium were clustered on their wooded hilltop at Paimio, Finland (1928–33). The sanatorium had been included in the 1938 Aalto show at the Museum of Modern Art, and there Kahn also seems to have encountered the auditorium of Aalto's Viipuri library, which he used as an example of the ideal neighborhood meeting room in the second Revere Copper pamphlet. But regardless of its sophistication, this design, too, was rejected because of its cost.

The Philadelphia Psychiatric Hospital was a member of the Federation of Jewish Charities, and Kahn's long work on the commission, despite its rocky moments, helped to cement his relationship in those circles. He also established a warm if combative friendship with Samuel Radbill, the president of the hospital board. During the time of the 1944–46 design, Kahn was simultaneously at work on alterations to the offices of the Radbill Oil Company and overseeing the installation of air-conditioning and the modernization of a bathroom in Radbill's house in Merion. The latter was subject to delays due to Kahn's increasingly famous perfectionism and procrastination, and Radbill, in frustration, canceled part of the work.[108]

The underlying strength of Kahn's relationship with his clients was sufficient for him to be called back in 1948 to direct the work that was finally executed for the hospital. Designed in 1949, this scheme consisted of a three-story, crook-necked block, attached at its bend to the existing hospital to create a Y-shaped building, and a separate, one-story auditorium and occupational therapy building. The new entrance facade of the Radbill Building, as the larger unit was named, was a serene modular composition, rendered in slate and stratified by horizontal sunshades (fig. 48). These shades were regularly perforated by what appeared to be ordinary flue tiles, but the terra-cotta inserts were actually custom-made. The entrance itself was sheltered by a triangular canopy—a piece of abstract collage

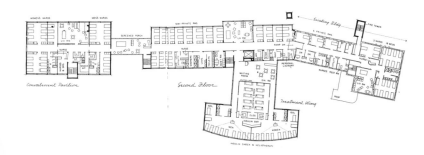

47

suggested by Anne Tyng.[109] The occupational therapy building, named the Pincus Building in honor of a major donor, was a simple structure whose flat roof was supported on exposed steel trusses (fig. 49). It employed a double-hung window/shutter system like that just devised for the Weiss house, allowing the careful adjustment of lighting and privacy.

Monumentality

Although the psychiatric hospital was Kahn's largest building to date and one with an important public face, it was essentially private and residential in character. It did not provide a testing ground for a final facet of the future-oriented speculation that had occupied him during the war. This was the question of how modern architecture, whose accomplishments in the prewar period had been concentrated in housing projects and houses, could embody public or institutional values and advance the larger aspirations of a human community. In the vocabulary of the day, how could modern architecture achieve "monumentality"?

Kahn's own work was a mirror of the problem he perceived. Since working for Cret and Zantzinger—and since giving up their modernized classical vocabulary—Kahn had devoted virtually all his energy to housing. He had spent years making, or trying to make, functional residential architecture, and, like George Howe, he had come to know the artistic limitations of functionalism, and to see that few transcendent ideas could be expressed with that vocabulary. Accordingly, as the end of the war approached and Kahn looked ahead to projects such as the United Nations that would demand distinctive treatment, he began to wonder aloud about the possibility of redirecting the course of modern architecture. This was a question that arose simultaneously in the minds of many during the war, and it had reached a kind of intellectual flash point by 1943, when the architectural historian Sigfried Giedion (whose *Space, Time and Architecture* had appeared in 1941), the architect José Luis Sert, and the painter Fernand Léger met in New York. They had each been invited to contribute to a publication planned by the pioneering American Abstract Artists, and they agreed that they should jointly address the fact that modernists in all media had achieved little outside the realm of domestic architecture and private art. What was needed was a "new monumentality," they decided, one capable of satisfying "the eternal demand of the people for translation of their collective force into symbols."[110] Giedion became a tireless champion of this idea, speaking on the subject on both sides of the Atlantic, and his 1946 lecture in

48

49

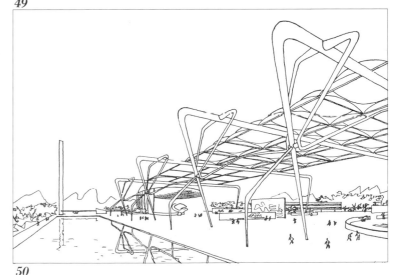

50

48. *Radbill Building, Philadelphia Psychiatric Hospital, Philadelphia, Pa., 1948–54. Front facade, ca. 1954 (entrance canopy now removed).*
49. *Pincus Building, Philadelphia Psychiatric Hospital, Philadelphia, Pa., 1948–54.*
50. *Model civic center illustrating "monumentality," 1944.*

London sparked the *Architectural Review* to take up the issue, eventually hosting a symposium and becoming one of the staunchest advocates of this redirection of modern design.[111]

When the planned publication by the American Abstract Artists failed to materialize, Giedion placed his essay in a volume assembled by Paul Zucker in 1944. This had an entire section called "The Problem of a New Monumentality," and it was here that Kahn also published his first extended theoretical paper, entitled simply "Monumentality."

Giedion and Kahn approached the question from opposite points of view. Whereas the Swiss scholar argued that the search for "emotional expression" demanded a recognition that "architecture is not exclusively concerned with construction," Kahn began by proclaiming that "monumentality in architecture may be defined as a quality, a spiritual quality inherent in a structure which conveys the feeling of its eternity, that it cannot be added to or changed."[112] Moreover, while Giedion lamented that the abusive eclecticism of the nineteenth century had poisoned the well of historical examples for the modern architect, Kahn forthrightly accepted the usefulness of history. The "monumental structures of the past," he wrote, "have the common characteristics of greatness upon which the buildings of our future must, in one sense or another, rely."[113]

In his twin fascination with structure and history, Kahn was returning to principles that he had been taught at the University of Pennsylvania. His teacher Paul Cret's philosophy had been developed on the side of the École des Beaux-Arts that favored the strong French tradition of structural rationalism, and Cret had also believed unswervingly that modern architecture could be made without rejecting the past.

What Kahn now proposed was that the starting point for monumental architecture could be discovered in history and then made modern by the application of new technology. In particular, he argued that the "spiritual quality" needed by monumental buildings was to be sought first in the "structural skeleton" of the Gothic and in the Roman dome, vault, and arch—forms whose influence had "etched itself in deep furrows across the pages of architectural history."[114] These forms were now to be modernized by the introduction of the steel frame. Kahn, who had taken a course in steel ship design in 1942, observed that "Beauvais cathedral

needed the steel we have," and he recommended special attention to the use of welded tubular construction, curved to imitate the "graceful forms which the stress diagrams indicated."[115] Thus would "the ribs, vaults, domes, buttresses come back again only to enclose space in a more generous, far simpler way and in the hands of our present masters of building in a more emotionally stirring way."[116] Kahn predicted that new materials would lead the modern architect to "the adventures of unexplored places."[117]

Despite the talk of Roman architecture, Kahn's recipe produced a kind of modernized Gothic. This was clearly prefigured by the work of Eugène-Emmanuel Viollet-le-Duc, whose Gothic rationalism had been admired in Cret's circle at the École, and it was also related to the analytical drawings of structure published by Auguste Choisy, another favorite of Cret's (see fig. 55). Kahn used Choisy's analysis of Beauvais as an illustration of his argument. Supporting Kahn's text were his own sketches for an urban cultural center, with a theater and a museum framed by the kind of sinuous steel skeleton he recommended (fig. 50).

This ferrous medievalism seems unrelated to the great masonry buildings, with their classical overtones, that were to dominate Kahn's mature work. But by then he had been diverted: the steel shortage of the postwar period helped to turn him back toward brick and concrete, and during that time he also rediscovered the power of ancient Rome at first hand. But although transmogrified, history and structure were to remain Kahn's watchwords.

The years immediately after the end of the war offered a few important opportunities for Kahn to develop this new vocabulary for monumental architecture. Together with Stonorov, he was appointed in October 1946 to the team of architects charged by the City Planning Commission with the creation of a master plan for the vast tract of central Philadelphia called the "Triangle" (see pp. 304–6). This was bordered on its three sides by the infamous "Chinese Wall" (the soon-to-be-demolished viaduct that had brought the Pennsylvania Railroad into the very heart of the city), the Schuylkill River (the western boundary of Center City), and Philadelphia's City Beautiful boulevard, the Benjamin Franklin Parkway (see fig. 408). Kahn provided the planning team with illustrations for their report, issued in January 1948, and he made some of the drawings that guided the builders of an enormous model of Philadelphia that was created for the "Better Philadelphia" exhibition at Gimbels Department Store in October 1947. The model contrasted conditions before and after the implementation of the master plan by means of large panels that flipped over dramatically to reveal the city of the future (fig. 51). It was the centerpiece of the exhibition and exceedingly popular, and the fact that Stonorov (who had already done a good deal of remodeling work for Gimbels) shunted Kahn aside in order to coordinate the show himself seems to have contributed to their falling-out. Most of the buildings drawn by Kahn—office blocks, apartment buildings, and low-rise cultural institutions alike—took the by then familiar form of the Le Corbusian prism supported on *pilotis* (figs. 52, 53). There was, however, some "monumental" use of steel in a sports arena suspended beneath four parabolic arches, and several large pieces of biomorphic sculpture embodied the "graceful forms" Kahn had recommended in 1944.

A simultaneous project with explicitly monumental content was Kahn's entry in the first phase of the Jefferson National Expansion Memorial competition, which led ultimately to the construction of Eero Saarinen's "Gateway Arch" in St. Louis. Kahn's design of 1947 would have covered both banks of the Mississippi River with a mixture of horizontally and vertically oriented slabs set atop an elaborate system of railroad and highway connections. There was to be more of the steel architecture foreseen in 1944, most notably a vast open-plan Laboratory of Education containing exhibition galleries and a theater and covered by a raking steel-frame roof. Kahn was not, however, selected to continue in the second phase of the competition, and this was a keen disappointment. Luckily, he began teaching at Yale in the same week the results were announced.

Yale

Kahn had actually been teaching for years; the members of the Architectural Research Group had hung on his words, and the large staffs assembled for Jersey Homesteads and the wartime housing projects had been treated like the malleable young artists they were. Before the fall of 1947, however, Kahn's natural talents as a teacher had not been formally employed. He had been invited a year earlier to teach at Harvard, then by far the leading school for modern architecture, but he turned down the appointment, largely because he could not bear to leave his native Philadelphia.[118] Yale was a different matter. Kahn was to be one of the visiting critics—they were the mainstay of studio instruction at Yale—with responsibilities limited to two days a week. That meant he could commute to New Haven by train. He accepted, and Yale became the forum for the ideas he had not yet been able to convert into real architecture.

Yale was an exciting place in 1947 (fig. 54).[119] A new dean,

51

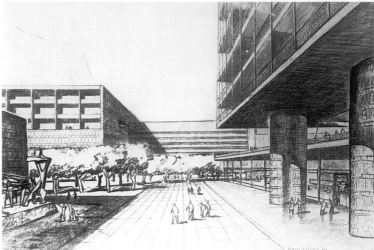

52

53

51. *Philadelphia model from the exhibition "A Better Philadelphia Within Your Grasp," Gimbels Department Store, Philadelphia, Pa., 1947.*
52. *Triangle Redevelopment Project, Philadelphia, Pa., 1946–48. Perspective of Civic Center. Inscribed Louis I. Kahn '47.*
53. *Triangle Redevelopment Project, Philadelphia, Pa., 1946–48. Bird's-eye perspective of Schuylkill River apartment buildings. Inscribed Louis I. Kahn '47.*
54. *Christmas card showing Kahn at Yale, by David Wisdom, 1947.*

Charles Sawyer, had just come on board in the summer before Kahn began to teach, and together with architecture chairman Harold Hauf he was working to consolidate the decisive turn toward modernism that had begun under Wallace Harrison, the chief critic in 1939–42. This was now being continued under Edward Durell Stone, who held the same position. Kahn undoubtedly came to their attention because of his well-published war work and his highly visible role in the American Society of Planners and Architects. At the same time, Sawyer had offered an associate deanship to Holmes Perkins, another prominent member of the ASPA, but Perkins had elected to remain with Gropius at Harvard.[120]

Kahn's appointment at Yale in the fall semester of 1947 was moved up because of the delayed arrival of another visiting critic, Oscar Niemeyer, the already renowned Brazilian disciple of Le Corbusier whose Communist sympathies had aroused the suspicions of immigration officials. Like most practicing architects who are part-time teachers, Kahn designed many of his studio problems to mirror his own work, and during his first stint he assigned a suburban shopping center like the one for which he was serving as a consultant in Greenbelt, Maryland.[121] Despite its relevance to postwar conditions, this was probably not a very challenging project for the Yale students, but Kahn's talent for teaching was evident, and Hauf asked him to return. He taught in both semesters in 1948–49 and took over the duties of coordinating the visiting critics from Stone. Among the visitors that year were Hugh Stubbins, Pietro Belluschi, and Eero Saarinen.

In his second year at Yale, Kahn was also put in charge of realizing Sawyer's favorite educational innovation, the "collaborative problem," for which student architects, painters, and sculptors were assembled into teams. Collaboration per se was also one of the hallmarks of Gropius's teaching at Harvard, where he organized his own private practice as The Architects' Collaborative in 1946. But teaming up with painters and sculptors was not usually attempted at Harvard, which had no real fine arts program. While such cooperation was achieved at specialized art schools like Cranbrook, the Yale system was rightly recognized as distinctive among university programs.

In the fall of 1948 the collaborative problem was the design of an exhibition hall for an imagined headquarters of UNESCO, the United Nations Educational, Scientific, and Cultural Organization.[122] Kahn located the project in Philadelphia's Fairmount Park, on the site he had promoted

for the entire UN two years earlier. (During the same semester he presented an advanced design problem that was even more directly related to his own practice—a suburban residence modeled, down to the client biography and street address, on the Genel house.[123]) Leaving the creation of a huge UNESCO mural to the painters and the treatment of "the vertical circulation element" (i.e., stairway) to the sculptors, he made the team architects responsible for the master plan and for engineering the vast exhibition hall— 200,000 unobstructed square feet beneath an 80-foot ceiling. Here was a chance to see his notions of monumentality fulfilled, for he specified that the skeleton frame of the exhibition hall be left undisguised. Several of the teams devised structures suspended on steel cable, while others cantilevered stupendous trusses over the hall. The project attracted national attention.[124]

Kahn's teaching in the spring semester of 1949 was interrupted by his trip to Israel. But his administrative involvement increased, and he championed the appointment of his old friend George Howe as chairman of architecture when Hauf resigned to become editor of *Architectural Record*. After Sawyer wired Yale's offer to Howe, who was then newly in love and very comfortably ensconced as resident architect at the American Academy in Rome, Kahn wrote his own powerful letter. "George, the school needs your personality and your kind of leadership," Kahn entreated, and he described the attractions of Yale:

The school is progressive, and in the state of constant change and development. There is no dictation from above. Everyone seems to like the results although there is no particular order or ideology followed. You can make the school what you want it to be and Ed [Stone] Chris [Tunnard, head of city planning] and I who know you best feel that you can give it the guidance which would continue the existing free spirit and better the results, thru your experience culture and wisdom.[125]

Howe accepted, agreeing to take up his new responsibilities in January 1950.

At the same time, Kahn and Sawyer convinced the former Bauhaus painter Joseph Albers (1888–1976), who had transplanted many Bauhaus ideals to America, to come as a visiting critic for the collaborative project in the fall of 1949. This time the program was an "Idea Center for Plastics," intended to serve the design staff of a manufacturer.[126] Albers liked Yale, and Sawyer, strongly supported by Kahn, liked him. They arranged for him to join the faculty permanently in the fall of 1950 as head of a newly organized department of design, subsuming and radicalizing the old

programs in painting and sculpture. Although Sawyer did not entirely succeed in creating what he had hoped would be a broad collaborative environment, framed by architecture under Howe and design under Albers, the almost simultaneous appointment of two artists of such high caliber moved Yale to the forefront of American art.

Albers had commenced the painstaking chromatic investigations of his "Homage to the Square" series just before his first teaching at Yale, and Kahn was evidently impressed. The painter's work may have helped to spark his own exploration of the underlying order of things, and Albers' aphoristic poems may also have shaped Kahn's later word compositions. In a typical poem Albers proclaimed:

To design is
to plan and to organize, to order, to relate and to control
in short it embraces
all means opposing disorder and accident.
Therefore it signifies
a human need
and qualifies man's
thinking and doing.[127]

When Kahn was designing a wall hanging for his First Unitarian Church in Rochester, New York, he turned to Albers's wife, Anni, a famous weaver, for its execution.

Architecture students did not study directly with Albers, however. For first- and second-year students (who were in the third and fourth years of the combined B.A./B.Arch. program), Howe created a separate basic design studio, headed by the almost mystical Eugene Nalle. Nalle's emphasis on personal discovery and on sensitivity to materials recalled the teaching of Johannes Itten during the earliest years of the Weimar Bauhaus. In the first volume of *Perspecta*, the Yale-based journal that Howe launched in 1952 as a vehicle for architectural debate, Nalle explicated his philosophy in typically opaque terms:

"Whole Design" in architecture, with its irrational complex yet deep roots of personal discipline, demands an extremely broad and viable outlook. It must encompass intuitive sensibility to the immediate situation observable in short range fact; this must be combined with a "moral behavior" (in the largest sense of the word) beyond egocentric sentimentality which demands a continual intellectual wrestling with theory—a philosophic study of relationships between the inner and outer worlds of reality.[128]

Kahn, who had his own streak of obscurantism, tolerated Nalle, but he concentrated with Howe on overseeing the advanced end of the program, where the established Yale model of visiting critics was continued. Philip Johnson and Buckminster Fuller were prominent visitors, and they were joined on juries by members of an art history faculty, notably Vincent Scully, who took their studio obligations seriously. Scully's passion for making students see the patterns of intention within the art of all periods served as a refreshing antidote to the kind of historical oblivion in which many young architects believed that modern architecture had to be created. This, of course, was entirely in keeping with Kahn's conviction about the necessity of history, and he and Scully became good friends. Yale students, who had this panoply of ideas before them, were watching the beginning of a new era in architecture.

Howe faced mandatory retirement at the end of the fall semester of 1953, and he may have considered Kahn as his own successor, but the chairmanship passed instead to Paul Schweikher, who had been an effective visiting critic. Schweikher lacked Howe's ability to keep a stable of visitors happy while ensuring that Nalle was properly appreciated by his sometimes jaundiced students. Kahn was uncomfortable under the new regime, and he quit in the spring of 1955. The architectural accrediting board smelled the blood of faculty dissension in the water, and it threatened loss of accreditation and put Yale on probation in 1955–56. Schweikher and Sawyer were compelled to resign.

Scully was among those who convinced Yale president Whitney Griswold to invite Kahn to become chairman in 1956, and Kahn was sorely tempted.[129] But he recognized that it was a decision that would keep him from at last expanding his architectural practice to match the size of his reputation as a teacher. Although he returned as a visiting critic in Yale's new master's program in the late fifties, he turned down the chairmanship. In a sense it was Yale itself that convinced him to reject the very position that it now offered, for the university had also given him the first great commission of his career, the Yale Art Gallery extension (1951–53). The enthusiasm for his built work that had begun with the completion of the new gallery gave Kahn the courage to say no.

D.B.B.

Notes

1. Details of Kahn's early life recounted by Esther I. Kahn, interview with Alessandra Latour, May 5, 1982, in *Louis I. Kahn: L'uomo, il maestro*, ed. Latour (Rome: Edizioni Kappa, 1986), 15–28; and interview with David B. Brownlee, April 27, 1990.

2. James Liberty Tadd, *New Methods in Education: Art, Real Manual Training, Nature Study* (Springfield, Mass., and New York: Orange Judd Company, 1898); Public Industrial Art School, *Statement of the Object of the School by the Director* (Philadelphia: Devine Publishing Company, 1904).

3. E. Kahn, interview with Brownlee. Kahn's text for Fleisher Memorial annual report, December 4, 1973, "Samuel S. Fleisher Art Memorial," Box LIK 45, Louis I. Kahn Collection, University of Pennsylvania and Pennsylvania Historical and Museum Commission, Philadelphia (hereafter cited as Kahn Collection).

4. Patricia McLaughlin, "'How'm I Doing, Corbusier?' An Interview with Louis Kahn," *Pennsylvania Gazette* 71 (December 1972): 19.

5. Quoted in, e.g., Vincent J. Scully, *Louis I. Kahn* (New York: George Braziller, 1962), 12.

6. Cret, "Modern Architecture," lecture presented to the T-Square Club, Philadelphia, October 25, 1923, Box 16, Cret Papers, Special Collections, Van Pelt Library, University of Pennsylvania. See also David B. Brownlee, *Building the City Beautiful: The Benjamin Franklin Parkway and the Philadelphia Museum of Art* (Philadelphia: Philadelphia Museum of Art, 1989), 8–12.

7. Ann L. Strong and George E. Thomas, *The Book of the School: 100 Years* (Philadelphia: Graduate School of Fine Arts, University of Pennsylvania, 1990), 34–36.

8. Kahn's college transcript, "Passport," Box LIK 57, Kahn Collection.

9. "Beaux-Arts Institute of Design," *American Architect* 125 (February 27, 1924): 207–10; 125 (April 9, 1924): 363–68; 125 (May 7, 1924): 443–46; 126 (September 24, 1924): 295–98.

10. Cret, "Modernists and Conservatives," lecture presented to the T-Square Club, Philadelphia, November 19, 1927, Box 16, Cret Papers, Special Collections, Van Pelt Library, University of Pennsylvania.

11. "Kahn on Beaux-Arts Training," ed. William Jordy, *Architectural Review* 155 (June 1974): 332.

12. Ibid.

13. John W. Skinner, "The Sesqui-Centennial Exposition, Philadelphia," *Architectural Record* 60 (July 1926): 1–17; John Molitor, "How the Sesqui-Centennial was Designed," *American Architect* 130 (November 5, 1926): 377–82.

14. "News of the World Told in Pictures," *Philadelphia Inquirer*, October 19, 1925, 15. For the doubts, see William H. Laird, "Records of Consulting Practice," vol. 12, Perkins Library, Fine Arts Library, University of Pennsylvania.

15. Passport, unmarked file, Box LIK 63, Kahn Collection.

16. Kahn, interview with Jaime Mehta, October 22, 1973, in *What Will Be Has Always Been: The Words of Louis I. Kahn*, ed. Richard Saul Wurman (New York: Access Press and Rizzoli, 1986), 225.

17. Job application questionnaire, December 30, 1949, "Housing Projects—Requests for Job," Box LIK 62, Kahn Collection.

18. Kahn's Italian itinerary may be reconstructed on the basis of his travel sketches. See: Kahn, "Pencil Drawings," *Architecture* 63 (January 1931): 15–17; Kahn, "The Value and Aim in Sketching," *T-Square Club Journal* 1 (May 1931): 18–21; Pennsylvania Academy of the Fine Arts, *The Travel Sketches of Louis I. Kahn* (Philadelphia: Pennsylvania Academy of the Fine Arts, 1978); and Jan Hochstim, *The Paintings and Sketches of Louis I. Kahn* (New York: Rizzoli, 1991).

19. Kahn, "Value and Aim," 21.

20. Scully, *Kahn*, 13.

21. Letter, Kahn to architectural fellows, American Academy in Rome, March 1, 1951, "Rome 1951," Box LIK 61, Kahn Collection.

22. Courtship recounted by E. Kahn, interview with Latour, 19–23; and interview with Brownlee.

23. The journal changed its name twice: to *T-Square* in January 1932, and to *Shelter* in April 1932. *Shelter* was briefly revived in New York, March 1938–April 1939.

24. Wisdom, interview with David B. Brownlee, David G. De Long, and Peter S. Reed, July 5, 1990.

25. Scully, *Kahn*, 15.

26. Piero Santostefano, *Le Mackley Houses di Kastner e Stonorov a Philadelphia, 1931–1935* (Rome: Officina Edizioni, 1982); Richard Pommer, "The Architecture of Urban Housing in the United States during the Early 1930s," *Journal of the Society of Architectural Historians* 37 (December 1978): 235–64.

27. "Slum Elimination Project on Display," *Philadelphia Record*, April 23, 1933, F3; "Prepare Plan for Slum Modernizing," *Philadelphia Inquirer*, April 23, 1933, W9; "Slum Modernizing Plan Unique Here," *Philadelphia Inquirer*, April 30, 1933, W11; "Air Castles Rise in 'Clinic,'" *Philadelphia Record*, May 14, 1934, 1.

28. Bernard J. Newman, "Northeast Philadelphia Housing Corporation," in *Housing in Philadelphia, 1933* (Philadelphia: Philadelphia Housing Association, 1934), 22–23; Pommer, "Urban Housing," 244–45.

29. St. Katherine's Village report, typescript, unmarked file, Box LIK 68, Kahn Collection; site plan (dated December 12, 1935), partial site plan (dated November 22, 1935), and first-floor plan for house type 2A, Magaziner Papers, Athenaeum of Philadelphia.

30. Ralph H. Danhof, "Jersey Homesteads," in *A Place on Earth: A Critical Appraisal of Subsistence Homesteads*, ed. Russell Lord and Paul H. Johnstone (Washington, D.C.: United States Department of Agriculture, Bureau of Agricultural Economics, 1942), 136–61; Paul Conkin, *Tomorrow a New World: The New Deal Community Program* (Ithaca, N.Y.: Cornell University Press, 1959), 256–76; Edwin Rosskam, *Roosevelt, New Jersey: Big Dreams in a Small Town and What Time Did to Them* (New York: Grossman Publishers, 1972); Gail Hunton, "National Register of Historic Places Inventory—Nomination Form . . . Jersey Homesteads," February 1983.

31. Drawings of the original designs, February–May 1935, by Lawrence and Callander, architects, "Hightstown N.J.," Box 35, Kastner Papers, American Heritage Center, University of Wyoming, Laramie (hereafter cited as Kastner Papers).

32. Noble autobiography, August 15, 1960, "Fellowships Jury of Fellows," Box LIK 57, Kahn Collection.

33. Weekly drafting room reports, December 21, 1935–May 23, 1936, notebook "11.(1938)," Box 45, Kastner Papers; personal history statement, January 9, 1939, "Housing," Box LIK 62, Kahn Collection.

34. Credit was assigned to H.D.M. [Michaelson or Martin?] for type A, to C.F.W[agner] for type B, to S.A.K[aufman] for type C, to L.H.M. [Michaelson or Martin?] for type E; photographs of lost drawings, "Hightstown, N.J.," Box 26, Kastner Papers.

35. Lewis Mumford, "The Sky Line: Houses and Fairs," *New Yorker*, June 20, 1936, 31.

36. "Tugwell Hands Out $1,800,000 for N.J. 'Commune,'" *Philadelphia Inquirer*, May 7, 1936, 1, 38.

37. Other designs, drawings 70.1, 70.3–7, "Hightstown School," Box LIK 62, Kahn Collection.

38. Blueprints of school as built, May 21–September 11, 1937, Box 25, Kastner Papers; "Schools: Community Building, Jersey Homesteads,

Hightstown, N.J., Alfred Kastner, Architect," *Architectural Forum* 68 (March 1938): 227–30.

39. "Steelox Details," "Misc II," "Philadelphia Housing Authority," Box LIK 68, Kahn Collection.

40. Timothy L. McDonnell, *The Wagner Housing Act: A Case Study of the Legislative Process* (Chicago: Loyola University Press, 1957).

41. For the story of twentieth-century housing in Philadelphia, see John F. Bauman, *Public Housing, Race and Renewal: Urban Planning in Philadelphia, 1920–1974* (Philadelphia: Temple University Press, 1987).

42. Elizabeth Mock, "What About Competitions," *Shelter* 3 (November 1938): 26–29.

43. "Housing Work of Kenneth Day," typescript, "Misc," Box LIK 63, Kahn Collection; "Lost: $19,000,000 for 3451 Dwellings," *Building Homes in Philadelphia: Report of the Philadelphia Housing Authority* (July 1, 1939–June 30, 1941), 36–37.

44. Bauman, *Public Housing*, 46.

45. Ibid.

46. "U.S.H.A. City of Tomorrow: Exhibit for New York World's Fair. Museum of Modern Art," Box LIK 68, Kahn Collection; Peter S. Reed, "Toward Form: Louis I. Kahn's Urban Designs for Philadelphia, 1939–1962" (Ph.D. diss., University of Pennsylvania, 1989), 13–35.

47. "City Wide Meeting," Box LIK 34, Kahn Collection.

48. Andrew Weinstein, "Americanizing Modernism: Housing by Louis I. Kahn during the Great Depression and World War Two" (M.A. paper, University of Pennsylvania, 1988).

49. Robert A. M. Stern, *George Howe: Toward a Modern American Architecture* (New Haven and London: Yale University Press, 1975).

50. Frederick Gutheim, ed., "Numero speciale dedicato all'opera di Oskar Stonorov (1905–1970)," *Architettura: Cronache e storia* 18 (June 1972).

51. McDonnell, *Wagner Housing Act*, 58–59.

52. Wisdom, interview with Brownlee, De Long, and Reed.

53. Howe, Stonorov, and Kahn, "'Standards' versus Essential Space: Comments on Unit Plans for War Housing," *Architectural Forum* 76 (May 1942): 308–11.

54. Letter, Stonorov to Arthur Johnson (president, United Steel Workers of America, Coatesville), August 19, 1942, "Correspondence—July–September, 1942," Box 49, Stonorov Papers, American Heritage Center, University of Wyoming, Laramie (hereafter cited as Stonorov Papers).

55. "What Housing for Willow Run?" *Architectural Record* 92 (September 1942): 51–54; Hermann H. Field, "The Lesson of Willow Run," *Task*, no. 4 (1943): 9–21.

56. Extensive correspondence, Box 48, Stonorov Papers.

57. Illustrated in Field, "Lesson," 21; and Howe, "The Meaning of the Arts Today," *Magazine of Art* 35 (May 1942): 165.

58. Letter, Saarinen to Stonorov, December 8, 1941, "Correspondence—October–December, 1941," Box 48, Stonorov Papers; letter, Stonorov to Saarinen, February 14, 1942, "Correspondence—January–March, 1942," Box 48, Stonorov Papers.

59. Letter, F. Charles Starr (National Housing Agency) to Stonorov and Kahn, August 5, 1942, "Correspondence—July–September, 1942," Box 49, Stonorov Papers.

60. "The Town of Willow Run: Neighborhood Unit 3," *Architectural Forum* 78 (March 1943): 52–54.

61. Letter, Stonorov to George Addes (UAW-CIO International secretary-treasurer), Walter Reuther, and William Nicholas (UAW), September 3, 1942, "Correspondence—July–September, 1942," Box 49, Stonorov Papers.

62. Addes to Stonorov, September 9, 1942, ibid.

63. Letter, Howe to Kahn, September 4, 1944, "Correspondence—July–

September 1944," Box 50, Stonorov Papers.

64. Stonorov tried repeatedly to enlist during this period, citing the lack of architectural work. But his request to be commissioned as an officer directly from civilian life was denied.

65. Letter, Stonorov to Maubert St. Georges (president, St. Georges and Keyes advertising agency), April 5, 1943, "Correspondence—April–June, 1943," Box 49, Stonorov Papers.

66. Letter, Stonorov to Richard K. Snively (St. Georges and Keyes), April 15, 1943, ibid.

67. Stonorov and Kahn, *Why City Planning Is Your Responsibility* (New York: Revere Copper and Brass, [1943]), 14, 5.

68. Letter, Donald F. Haggerty (Revere) to Stonorov and Kahn, August 10, 1943, "Correspondence—July–September, 1943," Box 49, Stonorov Papers.

69. Letter, St. Georges to Stonorov, February 11, 1944, "Correspondence—January–March 1944," Box 50, Stonorov Papers.

70. He repeated the house/city analogy in Kahn, "Architecture and Human Agreement" (lecture, University of Virginia, April 18, 1972), *Modulus*, no. 11 (1975): n.p.

71. Letter, Stonorov to Howard Myers, February 2, 1944, "Correspondence—January–March 1944," Box 50, Stonorov Papers.

72. Kahn, "Can Neighborhoods Exist?" Box 33, Stonorov Papers; letter, Elizabeth Mock (Museum of Modern Art) to Kahn, December 5, 1944, "Correspondence—October–December, 1944," Box 50, Stonorov Papers; letter, Stonorov to Richard Abbott (Museum of Modern Art), December 7, 1944, ibid.; letter, Mock to Stonorov, December 12, 1944, ibid.

73. "ICC," Box LIK 62, Kahn Collection.

74. "National Jewish Welfare Board," Box LIK 61, Kahn Collection.

75. "Seminar—Arch. Adv. Committee," "Architectural Advisory Com. Federal Public Housing Authority Louis I. Kahn," "Arch Adv. #2," Box LIK 63, Kahn Collection.

76. "PHA Advisory Committee Wash D.C.," Box LIK 61, Kahn Collection.

77. "Committee on Urban Planning A.I.A.," Box LIK 63, Kahn Collection.

78. "A.S.P.A.," "U.N.O.," Box LIK 63, Kahn Collection.

79. Howe, "Master Plans for Master Politicians," *Magazine of Art* 39 (February 1946): 66–68.

80. Victoria Newhouse, *Wallace K. Harrison, Architect* (New York: Rizzoli, 1989), 104–43.

81. Letter, Kahn to Phil Klutznick (Palestine Economic Corporation), March 13, 1949, "Correspondence Palestine Economic Corp," Box LIK 61, Kahn Collection.

82. Letter, George Shoemaker (secretary, Philadelphia Society for the Employment and Instruction of the Poor) to Kahn, February 18, 1947, "Correspondence January–March, 1947," Box 51, Stonorov Papers.

83. Letter, Ruth Goodhue (*Architectural Forum*) to Kahn, July 1, 1942, "Correspondence—July–September, 1942," Box 49, Stonorov Papers; telegram, Kahn to Goodhue, July 3, 1942, ibid.; letter, Stonorov to Goodhue, July 31, 1942, ibid.

84. "New Buildings for 194X: Hotel," *Architectural Forum* 78 (May 1943): 74–79.

85. Pittsburgh Plate Glass Company, *There Is a New Trend in Store Design* [Pittsburgh: Pittsburgh Plate Glass Company, 1945]. Also related was the "Business 'Neighborhood' in 194X" that Kahn sketched for a Barrett roofing ad in 1945: *Pencil Points* 26 (May 1945): 160; *Architectural Forum* 82 (June 1945): 179. Their postwar practice included some of exactly this kind of commercial work: the planned renovation of a Thom McAn shoe store in Upper Darby, the Coward shoe store in Philadelphia, and alterations to a Buten paint store in Camden.

86. Letter, Stonorov to *California Arts and Architecture*, May 19, 1943, "Correspondence—April–June, 1943," Box 49, Stonorov Papers; letter, John Entenza (*California Arts and Architecture*) to Stonorov and Kahn, September 7, 1943, "Correspondence—July–September, 1943," Box 49, Stonorov Papers. First- and second-floor plans in Kahn's hand, drawing 130.1, Kahn Collection.

87. "H. G. Knoll Assoc. Planning Unit," Box LIK 60, Kahn Collection; "Parasol House," Box LIK 33, Kahn Collection. The other architects were Serge Chermayeff, Charles Eames, Antonin and Charlotta Heythum, Joe Johannson, Ralph Rapson, and Eero Saarinen.

88. Letter, Stonorov to David Aarons (Gimbel Brothers), January 7, 1943, "Correspondence—January–March 1943," Box 49, Stonorov Papers.

89. Letter, G. P. MacNichol (Libbey-Owens-Ford) to Stonorov, August 25, 1945, "Correspondence—July–September, 1945," Box 50, Stonorov Papers.

90. Tyng, interview with David B. Brownlee, July 20, 1990.

91. Telegram, Earl Aiken (press relations manager, Libbey-Owens-Ford) to Stonorov, January 10, 1947, "Correspondence—January–March, 1947," Box 51, Stonorov Papers; telegram, Stonorov to Aiken, January 17, 1947, ibid.; telegram, Kahn to Aiken, January 17, 1947, ibid.

92. Maron Simon, ed., *Your Solar House* (New York: Simon and Schuster, 1947), 42–43.

93. Bill, Victory Storage Company to Stonorov and Kahn, March 4, 1947, "Veterans Administration," Box LIK 63, Kahn Collection.

94. Research assistance for the Oser house was provided by Marcia Fae Feuerstein.

95. Specifications, "Broudo Residence," Box LIK 61, Kahn Collection.

96. Chronology established from dated drawings in the Kahn Collection.

97. Research assistance for the Roche house was provided by David Roxburgh.

98. Tyng, interview with Brownlee, July 20, 1990.

99. Research assistance for the Weiss house was provided by David Roxburgh.

100. Kahn, quoted in Barbara Barnes, "Architects' Prize-winning Houses Combine Best Features of Old and New," *Evening Bulletin*, May 20, 1950.

101. Chronology established from dated drawings 305.1, 305.3, and office drawings, Kahn Collection.

102. Research assistance for the Genel house was provided by Marcia Fae Feuerstein.

103. Undated drawings 315.1–5, Kahn Collection, seem to belong to this phase.

104. Research assistance for the Philadelphia Psychiatric Hospital was provided by Peter S. Reed.

105. "Hospital to Cure the Mentally Ill," *Architectural Record* 90 (August 1941): 87–89.

106. Letter, Kahn to Rosenfield, August 2, 1945, "Correspondence—July–September, 1945," Box 50, Stonorov Papers.

107. Letter, Rosenfield to Stonorov and Kahn, February 13, 1946, "Correspondence January–March, 1946," Box 51, Stonorov Papers.

108. In response, Kahn protested, "I am sorry for the remarks you made about me personally. I hope I shall not have to reassure you of the earnestness of my intentions and efforts"; letter, Kahn to Radbill, September 11, 1945, "Correspondence—July–September, 1945," Box 50, Stonorov Papers.

109. Tyng, interview with Brownlee, June 5, 1990.

110. Sigfried Giedion, *Architecture You and Me: The Diary of a Development* (Cambridge, Mass.: Harvard University Press, 1958), 22–24, 48–51.

111. "In Search of a New Monumentality," *Architectural Review* 104 (September 1948): 117–28.

112. Sigfried Giedion, "The Need for a New Monumentality," in *New Architecture and City Planning*, ed. Paul Zucker (New York: Philosophical Library, 1944), 549, 551; Kahn, "Monumentality," ibid., 577.

113. Kahn, "Monumentality," 578.

114. Ibid., 578–79.

115. Ibid., 581, 580.

116. Ibid., 581.

117. Ibid., 587.

118. Letter, Kahn to Joseph Hudnut, May 15, 1946, "U.N.O.," Box LIK 63, Kahn Collection.

119. Robert A. M. Stern, "Yale 1950–1965," *Oppositions*, no. 4 (October 1974): 35–62; Stern, *Howe*, 210–25; William S. Huff, "Kahn and Yale," *Journal of Architectural Education* 35 (Spring 1982): 22–31.

120. Letter, Sawyer to Stern, February 9, 1974, Box VI, George Howe Papers, Avery Library, Columbia University, New York.

121. Program for "Suburban Shopping Center," "Yale University 1948–1949," Box LIK 60, Kahn Collection.

122. Program for "The National Center of UNESCO," "Yale—Professor 1950," Box LIK 61, Kahn Collection.

123. Program for "A Suburban Residence," "Yale University 1948–1949," Box LIK 60, Kahn Collection.

124. "3 Arts Combine in Architecture Project at Yale," *New York Herald Tribune*, February 27, 1949, 44; "Student Architects, Painters, Sculptors Design Together," *Progressive Architecture* 30 (April 1949): 14, 16, 18.

125. Draft of letter, Kahn to Howe [ca. July 1949], "Yale University 1948–1949," Box LIK 60, Kahn Collection.

126. Sawyer, draft program for collaborative project, "Yale—Professor 1950," Box LIK 61, Kahn Collection.

127. Albers, quoted in François Bucher, *Josef Albers: Despite Straight Lines* (New Haven and London: Yale University Press, 1961), 75.

128. Nalle, untitled text, *Perspecta*, no. 1 (Summer 1952): 6.

129. Letter, Scully to Kahn, February 15, 1956, "The Yale University, Correspondence," Box LIK 60, Kahn Collection; Scully, interview with Alessandra Latour, September 15, 1982, in Latour, *Kahn*, 151; Scully, conversation with David B. Brownlee and David G. De Long, August 16, 1990.

When in 1951 Louis Kahn received the commission for the Yale Art Gallery, he was a well-respected but hardly famous architect. Few besides those who worked with him sensed the potential that would, within the decade, lead to international acclaim. Yet in the relatively brief span of ten years following the Yale commission, he evolved an original vocabulary that responded to concerns being voiced by an entire generation of architects. And in the years remaining before his death in March 1974, he worked with that vocabulary to reshape architecture.

By no means was Kahn alone among his contemporaries in seeking change. But like Frank Lloyd Wright before him, he seemed to be the first of his generation to express through actual building what others had been able to suggest only through words, and Kahn, too, thus began a new architecture. In his persevering search for the very beginnings of architectural form, Kahn readily sacrificed visual charm. Considerations of site and materials—issues of primary importance to Wright—would for Kahn become secondary, although he used materials with an equal appreciation of their inherent qualities. He was less daring in his use of exotic geometries and innovative structure than Wright; in his determination to achieve the timelessness of great architecture, discovery became more important than invention. Whether the architecture that Kahn began should continue to be called modern or should be characterized by some other term would in itself have seemed of little consequence to Kahn—indeed, he once claimed, "there is no such thing as modern since everything belongs to architecture that exists in architecture and has its force"[1]— yet he wrought significant change of the sort that readily leads to such speculation.

When word came of the Yale commission, Kahn was a fellow of the American Academy in Rome, where, like so many architects before him, he no doubt welcomed the respite from practice to reconsider the direction of his work. His stay there was relatively brief—only three months—yet it seemed to have effect, for afterward the direction of his work began its decisive change. Clearly the physical presence of Rome, which offered fundamental lessons of history, was overwhelming. Shortly after his arrival he wrote to his office colleagues in Philadelphia:

I firmly realize that the architecture in Italy will remain as the inspirational source of the works of the future. Those who don't see it that way ought to look again. Our stuff looks tinny compared to it and all the pure forms have been tried in all variations. What is necessary is the interpretation of the architecture of Italy as it relates to our knowledge of building and needs. I care little for the restorations (that kind of interpretation) but I see great personal value in reading one's own approaches to the creation of space modified by the buildings around as the points of departure.[2]

Traveling the next month in Greece and Egypt, he remained enthusiastic as he visited sites suggesting the very beginnings of monumental architecture (see fig. 243).[3] Confirming his interest in history when other architects still tended to question its value, he later said, "The architect must always start with an eye on the best architecture of the past."[4]

Regarding specific impressions of Rome Kahn left few clues. Other than one or two tentatively identified sketches (fig. 56), no drawings of Roman ruins seem to exist. In his notebooks he wrote only that "the Romans introduced brick used elementally[?] with facing of marble."[5] As to specific monuments, he mentioned only two with any regularity: the Pantheon and the Baths of Caracalla.[6] Although his statements suggest it was the Pantheon to which he was most drawn, it was the Baths of Caracalla he formally identified as his favorite building: "It is ever a wonder when man aspires to go beyond the functional. Here was the will to build a vaulted structure 100 feet high in which men could bathe. Eight feet would have sufficed. Now, even as a ruin, it is a marvel."[7] Yet, however scant the evidence, Kahn's later work suggests that he benefited greatly from what he saw. Clearly he appreciated the massive, brick-faced ruins that so characterized the ancient city. With original decoration missing, Roman architecture was revealed as pure geometric volumes shaped by powerful walls and concrete vaults. Depictions of Rome that Kahn had long known no doubt strengthened his perceptions. Among these, as identified by Vincent Scully in his seminal monograph, were drawings by Auguste Choisy and Giovanni Battista Piranesi.[8] Choisy's illustrations reduced buildings to their structural and volumetric essence (fig. 55), and Piranesi's reconstructed views of Rome enlarged upon the fantastic geometries that lay beneath its ancient ruins.

Determining what Kahn actually read while in Rome, or, indeed, in any later period, is more problematic than determining what he saw. He always claimed never to have read, and there is no reason not to believe him.[9] For example, to a group of architecture students he once said, "I consider myself a rather interesting kind of a scholar because I don't read and I don't write."[10] Yet he constantly examined books and listened perceptively. At Yale he frequented Scully's classes on the history of architecture,

Chapter 2

The Mind Opens to Realizations

Conceiving a New Architecture, 1951–61

and at the American Academy he reportedly conversed at length with Frank E. Brown, the resident historian and archaeologist whose own appreciation of Roman architecture paralleled Kahn's.[11]

Kahn's travel sketches, even if not of Roman subjects, reveal a strong sense of ancient architecture that would also be reflected in his later work. Regarding travel sketches, he had written in 1931 that if such a drawing "discloses a purpose, it is of value," and, further, that following conventional rules of perspective or composition was unnecessary, for each drawing should reflect of its subject "that element of the feeling for its design, and the lyrical rhythm and counterpoint of its mass."[12] Kahn's later drawings of Greek columns (see fig. 245), done after his stay at the academy, render their mass with an animated vigor not apparent in earlier depictions, and his sketch of the Athenian acropolis (see fig. 246) signals a new appreciation of the mass and symbolic force of sacred terrain. The abstract, geometric power of architectural form is even more dramatically revealed by his sketches of Egyptian pyramids and temples (see fig. 244). Together these drawings reflected discoveries of ancient form that could still evoke the highest aspirations of humanity.

Reintroduction of Mass

Only a few weeks after returning from Rome, Kahn presented his first ideas for the Yale Art Gallery (fig. 57; see figs. 262–68 and pp. 314–17). By June 1951 his proposal was approved; essentially a loft building with entire walls either glazed or closed, it affirmed Kahn's adept handling of a modernist vocabulary and linked smoothly with his work before 1950. Yet it also gave evidence of his first major departure from that vocabulary, for in the subtle play of stringcourses along the brick plane of the main facade, and more emphatically in the almost three-foot-thick system of concrete floor slabs (fig. 58), Kahn had reintroduced the antique notion of mass with structure openly depicted as bearing weight. Certainly he was not the first to elect this course—Le Corbusier was one of several European contemporaries who had long since led the way—but in America the gallery's appearance had impact.

Kahn has often been described as approaching modernism uneasily, yet there is no record of his actually speaking against it. Instead he rethought it by dealing with its parts, and in so doing came ultimately to change it as a whole. Beginning with aspects of mass, he later examined aspects of spatial division, of openings, of interior and exterior correspondence, so that in the end nothing remained the

56

57

58

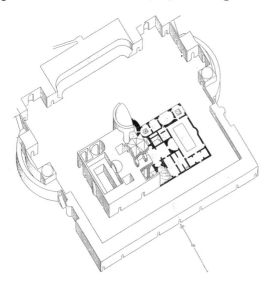

55. *Baths of Caracalla (ca.* A.D. *192–235), Rome, from Auguste Choisy,* Histoire de l'Architecture, *1899.*
56. *Interior sketch, Rome, 1951.*
57. *Yale University Art Gallery, New Haven, Conn., 1951–53. Perspective from southeast, before June 1951.*
58. *Yale University Art Gallery, New Haven, Conn., 1951–53. View from north, 1953.*

same. At this stage of his career, however, little of this was apparent, and the Yale Art Gallery, completed in 1953, held its own with such well-publicized American examples as Philip Johnson's glass house, completed in 1950; Mies van der Rohe's Lake Shore Drive Apartments, completed in 1951; and Gordon Bunshaft's Lever House, completed in 1952. That same year also saw the completion of Le Corbusier's Unité d'Habitation in Marseilles, which Kahn had visited during its construction. American practitioners of the time somewhat simplistically considered all these as manifestations of the International Style, and thus opposed to the school of Frank Lloyd Wright and his followers.

The hard, exposed structure of Kahn's gallery, which harbored exposed utilities, did not go unnoticed abroad as a departure from the smoother, seamless volumes of orthodox modernism. In England the gallery was seen as the best American example of New Brutalism, a briefly fashionable term that captured only a single dimension of Kahn's purpose.[13] Reflecting American bewilderment, Philip Goodwin, who had earlier proposed a design for the gallery and who, with Edward Durell Stone, had designed one of the icons of modernism in New York's Museum of Modern Art (completed in 1939), thought Kahn's building was "excellent, especially on the outside. I have some reservations on the ceiling treatment."[14] As these views suggest, Kahn had joined those architects of the 1950s wishing to free themselves from the constraints of the International Style without inclining toward the equally limiting approach of Wright. At the time, Eero Saarinen was regarded as more successful in this pursuit; Yale students were in fact unhappy that he had not gotten the gallery commission.[15] Like Kahn, Saarinen sought inspiration in both history and new building technologies, yet he approached those sources more as a means to surface decoration and superficial complication. By failing to question fundamental aspects of modernism, Saarinen, like so many of his equally restless contemporaries, romanticized architecture but did not change it.[16] That achievement lay with Kahn.

The ceiling treatment that had troubled Goodwin was, of course, crucial to Kahn's conception, for in answering both structural and mechanical needs in such an orderly manner as to leave structure and utilities exposed, he achieved architecture as basic and timeless as that which he had come to appreciate in Rome (fig. 61). Moreover, the insistent pattern of the ceiling's triangulated ribs suggested a differentiation of space below in a manner sympathetically aligned with Roman vaulting. In such ways Kahn brought fundamental aspects of history to bear on his architecture,

combining them with an image of advanced technology—in this case, the ceiling system—that spoke strongly of its own time. It was a system derived from Buckminster Fuller's space frames, which Kahn had transformed from a lightweight to a visually heavy structure, thus balancing history and technology, as Kenneth Frampton would note of his later buildings:

Kahn's work presents us with two complementary yet utterly opposed principles. The first is categorically anti-progressive and asserts the presence of a collective abstract architectural memory in which all valid compositional types are eternally present in their disjunctive purity. The second principle is vehemently progressive and pursues the renovation of architectural form on the basis of advanced technique. It seems that Kahn believed that this second principle, as it responded to new tasks and uses, would be able to lead, when combined with the first, to an appropriate architectural expression, resynthesizing fresh poetic and institutional values in terms of concrete form.[17]

On closer inspection, Kahn's approach seems characterized not so much by a pairing of history with advanced technique as by the pairing of history with a superimposed geometric order that gave the impression of advanced technique. In publications of his work Kahn favored the gallery's reflected ceiling plan (fig. 59), which indicated the stair enclosure as a pure cylinder, rather than plans showing the actual, only partly cylindrical form. And when compliance with local building codes forced Kahn to redesign the space frame so that it became a more conventional system of inclined "T"-beams, he complicated its appearance to preserve the dramatic look of the earlier system, leaving the hollow, three-sided pyramids—for Scully, a strong reminder of Kahn's recent Egyptian trip—intact as bracing elements.[18] Reinforcing the sense of this shape as an aesthetic choice is the dramatic stairwell, where the triangular plan of the stairs echoes the triangular coffer of the ceilings, thus amplifying the building's geometric theme (see fig. 268).

The ordered geometry of the Yale Art Gallery reflects the continuing critical influence of Anne Griswold Tyng (fig. 60).[19] She saw the gallery as a turning point in Kahn's career, one that she helped inspire and that sparked his awareness of "the archetypal order of geometry."[20] Something of Tyng's influence in this regard can be guessed from Kahn's reaction to Le Corbusier's Chapel at Ronchamp (1951–55): "I fell madly in love with it. . . . It is undeniably the work of an artist. . . . Anne is not satisfied . . . by form making not derived from an order. . . . [She] claims that if Le Corbusier had a growth concept of structure as I and she understand it, Le Corbusier himself would not be satisfied

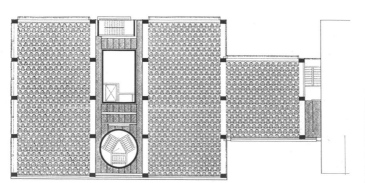

61

62

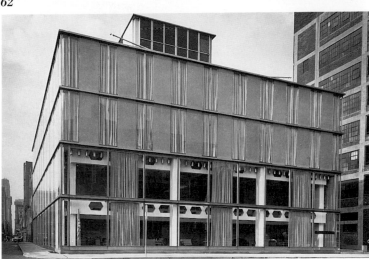

63

with his work."[21] Later he wrote that Tyng "knows the aesthetic implications of the geometry inherent in biological structures bringing us in touch with the edge between the measurable and the unmeasurable."[22] Tyng also formed an effective bridge between Kahn and Buckminster Fuller. She and Kahn had met Fuller in 1949,[23] and Fuller came to respect her ideas, praising her "superbly crafted and original scientific work which discloses her discovery of Golden-mean relationships between the whole family of Platonic solids. These relationships, according to the records, have not been previously known by man. . . . Anne Tyng has been Louis Kahn's geometrical strategist."[24]

Geometric order persisted in Kahn's work, as did an expressive use of masonry structure to impart a feeling of architectural mass. This can be seen in two somewhat conservative designs for Philadelphia begun in these years: the Mill Creek project (1951–56) and the American Federation of Labor Medical Services Building (1954–57). The Mill Creek project (to which a second component was added in 1956–63) embodied Kahn's ongoing efforts to design low-cost housing whatever the constraints, and the resulting complex of high-rise and low-rise units (with most of the latter added in 1956–63) reflected a long and bureaucratic process of compromise and is understandably subdued (fig. 62). The AFL building is the one other project in these years to link strongly with Kahn's pre-1950 work. Like the Yale Art Gallery, the AFL building made use of an exposed concrete structure to achieve a distinguishing appearance as well as to provide for an integrated system of mechanical services (fig. 63). The Vierendeel trusses that span between the widely spaced columns are cut with hexagonal openings, distantly recalling the geometry of the gallery, and inside, behind glass and stone panels sheathing the smooth, volumetric exterior, the resulting sense of mass was more appreciable. Yet by the time the AFL building was dedicated in February 1957, it was clearly out of phase with Kahn's other, more publicized work, and when in 1973 it was demolished to make way for a new expressway, there was little outcry.[25]

Differentiation of Space

Kahn's pursuit of an idealized geometric order, informed by his sense of historic architecture, seemed to draw him toward the differentiation of space, and the modernist ideal of spatial continuity was soon challenged. Traffic movement studies that he conceived for Philadelphia from late 1951 to mid-1953, while completing the design and supervising the construction of the Yale Art Gallery, forecast such ordered separation. Unbound by the sort of restraints that had so

59. *Yale University Art Gallery, New Haven, Conn., 1951–53. Reflected ceiling plan.*
60. *Kahn, Anne Tyng, and Kenneth Welch in Kahn office at 20th and Walnut Streets, ca. 1955.*
61. *Yale University Art Gallery, New Haven, Conn., 1951–53. Gallery, 1953.*

62. *Mill Creek Project, Philadelphia, Pa., 1951–56. Community center and high-rise apartment buildings, ca. 1956.*
63. *American Federation of Labor Medical Services Building, Philadelphia, Pa., 1954–57.*

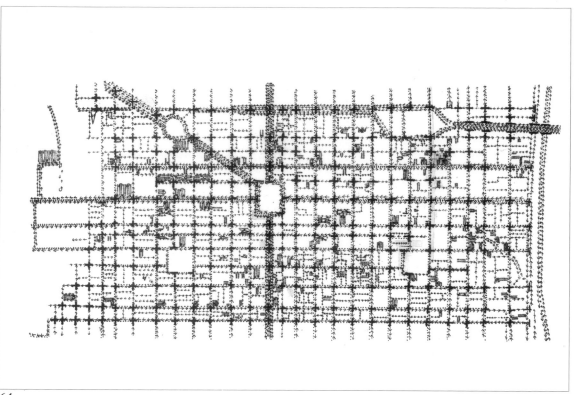

64

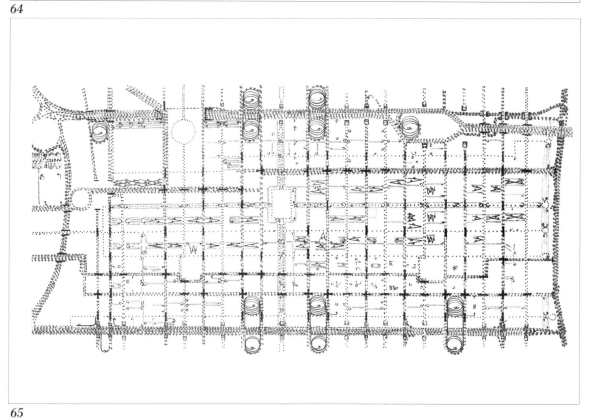

65

66

affected his design for the Mill Creek project, Kahn
prepared these visionary studies for a committee of the
Philadelphia Chapter of the American Institute of Architects
(see pp. 306–8). He began by differentiating individual
elements in his remarkable representations of urban
movement, following the long tradition of first analyzing a
problem by identifying its component parts, in this case
individual vehicles and people, each designated by an arrow
of different size or intensity to suggest relative scale and
speed (fig. 64). Next these elements were reassembled into a
more ordered totality that provided the appropriate harbor
or channel of flow for each component, so that a persuasive
unity was achieved without a loss of individual identity (fig.
65). Kahn's perspectives (see fig. 249) recall Le Corbusier's
idealized city images but happily lack the threatening
presence of hovering airplanes and death-defying landing
strips.

Anne Tyng recalled that "Lou always wanted a distinction
between things,"[26] referring primarily to his way of
detailing, but it was the same at a larger scale. For Kahn
such uncompromising reduction and reassembly was a viable
means of beginning, and he next applied it to architecture.
The plan of the H. Leonard Fruchter house (unbuilt, 1951–
54) shows this approach at a preliminary stage (fig. 67).
Commissioned by a New York businessman and his wife in
September 1951 as designs for the Yale Art Gallery ceiling
were being refined, it was not designed until spring of the
following year, with additional modifications in the first
months of 1953.[27] Each primary function was given an
independent geometric unit, yet in their reassembly Kahn
seemed less drawn to discovering unique relational order
than to amplifying his earlier configuration of the Yale
gallery stair. He must have found the plan device of a
triangle inscribed within a symmetrical enclosure
compelling, for within the next year three other projects
reflect its ordering pattern. Beneath their visual similarities
lie diverse unidentified sources.

In April 1953, not long after stopping work on the Fruchter
house, Kahn diagrammed a circular enclosure of hotel
rooms superimposed over a triangular department store as
part of his visionary Philadelphia Civic Center (fig. 68).
Claude-Nicolas Ledoux's project for an inn, ca. 1785,
published in a Philadelphia journal in 1952, must have
reinforced his fascination with this geometric combination
(fig. 70).[28] Next he exploited this device in the layout for the
Adath Jeshurun Synagogue and School Building (1954–55,
unbuilt), now assigning the triangular shape to the sanctuary
and placing it within a partially embanked, circular

68

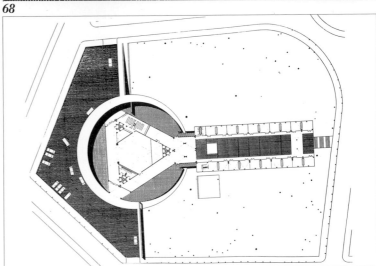

69

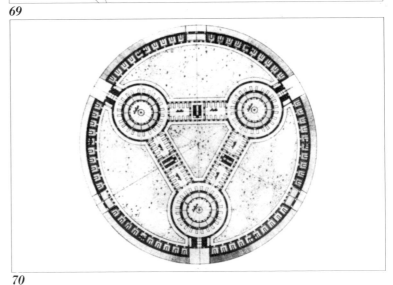

70

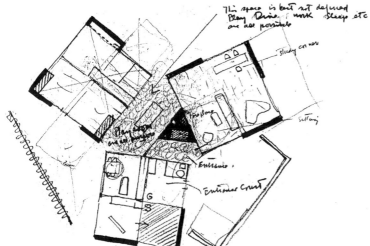

67

enclosure (fig. 69).[29] For its structure he envisioned an open, triangulated space frame that recalled the idealized structure he had drawn around 1953 to show how the Yale Art Gallery might have been (fig. 66); as he wrote to Walter Gropius: "My work on the Yale Art Gallery has led me to think about three-dimensional construction and its implications architecturally. I failed to command the forces which could have produced a truly significant building."[30] In the synagogue Kahn explored the potential of columns—sometimes angled in response to the frame—to be joined together in clusters that could define places for stairs within the larger volume.[31] Kahn's synagogue was planned for a site on York Road in North Philadelphia near Elkins Park, not far from the site where Frank Lloyd Wright's Beth Sholom synagogue (1954–59) would shortly rise. Kahn had kept clippings illustrating Wright's hexagonal plan;[32] in his own design he effectively rationalized Wright's romantic essay.

A third related design (developed in collaboration with Anne Tyng) exploited space-frame technology even more dramatically. For what came to be called the City Tower, Kahn and Tyng had first indicated a simple prismlike triangle, shown as a component of the Civic Center studies around 1952 (see fig. 412). In 1953 it was further developed as a triangular space frame with angled, faceted walls (fig. 71).[33] Its design might reflect the influence of the French engineer Robert Le Ricolais (1894–1977), who, like Tyng and Fuller, advocated such technology. Le Ricolais had written Kahn in April 1953, sending copies of two papers that explained his concepts. In these he argued poetically that hexagonal space frames could enhance spatial and structural efficiency in multistory buildings.[34]

Typically, Kahn sensed wide-ranging, less technological advantages, as he had earlier with his steel-frame experiments of the 1940s. In 1953 he wrote: "In Gothic times, architects built in solid stones. Now we can build with hollow stones. . . . The desire to express voids positively in the design of structure is evidenced by the growing interest and work in the development of space frames."[35] The clustered columns of Adath Jeshurun were a variation, with the void expanded to encompass circulation elements. Kahn's interest in space frames soon waned, but he continued to explore the interstitial spaces that he discovered within other structural systems. This became a means of defining relationships between spaces according to a visible, rational pattern, and a way of invigorating traditional, wall-bearing structure in a manner suitable to his own time. Ultimately he achieved the organic interrelatedness of parts that marks great architecture.

Kahn's preoccupation with the Yale Art Gallery extended to more than idealized amplifications of its structure and geometry, for his investigations into the rational division of space stemmed also from a growing dissatisfaction with how its open plan could be too freely changed. At first he thought his system of movable partitions had solved the problem by allowing controlled flexibility within the open plan of the gallery, explaining on the occasion of its opening, "A good building is one which the client cannot destroy by wrong use of space."[36] Inevitably other partitions were substituted; Kahn protested to Yale's president that his design was being compromised.[37] He had come to define architecture as "the thoughtful making of spaces"[38] and later said: "If I were to build a gallery now, I would really be more concerned about building spaces which are not used freely by the director as he wants. Rather I would give him spaces that were there and had certain inherent characteristics."[39] The Fruchter house had indicated the direction of this approach, yet its implications were at first left unexplored. In the Francis H. Adler house (1954–55, unbuilt), which he developed in September 1954, he initiated a more decisive course of action, one that led directly to a fully realized example of differentiated space in the Trenton Bathhouse of early 1955.[40]

The fall of 1954 was a time of relative calm in Kahn's office, encouraging concentrated effort. The Yale Art Gallery had been finished the previous year, the AFL building was at last under construction, the first phase of Mill Creek was very nearly done, and the final presentation of Adath Jeshurun had just been made. Kahn was rejoined by Anne Tyng, who was back from Rome, where their daughter, Alexandra Stevens Tyng, had been born. In these months Kahn's persistent questioning of his own beliefs seemed recharged. As he approached the design of smaller houses with new ideas, so he also began to formulate his distinction between ideal form, or what a building "wants to be," and design, or what actually emerges as a result of specific circumstance. At first he used the terms "order" and "design" to differentiate: "I believe that we are speaking about order when we are speaking about design. I think design is circumstantial. I think order is what we discover the aspects of."[41] No longer did he refer to order in the usual sense of superimposed geometric pattern, but rather as a preexisting, Platonic ideal. The measure of his designs depended, then, on the degree to which they participated in that discovered ideal.

Mrs. Adler had become impressed with Kahn while serving on the mayor's committee overseeing Philadelphia's Penn

72

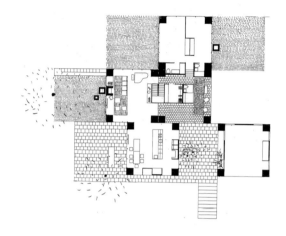

73

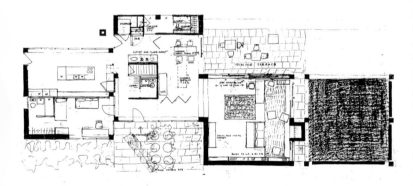

74

71. *Civic Center, Philadelphia,
Pa., 1952–57. Perspective
showing City Tower, ca.
1952–53.*
72. *Jewish Community Center,
Ewing Township, N.J.,
1954–59. Central courtyard of
bathhouse, ca. 1957.*
73. *Adler house, Philadelphia,
Pa., 1954–55. Plan, Fall 1954.*
74. *DeVore house, Springfield
Township, Pa., ca. 1954–55.
Plan, ca. 1955.*

Center, and she encouraged Kahn to break with convention
in the house she and her husband wished to build in the
Chestnut Hill section of the city.[42] This Kahn did in simple,
almost diagrammatic terms (fig. 73). Specified uses were
each housed in individual structural units so that spatial and
structural division corresponded; the open plan so
characteristic of modernism had been reconfigured. Walls
continued to be mostly glazed or solid, but the corner piers
themselves were planned as massive brick enclosures, left
hollow so that mechanical and structural elements could be
demonstrably integrated. In the visible joining of parts Kahn
seemed also to sense a potential for ornament; while
designing the Adler house he said:

The feeling that our present-day architecture needs embellishment
stems in part from our tendency to [furr] joints out of existence—
in other words, to conceal how parts are put together. If we were to
train ourselves to draw as we build, from the bottom up, stopping
our pencils at the points of pouring or erecting, ornament would
evolve out of our love for the perfection of construction and we
would develop new methods of construction.[43]

This statement, so indicative of Kahn's celebratory
articulation of parts, would continue to figure in his thinking
and was much repeated, with only minor variations. How
well he had come to understand the origins of ornament and
of the classical orders that apotheosized the joining of parts.

The clustered pavilion plan of the Adler house was hardly
new to the history of architecture. Its square, hipped-roofed
units in fact recalled ancient prototypes; one almost
identical to Kahn's had been added to the house of the Stags
at Herculaneum shortly before A.D. 79, and the type itself
was later much developed in the East. In the twentieth
century Frank Lloyd Wright had revived the idea with his
Jester house project of 1938, and Le Corbusier had
combined individually structured units in the Villa Sarabhai
(1952–55) and the Maisons Jaoul (1952–56). In later years
architects such as Aldo Van Eyck explored similar concepts,
as in his Children's Home (1957–60), and Charles Moore,
who had studied with Kahn at Princeton, was one of several
in America who tended to romanticize the concept, most
notably in his own house in Orinda, California, of 1962.
Closest to Kahn's design in these years was Philip Johnson's
Boissonnas house in New Canaan, Connecticut, of 1955–56;
during their encounters at Yale, Kahn could easily have
discussed his concept with Johnson in 1954. But ultimately it
was Kahn who most convincingly demonstrated the potential
of such a plan to reconfigure space.

When zoning problems caused the Adler project to falter

early in 1955,[44] Kahn adapted the concept for the Weber DeVore house in Springfield Township, Pennsylvania (ca. 1954–55). Again he composed the house of informally grouped pavilions, each a twenty-six-foot square, but now subdivided by two additional columns to better facilitate internal divisions (fig. 74). In both the Adler and DeVore projects, sketches record a variety of groupings as Kahn tried different relationships between each pavilion and the adjoining terrain. In both he also explored the use of hipped roofs, perhaps the better to shape the space within.

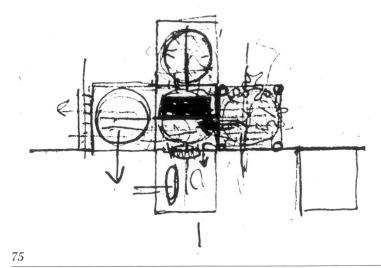

75

The DeVore project was apparently shorter lived than the Adler,[45] but the bathhouse that was part of the Jewish Community Center near Trenton, New Jersey, provided a third opportunity to develop a pavilion plan. Kahn received the commission in February 1955, and preliminary plans indicate a bathhouse of no particular distinction (see fig. 424 and pp. 318–23). Then, on February 15, he presented his Greek cross scheme of four symmetrically placed, pyramidal pavilions (see fig. 425). A simple structure, it was built rapidly, within a few months (fig. 72). There the balance of parts and the architectural hierarchy of what Kahn came to call "served" and "servant" space is clearly resolved, for the hollow piers of the Adler project have been enlarged, resulting in small, symmetrically placed rooms that contain toilet facilities or serve as vestibules. More extraordinary, perhaps, is the visual clarity of the building, for each functional unit is distinctly defined by its own structural volume.

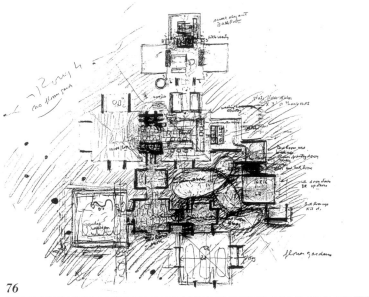

76

The Trenton Bathhouse became widely acknowledged as a key point of transition in Kahn's work. Looking back, Kahn reflected, "If the world discovered me after I designed the Richards towers building, I discovered myself after designing that little concrete-block bathhouse in Trenton."[46] At the time of its design in 1955 he had already begun to perceive its implications, recording in a section of his notebook titled "Compartmented Spaces": "Space made by a dome then divided by walls is not the same space. . . . A room should be a constructed entity *or* an ordered segment of a construction system."[47] He then commented on the great architects of his day in a way suggesting self-evaluation:

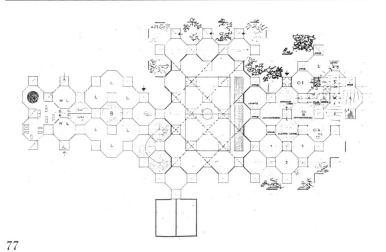

77

Mies's sensitivities with creation of space reacts to imposed structural order with little inspiration drawn from what a building 'wants to be.' Corbusier feels what a space 'wants to be,' passes through order impatiently and hurries to form. In Marseilles order was strong. . . . At Ronchamp order is only dimly felt in form born of dream. Mies's order is not comprehensive enough to encompass

acoustics, light, air, piping, storage, stairs, shafts, vertical and horizontal and other service spaces. His order of structure serves to frame the building but not harbor the servant space.

Next he praised Wright's early work as "the most wonderfully true architecture Amerique" but added, "The imitators of F.LL.W are of a lesser strata than imitators of Corbu. Wright is more arbitrary, personal, experimental and disdainful of tradition." In this same section he likened Le Corbusier to Beethoven, Mies van der Rohe to Clementi, and Wright to Wagner, adding, "We need a Bach in Architecture, like Brunelleschi, like Bramante." Kahn's comparisons were revealing. Clementi stood in contrast to the pioneering Beethoven and the tradition-defying Wagner; Mozart, in a well-known passage, had said of his contemporary: "He is an excellent cembalo-player, but that is all. He has great facility with his right hand. His star passages are thirds. Apart from this, he has not a farthing's worth of taste or feeling; he is a mere *mechanicus*."[48] Bach, who tempered the scale in a manner conceivably analogous to a rational division of architectural space, may have held special appeal.

Kahn concluded his notebook entry with a section titled "The Palladian Plan" that clarified his sense of historic precedent:

I have discovered what probably everyone else has found, that a bay system is a room system. A room is a defined space—defined by the way it is made. . . . To me that is a good discovery. . . . Someone asked me how one may carry out the room idea in the complex problems of house. I point to the DeVore house which is strictly Palladian in spirit, highly ordered for today's space needs. . . . The Adler house [is] stronger in order.[49]

Thus Kahn questioned the convention of open planning in light of a more antique sensitivity. To identify Palladio as the intermediary provides a clue to one source of this departure: Rudolf Wittkower's influential treatise *Architectural Principles in the Age of Humanism*, a book with which Kahn had earlier been familiar, even if, as colleagues claim, he mainly studied the illustrations.[50] Wittkower's diagram of Palladian villas, with clearly ordered "served" and "servant" spaces, would in itself account for his calling his own designs Palladian. Missing in the Adler and DeVore plans is the symmetrical balance of Palladio, yet in one of the first conceptual sketches for the Adler house (fig. 75), before specific circumstance reshaped its perfect symmetry, Kahn seemed to begin with a very Palladian plan indeed—what he would later use for the Trenton Bathhouse.

One final statement in Kahn's 1955 notebook linked the differentiated, Palladian plan with two later designs that he also began that year, the Lawrence Morris house in Mt. Kisco, New York (1955–58, unbuilt), and the intermediate scheme for the main building of the Jewish Community Center: "The community center in Trenton and the Morris house in Mt Kisco promise to be worthy variations of the room-space concept. There the supports are rooms serving the larger living spaces with the needed stairways, washrooms, closets, [illegible], entrances, etc."[51] Kahn began sketching his first scheme for the Morris house during the summer of 1955, but laid it aside during 1956. His preliminary plan (fig. 76), which corresponds to his notebook description, could almost be a conceptual sketch for the Richards Medical Research Building at the University of Pennsylvania (1957–65), his most noted example of differentiated space in these years, which he began in 1957.[52]

Reinforcing Kahn's Wittkowerian ties at mid-decade was a prolonged conversation late in December 1955 with one of Wittkower's most brilliant students, Colin Rowe.[53] The specific references to Palladio in Kahn's notebook may, in fact, have been entered after that meeting. Within a few weeks Rowe sent Kahn a new copy of *Architectural Principles*, saying, "I think that you may discover attitudes with which you are profoundly in sympathy."[54] Rowe may have had more in mind than Palladian parallels, for Kahn had earlier begun to differentiate ideal order from achievable shape in a manner recalling Wittkower's quotation of Barbaro: "The artist works first in the intellect and conceives in the mind and symbolizes then the exterior matter after the interior image, particularly in architecture."[55] Later, when Kahn came to speak of "the great event in architecture when the walls parted and columns became," he again recalled Wittkower's text, for he mythologized history in a manner not unlike Alberti as quoted by Wittkower: "A row of columns is indeed nothing else but a wall, open and discontinued in several places."[56] Both statements would have reinforced Rowe's appreciation, for he saw Kahn as a neo-humanist at the same time that Reyner Banham saw him as a New Brutalist; by then, however, Kahn had risen above both conventions.

The intermediate scheme for the Jewish Community Center that Kahn mentioned in his notebook and on which he worked from November 1955 into March 1956 is more startling in its diagrammatic rigidity than his other work of the time (fig. 77). Here the hand of Anne Tyng can again be sensed, and even more strongly in an elevation study

75. Adler house, Philadelphia, Pa., 1954–55. Sketch plan (detail of sheet), ca. 1955.
76. Morris house, Mt. Kisco, N.Y., 1955–58. First-floor plan, Summer 1955. Inscribed Lou.
77. Jewish Community Center, Ewing Township, N.J., 1954–59. Plan. Inscribed Louis I. Kahn–Architect/Nov. 3, 1955.

78. Jewish Community Center, Ewing Township, N.J., 1954–59. Elevation. Inscribed LIK '56.
79. Set of 14-hedra, from D'Arcy Wentworth Thompson, On Growth and Form, 1943 edition.

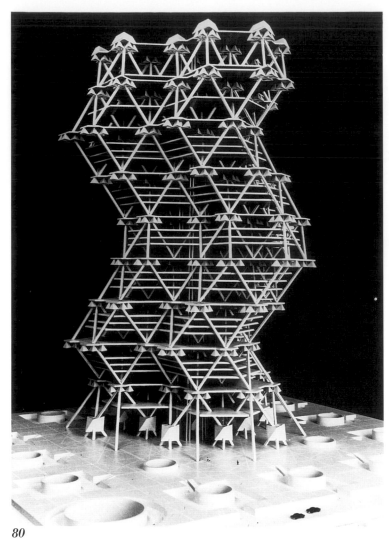

80

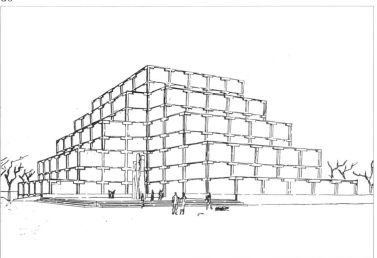

81

82

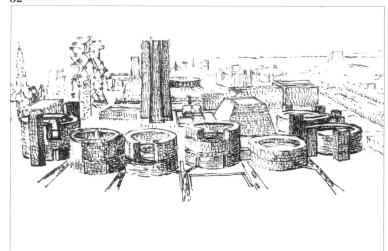

83

84

85

80. City Tower, Philadelphia, Pa., 1952–57. Model, 1956–57.

81. Washington University Library, St. Louis, Mo., 1956. Perspective, February–May 1956. Inscribed Lou K.

82. Research Institute for Advanced Science, near Baltimore, Md., 1956–58. Model.

83. Civic Center, Philadelphia, Pa., 1956–57. Bird's-eye perspective. Inscribed Lou K '57.

84. General Motors Exhibit, New York, N.Y., 1960–61. Bird's-eye perspective.

85. General Motors Exhibit, New York, N.Y., 1960–61. Plan.

86. Jewish Community Center, Ewing Township, N.J., 1954–59. Model, November 1956–June 1957.

(fig. 78) that resembles a drawing in D'Arcy Thompson's *On Growth and Form* (fig. 79). It seemed to illustrate her belief that architects should "conceive of forms in building which create their own *terrain* based on truly three dimensional relationships rather than on two dimensions simply extended upward. . . . From a comprehension of the geometries of close-packing may be developed forms which are most effective in creating spaciousness where populations are dense."[57] About similar polygonal solids Thompson had said that "in close-packed association" they could "enclose space with a minimum extent of surface."[58]

Tyng's collaboration was more openly acknowledged in the final version of the City Tower (1956–57), a 616-foot-high structure developed for Universal Atlas Cement as one of a series meant to stimulate far-reaching uses of concrete (fig. 80). A model of the highly articulated structure was exhibited at the Museum of Modern Art in 1960, where it was described by one critic as "a tottering, concrete Erector set."[59] The triangular geometry now seems firmly Tyng's, but Kahn's earlier sketch of San Marco (see fig. 248) records a sympathetic view of masonry frames. Other designs incorporating triangular geometries—like the Wharton Esherick Workshop addition (1955–56) or the Fred Clever house (1957–62)—were also much guided by Tyng.[60] And she contributed to the unbuilt design for the General Motors Exhibit at the 1964–65 New York World's Fair on which Kahn worked briefly between December 1960 and February 1961.[61] He experimented with centralized and even spherical structures, but settled on loosely grouped inflated pavilions (fig. 84). Tyng's own scheme brought to these the geometric regularity that she more consistently sought (fig. 85), for while Kahn absorbed such elements within a broader framework, Tyng remained more focused.[62]

In these years Kahn's commissions were so paced that he could focus on each individually, at least for a period of weeks. Thus as he was completing work on the octagonal scheme for the Jewish Community Center, an invitation came in February 1956 to enter the limited competition for the Washington University Library in St. Louis; when that was submitted in May, office records show that his attention turned to the Research Institute for Advanced Science near Baltimore, which had been commissioned in 1955 but awaited his efforts. When his final drawings for the research institute were completed in November 1956, he turned again to the Jewish Community Center, and between November and June 1957 he prepared his third and best-known proposal for that commission.

In both the library (fig. 81) and the research institute (fig. 82), Kahn continued to explore the Greek cross as a plan device appropriate to ordered, differentiated space, although now for programs of far greater complexity than that of the Trenton Bathhouse. The images that Kahn favored for publication minimized the necessary maze of partitions, particularly in the library. Such elimination of specifics reflected one means by which Kahn approached his universal truths: the program guided but did not command. As Kahn said of his design for Washington University, "A library should offer a system of spaces and their consequent form as a building should originate from broad interpretations of use rather than the satisfaction of a program for a specific system of operation."[63] Later he added, "It is the duty of the architect to find what is this thoughtful realm of space . . . not just take the program of the institution but try to develop something which the institution itself can realize is valid."[64] In this he became ever more firm: "I never read a program literally. . . . It's like writing to Picasso and saying, 'I want my portrait painted—I want two eyes in it—and one nose—and only one mouth, please.' You can't do that, because you're talking about the artist."[65] He approached his third proposal for the Jewish Community Center in the same way (fig. 86), for beneath the ordered, pyramidal pavilions are a variety of uses and spaces not always in congruence with the architectural shapes that contain them. Space was now particularized according to a general pattern of differently proportioned elements that facilitated minor shifts of function without impairing architectural character.

Unlike his commissions for actual buildings in these years, Kahn's visionary proposals for Philadelphia that he now initiated on his own (May 1956 through much of 1957; see p. 310) provided space for dreams. Perspectives of Philadelphia (fig. 83) show a fantastic landscape of powerful forms reminiscent of Piranesi's Rome. The Roman quality, in fact, seems stronger here than in earlier work and may reflect the influence of Robert Venturi. Kahn, impressed with Venturi's thesis at Princeton, had recommended him to Eero Saarinen, with whom he worked before going to the American Academy in Rome. Upon his return from the academy in 1956, Venturi joined Kahn's office; later, when he began to practice independently in 1957, they continued to exchange ideas.[66] Kahn's letters of recommendation for Venturi document close ties and deep appreciation,[67] and it was surely Venturi's perceptive comprehension of personal mannerisms and specificity in architecture that came to loosen Kahn's growing inclination toward highly controlled, even compulsively ordered

87

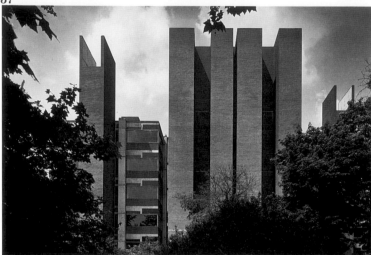

88

89

87. *Kahn teaching at the University of Pennsylvania, ca. 1967.*
88. *Richards Medical Research Building, University of Pennsylvania, Philadelphia, Pa., 1957–60. South facade, ca. 1959.*

89. *Richards Medical Research Building and Biology Building, University of Pennsylvania, Philadelphia, Pa., 1957–65. Perspective, ca. October 1957.*
90. *Richards Medical Research Building and Biology Building, University of Pennsylvania, Philadelphia, Pa., 1957–65. Typical floor plan.*

designs. Within the very shadow of the pure logic cast by the City Tower project, Venturi, in his sketch of the plaza, invoked the emotionally charged spirit of Michelangelo's Campidoglio. If Anne Tyng can be said to have strengthened Kahn's tendencies toward abstract geometric order, then surely Venturi provided the means by which that order could be made poetic.

Venturi was not alone among those who helped lead Kahn toward solutions. About his informally organized office much has been said in this regard,[68] for he benefited greatly from those who worked with him to develop his sketches into more finished drawings, and he depended heavily on a few more experienced colleagues who maintained some sense of conventional office routine. In a like manner he worked with students and faculty at Yale or the University of Pennsylvania or at other schools where he taught. After September 1955 his teaching was mainly at Penn, although he taught for short periods at both MIT and Princeton. He was recruited to Penn by G. Holmes Perkins, then dean of the school, as part of Perkins's farsighted development of that institution. There Kahn was primarily involved with advanced students working toward a second professional degree. He had begun to disengage from Yale just as Paul Rudolph began teaching. The problem of a "roadside frozen custard stand" that Rudolph assigned his studio may have contributed to Kahn's ultimate departure, especially when Kahn was curtly requested to serve on the reviewing jury.[69] Kahn's interest lay with deeper issues, and he identified problems accordingly. Often he assigned his own commissions, always in a spirit calculated to encourage wide-ranging inquiry. At Penn he organized his studio in the manner of a seminar, engaging in open discussion with both students and his fellow teachers, Robert Le Ricolais and a former classmate, Philadelphia architect Norman Rice. As Kahn said near the end of his life, "I come much more refreshed and challenged from the classes. I learn more from the students than I probably teach" (fig. 87).[70] He encouraged students to join with him in discovering the ideal form for each problem. In one instance the universal ideal was determined to be a sphere; how each student arrived at something approaching its shape was the measure of individual distinction.[71]

As Kahn's earlier connection with Yale led to the Yale Art Gallery commission, so his affiliation with the University of Pennsylvania led to the Richards Medical Research Building commission in February 1957 (fig. 88; see figs. 269–77 and pp. 324–29). By the time of his first presentation in June 1958, he had developed a basic scheme of three laboratory towers grouped asymmetrically about a fourth service tower. That summer the commission was expanded to include laboratory facilities for biology, and these Kahn added as two additional towers (fig. 90). Various fenestration patterns were proposed, some with arcuated elements recalling Roman motifs (see fig. 432), and the service towers were much studied as to profile and shape (fig. 89; see fig. 434); but the plan itself held, and ultimately its clear resolution honored both structural and compositional logic.

More fully than any of his previous designs, the Richards Building embodied Kahn's developing sense of differentiated space shaped by visible, rational, individualizing structure. By the time of the building's dedication in May 1960, critics sensed that a new synthesis was emerging, one that seemed to derive partly from Mies van der Rohe and the International Style, partly from Le Corbusier, and partly from Frank Lloyd Wright, but with an individual quality uniquely its own.[72] Kahn's clear articulation of separate components and his emphatic distinction between servant and served spaces were judged to be his strongest departures from accepted norms. These were generally explained as rational responses to specific demands of the program, in particular the need to designate separated areas for animals and to provide for the complicated systems of air supply and exhaust. In retrospect these demands seem almost incidental. Such pavilion plans were then well established as a theme in his work, and in the Trenton Bathhouse of 1955 his urge to clarify service elements had been made evident. It was a concept he readily acknowledged as stemming from his Beaux-Arts training.[73] He also wrote, "The nature of space is further characterized by the minor spaces that serve it. Storage-rooms, service-rooms and cubicals [sic] must not be partitioned areas of a single space structure, they must be given their own structure."[74] In the Richards Building Kahn's sensitivity to human feelings seems more crucial to his concept than functional need:

The Medical Research Building . . . is conceived in recognition of the realizations that science laboratories are studios and that the air to breathe should be away from the air to throw away. The normal plan of laboratories . . . places the work areas off one side of a public corridor [with] the other side provided with the stairs, elevators, animal quarters, ducts and other services. . . . The only distinction between one man's spaces of work from the other is the difference of the numbers on the doors.[75]

In his building Kahn not only provided for these differentiated areas that honored human effort, he also grouped them so that a sense of working among a community of scientists could be appreciated (fig. 91).

The Richards Building's concrete structure, elegantly expressed in juxtaposition to the visually more inert surfaces of red brick, was also much celebrated at the time of its completion. As in the Yale Art Gallery, an experimental system was exploited to order space, but now that order was more clearly defined and the spatial divisions within it more directly outlined by a system of interlocking precast, post-tensioned beams. Collaborating on its design was August Komendant, who since 1956 had been a frequent consultant.[76] Komendant, described by Kahn as "one of the rare engineers qualified to guide the architect to develop meaningful form,"[77] proved himself an able contributor. He recalled introducing Kahn to the structural potentials of precast concrete, and less generously said that Kahn "was completely ignorant of engineering. He lacked the basic knowledge of structures and structural materials. . . . He hid his lack of structural knowledge behind arrogance and his position. . . . Kahn's attitude about engineering changed drastically after close association with Robert Le Ricolais and myself."[78]

Various visual sources have been suggested for the Richards Building, ranging from the medieval towers of San Gimignano to facades by Mies van der Rohe.[79] Wright's Larkin Building (1904), which Scully suggested as an influence early on, provides a more convincing precedent and brings into sharper focus the question of Kahn's relationship to that architect.[80] Typical of his generation, Kahn had little praise for Wright's later designs, favoring instead the more rigorously intellectual work of Le Corbusier. Yet Kahn's work in these years suggests deeper understanding than is generally acknowledged.

Documented evidence of ties between Wright and Kahn is slight. His connection with Henry Klumb (1904–1984), a former associate of Wright's and a staunch supporter of his ideals, is noted in chapter 1.[81] In 1952 Kahn and Wright both attended a convention of the American Institute of Architects,[82] in 1955 (as previously noted) Kahn praised Wright's early work, and when Wright died in 1959 Kahn wrote in tribute, "Wright gives insight to learn/that nature has no style/that nature is the greatest teacher of all/The ideas of Wright are the facets of this single thought."[83] Scully recalls that later that same year Kahn made his first visit to a Wright building, the S. C. Johnson and Son Administration Building (1936–39), where, "to the depths of his soul, [he] was overwhelmed."[84] In view of the Richards Building, one further tie seems of special interest. In 1953, rebutting Pietro Belluschi's criticism that Wright's 1947 research tower for Johnson and Son did not function as a

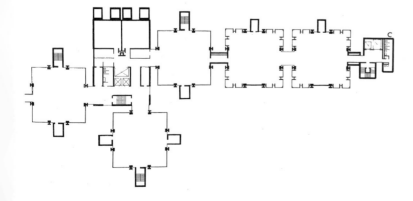

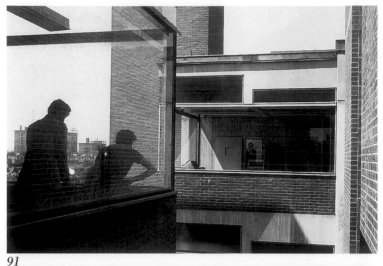

91

92

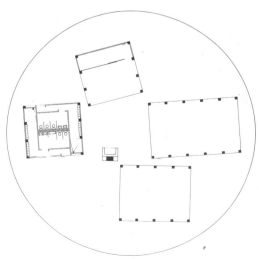

93

laboratory, Kahn said, "The Tower was done with love and I should say it is architecture. . . . Architecture should start a new chain of reactions. It shouldn't just exist for itself; it should throw out sparks to others. . . . If the Tower has this power . . . then I believe it functions."[85] Such could also be the defense for Kahn's similarly criticized research towers.

In seeking logical definition of spaces within, Kahn may also have respected Wright's approach to fenestration, for Wright varied openings systematically and effected dramatic balance between glazed and masonry surfaces. Nowhere is this better demonstrated than in the Richard Lloyd Jones house (Tulsa, Oklahoma, 1929), in which alternating bands of glass and masonry block reconfigure conventional enclosure. As one of Wright's most abstract and scaleless buildings, lacking the romantic contrivances typical of his later work, it may have held special appeal for Kahn, who seems to have taken it as his model for the reworked Morris house. At first its plan (see fig. 76) had anticipated the Richards Building, as noted. After putting the house project aside for more than a year, Kahn resumed work during the summer of 1957, while refining his design for Richards.[86] Drawings again reveal similarities between the two designs, and later perspectives of the Morris house closely resemble the towered massing of the Richards Building. But as the lower, more open pavilions and hipped roofs of earlier versions gave way to a stronger depiction of mass (fig. 92), it began to recall Wright's Jones house (fig. 93). In plan the two designs also drew together, for in the final version of the Morris house (fig. 98) the pavilions had coalesced, and volumetric divisions were achieved by internal piers.

However much Kahn may have drawn from Wright, the two remained divided in fundamental attitudes. Both believed in order as a fundamental principle, but they saw it as differently generated. As Scully summarized, Kahn believed that order was a "cultural construction and its archetypes are therefore to be found in human history";[87] or as Kahn said, "Architecture is what nature cannot make."[88] Wright believed that order was derived from nature. Both architects also sought ideal form, but Wright found patterns in earthly models, while Kahn searched for cosmic inspiration.

One last pavilion scheme, the day camp for the Jewish Community Center in Trenton, had been designed in June 1957, just as the Richards design was being readied for presentation and before work on the Morris house resumed. Designed and built with uncharacteristic speed, it is essentially a group of simple, open units that seem more like a quick sketch than a finished design. Of interest is the plan

91. Richards Medical Research Building, University of Pennsylvania, Philadelphia, Pa., 1957–60. View between towers, ca. 1961.
92. Morris house, Mt. Kisco, N.Y., 1955–58. Model, ca. 1957–58.
93. Frank Lloyd Wright. Richard Lloyd Jones house, Tulsa, Okla., 1929.
94. Jewish Community Center, Ewing Township, N.J., 1954–59. Plan of day camp, ca. June 1957.

95. Tribune Review Building, Greensburg, Pa., 1958–62.
96. Fleisher house, Elkins Park, Pa., 1959. Model.
97. Tribune Review Building, Greensburg, Pa., 1958–62. Elevation, before Fall 1959.
98. Morris house, Mt. Kisco, N.Y., 1955–58. Plan.
99. Fleisher house, Elkins Park, Pa., 1959. Plan, ca. January–March 1959.

94

95

96

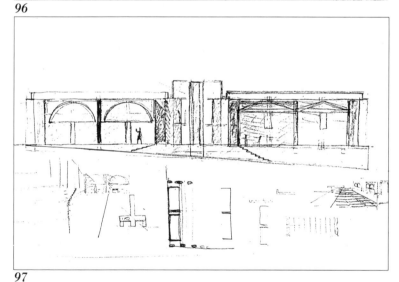

97

(fig. 94), for in the angled, informal play of the individual units an element of geometric complexity new to Kahn's work is suggested. This approach to planning would not be further explored until 1959, in the M. Morton Goldenberg house (unbuilt). But in the fall of 1958, when work on the Morris house had stopped and other projects were inactive, elevation studies that Kahn began for the Tribune Review Building show a similar sense of geometric freedom. It is tempting to link these variations as a group to ideas that Robert Venturi may have helped to stimulate, for in Kahn's immediate work to follow are even stronger reflections of what Denise Scott Brown has claimed: "Lou learned from Bob about Mannerist exception, distortion, and inflection in form. . . . Through Bob, he investigated the layering of enclosed spaces and the layered juxtaposition of walls and openings, and he discovered that windows could be holes in the wall again."[89]

Layered Juxtapositions

In the fall of 1958 Kahn began work on the Tribune Review Publishing Company Building, planned to accommodate a local newspaper in Greensburg, Pennsylvania (1958–62).[90] Its basically rectangular plan was relatively conventional, with two open bays joined by a central line of services, but in detailing its enclosing walls Kahn experimented with openings shaped in response to light. Only months before, Kahn had been forced to eliminate window blinds and other light-controlling devices in the Richards Building, and it was perhaps with this in mind that he sought a more integral control of natural light, conceiving devices less subject to elimination when the inevitable problems of cost arose. He studied windows with shapes that were foreign to modern architecture but suited to masonry walls, for whether arched or corbeled, such openings could be framed without steel lintels and were thus more natural to brick construction (fig. 97). By positioning the larger openings within the upper part of the wall and leaving only narrow slots below, he was able to moderate glare without blocking views. In appearance these windows recall Roman prototypes like those Kahn had seen at Ostia. Critics came to call them "keyhole" windows, and Kahn was not alone in using them; a simply grasped element, they soon became a cliché in the hands of other architects. By the fall of 1959, when construction began on the Tribune Review Building, other light-moderating elements that Kahn had proposed, including projecting bays and hoods, had been eliminated, but the keyhole windows, simplified in shape, remained (fig. 95).[91]

Kahn developed his keyhole windows more extensively in the

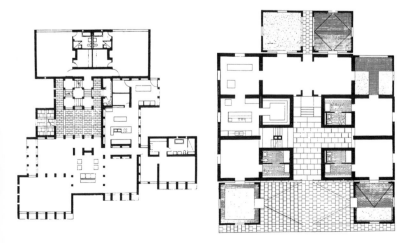

98   99

Fleisher and Goldenberg projects, both designed in the first months of 1959, while he was simplifying the Tribune Review Building in an effort to lower costs. The Robert H. Fleisher house for Elkins Park, Pennsylvania (1959, unbuilt), is a complete essay in the keyhole, with arcuated openings defining each of its square bays (figs. 96, 99).[92] At each end of the house, terminating units are left unroofed to serve as walled gardens. As if subjected to compacting pressure, the loosely arranged pavilions of the earlier Adler and DeVore projects are now densely ordered, and the Palladian aspect is made more apparent. In this design Kahn suggested two further departures from modernist norms that he would later examine in greater detail: exaggeratedly thick walls—for here his plan inclines away from the planar modularity of Brunelleschi toward the more three-dimensional units employed by Alberti—and the visual separation of outer layers of enclosure, signaled in the Fleisher house by the hypaethral garden rooms abutting the ends of the house.

In the M. Morton Goldenberg house, Rydal, Pennsylvania (1959, unbuilt), Kahn again relaxed the plan, not by dispersing individual elements but by exploring radiating, 45-degree diagonals as a means to less constrictive unity (figs. 100, 101).[93] For Kahn, such expressive reconfiguration of a square enclosure went beyond artistic choice: "I felt this was rather a discovery in the desires of interiors—interior spaces . . . a house is a building which is extremely sensitive to internal need. In this satisfaction there was an *existence will* of some kind . . . but there was an *existence will* for this house not to be disciplined within a geometric shape."[94] On one level, the diagonal framing elements satisfied Kahn's demand for variety based on demonstrable logic rather than personal choice (fig. 105). As something generated more readily by square rather than polygonal geometry, the 45-degree diagonal was also in sympathy with a preference he later stated: "I always start with a square, no matter what the problem is."[95] In the hands of other architects, such diagonals became an architectural cliché of the 1960s. As with certain of H. H. Richardson's details some eighty years earlier, the appropriation of Kahn's more obvious elements gave an impression of newness, however shallow the thought behind their use.

The First Unitarian Church and School in Rochester, New York (1959–69), which Kahn began to design in June 1959 after work on the Fleisher and Goldenberg projects was largely completed, also, like the latter, began as a square, or so he claimed (see figs. 293–301 and pp. 340–45). Before his final scheme was approved in early 1961 he had tried several

variations, but the centralized form that Kahn believed to be essential was ultimately honored (fig. 106). It was Kahn's first commission for a church, and Wittkower's discussion of ideal Renaissance churches must have been of interest. Wittkower had explained that Alberti recommended nine symmetrical shapes, beginning with the circle and the square, and further demonstrated the importance of centralized planning as honoring geometrical perfection: "No geometrical form is more apt to fulfill this demand than the circle or forms deriving from it. In such geometrical plans the geometrical pattern will appear absolute, immutable, static and entirely lucid. Without that organic geometrical equilibrium where all parts are harmonically related like the members of a body divinity cannot reveal itself."[96] Kahn's first known drawing for the Unitarian Church conforms remarkably with Wittkower's illustrations of centralized churches by Leonardo da Vinci (figs. 102, 103). Centralized planning itself was hardly new to Kahn's work—Adath Jeshurun was one of several earlier designs in which such rules had been followed. What was new was the extension of that centralized shape through juxtaposed units of sympathetic, but distinctly different, configuration. For the first time in his post-1950 phase Kahn seems to be dealing with supporting elements of the program in a more exploratory manner, dissolving thereby the modernist expectation of conventional geometric coherence. It marks an advance from the subdivided bays of the Washington University Library scheme, and also from the simple duplication of identical shapes that characterizes so many earlier projects. Different variations were developed for the Rochester commission, some as fully symmetrical as his first drawing (see fig. 448), and others sympathetic to Wright's Unity Temple (see fig. 449), as recorded in his conceptual diagrams (fig. 106). With each developed version Kahn provided ambulatories that enriched the Renaissance prototype:

The ambulatory I felt necessary because the Unitarian Church is made up of people who have had previous beliefs. . . . I drew the ambulatory to respect the fact that what is being said or what is felt in a sanctuary was not necessarily something you have to participate in. And so you could walk and feel free to walk away from what is being said. And then I placed a corridor next to it—around it—which served the school which was really the walls of the entire area.[97]

The bottom image of Kahn's conceptual diagrams for the Unitarian Church corresponds most closely to the built version (see fig. 452) and introduces another, more passive kind of geometric juxtaposition. The shapes no longer conform to a preconceived pattern but rather reflect specific

100. Goldenberg house, Rydal, Pa., 1959. Model.
101. Goldenberg house, Rydal, Pa., 1959. Plan.
102. First Unitarian Church and School, Rochester, N.Y., 1959–69. Sketch plan and elevation, June–July 1959.
103. Detail of church designs by Leonardo da Vinci, as published by Rudolf Wittkower in 1952.

104. Plan of S. Sebastiano, Rome, ca. A.D. 320.
105. Goldenberg house, Rydal, Pa., 1959. Plan diagrams.
106. First Unitarian Church and School, Rochester, N.Y., 1959–69. Plan diagram, ca. January 1961.

100

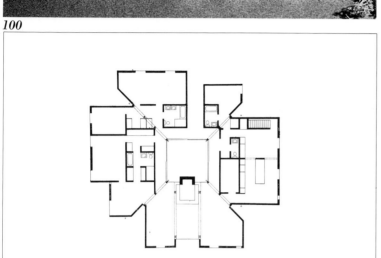

101

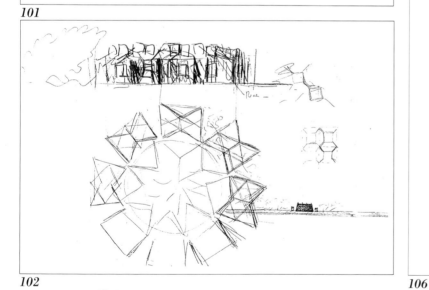

102

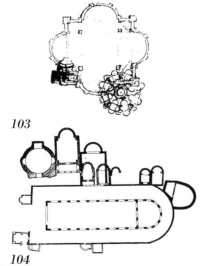

103

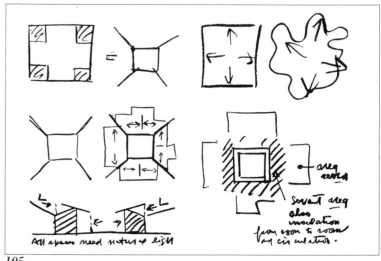

105

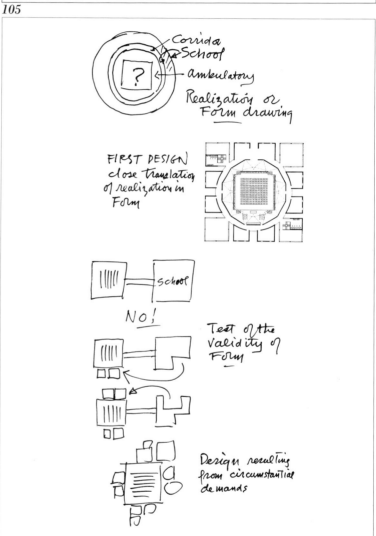

106

104

demands of individual use, and the resulting profile seems more distant still from conventional modernist planning. The precedents now are not Renaissance as much as late Roman, or more specifically Early Christian, for in plan Kahn's design recalls fourth-century funerary basilicas (fig. 104). Such basilicas were a relatively new archaeological discovery, only fully identified after the Second World War.[98] Given his fascination with beginnings, it seems possible that Kahn, perhaps through Frank Brown, was familiar with this early, short-lived building type.

In his final schemes for the Unitarian Church, designed during the spring and summer of 1960, Kahn not only reestablished the central focus of his first scheme but also conceived the enclosing walls in terms of a perceivable, faceted thickness, infusing his building with a quality of exaggerated mass that was new even to his work (figs. 109, 110). His design of the Margaret Esherick house in Chestnut Hill (1959–61) may have contributed to this result, for its walls, designed just before those of the Unitarian Church, are similarly conceived though less emphatically massive (see figs. 250–53).[99] A single-person dwelling, the house was designed for the niece of the sculptor Wharton Esherick, whose studio Kahn had designed in 1955. In his first plan of late 1959 Kahn had combined square units in a manner recalling the Adler project, but in the first months of 1960 he consolidated these into a compact rectangular enclosure.[100] Both the Esherick house and the Unitarian Church reflected Kahn's continued study of openings that moderated light, and in each instance built-in furniture was inserted to justify the extra thickness: bookcases in the house (fig. 107; see fig. 252) and window seats in the church. He described the effect in Rochester as "very Gothic," and in February 1961—the very month he completed the design of the facades—he said:

Before [in the second scheme] the window's punched out of the walls. We felt the starkness of light again, learning also to be conscious of glare every time. . . . This [final scheme] is the beginning of a realization that the reveals are necessary. And this came about also because there was a desire to have some window seats. . . . This window seat had a lot of meaning and it became greater and greater in my mind as meaning associated with windows.[101]

The Unitarian Church may also owe something to Kahn's well-known fascination with plans of Scottish castles (fig. 108), a source more often linked to his later design for the Erdman dormitory (1960–65). Recalling his interest in 1973, he wrote: "The Scottish Castle. Thick, thick walls. Little openings to the enemy. Splayed inwardly to the occupant. A place to read, a place to sew. . . . Places for the bed, for the

stair. . . . Sunlight. Fairy tale."[102] The result indeed recalls images of another time, its already complicated profile further exaggerated by light hoods rising above the parapet. Kahn had made these light-giving elements an integral part of the roofing structure, which was further enriched by inclined ceiling planes that configured the space below (see fig. 301). Typically Kahn's rejection of the conventional and more readily achievable flat roof reflected a pervasive rethinking of how spaces might be more expressively shaped. Frank Brown's lucid discussion of Roman vaulting may have encouraged Kahn in his own search.[103]

During 1960, as Kahn realized his thick walls in the Esherick and Unitarian Church commissions, he took the momentous step of consciously separating interior and exterior surfaces in his project for the Luanda Consulate. He had begun discussions with the State Department in October of the previous year and signed a contract for the consulate's design in December. In January 1960 he traveled to Angola to study conditions in accord with State Department policy, which urged some visible reflection of local climate and site.[104] Still, Kahn delayed in designing, and in March 1960 he had only his sketches of the site to submit as proof of work. Over the next three months he conceived his approach: to protect against intense glare, the chancellery and adjoining residence would each be enclosed by a second system of walls, and to help cool the buildings a second roof would be erected to provide a ventilating layer of shade (fig. 112). Officials at the State Department were alarmed by Kahn's first drawings, finding the roof "bizarre" and fearing the buildings would seem "windowless," adding, "the whole concept is rather cold and formidable."[105] During the fall Kahn refined his design (fig. 113); keyhole windows that he had added to the outer wall, a simplified roof structure, and clarified plan arrangements were more favorably received, but his seeming inability to meet deadlines, together with the State Department's changing political objectives, led to the cancellation of the commission in August 1961.[106] Kahn clung to the project; a model was completed later that same month (fig. 111), while formal termination of the contract was pending, and Kahn did not submit his final bill until December 1962.[107]

The Luanda plans are clearly organized but not particularly remarkable. In the separation of walls and roofs, however, Kahn initiated an approach that for the time was revolutionary. Again work by Le Corbusier provided a precedent, for example the sunscreens shading the High Court at Chandigarh (1951–56), but a more remote and, for Kahn, less agreeable precedent, as he felt the problem of

107

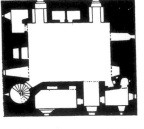
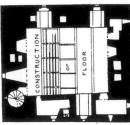
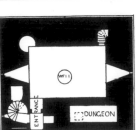
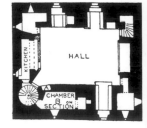

108

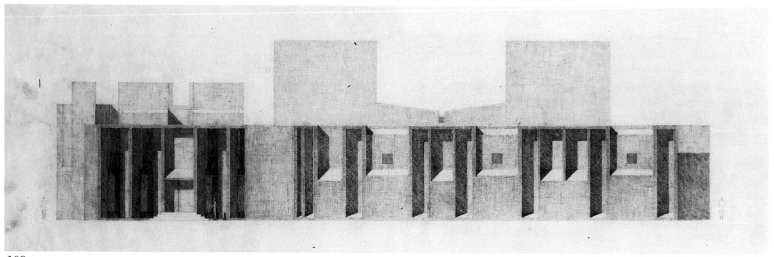

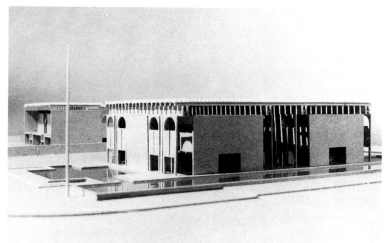

110   111

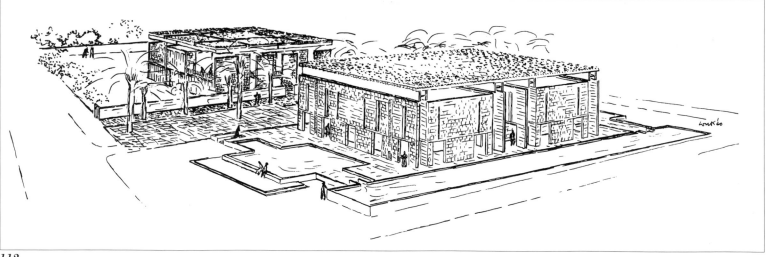

112

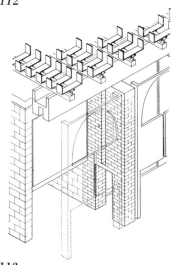

107. Esherick house,
Philadelphia, Pa., 1959–61.
First-floor plan, redrawn 1990.
108. Comlogan Castle,
Dumphriesshire, Scotland.
Plans.
109. First Unitarian Church
and School, Rochester, N.Y.,
1959–69. North elevation,
ca. January 1961.
110. First Unitarian Church
and School, Rochester, N.Y.,
1959–69.

111. U.S. Consulate, Luanda,
Angola, 1959–62. Model, ca.
August 1961.
112. U.S. Consulate, Luanda,
Angola, 1959–62. Bird's-eye
perspective. Inscribed Lou K
'60.
113. U.S. Consulate, Luanda,
Angola, 1959–62. Isometric
diagram of wall and roof
detail, Fall 1960.

glare was unresolved by such devices. Even more emphatically he reacted against the sort of filigreed sunscreens popularized by Edward Durell Stone in the mid-1950s, for he sought an architectural rather than decorative solution. As he explained, "I thought of the beauty of ruins . . . the absence of frames . . . of things which nothing lives behind . . . and so I thought of wrapping ruins around buildings."[108] What began as the addition of one series of walls to another Kahn soon came to regard as one irreducible element, a hollow wall with the potential of two quite distinct interior and exterior profiles. This he first demonstrated in the Salk Institute for Biological Studies (1959–65; see figs. 278–92 and pp. 330–39).

Resolutions of Form and Design

Rarely has the beneficial effect of a sympathetic, collaborative client been better demonstrated than in the extraordinary commission given to Kahn by Jonas Salk. It was Kahn's first real opportunity to conceive the very nature of an institution itself, the tabula rasa he had long sought, and with his resulting design it is possible to define the beginning of a later, more mature phase of his career. In this context the commission will be more fully discussed in chapter 4. But the design for the unbuilt meeting house that Kahn initiated in the fall of 1960 (fig. 115; see figs. 155, 156) also brought to a conclusion the development of a formal vocabulary that Kahn had initiated with the Yale Art Gallery in 1951, for disparate elements of earlier work were now joined in one project. The meeting house is strongly, almost aggressively massive. Its interior spaces are differentiated according to use and defined by individualizing structure. These units of varied shape are juxtaposed in plan without an extrinsic management of form, resulting in a geometrically varied profile. This profile is further complicated by portions of walls enclosing differently shaped interior volumes, for in addition to passively juxtaposed shapes, other, more complicated shapes are juxtaposed through superimposition: squares enclosing circles, circles enclosing squares.[109] Although the similarity is surely coincidental, these configurations recall Renaissance diagrams of the Vitruvian man. Wittkower had described how these diagrams, inscribed within a superimposed square and circle, served "as a proof of the harmony and perfection of the human body . . . [and] seemed to reveal a deep and fundamental truth about man and the world."[110] What better symbol for Salk? For Kahn, the double layers generated by these superimposed shapes illustrated the different natures of inside and outside surfaces, which he diagrammed to accompany the first publication of the design in April 1961 (see fig. 442).[111] A few

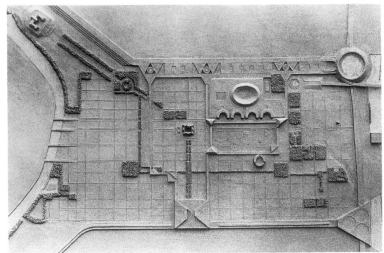

114

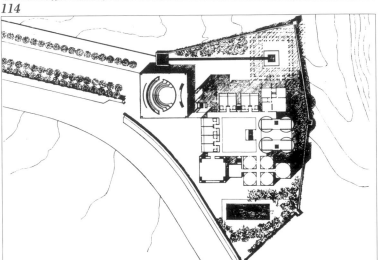

115

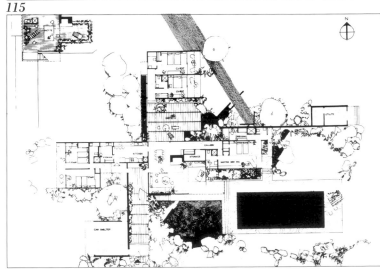

116

114. *Market Street East Studies, Philadelphia, Pa., 1960–63. Model, ca. January 1962.*
115. *Salk Institute for Biological Studies, La Jolla, Calif., 1959–65. Plan of meeting house, Fall 1960– Spring 1961.*
116. *Richard Neutra. Kaufmann house, Palm Springs, Calif., 1946. Plan.*

months later he wrote: "Because a wall has an interior which is different from an exterior . . . we have come to the point where this realization now can separate an exterior wall from an interior wall . . . and create space between them that you could walk between, that which you couldn't do with a solid stone wall."[112]

A comparison of the meeting house plan with Richard Neutra's Kaufmann house (Palm Springs, California, 1946, fig. 116) shows how far Kahn had progressed in the fourteen-year period since that much-praised example of American modernism had been completed. Kahn's plan is rendered to emphasize an ordered assembly of separate spaces, each firmly and clearly enclosed, while Neutra's emphasizes the opposite effect of freely disposed, flowing spaces with lines of enclosure purposely obscured. No governing logic seems to guide dimension or shape in Neutra's design; rather, the scheme reflects an unstructured freedom of what was rapidly becoming another age.[113] Wright's plans in these years exhibited more rigorous organization, but the differentiation of space was implied rather than explicit, and shapes were woven into unified, concordant tapestries.

Major periods of architectural history have often been defined by alternating manifestations of massive or volumetric shape, differentiated or open space, juxtaposed or unified geometries, and layered or exposed profiles. Similar characteristics, differently balanced, have been cited to demonstrate stylistic shifts from imperial Roman to Late Antique architecture, from Renaissance to Baroque, from premodern to modern, and so on. It could be argued that Kahn, beginning with the meeting house, redirected architectural style in the twentieth century through similar means. Yet to judge his work solely in physical terms obscures its deeper meanings, even if at this secondary level his measurable influence has been more immediate. But like Wright before him, Kahn projected an influence so pervasive as to defy concise summary. By reconnecting architecture with the fundamentals of history, he revitalized its primary forms and principles, and he awakened an entire generation of architects who followed. For some of those architects, less drawn to principles, this encouraged an almost picturesque application of specific historic motifs; for others, it led toward a profound exploration of spatial configuration. It would be premature to judge the former as a secondary phenomenon; work by Michael Graves and Robert A. M. Stern, among others, exhibits a warmth that comes from the familiarity of historic associations and should not be denied. But in the architecture of such diverse figures as Mario Botta and Arata Isozaki, a deeper influence can be detected, one rooted in the freedom to reconsider the underlying aspects of design in the light of history.

Before Kahn's debt to history was openly acknowledged, critics tended to praise his work to the degree that it upheld standards of modernism, and they hesitantly excused his unusual, expressive forms as specific responses to tightly defined, conventionally narrow functions. They soon saw otherwise, among them Sibyl Moholy-Nagy, who wrote after visiting Kahn's office: "I was very much impressed with the first sight of the Philadelphia sketches till I realized . . . that these . . . towers are *not* the uniquely adequate solution of this and no other building, but are your trademark now: impartially imposed on everything you design. That is when I liked the [Mikveh Israel] Synagogue less."[114] Kahn indeed imposed inventive, sometimes historically inspired devices— keyhole windows, diagonal elements, circular towers—on whatever commission he was designing at any given time, irrespective of specific function. As he evolved his approach he was not bound by standard typologies. Historic precedents could suggest physical patterns and provide models for organizing space that were new to the twentieth century, but they were a means rather than an end.

The seriousness of Kahn's intent can be sensed in his brief, often repetitive writings. One article in particular stands out as summarizing his attitudes in the 1950s: "Form and Design," which he presented in an early form at the 1959 CIAM conference, then revised for delivery in California in April 1960, and further revised for a Voice of America broadcast in November 1960. With minor revisions this last version was much published, first by the Voice of America and shortly after by *Arts and Architecture* and *Architectural Design*.[115] To those requesting copies of his writings, "Form and Design" was most often sent; as a colleague explained, "It was worked on painstakingly by him over a period of several months and embodies, as nothing else he has written, his current thinking and ideas."[116]

In "Form and Design" Kahn described his work more as the discovery of some ideal, preexisting "form" than as the invention of something new:

When personal feeling transcends into Religion (not *a* religion but the essence of religion) and Thought leads to Philosophy, the mind opens to realizations. Realization of what may be the *existence will* of, let us say, particular architectural spaces. Realization is the merging of Thought and Feeling at the closest rapport of the mind with the Psyche, the source of *what a thing wants to be*.[117]

Kahn's distinctions between "form" and "design," now matured from his first statements of 1953, thus offered a means of disciplining personal choice: "Form has no shape or dimension. . . . Form is 'what'. Design is 'how'. Form is impersonal. Design belongs to the designer. Design is a circumstantial act. . . . Form has nothing to do with circumstantial conditions."[118]

Until he discovered the Platonic image for any given problem, questions of materials and site remained secondary in importance, as he explained in an earlier version of "Form and Design": "What material you use is circumstantial; it is a design problem. . . . The realization of what is an auditorium is absolutely beyond the problem of whether it is in the Sudan, or in Rio de Janeiro."[119] He reinforced this neo-Platonic view by likening form and design to ideas of "spoon" versus "a spoon," "house" versus "a house," and "school" versus "a school": "A School or a specific design is what the institution expects of us. But School, the spirit school, the essence of the existence will, is what the architect should convey in his design. And I say he must, even if the design does not correspond to the budget."[120] Regarding sources and extensions of Kahn's neo-Platonism there has been much thought, most of it necessarily speculative, as Kahn left few specific references. How he came to these ideas is thus somewhat uncertain, although such sources as Egyptian hieroglyphics and German romanticism have been suggested.[121]

Elsewhere in "Form and Design" Kahn partly explained his urge to differentiate space, and to relate that space to structure:

A teacher or a student is not the same when he is with a few in an intimate room with a fireplace as in a large high room with many others. . . . Space has power and gives mode.

. . .

Each space must be defined by its structure and the character of its natural light. . . . An architectural space must reveal the evidence of its making by the space itself.[122]

After mentioning selected projects, Kahn concludes "Form and Design" by discussing his unified vision of the city:

The motor car has completely upset the form of the city. I feel that the time has come to make the distinction between the Viaduct architecture of the car and the architecture of man's activities. . . . The Viaduct architecture includes the street which in the center of the city wants to be a building. . . . The distinction between the two architectures, the architecture of the Viaduct and the architecture of the acts of man's activities, could bring about a logic of growth and a sound positioning of enterprise.[123]

The designs for viaduct architecture that he envisioned for Philadelphia from 1959 to 1962 (see pp. 310–11) provided an outlet for explorations parallel to his writings. As rendered, they reflect an abstract mastery of Roman forms parallel to the much smaller Salk meeting house (fig. 114; see fig. 417). Like Piranesi, Kahn had reconfigured reality. But unlike Piranesi, he would in the years to follow transfer these monumental urban images to other, more realistic commissions.

Others besides Kahn were reexamining history at this time. Buildings by Philip Johnson, Eero Saarinen, and Minoru Yamasaki were among those in America sporting various historic motifs, but these motifs were applied primarily as surface decoration without ties to deeper principles of spatial configuration or structural integrity.[124] Kahn alluded to this issue in criticizing Saarinen's MIT Chapel (1950–55) in "Form and Design."[125] Elsewhere Kahn was critical of what he characterized as "chaotic permissiveness," and he spoke of the need for "an anchoring course of logic."[126] By 1961, following his critical decade of development, his innovative forging of that logic was beginning to be widely recognized, and he came to be acknowledged as the leader of what was termed the Philadelphia School. Referring to this school, which included such architects as Robert Venturi, Romaldo Giurgola, and Robert Geddes, all loosely allied through affiliations at the University of Pennsylvania, one writer stated: "The sixties, it appears, began without any coherent ideologies and systematic disciplines; instead, a strange free-for-all is the admitted, accepted, and defended design approach. There are indications, however, that among this confusion there is already in existence a new design movement with a powerful ideology and a clearly defined design approach."[127]

Kahn's dedication to conceiving buildings that symbolized human beliefs and aspirations, and to providing places where such values could flourish, guided later achievements. As he advised the Kennedy family in their planning for the John F. Kennedy Memorial Library:

Every building that is built is dedicated to the man. It is a way of life. It is the first duty of an architect in order to know in what way to express this. I am hoping that a commitment here will be made to the well being of man. There are many ways to express this. Buildings are based on beliefs—that is the material you need to know, to know how to express it. This is the most important thing.[128]

As these words imply, Kahn believed it was imperative to

identify human beliefs in order to discover ideal form, and to this end he rejected conventional typologies, which he suspected of subverting such investigation by supporting a routine response. As he had earlier observed: "The Air Force Academy [Skidmore, Owings, and Merrill, 1957ff] is a design based on building types accepted by the profession to date as appropriate. In a phenomenally short time the Academy was given form. . . . It would have taken Corbusier many months more than was apparently allowed the architects to conceive the Academy."[129]

As has been much noted, Kahn sought beginnings, designing each building as if it were the first of its kind. His often-cited example was that of the first school:

Schools began with a man under a tree. . . . Soon spaces were erected and the first schools became. The establishment of school was inevitable because it was part of the desires of man. Our vast systems of education, now vested in Institutions, stem from these little schools but the spirit of their beginning is now forgotten. The rooms required by our institutions of learning are stereotype and uninspiring.[130]

He later added, "So I believe the architect somehow must hark back to the time of the beginning."[131] In the Salk Institute Kahn had the rare opportunity to actually conceive a new institution, but in other instances he simulated the effect of origination by reducing programs to their most basic human elements. This process of reduction seemed to relate very much to concerns for the single, essential use that gave meaning to any building. By examining these aspects it is possible to suggest a broad pattern of less conventional typologies that draw closer to Kahn's own objectives. Sharp divisions are necessarily arbitrary, for such typologies lack exclusivity. Yet in the 1960s, as Kahn's commissions increased to a degree not experienced in his earlier years, the linear development of an evolving vocabulary that characterized his work in the 1950s seemed to give way to parallel campaigns devoted to these typologies of use, and differences were clarified.

When Kahn wrote, "space has power and gives mode," and discussed how that power could impose patterns of use, he provided one clue to his manner of conceiving typologies: spaces providing for one person differed fundamentally from those for many. One typology seemed, then, to derive from the creation of individual places, or studies, which were strongly related whether they served laboratories or monasteries. These will be discussed in chapter 4. An opposite typology was guided by the need to create places for meeting or assembly, conceptually similar whether secular

or religious, as examined in chapter 3. Kahn discussed ideal images of each: for study, the St. Gall plan, which diagrammed a series of extended, separated spaces for a monastery; and for assembly, the Pantheon, with its single holistic space.[132] Each defined the terminus of a continuum of possible spatial configurations.

A third typology, the subject of chapter 5, dealt with more complicated problems, with assemblages of components lacking any simple, single focus. For Kahn these resulting complexes were analogous to cities, and like cities they were meant to provide frameworks for more varied human use, for individual choice, and for the resources that he often termed "availabilities." In this way he seems to have rethought such ubiquitous problems as fine arts centers and commercial developments, finding within them unexpected bonds of human endeavor.

Near the end of his career, when Kahn defined the three major human inspirations as "learning, meeting, and well being," the basic typologies relating to study, assembly, and the availabilities seemed firmly established.[133] By then his richly complex, almost baroque solutions had been much publicized. At about this time he seems also to have considered a fourth typology, one that honored both ideas and things and that led him to simpler resolutions. Related in this way were libraries and museums as well as commemorative monuments, all providing spaces for experiencing the achievements of others. Perhaps his commitment to the Kennedy Memorial Library had first inspired the joining of these otherwise disparate types.[134] Later he used the term "treasury space" to characterize his project for the De Menil museum, again enlarging meaning.[135]

Very much a part of these honorific designs were Kahn's later writings relating silence and light, as discussed in chapter 6. How appropriate, then, that he sketched his concept for the Franklin Delano Roosevelt Memorial (1973–74) at the bottom of notes for a talk on silence and light.[136] For in conceiving his design together with ideas of eternity and creation, he reminds us that the simple placement of stones, like the room, is a beginning of architecture.

D.D.L.

Notes

1. Kahn, "Address by Louis I. Kahn, April 5, 1966," *Boston Society of Architects Journal*, no. 1 (1967): 5–20; quoted from typescript, "Boston Society of Architects," Box LIK 57, Louis I. Kahn Collection, University of Pennsylvania and Pennsylvania Historical and Museum Commission, Philadelphia (hereafter cited as Kahn Collection).
2. Letter, Kahn to Dave [Wisdom], Anne [Tyng], and others, December 6, 1950, "Rome 1951," Box LIK 61, Kahn Collection.
3. He wrote, "I now know that Greece and Egypt are musts"; card, Kahn to office, n.d., "Letters to L.I. Kahn," Box LIK 60, Kahn Collection.
4. "Training the Artist-Architect for Industry," in *Impressions* (proceedings of the Design Conference, Aspen, Colorado, June 28–July 1, 1951), ed. R. Hunter Middleton and Alexander Ebin, Box LIK 63, Kahn Collection.
5. Kahn, notebook (K12.22), ca. 1966–72, Kahn Collection.
6. Among early references to the Pantheon in Kahn's writings is a mention in Kahn, "Law and Rule in Architecture" (lecture, Princeton University, November 29, 1961), typed transcript, "LIK Lectures 1969," Box LIK 53, Kahn Collection.
7. Kahn, quoted in Ada Louise Huxtable, "What Is Your Favorite Building," *New York Times Magazine*, May 21, 1961; filed in "Misc.," Box LIK 64, Kahn Collection.
8. Vincent J. Scully, *Louis I. Kahn* (New York: George Braziller, 1962), 10, 12–13, 37.
9. For example, after recommending D'Arcy Wentworth Thompson's *On Growth and Form* to his nephew Alan Kahn as the single book that would explain architecture, he later admitted that he had never read it; Alan Kahn, " 'Conversation about Lou Kahn,' Los Angeles, California, June 20, 1981," in *Louis I. Kahn: L'uomo, il maestro*, ed. Alessandra Latour (Rome: Edizioni Kappa, 1986), 65. Also, to a former student and office colleague he wrote in reference to an article he had been sent, "without reading a word I can feel its significance"; letter, Kahn to William S. Huff, November 4, 1965, "Huff, William, Correspondence," Box LIK 57, Kahn Collection.
10. Kahn, "Space-Order in Architecture" (lecture, Pratt Institute, November 10, 1959), transcript. The transcript was mailed to Kahn on March 28, 1960; letter, Olindo Grossi (Pratt Institute) to Kahn, March 28, 1960, "LIK Lectures 1960," Box LIK 54, Kahn Collection.
11. Scully, interview with Alessandra Latour, in Latour, *Kahn*, 155. Among Brown's publications is Frank E. Brown, *Roman Architecture* (New York: George Braziller, 1961).
12. Kahn, "The Value and Aim in Sketching," *T-Square Club Journal* 1 (Philadelphia, May 1931): 18–21.
13. Reyner Banham, "New Brutalism," *Architectural Review* 118 (December 1955): 357.
14. Letter, Goodwin to Kahn, May 13, 1954, "Personal," Box LIK 66, Kahn Collection.
15. As recounted in William Huff, "Louis Kahn: Sorted Recollections and Lapses in Familiarities," interview with Jason Aronoff, *Little Journal* 5 (September 1981), reprinted in Latour, *Kahn*, 407.
16. For a general description, see David G. De Long, "Eliel Saarinen and the Cranbrook Tradition in Architecture and Urban Design," in *Design in America: The Cranbrook Vision, 1925–1950* (New York: Harry N. Abrams, 1983), 47–89.
17. Kenneth Frampton, "Louis Kahn and the French Connection," *Oppositions*, no. 22 (Fall 1980), reprinted in Latour, *Kahn*, 249.
18. Scully, interview with Latour, 147.
19. Among several accounts of Tyng's association with Kahn is Anne Griswold Tyng, "Architecture Is My Touchstone," *Radcliffe Quarterly* 70 (September 1984): 5–7.
20. Tyng, interview with Alessandra Latour, in Latour, *Kahn*, 51.
21. Kahn, notebook (K12.22), ca. 1955, Kahn Collection.
22. Letter, Kahn to John D. Entenza (director, Graham Foundation), March 2, 1965, "Letters of Recommendation, 1964," Box LIK 55, Kahn Collection.
23. Anne G. Tyng, "Louis I. Kahn's 'Order' in the Creative Process," in Latour, *Kahn*, 285. Fuller recalled speaking with Kahn during train trips between Philadelphia and New Haven; telegram, Fuller to Esther Kahn, March 20, 1974, in Latour, *Kahn*, 179.
24. Letter, Fuller to Entenza, April 5, 1965, "Fuller, R. Buckminster Correspondence, 1965," Box LIK 55, Kahn Collection.
25. Kahn began work on the project in May 1954; summary of expenses, "A.F. of L. Health Center (Melamed) Architects Fee," Box LIK 83, Kahn Collection. The building dedication in February 1957 is reported in "AFL-CIO Center Dedicated Here," *Philadelphia Inquirer*, February 17, 1957. The demolition was reported in "Kahn Finds Lesson in Ruins of His Work," *Philadelphia Inquirer*, August 27, 1973. At that time he reasserted his dislike of the penthouse projection, confirming David Wisdom's account of Kahn's initial reaction when the building was built; Wisdom, interview with David B. Brownlee, Peter S. Reed, and David G. De Long, July 5, 1990. I am grateful to Peter Reed for his research report on this project.
26. Tyng, interview with Latour, 43.
27. Letter, Fruchter to Kahn, September 10, 1951; time sheets, April 25–June 13, 1952; and letter, Kahn to Fruchter, January 30, 1953; "Fruchter," Box LIK 34, Kahn Collection. I am grateful to Peter S. Reed for his research report on this project.
28. Emil Kaufmann, "Three Revolutionary Architects, Boullée, Ledoux, and Lequeu," *Transactions of the American Philosophical Society* 42 (October 1952): 510, fig. 135. Kenneth Frampton notes the similarity between the Ledoux plan and later designs by Kahn; Frampton, "Kahn and the French Connection," 240–41.
29. Kahn received the program and a retainer in June 1954; letter, Benjamin F. Weiss (chairman, building committee) to Kahn, June 29, 1954, "Synagogue & School Bldg . . . Adath Jeshurun," Box LIK 60, Kahn Collection. I am grateful to Peter S. Reed for his research report on this project.
30. Handwritten draft of a letter, Kahn to Gropius, n.d., responding to a letter from Gropius to Kahn, March 16, 1953, "Louis I. Kahn (Personal) 1953," Box LIK 66, Kahn Collection.
31. Kahn had completed preliminary sketches by July 1954; letter, Edward C. Arn (American Seating Company) to Kahn, July 19, 1954, "Synagogue & School Bldg . . . Adath Jeshurun," Box LIK 60, Kahn Collection. Preliminary schemes were submitted in August; letter, Kahn to building committee, August 16, 1954, ibid. His design was rejected as "out of spirit with the type of building wanted by the Board" in April 1955; letter, Weiss to Kahn, April 29, 1955, "LIK Miscellaneous 1954–56," Box LIK 65, Kahn Collection.
32. "Frank Lloyd Wright Plans Synagogue Here," *Sunday Bulletin*, May 23, 1954; filed in "Personal," Box LIK 66, Kahn Collection. The design was also published in "Frank Lloyd Wright Has Designed His First Synagogue . . . ," *Architectural Record* 66 (July 1954): 20.
33. Published in "First Study of the City Hall Building," *Perspecta*, no. 2 (1953): 27. I am grateful to Peter Reed for his research report on this project.
34. Letter, Le Ricolais to Kahn, April 3, 1953, "Louis I. Kahn (personal)—1953," Box LIK 60, Kahn Collection. In the first paper, "Structural Approach in Hexagonal Design" (February 1953), it was claimed that hexagonal planning could also be applied to city traffic patterns; "Le Ricolais," Box LIK 56, Kahn Collection. Le Ricolais was

later invited to Penn, where, beginning in 1955, he and Kahn taught together.

35. Kahn, "Toward a Plan for Midtown Philadelphia," *Perspecta*, no. 2 (1953): 23.

36. Kahn, quoted in Henry S. F. Cooper, "Dedication Issue; The New Art Gallery and Design Center," *Yale Daily News*, November 6, 1953.

37. Letter, Kahn to A. Whitney Griswold, July 30, 1958, "Yale Univ., Correspondence," Box LIK 60, Kahn Collection.

38. Kahn, "Architecture is the Thoughtful Making of Spaces," *Perspecta*, no. 4 (1957): 2–3.

39. Kahn, "Talk at the Conclusion of the Otterlo Congress," in *New Frontiers in Architecture: CIAM '59 in Otterlo*, ed. Oscar Newman (New York: Universe Books, 1961), 213.

40. Kahn had been retained to design the house by June 1954; letter, Mrs. Adler to Kahn, June 14, 1954, "Adler," Box LIK 32, Kahn Collection. Time sheets document work from August to February 1955, most intensely in September; time sheets, ibid. I am grateful to David Roxburgh for his research report on this project.

41. Kahn, quoted in "Louis Kahn Places Design as a Circumstance of Order," *Architecture and the University* (proceedings of a conference, Princeton University, December 11–12, 1953; Princeton, N.J.: School of Architecture, 1954), 29–30.

42. Letters, Mrs. Adler to Kahn, December 3 and 4, 1953, "Louis I. Kahn (personal)—1953," Box LIK 60, Kahn Collection.

43. Kahn, quoted in "How to Develop New Methods of Construction," *Architectural Forum* 101 (November 1954): 157. Kahn's remarks had been made at a conference on architectural illumination at the School of Design, North Carolina State College.

44. Letter, Constance H. Dallas (City Council) to Francis Adler, February 18, 1955, "Adler," Box LIK 32, Kahn Collection. Later, during the summer of 1955, Kahn undertook to remodel a kitchen in their existing house; letter, Kahn to Francis Adler, October 24, 1955, ibid.

45. Scully cites the beginning date as 1954; Scully, *Kahn*, 47. There are no records yet discovered in the Kahn Collection that confirm this. Drawings carry dates only from February 3 to 8, 1955. I am grateful to David Roxburgh for his research report on this project.

46. Kahn, quoted in Susan Braudy, "The Architectural Metaphysic of Louis Kahn," *New York Times Magazine*, November 15, 1970, 86.

47. Kahn, notebook (K12.22), 1955–ca. 1962, Kahn Collection.

48. Letter 441, Mozart to his father, January 16, 1782, in *The Letters of Mozart and His Family*, 2d ed., trans. and ed. Emily Anderson (London: Macmillan; and New York: St. Martin's Press, 1966), 2:793. I am grateful to Eugene K. Wolf and Jean K. Wolf for their assistance in locating this quote.

49. Kahn, notebook, 1955–ca. 1962.

50. Rudolf Wittkower, *Architectural Principles in the Age of Humanism* (London: Alec Tiranti, 1952); Tyng, interview with David G. De Long, October 11, 1990.

51. Kahn, notebook, 1955–ca. 1962.

52. Kahn had been retained to design the Morris house by July 1955; letter, Lawrence Morris to Kahn, July 8, 1955, "Morris House," Box LIK 80, Kahn Collection. There are no time reports or dated records of any sort in the archive for 1956.

53. Letter, Rowe to Kahn, February 7, 1956, "Correspondence from Colleges and Universities," Box LIK 65, Kahn Collection.

54. Ibid. Two articles including a brief discussion of Kahn in the context of the 1950s that Rowe wrote in 1956–57 were published under the title "Neoclassicism and Modern Architecture," *Oppositions*, no. 1 (September 1973): 1–26.

55. Wittkower, *Architectural Principles*, 61.

56. Ibid., 30.

57. Letter, Tyng to Entenza, February 28, 1965, "Letters of Recommendation 1964," Box LIK 55, Kahn Collection. Tyng was applying for a grant to complete a book, *Anatomy of Form*.

58. D'Arcy Wentworth Thompson, *On Growth and Form*, abridged and edited by John Tyler Bonner (Cambridge: Cambridge University Press, 1943; 1961), 119–20, describing fig. 14.

59. "The Dream Builders," *Time*, October 17, 1960, 86. Kahn confirmed Tyng's collaboration on the design in a letter to G. Holmes Perkins, June 21, 1968, "Perkins, Dean G. Holmes, Correspondence," Box LIK 57, Kahn Collection.

60. Tyng, interview with De Long, January 24, 1991.

61. Letter, William Mitchell (vice president, styling staff, General Motors Corporation) to Kahn, December 5, 1960, "General Motors—Contract," Box LIK 32, Kahn Collection. Kahn was expected to finish by late December; the last date carried on the drawings is February 17, 1961. I am grateful to David Roxburgh for his research report on this project.

62. Tyng remained associated with the office until Kahn's death, her position evolving from that of employee to consultant, and she continues, in 1991, to practice independently and teach at the University of Pennsylvania; Tyng, interview with De Long, February 15, 1991.

63. Kahn, "Space Form Use—A Library," *Pennsylvania Triangle* 43 (December 1956): 43.

64. Kahn, quoted in "On Philosophical Horizons" (panel discussion), *AIA Journal* 33 (June 1960): 100.

65. Kahn, "Louis I. Kahn: Talks With Students," *Architecture at Rice*, no. 26 (1969): 26–27.

66. Denise Scott Brown, "A Worm's Eye View of Recent Architectural History," *Architectural Record* 172 (February 1984): 73.

67. For example, letters, Kahn to the Philadelphia Art Alliance, June 23, 1961, "Master File, June 1, 1961 through July 31, 1961," Box LIK 9, Kahn Collection; Kahn to National Council of Architectural Registration Boards, May 20, 1963, "Venturi, Bob," Box LIK 59, Kahn Collection; Kahn to Gordon Bunshaft, February 17, 1971, "Master File, 1 Jan 1971 thru 30 August 71," Box LIK 10, Kahn Collection.

68. For example, in interviews with Alessandra Latour, in Latour, *Kahn: Sue Ann Kahn*, 35; Anne Tyng, 41–49; and Marshall D. Meyers, 77.

69. Memorandum, Paul Schweikher (chairman, department of architecture) to Messrs. Hansen, Kahn, Nalle, and Wu, April 14, 1955, "Yale University—LIK Classes," Box LIK 63, Kahn Collection.

70. Kahn, "1973: Brooklyn, New York" (lecture, Pratt Institute, Fall 1973), *Perspecta*, no. 19 (1982): 94.

71. For the Lawrence Hall of Science, a limited competition in which Kahn had participated and which he gave as a class problem in September 1962, while I was in the studio.

72. For example, Wilder Green, "Louis I. Kahn, Architect Alfred Newton Richards Medical Research Building," *Museum of Modern Art Bulletin* 28 (1961). An exhibition on the Richards Building was held at the Museum of Modern Art from June 6 to July 16, 1961.

73. "Kahn on Beaux-Arts Training," ed. William Jordy, *Architectural Review* 155 (June 1974): 332.

74. Kahn, "Architecture is the Thoughtful Making of Spaces," 2.

75. Kahn, "Form and Design," *Architectural Design* 31 (April 1961): 151. Kahn had first used these terms of description at the CIAM conference in Otterlo in September 1959.

76. August E. Komendant, *18 Years With Architect Louis I. Kahn* (Englewood, N.J.: Aloray, 1975).

77. Letter, Kahn to Eero Saarinen, March 23, 1959, "Master File, September 8, 1958–March 31, 1959," Box LIK 9, Kahn Collection.

78. August Komendant, "Architect-Engineer Relationship," in Latour, *Kahn*, 317.

79. For example, in Scully, *Kahn*, 28; and Scott Brown, "A Worm's Eye View of History," 71.

80. Scully, *Kahn*, 30.

81. Klumb (born Heinrich Klumb) later practiced in Puerto Rico; his work is mentioned in Henry-Russell Hitchcock, *Architecture, Nineteenth and Twentieth Centuries*, 3d rev. ed. (Baltimore and Harmondsworth: Penguin Books, 1968), 422, 465; and Edgar Tafel, *Apprentice to Genius: Years With Frank Lloyd Wright* (New York: McGraw-Hill, 1979), 37–38, 94.

82. "1952 A.I.A. Convention," *Architectural Record* 112 (August 1952): 204.

83. Letter, Kahn to Joseph Hazen, n.d., in response to a request from *Architectural Forum* for a testimonial; and telegram, April 10, 1959, Hazen to Kahn, "Architectural Forum—Louis I. Kahn," Box LIK 61, Kahn Collection.

84. Scully, *Kahn*, 30–31.

85. Kahn, quoted in "On the Responsibility of the Architect" (panel discussion), *Perspecta*, no. 2 (1953): 47.

86. The resumption of work is noted in a letter, Morris to Kahn, June 17, 1957, "Morris House, Mount Kisco, New York," Box LIK 32, Kahn Collection. Early design drawings in the Kahn archive are dated August 6, 1957. Time sheets record design activity from February to October 1958, with the greatest intensity of effort between April and July; "Morris House," Box LIK 80, Kahn Collection. Kahn's final bill is dated October 1, 1958; letter, Kahn to Morris, October 2, 1958, ibid. I am grateful to David Roxburgh for his research report on this project.

87. Vincent Scully, Introduction to *The Louis I. Kahn Archive: Personal Drawings*, 7 vols. (New York: Garland Publishing, 1987), 1:xviii.

88. Kahn, "Remarks" (lecture, Yale University, October 30, 1963), *Perspecta*, no. 9/10 (1965): 305.

89. Scott Brown, "A Worm's Eye View of History," 73.

90. The building was commissioned by Mrs. Robert B. Herbert, whose nephew, William Huff, had been a student of Kahn's at Yale. Huff was working in Kahn's office when the building was commissioned and became chief assistant for the design. Kahn visited the site in August 1958 and signed a contract for design services on September 8; "Greensburg Tribune-Review Publishing Company," Box LIK 35, Kahn Collection. Drawings dated November 7, 1958, show its compact form. I am grateful to P. Bradford Westwood for his research report on this project.

91. Construction began in November 1959; letter, David W. Mark to William Huff, November 11, 1959, "Greensburg Tribune-Review Publishing Company," Box LIK 35, Kahn Collection. It was completed by December 1960, but later additions have altered its appearance.

92. A survey of Fleisher's property was requested in March 1959; letter, Kahn to George Mebus, Inc., March 19, 1959, "Robert H. Fleischer Residence," Box LIK 34, Kahn Collection. Fleisher asked Kahn to stop work in May; letter, Fleisher to Kahn, May 16, 1959, ibid. I am grateful to David Roxburgh for his research report on this project.

93. Kahn signed a design agreement with Goldenberg on January 12, 1959; time sheets record design activity beginning in February; contract documents were complete by late June; "Goldenberg House," Box LIK 80, Kahn Collection. Because of excessive bids the client terminated the contract in August; letter, Goldenberg to Kahn, August 18, 1959, ibid. I am grateful to Peter S. Reed for his research report on this project.

94. Kahn, quoted in "Kahn" (transcribed discussion in Kahn's office, February 1961), *Perspecta*, no. 7 (1961): 13.

95. Kahn, quoted in Heinz Ronner and Sharad Jhaveri, *Louis I. Kahn: Complete Work, 1935–1974*, 2d ed. (Basel and Boston: Birkhäuser, 1987), 98.

96. Wittkower, *Architectural Principles*, 7.

97. Kahn, "Kahn," 15.

98. Funerary basilicas are discussed in Richard Krautheimer, *Early Christian and Byzantine Architecture* (Baltimore and Harmondsworth: Penguin Books, 1960), esp. 30–32.

99. Kahn signed a design agreement on October 1, 1959; "Margaret Esherick Finance File," Box LIK 80, Kahn Collection. I am grateful to David Roxburgh for his research report on this project.

100. Its design was discussed in November; letter, Kahn to C. Woodard, November 12, 1959, "Master File November 2 1959," Box LIK 9, Kahn Collection. Revised plans had been sent by March 1960; letter, Margaret Esherick to Kahn, March 16, 1960, "Miss Margaret Esherick's House, Correspondence," Box LIK 34, Kahn Collection. Construction began in November 1960; agreement with Thomas Regan for Ross and Co., Contractors, November 2, 1960, "Esherick House, Philadelphia, Pennsylvania," Box LIK 139, Kahn Collection. Construction was essentially complete by the following November; letter, Kahn to Ross and Co., November 22, 1961, "Esherick Miscellaneous," Box LIK 34, Kahn Collection.

101. Kahn, "Kahn," 16–17.

102. Letter, Kahn to Richard Demarco (Richard Demarco Gall Ltd., Edinburgh), August 28, 1973, "Master File 1 July 1973 to 31 October 1973," Box LIK 10, Kahn Collection.

103. For example, Brown, *Roman Architecture*, 33. Kahn's conversations with Brown at the American Academy would have provided opportunities to exchange views.

104. The U.S. Department of State program for building embassies and consulates during the 1950s is discussed in Jane C. Loeffler, "The Architecture of Diplomacy: Heyday of the United States Embassy-Building Program, 1954–1960," *Journal of the Society of Architectural Historians* 49 (September 1990): 251–78.

105. Kahn described his ideas for the building at a meeting on June 24, 1960. The perspective illustrated was apparently one of the sketches resulting from that meeting, and was probably one of those being criticized. Letter, William P. Hughes (director, Office of Foreign Buildings, U.S. State Department) to Kahn, August 26, 1960, "Communications and Correspondence," Box LIK 34, Kahn Collection.

106. Letters and memoranda, including letters, R. Stanley Sweeley (supervising architect for residences, Office of Foreign Buildings, U.S. State Department) to Kahn, August 30 and October 19, 1960, and D. Merle Walker (acting director, Office of Foreign Buildings, U.S. State Department) to Kahn, August 4, 1961, "Communications and Correspondence," Box LIK 34, Kahn Collection; memorandum of meeting with a Mr. Chappellier, September 20, 1960, "Program, Luanda, Angola," Box LIK 34, Kahn Collection. I am grateful to David Roxburgh for his research report on this project.

107. The construction of a model is documented by a card, August 26/27, 1961, "Luanda, Africa," Box LIK 80, Kahn Collection. Later drawings are described in a letter, Kahn to Walker, August 30, 1961, "Program, Luanda Angola," Box LIK 34, Kahn Collection. Kahn's final bill is included in a letter, Kahn to Earnest J. Warlow (assistant director for architecture and engineering, Office of Foreign Buildings, U.S. State Department), December 19, 1962, "Luanda, Africa," Box LIK 80, Kahn Collection.

108. Kahn, "Kahn," 9.

109. Anne Tyng has indicated what she believes are roots of this motif in Kahn's earlier work to which she contributed; Tyng, interview with Latour, 55.

110. Wittkower, *Architectural Principles*, 13.

111. Jan C. Rowan, "Wanting to Be: The Philadelphia School," *Progressive Architecture* 42 (April 1961): 141.

112. Kahn, typed transcript of a November 14, 1961, talk to the Board of Standards and Planning for the Living Theater, "Board of Standards & Planning—N.Y. Chapter—ANTA," Box LIK 57, Kahn Collection.

113. Neutra later praised Kahn's nearly completed laboratories at Salk; letter, Neutra to Kahn, May 12, 1965, "Neutra, Richard," Box LIK 57, Kahn Collection. For a discussion of Kahn's theories in relation to the modernism of his day, see Romaldo Giurgola and Jaimini Mehta, *Louis I. Kahn: Architect* (Zurich: Verlag für Architektur, 1975; English ed., Boulder, Colo.: Westview Press, 1975), 216–23.

114. Letter, Sibyl Moholy-Nagy to Kahn, January 22, 1964, "Sibyl Moholy-Nagy Correspondence, 1964," Box LIK 55, Kahn Collection.

115. Bibliographic information on these versions is contained in the annotated bibliography, pp. 433–39. Kahn's quotes that follow in the text are from the version "Form and Design," *Architectural Design* 31 (April 1961): 145–54.

116. Letter, Tim Vreeland to Monica Pidgeon (editor, *Architectural Design*), January 11, 1961, "Master File, November 1 through December 30, 1960," Box LIK 9, Kahn Collection.

117. Kahn, "Form and Design," 145, 148.

118. Ibid., 148.

119. Kahn, "Talk at the Otterlo Congress," 213.

120. Ibid.

121. For example, in Joseph Burton, "Notes from Volume Zero: Louis Kahn and the Language of God," *Perspecta*, no. 20 (1983): 69–90.

122. Kahn, "Form and Design," 148–49.

123. Ibid., 151–52.

124. For a discussion of these examples, see Vincent Scully, *American Architecture and Urbanism* (New York and Washington: Praeger, 1969), 190–212.

125. Kahn, "Form and Design," 148. The chapel had been identified by name in the 1959 version.

126. Kahn, quoted in "The Sixties; A P/A Symposium on the State of Architecture," *Progressive Architecture* 42 (March 1961): 123; and "The New Art of Urban Design—Are We Equipped?" *Architectural Forum* 114 (June 1961): 88.

127. Rowan, "Wanting to Be," 131.

128. Kahn, quoted in the minutes, "Summary of Preliminary Meeting of Committee on Arts and Architecture for the Kennedy Library," n.d., "Mrs. John F. Kennedy Correspondence," Box LIK 56, Kahn Collection. Kahn was invited to serve on the Arts and Architecture Committee for the Kennedy Library in February 1964; letter, Jacqueline Kennedy to Kahn, February 4, 1964, ibid. The selection of I.M. Pei as architect was announced in December 1964; letter, Jacqueline Kennedy to Kahn, December 8, 1964, ibid.

129. Kahn, notebook (K12.22), 1955–ca. 1962, Kahn Collection.

130. Kahn, "Form and Design," 148.

131. Kahn, "Law and Rule in Architecture" (annual discourse, Royal Institute of British Architects, March 14, 1962), typed transcript, "LIK Lectures 1969," Box LIK 53, Kahn Collection.

132. Among his own commissions that he gave his Penn studio as problems, two in the 1962–63 academic year reflect these types: St. Andrew's Priory (1961–67) and Sher-e-Bangla Nagar, the assembly complex at Dhaka (1962–83). The ideals of St. Gall and the Pantheon were much discussed in that year's studio.

133. Letter, Kahn to Stephen S. Gardner (chairman, Bicentennial Site Committee), January 16, 1972, "1972 Bicentennial Corporation Correspondence," Box LIK 50, Kahn Collection.

134. The Turkish architect Gönül Aslanoğlu Evyapan, a former student who was in regular touch with Kahn at the time, recalled Kahn telling her that never had he felt more sympathetic to a commission and never had he wanted one more. I often saw Ms. Evyapan after her meetings with Kahn in 1964 and 1965, when her impressions were particularly strong.

135. Kahn, quoted in Patricia Cummings Loud, *The Art Museums of Louis I. Kahn* (Durham, N.C., and London: Duke University Press, 1989), 258.

136. The talk was given when he was inducted into the American Academy of Arts and Letters. Kahn's notes are undated but are filed with the letter informing Kahn of his election; letter, Aaron Copland to Kahn, November 23, 1973, "The American Academy of Arts & Letters (1972)," Box LIK 44, Kahn Collection.

Buildings dedicated to assembly provided Louis Kahn with extraordinary opportunities to express his beliefs. For him, places of meeting shared essential qualities that rendered differences between secular and religious use secondary in importance, and commissions as diverse as the Mikveh Israel synagogue in Philadelphia (1961–72, unbuilt), the National Assembly Building at Sher-e-Bangla Nagar in Dhaka (1962–83; fig. 118), and the Palazzo dei Congressi in Venice (1968–74, unbuilt) thus drew together as a common endeavor. Few of these designs were realized, but in those that were, his visions of eternal, timeless principles assumed tangible form, and the promise of a new architecture, so fervently sought by his fellow architects, was fulfilled. This he accomplished despite the demands of more commissions than he could readily manage, commissions often made difficult by bureaucratic complexity and extensive travel to unfamiliar climes. With his growing fame, invitations to speak came even more frequently than in the previous decade, and these he continued to accept, for, however pressed, he remained unremittingly generous in sharing his ideas. Perhaps this very activity also proved stimulating, for it required that he focus on essentials and seemed to encourage a clarification of differences.

Kahn had first recorded his thoughts about assembly in 1955 when speaking of his design for the Adath Jeshurun synagogue (1954–55, unbuilt): "It is what the space wants to be: a place to assemble under a tree" (see fig. 69).[1] This sense of the historic origin of assembly he later elaborated by explaining his triangular synagogue as "free from a single traditional plan, free from a space everyone remembers as typical."[2]

In his next design for assembly—the First Unitarian Church in Rochester (1959–69), designed while he was still developing his mature vocabulary—he discarded the triangular shape, but not the centralized plan, which remained a constant. Theaters or lecture halls Kahn approached differently; performance—whether speech or music—differed by nature of its predictability, and a passive audience did not constitute true assembly: "With only one other person one feels generative. The meeting becomes an event. The actor throws aside the lines of his performance. The residue from all his thoughts and experiences meets the other on equal terms."[3]

Beginning in 1961, within a few weeks of receiving the commission for Mikveh Israel, Kahn began to speak more frequently of assembly and of beliefs that transcended conventional religion. Declining to enter the proposed competition for the state capital of Gandhinagar in India, he explained: "The beginning of any work must start from Belief. . . . I distrust competitions because the design is unlikely to stem from Belief which is of religious essence out of a commonness sensed from other men."[4] Whether a particular use was religious or secular became incidental to the nature of assembly, which Kahn believed embodied a broader concept than either alone could command. This view was reflected in his frequent references to the Pantheon, for him an archetypal image: "It was a kind of conviction, a belief on the part of a man who said that this, because of its shape, presents a statement in form of what may be a universal religious space."[5] Later he described the Pantheon as "a kind of institution"[6] and then as "a world within a world. The client . . . saw the demand of this pantheonic requirement of no religion, no set ritual, only inspired ritual."[7] Centralized shapes—preferably circular rather than triangular—best served this end; thus the Pantheon was "a circular building from which one could not derive a formalistic ritual."[8] Kahn developed his ideal prototype by adding an ambulatory. As eloquently explained in regard to the design of the Unitarian Church, the form of centralized volume was thus modified to allow participants to elect degrees of commitment. Kahn seemed drawn less to centralized churches of the fourth and fifth centuries than to their pagan prototypes; perhaps the particularized provisions for religious ritual and established axial hierarchies of those churches defeated the participatory experience he sought to foster.

In his first proposal for Mikveh Israel, presented in December 1961, Kahn began with a square sanctuary (see fig. 473 and pp. 362–67). Its ambulatory, slight at first, gradually expanded in later proposals until it came to have its own definition. From the outset he firmly separated the place for religious assembly from places for other uses, resisting the creation of any multipurpose spaces, however much later economy would seem to dictate. In Kahn's mind, space dedicated to a single, elevating purpose was evidently essential to assembly, and in this he did not waver.

As a specific design, Mikveh Israel is better known for its "window rooms," the extraordinary cylindrical, open towers that Kahn derived from diverse sources but persuasively synthesized, so that ultimately they came to characterize one aspect of his inventive genius. They first appeared in plans dating from August 1962, spaced along the perimeter of a square sanctuary (see fig. 477). Undated pages from Kahn's notebook suggest how he began their

Chapter 3

Assembly... a Place of Transcendence

Designs for Meeting

118

122

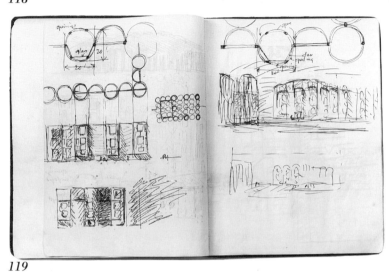

119

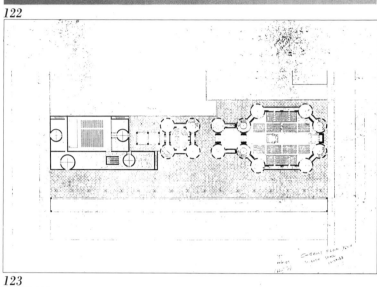

123

120

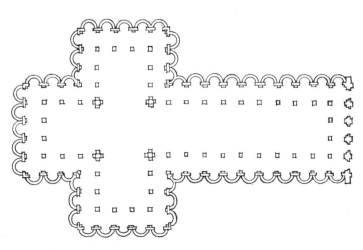

121

117. Tree of Sefiroth from
Paulus Ricius, Portae Lucis,
1516.
118. Sher-e-Bangla Nagar,
Dhaka, Bangladesh, 1962–83.
National Assembly Building
from northwest, 1987.
119. Mikveh Israel Synagogue,
Philadelphia, Pa., 1961–72.
Sketchbook studies, ca. August
1962.

120. Mikveh Israel Synagogue,
Philadelphia, Pa., 1961–72.
South elevation, October 1962.
121. Filippo Brunelleschi.
Santo Spirito, Florence,
1434–82. Plan.
122. Mikveh Israel Synagogue,
Philadelphia, Pa., 1961–72.
Model, January 1964.
123. Mikveh Israel Synagogue,
Philadelphia, Pa., 1961–72.
Plan. Inscribed 10-29-63.

design: as light-filtering elements generated by a plan fully regulated according to circular modules (fig. 119). Brunelleschi's plan of Santo Spirito (Florence, 1434–82), although emphatically longitudinal, was similarly planned, and was originally to be bounded by continuous, semicircular niches that were meant to be seen from outside (fig. 121).[9] Kahn's own design for the Salk meeting house of 1960 offered a closer precedent, both for cylindrical elements serving to modulate light and for the concept of separating interior and exterior walls (see figs. 155, 156). With Mikveh Israel, Kahn developed the circular unit as a space in itself, opened to the inside and linked by passages so that the ambulatory assumed an architectural presence.

When Kahn gave the sanctuary an octagonal configuration in October 1962, he intensified its centralized focus (fig. 120; see fig. 479). Its shape was slightly elongated in his scheme of the following year, but without a loss of centrality (fig. 123), and it was this version and its model (fig. 122) that Kahn preferred to illustrate in publications of his work.[10] As others have noticed, the plan resembles a cabalistic image of a Tree of Life that depicts ten aspects of God (fig. 117);[11] its symbolism would have been appropriate, but Kahn's knowledge of the image remains uncertain. Regarding the architect's approach to such obscure sources he stressed visual aspects alone: "He doesn't *read* the thing anyway. If it is in Latin, it is just the same as if it was in English, because he will see the pictures. He will see what he sees, what his mind tells him it is. . . . What you *think* it is, is absolutely as important as what the man *writes* it is."[12]

In appearance, Mikveh Israel understandably elicited comparisons with various medieval fortifications, yet the familiar gateways of ancient Rome's Aurelian walls would have provided an even earlier antecedent (fig. 124). Other buildings that Kahn designed also bore something of a castle air, and many of these were for assembly. Kahn admitted fascination with castles (see chapter 4), and the layered composition he defined for the synagogue visually ennobled its broader purpose as perceived from without. Perhaps more essentially, it strengthened the creation of the "world within a world" that Kahn so admired in the Pantheon and that he seemed to envision for Mikveh Israel (fig. 125). There, apart from the outer world yet within natural light seemingly generated by the building itself, assembled members of the congregation appear not as mute spectators but as participants actively seeking common understanding.

As with Jonas Salk, Kahn again benefited from an understanding client in Mikveh Israel, and while Dr.

Bernard Alpers (for whom Esther Kahn worked) chaired the building committee, the design progressed. Kahn's proposals for Salk and Mikveh Israel—both resulting in construction estimates far beyond the original amounts available—were part of a pattern from which he rarely deviated: the refusal to be bound by conventional economic restraints. For Kahn, such restraints had no bearing on the ideal form each building should approximate. By discovering that form and giving it tangible shape, he understandably felt that he had fulfilled a primary obligation, and that somehow the means to realization would be found. Yet the degree of client support necessary to assemble the vast sums that were usually required was seldom sustained. Inspired by such commitment, Salk heroically jeopardized his institution and proved the rightness of their shared vision. With committees Kahn was ordinarily less fortunate, and at the very least defeating compromises resulted. Two extraordinary exceptions—both commissioned in the fall of 1962—were the Indian Institute of Management in Ahmedabad (1962–74; discussed in chapter 4), and Sher-e-Bangla Nagar in Dhaka (1962–83), originally commissioned as the legislative capital of East Pakistan (see figs. 337–59 and pp. 374–83). On the subcontinent Kahn's philosophic approach seemed more widely appreciated than in his own country. In the latter commission that appreciation was facilitated by the firm and continuing support of Dhaka's preeminent architect, Mazharul Islam, who actively supported Kahn's design throughout its long course.

Kahn received the Ahmedabad and Dhaka commissions at a time of unusual activity in his career. Only months before, in March 1962, he had moved his Philadelphia office for what would be the last time, from 138 South 20th Street to a more central location at 15th and Walnut. In addition to Mikveh Israel and Salk, Kahn was already involved with designs for the Erdman dormitory, the Fort Wayne cultural center, and the Levy Memorial Playground, as discussed in later chapters. His schedule was further complicated by the birth of a son, Nathaniel Alexander Phelps Kahn, in November of that same year. Robert Venturi had introduced Kahn to Nathaniel's mother, Harriet Pattison, around 1959. She had a diverse background in theater, philosophy, and music, and had studied at Yale and in Edinburgh.[13] She and Kahn developed a close relationship that was to last until his death and that was to involve her as a professional associate, for after Nathaniel's birth she studied landscape architecture— first as an apprentice to Dan Kiley, then at the University of Pennsylvania. During the last years of Kahn's life, she described herself as a "companion for his thoughts," and continued to offer influential support as he developed his

124. *Porta Asinaria, Aurelian wall, Rome, ca. A.D. 275.*
125. *Mikveh Israel Synagogue, Philadelphia, Pa., 1961–72. Perspective of sanctuary, 1963.*
126. *Sher-e-Bangla Nagar, Dhaka, Bangladesh, 1962–83. Site model, ca. March 1963.*
127. *Claude-Nicolas Ledoux. Chaux Saltworks, Arc-et-Senans, France. First project plan, ca. 1773–74, as published in* Transactions of the American Philosophical Society, *1952.*

124

125

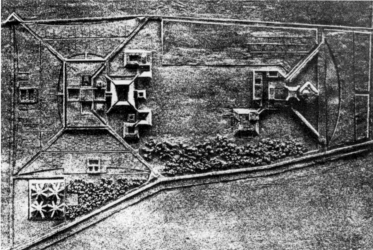

126

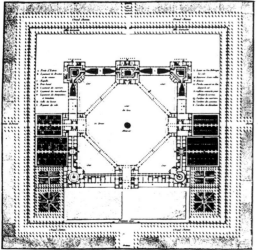

127

ideas.[14] His sensitivity to the landscape grew, and he sought intellectual parallels between their relationship and that between Edwin Lutyens and Gertrude Jeckyll: "When I think of how sensitive a person must be in regard to human agreement, I think of Gertrude Jeckyll, who was a great landscape architect who worked with Lutyens, who was a great architect. . . . She was . . . very responsive to what would sympathize with his architecture."[15]

Kahn deferred work on the Dhaka commission until January 1963, when he traveled to the subcontinent to inspect the site and began designing one of his most important works: the capital district of what later became the independent nation of Bangladesh. Distinguished by the name Sher-e-Bangla Nagar, meaning "the city of the Bengal tiger," it lies on the outskirts of the city of Dhaka. He was to be occupied with this commission for the remainder of his life, yet when he returned from his first trip to Dhaka in early 1963, he already had the guiding idea in mind. Referring to its beginnings, he explained to his students at the University of Pennsylvania:

On the night of the third day, I fell out of bed with the idea which is still the prevailing idea of the plan. This came simply from the realization that assembly is of a transcendent nature. Men came to assemble to touch the spirit of commonness, and I thought that this must be expressible. Observing the way of religion in the living of the Pakistani, I thought that a mosque woven into the space fabric of the assembly would have such effect.[16]

From a long list of building requirements that he had been given, Kahn had already identified those essential components that could give meaning to his design:

The relationship of the assembly, mosque, [supreme] court, and hostels in their interplay psychologically is what expresses a nature. The institution of Assembly could lose its strength if the sympathetic parts were dispersed. The inspirations of each would be left incompletely expressed.

. . .

What I'm trying to do is establish a belief out of a philosophy I can turn over to Pakistan so that whatever they do is always answerable to it.[17]

Kahn's dedication to the Dhaka commission was intense, and within a matter of days following his return he assigned it to his class as their studio problem. Forgotten was the earlier assignment of a new design for Market Street East that the dean of the school had urged Kahn to undertake; the greater and more realistic challenge of significant, city-scaled design in Dhaka now eclipsed hypothetical reworkings of

Philadelphia.[18] With the class he continued to explore the underlying meaning of assembly, speaking of it as having "a religious atmosphere" and defining the sense of religion as "a realization that you are responsible beyond your own selfish self—the kind of thing that makes people group together to form a mosque or form a legislature. . . . Kinship, a simpler word than religion, comes from the same inspiration. . . . Because architecture has enclosure, it has the power to evoke a feeling of kinship when [one] enters the spaces."[19] Kahn's belief in the sacral meaning of secular assembly remained firm; he later said, "A house of legislation is a religious place,"[20] and, of the commission as a whole, "The stimulation came from the place of assembly. It is a place of transcendence for political people. . . . The assembly establishes or modifies the institutions of man."[21]

On the program he received during his first trip to Dhaka in early 1963 Kahn sketched his ideas (see fig. 488).[22] He indicated positions for major elements within the site and, in the lower left-hand corner, emphasized with heavy lines the geometric motif that would shape the joined assembly and mosque: two squares, one turned obliquely to the other. In March, during the spring break at the university, he returned to Dhaka to make his first presentation. The obliquely placed square of the assembly was diagrammed with a low dome near its center, and angled spurs representing minarets expanded the square mosque it touched (fig. 126). To give some shape to the largely featureless terrain and to guard against floods, Kahn proposed embanked roadways and geometrically shaped mounds of earth; on these he placed related elements, partly framed by a lake that he "employed . . . as a discipline of location and boundary."[23] At the opposite end of the expansive site he located schools, libraries, and other facilities, grouped as his Citadel of Institutions to balance the Citadel of Assembly.

Le Corbusier's work at Chandigarh (1951–63) must have been in Kahn's mind. He had visited that new capital during his first trip to India in November 1962, when he began work on the Indian Institute of Management, and later he urged his students to study it as they began their individual designs for Dhaka.[24] Yet however much he admired Le Corbusier, he also harbored doubts about Chandigarh. Earlier he had praised Le Corbusier's buildings for their beauty, but he had also claimed that they were "out of context and had no position."[25] At Dhaka, Kahn's buildings were emphatically positioned so they formed a single, interconnected composition; an urge for connection seemed basic to his approach.

128

129

128. Sher-e-Bangla Nagar,
Dhaka, Bangladesh, 1962–83.
Ambulatory of National
Assembly Building.
129. Sher-e-Bangla Nagar,
Dhaka, Bangladesh, 1962–83.
Plan of National Assembly
Building, 1966.
130. Sher-e-Bangla Nagar,
Dhaka, Bangladesh, 1962–83.
Section through National
Assembly Building facing west.
Inscribed July 6, 1964.

Nowhere was Kahn's urge for architectural connection more apparent than in the joining of mosque and assembly, the central focus of his plan for Dhaka. As a conscious motif, the linking of one square at its corner to a second, diagonally aligned figure had no exact parallel in his earlier work, nor was it a familiar plan elsewhere. At Dhaka, Kahn devised a forceful, active juxtaposition of parts that differed from both the more passive and the more sympathetic juxtapositions discussed in the previous chapter, for they were neither a loosely joined arrangement of differing shapes, as in later plans for the Unitarian Church (see fig. 452), nor a more formal grouping of similarly shaped, hierarchically stabilized units, as in an earlier scheme for that same project (see fig. 102). Dhaka's strongly wrought exterior differed also from cohesive shapes that Kahn had juxtaposed through superimposition, as in the Salk meeting house (see fig. 115). This geometric motif of active juxtaposition came to figure prominently in Kahn's work to follow immediately after. In such Roman precursors as Hadrian's Villa, such juxtapositions remained passive, for they lacked symmetrical disposition and were not planned together from the viewpoint of exterior presentation. Piranesi's reconstructed plan of the Campus Martius in Rome contained individual elements that more closely anticipate Kahn's, yet they had remained undeveloped as three-dimensional images. A closer antecedent to Kahn's design is Ledoux's first project for the Saltworks at Chaux (fig. 127), yet the superimposition of the two squares in that design neutralizes their visible interaction. Appropriately, Ledoux's compositions have been cited for leading the way from a classical toward a juxtapositional composition.[26] Out of such diverse sources, Kahn forged angular compositions quite unlike those of his contemporaries, for there was no longer any real resemblance to the relaxed meanderings best typified by Alvar Aalto's work, and even less to the cohesive triangular essays of Frank Lloyd Wright.

Kahn's plan for the Erdman dormitory at Bryn Mawr, with three parallel squares joined at their corners, lies at the threshold of the Dhaka proposal. Its difficult resolution in December 1961 (see pp. 352–57) came a few days after Kahn had defined a central and troubling issue: "The architecture of connection . . . that which connects the usable space. . . .This is the measure of the architect— the organization of the connecting spaces—that which gives the man walking through the building . . . a feeling of the entire sense of the institution."[27] During ensuing months Kahn cited his plan for Bryn Mawr as resolving the issue: "It never occurred to me that I could take the square and turn it . . . so that it made its own connection."[28] Anne Tyng's Bryn

Mawr proposal (see fig. 467) had surely been the catalyst for this change; connecting its angled, central squares to surrounding rooms were linear walkways much like the angled corridors of Ledoux's plan for Chaux.

In his first scheme for Dhaka, Kahn effected a still more powerful connection than in the Erdman dormitory. By angling the mosque against the assembly building, he brought into dynamic balance places for two kinds of assembly, with the contemplative holding the active in check. In such angled geometries Kahn found a principle of broad meaning and wide applicability, for Dhaka's plan seemed to inspire other designs, like the Norman Fisher house (1960–67). The early date of the Fisher commission would suggest otherwise, but in January 1963 Kahn admitted that it was still undesigned and assigned it to his students at the university while he made his first trip to Dhaka. As documents show, it was only later in 1963 that he reached a solution. It was also after his return from Dhaka that he added similar shapes to his Levy Memorial Playground plan (1961–66). Likewise resolved were the Indian Institute of Management and the University of Virginia Chemistry Building (1960–63). Sketches for the former had included angled lines representing prevailing breezes and suggesting angled orientation, but it was only in March 1963 that Kahn resolved its plan with juxtaposed squares. It was also in March that the towered, fortresslike auditorium of the chemistry building gave way to an angled square joined at its corners to surrounding wings. During the summer of 1963 he began to incorporate similar geometrics in studies for the Fort Wayne Fine Arts Center.

After his March presentation in Dhaka, Kahn reduced the size of the mosque and incorporated it more fully within the assembly building. Yet the richly curvilinear structure he ultimately designed (see fig. 497), with cylindrical light-giving elements at the corners (see fig. 348), was resolutely angled away from the main axis and toward Mecca (fig. 129), maintaining a visible presence. The Mosque of the Shah in Isfahan (1612–38) had been similarly angled away from the axis of the Royal Square, but its site was constrained in a way that Dhaka's was not, and Kahn could easily have eliminated the angle through a slight realignment of the entire complex. Again it seemed a willful means of strengthening identity; as Kahn described, "I made it differently that way so that you could, in fact, express [the mosque] differently."[29]

Other, more separate elements of the program were either eliminated or brought toward the assembly, juxtaposed in a

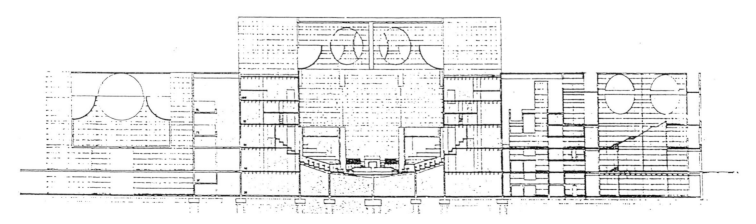

manner emphasizing centralized focus (fig. 130). Hostels flanking the assembly remained at each side, visually supporting the central structure. Their original purpose of providing places of temporary residence for the legislators was thus demonstrated. Within the assembly building itself, an ambulatory of grandly sublime scale further amplified the assembly's elevated purpose while providing a less formal space for related activity (fig. 128). To bring natural light to the interiors of the vast structure, Kahn developed "hollow columns"—something akin to light wells, but in his mind having greater architectural purpose:

In the plan of the assembly I have introduced a light giving element to the interior of the plan. Consider if you see a series of columns you can say that the choice of columns is a choice in light. The columns as solids frame the spaces of light. Now think of it just in reverse and think that the columns are hollow and much bigger and their walls can themselves give light, then the voids are rooms, and the column is the maker of light and can take on complex shapes and be the supporter of spaces and give light to spaces.[30]

In study models these "hollow columns" were given clear geometric definition (fig. 131); as realized, they were shaped by the volumes they adjoined, and they brought light to the outer offices rather than to the assembly itself. There Kahn struggled to find the ideal roof for this most important of spaces, a structural solution that would sustain the abstract geometry of his design and, perhaps most importantly, bring light from above (fig. 132). Kahn had praised the Pantheon's oculus as a source of light "that is most transcending" and "an expression of a world within a world";[31] now that ideal seemed likely to elude him. He disagreed with August Komendant, his consulting engineer, who saw no structural logic in what he sought,[32] and ultimately settled for a melon-shaped vault that lacked the visual strength of his earlier proposals (see fig. 349).

Elsewhere on the site Kahn's design was subject to the vicissitudes of a complicated and ever-developing program. As more components were added, the simple clarity of his early schemes gave way to greater crowding, and outside the area of governmental buildings his controlling concept became more difficult to perceive (fig. 133). Of necessity, associates assumed responsibility for much of the housing and some related structures, although Kahn oversaw even these smaller elements to the degree possible during his visits to the site.[33] Evidence suggests he was more closely involved with the design of the observatory (added to the program in September 1963) and of the higher categories of housing. But it is in the assembly and related hostels that his hand remained most sure.

During construction (fig. 135), views of the assembly suggested the timeless geometry of the observatories of the Maharajah Sawai Jai Singh II at Jaipur and Delhi (fig. 134), as do views of the members' hostels (see fig. 351). Kahn would have noticed Isamu Noguchi's photographs of the observatories published in *Perspecta*,[34] and surely he visited the Jantar Mantar in Delhi. Sympathetic to those eighteenth-century observatories, Kahn's building, too, seems to chart cosmic order. In the assembly building itself, the elemental forms that surround the central chamber sustain this image, as do the unglazed openings in the outer walls (see fig. 341). Echoes of antiquity—at least antiquity as it was imagined—seem to lie behind even the most abstract of these shapes. Like eyes looking in both directions toward wider realms that lie beyond, they also recall Ledoux's famous drawing of the proscenium in his Théâtre Besançon (1771–73). By limiting himself to basic Euclidian shapes, Kahn disciplined sentiment and achieved that rare level of abstraction wherein each individual could discover personal meaning. Thin lines of white marble accent the joints, ennobling the exposed concrete of the walls while marking increments of construction and also tracing an element of human scale. The red brick of adjoining terraces and of the hostels further reinforces the special nature of the assembly. Everywhere are marks of local effort in building so mighty a structure, and they enlarge its already heroic scale (see fig. 342).

For some, the assembly building recalls such Italian fortifications as the Castel del Monte.[35] Others have likened its plan to the centralized traditions of Islamic and Buddhist architecture, believing that Kahn fused Eastern and Western traditions.[36] In 1990, observant of the building's power to generate national pride, one writer said:

This cosmo-geographical macrocosm, whose microcosms are those of the city, the mosque, the house and the garden, distills a concept of divine essence which leads us by specific ways and paths in an earth-paradise ascension. . . . This is architecture which restores something to those who have no heritage, who find in it an image of their dignity, and who—for lack of anything better—see in it a vision of a different life.[37]

More simply, Kahn himself said, "The image is that of a many-faceted precious stone, constructed in concrete and marble."[38] Some have criticized the building for lacking human scale,[39] yet partly this may have been Kahn's purpose, at least from distant viewpoints. By avoiding such conventions, he stressed the "transcendent nature" of assembly rather than the smaller dimension of the individual. For those who assemble within, and for the

131

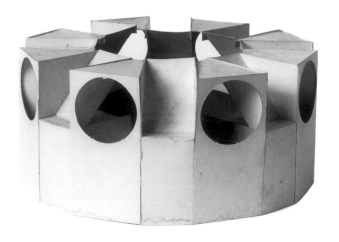

132

133

134

135

larger populace who gather peacefully on its broad terraces, the building surely fulfills its purpose.

The architectural representation of assembly must have been compelling as an idea, for it seemed to guide Kahn's parallel work in Islamabad, the new capital of West Pakistan. This was designated as the executive capital of the country, balancing the legislative capital in East Pakistan. The government selected Constantine Doxiadis to devise the master plan, which was published in May 1961, and various prominent architects were assigned major buildings, including Gio Ponti and Alberto Rosselli for a central secretariat and Arne Jacobsen for a second, supplementary assembly.[40] In July 1963, while refining his master plan for the east capital in Dhaka, Kahn was selected as the architect for the President's Estate in Islamabad, intended as a residential and administrative complex.[41] Gradually he assumed responsibility for other components of the capital as well, including the assembly when Jacobsen's design was judged unsatisfactory.

There is no evidence of any design effort on Kahn's part before December 1963, and sketches made during ensuing months show little more than preliminary effort, with juxtaposed geometries portraying an active engagement of interrelated parts. Beginning in September of the following year, while Kahn was being pressured to present some indication of his design, his sketches suggest a firmer sense of architectural composition (fig. 136).[42] The President's Estate, shown as a linear complex along the left, is linked by an angled square containing administrative offices to a triangular element designated as a center for Islamic studies. These three elements enclose one corner of what came to be known as Presidential Square; at the top of the drawing, Kahn, beginning to take over from Jacobsen, sketched his first diagrammatic indication of the assembly building for Islamabad, shown as a circular building much like the hollow-column study for Dhaka. By the time of his first presentation in October 1964, this had taken the form of a truncated pyramid; at its center was a circular opening, and within that, an obliquely placed cube. By January 1965 Kahn was also designing a national monument on the square, apparently developed as part of the President's Estate. Describing his initial idea to Robert Matthew, the architectural coordinator for the Administrative Sector of Islamabad, he said, "It could be a new concept of Minaret embodying a small chapel raised above the level of the square, and a special platform from where one could preach facing Mecca. . . . The square is being suggested as a roofless Hall of Meeting. . . . The Assembly Building has remained

131. Sher-e-Bangla Nagar, Dhaka, Bangladesh, 1962–83. Study model of National Assembly Building, ca. 1964.
132. Sher-e-Bangla Nagar, Dhaka, Bangladesh, 1962–83. Study model of National Assembly Building, ca. 1964.
133. Sher-e-Bangla Nagar, Dhaka, Bangladesh, 1962–83. Site model, January 1973.

134. Rasi Valaya Yantra, Jaipur, India, early 18th century.
135. Sher-e-Bangla Nagar, Dhaka, Bangladesh, 1962–83. National Assembly Building under construction, ca. 1967.

essentially the same. Its shape was praised by Noguchi."[43] By March 1965 Kahn had further refined the assembly building, shown at the left of a site model (fig. 137) as a cube atop a square platform with towerlike elements at the corners. At the bottom of the model the linear President's Estate is elaborated with monumental apses, and at the top the National Monument appears as a truncated obelisk. The triangular center for Islamic studies defines the fourth side of Presidential Square, and behind it Ponti's administrative buildings are indicated as low rectangles.

At what point Kahn was invited to design the assembly building, and how definite its commission, remain uncertain. Jacobsen's design for the assembly, with facades of anodized aluminum and glass, had been rejected sometime after its presentation in January 1964, and reports identified Kahn as its new architect.[44] Yet in Kahn's much-delayed contract of January 1965 there is no mention of any responsibility for the assembly, and following his presentation in March he was criticized for not restricting his efforts to the President's Estate and the related monument.[45] Kahn apparently began to study the problem without an official invitation, believing its sympathetic design critical to his own efforts and to the entire venture of the new capital. Kahn's own notes at the time allude to this, for he wrote, "The master plan and the spirit of its architecture are one," explaining that the "establishment of a building order" was essential to the city as a whole and that "the buildings of the higher institutions must be the inspiration for the continuance of . . . buildings designed by many architects."[46]

After March 1965 Kahn's invitation to design the assembly must have been more legitimized, for during the summer he focused on its design without further complaint from Matthew, and a developed scheme resulted. By August it had attained a clear definition that made the rambling shapes of the President's Estate seem unplanned by comparison (fig. 139). In place of the generalized form of his earlier cube, Kahn now proposed a shallow dome resting on an elongated drum that rose from its base like Choisy's idealized drawings of the Pantheon (fig. 138).[47] Ambulatories enclose the central chamber, where the rotated squares, indicated as generating the plan, emphasize centrality (fig. 141). The low wings of the outer enclosure are geometrically less complicated than Dhaka's, but only slightly less protective. Government officials had stipulated "that the architecture be given an Islamic touch,"[48] and this accounts in part for both the dome and the plan; Kahn had written, "The insistence of the Islamic touch is plaguing . . . but in spite of this, it can stimulate resources not called on before."[49]

Ultimately the Pakistani government rejected Kahn's designs for both the assembly and the President's Estate, diverting the commission to Edward Durell Stone.[50] He designed a predictable confection of no apparent distinction (fig. 140); without the guiding intellect of Dhaka's Mazharul Islam, government officials were apparently unwilling to gamble with genius. Yet however distinctive Kahn's proposals were by comparison with Stone's, they seemed to lack the conviction of his work at Dhaka. His simplified Islamabad assembly may have represented a conscious effort to distill essential components—a powerfully centralized form with the pressure of its single vaulted chamber relieved by ambulatories—yet without the firm positioning established by Dhaka's hostels and terraces, its presence was not fully appreciable. And the President's Estate seemed never to have achieved fixed location or perceivable form. Kahn had insisted on full control of the master plan at Dhaka; at Islamabad there was no such opportunity, and the results were telling.

Cooperative ventures did not elicit Kahn's best work, especially when major elements were assigned to other architects. While he may have been free to design his own part, he was hampered by the fact that he was not able to determine the philosophy that could guide the endeavor. Illustrating this are his efforts on behalf of the regrettably named Interama, imagined as a permanent international fair for North and South America. Not only did this project involve an awkwardly balanced group of architects, but Kahn's work was limited to a secondary element of housing and exhibition space (Interama Community B, 1963–69, unbuilt) within the very shadow of the major assembly building, for which he must have felt best qualified. His fellow architects were among America's leading practitioners of the time: Marcel Breuer, Paul Rudolph, Jose Luis Sert, Edward D. Stone, and Harry Weese. This ambitious scheme of six major building complexes was federally financed and was planned for a 680-acre site near Miami.[51] At first Kahn had been understandably reluctant to participate, but in November 1964 he accepted the commission for the seven national houses of Community B together with an exhibition hall and auditorium.[52] Breuer had been given the adjacent parliamentary center. Kahn strove to elevate the purpose of the otherwise commercially focused enterprise, expanding upon the program to identify three "inseparable parts": the meeting enclave, the university enclave, and the enclave of industry; he defined his own segment as a place of "minor assembly" in relation to Breuer's "major assembly."[53] In each of three versions he presented, his part remained an uncompleted segment (fig. 143).[54] Flanked by the national

136. President's Estate, First Capital of Pakistan, Islamabad, 1963–66. Site plan. Inscribed LIK September 30, 64.
137. President's Estate, First Capital of Pakistan, Islamabad, 1963–66. Site model, ca. March 1965.
138. President's Estate, First Capital of Pakistan, Islamabad, 1963–66. Site model, September 1965.

139. President's Estate, First Capital of Pakistan, Islamabad, 1963–66. Elevation and partial section, ca. August 1965.
140. Edward Durell Stone. President's Residence, Islamabad, Pakistan, 1966.
141. President's Estate, First Capital of Pakistan, Islamabad, 1963–66. First-floor plan of Assembly Building, after March 1965.

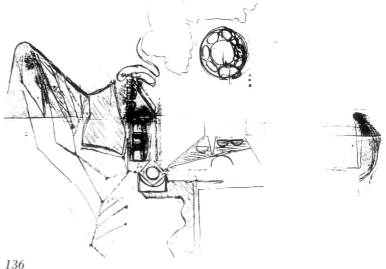

137

138

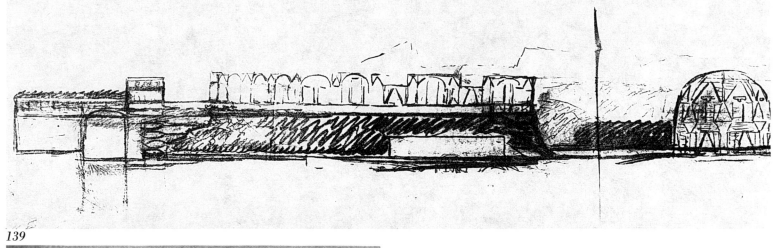

139

140

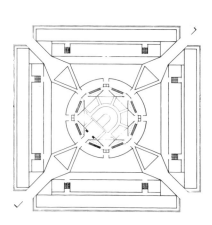

141

houses, his exhibition hall was shaped in the manner of grand, theater-like stairs and overlooked a ceremonial plaza that recalled the north ceremonial plaza at Dhaka. Given the improbable nature of Interama, its demise for lack of support is hardly surprising.

Of Kahn's three remaining commissions focused on assembly, only the smallest and least consequential was realized: Temple Beth-El in Chappaqua, New York (1966–72). Yet even with so small a commission he conceived a strongly centralized structure symbolic of its purpose (fig. 144). Kahn was selected as architect in July 1966, but he deferred its design until after a contract was signed in March of the following year.[55] From the outset he urged that an ambulatory be added to the program, justifying it as a place for extra seating.[56] Well before he reduced Beth-El's final design to the relatively simple wood-framed structure that was built from 1970 to 1972,[57] he had initiated proposals for assemblies that were less realistic yet more stimulating: the Hurva Synagogue in Jerusalem and the Palazzo dei Congressi in Venice.

With the Hurva Synagogue, Kahn had his first opportunity to build within the archaeological boundaries of the ancient world that had so moved him during his earlier travels. In August 1967 he was asked to rebuild a smaller synagogue that had once stood on the site,[58] which he visited in December, but he did not begin concentrated effort on its design until July of the following year, a few days before returning to Jerusalem to present his proposal.[59] The rich architectural heritage of the site must have charged the commission with special meaning. As Kahn worked on the design, he spoke of the honor of expressing "the spirit of history and religion of Jerusalem,"[60] recalling his earlier statement, "The ancient building still vigorous in use has the light of eternity."[61] His early studies reinforce this caring attitude, for they show a proposal that is in a sympathetic relationship with the ancient city. The broader setting of the synagogue included two of the world's most significant religious monuments, the Dome of the Rock (A.D. 688–691) and the Church of the Holy Sepulchre (ca. A.D. 326ff); Kahn conceived his design in relation to these, sensing its potential to symbolize a third religion. Drawings suggest how these buildings also related to the still more ancient terrain of their setting (fig. 142); as he had once depicted the weight of human history in his drawing of the Athenian acropolis (see fig. 246), so Kahn also evoked it in Jerusalem, though now with the added dimension of his own creation.

Kahn's monumental vision exceeded the expectations of his patrons, who had thought of the structure in more modest terms, yet they came to support it. After the first presentation, Mayor Teddy Kollek of Jerusalem described the design as a "world synagogue," saying, "It's an idea that a beautiful synagogue should be built in Jerusalem."[62] The scheme also reinforced Kahn's ideas of assembly. Four hollow piers defined the corners of a centrally focused, square sanctuary (fig. 146). Surrounding the piers, an ambulatory separated the sanctuary from an outer enclosure of sixteen square niches. These were provided—or, more likely, were justified—as spaces for a special candle service. Stairways at the centers of the outer enclosure led to an upper gallery, and the corners were left open as entrances. The four central piers flared out near the top as a roof for the cubical space, and the niches tapered inward, rising above the roof like fortifying pylons (fig. 147). Shown unglazed and composed of simple, almost neutral elements, the building bore the air of an occupied ruin from some ancient yet unspecifiable epoch.

Kahn's primitivistic plan recalls such conjectural reconstructions of the Temple of Solomon as in Fergusson's *History of Architecture* (fig. 148), a resemblance that was soon noted.[63] Seeking information on early synagogues from New York's Jewish Theological Seminary, Kahn had been sent a copy of an article which emphasized the importance of Solomon's Temple;[64] filed with slides of his first proposal was an unidentified reconstruction of its ancient precinct. The temple would have been an appropriate inspiration, for it not only marked a beginning of Jewish architecture, but also, as recounted by Wittkower, embodied cosmic ratios transmitted by God to Moses.[65]

While Kahn altered details in later variations of the Hurva Synagogue, his basic concept remained unchanged. The version he presented in July 1969 substituted a curved shell with perimetral supports for the hollow piers of his first design and moved the ark and the bema to an outer location.[66] In a final version of July 1972 the ark and the bema had regained a more central position where they might more effectively interact as a focus of participatory assembly, and four hollow piers were again located at the corners of the sanctuary, now with capitals enriched by oval openings (fig. 145).[67] The calm symmetry of the design contrasts with the more active shapes of Dhaka and corresponds appropriately to Kahn's later work of a more commemorative nature. Kollek remained supportive but was unable to convince the congregation to build Kahn's design.[68] Thus the "light of eternity" Kahn sought remained all too elusive.

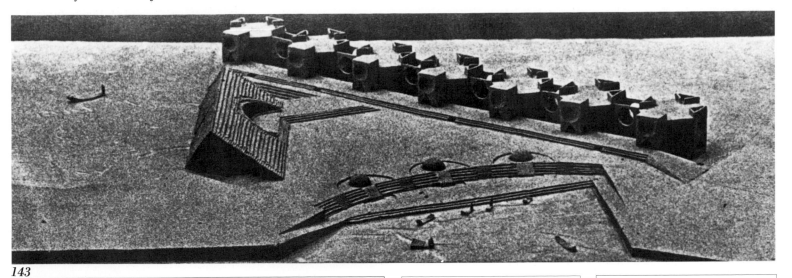

143

144

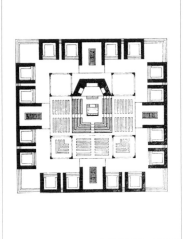

146

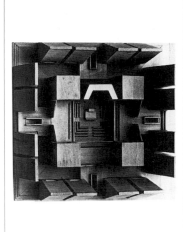

147

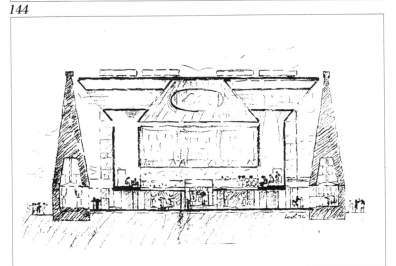

145

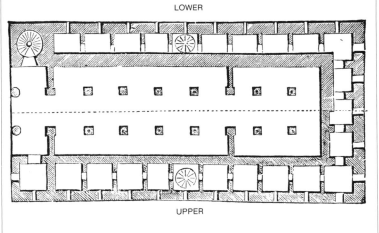

LOWER

UPPER

148

142. Hurva Synagogue,
Jerusalem, Israel, 1967–74.
Site section, ca. July 1968.
143. Interama Community B,
Miami, Fla. 1964–69. Model,
October 1965.
144. Temple Beth-El
Synagogue, Chappaqua, N.Y.,
1966–72. Perspective.
Inscribed Lou K '68.
145. Hurva Synagogue,
Jerusalem, Israel, 1967–74.
Section of third scheme.
Inscribed Lou K '72.

146. Hurva Synagogue,
Jerusalem, Israel, 1967–74.
Plan, ca. July 1968.
147. Hurva Synagogue,
Jerusalem, Israel, 1967–74.
Model for first scheme, ca.
July 1968.
148. Temple of Solomon,
Jerusalem, Israel, 1015 B.C.
Conjectural plan of lower and
upper levels.

In Venice, as in Jerusalem, Kahn found a city rich in the evidence of its beginnings. The idea of a hall for meeting with which he was presented in April 1968 (see pp. 404–9) seemed clear enough, but its functional necessity within the Biennale and its larger purpose were both sufficiently vague to stimulate Kahn's imagination. With the Palazzo dei Congressi commission came an opportunity to shape an institution that would be experienced and judged in close proximity to examples of great architecture, and in the noted Venetian professor Giuseppe Mazzariol he again found an understanding intellect who would guide and support his proposals. Kahn offered to work without his usual fee as a gift to the city.

The Palazzo dei Congressi was less tied to ritualistic or procedural requirements than were Kahn's earlier designs for assembly, and he seemed to begin, as he had with Adath Jeshurun some fifteen years earlier, by recalling early places of meeting. At the time of his initial presentation he described his design as "a place of happening," continuing, "In the Congress Building in Venice . . . I am thinking of building a place which is the meeting of the mind and a place where expressions of the meeting of the mind can take place."[69] Its form, however, was more structured, perhaps in the way Kahn imagined the first architecturally defined places for assembly to have developed, and in it he drew a fine distinction between passive and participative assembly: "I can see the Congress Hall as if it were a theater in the round—where people look at people—it is not like a movie theater where people look at a performance. My first idea, regardless of the shape of the site, was to make so many concentric circles with a nucleus in the middle."[70]

Restrictive site conditions worked against Kahn's ideal form. To avoid existing trees while staying within the portion of the garden he was assigned, it was necessary for him to give the building a long and narrow shape, and to simplify foundation problems in the spongy soil, he elected to support the building in the manner of a bridge, with only a minimal number of supports at each end (see fig. 523). The idea of a bridge held special meaning in Venice, and Kahn's design has been compared to the Rialto, described as "the most effective stage of the theater of Venetian life."[71] In contrast to the massive piers supporting each end of the building, the visually light suspension structure of the hall itself would have sustained the spirit of celebration he felt essential to its purpose.[72] Early sketches (probably done before his first informal presentation to Mazzariol in October 1968) suggest the design's evolution. Near both the upper and lower right, amidst hammock-like diagrams, are sections showing a

149

150

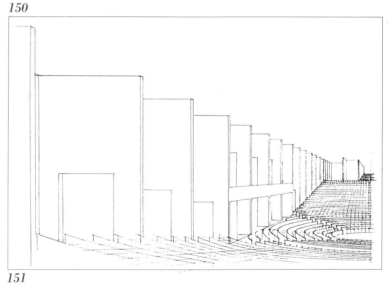

151

149. Palazzo dei Congressi, Venice, Italy, 1968–74. Model for Giardini Pubblici site, January 1969.
150. Palazzo dei Congressi, Venice, Italy, 1968–74. Model for Arsenale site, May 1973.
151. Palazzo dei Congressi, Venice, Italy, 1968–74. Interior perspective.

theatrical cavea within a suspended frame. He further narrowed this form, explaining as he presented his design in Venice in January 1969: "Because the site is long and narrow, I simply sliced the theater in the round with two parallel cuts . . . the impression in the hall will be of people seeing people. The curve of the meeting hall is slight in order to retain the sense that it is really a street-like-piazza gently sloping. One could be reminded of the Palio Square in Siena."[73] Kahn's travel sketch of Siena had been one of his most powerful images (see fig. 247), an agora molded advantageously for assembly.

To the ideal form of a theater in the round Kahn also added an ambulatory-like space (fig. 151), bringing his design more into alignment with his other designs for assembly. As he explained, "to each side . . . are two streets . . . which lead to the seating place . . . provided with niches where people can go away from the congress and discuss things separately."[74] His model (fig. 149) showed the sensitive positioning of the Palazzo dei Congressi on its site and its relation to the added elements, which he kept distinct: an entrance pavilion in the shape of a cube, and another cubical structure containing galleries and studios behind (see fig. 525). In these, as in the meeting hall itself, he seemed to work mainly with simple, whole numbers, maintaining basic modular relationships.[75] Komendant again served as Kahn's consultant, insuring structural efficiency. In 1970, at his insistence, segmentally arched openings were removed from the parapet and replaced with balusters that Kahn rendered in the manner of an Archaic stoa.

In typical fashion, Kahn continued to design even when the commission was uncertain, for political debate made realization unlikely. And later, in 1972, he willingly revived his design for a new site near the Arsenale; there the building would actually bridge a canal (fig. 150; see fig. 526). As with Mikveh Israel, Islamabad, and Hurva, he clung tenaciously to a concept that had assumed real existence in his mind and seemed too vitally a part of his thinking to abandon. And he remained steadfast in seeking to build his ideas, no doubt partly as proof of their validity and as a measure of his accomplishment. In his designs for assembly, he gave shape to universal qualities of meeting that enlarged individual worth.

D.D.L.

Notes

1. Kahn, "A Synagogue," *Perspecta*, no. 3 (1955): 62.
2. Kahn, "Places of Worship" (review of *Synagogue Architecture in the U.S.*, by Rachel Wischnitzer), *Jewish Review and Observer*, clipping stamped February 17, 1956, Louis I. Kahn Collection, University of Pennsylvania Historical and Museum Commission (hereafter cited as Kahn Collection). Kahn had written the review before December 2, 1955; see annotated bibliography, pp. 433–39.
3. Kahn, "Architecture: Silence and Light" (lecture, Solomon R. Guggenheim Museum, December 3, 1968), in Guggenheim Museum, *On the Future of Art* (New York: Viking Press, 1970), 25.
4. Letter, Kahn to Balkrishna V. Doshi, May 26, 1961, "Master File 3/1/61 thru 5/31/61," Box LIK 9, Kahn Collection.
5. Kahn, "Law and Rule in Architecture" (lecture, Princeton University, November 29, 1961), typed transcript, "LIK Lectures 1969," Box LIK 53, Kahn Collection.
6. Kahn, "Law and Rule in Architecture" (annual discourse, Royal Institute of British Architects, March 14, 1962), typed transcript, "LIK Lectures 1969," Box LIK 53, Kahn Collection.
7. Kahn, lecture at the International Design Conference, Aspen, Colorado, June 1962, typed transcript, "Aspen Conference—June 1962," Box LIK 59, Kahn Collection.
8. Kahn, "Louis Kahn: Statements on Architecture" (lecture, Politecnico di Milano, January 1967), *Zodiac*, no. 17 (1967): 55.
9. Peter Murray, *The Architecture of the Italian Renaissance* (New York: Schocken Books, 1963), 42–44.
10. For example, Kahn, "Remarks" (lecture, Yale University, October 30, 1963), *Perspecta*, no. 9/10 (1965): 320.
11. This parallel was identified by J. Kieffer, *Louis I. Kahn and the Rituals of Architecture* (privately published, 1981), later cited by Joseph Burton, "Notes from Volume Zero: Louis Kahn and the Language of God," *Perspecta*, no. 20 (1983): 80–83, among others.
12. Kahn, "Louis I. Kahn: Talks with Students" (lecture and discussion, Rice University, ca. 1969), *Architecture at Rice*, no. 26 (1969): 44.
13. Pattison, interview with David B. Brownlee, December 20, 1990.
14. Pattison, interview with David G. De Long, January 29, 1991.
15. Kahn, "Architecture and Human Agreement" (lecture, University of Virginia, April 18, 1972), *Modulus*, no. 11 (1975): n.p.
16. I was a student in Kahn's studio at the University of Pennsylvania during the 1962–63 academic year. According to my class notebook, Kahn's first meeting with our class after his return from Dhaka was February 11, 1963. His words then, which he further embroidered in later meetings, corresponded closely to his later talk at Yale in the fall of 1963. This talk, from which the quotations are taken, was subsequently published: "The Development by Louis I. Kahn of the Design for the Second Capital of Pakistan at Dacca," *Student Publication of the School of Design, North Carolina State College, Raleigh* 14 (May 1964): n.p.
17. Ibid.
18. According to my class notebook, Kahn assigned the Dhaka problem on February 25.
19. These remarks by Kahn on April 1, 1963, I had enclosed in quotation marks as I took notes of his discussion of Dhaka.
20. Kahn, lecture at Princeton University, March 3, 1968, quoted in Bruno J. Hubert, "Kahn's Epilogue," *Progressive Architecture* 65 (December 1984): 61.
21. Kahn, "Talks with Students," 28–29.
22. The drawings identified as dating from 1962 in Heinz Ronner and Sharad Jhaveri, *Louis I. Kahn: Complete Work, 1935–1974*, 2d ed. (Basel and Boston: Birkhäuser, 1987), 234–35, SNC.3–6, seem instead to have followed his first trip to Dhaka in 1963. There is no evidence of any design activity before that trip, when he first received information on the site and the program. The model that Ronner illustrates as first in the sequence (234, SNC.1) seems to predate the model presented in March 1963, but it could have been a study model done after Kahn's return and before his next presentation model was begun.
23. Kahn, quoted in "The Development of Dacca," n.p.
24. Kahn was in Chandigarh on November 11, 1962; hotel receipt, Oberoi Mount View, "National Institute of Design Incidentals," Box LIK 113, Kahn Collection.
25. Kahn, "Form and Design," *Architectural Design* 31 (April 1961): 152.
26. Ignacio de Sola-Morales i Rubio, "A Lecture in San Sebastian" (1982), reprinted in *Louis I. Kahn: L'uomo, il maestro*, ed. Alessandra Latour (Rome: Edizioni Kappa, 1986), 219. This thesis was earlier developed in Emil Kaufmann, "Three Revolutionary Architects, Boullée, Ledoux, and Lequeu," *Transactions of the American Philosophical Society* 42 (October 1952).
27. Kahn, "Law and Rule" (Princeton).
28. Kahn, "Law and Rule" (RIBA). Also recounted in "The Architect and the Building," *Bryn Mawr Alumnae Bulletin* 43 (Summer 1962): 2–3.
29. Kahn, address to the Boston Society of Architects, April 5, 1966, typed transcript, "Boston Society of Architects," Box LIK 57, Kahn Collection. It was later published: "Address by Louis I. Kahn," *Boston Society of Architects Journal*, no. 1 (1967): 5–20.
30. Kahn, quoted in "The Development of Dacca," n.p. In the fall of 1963 Kahn added similar "hollow columns" to the school component of Mikveh Israel, later relating them to Dhaka; Kahn, "Remarks," 320.
31. Kahn, lecture in Aspen, 1962; Kahn, "Law and Rule" (Princeton).
32. As recounted in August Komendant, "Architect-Engineer Relationship," in Latour, *Kahn*, 319.
33. Roy Vollmer, an architect in Kahn's office assigned to Dhaka, designed a portion of the housing; reference is made in a letter quoting Kahn, Louise Badgley (Kahn's secretary) to James K. Merrick (Philadelphia Art Alliance), May 23, 1968, "April 1968 Master File, May & June 1968 & July 1968," Box LIK 10, Kahn Collection.
34. "The Observatories of the Maharajah Sawai Jai Singh II," *Perspecta*, no. 6 (1960): 68–77.
35. Marco Frascari (associate professor of architecture, University of Pennsylvania), interview with David G. De Long, November 15, 1989.
36. For example, William J. R. Curtis, "Authenticity, Abstraction and the Ancient Sense: Le Corbusier's and Louis Kahn's Ideas of Parliament," *Perspecta*, no. 20 (1983): 191.
37. Darah Diba, "Return to Dacca," *L'architecture d'aujourd'hui*, no. 267 (February 1990): 11.
38. Kahn, "Remarks," 313.
39. For example, Michael Graves, revised interview with Kazumi Kawasaki (1983), reprinted in Latour, *Kahn*, 167.
40. Monthly bulletin, Doxiadis Associates, "The Administrative Sector of Islamabad," May 1, 1961, "President's Estate, West Pakistan Gen. Correspondence," Box LIK 82, Kahn Collection. Among articles recounting the early history of Islamabad are B. S. Saini, "Islamabad; Pakistan's New Capital," *Design* 9 (May 1964): 83–89; C. A. Doxiadis, "Islamabad: The Creation of a New Capital," *Ekistics* 20 (November 1965): 301–5; Maurice Lee, "Islamabad—The Image," *Architectural Design* 37 (January 1967): 47–50; and Leo Jamoud, "Islamabad—The Visionary Capital," *Ekistics* 25 (May 1968): 329–35.
41. Kahn's selection as architect is confirmed in a letter, Masoodur Rouf (Capital Development Authority) to Robert Matthew (coordinating architect for the Administrative Sector, Islamabad), July 26, 1963, "Prespak Capital Development Authority Correspondence," Box LIK 82, Kahn Collection. The basic components of the complex are contained in

the document "Revised Space Requirements in Respect to the President's Estate . . . April 1963," "President's Estate, Islamabad, Program," Box LIK 82, Kahn Collection. I am grateful to David Roxburgh for his research report on this project.

42. Kahn had been expected to present his preliminary designs in June 1964; letter, Sarfraz Khan (deputy director of planning, Capital Development Authority) to Kahn, July 13, 1964, "President's Estate, Islamabad, Corres. Cap. Dev. Auth," Box LIK 82, Kahn Collection. Kahn promised something by September; letter, Matthew to Zahir ud-Deen (director of planning, Capital Development Authority), August 13, 1964, "President's Estate . . . Correspondence, Sir Robert Matthew," Box LIK 82, Kahn Collection.

43. Letter, Kahn to Matthew, January 8, 1965, "Master File—January 1965–February," Box LIK 10, Kahn Collection.

44. Ajaz A. Khan, *Progress Report on Islamabad (1960–1970)* (Islamabad: Capital Development Authority, 1970), 26.

45. Letter, Matthew to Kahn, March 3, 1965, "President's Estate . . . Correspondence, Sir Robert Matthew," Box LIK 82, Kahn Collection.

46. Kahn, notebook (K12.22), ca. 1963, Kahn Collection. Following these notes are sketches for the final version of the assembly building in Islamabad.

47. Auguste Choisy, *Histoire de l'architecture* (Paris: Edouard Rouveyre, [1899]), 1:529, fig. 15.

48. Among several documents emphasizing this are a letter, N. Faruqi (newly appointed chairman, Capital Development Authority) to Matthew, Kahn, and Ponti, May 11, 1965, "Prespak, Capital Development Authority Correspondence," Box LIK 82, Kahn Collection.

49. Letter, Kahn to Matthew, August 27, 1965, "Master File, June 1965 July . . . October," Box LIK 10, Kahn Collection.

50. Cable, Kahn to his Philadelphia office, January 11, 1966, "Cablegrams—Pak. Estate," Box LIK 82, Kahn Collection.

51. "Interama Exposition Hailed as 'Full-Scale Experiment in Urban Design,'" *Architectural Record* 141 (March 1967): 40–41.

52. Letter, Kahn to Robert B. Browne (architect in charge), November 14, 1964, "Interama Contract," Box LIK 116, Kahn Collection. Kahn had first been contacted in December 1963; letter, Browne to Kahn, December 18, 1963, "Interama Correspondence Browne, Robert B.," Box LIK 21, Kahn Collection. He expressed reservations in April; letter, Kahn to Browne, April 17, 1964, "Interama Contract," Box LIK 116, Kahn Collection.

53. Letter, Kahn to Browne, May 5, 1965, "Interama," Box LIK 21, Kahn Collection. Kahn introduced his comments with the statement, "My thought behind this note is to arrive at a sense of the institutional construction of INTERAMA."

54. His second version, presented in October 1965, is illustrated; its presentation is recorded in minutes, June 7, 1965, "Interama Correspondence Browne, Robert B.," Box LIK 21, Kahn Collection. An earlier scheme, with elements enclosing three sides of the triangular parcel, had been presented in September; minutes, September 19, 1965, "Interama Meeting Notes," Box LIK 21, Kahn Collection. A final version, with all elements linked along one side, was completed by April 1967; letter, Kahn to Browne, April 28, 1967, "Interama Arch. & Eng. Est.," Box LIK 21, Kahn Collection.

55. Letters, S. Budd Simon (chair, architect selection committee) to Kahn, July 15, 1966, and David Wisdom (Kahn's office) to Morton Rosenthal (first chair, building committee), March 20, 1967, "Temple Beth El Correspondence Client," Box LIK 38, Kahn Collection. I am grateful to Marcia Fae Feuerstein for her research report on this project.

56. Letter, Simon to Kahn, May 29, 1966, ibid.

57. Construction report, Guzzi Bros. & Singer, Inc., August 31, 1970, "I

Temple Beth El Cuzzi Bros. & Singer, Inc. All Corres.," Box LIK 38, Kahn Collection; invitation to dedication, May 5, 1972, "Temple Beth El Correspondence Client," Box LIK 38, Kahn Collection.

58. Letter, Yacoov Salomon (holder of the synagogue property lease) to Kahn, October 9, 1967, "Hurva Synagogue," Box LIK 39, Kahn Collection. An original synagogue, built in 1700 by an Ashkenazic sect, had been destroyed in 1720; a second synagogue on the site, built in 1857, had been destroyed in 1948. Nahman Avigad, *Discovering Jerusalem* (New York: Nelson Publishers, 1980), 18; Pierre Loti, *Jerusalem* (Philadelphia: David McKay, 1974), 20.

59. Telegram, Kahn to Salomon, July 8, 1968, "Hurva Synagogue," Box LIK 39, Kahn Collection. The feverish work on the first proposal was described by Marvin Verman in an unpublished interview with Maria Isabel G. Beas in the fall of 1989; Verman, Kahn's employee at the time, had been in charge of the first presentation. I am grateful to Maria Beas for her research on this project.

60. Letter, Kahn to Yehuda Tamir (prime minister's office), March 28, 1969, "Hurva Synagogue," Box LIK 39, Kahn Collection.

61. Letter, Kahn to Harriet Pattison, September 15, 1964, published in Alexandra Tyng, *Beginnings: Louis I. Kahn's Philosophy of Architecture* (New York: John Wiley & Sons, 1984), 166.

62. Kollek, quoted in J. Robert Moskin, "Jewish Mayor of the New Jerusalem," *Look*, October 1, 1968, 71. Controversy surrounding Kahn's first presentation is noted in a letter, Kollek to Kahn, August 29, 1968, "Hurva Synagogue," Box LIK 39, Kahn Collection.

63. For instance, Robert Coombs, "Light and Silence: The Religious Architecture of Louis Kahn," *Architectural Association Quarterly* 13 (October 1981): 32, 34.

64. Letter, Kahn to Mrs. Serata (librarian, Jewish Theological Seminary), July 2, 1968, "Hurva Synagogue," Box LIK 39, Kahn Collection. The article was Louis Finkelstein, "The Origin of the Synagogue," *Proceedings of the American Academy for Jewish Research* 1 (1928–30): 49–59.

65. Rudolf Wittkower, *Architectural Principles in the Age of Humanism* (London: Alec Tiranti, 1952), 91.

66. Letter, Kollek to Kahn, June 6, 1969, "Jerusalem Committee," Box LIK 39, Kahn Collection. This version is sometimes identified as the third rather than the second, but dated drawings show otherwise.

67. Letter, Kollek to Kahn, April 23, 1972, ibid.

68. Letter, Kollek to Kahn, December 28, 1973, "Hurva Garden," Box LIK 39, Kahn Collection.

69. Kahn, "Silence and Light" (lecture, School of Architecture, ETH Zurich, February 12, 1969), in Ronner and Jhaveri, *Complete Work*, 8.

70. Kahn, lecture at the Sala dello Scoutinio, Venice, January 30, 1969, typed transcript, "Venezia," Box LIK 55, Kahn Collection.

71. Neslihan Dostoglu, Marco Frascari, and Enrique Vivoni, "Louis Kahn and Venice: Ornament and Decoration in the Interpretation of Architecture," in Latour, *Kahn*, 307.

72. Pattison, interview with De Long, January 29, 1991.

73. Dostoglu, Frascari, and Vivoni, "Kahn and Venice," 307.

74. Kahn, lecture in Venice, 1969.

75. In addition to the simple dimensions of the related buildings, drawings in the archive of the Canadian Centre for Architecture repeatedly contain simple numerical notations, such as 40, 60, 100 (CCA DR 1982.0006); 20, 40, 80 (CCA DR 1982.0007); and 15, 30, 120 (CCA DR 1982.0009).

At the same time that Louis Kahn was devising an architecture to accommodate the human desire to assemble, he was also at work making an architecture for the complicated mixture of collective and individual activity that occurred in schools, research centers, and monasteries. These institutions were among those that he called "the houses of the inspirations"—places defined by the fundamental inspiration to learn and by the concomitant need to shelter learning within a supportive community.[1] Such idealistic clients brought him many of the commissions that poured into his office in the early 1960s, projects that seemed to bring with them the optimism and commitment that radiated from John F. Kennedy's presidency. For these institutions, Kahn created an architecture rooted in natural order and human tradition.

Learning was for Kahn an existential quest. It was at heart an exploration of life itself, as he told a medical school conference in 1964:

I believe that the institution of learning actually stems 'way back from the nature of nature. Nature, physical nature, records in what it makes how it was made. Within us is the complete story of how we were made, and from this sense, which is the sense of wonder, comes a quest to know, to learn, and the entire quest, I think, will add up to only one thing: how we were made.[2]

Community making was also one of mankind's—and the architect's—chief responsibilities. Kahn proclaimed to an interviewer in 1961, "I wanted very much . . . to demonstrate to the man on the street a way of life."[3] Three years later he was even more emphatic about the task: "I don't believe that society makes the man. I believe that man makes the society."[4] The combined challenges of supporting learning and making model communities generated three of Kahn's most successful built works—the Salk Institute for Biological Studies in La Jolla, California, Erdman Hall at Bryn Mawr College, and the Indian Institute of Management in Ahmedabad (fig. 152)—as well as a large handful of extraordinary unbuilt projects.

Work on many of these similar problems began in a rush. Late in 1959, with the Richards Building under construction, Kahn was contacted about designing the Salk Institute and an arts center in Fort Wayne. In 1960, while the design of the Rochester church was being developed, commissions were received from Bryn Mawr College, the University of Virginia, and the Philadelphia College of Art. The following year brought Wayne State University and St. Andrew's Priory into the office—contemporaries of Mikveh

Israel synagogue—and 1962 saw the start of the Indian Institute of Management, in the same year that the commission for the new capital of East Pakistan was assigned. After a lapse, three similarly motivated clients hired Kahn in 1965: St. Catherine's convent, the Maryland Institute College of Art, and Phillips Exeter Academy, followed by Rice University in 1969. Because Kahn's work defies ordinary typological classification, two of these functionally related commissions—Fort Wayne and the Philadelphia College of Art—will be treated in chapter 5 with Kahn's urban design work of this period. For the same reason, his library and dining hall for Exeter will find their place in chapter 6, with the commemorative and honorific buildings that occupied much of his time during the last years of his career. But all need to be tabulated here to portray the full impact this species of work had on his practice.

The first step of Kahn's planning, as always, was to strip his clients' architectural programs down to the essence of the human activity they contained. It was thus that he established the character of a building, based more on his own feelings than the conditions stated by his employers. His consideration of these institutions devoted to study and contemplation was defined by his knowledge of education, his imaginings about monastic life, and his commitment to activist, social architecture.

Kahn's educational experience had begun with years as a commuting student, crisscrossing Philadelphia to public school, to special art classes, and finally to the University of Pennsylvania. Then, as a teacher, he had first worked informally, outside the academic establishment, and subsequently as a part-time critic who commuted to Yale and Penn. This peripatetic pattern produced an anti-establishment view of education and inspired one of his most repeated architectural fables:

Schools began with a man under a tree, who did not know he was a teacher, discussing his realizations with a few others, who did not know they were students. The students reflected on the exchanges between them and on how good it was to be in the presence of this man. They wished their sons, also, to listen to such a man. Soon, the needed spaces were erected and the first schools came into existence. The establishment of schools was inevitable because they are part of the desires of man.[5]

In Kahn's idealization of the programs for these buildings, he combined this hazy image of the collective work of education with an even more abstract vision of monastic solitude. Like Le Corbusier before him, he revered the

Chapter 4

The Houses of the Inspirations

Designs for Study

monastery as a model habitat, and he often spoke with admiration of the famous monastery plan of St. Gall. Although Kahn designed a number of synagogues, churches, and mosques, he was personally more inclined toward private reflection, like that of monks, than public manifestations of religion. He admired the Pantheon in part because its great circular form was "a non-directional space, where only inspired worship can take place. Ordained ritual would have no place."[6] Contemplation, it seemed to him, was of universal educational significance, and it was thus a relevant model for the complementary, independent part of learning.

The obvious pleasure that Kahn took in working on programs of this kind also derived from his long-standing interest in the making of human communities. During his early career this concern had been focused on the challenges of public housing, a field that was nourished by a national enthusiasm for social action during the Depression and then accelerated by the urgency of wartime needs. But after World War II, American public housing drifted downward, providing only minimal shelter for the poorest of the poor. Kahn himself witnessed this dispiriting spiral in working on the two phases of housing at Mill Creek in West Philadelphia (1951–63). By the time he received this new wave of commissions, he was looking for renewed inspiration.

Despite the apparent vagueness of Kahn's reinvented, composite program for these educational institutions—the sheltering tree and the monastery—his thinking rapidly assumed concrete form when it came into contact with his strong and mature visual preferences. His ideas were handily captured by his favorite shapes. In plan, the pavilions of the Richards Building and the concentric served and servant hierarchy of the Rochester Unitarian Church were useful starting points. In elevation, there continued the drama of historic rediscovery that had begun in his towered and seemingly thick-walled buildings of the late fifties, full of allusion to the power of medieval and ancient monuments. Created at the point of intersection between Kahn's poetic understanding of human life and such lively visual desiderata, these were works whose genesis was sometimes stormy. Compromise seemed impossible; it was a matter of adjusting conditions perfectly until fusion could occur. Many of the projects remained unbuilt.

Kahn's solutions for the first two of these projects—the Salk Institute and Erdman Hall, a dormitory for Bryn Mawr College—translated the abstract problem into convincingly material terms. In both cases, a powerful but sympathetic

client demanded the best from Kahn and wrested an excellent design from his sometimes too reluctant fingers. He liked dealing with individuals who were intelligent and could hold up their side of the client-architect relationship. In 1963 he told a Yale audience: "It's the man, the man only, not a committee, not a mob—nothing makes anything but a man, a single, single man."[7] Naturally, he thought he was describing himself at the same time.

Jonas Salk, the inventor of the first effective polio vaccine, was the most impressive intellectual Kahn ever had as a client (see figs. 278–92 and pp. 330–39). Fortunately, their thinking converged on the challenge of repairing the modern schizophrenia that had divorced human intellect from spirit, and they became friends and collaborators. As no one else might have, Salk could reject Kahn's proposals without deadening the architect's interest in the project, and he did so on two significant occasions. Kahn, who met Salk in December 1959, called him "my most trusted critic."[8]

What Salk wanted was nothing less than a recombination of science and the humanities. To mend the rift that had split modern life between the "two cultures" C. P. Snow had described in 1959, Salk foresaw a facility that would both support scientific research and foster the exchange of ideas between scientists and other cultural leaders.[9] "Instead of writing a book, I decided to make the statement architecturally," he later recalled.[10] The test of this architecture, as he often said, was that it should be a place where he could entertain Pablo Picasso.[11]

Kahn translated Salk's description of the two cultures into the "measurable" and the "unmeasurable," a vocabulary that was obviously congruent with his own concept of "design" and "form," and he accepted the challenge of fulfilling Salk's holistic vision as part of his own architectural quest.[12] He was sincere, seeing to it that Snow was invited to the dinner party following Kahn's presentation of the annual discourse of the Royal Institute of British Architects in London in 1962, but, being an artist, Kahn did not always describe the two cultures in morally equal terms. "Science finds what is already there," he told an audience in 1967, "but the artist makes that which is not there."[13]

Kahn first visited Salk's spectacular site atop the Pacific cliffs at La Jolla in January 1960. His initial sketches, and the model worked up from them during the next few months, reflected his own formulation of the program (Salk had given him only the barest outline), with a tripartite division of the

152. Kahn and Balkrishna V. Doshi at the Indian Institute of Management, Ahmedabad, India, March 1974.

facility into laboratories, residences, and a meeting house for the exchange of ideas among researchers and with the wider world (figs. 153, 154; see fig. 436). Salk accepted the three-part *parti*, but he immediately rejected the planned laboratories, which Kahn proposed to assemble at the inland end of the site in studio towers like those of the Richards Building. Although the Richards design was already famous, Salk insisted on the kind of practical, open-plan building that was usual for laboratories. This open planning was what Kahn himself had created in the Yale Art Gallery, but he now saw it as an old-fashioned modernist cliché. He could not, however, reject Salk's directive.

Salk also explicitly suggested to Kahn that his scientific community might be modeled on the monastery of San Francesco in Assisi. Salk had visited the monastery in 1954, and Kahn had sketched it in 1929.[14] That the architect accepted this suggestion as a friendly one does not need to be questioned, given the repeated praise for historical sources that had dotted his utterances since the 1940s and his specific interest in monasteries. But that does not mean that the Salk Institute was created as a medievalist romance. Its design was an imbricated pattern of historical and modern thinking of the kind that was now natural to Kahn.

The labs themselves were reworked during 1960–62 as four large, two-story buildings, spanned by a prodigious system of folded plates and box girders that provided a walk-through space for plumbing and ventilation (what Kahn called servant space) (fig. 157; see fig. 440). This heroic structural honesty made amends for the cunning deceit of the Yale Art Gallery, where the elaborate ceiling pattern, so suggestive of a space frame, was actually composed of relatively simple tilted beams. Kahn, although ultimately willing to sacrifice material demands to the logic of the eye, as he had at Yale, always tried to avoid doing so. In the Salk solution, he proudly confided, "I thought I had something pretty hot."[15]

While the laboratory spaces were very flexible, in keeping with Salk's directive, they were not designed to contain all of the research activity of the building. Kahn also proposed small studies for each of the principal scientists, which were attached to the sides of their open-plan laboratories. These studies were grouped into towers that rose in the two courtyards between the paired laboratory blocks, and they thus re-created some of the studio-like environment of the Richards Building. The researchers at first professed no desire for these refuges from the noise of the lab; they were willing to remain all day beside their apparatus, even eating

lunch on a work bench "after a few microbes were swept away." But Kahn seduced them and Salk with the image of "an architecture of the oak table and the rug," separate from the hard, "clean architecture" of the laboratory.[16] This divided organization permitted him to create the functional individuation of space that had become a central theme in his work of the fifties, and the type of environment created by the studies—solitary retreats overlooking the gardens—was very like the monastic setting that had interested Salk and him from the start.

The broader division of the Salk Institute program into three buildings was a more general indication of Kahn's desire to mark each function with a specific architectural character. Utterly unlike the laboratories, the residences and the meeting house, although never built, were provocative expansions of his new, allusion-rich vocabulary.

Kahn planned a meandering "little village" of houses for the visiting fellows on the south brink of the ravine that cut into the site from the sea (see figs. 444, 445).[17] The residences must be seen in the context of the medieval-inspired urbanism that had won a broad following in America during the late fifties and sixties. Among its most familiar monuments were Stiles and Morse Colleges (1958–62), the pair of craggy dormitories that Eero Saarinen built on either side of a curving pathway at Yale shortly after Kahn had shifted his teaching to Philadelphia. Saarinen's colleges rejected the orthogonal rationalism and the sleekness of the modern movement in favor of sentimental associations and varied texture, and Kahn's design showed that he, too, was intrigued by this alternative view of urban development. He had, of course, enthusiastically recorded the hill and coastal towns of Italy in his youth, and the towered skyline of his Richards Building already suggested the endurance of his memories of those places. But while the Salk village was an accomplished design, its sweet neo-picturesqueness, so different from the crisp rectilinearity of Richards, stood out as an exception among his works. Kahn's larger urban designs, with which it might properly be compared, had advanced since the forties from the heroic ambitions of the Triangle redevelopment to the visionary monumentalism of his later plans for central Philadelphia and Dhaka (see figs. 52, 53, 83, 126). These all possessed a more profound sense of geometric order than his La Jolla design. His remarks regarding another project, recorded after he had worked for Salk for a year, might be taken as the summation of his more usual, tougher attitude: "I didn't want anything pretty; I wanted to have a clear statement of a way of life."[18]

153. Salk Institute for Biological Studies, La Jolla, Calif., 1959–65. Perspective of site, ca. January 1960.
154. Salk Institute for Biological Studies, La Jolla, Calif., 1959–65. Site plan, ca. January 1960.
155. Salk Institute for Biological Studies, La Jolla, Calif., 1959–65. Model of meeting house, ca. 1960–61.
156. Salk Institute for Biological Studies, La Jolla, Calif., 1959–65. Perspective of meeting house, 1961.

153

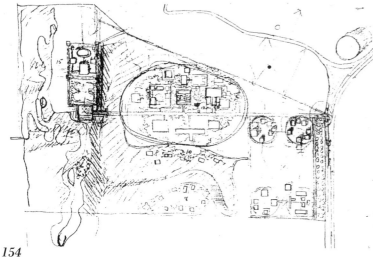

154

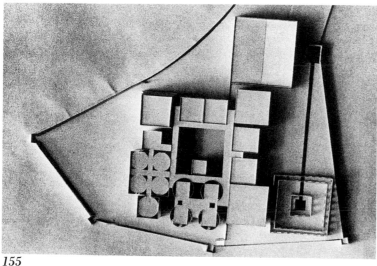

155

156

Kahn came closer to attaining this objective in the meeting house planned for the promontory north of the ravine. It was here that Salk hoped to accomplish the remarriage of the two cultures: the extraordinary setting where Picasso and the rest of the nonscientific world would encounter the community of science, in spaces to which Kahn refused to assign conventional labels. He described the cloistered garden of the meeting house, for instance, as "a religious place—a place which has no other meaning but is just a good place to go."[19]

The meeting house program was expanded to contain everything that Salk and Kahn could imagine would be useful, including a large library, quarters for unmarried scientists, an auditorium, and all sorts of facilities for casual mingling and talk. Kahn elaborated:

It was a place where one had his meal, because I don't know of any greater seminar than the dining room. There was a gymnasium. There was a place for the fellows who were not in science. There was a place for the director. There were rooms that had no names, like the entrance hall, which had no name. It was the biggest room, but it was not designated in any way. People could go around it, too; they didn't have to go *through* it. But the entrance hall was a place where you could have a banquet if you wanted to.[20]

The architectural vocabulary of the meeting house was as unusual as the agenda mapped out for it (figs. 155, 156, 159; see fig. 443). Kahn adopted an additive plan of strongly individualized units that was consonant with the building's use for conferences and entertainment at a variety of scales and in differing formats. The layout bore more than a passing resemblance to the great suburban villas of imperial Rome and to the haunting geometries of Piranesi's imaginary reconstructed plan of the Campus Martius, which hung over Kahn's desk.[21] Moreover, the elevations, with glare walls pierced by giant openings encircling the meeting and dining rooms, looked like nothing so much as the masonry carcass of a Roman ruin. This was not by chance. The ancient ruin, Kahn reasoned, was a symbol of the enduring values upon which art was founded, but it was a symbol that had been cleansed of the narrow and specific meanings brought to it by prior occupation. It was thus ready to serve the new purposes that a Jonas Salk might invent in order to heal the world. As Kahn said in 1963, "A building that has become a ruin is again free of the bondage of use."[22]

Of course, neither the residences nor the meeting house were constructed, and only the laboratories, designed from the start to be unlike the other two parts, stand today to represent Salk and Kahn's grandiose vision. Before they

157

158

159

157. *Salk Institute for Biological Studies, La Jolla, Calif., 1959–65. Model, ca. March 1961.*
158. *Salk Institute for Biological Studies, La Jolla, Calif., 1959–65. Model, Summer 1962.*
159. *Salk Institute for Biological Studies, La Jolla, Calif., 1959–65. Bird's-eye perspective with meeting house in foreground, ca. 1962.*

160. *Salk Institute for Biological Studies, La Jolla, Calif., 1959–65. Perspective of courtyard with poplars, before December 1965.*
161. *Salk Institute for Biological Studies, La Jolla, Calif., 1959–65. Model of study tower, ca. 1963.*

were completed, Salk once again rerouted Kahn's design, shifting it to a trajectory that converged with the architect's Beaux-Arts training.

It was in the spring of 1962, with construction of the labs about to start, that Salk had a swift change of heart. He and Kahn were flying back to San Francisco after signing the construction contract when he told the architect that he had suddenly realized that the four-laboratory solution, with the buildings organized in pairs around two courtyards, did not represent the wholeness that he desired for his institution.[23] Two buildings, facing each other across a single common space, would be better, and he paced off the dimensions of such a layout in a park when he reached his destination. Kahn was not at first sympathetic. He was especially pleased with the integrated structural truss and servant space system of the four-lab design, and he called the new solution "much dumber than the building I originally conceived."[24] But, never one to shy away from last-minute changes himself, he came to appreciate the logic of Salk's point of view. In this, his classical sense may have been decisive, for it naturally predisposed him to favor a single axis. Later he explained: "I realized that two gardens did not combine in the intended meaning. One garden is greater than two because it becomes a place in relation to the laboratories and their studies. Two gardens were just a convenience. But one is really a place; you put meaning in it; you feel loyalty to it."[25] The design was reworked very quickly, and construction began that summer (fig. 158).

As built, the taller, three-story laboratory buildings preserved much of the structural and functional logic of the earlier, two-story version. Although the trusses were less elaborate, they still created a walk-through space for tending mechanical services (see fig. 439). And the separate studies were still clearly delineated, grouped in towers that rose on either side of the courtyard and only connected to the laboratories by bridges (fig. 161; see fig. 282). Beneath the towers, a sheltered walkway circled the courtyard.

The airy study towers, consisting of concrete frames with teak cubicles inserted on two of their four floors, were the subject of much loving attention. Here, in monastic cells overlooking a cloistered court, Kahn was able to bring his own feelings to bear on the design with a directness that was not possible in those parts of the building that were saddled with complex technical specifications. Seemingly animated by the innate "existence will" that he always postulated for his designs, each little cabin craned its neck to catch a glimpse of the Pacific. This required a slight staggering of

the paired studies and interrupted the apparent regularity of the facades with an idiosyncrasy born of need. The interiors were plainly finished with unstained teak, and their rustic air intensified the distinction between this territory of "the oak table and the rug" and the sterile laboratories. There was inevitably something of the simple air of a beach house in these domestic-scale units, perched on their sun-washed clifftop above the sea.

Because the lowest laboratories were at the level of a conventional basement, Kahn provided long, sunken courtyards on either side of the main plaza to bring them light. Generously scaled and bridged by the study towers, these were more like streets than light wells (see fig. 283). Similar streetlike courts ran along the outer facades of the laboratories, spanned by the sober service blocks that carried the mechanical systems up into the buildings (see fig. 290). The severe, repetitive vocabulary of the towers was like that being adopted at the same time by minimalist sculptors, but although Kahn shared their interest in reinvesting modern art with dignity and meaning, there is no evidence that he was aware of their work.

At the Salk Institute, Kahn's lifelong care for construction materials flowered into an absolute passion for scrupulous detailing and excellent finish. The standards that were set there for poured-in-place concrete have never been surpassed and have rarely been equaled. Transformed into an elegant material, the concrete overshadowed even the beauties of the travertine paving. To attain this high state of finish, Kahn established a branch office in San Diego. His resident staff inspected the concrete as it was colored, mixed, compacted, and cured, insuring that it received an unusually hard surface and that it was patterned exactly as intended, with formwork edge markings laid out with thoroughgoing calculation (see fig. 289). Kahn, indeed, saw concrete as the near equivalent of ashlar masonry, observing in 1972 that "Concrete really wants to be granite." But he also recognized its own unique qualities: "Reinforcing rods are the play of a marvelous secret worker that makes this so-called molten stone appear wonderfully capable—a product of the mind."[26]

It was also at the Salk Institute that Kahn designed extensive woodwork for the first time since building houses in the late 1940s. He adopted a new vocabulary for the occasion, with doors and shutters of timeless paneled construction, assembled out of teak, a wood that needed only to be cleaned and oiled regularly to resist deterioration (see fig. 279). It is perhaps the greatest tribute to Kahn's comprehensive design

160   161

sense that concrete and wood, often conceived as materials of opposite character, complemented each other at the Salk Institute. Both were provocatively detailed in a way that moved back and forth between abstraction and structural description; neither was allowed to stand in the background.

Most of the laboratory construction had been completed when Kahn made his final, long-postponed decision about landscaping the courtyard. This central space, the axis of his quasi-classical plan, demanded special attention, but, like the best Beaux-Arts work, this apparently straightforward demand was complicated by an underlying ambiguity. Here the peculiarity stemmed from the absence of any architectural feature on axis, such as the stereotypical domed pavilion.

Guided by the monastic imagery that both he and Salk associated with the project, he had initially imagined this central courtyard as a verdant garden, a thing apart from the arid surrounding landscape. He had experimented with various types and patterns of plantings, coming in the end to favor an allée of poplar trees, although never fully accepting this solution (fig. 160; see figs. 158, 438). The somewhat contrived appearance of these possible garden configurations was weighing on Kahn's mind when he visited Mexico City in December 1965 and saw the house and garden of Luis Barragan. Kahn was impressed by Barragan's austere vocabulary, with its strong connections to vernacular patterns, and he invited the Mexican architect to come to La Jolla and offer advice about the courtyard. Barragan's famous suggestion was often recounted by Kahn:

When he entered the space he went to the concrete walls and touched them and expressed his love for them, and then he said as he looked across the space and towards the sea, "I would not put a tree or blade of grass in this space. This should be a plaza of stone, not a garden." I looked at Dr. Salk and he at me and we both felt this was deeply right. Feeling our approval, he added joyously, "If you make this a plaza, you will gain a facade—a facade to the sky."[27]

Kahn ultimately designed the courtyard with a central channel through which water flowed, beneath the axis of the sun, toward an artificial cascade at the seaward end. This was a conceit certainly borrowed from the Mughal gardens with which he had become familiar through his work in India. But more than any particularity of inspiration, the hard-surfaced courtyard was a general statement about the essential distance an artist had to establish between his work and nature (see fig. 278). "Architecture is what nature cannot make," Kahn preached to a Yale audience in 1963.

"Nature cannot make anything that man makes. Man takes nature—the means of making a thing—and isolates its laws."[28]

Beginning in 1961 and continuing throughout the period that Kahn was isolating the laws of nature for the Salk Institute, he was also occupied with a dormitory for Bryn Mawr College, a women's school in the western suburbs of Philadelphia (see figs. 305–13 and pp. 352–57). Eleanor Donnelley Erdman Hall was a project with a more conventional program, but its design was not easy for Kahn. It became a battleground between what had been the twin objectives of his architecture throughout the fifties: clearly expressed structure and geometric order. These had gradually come to resemble antagonists. Although he had found that structure could generate pleasantly simple geometry at a small scale, like that of the Trenton Bathhouse, the necessarily complex structural systems of larger works, like the City Tower project, seemed to demand formal solutions of equal complexity (see figs. 72, 80). Kahn was never entirely happy with such visual complication, and at Bryn Mawr he sublimated his interest in heroically expressed structure to allow geometric order to win a decisive victory.

His patron at Bryn Mawr was another formidable personality, college president Katharine McBride. She was not one to accept lame excuses, as Kahn apparently learned the hard way; he observed, "If you took a position that someone else was responsible for what went wrong, her whole point of view changes."[29] Indeed, he gave McBride every reason to doubt his sense of responsibility, making little effort to conceal the fact that he was torn between two design solutions and carrying out their testing before her eyes.

Kahn had reformulated the Bryn Mawr program in his usual way, replacing the particulars provided by the college with his own perception that a women's dormitory needed to evoke "the presence of a house."[30] He interpreted this to require the familiar domestic separation of public areas (living room, dining room, and entrance hall) from sleeping quarters, just as in his binuclear house plans of the forties, albeit at a larger scale. In order to achieve a sense of domestic completeness within this all-female environment, he placed fireplaces in the major rooms to give "the feeling that a man is present, because somehow you associate the fireplace with a man."[31]

As envisioned by Kahn as a giant house, the Bryn Mawr

162

163

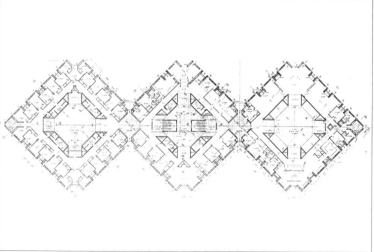

164

162. *Erdman Hall, Bryn Mawr College, Bryn Mawr, Pa., 1960–65. Model, 1960.*
163. *Erdman Hall, Bryn Mawr College, Bryn Mawr, Pa., 1960–65. Aerial view.*
164. *Erdman Hall, Bryn Mawr College, Bryn Mawr, Pa., 1960–65. Second-floor plan, February 23, 1963–May 21, 1963.*

dormitory posed two great problems of organization—problems in what he called "the architecture of connection," a phrase reminiscent of his training in plan composition under Paul Cret. In question were the connections between the three large public spaces and between those spaces and the much smaller bedrooms.

For these problems, Anne Tyng was eager to put forward a structural solution: a concrete honeycomb that could enfold spaces of all sizes and wrap them in aggregated polyhedra (fig. 162; see fig. 465). The design was the sophisticated outgrowth of her continuing exploration of the relationship between architectural structure and visual order, an exploration that was now shaped by her newly gained insights into the Jungian interpretation of human creativity and the collective unconscious. But the animated elevations generated by such systems had lost much of the appeal they had had for Kahn, who increasingly preferred an ancient kind of monumentality. He and Tyng debated openly about the Erdman design throughout 1961, bringing forward their alternative proposals in a succession of meetings with McBride. She allowed the competition to take its natural course. At the end of the year Kahn established the final *parti* of three concatenated diamonds, each with a central public room (living room, dining room, or entrance hall) enveloped by bedrooms (figs. 163, 164). This echoed the visual pattern but not the functional logic of a concentric served-servant hierarchy, and its majestic orderliness marked a turning point in Kahn's career. It was not that he subsequently ignored matters of construction and structure, but composition in plan—the centerpiece of his Beaux-Arts training—was never again challenged as the foremost of his priorities.

Although Erdman's three diamonds at first appear to be willfully unconventional, Kahn developed them at the end of a long line of compositional experiments with pavilion plans that stretched back into the 1950s. For years he had explored an architecture of connected pavilions, alternately testing picturesque groupings, like those of the Richards Building and the Adler and DeVore houses, and seeking to assert an axial order over the composition, as seen most dramatically in the Trenton Bathhouse (see figs. 90, 73, 74, 425). Despite its apparently arcane geometry, Erdman Hall falls in the latter group, disciplined by the underlying classicism of Kahn's compositional sense.

The diagonality of the Erdman design allowed Kahn to achieve classical balance without the artificiality inherent in conventional axial planning, in which useless elements were retained and held in position for the sake of symmetry. By rotating the three squares, he converted their otherwise dead corners into connectors, making each square "its own connection" with an unorthodox logic that would be impossible in an orthogonal arrangement.[32] In part, this was the same kind of ad hoc, "circumstantial" diagonal that he had discovered to be useful in the Goldenberg house (see fig. 101).[33] Kahn was delighted to find a solution emerging in this way: "It is always the hope on the part of the designer that the building in a way makes itself rather than be composed with devices that tend to please the eye. It is a happy moment when a geometry is found which tends to make spaces naturally, so that the composition of geometry in the plan serves to construct, to give light, and to make spaces."[34] Once the entire system of planning had been realigned along the diagonals, however, the ad hoc quality of the design vanished, and a majestic sense of classical order settled over the composition. This order was celebrated by the great stairways of the central hall, accenting the new axis that skewered the squares through their corners (see figs. 310, 313).

Although important to Kahn, he did not feel that the powerful planning logic of Erdman Hall's three great diamonds had to be revealed to average visitors. Their experience of the building was not confined to the two dimensions of plan; it was strongly shaped by Kahn's other, seemingly contradictory interest in monumental massing and ancient resonances. At Bryn Mawr, this produced an active, towered skyline—without apparent symmetry—that echoed the silhouettes of the Middle Ages and the college's own historic neo-Tudor campus (see fig. 307). On the uphill, entrance front, the clear plan was so obscured by this picturesque impression that even the central door was hard to find (see fig. 305). The historical allusion was furthered by the cladding of slate panels (the material Kahn would have used for the Salk Institute if travertine had not been cheaper), whose color closely matched the masonry of Bryn Mawr's older buildings (see fig. 308). It was also to be seen in the cavernous living and dining rooms, lit from above and hung with tapestries (see fig. 312).

Kahn admitted that his perennial interest in medieval architecture could be detected in the Bryn Mawr dormitory, whose plan might be "compared to that of a Scottish castle" (see fig. 108).[35] But, wary of being branded a historicist, he was always a little sheepish about allowing this connection to be drawn. "I have a book on castles and I try to pretend that I did not look at this book," he confessed in 1962, "but everybody reminds me of it and I have to admit that I looked

165. *Chemistry Building, University of Virginia, Charlottesville, Va., 1960–63. Model of towered lecture hall, 1962.*
166. *Lawrence Memorial Hall of Science Competition, University of California, Berkeley, Calif., 1962. Model.*

very thoroughly at this book."[36] He did make a flying visit to Scotland to see castles in March 1961, when he was called to London by another job while in the midst of the Erdman design.[37]

Kahn often defended his enthusiasm for castles by claiming that it stemmed strictly from the fact that castles demonstrated served-servant planning, with great central living halls and auxiliary spaces nestled into thick outside walls. It is true that this arrangement was successfully adapted in Erdman Hall (as it was earlier in the Rochester Unitarian Church), but Kahn's fascination with castles was not limited to their interesting plan typology. A lover of fairy tales, he was not immune to the broader power of these— and all—historical monuments, and he very movingly explained to several audiences in the mid-sixties how art outlived the particular circumstances of its making and exerted an enduring influence over human experience. In response to the question "What is tradition?" he began his answer with an imagined visit to Elizabethan England:

"My mind goes back to the Globe Theatre in London." Shakespeare had just written "Much Ado About Nothing" which was to be performed there. I imagined myself looking at the play through a hole in the wall of the structure, and was surprised to see that the first actor attempting his part fell as a heap of dust and bones under his costume. To the second actor the same thing happened, and so to the third and fourth, and the audience reacting also fell as a heap of dust. I realized that circumstance can never be recalled, that what I was seeing then was what I could not see now. And I realized that an old Etruscan mirror out of the sea, in which once a beautiful head was reflected had still with all its encrustation the strength to evoke the image of that beauty. It's what man makes, what he writes, his painting, his music, that remains indestructible. The circumstances of their making is but the mould for casting. This led me to realize what may be Tradition. Whatever happens in the circumstantial course of man's life, he leaves as the most valuable, a golden dust which is the essence of his nature. This dust, if you know this dust, and trust in it, and not in circumstance, then you are really in touch with the spirit of tradition. May be then one can say that tradition is what gives you the powers of anticipation from which you know what will last when you create.[38]

It was with such an eye to future appreciation that Kahn argued in 1964 for the creation of "very archaic looking buildings, buildings that will be considered archaic in the future."[39]

Of course, not every client agreed with Jonas Salk and Katharine McBride that Kahn's ancient imagery was appropriate. In 1961–62, while at work for them, he lost or

failed to win three commissions for university research buildings because his designs differed so radically from the expected architecture of modern science. The Chemistry Building for the University of Virginia, whose *parti* was a freestanding lecture hall in a courtyard surrounded by laboratories, was much studied and restudied, with the auditorium successively conceived as an antique semicircular theater and a towered, irregular hexagon (fig. 165).[40] The latter design, related to Kahn's contemporary "window room" towers for Mikveh Israel synagogue, was flatly rejected by the university president as "rather cold and forbidding."[41] Perceptively, but without sympathy, he added, "I am reminded of a Norman castle with its formidable towers." Shapero Hall of Pharmacy at Wayne State University, which Kahn proposed to wrap in a circular "ruin" like the Salk meeting house, met with a similar reaction.[42] The university declined to approach donors for additional money, judging that they were "accustomed to more conventional buildings."[43] And Kahn was also undone by the unorthodoxy of his submission in the invited competition for the Lawrence Memorial Hall of Science at the University of California, Berkeley.[44] His earthwork-encircled citadel, designed to contain a memorial to the inventor of the cyclotron and a center for science education, was passed over by the judges in favor of something less unusual (fig. 166). It was sometimes difficult for patrons to believe that Kahn's ancient-looking monuments could represent the future of their institutions.

There was no such lack of understanding on the part of those who called Kahn to India in 1962 to design—and build—the Indian Institute of Management in Ahmedabad (see figs. 314–36 and pp. 368–73). Here, in a graduate school of business administration, he was able to create a complete environment for learning—the type of ideal campus of which Erdman Hall and the Salk laboratory were only fragments. This was the environment he had described in 1959: "It is . . . a realm of spaces which may be connected by ways of walking, and the walking is a protected kind of walking. . . . You consider it as high spaces together with low spaces, and various spaces where people can sort of find the place where they can do what they want to do."[45] With the commencement of the Ahmedabad project, the subcontinent became the most receptive testing ground for Kahn's art, as reinforced by the even more far-reaching commission for the new capital at Dhaka that arrived in his office at almost the same time.

The Indian Institute of Management was created with the support of the state and national governments and under the sponsorship of the Sarabhai family, who had earlier brought Le Corbusier to their city to build houses, a museum, and a grandiose clubhouse for themselves and the other prosperous leaders of the textile industry. Kahn threw himself into the project with enormous energy, making the long, uncomfortable journey to India for the first time in November 1962 and returning on more than a score of occasions.

In mystical, timeless India, Kahn discovered that the unchanging essence he sought in all things seemed to lie closer to the surface, and he was in turn discovered by Indian admirers who were immediately receptive to his way of looking at the world. For the rest of his life, Indian students flocked to the University of Pennsylvania to study in his master's studio. His great friend and the engineer of his appointment, the Ahmedabad architect Balkrishna Doshi, spoke for many of them when he said, "Lou appeared to me a Yogin [yogi] because of his 'Samadhi' [heightened consciousness] to discover the value of the eternal—the Truth—the Atman—the Soul" (see fig. 152).[46]

India was also full of rich architectural experiences, from the powerful medieval buildings of her Mughal rulers to the twentieth-century work of Lutyens in New Delhi and Le Corbusier in Chandigarh and Ahmedabad. Kahn drank in all of this from the past, enjoying, too, the energy of Ahmedabad's contemporary artists and architects. Most of all, in Ahmedabad (as in Dhaka), he found ambitions that were large enough and support that was deep enough to build on a scale nearly equal to his vision, despite the limited resources of his clients.

As usual for Kahn, his thinking about the Indian Institute of Management began with its overall plan, one that could unite the required classrooms, offices, library, dining hall, dormitories, faculty residences, workers' housing, and market. The recently finalized design for Erdman Hall apparently inspired him to base his plan on diagonals, with long, interconnected dormitory blocks stretching outward like fingers from the main instructional building, ending at the edge of a lake (fig. 167). Across the lake, houses for faculty were arranged in chevrons. As at Bryn Mawr, Kahn found this diagonal system to be a powerful "architecture of connection." It could cope with the exigencies of the program and at the same time impose his sense of order over the multipart plan, doing both far better than an orthogonal scheme in which "everything is . . . answerable to a square."[47]

166

The diagonal layout had the particular advantage of responding well to the requirement that the buildings be oriented toward the southwesterly breezes, a matter that required several readjustments and Doshi's assistance before Kahn got it right. In the course of this revision he also subdivided the dormitories into twenty-bedroom units (fig. 168). As in the Richards Building, the importance of air circulation was probably overstated, and in the end it was clearly abstract pattern that governed the placement of units. But, for a time at least, Kahn saw proper orientation to the wind as the key to building in the tropics. This had been brought home to him by a magical but uncomfortable experience:

I was impressed with the need for air when I happened, with twenty other people, in the palace in Lahore, where the guide showed us the ingenuity of craftsmen who had covered an entire room with multi-colored mirrored mosaics. To demonstrate the mystery of the reflections, he closed all the doors and lit a match. The light of the single match gave multiple and unpredictable effects but two people fainted for lack of air in the short moment that the room was shut off from the breeze. In that time, in that room, you felt that nothing is more interesting than air.[48]

Ultimately, Kahn's scrupulous attention to the use of local brick, the material prescribed to him by the client because of its economy, was more effective in attaching the school design to its Indian environment than his concern for ventilation (fig. 170). In brick Kahn seemed to have discovered a friend, a simple and robust building system that invited honest exposure without the distracting visual complications that came with more sophisticated technology. Although he had frequently employed brick veneer before, in Ahmedabad he was committed to using brick as a structural material, and he gave himself over completely to a study of its properties. The almost painful straightforwardness of his arched forms bore witness to the sincerity of this investigation. Kahn often dramatized the earnest dialogue with brick that he claimed lay at the heart of his use of the material: "You say to brick, 'What do you want, brick?' And brick says to you, 'I like an arch.' And you say to brick, 'Look, I want one too, but arches are expensive and I can use a concrete lintel over you, over an opening.' And then you say, 'What do you think of that, brick?' Brick says, 'I like an arch.'"[49]

Kahn himself pointed out that arcuated brick construction made his buildings look "old-fashioned," by now a highly complimentary description.[50] His point of comparison was probably utilitarian Roman brickwork, like that which mounted skyward in the Basilica of Constantine or on the

rear slope of the Palatine Hill, but Doshi also saw references to the medieval architecture of India in Kahn's design, specifically the thickset twelfth-century monuments of Mandu.[51] He had succeeded in creating forms of such elemental authority that they resisted any single identification.

Brimming with primitive tectonic energy, the Indian Institute of Management derived another kind of power from the academic life that it so effectively promoted. "When one walks around the complex silently," Doshi reported, "either in cool winter or hot and stark summer, one gets the vibrations of conversations, dialogues, meetings and activities. The spaces that are created for these activities link the entire complex."[52] That is exactly how Kahn had hoped the school would work, for even before receiving the commission, he had maintained that the best education was informal, like the gathering of students under his proverbial tree. He argued eloquently against the arrangement of classrooms along ordinary hallways—what he called "sneak passage[s]"—and in favor of substituting places for impromptu gathering—"spaces of no obligation."[53] He explained this ideal school in some detail in 1960:

The corridors, by the provision of greater width and alcoves overlooking gardens, would be transformed into classrooms for the exclusive use of the students. These would become the places where boy meets girl, where student discusses the work of the professor with fellow student. If classroom time were allotted to these spaces instead of only the passage time from class to class, they would become not merely corridors but meeting places— places offering possibilities in self learning. In this sense they would become classrooms belonging to the students.[54]

This accurately forecast the shape taken by the main building at Ahmedabad, in which freestanding lecture rooms and blocks of faculty offices stood on opposite sides of a great central courtyard, linked not by corridors but by shady walkways that offered many places to stop and talk (fig. 169; see figs. 325, 328, 330). Presiding over the courtyard at one end was the austere face of the library, illuminated by two vast glazed circles set within a shady recess. At the other end Kahn planned to build the dining hall, its attached kitchen set within a smell-confining truncated cone, and for the center of the courtyard he designed an amphitheater. Reflecting on the usefulness of this kind of plan for schools in general, Kahn said, "The court is the meeting place of the mind, as well as the physical meeting place."[55]

The life of learning and self-instruction was also integral to

167. Indian Institute of Management, Ahmedabad, India, 1962–74. Model, ca. 1963.
168. Indian Institute of Management, Ahmedabad, India, 1962–74. Model, ca. November 1964.
169. Indian Institute of Management, Ahmedabad, India, 1962–74. Classroom building, entrance stairway, and office wing.
170. Indian Institute of Management, Ahmedabad, India, 1962–74. Classrooms seen from dormitory terrace.

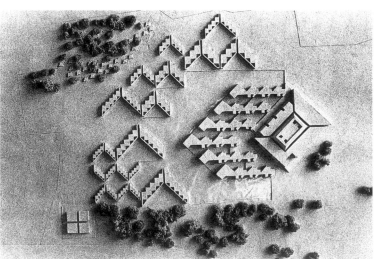

167

168

169

170

the design of the residential part of the complex, which was closely linked to the main building. This pattern, Kahn believed, was demanded by the particular mode of teaching at the institute, the "case study" method borrowed from the Harvard Business School, with its emphasis on the analysis of sample business cases by teams of students, under faculty guidance. As Kahn somewhat incorrectly explained it: "[There are] no lectures, the lectures are just inspired out of case studies. All the dormitories are also places where people can meet. So the dormitories and the school are really one; they are not separated."[56] Such an integrated environment suggested an obvious and familiar model; in explaining the Indian Institute of Management, Kahn declared, "The plan comes from my feelings of monastery."[57]

This thinking generated a wonderfully rich arrangement of public, semiprivate, and private spaces in and around the eighteen dormitory units that grouped themselves on two sides of the main building (figs. 171, 172; see figs. 314, 317). Each four-story block accommodated twenty private rooms, arranged on the two upper floors around triangular lounges or "tea rooms" that opened to the outside through gigantic circular perforations. Serving kitchens and toilets were contained within a square tower attached to the long face of the overall triangular plan. The lower floors were entirely devoted to communal space, intended to serve as meeting rooms for student organizations and for the kind of unchoreographed interaction that Kahn wished to promote. Among the dormitories was woven a network of small courtyards, interconnected by partially unenclosed ground floors. While these spaces read in plan as an orderly grid, Kahn's activating diagonality and the rapid and continuous transition from sunny exterior to shady interior would quickly disorient the casual visitor (see figs. 319–24). For the resident, however, the environment was a private realm of special personality and charm, like the medieval colleges of Oxford and Cambridge.

Kahn planned for the dormitories to be surrounded on two sides by a shallow lake, with more elaborate clubrooms in the strongly buttressed ground floors of the buildings adjacent to the water (see fig. 484). The lake would separate the dormitories from the houses of the faculty and staff, providing privacy for the older members of the community without moving them very far from the students. Although concern about malarial mosquitoes kept the lake from being filled, Kahn insisted to the end that it was an essential part of the plan.

The simple faculty housing that lay to the south and east

contrasted sharply with the robust and sculptural dormitories (fig. 173; see figs. 331–35). The fifty-three houses were articulated by little more than Kahn's "composite order"—the system of shallow brick arches and concrete tie beams that he invented for Ahmedabad—and, indeed, Kahn said that "houses should be dumb looking so that the families and children can have their own say."[58] But for all their simplicity, the houses possessed a variety of wonderful amenities, including enclosed upper floor terraces (really outdoor rooms) and a staggered siting scheme that secluded each house from its neighbors. The even plainer one-story houses for the school's workers were joined together in straight blocks at the southern edge of the site.

Construction in Ahmedabad proceeded with excruciating slowness, due in part to a shortage of funds and in part to Kahn's penchant for procrastination and reconsideration. Responsibility was increasingly shifted to Doshi and Anant Raje, a younger architect who worked on the project for a time in Kahn's Philadelphia office. Upon Kahn's death, Raje assumed responsibility for designing the dining hall, as well as the executive education center and married-student housing, which had been later additions to the program. Despite this, the Indian Institute of Management possesses a completeness and a unity of vision that is rare for works of this scale. It is the nearest the twentieth century has come to creating a successor to Thomas Jefferson's great academic village at the University of Virginia. There, as in Ahmedabad, the essential elements are an integrated environment for faculty and student life, interwoven by covered walkways and dominated by a great library.

In Ahmedabad and La Jolla monastic images had inflected Kahn's thinking, and in 1966 he finally got to design two real religious communities: a monastery in California and a convent in Pennsylvania. This must have seemed like the fulfillment of a dream, for he had long challenged himself and his students to consider the monastery as the model for communal life. He had also frequently described the invention of the primordial monastery as an example of the kind of fundamental searching on which all institutional architecture should be based: "Why must we assume that there cannot be other things so marvelous as the emergence of the first monastery, for which there was no precedence whatsoever? It was simply that some man realized that a certain realm of spaces represents a deep desire on the part of man to express the inexpressible in a certain activity of man called a monastery."[59] As it happened, neither of these actual commissions lived up to his expectations about the cloistered life, although, as planning exercises, they gave

171

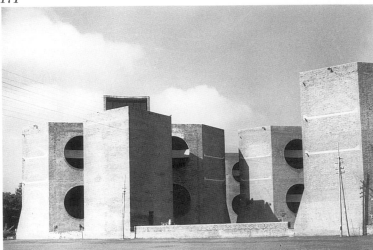

172

173

171. Indian Institute of Management, Ahmedabad, India, 1962–74. Dormitories with classroom and administration building foundations in foreground, ca. 1969.
172. Indian Institute of Management, Ahmedabad, India, 1962–74. Dormitories.
173. Indian Institute of Management, Ahmedabad, India, 1962–74. Dormitories and faculty houses.

him an opportunity to test some of his more radical ideas about juxtapositional composition to their maximum.

Kahn's first, tentative contact with Saint Andrew's Priory in Valyermo, California, had been in 1961, when he visited its extraordinary hilltop site in the high desert north of Los Angeles.[60] He was impressed by the arid vastness of the place and intrigued by the remarkable prior, Father Raphael Vinciarelli, who had founded Saint Andrew's and made it a center for the arts and ecumenicalism after his monastery in China was closed by the Communists.[61] Kahn sketched out for Vinciarelli a poetic design that would begin with the building of a fountain at the place where precious water had been discovered, because "something must be done to show your appreciation." Next would come a system of aqueducts, and "only then should you think in terms of placing your buildings, your chapel and your church and the place of meditation and rest."[62] These were never more than word pictures, however, for the abbey had already retained another architect and Kahn was prevented by his scruples (and the strict professional code of the American Institute of Architects) from accepting the monks' invitation to go further.[63]

Late in 1965, with the other architect long out of the picture, Vinciarelli's successor inquired if Kahn would now consider taking up the commission. He replied with delight, "It is rare that the client of an architect feels the inspiration to express in the realm of architecture," and he waived his usual fee.[64] Kahn returned to Valyermo in March 1966 and developed the design over the summer, in time to unveil a model to the tens of thousands who came to the monastery's annual fall festival in late September (fig. 174). The gathering was described by the *Los Angeles Times* as "a true fiesta of art, music and spiritual excitement."[65]

The collagelike monastery plan reflected the continuing evolution of Kahn's thinking about juxtapositional, diagonal composition. Whereas at Bryn Mawr and Ahmedabad he had used a diagonal armature to reaffirm the authority of Beaux-Arts plan-making (purging it in the process of some of its artificiality), the more varied diagonals of the Valyermo design were related to another line of development, in the direction adumbrated by his energetic World War II community buildings (see figs. 18, 19). This avenue toward freer composition had been followed in his mature period by the day camp for the Trenton Jewish Community Center and, most recently, by the mosque/assembly complex at Dhaka and the 1964 redesign of the Fisher house (see figs. 94, 129, 205). Nominally dependent on the imagined programmatic demands of adjacency between units, these designs were defined in the final analysis by Kahn's visual sensitivity—a kind of modern baroque that, like David Smith's "Cubi" sculptural series, broke down static paradigms with an affection for gestural placement. The independent units of the monastery plan seemed to come together of their own free will, creating the democratic plan type that Kahn would call "a society of rooms."[66]

To describe the dynamic equipoise of part to part in this kind of planning, Kahn employed eloquence that he ascribed to the students in his master's studio at the University of Pennsylvania. He had assigned them the Valyermo monastery as a project, and he recounted that they had spent the first two weeks, without a program, discussing "nature." Then, he said,

An Indian girl gave the first remark of significance. She said, "I believe that this place should be so that everything stems from the cell. From the cell would come the right for the chapel to exist. From the cell would come the right for the retreat, and for the workshops to exist." Another Indian student (their minds work in most transcendent ways) said, "I very much agree, but I would like to add that the refectory must be equal to the chapel, and the chapel must be equal to the cell, and the retreat must be equal to the refectory. None is greater than the other."[67]

Working thus, without programmatic constraints, it is not surprising that the students confounded a "merry monk" from Pittsburgh who came to the studio to advise them about monastic life. An artist himself and a modern, worldly man, he preferred a big studio to a cell, and, when some of the students proposed placing the refectory a half-mile away in order to create a proper sense of ceremony, he horrified them by saying that he would rather have his meals in bed. "We were dejected when he left," Kahn recalled. But he was used to clients who failed to appreciate the new directions that he mapped out for them, and he added, "But then we thought, '*Well, he's only a monk—He doesn't know any better.*'"[68]

The lively public life of the monks at Saint Andrew's must have disappointed Kahn in similar ways, but it was their lack of resources that halted his work. Before the end of their relationship early in 1967, he had, however, sketched elevations for the priory. The attached chapel and refectory were lit through huge circular openings like those he was using in south Asia, and at the center of the composition rose a faceted reception tower, containing the administrative offices and library and topped by the symbolically and functionally important water tank.

174

177

175

178

176

174. St. Andrew's Priory,
Valyermo, Calif., 1961–67.
Model, September 1966.
175. Dominican Motherhouse,
Media, Pa., 1965–69. Plan, ca.
April 1968.
176. Dominican Motherhouse,
Media, Pa., 1965–69.
Elevation, ca. 1968.

177. Dominican Motherhouse,
Media, Pa., 1965–69. Model,
ca. October 1966.
178. Rice University Art
Center, Houston, Tex.,
1969–70. Site plan, late Spring
1970.

Shortly after he began work on the Valyermo project in 1966, Kahn undertook a very similar commission for the Dominican Motherhouse of St. Catherine de Ricci, at Media, in the southwestern suburbs of Philadelphia (see pp. 384–89). At a slightly slower pace, it followed the same route that had been charted by St. Andrew's toward eventual disillusionment and disappointment, owing to the worldliness and poverty of the sisters. But along the way, Kahn created for the convent an even more incandescent realization of the planning principles that he had adopted for the monastery.

Those principles were emblematized by a design method adopted by Kahn's office early in the fall of 1966, when they were at work on the convent. His staff decided to study the design by cutting up an existing drawing so that the component parts of the program could be shifted and reassembled like a real collage (see fig. 503). Kahn could thus experiment with relationships while preserving the integrity of the separate elements, each of which was really a room, for him the infrangible unit of architectural design. It may have been this method that Kahn had in mind in 1972 when he said, "The rooms talk to each other and they make up their minds where their positions are."[69] On another occasion he offered a variant wording: "I think architects should be composers and not designers. They should be composers of elements. The elements are things that are entities in themselves."[70]

The resulting plan, a model of which was ready for presentation on October 10, 1966, had a wiry energy even greater than that of the just-completed scheme for St. Andrew's (fig. 177). This strong vision was expensive to realize, however, and Mother Mary Emmanuel asked Kahn to reduce the size of the building, reminding him that he had to deal with the contemporary realities of an outward-oriented church, not some gentle fantasy of Trappist spirituality in the Middle Ages.[71] During the first months of 1967 he made sharp reductions, and economizing continued into 1968, when working drawings were prepared. The more compact plan compressed most of the energy of its predecessor into a smaller space (fig. 175). Elevations were also developed during this period, and they showed the same variety of forms employed in Valyermo (fig. 176). In the end, however, no common meeting ground could be found for the convent's budget and Kahn's architecture.

The consideration of these projects for communities devoted to education and contemplation can properly conclude with two further academic commissions that Kahn received

toward the end of this period. His proposals for the Maryland Institute College of Art, in Baltimore, and the Art Center for Rice University, in Houston, were both defined by his vision of a life of learning, and both were undermined by his rewriting of the programs at a scale beyond the means of his clients.

In Baltimore the assignment was to accommodate studios, an artists'-supply store, and an auditorium on a narrow site that lay across the railroad tracks from the old Mt. Royal railroad station (1896), recently occupied by the school.[72] Kahn proposed a very slender building whose plan was riven by diagonals and whose austere facades were punctuated by circular and triangular openings. He planned to cover the tracks and connect the new and old buildings with a pedestrian mall. There was some uncertainty on the part of the College of Art about the extent of its needs, and during the first design phase in 1966–67 the program was adjusted upward from roughly 22,000 to 39,000 square feet. But they expressed no uncertainty when Kahn presented a model for a 100,000-square-foot building in March 1967. College president Eugene Leake wrote that the "model presentation did nothing but put everybody in deep shock for, I guess, at least five or ten years."[73] Over the next months Kahn's office struggled to reduce the size of the building while retaining, as they explained, "a long 'wall' shape very much in the spirit of our first studies."[74] Despite these problems, relations remained cordial. Kahn was awarded an honorary doctorate by the college in 1968, and Leake seemed to be genuinely grateful that he was still interested in working for them after his dream of a gigantic building was dashed. "Thanks for your continued interest—we're *lucky*," he wrote. "We believe that a Kahn building is a must and that it would make us the best art school in the country."[75] The project was finally killed by cutbacks in federal education support made during the Nixon administration.

Kahn's proposal for the Art Center at Rice University encompassed the programs in architecture, theater, art history, music, and fine arts, as well as a large performance hall and a new gallery for the Institute of Art (to be relocated from the University of St. Thomas by its director, Dominique de Menil).[76] He was asked to prepare only a preliminary report, and his site plan and model were readied during the late spring of 1970 and presented to the university on June 29 and 30. West of the main library Kahn created a large courtyard, nearly equal in size to the handsome main quadrangle that lay to the east, a truncated version of the one planned by Ralph Adams Cram and Bertram Grosvenor Goodhue in 1909–10 (fig. 178). Because construction of the Art Center would necessitate the demolition of the existing student center, a replacement facility was also part of the program. Kahn showed it standing within the new courtyard, surrounded by buildings for the various art departments. None of this was worked out in detail, and the university never called on Kahn to go further, but his image of the ensemble, functioning as a school, was strong. In a discussion with Rice students, he explained how he had chosen between two possible planning approaches, rejecting a linear arrangement and choosing a courtyard, like that at Ahmedabad:

Suppose you had a great kind of alley, or gallery, and walked through this gallery, and connected to this gallery are the schools which are associated in the fine arts, be it history, sculpture, architecture, or painting, and you saw people at work, in all these classes. It was designed so that you felt always as though you were walking through a place where people are at work.

Then I present another way of looking at it, say as a court, and you enter this court. You see buildings in this court, and one is designated as painting, one as sculpture, another as architecture, as history. In one, you rub against the presence of the classes. In the other, you can choose to go in if you want to.

. . .

I think the latter is the greater by far.

. . .

There is something that has to do with the feeling of association which is remote, rather than direct, and more remote association has a longer life and love.[77]

This diffidence toward involuntary contact with the resources of education seemed to preserve a memory of Kahn's own early experience as a commuting student, choosing carefully among the many opportunities offered by his urban boyhood. For him the perfect school was a courtyard of institutional opportunities—or "availabilities," as he called them late in his career— combined with monastic cells for individual contemplation. Students were free in such a setting to establish their own relationships with each other and with the available resources, creating a human collage, just as the architectural elements in Kahn's "society of rooms" found their own points of contact and established their own equilibriums. Design was the overlaying of these human and architectural patterns, whether at the scale of a house, a public institution, or a city.

D.B.B.

Notes

1. Kahn, "Remarks" (lecture, Yale University, October 30, 1963), *Perspecta*, no. 9/10 (1965): 310. A second often-cited inspiration was "to meet," and he sometimes added a third, variously called "to express" and "well-being"; e.g., Kahn, interview with Karl Linn, May 14, 1965, typed transcript, "Linn, Karl," Box LIK 58, Louis I. Kahn Collection, University of Pennsylvania and Pennsylvania Historical and Museum Commission, Philadelphia (hereafter cited as Kahn Collection); Kahn, *Architecture: The John Lawrence Memorial Lectures* (New Orleans: Tulane University School of Architecture, 1972), n.p.
2. Kahn, quoted in University of Pennsylvania, School of Medicine, *Report of the Proceedings, Sixth Annual Conference on Graduate Medical Education: Medicine in the Year 2000. Philadelphia, Pennsylvania, December 1964* (Philadelphia: University of Pennsylvania, 1965), 149.
3. Kahn, quoted in "Kahn" (interview, February 1961), *Perspecta*, no. 7 (1961): 10.
4. Kahn, "Our Changing Environment" (panel discussion, June 18, 1964), in American Craftsmen's Council, *First World Congress of Craftsmen, June 8 through June 19, 1964. Columbia University, New York* (New York: American Craftsmen's Council, [1965]), 120.
5. Kahn, lecture recorded November 19, 1960, and broadcast November 21, 1960; published as *Structure and Form*, Forum Architecture Series, no. 6 (Washington, D.C.: Voice of America, [1961]), 2. The tree metaphor was introduced at least as early as 1955; see Kahn, review of *Synagogue Architecture in the U.S.*, by Rachel Wischnitzer, MS, ca. November 1955, "Descriptions of Buildings," Box LIK 54, Kahn Collection.
6. Kahn, "Space and the Inspirations" (lecture, New England Conservatory of Music, Boston, November 14, 1967), *L'architecture d'aujourd'hui* 40 (February–March 1969): 15.
7. Kahn, "Remarks," 305.
8. Ibid., 332.
9. C. P. Snow, *The Two Cultures and the Scientific Revolution*, The Rede Lecture 1959 (Cambridge: Cambridge University Press, 1959).
10. Salk, interview with David B. Brownlee and David G. De Long, May 24, 1990.
11. Salk, interview with David B. Brownlee et al., April 18, 1983.
12. Kahn, "Law and Rule in Architecture" (lecture, Princeton University, November 29, 1961), typed transcript, "LIK Lectures 1969," Box LIK 53, Kahn Collection.
13. Letter, Monica Bromley (RIBA) to Kahn, February 21, 1962, "Discourse for R.I.B.A. 1962 Correspondence," Box LIK 55, Kahn Collection; Kahn, "Louis I. Kahn: Talks with Students" (lecture and discussion, Rice University, ca. 1969), *Architecture at Rice*, no. 26 (1969): 13.
14. Esther McCoy, "Dr. Salk Talks about His Institute," *Architectural Forum* 127 (December 1967): 31–32.
15. Kahn, *Medicine in the Year 2000*, 150.
16. Kahn, "Law and Rule" (Princeton).
17. Kahn, *Medicine in the Year 2000*, 153.
18. Kahn, "Kahn," 11. The project under discussion was the consulate in Luanda.
19. Kahn, "Law and Rule in Architecture" (annual discourse, Royal Institute of British Architects, March 14, 1962), typed transcript, "LIK Lectures 1969," Box LIK 53, Kahn Collection.
20. Kahn, "Talks with Students," 13–14.
21. Vincent J. Scully, *Louis I. Kahn* (New York: George Braziller, 1982), 37.
22. Kahn, "Remarks," 330.
23. Salk, interview with Brownlee and De Long.
24. Kahn, *Medicine in the Year 2000*, 151.

25. Kahn, "Remarks," 332.

26. Kahn, "I Love Beginnings" (lecture, International Design Conference, "The Invisible City," Aspen, Colorado, June 19, 1972), *Architecture + Urbanism*, special issue "Louis I. Kahn," 1975, 282.

27. Kahn, "Silence," *Via* 1 (1968): 89.

28. Kahn, "Remarks," 305.

29. Kahn, interview with Linn.

30. Kahn, "The Architect and the Building," *Bryn Mawr Alumnae Bulletin* 43 (Summer 1962): 2.

31. Kahn, unidentified discussion, International Design Conference, "The Invisible City," Aspen, Colorado, June 1972, quoted in *What Will Be Has Always Been: The Words of Louis I. Kahn*, ed. Richard Saul Wurman (New York: Access Press and Rizzoli, 1986), 170.

32. Kahn, "Law and Rule" (RIBA).

33. Kahn, "Kahn," 12–13.

34. Kahn, "Architect and Building," 5.

35. Ibid., 3.

36. Kahn, "Law and Rule" (RIBA). Peter S. Reed suggests that the book was probably William Douglas Simpson, *Castles from the Air* (London: Country Life; New York: Charles Scribner's Sons, 1949). Alexandra Tyng notes that in 1962 he was given Stewart Cruden, *The Scottish Castle* (Edinburgh: Spurbooks, 1962); Tyng, *Beginnings: Louis I. Kahn's Philosophy of Architecture* (New York: John Wiley & Sons, 1984), 19.

37. Susan Braudy, "The Architectural Metaphysic of Louis Kahn: 'Is the Center of a Column Filled with Hope?' 'What Is a Wall?' 'What Does This Space Want To Be?'" *New York Times Magazine*, November 15, 1970, 80. Comlongan Castle, Dumphriesshire, is illustrated in Scully, *Kahn*, fig. 116, and Kahn, "Remarks," figs. 42–45. Both were published with Kahn's consultation.

38. Kahn, "Space and the Inspirations," 16; for another version, see Kahn, "Address by Louis I. Kahn, April 5, 1966," *Boston Society of Architects Journal*, no. 1 (1967): 8.

39. Kahn, *Medicine in the Year 2000*, 151.

40. Research assistance for the Chemistry Building, University of Virginia, was provided by Peter S. Reed.

41. Letter, Edgar F. Shannon to Kahn, November 19, 1962, "UVA—University Correspondence," Box LIK 33, Kahn Collection.

42. Research assistance for Shapero Hall, Wayne State University, was provided by Peter S. Reed.

43. Memo, Douglas R. Sherman (president, Wayne State University) to Arthur Neef (vice president and provost, WSU), Stephen Wilson (dean, College of Pharmacy, WSU), and Mark Beach, February 5, 1962, "Wayne University Correspondence," Box LIK 33, Kahn Collection.

44. Research assistance for Lawrence Memorial Hall, University of California, Berkeley, was provided by Peter S. Reed.

45. Kahn, "Talk at the Conclusion of the Otterlo Congress," in *New Frontiers in Architecture: CIAM '59 in Otterlo*, ed. Oscar Newman (New York: Universe Books, 1961), 212.

46. Balkrishna V. Doshi, "Louis Kahn in India," *Architecture + Urbanism*, special issue "Louis I. Kahn," 1975, 313.

47. Kahn, "Remarks," 324.

48. Ibid., 327.

49. Kahn, "1973: Brooklyn, New York" (lecture, Pratt Institute, Fall 1973), *Perspecta*, no. 19 (1982): 92; another version: Kahn, "I Love Beginnings," 281.

50. Kahn, quoted in James Bailey, "Louis Kahn in India: An Old Order at a New Scale," *Architectural Forum* 125 (July–August 1966): 40.

51. Doshi, "Louis Kahn in India," 312.

52. Ibid., 311.

53. Kahn, "Architecture and Human Agreement" (lecture, University of Virginia, April 18, 1972), *Modulus*, no. 11 (1975): n.p.

54. Kahn, *Structure and Form*, 3

55. Kahn, "Talks with Students," 40.

56. Kahn, "Address," 17.

57. Kahn, "Remarks," 322.

58. Kahn, quoted in Doshi, "Louis Kahn in India," 311.

59. Kahn, "Remarks," 305.

60. Research assistance for St. Andrew's Priory was provided by Peter S. Reed.

61. Shari Wigle, "The World, the Arts, and Father Raphael," *Los Angeles Times West Magazine*, September 18, 1966, 32–33, 46–51.

62. Kahn, "Law and Rule" (RIBA).

63. Letter, Kahn to Father Vincent Martin, September 25, 1961, "Master File—August 1-61 through 9/28/61," Box LIK 9, Kahn Collection. The architect was Foster Rhodes Jackson.

64. Letter, Kahn to Father Philip Verhaegen (prior, St. Andrews Priory), November 26, 1965, "St. Andrew's Priory Valyermo, California," Box LIK 81, Kahn Collection; letter, John Duncan (priory's attorney) to Father de Morchoven, April 26, 1966, ibid.

65. Wigle, "Father Raphael," 32.

66. Kahn, "Architecture and Human Agreement," n.p.

67. Kahn, "Talks with Students," 7–8.

68. Ibid., 8.

69. Kahn, *Architecture*, n.p.

70. Kahn, "Address," 13.

71. Letter, Mother Emmanuel to Kahn, December 16, 1966, "Mother Mary Emmanuel Motherhouse—Media," Box LIK 32, Kahn Collection.

72. Research assistance for the Maryland Institute College of Art was provided by Peter S. Reed.

73. Letter, Leake to David Wisdom, March 30, 1967, "Maryland Institute College of Art Correspondence," Box LIK 33, Kahn Collection.

74. Letter, Wisdom to Leake, April 6, 1967, ibid.

75. Letter, Leake to Kahn, April 9, 1969, ibid.

76. Research assistance for the Art Center, Rice University, was provided by Peter S. Reed.

77. Kahn, "Talks with Students," 39–40.

When Louis Kahn spoke of "architecture and human agreement,"[1] he expressed a belief in the social nature of humanity. He viewed architecture as supportive of this nature and strove to provide a framework for human interaction within which each individual could realize a greater degree of worth. For Kahn, a sense of self-determination through choice was essential to such realization, and thus he maintained a certain degree of neutrality in his designs, feeling that the architect's imposition of rigid patterns could suppress spontaneity. Balancing structured order with provisions for individual choice seemed to incline him toward complex geometric patterns that could demonstrate opportunities for varied use. Instead of being formally aligned, his shapes were more often joined in complicated ways to suggest what he began to call "availabilities." This term he favored in alluding to his objectives: "The architect's job, in my opinion . . . is to find those spaces . . . where the availabilities, not yet here, and those that are already here, can have better environments for their maturing into."[2] He found effective vehicles in a broad range of commissions that were not dedicated to a single purpose of study or assembly, but were more inclusive of varied pursuits. Most of these were institutional complexes within cities, or speculative urban complexes, which Kahn studied to discover some deeper purpose. But they could also include more remotely located complexes and even individual houses wherein a "society of rooms"[3] provided diverse yet mutually supportive activities, like those of a small city.

Kahn continued to speak about cities even as he became less involved in their overall design; in one of his last public lectures he spoke of their potential: "Probably the measure of a city is the degree or the quality of the availabilities. . . . If I were to make a city plan, I think I would say, 'In what way can I make the architecture of connection which would enliven the mind as to how the availabilities can be even more enriched than they are?'"[4] He came to distrust conventional urban planning as superficial in its consideration of human aspiration, once saying, "If I had to give lectures on town planning I should not want to call them that, but rather 'architecture of high intention.'"[5] He particularly disliked popular jargon, for him a substitute for thought. He once said, "'Urbanism' immediately makes all minds as heavy as lead. You don't think anymore because it's all finished."[6]

During his mature years of practice, Kahn tended to define the city as "the place of the assembled institutions" and as something "measured by the character of its institutions."[7] An institution he described as "that which can be called *availability*. You might say the city street is actually an institution because it is an availability."[8] Institutions were brought into being by "inspirational sources" that he came to define as "the inspiration to learn, the inspiration to meet, and the inspiration to express."[9] The first led to places of study and the second to places of assembly. The third was both more general and more profound: "The reason for man's living is to express. . . . The inspiration to express is that which sets up man's urge to seek shapes and forms which are not in nature."[10] He had movingly described this inspiration as "a revolt against that approximation of nature which makes us live for only a short time. It is the most numbing revolt we have."[11] Its architectural embodiment assumed special significance.

Of Kahn's commissions in the 1960s, none seemed more dedicated to the "inspiration to express" than those complexes he designed for performing and visual arts, perhaps most effectively envisioned in the Philadelphia College of Art (1960–66, unbuilt; fig. 180). Unlike some of his other academic architecture, these complexes dealt less with independent studies tied to libraries or cloistered spaces and more with the interaction associated with theaters and galleries. His first opportunity came with the Fine Arts Center for Fort Wayne, Indiana (partly built), which had been formally commissioned in 1961 but on which he delayed work until the following year, when he advised the city in its selection of an appropriate site (see figs. 302–4 and pp. 346–51). Early studies show parking structures related to an existing viaduct, recalling the viaduct studies for Philadelphia that he had completed the month before (compare figs. 417 and 457). Only after the site was selected in April 1963, following his second presentation in Dhaka, did Kahn begin to plan more intensively. The means to urban expression that he had initiated at that remote site he now exploited more fully in his proposals for Fort Wayne.

Less hierarchically bound than the elements at Dhaka, the component parts of the Fine Arts Center were also less defined in terms of functional relationships. This is clear in Kahn's sketches of mid-1963 (fig. 179): actively juxtaposed shapes engage to define variously bounded courts, and conventional, orthogonal relationships seem avoided with purpose, almost as if the unresolved geometries symbolized the activity of ideas within. By the fall of 1963 the philharmonic hall, the theater, the art school, the art alliance, and the historical museum had assumed positions that would remain basically unchanged (fig. 182). Even

Chapter 5

The Forum of the Availabilities

Designs for Choice

after the historical society withdrew from the proposed complex in early 1964, Kahn managed to retain essential features of connection (fig. 181). An entrance garden would serve as a gateway linking the center with the city beyond, and within, a Court of Entrances would provide the sense of choice so essential to Kahn's concept. Like the shapes of the buildings themselves, it encouraged spontaneity rather than formal movement. Within such complexes, as the Fine Arts Center illustrates, Kahn's avoidance of rigid patterns was intentional. In criticizing a student's proposal to link similar elements with a hall-like bridge rather than a court, he later said:

In [the bridge] you rub against the presence of the classes. In [the court], you can choose to go in if you want to. . . . If you can choose to go there, even if you never do, you can get more out of that arrangement than you can of the other. There is something that has to do with the feeling of association which is remote, rather than direct, and the remote association has a longer life and love.[12]

At Fort Wayne, as at Dhaka, Kahn argued passionately for the entirety of the complex, believing that wholeness was essential to its meaning. Yet as proposed the center was vastly more expensive than its backers had expected; confidence in Kahn's ideas and in the ability to raise the needed funds waned, and elements began to drop away. By October 1966 only the theater, expanded to accommodate the philharmonic, remained as an immediate reality. From the beginning Kahn had conceived both the philharmonic hall and the theater as essentially rectangular volumes, for unlike places of interactive assembly each was frontally rather than centrally focused, and each conformed to Kahn's earlier description of an ideal theater as "something which presents a building in which people gather to see something which has an inevitable kind of nature."[13] In appearance the theater was very much the incomplete fragment that one would expect, designed no doubt with little spirit (see fig. 303). Construction began in 1970 and was completed in 1973 (see fig. 302).

Kahn's suggestion of spontaneity by means of unconventional geometric arrangements came into stronger focus with the Levy Memorial Playground (1961–66, unbuilt), which in turn led to the Philadelphia College of Art. Both, like Fort Wayne, seemed driven by an urge to stimulate creative energy, thus honoring Kahn's "inspiration to express." With the Levy Playground such effort was directed toward children, but it was no less seriously considered. Designed for a New York City site along Riverside Drive between 102nd and 105th Streets, it

180

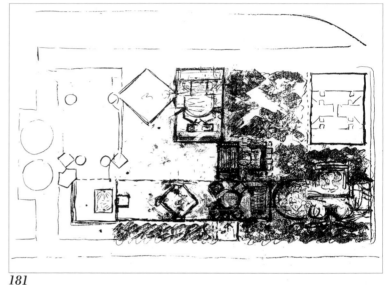

181

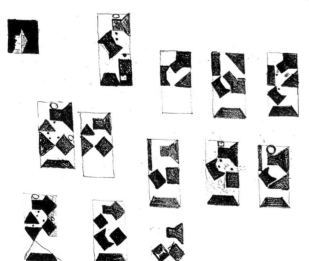

182

179. *Fine Arts Center, School, and Performing Arts Theater, Fort Wayne, Ind., 1959–73. Site plan diagrams, ca. October 1963.*
180. *Philadelphia College of Art, Philadelphia, Pa., 1960–66. Model, ca. December 1964.*

181. *Fine Arts Center, School, and Performing Arts Theater, Fort Wayne, Ind., 1959–73. Site plan. Inscribed January 2 1965 Louis I. Kahn.*
182. *Fine Arts Center, School, and Performing Arts Theater, Fort Wayne, Ind., 1959–73. Model, Fall 1963.*

179

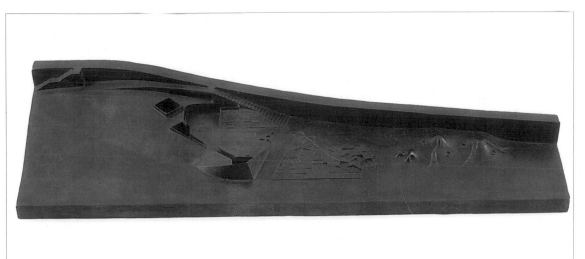

183

184

185

186

183. *Levy Memorial Playground, New York, N.Y., 1961–66. Model, before February 28, 1963.*
184. *Levy Memorial Playground, New York, N.Y., 1961–66. Model, October 1963.*
185. *Levy Memorial Playground, New York, N.Y., 1961–66. Bird's-eye perspective, ca. January 1965.*
186. *Philadelphia College of Art, Philadelphia, Pa., 1960–66. Site plan, December 1964–March 1965.*
187. *Philadelphia College of Art, Philadelphia, Pa., 1960–66. Plan, final version, January 19, 1966.*
188. *Philadelphia College of Art, Philadelphia, Pa., 1960–66. Section facing west. Inscribed January 19, 1966.*

was supported by the estate of Adele Levy, who had been active in funding earlier playgrounds.[14] Isamu Noguchi was commissioned to begin its design in 1961, and he sought the collaboration of Kahn in August of that year.[15]

Kahn worked intermittently on the Levy project, producing that fall a preliminary scheme of discrete circular elements that lacked strong form, but he did little more during the following year, and in January 1963, sponsors complained that proposals were insufficiently developed for presentation to the mayor.[16] By late February matters had changed. Within three weeks of Khan's return from Dhaka he presented a design rigorously shaped by monumental steps and broad terraces; these gave position to play mounds and other elements (fig. 183). Recalling in its geometry his design for Dhaka, an obliquely turned square at one end was developed as a skylight for a grottolike enclosure below. Kahn lessened the severity of this scheme in a third version, designed by October 1963 (fig. 184),[17] and in a final version, completed by January 1964, he created an archaic landscape of ramped and staired elements that recalled Minoan ruins (fig. 185).[18] Noguchi complained that "the architecture is now in ascendancy over the playground. I had hoped it might be the other way around."[19] Kahn, in turn, seemed dismayed by the overly particularized elements contributed by Noguchi: "The spontaneity of participation . . . if you sense this, you also sense that a thing is *made* to be incomplete for play. This sense of incompleteness has to be affirmed. I'll have to speak to Noguchi; there are many things that need tremendously harsh criticism."[20] By then local opposition to the project had grown, for the playground would have taken part of the open space of Riverside Park, and by October 1966 the mayor's office had withdrawn the necessary support, dooming the proposal.[21]

In April 1964, while refining proposals for Fort Wayne and the Levy Playground, Kahn received a commission from the Philadelphia College of Art to design a major addition adjoining their existing buildings on Broad Street. The design evolved through several phases. His final scheme was publicized by university officials in March 1966 (see fig. 180 and pp. 358–61); it gave tangible form to Kahn's belief in the inspiration to express within the supporting framework of an urban matrix. How sad that the university president— appointed in 1965, after Kahn had begun to work—lacked the courage to realize Kahn's vision.

The complex program of related parts, including a theater, a library, an exhibition hall, and studios as well as other elements, was not unlike Fort Wayne's, yet it focused on visual arts rather than performance and was closely contained within the dense center of the city (fig. 186). Again Kahn resisted demands that it be built in phases, believing the totality of parts essential to its very being. Its entrance courts opened more fully to the city than the entrance at Fort Wayne, and they led as well to interior courts and gardens within the complex, so that compelling unity was achieved. As Kahn said, "The campus is interwoven into the building. . . . The roof is a landscape, too."[22] Adjoining the entrance court, the multistory library and exhibition hall, in plan a square turned like the assembly building in Dhaka, served as both gateway and citadel of precious objects, linked at the back to the more actively shaped studios (fig. 187). Their outer, north-facing walls, dramatically battered, were stepped to create skylights (fig. 188), and inside, connecting passages were varied in dimension and direction, reflecting Kahn's dislike of monotonous corridors and avoiding what he now characterized as the "bondage of use."[23]

Rarely had Kahn's designs offered greater promise of new urban form. A massive composition of juxtaposed shapes and layered enclosures, with spaces differentiated according to use and structural definition, the design sustained those departures from convention that he had earlier initiated. Yet individual shapes were more obviously distorted by extrinsic demands of connection and approach, rendering the geometry more rational and less Euclidian than such earlier work as the capitol at Dhaka. By these means Kahn provided protectively framed openings to the wider availabilities of the city itself, for which the Philadelphia College of Art was a microcosm.

Like Dhaka, so large a complex as the Philadelphia College of Art lacks an exact historical parallel in its cohesive unity. It departs more radically than Dhaka from the carefully balanced manner advocated for such complexes by followers of the École des Beaux-Arts, an approach Kahn never fully endorsed in his mature work. With few exceptions the achievement of such compositional unity eluded modern practitioners of the twentieth century, for, as exemplified in Mies van der Rohe's campus for the Illinois Institute of Technology (begun 1939), isolated elements were rarely joined to form some greater whole. Le Corbusier's proposal for the Palace of the League of Nations, Geneva, 1927–28 (fig. 189), was among his designs offering an exception; in light of Kahn's intense admiration for that architect, it might be regarded as a point of departure, but its more neutral, orthogonal elements speak of an earlier phase of the

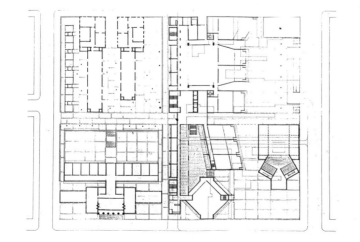

187

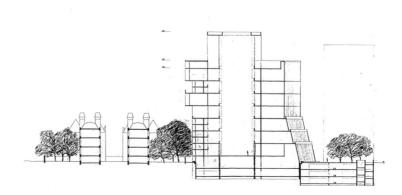

188

twentieth century. Closer in spirit to Kahn's designs of the mid-1960s are two unbuilt examples by Frank Lloyd Wright that Kahn must have noticed: Florida Southern College in Lakeland (begun 1938, fig. 190) and the Crystal Heights hotel, shops, and theater complex in Washington, D.C. (1940). As published they were readily accessible and reflected Wright's more rational side, which Kahn favored. Both contain complexly angled elements that are architecturally unified without recourse to conventional symmetries, and the former approximates Kahn's plan for the Dominican Motherhouse at Media (1965–69, unbuilt), but both also answer to underlying systems of triangular geometry that isolate them from Kahn's freer approach. Yet until Kahn, Wright's achievement of monumental unity had not been surpassed, and however much Kahn may have favored Le Corbusier, it was Wright who more fully prepared the way. As noted in chapter 4, only certain contemporary examples of painting and sculpture—works by Franz Kline or David Smith, for example—seemed to express a comparable spirit. From Kahn's beginning stem major works of late-twentieth-century architecture.

Researchers examining office documents have found it difficult to identify the intended materials of the Philadelphia College of Art, for its structural concrete walls and extensive areas of glazing, while mentioned in newspaper accounts, were not a matter of obvious record. By this stage Kahn had evolved his own approach to structural design, employing concrete slabs, walls, and columns in a manner derived largely from Le Corbusier. Specific representation of structural devices or materials was unnecessary unless some special condition governed, as in the Palazzo dei Congressi. He seemed past the more dramatic but complicated structural displays of the Yale Art Gallery or the City Tower, and he disdained Wrightian essays shaped by new or unusual materials. Particular shapes and exact dimensions came later, guided by Komendant or other engineers with whom he consulted. Yet what seemed obvious and easily attainable to Kahn and efficient to Komendant did not always satisfy the more restricted criteria of clients, especially those engaged in speculation.

Kahn was ill-attuned to the pragmatic demands of developers, yet on several occasions he strove to supply proposals that met their needs, no doubt spurred by the chance to contribute to the urban fabric he found so enthralling. His ventures also revealed an interest in skyscrapers that would otherwise have gone largely unfulfilled. The first of three such commissions for which

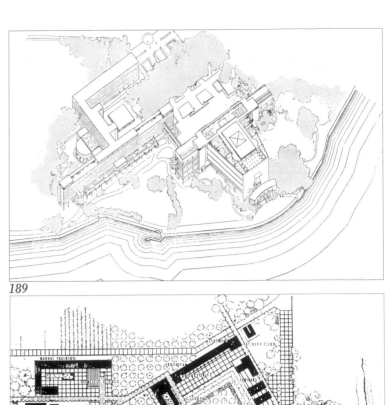

189

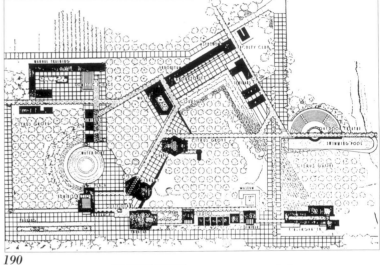

190

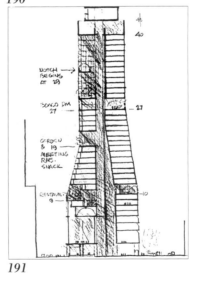

191

192

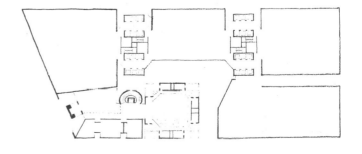

designs were prepared—each for speculative office buildings incorporating elements that were calculated to enhance their civic appeal—was for the Broadway United Church of Christ and Office Building in New York (1966–68, unbuilt), and it was followed within only a few days by the second, an office building in Kansas City (1966–73, unbuilt). The two were intertwined in terms of their design, and while still working on the latter Kahn was commissioned to design the third, the Inner Harbor development in Baltimore (1969–73, unbuilt). Yet however drawn he might have been to these opportunities to express new ideas about urban space, in the end his efforts came to nothing.

The Broadway Church and Office Building was an early example of collaboration between a tax-exempt institution—the Broadway United Church of Christ—and a developer, the Carlyle Construction Company, represented by its own architect, Emery Roth & Sons.[24] Kahn had been contacted by the church in late June of 1966, and by mid-July he was charged as its representative in the venture and expected to coordinate design for the development as a whole.[25] The site, occupying much of the block bounded by Broadway, Seventh Avenue, 56th Street, and 57th Street, was well placed in relation to a developing area of the city.

The prospect of incorporating a church and various commercial functions within an office tower must have stimulated Kahn's imagination, for preliminary sketches show a skyscraper unlike any of its time. Closely resembling the Philadelphia College of Art, which Kahn had ceased work on only a few months before, its plaza was depicted as a landscape of actively juxtaposed shapes; the tower above, rising like an all-encompassing master roof, tapered inward and was enriched by a similarly complicated geometry (figs. 191, 193).[26] The tower itself, like the plaza level, was envisioned as a series of interrelated segments defined by giant "notches" (as termed on the drawing) that opened to a central court within. Receiving the light below was the church, nestled beneath the tower like some ancient foundation of another age. Instead of a single, sharply defined building, Kahn had proposed a complex of parts; lacking a clear line of boundary, they could open more freely to the city they served, and their "availabilities" would be more inviting.

The battered walls of the Broadway project, in form so like those of the Philadelphia College of Art, seemed in New York to be generated first by zoning, and second by Kahn's belief in legible structure. As office drawings record, Kahn had studied New York's building regulations governing site

coverage and wall planes, and the receding plane they dictated for upper floors—conventionally realized as stepped setbacks—Kahn adapted without modification. Hugh Ferriss had long before rendered similar profiles to illustrate these same regulations (fig. 192), but surely not with the expectation of such literal interpretation. No doubt the battering also reflected Kahn's concern with structural clarity; he had criticized architects such as Mies van der Rohe for failing (as in the celebrated Seagram Building, 1956–58) to express the different structural requirements of a tall building's lower floors, where both wind bracing and concentrated loads made added structure necessary.[27]

Representatives of the church supported Kahn's proposal, but the developers were uneasy and urged a more routine solution.[28] Market forces were not yet supportive of such architectural complication: John Portman's profitable, self-financed Atlanta Hyatt Regency was completed only in 1967, and such later examples as New York's Citicorp Building, which also incorporated a church within its base and for which Kahn was briefly considered as architect, were not yet conceived.[29]

Before returning with a second proposal for the Broadway Church and Office Building, Kahn turned his attention to the Kansas City office building. A more typical commission of the time, it was to include underground parking, street-level shopping, a health club and a restaurant on the upper floors, and, for a while, even a heliport. It had been under discussion since July 1966, when its developers, Richard Altman and Arnold Garfinkel, visited Kahn in Philadelphia to engage him in what they hoped would be a building of special quality for their city.[30] It was not until January 1967 that Kahn presented his preliminary sketches, and only in May that his first model followed.[31] Again Kahn began by reexamining the very nature of the problem, and his unexpected proposal reflected structural determinism: at each corner, four hollow, room-sized columns were to support a multistory truss at the top of the building, and from this height intermediate floors would be suspended (fig. 199). Komendant, working with Kahn, devised an elaborately choreographed operation for the building's construction; using slip forms, the corner columns and the truss were to be erected first, followed by the pouring of the individual floor slabs, beginning at the top. Kahn embellished the hollow columns with round openings to light the corner offices, and segmental arches defining the top truss lit the restaurant and club contained within. Distinctive form was thus achieved through rational means, at least as Kahn defined it. As an associate said, "It was a

189. *Le Corbusier. Palace of the League of Nations, Geneva, Switzerland, 1927–28. Axonometric.*
190. *Frank Lloyd Wright. Florida Southern College, Lakeland, Fla., 1938. Site plan.*

191. *Broadway United Church of Christ and Office Building, New York, N.Y., 1966–68. Sections, August–September 1966.*
192. *Hugh Ferriss. Zoning study, 1922.*
193. *Broadway United Church of Christ and Office Building, New York, N.Y., 1966–68. Plan, August–September 1966.*

wonderful project to work on because he was thinking of new ways of building and expressing the nature of the elements of a skyscraper."[32]

Within the next year both the Broadway and Kansas City projects were redesigned, and clearer statements of slip-form construction emerged. Giving in to client pressure for a less complicated floor plan and a single elevator core—both considered essential to profitability—Kahn first revised his proposal for New York, presenting his second scheme for that commission in September 1967.[33] Gone were the richly complicated profile and the elaborate plan, which were replaced by a simple structure of rectangular floors supported by hollow cylindrical columns (figs. 194, 196). Only the church, partly projecting beyond the overhanging slabs, escaped rigid discipline.[34] Kevin Roche's Knights of Columbus Headquarters in New Haven (1965–69), then under construction, seems to have inspired its structural form (fig. 195),[35] yet Kahn's earlier travel sketches of Albi are also similar. The Broadway tower's slip-form construction still alarmed New York developers, and the project languished.[36] Work on the Kansas City project, however, continued. By the fall of 1968 a revised model had been completed, and it, too, had been greatly simplified, though without a sacrifice of unusual construction (fig. 200). The roof truss was now reduced to an elegant inverted arch, and the corner columns, no longer hollow, had become fluted stems. Kahn's proposal was well received, but before financial arrangements could be completed a new, more advantageous site became available, and he again revised his design.[37] In March 1972 Kahn depicted the final version of his building as it would appear during construction; it had been extended by more than ten floors, resting on a square plinth that held related facilities, and its corner columns were made square (fig. 197). But however compelling the image and however supportive the clients, its unusual structure proved impossible to finance. Komendant then produced a version of his own, but it, too, went unrealized.[38]

The 1971 commission for the Baltimore Inner Harbor development provided Kahn with an opportunity of greater scale, for the expansive site overlooking the waterfront was to contain an urban nucleus of office buildings, apartments, a hotel, and a broad range of shops.[39] The progress of the complex, part of Baltimore's ambitious, comprehensive plan, was closely monitored; developers were expected to select distinguished architects in return for receiving the city's permission to build on newly assembled sites, and strict guidelines, including a seventy-five-foot height limit,

194. Broadway United Church of Christ and Office Building, New York, N.Y., 1966–68. Elevation. Inscribed Louis I. Kahn '67.
195. Kevin Roche, John Dinkeloo and Associates. Knights of Columbus Headquarters, New Haven, Conn., 1965–69. Elevation.

196. Broadway United Church of Christ and Office Building, New York, N.Y., 1966–68. Plan. Inscribed November 13, 1967.
197. Kansas City Office Building, Kansas City, Mo., 1966–73. Perspective of third version. Inscribed Lou K '72.

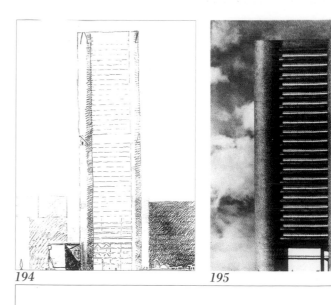

194   195

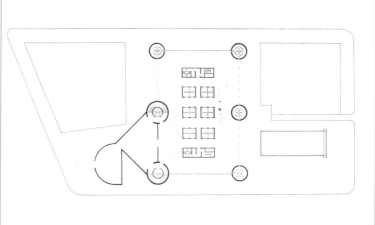

196

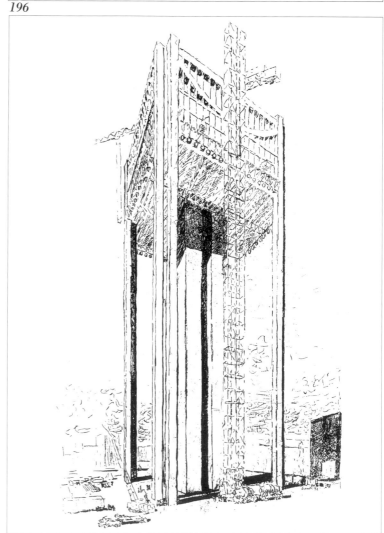

197

were imposed. Kahn's first ideas for its plan brought to the project an active play of juxtaposed shapes corresponding to his proposals elsewhere. By the time of his first presentation in November 1971, these shapes were further sharpened without an apparent loss of spontaneity (fig. 198). Rather than re-creating the experimental structures of his earlier skyscrapers, Kahn worked pragmatically with conventionally framed yet still distinctively shaped buildings, expressing the diagonal lines of their wind bracing and adding pyramidal tops to gain additional rentable area while still honoring the spirit of the height limit. He joined the individual structures with monumental stairways and broad bridges in a manner gauged to generate a sense of urban vitality, exploiting the master plan's requirement that upper-level walkways be incorporated and the developer's demand that a high podium be provided to minimize problems created by the harbor site's high water table (figs. 201, 202). As Kahn explained, "The main idea was to develop a richness of place, full of availabilities.... We wanted an interlocking relationship between buildings so the view would not be obstructed. In turn, that caused the buildings to be multi-faced instead of four sided; the hotel, the apartment and office buildings respect each other."[40] As was typical of such complicated enterprises and even more to be expected of Kahn, many variations were explored. By the summer of 1972, although the major elements had retained their positions, the parts were reduced in number and the shapes were somewhat simplified. By then office associates were discouraged about the prospects of the development and felt Kahn's talent was being unfairly exploited by the developer.[41]

In March 1973 Kahn's contract for the Inner Harbor was terminated.[42] That same month he had presented a final schematic study for the apartment and hotel complex of the Government House Hill Development in Jerusalem (1971–73), which also came to nothing (fig. 203).[43] In Paris two months later he seemed to air his displeasure with developers when he characterized speculative office towers like the Tour Montparnasse as "related only to money," continuing, "ours [in the United States] seem high in a financial sense. The latter [in Europe] are 'anarchitectural,' they are just heaps of masonry."[44] Yet at the time of his death Kahn was again engaged in a speculative venture, this time in Iran, where in association with Kenzo Tange he was to devise the master plan for Abbasabad, an extensive commercial and residential development on the northern outskirts of Tehran (1973–74, unbuilt).[45] Perhaps, to judge by a letter of appreciation to the shah's wife, Kahn felt royal patronage would assure a better outcome, and, inspired by

199 *200*

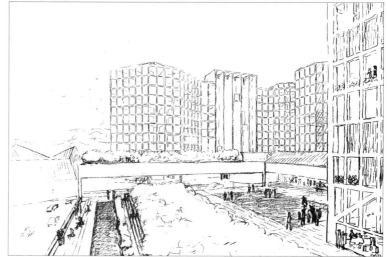

201

202

198. Inner Harbor, Baltimore, Md., 1969–73. Site plan, November 1971.
199. Kansas City Office Building, Kansas City, Mo., 1966–73. Model of first version, April–May 1967.
200. Kansas City Office Building, Kansas City, Mo., 1966–73. Model of second version, September 1968.

201. Inner Harbor, Baltimore, Md., 1969–73. Perspective from northeast. Inscribed Lou K '71.
202. Inner Harbor, Baltimore, Md., 1969–73. Perspective from east, 1971.

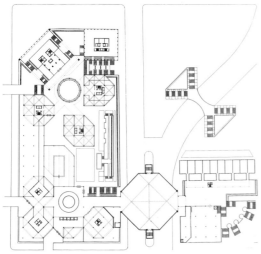

198

203

204

203. *Government House Hill Development, Jerusalem, Israel, 1971–73. Model, January 1973.*
204. *Abbasabad Development, Tehran, Iran, 1973–74. Site plan diagram (with later annotations), February 1974.*
205. *Fisher house, Hatboro, Pa., 1960–67. First-floor plan, redrawn 1990.*

the "strength and beckoning of this ancient land,"[46] he tried to find meaning when apparently little was expected. Following his first visit to the site in November 1973 he began to plan, but his drawings of the next few months fell short of his words. Lacking a detailed program, he incorporated a broad range of governmental and cultural institutions, even including a "Palazzo dei Congressi" (fig. 204). Among images filed with Kahn's project papers are plans for Persepolis, Isfahan, Vatican City, and several chessboards—the latter perhaps the inspiration for the lower portion of his preliminary scheme for Abbasabad.[47]

During the years of demanding involvement with projects of almost unchartable complexity, the design of private dwellings may have offered Kahn some sense of relief. With these Kahn related to people he knew as friends, fewer pressures for production were imposed, and there was greater likelihood of realization. Yet the houses carried their own frustrations; in 1963 Kahn expressed dissatisfaction with his ability to design houses and admitted being unable to conceive a suitable design for the Norman Fisher house (1960–67), commissioned by a physician and his wife some three years before for a suburban site near Philadelphia.[48] As noted in chapter 3, its solution a few months later (fig. 205; see figs. 254–57) recalls in its geometry the first plan he proposed for Dhaka and later exploited more fully in proposals for urban complexes.[49] Some twenty years earlier Kahn had characterized houses as each being a "society of rooms," parallel to the city;[50] now, it seems, he sought to provide a parallel sense of "availabilities." In his later designs for houses, of which the Fisher was the first, there was a similar lack of symmetrical balance, and separately articulated elements were actively juxtaposed so that no single one dominated. A framework more supportive of individual choice would result from this obscuring of conventional hierarchies and the invitation of personal selectivity. These designs for actual houses differed from the idealized domesticity of such designs as the Kimbell Art Museum (1966–72), where a calmer order prevailed.

Kahn tried to resist imposing his own choices in the houses he designed. Neutral finishes—most typically vertical wood siding—clarified volumetric definition, and details were restrained. The detailing attests to his care with even the smallest of parts, and it possesses an elegant spareness that can only be imagined in the larger, unbuilt projects. Kahn's first plans for the Steven Korman house (1971–73), designed near the end of his life for a young developer and his family in suburban Philadelphia, contain angled elements like those of the Fisher house (fig. 208).[51] By August 1972 Kahn

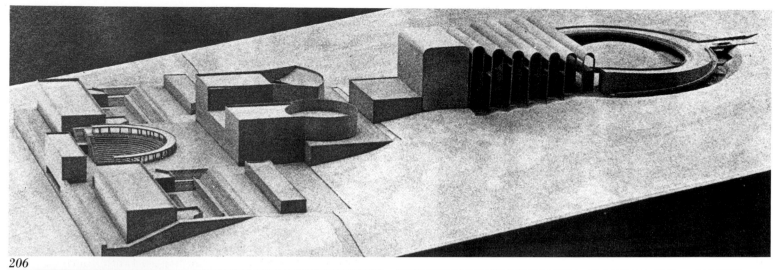

206

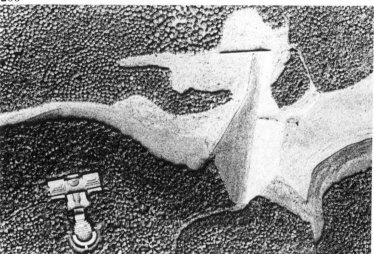

207

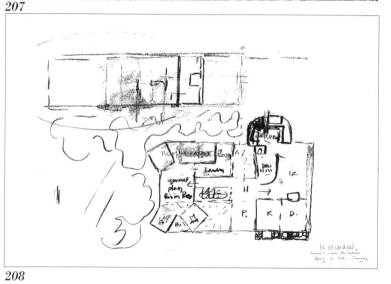

208

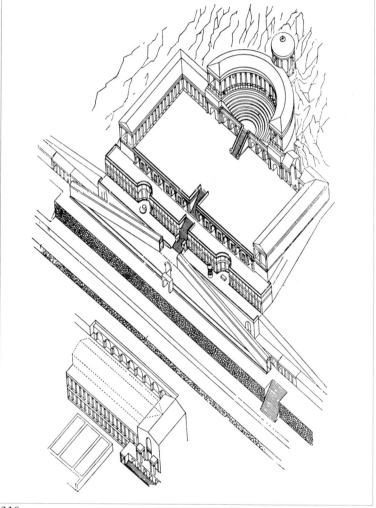

210

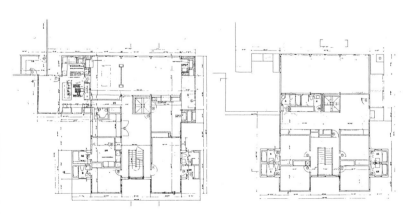

209

206. Pocono Arts Center, Luzerne County, Pa., 1972–74. Model, April 1974.
207. Pocono Arts Center, Luzerne County, Pa., 1972–74. Site model, January 1973.
208. Korman house, Fort Washington, Pa., 1971–73. First-floor plan. Inscribed Louis I. Kahn Architect August 10, 1971.

209. Korman house, Fort Washington, Pa., 1971–73. Second-floor plan. Inscribed October 3, 1972, rev. April 13, 1973.
210. Sanctuary of Fortuna, Praeneste, ca. 80 B.C. Axonometric.

had simplified the design, yet he retained the clear definition of rooms for individual family members (fig. 209; see figs. 258–61). As realized, the Korman house, too, reflected Kahn's sensitivity to detail.[52] The Korman house stands as Kahn's last realized design in the Philadelphia area or even in his home state of Pennsylvania; other, more ambitious designs—the Pocono Arts Center (1972–74) and the Philadelphia Bicentennial Exposition (1971–73)—remained unbuilt.

Like the Fort Wayne project begun more than a decade earlier, the Pocono Arts Center was intended as a center for visual and performing arts, and it was also to be supported by public funds, in this instance provided by the Commonwealth of Pennsylvania. To be located in the foothills of the Pocono Mountains about five miles from Whitehaven, it was meant to include both indoor and outdoor theaters, art galleries, and artists' studios, for in addition to housing the Philadelphia and Pittsburgh orchestras during the summer, it was seen as providing year-round facilities for artists. Rich in promise and loosely programmed, it was the sort of challenge that stimulated Kahn. He began designing in July 1972 well before his appointment was confirmed in November.[53] By the time a formal agreement was signed in January of the following year, Kahn had submitted a model of his first design (fig. 207). His image of monumental terraces remained essentially unchanged during the months that followed (fig. 206).

While Governor Milton Shapp struggled to convince the state legislature of the project's value, Kahn said, "Some of our institutions may have lost their inspiration but their potentials—what I would call their 'availabilities'—remain. The Art Center in the Poconos would be a jewel of availabilities in the arts."[54] At the top of the complex Kahn located the major concert hall, roofed but left open at the sides and approached by a gracefully curved entrance arcade. Along the axis below lay two smaller theaters, enclosed for year-round use. An open-air theater flanked by enclosed studios and related facilities terminated the axis below.

Within the arts center's pastoral setting, the active, unresolved geometries that Kahn had favored for urban complexes gave way to balanced order, and like other examples of his late work it seemed to assume an almost honorific aspect. In its monumental embankment of the landscape it recalls some late Hellenistic acropolis, or more closely the great Roman complexes erected during the last years of the Republic, like the Sanctuary of Fortuna at Praeneste (fig. 210).[55] There, on eight descending levels linked by stairways and broad ramps, a temple, a theater, and shops were all included, and the open-air theater, like Kahn's, was relatively small in comparison to the whole. Whether or not Kahn was aware of this prototype seems of less consequence than what the physical resemblance alone reveals: his continued sympathy with the spirit of the ancient world and with the timeless principles that underlie its noble monuments.

Perhaps no design better reflects Kahn's belief in architecture as a social art than one that may be his least architectural: the Philadelphia Bicentennial Exposition (1971–73), in which he still held hope of participation at the time of his death. Although Kahn's formal involvement with the bicentennial started only in 1971 (see pp. 414–17), he had begun to consider its possibilities by 1968, when he was asked to contribute ideas for publication.[56] He urged that the bicentennial's qualities as an event be emphasized rather than the creation of permanent, monumental buildings: "This will not be an exposition of accomplished work. It will be the wonder of the yet unmade thing . . . the meeting [of] people [in] the realm of its spaces which offer all communication means, all meeting places, the places of expression."[57] When he was later asked to provide an actual design, it was just such a place of unstructured meeting that he seemed to seek. The design was conceived as a loosely defined street linking buildings of unspecified shapes, and he called it the Forum of the Availabilities (fig. 211). Urged by Harriet Pattison, he incorporated a canal as a mode of transportation appropriate to the event and provided gardens as a matrix for the individual pavilions that participating nations would erect.[58] To sponsors both the drawing and the model that followed (fig. 212) must have lacked the architectural bombast they sought. But ultimately his design had effect, for no special structures were erected to commemorate the bicentennial, and Kahn's ideas, uncontaminated by material limitations, retain their presence. Yet he did not claim these ideas as his personal inventions any more than he did the others of his all too brief career; as he said only a few months before his death, "I believe that a man's greatest worth is in the area where he can claim no ownership."[59] This may have been his greatest accomplishment: not the specific shapes, which have inspired an entire generation of architects, but the ideas that knew no shape and would endure.

D.D.L.

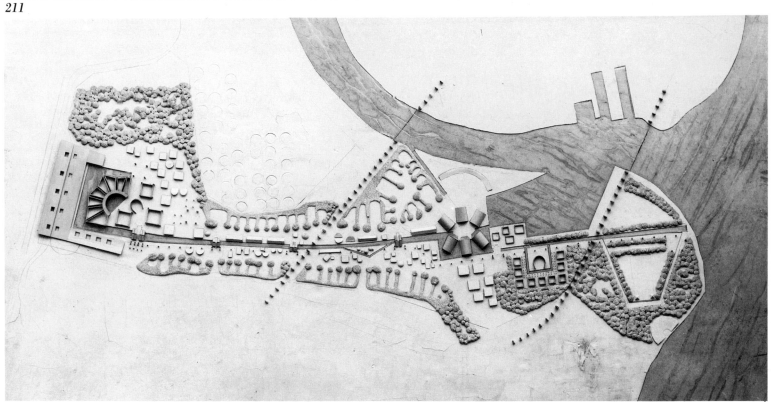

The Forum of the Availabilities

The courts
of the Physical
Resources

The Houses of the Nations

The Houses of the Nations

The courts
of The
Expressions

The Places of the Human & Physical Resources
(Street)

The Thresholds
The Inspirations

Where the urges to express
Meet the possible
The Themes

The building has the
Many Facets of Enclosure
It is the Street enclosed
made like an Unfolding
Flower Morning & Night.

211

212

211. *Bicentennial Exposition,
Philadelphia, Pa., 1971–73.
Site plan, February–March
1972.*
212. *Bicentennial Exposition,
Philadelphia, Pa., 1971–73.
Site model, April–May 1972.*

Notes

1. Kahn, "Architecture and Human Agreement" (lecture, University of Virginia, April 18, 1972), *Modulus*, no. 11 (1975): n.p.
2. Kahn, "1973: Brooklyn, New York" (lecture, Pratt Institute, Fall 1973), *Perspecta*, no. 19 (1982): 100.
3. Kahn, "The Room, the Street and Human Agreement" (AIA Gold Medal acceptance speech, Detroit, June 24, 1971), *AIA Journal* 56 (September 1971): 33.
4. Kahn, "1973: Brooklyn," 100.
5. Kahn, "Harmony Between Man and Architecture" (lecture, Paris, May 11, 1973), *Design* 18 (Bombay, March 1974): 25.
6. Kahn, interview with Karl Linn, May 14, 1965, typed transcript, "Linn, Karl," Box LIK 58, Louis I. Kahn Collection, University of Pennsylvania and Pennsylvania Historical and Museum Commission, Philadelphia (hereafter cited as Kahn Collection).
7. Kahn, "The Room, the Street and Human Agreement," 33–34.
8. Kahn, "Architecture and Human Agreement," n.p.
9. Ibid.
10. Kahn, address to the Boston Society of Architects, April 5, 1966, typed transcript, "Boston Society of Architects," Box LIK 57, Kahn Collection. It was later published: "Address by Louis I. Kahn," *Boston Society of Architects Journal*, no. 1 (1967): 5–20.
11. Kahn, interview with Linn. At this point he referred to the "inspiration to live," later redefined as the "inspiration to express"; explained in "Architecture and Human Agreement."
12. Kahn, "Louis I. Kahn: Talks With Students," *Architecture At Rice*, no. 26 (1969): 40.
13. Kahn, lecture for the Board of Standards and Planning for the Living Theatre, New York, November 14, 1961, transcript, "Board of Standards and Planning, N.Y. Chapter—ANTA," Box LIK 57, Kahn Collection.
14. "Group Abandons Levy Memorial," *New York Times*, October 7, 1966. I am grateful to David Strauss for his research report on this project.
15. Letter, Noguchi to Kahn, August 2, 1961, "Levy Memorial Playground," Box LIK 33, Kahn Collection.
16. Letter, David Wisdom (Kahn's office) to Noguchi, January 10, 1963, ibid.
17. "Model Play Area for Park Shown," *New York Times*, February 5, 1964.
18. A model conforming to this "final version" was photographed by George Pohl on January 21, 1965; Pohl records, Kahn Collection.
19. Letter, Noguchi to Arthur W. Jones, Jr. (Kahn's office), December 3, 1964, "Levy Memorial Playground," Box LIK 33, Kahn Collection.
20. Kahn, interview with Linn.
21. "Court Battles and Confusion Over Playground," *New York Herald Tribune*, February 27, 1965; "Fight Over Park Nearing Climax," *New York Times*, February 13, 1966; "Group Abandons Levy Memorial."
22. Kahn, quoted in "Kahn Designs a 'Non-College,'" *Philadelphia Inquirer*, March 29, 1966.
23. Ibid.
24. Lines of responsibility are not always made clear in surviving correspondence, and later at least one other developer—Leonard G. Styche and Associates, Incorporated—was also involved; letter, Leonard G. Styche to Kahn, September 1, 1966, "Broadway Church," Box LIK 33, Kahn Collection. I am grateful to Peter S. Reed for his research report on this project.
25. Notes, June 30, 1966, "Broadway Church," Box LIK 33, Kahn Collection; letter, William J. Conklin to Kahn, July 13, 1966, "Broadway United Church of Christ," Box LIK 85, Kahn Collection. Conklin, a noted New York architect who with James Rossant had designed the new town of Reston, Virginia, was then president of the board of trustees for the church.
26. A gray chipboard model of this version was presented but evidently no longer exists; I saw the model when William Conklin brought it back to his office (where I was working at the time) after Kahn had presented it to the board.
27. Kahn, "Talk at the Conclusion of the Otterlo Congress," in *New Frontiers in Architecture: CIAM '59 in Otterlo*, ed. Oscar Newman (New York: Universe Books, 1961), 214.
28. Letter, Conklin to Kahn, September 19, 1966, "Broadway United Church of Christ," Box LIK 85, Kahn Collection; letter, Styche to Kahn, September 1, 1966, "Broadway Church," Box LIK 33, Kahn Collection.
29. Letters, James A. Austrian (James D. Landauer Assoc., Inc., Real Estate Consultants) to Kahn, March 13, 1970; Kahn to Austrian, April 23, 1970; Austrian to Kahn, June 22, 1970; and John R. White (Landauer Assoc.) to Kahn, September 10, 1970; "Saint Peter's Lutheran Church," Box LIK 13, Kahn Collection. Again the church was supportive of Kahn's involvement as architect, but the First National City Bank engaged another architect instead.
30. Letter, Altman to Kahn, July 11, 1966, "Kansas City Office Building Client Correspondence I," Box LIK 39, Kahn Collection. I am grateful to Arnold Garfinkel for discussing this commission with me on several occasions, especially on May 23, 1990, when David B. Brownlee and I interviewed him in his Kansas City office.
31. Meeting notes, January 5, 1967, and letter, Altman to David Polk (Kahn's office), May 8, 1967, "Kansas City Office Building Correspondence," Box LIK 39, Kahn Collection. I am grateful to Peter S. Reed for his research report on this project.
32. Polk, revised interview with Kazumi Kawasaki (1983), reprinted in *Louis I. Kahn: L'uomo, il maestro*, ed. Alessandra Latour (Rome: Edizioni Kappa, 1986), 95.
33. Minutes of a meeting in the office of Emery Roth, September 19, 1967, "Broadway Church; Komendant's Information; Late Meeting Notes," Box LIK 33, Kahn Collection.
34. A variation of this scheme showed the tower as L-shaped, with two additional columns straddling the outer corner of the church; Heinz Ronner and Sharad Jhaveri, *Louis I. Kahn: Complete Work, 1935–1974*, 2d ed. (Basel and Boston: Birkhäuser, 1987), 316–17, BCA.9 and BCA.10.
35. As first claimed by Polk, interview with Kawasaki, 95.
36. Kahn submitted his final invoice the following year; letter, E. J. Sharpe (Kahn's accountant) to Conklin, July 17, 1968, "Broadway United Church of Christ," Box LIK 85, Kahn Collection.
37. The possibility of a new site was discussed in several letters during the spring and summer of 1970, including Richard Altman to Carles Vallhonrat (Kahn's office), July 9, 1970, "Kansas City Office Building Client Correspondence I," Box LIK 39, Kahn Collection. The original site, on property partly held by Altman, was bounded by Walnut, Grand, and 11th Streets; the new site was bounded by Main, Baltimore, 11th, and 12th Streets.
38. Komendant's scheme is identified as being by Kahn in Ronner and Jhaveri, *Complete Work*, 321, AOT.24 and AOT.25. Kahn's final invoice was submitted in December 1973; letter, Wisdom to Garfinkel, December 21, 1973, "Master File," Box LIK 20, Kahn Collection.
39. The six-and-a-half-acre site was located south of Pratt and Light Streets, and the developer was the Hammerman Organization; memorandum, Abba Tor (structural engineer) to file, February 18, 1971, "Engineer's Resumes," Box LIK 12, Kahn Collection; letter, Kahn to I. H. Hammerman/S.L., June 14, 1971, and contract for architectural services, June 18, 1971, "Miscellaneous," Box LIK 11, Kahn Collection.

By late 1972 the Ballinger Company, Architects and Engineers, was also engaged to collaborate with Kahn; letter, Louis deMoll (vice president, Ballinger) to Thomas Karsten (president, Thomas L. Karsten Associates), November 6, 1972, "BIHP 1/Ballinger," Box LIK 12, Kahn Collection. I am grateful to Joan Brierton for her research report on this project.

40. Kahn, quoted in Ronner and Jhaveri, *Complete Work*, 393.

41. Abba Tor, "A Memoir," in Latour, *Kahn*, 127.

42. Letter, I. H. Hammerman II to Kahn, March 13, 1973, "Hammerman Correspondence," Box LIK 12, Kahn Collection.

43. Ronner and Jhaveri, *Complete Work*, 408–11.

44. Kahn, "Harmony Between Man and Architecture," 23.

45. Kahn was contacted in October 1973; in addition to Tange, the Teheran architect Nader Ardalan was to coordinate local efforts. John Reyward was named as developer. Letter, Kahn to Aaron, October 9, 1973, and undated note, "Prospective, Tehran," Box LIK 106, Kahn Collection. I am grateful to David Roxburgh for his research report on this project.

46. Letter, Kahn to Farah Pahlavi Shahbanan, November 13, 1973, ibid.

47. As suggested by David Roxburgh. These and other images are contained in "Teheran Studies," Box LIK 106, Kahn Collection.

48. From my class notes, January 1963, master's studio, the University of Pennsylvania.

49. The Fisher house was commissioned in August 1960; agreement, August 23, 1960, "Fisher Residence . . . ," Box LIK 83, Kahn Collection. A preliminary, H-shaped scheme, developed between January and April 1961, was left undeveloped; drawings and time sheets, January 5 to April 30, 1962, ibid. Construction of the final scheme, designed between June and December 1963, began in October 1964 and was completed in June 1967; drawings and time sheets, June 4 to December 10, 1963, and contract for construction, October 24, 1964, ibid.; final certificate of payment, June 26, 1967, "Dr. and Mrs. N.J. Fisher Res Certificates of Payment," Box LIK 83, Kahn Collection. Minor additions were made later, including a bridge over the backyard stream in 1969; transmittal, Vincent Rivera (Kahn's office) to Fisher, April 25, 1969, "Dr. Norman Fisher Corres. 1968–1969," Box LIK 69, Kahn Collection. I am grateful to Peter S. Reed, who completed the research report begun by Elizabeth D. Greene Wiley.

50. Oscar Stonorov and Louis I. Kahn, *You and Your Neighborhood: A Primer for Neighborhood Planning* (New York: Revere Copper and Brass, 1944), n.p.

51. The house was commissioned before May 10, 1971, when plot plans were sent to Kahn together with the Kormans' program; letter, Steven H. Korman to Kahn, May 10, 1971, "Korman Res. Client Correspondence," Box LIK 36, Kahn Collection. I am grateful to Stephen G. Harrison for his research report on this project.

52. Construction began in October 1972 and was nearly completed by November 1973; agreement between owner and builder, October 18, 1972, and site inspection reports, September 28, 1973, "Korman Residence," Box LIK 36, Kahn Collection.

53. Letter, Herbert Fineman (chairman, Architects/Engineers Committee, General State Authority) to Kahn, November 30, 1972, "Pocono Arts Center Appointment Letter," Box LIK 121, Kahn Collection. Kahn's first drawings carry the date of July 1972. I am grateful to David Roxburgh for his research report on this project.

54. Kahn, quoted in Gerard J. McCullough, "Foes in Legislature Gird to Fight Shapp's Pocono Arts Center Plan," *Sunday Bulletin*, December 16, 1973, section 5, 3.

55. This complex was fully revealed only as a result of the Second World War, when modern buildings above it were destroyed. Published sources include Frank E. Brown, *Roman Architecture* (New York: George Braziller, 1961), fig. 18.

56. Letter, Leslie M. Pockell (articles editor, *Avant Garde*) to Kahn, November 18, 1968, "Avant Garde," Box LIK 69, Kahn Collection.

57. Kahn, undated manuscript prepared in response to November 18, 1968, request, "Avant Garde," Box LIK 69, Kahn Collection.

58. Pattison, interview with David G. De Long, January 29, 1991.

59. Kahn, "1973: Brooklyn," 89.

By the middle of the 1960s, Louis Kahn had taught for nearly twenty years, and his buildings were being built around the world. He had made modern architecture seem morally important and artistically challenging again, at a time when many had come to regard it as a simple utilitarian device.

In the last decade of Kahn's life, the importance and difficulty of all creative work seemed to become even greater. America staggered under the burden of its power, divided by racial strife and sapped by the ethical and material losses of Vietnam. Kahn, who had long argued that architecture was the servant of human institutions, recognized that his country was in crisis, and in November 1967 he lamented that "all our institutions are on trial."[1] However, in this time of frightening ambiguities, he created the simplest and strongest architecture of his career: the library for Phillips Exeter Academy, the Kimbell Art Museum, the Yale Center for British Art, the Memorial for the Six Million Jewish Martyrs, and the Franklin D. Roosevelt Memorial.

The power of most of these last buildings derived from their almost alchemical integration of mass and space—Kahn's long-sought wedding of the fundamental and apparently antithetical elements out of which architecture was made. For Kahn, mass was always analyzed rationally as a question of structure—the substance of building—while space was defined more mystically in terms of natural light—the energy that brought space to life. The manipulation of both structure and light was essential in making "the room," which Kahn had long maintained was the basic compositional element of architecture, and he believed that they could be made to work together. He loved to say that architecture itself had begun "when the walls parted and the columns became," admitting light and creating a system of support at the same time.[2] It was thus that the earliest Greek temples had come into being (fig. 213), and in 1971 he summed up: "The room is the beginning of architecture. It is the place of the mind. You in the room with its dimensions, its structure, its light respond to its character, its spiritual aura, recognizing that whatever the human proposes and makes becomes a life. The structure of the room must be evident in the room itself. Structure, I believe, is the giver of light."[3] This was a concept that he frequently discussed with his students and tried to draw (figs. 214, 215).

At a tiny scale and without having to worry about glazing, Kahn had been able to achieve the room-making integration of structure and light in the Trenton Bathhouse, where the wooden pyramidal roofs were carried by load-bearing concrete-block walls in such a way that light washed into the building through the construction (see fig. 72). Since then, he had experimented with systems that could work in larger, more complex buildings, like the great perforated screen walls he devised for use in tropical countries and the towering light rooms he created for Mikveh Israel synagogue and the mosque at Dhaka. By the late sixties he was able to put forward several extraordinary solutions to this vexing problem almost simultaneously. His success is to be seen in the silver-lit barrel vaults of the Kimbell Museum, the interfingering light patterns that reach through the gridded exterior of the Exeter library, the luminous coffers of the Yale Center for British Art, and the glowing glass pylons of the monument for the Jewish martyrs.

Not coincidentally, the achievement of a space-defining alliance between structure and light quieted Kahn's planning. The dynamic asymmetries of the monastery plans and the baroque diagonals of his buildings in Asia dropped out of his latest works, which recentered themselves around strong interior spaces and in compact, symmetrical arrangements. In this way, the original decorum of the Beaux-Arts plan was restored after decades of Kahn's strenuous testing, and the attention to structural truth and lighting that effected this restoration was, of course, also part of his Beaux-Arts heritage. He became fond of saying about architecture that "what will be has always been," words that applied to his own recursive habits as well.[4]

The serenity of this last group of designs depended on what was even for Kahn a low level of programmatic specificity. The museums for the Kimbell collection in Fort Worth and Paul Mellon's collection at Yale were similarly and simply imagined as large houses filled with art, or, alternatively, as monuments to human creativity with few ordinary functional responsibilities. "A museum," Kahn said in 1972, "seems like a secondary thing, unless it is a great treasury."[5] Much of the same mixture of domestic and honorific imagery pervaded the Exeter Academy library; and, of course, memorials like those for victims of the Holocaust and for Franklin Roosevelt were truly "free of the bondage of use," like the ruins of antiquity Kahn most admired.[6] Uncomplicated by the demanding program considerations that had inflected his plans for the big institutions of the early sixties, these buildings were free to be simple.

This evolution toward an almost classical coherence was not readily apparent to those who were looking at Kahn's work at the time. For one thing, the visible fruits were slow to

Chapter 6

Light, the Giver of All Presences

Designs to Honor Human Endeavor

ripen. Although the commissions in which this process occurred had begun to occupy Kahn's office fully in 1967–68, the first of these last great projects to be completed, the Exeter library and the Kimbell Museum, were dedicated only in October 1972, less than a year and a half before Kahn died. The Yale Center was finished posthumously, and the Jewish martyrs' and Roosevelt monuments were never built.

What observers had to go on suggested that a very different evolution was under way, for in the long, rambling speeches that Kahn was now invited to give ever more often, he rarely talked about his most recent work. Revisiting instead the commissions of the fifties and early sixties, he veiled his methods with increasingly inscrutable vocabulary. Those who liked him best were alarmed by this tendency. Vincent Scully recalled:

Sometimes even I and the people who loved him most found it hard to let him do it, to listen to him talking this terribly vague stuff—and even slightly sort of false stuff. Then, to hear so many people pick it up as gospel, the sort of philosophical gospel of Lou, was distressful because in his later years it had become more of a smoke screen around his actual methods than anything else.[7]

Even someone who first met Kahn during this time, like Jules Prown, who represented Yale's client interests in building the Center for British Art, could detect the disjunction between the "very factual, very direct" man he dealt with on the job and the man who spoke "more abstractly, more poetically" when he was nervous and trying to impress. When Kahn and he met with Paul Mellon or Yale president Kingman Brewster, Prown found himself "acting as a kind of intermediary between him and them, trying to convince them that this guy wasn't some kind of mad poet."[8] Kahn's longtime assistant Marshall Meyers, who returned to the office in 1967 when work on these commissions was beginning, dealt with this behavior on a day-to-day basis. He complained, "In the later years, one of the difficulties was that he seemed to have too many people in his office who almost deified him."[9]

In fact, little had changed in what Kahn thought. He continued to believe in an idealist architecture, oriented toward the durable essence of things, and what he said was still informed by the fundamental Platonic distinction between "form" and "design," worked out with care and expressed with simple power in the much-reprinted Voice of America broadcast of 1960. What *had* changed, however, was the vocabulary with which he expressed this versatile

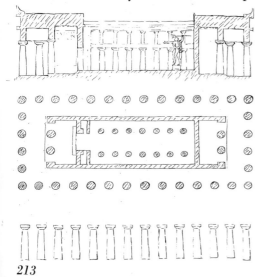

213

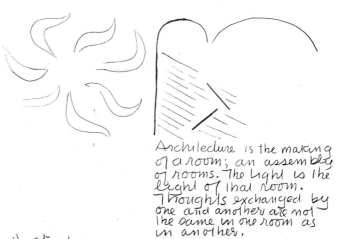

Architecture is the making of a room; an assembly of rooms. The Light is the light of that room. Thoughts exchanged by one and another are not the same in one room as in another.

A street is a room; a community room by agreement. Its character from intersection to intersection changes and may be regarded as a number of rooms

214

Architecture comes from The Making of a Room
The Plan A society of rooms is a place good to live work learn

The Room

A great American Poet once asked the Architect "What slice of the sun does your building have, what light enters your Room as if to say the sun never knew how great it is until it struck the side of a building.

is The place of the mind. In a small room one does not say what one would in a large room. In a room with only one other person could be generative The vectors of each meet. A room is not a room without natural light. natural light gives the time of day and the mood of the seasons to enter.

215

213. Second Temple of Hera, Paestum, from sketchbook, ca. 1969.
214. Page from sketchbook, ca. 1969.
215. "The Room." Inscribed Lou K '71.

idealism, and the increasing allusiveness of his words led some to believe that he was saying something different.

Having successfully rechristened underlying "form" and pragmatic "design" as "law and rule" (1961),[10] "belief and means" (1963),[11] and "existence and presence" (1967),[12] by the late sixties Kahn had come upon a favorite formulation that was more mysterious: silence and light. In November 1967, in what may have been his first public explanation of these newest terms, he told a Boston audience that architecture was created at a point that lay between a silent ideal and the illumination of the real, a place that he called "the threshold where Silence and Light meet, Silence with its desire to be, and Light, the giver of all presences." This artistic workplace was also "the sanctuary of all expression, which I like to call the Treasury of the Shadows."[13] A year later, at the Guggenheim Museum, Kahn elaborated on this theme. Silence was the realm of ideal truth which had existed even before the pyramids had been built—"before the first stone was laid." Light, on the other hand, was the energy of the real: "I sense Light as the giver of all presences, and material as spent Light. What is made by Light casts a shadow, and the shadow belongs to Light. I sense a Threshold: Light to Silence, Silence to Light—an ambiance of inspiration, in which the desire to be, to express crosses with the possible."[14] In preparing the Guggenheim lecture for publication, Kahn drew a series of illustrations of this architectural universe. The reflexive discourse between silence and light was expressed in mirror writing and presided over by a pyramid (fig. 216). The twin character of reality was explained as that of "two brothers" and portrayed as a burst of light (fig. 217). And light's making of tangible things was shown as a dance of flame (fig. 218).

Although few observers seem to have noticed, even this most poetic rendering of "form" and "design" was strongly grounded in the vocabulary that Kahn had used ever since the fifties. He had long assigned light a key role in the making of architecture, maintaining that "no space is really an architectural space unless it has natural light."[15] The notion that art was created at a "threshold" between real and ideal had also been expressed earlier, in simpler terms. "A great building must, in my opinion, begin with the unmeasurable and go through the measurable in the process of design," Kahn wrote in introducing a publication of his drawings in 1962, "but [it] must in the end be unmeasurable."[16] Largely unrecognized, too, was the degree to which this new vocabulary was fortified by allusions to respected authority. Most fundamentally, the role played by light and shadow in differentiating the ideal world from the

216

217

218

216–18. Pages from sketchbook, ca. 1969.
219. Phillips Exeter Academy Library, Exeter, N.H., 1965–72. Central hall.
220. Phillips Exeter Academy Library, Exeter, N.H., 1965–72. Perspective of reading room with carrels. Inscribed Lou K '67.
221. Phillips Exeter Academy Library, Exeter, N.H., 1965–72. Third-floor plan.

219

world of daily experience was an echo of the famous discussion of the same subject in Plato's *Republic:* the parable of the prisoners whose only glimpse of the outside was the shadow it projected on the wall of their cave. And Kahn's seemingly eccentric identification of ideal architecture with silence depended, as he said, on one of the most widely read postwar analyses of visual culture, André Malraux's *Voices of Silence* (1953).[17]

In the end, however, Kahn's poetry was his own. He toiled over the making of words with the same indefatigable energy that he devoted to architecture, crossing out and rubbing out and remaking a phrase or a plan. If, after all this labor, his words had failed to elevate and illuminate his subject, he might have been justly accused of succumbing to a cantankerous mysticism. And if his architectural creativity had faltered in his last years, it could have been said that he was preaching what he could not perform. But his words were eloquent, and his architecture was ever more profound.

The first building in which the traits of Kahn's final style could be clearly seen was the library for Phillips Exeter Academy, designed in 1966–68 (see figs. 360–68 and pp. 390–95). There, upon a simple plan, he erected a great room filled with light. Functionally a library, it was spiritually a sanctuary. Kahn had always loved books, browsing in bookshops, paging through volumes, and buying books with unaffected reverence, but, as he freely admitted, rarely reading more than the first pages of anything. A book was therefore not an ordinary useful object. "A book is tremendously important," he told a design conference at Aspen in 1972. "Nobody ever paid for the price of a book, they pay only for the printing. But a book is actually an offering and must be regarded as such. If you give honor to the man who writes it, there is something in that which further induces the expressive powers of writing."[18] A library was therefore a place of piety.

So powerful was Kahn's vision of books as objects of reverence that he felt it was appropriate to adapt the terraced, closely planted mausoleums of the Roman emperors in his later, unbuilt design for the Graduate Theological Union Library at Berkeley (1971–74).[19] For Exeter, however, no such monumentalism was ever contemplated; the program called instead for an almost domestic environment that would "encourage and insure the pleasure of reading and study."[20] That, perhaps, was all the reverence that books required.

Kahn's first thinking about the Exeter library showed the influence of his contemporary monastery projects, wrapped in allusions to the Middle Ages in general and monasteries in particular. Corner towers and interior and exterior arcades imparted a castellar feeling to the first design of May 1966, and Kahn explained that his work had been influenced by the example of monastic libraries (see figs. 506, 507).[21] When the Exeter commission was expanded early in the design development phase to include an adjacent dining hall, he established their relationship with the kind of casual, conversational angularity that he was employing in the Valyermo monastery and the Media convent at the same time.

However, as work continued into 1967, the towers and arcades of Kahn's personal kind of medievalism disappeared, and they were replaced by a contained, regular, and symmetrical vocabulary. The result was a much more classical design that faced inward to one of Kahn's primordial rooms (figs. 219, 221; see fig. 361). Here, one level above the ground, the reader was introduced to the building by a square space, confidently defined by structure and light: circles of concrete framed each interior elevation, bracing the main piers at the corners, and the sun entered from above to bathe the whole in quiet brightness. Still and balanced, the central hall took the circle-in-square as its leitmotif—an inversion of the venerable square-in-circle paradigm of natural order cited by the Roman architect Vitruvius and echoed before in Kahn's plan for the Salk meeting house.

Arrayed around the central space on all sides were the book stacks, their floors suspended like the shelves of a giant bookcase between the corner piers. Although the bold display of shelving within the circular openings accomplished Kahn's desired "invitation of books," the books themselves were kept in relative darkness.[22] Only beyond the stacks, at the perimeter of the building, did the walls part to admit natural light to the double-height reading areas. In each, a mezzanine balcony created an upper work level next to the stacks, and a row of wooden carrels, each with its own shuttered, desk-level window, lined the exterior wall (fig. 220; see fig. 364). This environment responded to what Kahn considered the instinctive behavior of the reader: "A man with a book goes to the light./A library begins that way."[23] The carrels, which gave students the ability to let in the view or close it out, also afforded them an essential autonomy. Kahn said about schools in general, "The windows should be made particular to suit a student who wants to be alone even when he is with others."[24]

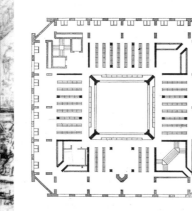

220   221

In plan, the concentric arrangement of great hall, book stacks, and reading areas seemed to echo the earlier served/servant hierarchies of the Richards Building and the Rochester Unitarian Church (see figs. 90, 452). This time, as in Erdman Hall, the authentic service functions (elevators, secondary stairs, toilets, photocopying, etc.) were concentrated in the corners, and Kahn quite forthrightly adopted the concentric pattern for the sake of its visual clarity. His pursuit of order was even more obvious in the bilateral symmetry of the Exeter dining hall, with each elevation rising to a central chimney (fig. 222).

The rectilinear brick elevations of the library paid homage to the surrounding neo-Georgian architecture of the campus, for Kahn said that he "didn't try to make something that stands out" (see fig. 360).[25] But the load-bearing exterior walls also reflected his continuing love affair with honest brick construction, which he had originally hoped to use both inside and out. Openings were spanned by versatile jack arches, and Kahn thickened the walls as they reached downward and narrowed the piers between the windows as they rose, clearly portraying the varying loads carried at different levels of the facade. In typical language, he explained that he had reached his construction decisions after consulting the material: "The brick was always talking to me, saying you're missing an opportunity. . . . The weight of the brick makes it dance like a fairy above and groan below."[26]

The truth telling of the facade included the external expression of the wooden carrel units, but there was nothing to signal other functional elements, most notably the location of the entrance. This was to be found within the low, covered passage that circled the building, and Kahn made a rather lame effort to describe its ambiguity as an advantage: "From all sides there is an entrance. If you are scurrying in a rain to get to a building, you can come in at any point and find your entrance. It's a continuous campus-type entrance."[27] It was plain that he simply declined to interrupt the taut, repetitive rhythms of his facades with a monumental entrance. Rather than compromise, he banished the problematic element.

In a similar way, Kahn cropped off the corners of the library instead of papering over the collision of adjacent elevation systems or finding another compromise solution to the age-old, classical problem of "turning a corner." He had solved this dilemma at Bryn Mawr with similar radicalism, tucking the corners of the three dormitory units into each other, and he was forthright about his return to this contentious arena

of Beaux-Arts debate at Exeter: "It's always a problem to know how to treat a corner. Do you suddenly introduce diagonal members, or make some kind of exceptional rectangular structure at this point? So I thought why not eliminate the problem?"[28] Such iconoclasm preserved the purity of the design.

The final design of the Exeter library was taking shape in 1967 when Kahn began to turn his attention to what was to become his most universally admired and loved building, the Kimbell Art Museum in Fort Worth, Texas (see figs. 369–91 and pp. 396–99). His client was the museum's first director, Richard Brown, who was entrusted with comprehensive responsibility for the project by an unusually tolerant board of directors. Kahn was already on the short list of architects Brown recommended at his own job interview.[29]

Brown conducted himself like an ideal client within Kahn's system of "form" and "design," beginning, before Kahn was hired, by composing a conceptual, "Pre-Architectural Program." This defined the spirit of the institution as much as it detailed its functioning, and in its call for natural light in the galleries and a comfortable, human scale, it was already steering the commission in a direction that Kahn was eager to pursue.[30]

In large measure, the Kimbell design was Kahn's reconsideration of the open planning of his own Yale Art Gallery. There, the flexible plan had allowed for such freedom that a subsequent director of the museum had been able to denature Kahn's interiors. Moreover, Kahn's commitment to open planning had declined as he came to see the discrete "room" as the basic architectural unit. By 1959, when the Yale Art Gallery had been open for only a few years, he was already announcing that his next museum would be divided into spaces with "certain inherent characteristics."[31] One of those characteristics would be natural light.

Kahn's conception of an architecture of skylit rooms accorded well with Brown's intentions for the new museum, and together they produced a building of domestic scale that was closely attuned to Kay and Velma Kimbell's collection of moderate-size paintings. They shared a distaste for gigantic exhibitions and tiresome didacticism, and they banished both. Echoing Brown's worries about the fatigue induced by the usual, bombastic displays, Kahn admitted, "The first thing you want in most museums is a cup of coffee. You feel so tired immediately."[32]

222. Phillips Exeter Academy Dining Hall, Exeter, N.H., 1965–72. North facade.
223. Kimbell Art Museum, Fort Worth, Tex., 1966–72. Sketch section. Inscribed September 22, 1967.

222

From the start, Kahn conceived of the basic unit (or room) of the design as a barrel-vaulted space—an idea that Brown remembered "was already in Lou Kahn's mind and had been for a long time."[33] Although he first experimented with polygonal vaulting of folded plate construction, most of the design development concentrated on segmental vaults, for which Marshall Meyers, Kahn's project captain for the museum, invented a cycloidal section (fig. 223; see figs. 513, 514). It may have been the example of ancient Roman warehouses like the Porticus Aemilia, with their concatenated barrel vaults, that had implanted this form in Kahn's imagination, but Le Corbusier had also regularly employed shallow vaulting in his domestic architecture of the fifties, most notably the villa of Manorama Sarabhai at Ahmedabad (1951–55). Kahn was often entertained by the Sarabhais while working on the Indian Institute of Management. Moreover, Kahn's assembly of many such independently roofed elements to create a large building had been proposed by Le Corbusier at an even greater scale in projects like his Usine Verte (1944), published in the fourth volume of the *Oeuvre complète*. A few months before his death, Kahn spoke candidly of the lasting impression of such designs: "Somebody asked me, *Hasn't the image of Le Corbusier faded in your mind?* I said, *No, it hasn't faded, but I don't turn the pages of his work any more*."[34] He did not need to turn the pages to remember.

Composing the Kimbell Museum out of independently vaulted units was not unrelated to the assembly of elements that Kahn had practiced in most of his major projects, from the Richards Building and Erdman Hall to the monasteries. But in contrast to those earlier exercises in the picturesque or diagonal grouping of pavilions, the Kimbell was an orthogonal project from the start, even in the grandiose early version that Brown had to reject as too large for the intimate museum that he wanted (see fig. 513). Shorn of the round-arched portico that had encircled that first developed design, the modular vaulting system of Kahn's second, smaller proposal was exposed on all elevations and allowed to assert an increasing measure of classical control (fig. 224; see fig. 515). This authority increased when the smaller plan was in turn abandoned in the fall of 1968, after Brown realized that its layout would compel visitors to pass the often-empty temporary exhibition gallery as they entered the building. Starting almost from scratch, Kahn created a C-shaped, forecourt-centered design that was even more inherently classical, although he avoided the clichéd accentuation of the central axis (fig. 225). Before construction, one bay was eliminated from the plan to save costs, and this strengthened the clarity with which the parts

announced their presence and interrelationships (see figs. 373, 517). Here was a crystalline composition quite unlike the rough-hewn Le Corbusian designs to which it was most closely related.

Small in size and breathtakingly straightforward in the organization of its public spaces, the Kimbell achieved the domestic spirit that Brown had wanted. Like the entrance hall of a rich collector's house, the lobby afforded views of virtually all of the public parts of the building: the café where Kahn's sleepy visitor could find a cup of coffee (analogous to the dining room of the house); the bookstore (akin to the library); and, on both sides, the galleries (surrogates for the picture-filled entertaining rooms) (see figs. 384, 391). Kahn called the museum "a friendly home."[35]

In part to lessen the fatigue of the museumgoer, Kahn planted the forecourt with a regimented grove of miniature Yaopon holly trees, centered between two reflecting pools that spilled continuously over their curbing (see figs. 369, 372). This setting was needed, he explained shortly before the Kimbell opened, because "a museum needs a garden. You walk in a garden and you can either come in or not. This large garden tells you you may walk in to see the things or you may walk out. Completely free."[36] But the forecourt planting also represented the orderly natural world within which Kahn imagined that all human labor was accomplished, most especially the making of idealist architecture such as his own. The visitor was to be physically oriented to this view of nature before the building itself, hidden by the trees, was easily visible. (Kahn, who did not drive, never accepted the fact that Texans would arrive by car, crossing the parking lot to the back door of the museum.) Like most of his landscape and site-planning work during the sixties and seventies, this carefully articulated procession through a landscape was created in consultation with Harriet Pattison, who delighted in making calculated juxtapositions of environmental effects. She was then working for George Patton, Kahn's landscape architect for the project.

Inside, the Kimbell Museum was conceived as a succession of rooms defined by an integrated system of structure and lighting. Nowhere did Kahn better achieve his intentions in this respect. The supporting system was guilelessly explained to the visitor by the three unwalled front bays of the building, which formed a generous portico that echoed the familiar colonnades of classical museums (see fig. 370). Here, Kahn said, "how the building is made is completely

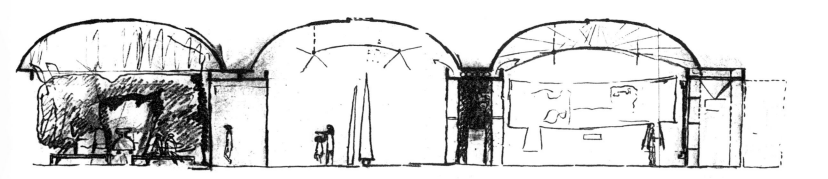

clear before you go into it," and everything could be inspected: four concrete piers supported an exquisitely elongated concrete shell, whose shape was that of a cycloidal vault.[37] Comparison with the adjacent, enclosed bays revealed that the travertine walling was non-load-bearing, its role carefully choreographed in relation to the concrete (see fig. 375). As at the Salk Institute, where travertine was also used, the detailing of the poured concrete resulted from a combination of painstaking formwork design and the unpredictable (but expected) accidents of coloration and texture (see fig. 374).

Thus announced on the outside, the same structural system continued within. Kahn's dictum that "space is not a space unless you can see the evidence of how it was made" was obeyed, rejecting the infinitely divisible open planning of the Yale Art Gallery, a system now epitomized for him by the work of Mies van der Rohe.[38] From the entrance, the 100-by-23-foot vaults swept away in all directions, each exposing its four supporting piers and each cupping beneath it a spatial unit that had a "room-like quality" and "the character of completeness," despite the fact that the overall plan was quite open and capable of subdivision with movable panels (see fig. 382).[39] Even the library and the auditorium were adjusted for enclosure under single vaults, while the lower, flat-ceilinged spaces between the vaults were rather vaguely assigned to servant duty within Kahn's served/servant hierarchy (see figs. 381, 383, 389).

Reinforcing the sense of totality possessed by each gallery room was its integral natural lighting. In Fort Worth, Kahn created a skylight system without peer in the history of architecture, opening the building to the sun in just the way that he had long recommended—by parting the structure and thus weaving support and illumination together. As he explained in 1972, "structure is the maker of light, because structure releases the spaces between and that is light giving."[40] But whereas Kahn believed that the first architecture had been made when the opaque, primordial walls were broken apart to make columns, at the Kimbell it was not the walls but the roofs that were parted, each vault split along the full length of its crown (fig. 226). Of course, the positioning of this skylight where the keystone should have been demonstrated that the structures were not true vaults, but curved poured-in-place, post-tensioned concrete beams, each 100 feet long. As had often been the case, Kahn was willing to obscure the real complexity of a structure for the sake of visual clarity.

The splinters of sun that penetrated the concrete of the

Kimbell danced as images through many of Kahn's later lectures, as he tried to explain the ability of natural light to imbue space with meaning—to make rooms. He often misquoted a scrap of uncannily apposite poetry that Harriet Pattison had shown him:

The great American poet Wallace Stevens prodded the architect, asking, "What slice of the sun does your building have?" To paraphrase: What slice of the sun enters your room? What range of mood does the light offer from morning to night, from day to day, from season to season and all through the years?

Gratifying and unpredictable are the permissions that the architect has given to the chosen opening on which patches of sunlight play on the jamb and sill and that enter, move, and disappear.

Stevens seems to tell us that the sun was not aware of its wonder until it struck the side of a building.[41]

In the spirit of this exposition, Kahn predicted that the skylighting of the Kimbell galleries would "give the comforting feeling of knowing the time of day."[42] This effect was diminished, however, by the diffusers that Kahn called "natural light fixture[s],"[43] employed to reduce the damaging intensity of the Texas sun. These transformed all daylight into an even, silvery luminosity that washed the undersurfaces of the vaults. More successful in conveying the natural variety of light were the tiny, glass-walled courtyards with which Kahn brought the outside world directly into the galleries (see figs. 376–80). He spoke of "a counterpoint of courts, open to the sky, of calculated dimensions and character, marking them Green Court, Yellow Court, Blue Court, named for the kind of light that I anticipate their proportions, their foliation, or their sky reflections on surfaces, or on water will give."[44]

So successful were most of these lighting devices that the Kimbell Museum disarmed virtually every potential critic, and Kahn told those closest to him that it was his favorite building.[45] The cycloidal vaults fulfilled his greatest dream, defining spaces through the unification of light and structure (albeit with some deceit about the nature of the structure), and he found it hard to resist copying his success. He proposed variations on the same kind of vaulting for the galleries of the Yale Center for British Art (1970), the laboratories of the Wolfson Center for Engineering at the University of Tel Aviv (1971), and the De Menil Foundation in Houston (1973); the formula was later rejected at Yale and the De Menil project was unbuilt, but part of the Wolfson Center was completed after Kahn's death, without supervision from America.

224

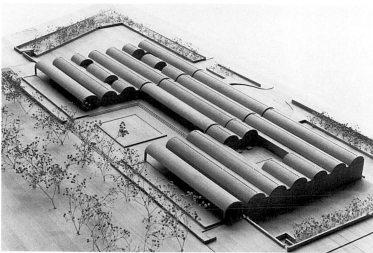

225

226

224. *Kimbell Art Museum, Fort Worth, Tex., 1966–72. Plan, Summer 1968.*
225. *Kimbell Art Museum, Fort Worth, Tex., 1966–72. Model, September 1968.*
226. *Kimbell Art Museum, Fort Worth, Tex., 1966–72. Gallery.*

Despite the celebrity of the Kimbell vaulting formula, it was not Kahn's only successful space-making combination of light and structure. In 1967, at the same time that he was developing the Kimbell design, he created another solution based on entirely different principles for the Olivetti-Underwood business machine factory near Harrisburg, Pennsylvania. Here the problem was again to give spatial texture to an interior without losing the practical advantages of an open plan, for the building had to be "ready to jump and change, overnight."[46] After considering a grid of pyramidal roofs, skylit at their apexes, Kahn worked out a solution with his engineering consultant, August Komendant, that consisted of self-supporting concrete roof sections, each balanced on a single pier in a manner reminiscent of his own Parasol Houses and Wright's Johnson Wax Administration Building (fig. 227; see fig. 30). The meeting of the cropped corners of the roof units defined diamond-shaped skylights that were integral to the overall system. Kahn explained this in now familiar terms: "We wanted to achieve a structure that was the giver of light. Normally the column is dark. But we made it, in this case, the Maker of Light. It embraced the clearstories, which are really our windows."[47]

The spatial control exerted by this roof system was strong, even though it left the work floor almost entirely unobstructed. Rather than follow the orthogonal grid established by the placement of the piers, the space was reoriented obliquely, in obedience to the diagonal pattern established by the clerestories and reinforced by the suspended lighting (fig. 228). The Olivetti factory thus retained some of the baroque planning energy of Kahn's mid-sixties work, although here it was contained within a calm, rectangular envelope.

A third system for modulating spaces with a structural roofing system and natural light was developed for the Yale Center for British Art, a building that was nearing completion when Kahn died (see figs. 392–407 and pp. 410–13). This commission presented another, even more poignant opportunity for Kahn to reconsider the design of the Yale Art Gallery, which faced the site of the new building from across Chapel Street.

Like the Kimbell Museum, the Yale Center was created under the leadership of a powerful director, Jules Prown, who envisioned a naturally lit, houselike setting for a private collection. However, unlike the Kimbell, the site was decidedly urban, and the program was complicated by the nature of the collection (that of Paul Mellon) and the

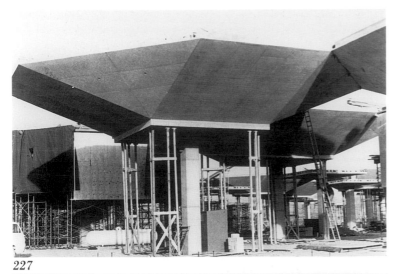

227

228

229

227. *Olivetti-Underwood
Factory, Harrisburg, Pa.,
1966–70. Construction of pier,
ca. 1968–69.*
228. *Olivetti-Underwood
Factory, Harrisburg, Pa.,
1966–70. Aerial view, 1970.*
229. *Yale Center for British
Art, New Haven, Conn.,
1969–74. North elevation, June
1970. Inscribed Palazzo
Melloni.*

educational mission of the center. The building was to include large facilities for the study of prints and drawings, painting galleries, and a library—for a time expanded to include the main art library of the university. Moreover, in a deal with the city of New Haven, it was agreed to insert retail space on the ground floor to provide the city with tax income.

These conditions suggested a *parti* for the building, which Kahn began to sketch early in 1970: a block with skylit galleries on top, commercial space on the bottom, and everything else in between arranged around two courtyards (see fig. 530). An obvious historical analogy for this kind of building could be found in the great town houses of the Italian Renaissance, courtyard-centered palaces whose ground floors were rented out to shopkeepers. Kahn acknowledged this allusion, labeling an early facade study "Palazzo Melloni" (fig. 229).

The same elevation showed his powerful first proposal for an integrative system of structure and light, with two long, low arches leapfrogging the entire length of the building and turning clerestory windows to the north (see fig. 531). Prown was worried, however, that this mighty architecture would overwhelm the small works of the Mellon collection—just what Brown had also feared when contemplating Kahn's huge first proposal for the Kimbell. Prown recalled, "We finally just had to say, 'No.'"[48]

Kahn's second design, worked out in the winter of 1970–71, adopted a variant of the Kimbell barrel vaults, this time glazed on their north-facing surfaces rather than split along their crowns (fig. 230). Mechanical services were to be contained within four semicircular corner towers, clad in steel to symbolize their contents, and in the entrance courtyard (now also covered with barrel vaults) Kahn placed a great curved stairway (fig. 231). This design was far advanced in April 1971 when it, too, was abandoned—a victim of inflation at a time when Mellon was also paying for I. M. Pei's vastly more expensive East Building of the National Gallery in Washington, D.C.

After the Yale program was reduced by about one third, work on the realized design began. Based on the same *parti*, this revolved around two covered courtyards. The first, with its floor at ground level, served as the lobby (see fig. 398). The second, one floor up at the level of the library, was connected to the first court by the main stairway, and the stair in turn rose through the volume of this "library court" to serve the upper floors. Having abandoned the great

230

231

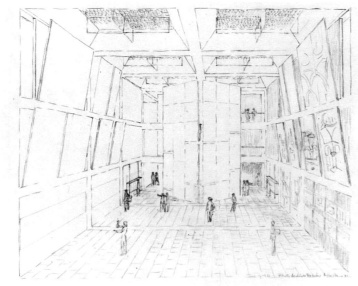

232

semicircular staircase that was possible within the original program, Kahn experimented with a diamond plan before settling on a circle (fig. 232; see figs. 399, 400). These courtyard spaces, encircled by the galleries that looked out into them through large windows, were transformed by paneling and paintings into something approximating the receiving rooms of a country house. Shifting now from an Italian metaphor to one in keeping with the British art that was to hang on the walls, Kahn explained: "I think of the Mellon Gallery as an English hall. When you walk into the hall, you're introduced to the whole house. You can see how the interior is laid out, how the spaces are used. It's as though you can walk into the house and meet the whole house and say, 'Gee whiz, I think you're great.' "[49] In fact, the planning clarity that was apparent on paper was obscured in reality by one major barrier, the impossibility of looking directly from one courtyard into the other and thus understanding the armature of the design.

In the small upper-floor galleries, the domestic imagery was continued in a series of twenty-by-twenty-foot "rooms" that were defined by the strong concrete framing of the square skylights (see figs. 401–4). Here the challenge of providing a naturally lit environment for art, nestled within a clearly expressed structural system, was met again. As at the Kimbell, it was necessary to accommodate a fundamental dichotomy: "Of course," Kahn said, "there are some spaces which should be flexible, but there are also some which should be completely inflexible."[50] The result was a strongly figured ceiling beneath which neutral wall panels could be placed with some freedom (fig. 233). The system of diffusers in the skylights, although long studied before Kahn died, was not worked out until afterward by Marshall Meyers.

The exterior of the Yale Center, shorn of the service towers that were part of the earlier design, became a mute prism, inherently classical in its containment and modularity, yet clearly inflected by complex meanings. The concrete skeleton was revealed in the facades, the piers narrowing floor by floor as they rose and as the superincumbent weight of the building decreased, like the piers at Exeter. The infill walling—the selection of which, like most details of the exterior, was delayed by Kahn until the last possible moment—was dark, unpolished stainless steel. Kahn chose this material over the objections of Jules Prown, perhaps influenced by Paul Mellon's stated preference for gray granite and by the prevailing gray tonalities of Yale's nearby neo-Gothic buildings.[51] Kahn had become familiar with the properties of stainless steel while working on earlier projects, where it was used as trim, and from the start it had

230. *Yale Center for British Art, New Haven, Conn., 1969–74. Model, December 1970.*
231. *Yale Center for British Art, New Haven, Conn., 1969–74. Library court with semicircular stair, December 1970.*

232. *Yale Center for British Art, New Haven, Conn., 1969–74. Library court with diamond stair, ca. August 1971. Inscribed Lou Kahn.*
233. *Yale Center for British Art, New Haven, Conn., 1969–74. Section of upper gallery, Summer 1971.*

been his chosen material for the ultimately abandoned service towers of the Yale Center. He liked the fact that its textures and coloration varied perceptibly, admiring, too, the way its slight reflectivity mirrored the variety of the environment. To Prown he predicted, "On a grey day it will look like a moth; on a sunny day like a butterfly."[52] He sought to ennoble steel (perhaps for Prown's benefit) by likening it to lead and pewter.

Windows replaced the steel panels on the facades where interior usage called for daylight, and two-story spaces on the inside were represented by two uninterrupted stories of steel and glass on the outside (see fig. 394). By no means, however, did this modest external expression make the Yale Center seem extroverted, and although the first-floor shops did bring the life of the street to the building, it replied only with reserved urban mannerliness. Like Exeter, the final design did little to reveal its entrance, which was tucked under a corner (see fig. 392). Nothing was allowed to disturb the prismatic completeness of the building. Vincent Scully, who had thought that Robert Venturi or another younger architect should have been given the commission in preference to his now well-established friend, was delighted by this final effect. "I think it is wonderful," he said in 1982, "so quiet, so soundless, so timeless. It is really silence and light and that is what Lou was always talking about."[53]

Construction of the Yale Center was beginning in 1973 when Kahn undertook preliminary studies for a third museum designed for a private collection—or, more properly, the several collections (including surrealist painting, Greek antiquities, and African sculpture) of John and Dominique de Menil. He had come to know them in 1967 when Dominique de Menil organized the "Visionary Architects" exhibition at the University of St. Thomas in Houston, for which Kahn contributed a poetic catalogue introduction. She had also had a hand in the abortive Art Center project for Rice University on which he worked in 1969–70.

The program for the De Menil Foundation was complicated and loosely stated, including not only a museum (designed to allow easy, informal access to works in storage) but also a conference center and housing. All was to be located adjacent to the Rothko Chapel and close to Philip Johnson's campus for the University of St. Thomas. For Kahn, this kind of comprehensive project was hugely exciting, and he proceeded with a site plan that showed his proposed museum, with parallel vaulted galleries, and the Rothko Chapel occupying opposite sides of a central lawn. The new residential buildings and meeting halls were located to the

234

235

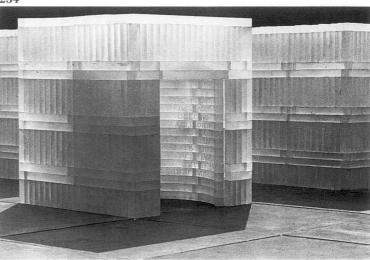

236

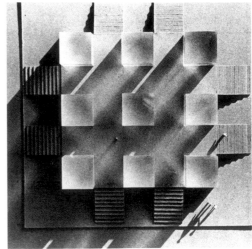

237

west, while existing St. Thomas dormitories occupied the eastern part of the master plan. The death of John de Menil in March 1973 slowed the project, and it was halted by Kahn's death a year later. After several years of delay, the museum was built to the design of Renzo Piano.

Among the most powerful works that Kahn created during this period were a pair of memorials in New York City—both as yet unbuilt. They were to commemorate the victims of the Holocaust and Franklin Delano Roosevelt. Kahn was thus occupied with representing both the tragedy and the aspirations of twentieth-century life in the last years of his own life.

Although both projects were compromised by the addition of descriptive or pictorial elements, they started by affording Kahn the chance to create something almost purely architectural, unfettered by ordinary and practical restrictions. Kahn described this precious field of opportunity in Platonic terms:

Architecture has little to do with solving problems. Problems are run-of-the-mill. To be able to solve a problem is almost a drudgery of architecture. Though it is tremendously delightful, there is nothing equal to the delight of coming to realizations about architecture itself. There's something that pulls on you as though you were reaching out to something primordial, something that existed before yourself. You realize when you are in the realm of architecture that you are touching the basic feelings of man and that architecture would never have been part of humanity if it weren't the truth to begin with.[54]

He could also explain this with vivid concreteness: "In the mind . . . is the temple, yet not made. A manifestation of desire, not need. Need is so many bananas. Need is a ham sandwich."[55]

The Memorial to the Six Million Jewish Martyrs was a project defined by human feelings of such magnitude and complexity that they resisted expression (see pp. 400–403). Indeed, several designs had been proposed and abandoned before 1966, when Kahn was asked to join a new memorial advisory committee by its energetic chairman, David Kreeger, a philanthropist and collector. A few months later Kahn was awarded the commission, and over the winter of 1967–68 he did his best to create an architectural solution for the spectacular site in Battery Park at the southernmost extremity of Manhattan.

Kahn decided almost at the start that the memorial should be a group of pylons formed out of clear glass, a material of great purity. Lighting was a vital part of this design, just as it was in the contemporary vaults of the Kimbell Museum, and he explained its effect on the memorial in similar words: "Changes of light, the seasons of the year, the play of weather, and the drama of movement on the river will transmit their life to the monument."[56] Even more than the concrete vaults of the Kimbell, however, a glass structure could literally be "the maker of light," a phrase he began to use at exactly this time.[57] Here at last was an effective expression of "the spiritual quality inherent in a structure" that he had spoken of in defining "monumentality" in 1944.[58]

The first plan for the memorial, developed in the fall of 1967, was the least compromised: a three-by-three matrix of pylons standing on a pedestal (figs. 234, 237). The gridded arrangement bespoke the classical discipline that prevailed in Kahn's late work, but, as usual, this was a discipline that his Beaux-Arts sophistication prevented from descending into banal predictability. Thus the central axes were occupied by pylons rather than the expected circulation passages, and the spacing between the pylons equaled the dimensions of the pylons themselves. The latter established a disconcerting equality of solid and void, like that sometimes seen in contemporary Op Art and also seen in early Doric temples, where the intercolumnar spacing nearly matched the diameter of the columns.

Transmitting light by day and radiating light by night, the memorial seemed to afford a glimpse into the usually invisible order of pure architecture. It was an ineffably poignant symbol of the human idealism exterminated by the Nazis' terrible reality. But it was too abstract for those members of the committee who had witnessed the grisly particulars of the Holocaust, and in response to their suggestions, Kahn revised the design in December 1967. He replaced the nine identical piers with a more complicated pattern of seven: six around the edge of the platform to symbolize the six million dead and a seventh at the center, bearing an explanatory inscription. This arrangement set forth the meaning of the monument without ambiguity (fig. 236). Several variations were tested with models, with the central pylon evolving into a chapel-like structure (see figs. 518, 521). At the end of this development, the chapel had a circular interior, as shown in a large and elaborate model that was assembled out of miniature plexiglass bricks and mounted on a lead-sheathed plinth (fig. 235). This was exhibited at the Museum of Modern Art in November 1968, but the project failed to kindle enthusiastic support in the Jewish community. Although Kahn revised his design again

234. Memorial to the Six Million Jewish Martyrs, New York, N.Y., 1966–72. Model, Fall 1967.
235. Memorial to the Six Million Jewish Martyrs, New York, N.Y., 1966–72. Model showing chapel, Fall 1968.
236. Memorial to the Six Million Jewish Martyrs, New York, N.Y., 1966–72. Detail of perspective. Inscribed LIK 3 Dec '67.
237. Memorial to the Six Million Jewish Martyrs, New York, N.Y., 1966–72. Model, Fall 1967.

238. *Roosevelt Memorial, New York, N.Y., 1973–74. Plan, April 1973.*
239. *Roosevelt Memorial, New York, N.Y., 1973–74. Perspective, ca. August 1973.*
240. *Roosevelt Memorial, Washington, D.C., 1960. Section (detail of sheet), Summer 1960.*
241. *Roosevelt Memorial, Washington, D.C., 1960. Partial plan (detail of sheet), Summer 1960.*

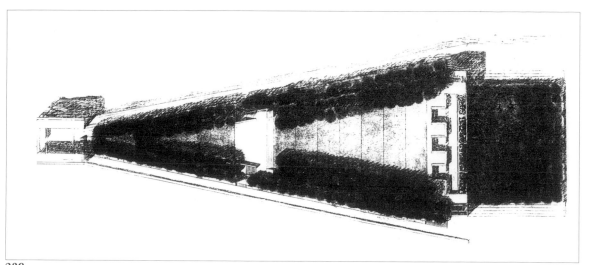

238

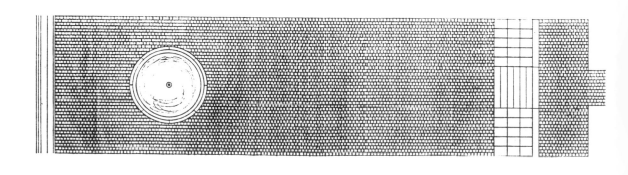

239

240

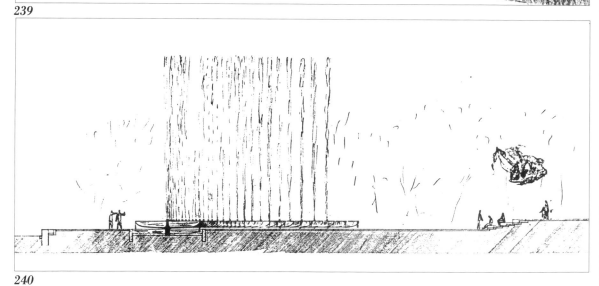

241

in 1972, substituting a cheaper construction method, the memorial was not built (see fig. 520).

By chance, the end of the project for the Holocaust memorial preceded by only a few months the commission for another monument on another breathtaking waterfront site in New York City. This was a memorial to Franklin Delano Roosevelt, and the location was the southern tip of Welfare Island (renamed Roosevelt Island) in the East River. The United Nations Building was only a few hundred yards away across the water. The commission came from the New York State Urban Development Corporation, which was then demolishing Welfare Island's public hospitals and launching a new urban community, the master plan for which had been drawn by Philip Johnson and John Burgee in 1968–69.

Kahn worked on the Roosevelt Memorial throughout 1973, returning to a subject that had occupied him once before, when, in 1960, he had submitted an unsuccessful entry in the first stage of the competition for a Roosevelt monument in Washington, D.C.[59] That monument was to be located in West Potomac Park, a peninsula lying between the Potomac River and the cherry tree–encircled Tidal Basin. As demanded by the instructions, Kahn's design deferred in size and spirit to the nearby Lincoln and Jefferson Memorials (figs. 240, 241). Rather than a building, it consisted of sixty traditional-looking fountain basins—each sending a jet of water fifty feet into the air and arranged in a giant arc, nearly half a mile long. The result would have been a curved screen of water, abstract in effect yet conservative in architectural detail.

For Roosevelt Island thirteen years later, Kahn strove to solve the problem on his own architectural terms.[60] It was an important commission for him, for he had been an ardent supporter of the New Deal who "loved Roosevelt and knew much more about him than most of us," according to Theodore Liebman, director of design for the Development Corporation.[61] Kahn conceived of the memorial as a combination of two suitably archetypal forms: "I had this thought that a memorial should be a room and a garden. That's all I had. Why did I want a room and a garden? I just chose it to be the point of departure. The garden is somehow a personal nature, a personal kind of control of nature, a gathering of nature. And the room was the beginning of architecture."[62] Again collaborating closely with Harriet Pattison, Kahn placed this ideal room at the tip of the island, to be approached across a controlled landscape of lawn framed by closely planted trees. At first he imagined the room defined by huge slabs, at a relative scale worthy of

Ledoux or Boullée, but by the time a model was presented on April 26, 1973, it had been reduced to a paved platform with shelters on two sides (fig. 238).[63] This, in turn, yielded by the end of the summer to an outdoor room with two simple ashlar walls, in which the required statues of Roosevelt were to stand in company with two rows of four pillars, representing the "Four Freedoms" (of speech and worship, and from fear and want) that Roosevelt had proclaimed as the bases of American life in January 1941 (fig. 239). The walls were to be constructed out of the largest possible blocks, through which precisely aligned slits would admit sunlight at dawn on the anniversary of Roosevelt's birth and at sundown on the anniversary of his death.[64] This alluded unmistakably to Kahn's description of the beginning of architecture as the parting of walls.

The final design, worked out in the months immediately before Kahn's death, was a further simplification. The markers of the Four Freedoms were removed, and after traversing Pattison's successive funnel-shaped gardens, the visitor entered Kahn's room: his architecture reduced to a primitive quintessence that he called a "pre-Grecian temple space."[65] Walled by masonry of unquestionable tectonic honesty and ceiled by the light of the sky itself, the memorial room allowed outward views only to the south, down the river and past the UN toward the Williamsburg Bridge. The nearby tumult of Manhattan and its spiky midtown skyline were screened from sight. Here was quiet at the end of a journey.

The last years of Louis Kahn's life were especially full of accomplishment and honor. Temple Beth-El, the Kimbell Museum, and the Exeter library were dedicated in 1972, followed by the theater at Fort Wayne in 1973. The museum and the library were among his greatest works and among the greatest buildings of the twentieth century. Kahn's architecture was the subject of retrospective exhibitions at the Museum of Modern Art in New York (1966) and the Eidgenössische Technische Hochschule in Zurich (1969), and it was comprehensively surveyed in special issues of *L'architecture d'aujourd'hui* (1969), *Architectural Forum* (1972), and *Architecture + Urbanism* (1973). In the year before he died, two teams of authors were preparing books about him, completed as Romaldo Giurgola and Jaimini Mehta's *Louis I. Kahn* (1975) and Heinz Ronner, Sharad Jhaveri, and Alessandro Vasella's *Louis I. Kahn: Complete Work, 1935–1974* (1977).

All of the highest awards of Kahn's profession also arrived in a rush during these years: the gold medals of the

Philadelphia and New York chapters of the American Institute of Architects in 1969 and 1970, the AIA's national gold medal in 1970, and the gold medal of the Royal Institute of British Architects in 1971. Not to be overshadowed by this architectural recognition was the 1971 Philadelphia Award, called the "Bok Award" for its donor, Edward W. Bok. This was usually seen as the highest honor accorded to a citizen of Kahn's native city.

The architectural work, of course, continued, and much of it was exhaustingly far away. The school in Ahmedabad and a family planning center in Kathmandu required supervision. Construction in Dhaka resumed with a revised program after the war for Bangladesh independence, and new commissions arrived from Morocco, Israel, and Iran. Closer to home, Kahn taught as much as ever at the University of Pennsylvania, although he was now technically an emeritus professor. And the invitations to lecture poured in.

With his eyesight saved by a cataract operation in 1966 and a hernia repaired in 1972, Kahn entered his seventies in apparent good health. Indeed, he usually seemed to be energetic and robust, even on the grueling trips that took him across Europe to Asia, often with several lecture or business stops along the way, and returned him to Philadelphia just in time to teach a class or meet an American client in a far-off city. He had, however, begun to consult a doctor about a worrisome heart condition, and friends and family noted that he occasionally looked gray and tired.

There was, amidst all of this honor and tiring activity, some disappointment, too. While Kahn was honored as an "architect's architect" by his colleagues and adored by many students, his influence remained rather narrow. He had difficulty winning the type of support he wanted most, from the large, often public institutions that controlled what he thought was the architect's most important work. Although he had been respected by discerning individuals like Jonas Salk, Richard Brown, and Jules Prown, this kind of personal backing could not secure the success of his largest plans. Numerous ambitious projects were thus abandoned: the President's Estate in Islamabad, the new city of Gandhinagar, the Hill Area Redevelopment in New Haven, the convention hall in Venice, the Art Center for Rice University, and (except for a fragment) the arts complex at Fort Wayne. In the year before he died, he faced increasing frustration in elevating Philadelphia's planned celebration of the bicentennial of American independence to an appropriate level, and two large commercial

developments in which he had invested much energy were abandoned: the Inner Harbor in Baltimore and the skyscraper in Kansas City. Only in India and Bangladesh was he able to complete large projects, and there the work was forcefully advanced by local representatives to whom Kahn was compelled to grant much discretion.

Even among the colleagues and students who admired Kahn, few recognized that his philosophy demanded that each architect seek his own understanding of human institutions and then test for himself the natural laws that established the limits of design. What they could see clearly was only the example of Kahn's own powerful architecture, and it was this that they emulated. The results were often unhappy, for no one could equal his ability to infuse hard materials with humanity or to lift complex planning above formalist pattern making. Only in south Asia (again an exception) and in some other parts of the developing world did Kahn's work seem to inspire a vibrant brick vernacular style; elsewhere the architecture that was most obviously indebted to his example frequently looked derivative or worse: brutal in elevation and artificial in plan. It was thus with many unfulfilled dreams—as well as the knowledge of his great success—that Kahn made his final trip to India in March 1974.

In retrospect, many thought that the time before his departure had been full of signs. Esther Kahn remembered that his chronic indigestion had gotten worse, and his daughter Sue Ann had remarked on his tiredness.[66] On the evening before his trip there had at last been time to look through the photographs of a big family party held in his honor several months earlier, and just a few days before that he and Esther had had dinner with Steven and Toby Korman in the sumptuous, recently completed house that Kahn had designed for them (see fig. 261). The Kormans recalled that their guests had stayed late, talking in the end as though they were alone.[67]

Kahn flew to India for a week to lecture under the auspices of the Ford Foundation and to inspect the Indian Institute of Management and see his friend Balkrishna Doshi in Ahmedabad. At the end of the visit Doshi put Kahn on the 1:15 A.M. flight from Ahmedabad to Bombay on Saturday, March 16.[68] In Bombay, Kahn boarded an Air India plane en route to London via Kuwait, Rome, and Paris, expecting to connect with TWA in London and fly on to Philadelphia Sunday afternoon. He was scheduled to teach on Monday. In the event, he missed the TWA flight and had to rebook with Air India into New York.

This had turned into a very long journey, and Kahn had reason to be weary. He had flown out and back to Teheran in February, to Dhaka in January, to Tel Aviv in December, and in the previous twelve months he had made four other long trips abroad, visiting Dhaka, Brussels, Paris, Tel Aviv, Rabat, and Kathmandu one or more times. Doshi remembered him being lively and full of fun during his stay in Ahmedabad, but by the time he reached Heathrow Airport in London on Sunday he was evidently in distress. Stanley Tigerman, a pupil from Kahn's last years at Yale, was traveling to inspect his own work in Bangladesh. Tigerman encountered him in the waiting room at Heathrow:

I'm at the airport and I see this old man, who looks like he has detached retinas, is really raggy and looks like a bum. It was Lou. . . . We had two hours together. We talked mostly about this friend of mine who got me into Bangladesh, Muzharul Islam, who later gave up architecture. He was the one responsible for Lou getting the capital [project]. . . . Lou and I were sitting talking and he couldn't figure out why Islam had given up architecture. We were reminiscing. We had a nice talk. He seemed exhausted, depressed. He looked like hell. . . . He talked mostly about the state of Muzharul Islam, that he had done such a wonderful thing for Lou and then how he gave up architecture because of politics. Lou said *There's so few things I know in life. I could never do anything but be an architect because that's all I know how to do.*[69]

After talking with Tigerman, Kahn boarded an Air India jet bound for New York. He passed through customs at Kennedy Airport at 6:20 P.M., and made his way to Pennsylvania Station to catch a train to Philadelphia. There, in the station men's room, Louis I. Kahn died of a heart attack at about 7:30 on Sunday, March 17, 1974.

The New York police advised Philadelphia authorities of Kahn's death by teletype almost immediately, but they supplied only his business address, and no further effort was made to locate his family when, on that Sunday evening, no one was found at the office.[70] On Monday concern deepened into alarm among his staff and family when he failed to arrive, and they began to retrace his itinerary. His changed routing and the lack of some passenger manifests made this inquiry difficult, but on Tuesday they at last learned from U.S. Customs that he had reached New York City on Sunday evening. Their attention now shifted to hospitals and morgues in New York. Kahn was at Missing Persons in Manhattan, and it was there that his widow identified the body.

Funeral services were conducted in Philadelphia on Friday, March 22, followed that day by a memorial meeting for students and office staff in his studio at the University of Pennsylvania. On April 2 there was a more public service for the university community. A recurrent theme in all that was said of him was that he was a very young man of seventy-three. Because the start of his career had been slowed by the Depression and the war, Kahn's most memorable architecture had been done rather recently and in an enormous rush of creative energy. Moreover, he had always seemed like a boyish enthusiast who had newly fallen in love with his lifework. Jonas Salk said, "For five decades he prepared himself and did in two what others wish they could do in five."[71] Peter Shepheard, Holmes Perkins's successor as dean of fine arts, recounted simply, "After that dry period when so many of us thought the fun had gone out of architecture, Lou brought it back."[72]

Along with the pleasure of making architecture, Kahn had also restored its importance. He rescued modernism from the banality induced by its commercial success and reattached it to serious themes: the sheltering of human institutions and the definition of space by structure, mass, and light. It was not, of course, that these fundamental matters had been ignored in the earlier years of the twentieth century. In the work of Gropius and those first Americans who had fought for public housing, Kahn had seen and known social activism in architecture. And he had recognized Le Corbusier as a sculptor of powerful structures and a magician of light. In a sense, Kahn had restored the moral and artistic importance that the modern movement had embraced at its start.

But Kahn could also do what those of an earlier generation could not. No longer fearful that creativity would be frozen by anything more than an occasional backward glance into the past, he could freely enrich his architecture by drawing on history's artistic and philosophical treasury. This had two important consequences. He was able to increase the visual range of twentieth-century architecture just as it was teetering into self-parody, and he could broaden and ennoble the sometimes arcane rhetoric of abstract art by explicitly connecting it to its neo-Platonic and classical roots.

Louis Kahn thus reassigned modern architects the most difficult work in the world, but he also opened up to them all the world's resources. He offered them daunting responsibility and terrifying liberty. As Vincent Scully said, "He broke the models and set his strongest students free."[73]

D.B.B.

Notes

1. Kahn, "Space and the Inspirations" (lecture, New England Conservatory of Music, Boston, November 14, 1967), *L'architecture d'aujourd'hui* 40 (February–March 1969): 16.

2. Kahn, "Architecture is the Thoughtful Making of Spaces," *Perspecta*, no. 4 (1957): 2.

3. Kahn, "The Room, the Street and Human Agreement" (AIA Gold Medal acceptance speech, Detroit, June 24, 1971), *AIA Journal* 56 (September 1971): 33.

4. Kahn, *Architecture: The John Lawrence Memorial Lectures* (New Orleans: Tulane University School of Architecture, 1972), n.p.

5. Kahn, unidentified discussion, International Design Conference, "The Invisible City," Aspen, Colorado, June 1972, in *What Will Be Has Always Been: The Words of Louis I. Kahn*, ed. Richard Saul Wurman (New York: Access Press and Rizzoli, 1986), 159.

6. Kahn, "Remarks" (lecture, Yale University, October 30, 1963), *Perspecta*, no. 9/10 (1965): 330.

7. Scully, interview with Alessandra Latour, September 15, 1982, in *Louis I. Kahn: L'uomo, il maestro*, ed. Latour (Rome: Edizioni Kappa, 1986), 149.

8. Prown, interview with Alessandra Latour, June 23, 1982, in Latour, *Kahn*, 137.

9. Meyers, quoted in "Louis I. Kahn, Yale Center for British Art, Yale University, New Haven, Connecticut," in Hayden Gallery, Massachusetts Institute of Technology, *Processes in Architecture: A Documentation of Six Examples*, published as *Plan*, no. 10 (Spring 1979): 34.

10. Kahn, "Law and Rule in Architecture" (lecture, Princeton University, November 29, 1961), typed transcript, "LIK Lectures 1969," Box LIK 53, Louis I. Kahn Collection, University of Pennsylvania and Pennsylvania Historical and Museum Commission, Philadelphia (hereafter cited as Kahn Collection).

11. Kahn, "Remarks," 304.

12. Kahn, "Space and the Inspirations," 14.

13. Kahn, ibid., 13–14.

14. Kahn, "Architecture: Silence and Light" (lecture, Solomon R. Guggenheim Museum, December 3, 1968), in Guggenheim Museum, *On the Future of Art* (New York: Viking Press, 1970), 21.

15. Kahn, "Talk at the Conclusion of the Otterlo Congress," in *New Frontiers in Architecture: C.I.A.M. '59 in Otterlo*, ed. Oscar Newman (New York: Universe Books, 1961), 210.

16. Kahn, quoted in *The Notebooks and Drawings of Louis I. Kahn*, ed. Richard S. Wurman and Eugene Feldman (Philadelphia: Falcon Press, 1962), n.p.

17. Patricia McLaughlin, "'How'm I Doing, Corbusier?' An Interview with Louis Kahn," *Pennsylvania Gazette* 71 (December 1972): 23.

18. Kahn, "I Love Beginnings" (lecture, International Design Conference, "The Invisible City," Aspen, Colorado, June 19, 1972), *Architecture + Urbanism*, special issue "Louis I. Kahn," 1975, 283–84.

19. Peter Kohane, "Louis I. Kahn and the Library: Genesis and Expression of 'Form,'" *Via* 10 (1990): 119–29.

20. Quoted in Rodney Armstrong, "New Look Library at Phillips Exeter Academy," *Library Scene* 2 (Summer 1973): 23.

21. Robert Hughes, "Building with Spent Light," *Time* 101 (January 15, 1973): 65.

22. Kahn, quoted in "The Mind of Louis Kahn," *Architectural Forum* 137 (July–August 1972): 77.

23. Kahn, "The Continual Renewal of Architecture Comes from Changing Concepts of Space," *Perspecta*, no. 4 (1957): 3.

24. Kahn, "Architecture and Human Agreement" (lecture, University of Virginia, April 18, 1972), *Modulus*, no. 11 (1975): n.p.

25. Kahn, quoted in Israel Shenker, "Kahn Defines Aim of Exeter Design," *New York Times*, October 23, 1972, L40.

26. Kahn, quoted in Ada Louise Huxtable, "New Exeter Library: Stunning Paean to Books," *New York Times*, October 23, 1972, L33.

27. Kahn, "Comments on the Library, Phillips Exeter Academy, Exeter, New Hampshire, 1972" (from unidentified source at Phillips Exeter Academy), in Wurman, *What Will Be Has Always Been*, 178.

28. Kahn, quoted in William Jordy, "The Span of Kahn: Criticism, Kimbell Art Museum, Fort Worth, Texas; Library, Philips [sic] Exeter Academy, Exeter, New Hampshire," *Architectural Review* 155 (June 1974): 334.

29. Patricia Cummings Loud, *The Art Museums of Louis I. Kahn* (Durham, N.C., and London: Duke University Press, 1989), 103.

30. Ibid., 105–6.

31. Kahn, "Talk at the Otterlo Congress," 213.

32. Kahn, unidentified discussion, International Design Conference, 159.

33. "Kahn's Museum: An Interview with Richard F. Brown," *Art in America* 60 (September–October 1972): 48.

34. Kahn, interview with Jaime Mehta, October 22, 1973, in Wurman, *What Will Be Has Always Been*, 230.

35. Kahn, quoted in Latryl L. Ohendalski, "Kimbell Museum To Be Friendly Home, Says Kahn," *Fort Worth Press*, May 4, 1969, as quoted in Loud, *The Art Museums*, 264.

36. Kahn, unidentified discussion, International Design Conference, 159.

37. Kahn, quoted in "Mind of Kahn," 57.

38. Kahn, quoted in "Louis Kahn," *Conversations with Architects*, ed. John W. Cook and Heinrich Klotz (New York: Praeger, 1973), 212.

39. Kahn, interview with William Marlin, June 24, 1972, typed transcript, Kimbell Art Museum Files, quoted in Loud, *The Art Museums*, 156; Kahn, "Mind of Kahn," 59.

40. Kahn, "I Love Beginnings," 285.

41. Kahn, "The Room," 33. The misquotation is apparently from Wallace Stevens, "Architecture," in Stevens, *Opus Posthumous*, rev., enl., and corrected ed., ed. Milton J. Bates (New York: Alfred A. Knopf, 1989), 37–39. Alan Filreis brought this poem to my attention. Pattison, interview with David B. Brownlee and Peter S. Reed, December 20, 1990.

42. Kahn, "Space and the Inspirations," 16.

43. Kahn, quoted in Shenker, "Kahn Defines," L40.

44. Ibid.

45. Esther Kahn, remarks at a symposium sponsored by the Architectural League of New York, January 22, 1990.

46. Kahn, quoted in Heinz Ronner and Sharad Jhaveri, *Louis I. Kahn: Complete Work, 1935–1974*, 2d ed. (Basel and Boston: Birkhäuser, 1987), 322.

47. Ibid., 323.

48. Prown, interview with Latour, 141.

49. Kahn, quoted in Susan Braudy, "The Architectural Metaphysic of Louis Kahn: 'Is the Center of a Column Filled with Hope?' 'What is a Wall?' 'What Does This Space Want To Be?' " *New York Times Magazine*, November 15, 1970, 96.

50. Kahn, "Louis I. Kahn: Talks with Students" (lecture and discussion, Rice University, ca. 1969), *Architecture at Rice*, no. 26 (1969): 14.

51. Prown, interview with Latour, 137, 141.

52. Kahn, quoted in Jules David Prown, *The Architecture of the Yale Center for British Art*, 2d ed. (New Haven: Yale University, 1982), 43.

53. Scully, interview with Latour, 151.

54. Kahn, "Lecture, Drexel (University) Architectural Society, Philadelphia, PA, 5 November 1968," in Wurman, *What Will Be Has Always Been*, 27.

55. Ibid., 29.

56. Kahn, quoted in "Memorials: Lest We Forget," *Architectural Forum* 129 (December 1968): 89.

57. Kahn, "Space and the Inspirations," 15.

58. Kahn, "Monumentality," in *New Architecture and City Planning*, ed. Paul Zucker (New York: Philosophical Library, 1944), 577

59. Research assistance for the Roosevelt Memorial, Washington, D.C., was provided by Peter S. Reed. Hélène Lipstadt, "Transforming the Tradition: American Architectural Competitions, 1960 to the Present," in *The Experimental Tradition: Essays on Competitions in Architecture*, ed. Lipstadt (New York and Princeton: Architectural League of New York and Princeton Architectural Press, 1989), 97–98, 158–59.

60. Research assistance for the Roosevelt Memorial, New York City, was provided by David Roxburgh.

61. Liebman, quoted in Paul Goldberger, "Design by Kahn Picked for Roosevelt Memorial Here," *New York Times*, April 25, 1974, L45.

62. Kahn, "1973: Brooklyn, New York" (lecture, Pratt Institute, Fall 1973), *Perspecta*, no. 19 (1982): 90.

63. Invoice, October 25, 1973, "Roosevelt Island Xerox Copies of Billing," Box LIK 121, Kahn Collection; schematic plans estimate, May 4, 1973, "Master File 1 May 1973 to 30 June 1973," Box LIK 10, Kahn Collection.

64. Laurie Johnston, "Plans for Memorial at Roosevelt Island Announced During Dedication Ceremony at Site," *New York Times*, September 25, 1973, L25.

65. Kahn, quoted in Wolf Von Eckardt, "Famed Architect Louis Kahn Dies," *Washington Post*, March 21, 1974, C13.

66. Esther Kahn, unidentified interview, in Wurman, *What Will Be Has Always Been*, 283.

67. Steven and Toby Korman, interview with David B. Brownlee, Julia Moore Converse, and David G. De Long, August 1, 1990.

68. The details of Kahn's itinerary are from a log of the events of March 18 and 19, 1974, maintained by Kathleen Condé, his secretary; Kahn Collection.

69. Tigerman, unidentified interview, in Wurman, *What Will Be Has Always Been*, 299.

70. Jim Mann, "Police Here Failed to Notify Wife of Kahn's Death," *Philadelphia Inquirer*, March 21, 1974, 1.

71. Jonas Salk, "An Homage to Louis I. Kahn," *L'architecture d'aujourd'hui* 45 (May–June 1974): vi.

72. Shepheard, eulogy quoted in Wurman, *What Will Be Has Always Been*, 304.

73. Vincent J. Scully, "Education and Inspiration," *L'architecture d'aujourd'hui* 45 (May–June 1974): vi.

Portfolio

Travel Sketches

1928–59

242

242. *Amalfi, Winter 1928–29.*
243. *Pyramids, Giza, January 1951.*
244. *Temple interior, Karnak, January 1951.*

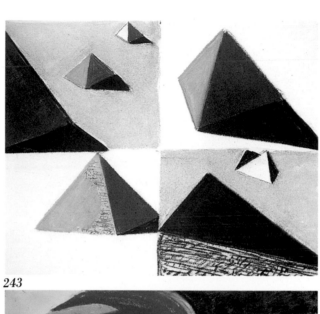

243

244

245

245. Columns, Temple of
Apollo, Corinth, January 1951.
246. Acropolis, Athens,
January 1951.
247. Campo, Siena, Winter
1951.
248. San Marco, Venice,
Winter 1951.

246

247

248

Traffic Studies

Philadelphia, Pennsylvania, 1951–53

249. Perspective, ca. 1953.

Margaret Esherick House

Philadelphia, Pennsylvania, 1959–61

251

252

Dr. and Mrs. Norman Fisher House

Hatboro, Pennsylvania, 1960–67

254. Rear facade.
255. Side facade.
256. Entrance hall and living
room.
257. Living room.

255

256

Mr. and Mrs. Steven Korman House

Fort Washington, Pennsylvania, 1971–73

258. *Front facade.*
259. *Side facade.*
260. *Side facade at dusk.*
261. *Living room.*

259

260

Yale University Art Gallery

New Haven, Connecticut, 1951–53

262. Rear garden.
263. Entrance.
264. Side facade.

264

265. Gallery.
266. Gallery, *looking toward stairwell.*
267. Stairwell.
268. Stairwell, *looking up.*

266

267

Alfred Newton Richards Medical Research Building, University of Pennsylvania

Philadelphia, Pennsylvania, 1957–65

*269. Richards Building towers
from northeast.
270. Biology Building towers.
271. Richards Building, view
toward entrance.*

271

272. Richards Building, view
from entrance.
273. Biology Building
entrance.
274. Richards Building
entrance tower, corner detail.

272

273

275. Biology Building tower.
276. Richards Building
ventilation towers.
277. Biology Building from
west.

276

277

Salk Institute for Biological Studies

La Jolla, California, 1959–65

THEODORE

ED COURT

280

281

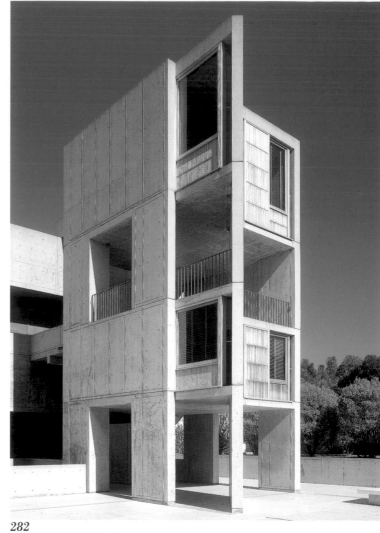

282

283

278–79. *Courtyard, looking west.*
280–82. *Study towers.*
283. *Study tower and lower courtyard.*
284. *Study towers.*

284

285. Walkway beneath study
towers.
286–87. South facade.

285

286

287

288

289

288. Ventilation intakes.
289–90. South facade.
291. Study towers.
292. Courtyard, looking east.

290

291

First Unitarian Church and School

Rochester, New York, 1959–69

294

295

293. Rear facade of church.
294. School.
295. Entrance and light towers.
296. Entrance.

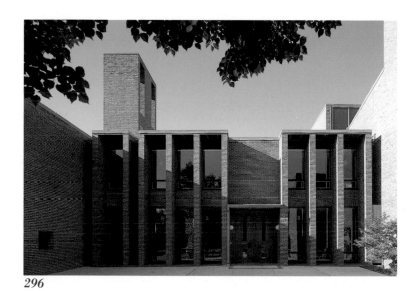

296

298

299

297. Rear facade of church.
298. View from school toward church.
299. Front facade of church.
300. Windows of school.
301. Auditorium.

300

Performing Arts Theater

Fort Wayne, Indiana, 1959–73

303

302. *Front facade.*
303. *Perspective of theater.*
Inscribed Lou K '70.
304. *Perspective of theater*
lobby. Inscribed Lou K '70.

304

Eleanor Donnelley Erdman Hall,
Bryn Mawr College

Bryn Mawr, Pennsylvania, 1960–65

305. Entrance.
306–7. Rear facade.
308. Detail of rear facade.

306

307

309. *Central hall from entrance.*
310. *Central hall.*
311. *Stair.*

310

311

312. *Living room.*
313. *Upper central hall.*

312

Indian Institute of Management

Ahmedabad, India, 1962–74

315

316

319

321

320

322

323

324

325. *Classroom building, main courtyard.*
326. *Classroom building, faculty office wing.*
327. *Classroom building, loggia.*
328. *Classroom building, faculty office wings.*

326

327

329. Water tower.
330. Classroom building,
classrooms.

329

331–35. Faculty houses.
336. Dormitories.

331

332

333

334

Sher-e-Bangla Nagar, Capital of Bangladesh

Dhaka, Bangladesh, 1962–83

339

341. *National Assembly Building, view from east.*
342. *National Assembly Building, west detail.*

343. *Bridge from South Plaza to prayer hall.*
344. *National Assembly Building, seen from east hostels.*

343

344

345

345. Prayer hall.
346. National Assembly
Building ambulatory.
347. North entrance staircase.

346

348. Prayer hall.
349. Assembly chamber.
350. Ceiling of assembly chamber.

348

351. East hostels.
352. East hostels, seen from
Presidential Square.
353. Aerial view of east hostels.

352

354

356. Entrance veranda and
waiting hall of hospital.
357. Vaults under National
Assembly Building South
Plaza.

358. Hospital veranda.
359. National Assembly
Building, seen from west
hostels.

356

357

Library, Phillips Exeter Academy

Exeter, New Hampshire, 1965–72

360. *View from northwest.*
361–62. *Central hall.*

362

363. *Librarian's office.*
364. *Carrels.*
365. *Corner of central hall.*

364

365

366–67. Stair.
368. Central hall, looking up.

366

367

369. Grove of Yaopon holly
trees, seen from entrance
portico.
370. North portico.
371. Entrance portico.
372. South portico with
reflecting pool.
373. South garden with
sculpture by Isamu Noguchi.

374. Detail of south garden
court.
375. Detail of entrance portico.

375

376

378

377

379

381

383. Auditorium.
384. Stair and lobby.
385. Café.

384

385

386

387

388

389

390

Yale Center for British Art

New Haven, Connecticut, 1969–74

392. North facade.
393. Detail of rear facade.
394. Exterior from northwest.
395. Yale University Art
Gallery (foreground) and Yale
Center for British Art.

394

395

396. Entrance.
397. View into entrance court.
398. Entrance court, looking up.

396

397

399. Library court.
400. Stair in library court.

400

401. Upper gallery, looking into court.
402–4. Upper galleries.

403

404

405

406

405. Library.
406. Auditorium.
407. Upper gallery level,
looking toward stair.

407

Selected Buildings and Projects

Philadelphia, where Louis Kahn lived nearly his
entire life, enjoyed an urban renaissance after
World War II. Kahn was at the forefront of these
large-scale redevelopments, and the remarkable
series of unrealized urban designs he drafted between 1947
and 1962 record the unfolding of an architectural vision that
was fulfilled in his later masterpieces. A self-described
architect-planner who claimed that an architect could design
a house and a city "in the same breath,"[1] Kahn used
principles in his urban designs that were pervasive in all of
his work, regardless of scale—from a room to the most
monumental and symbolic city center.

The principal area of this transformation and the subject of
Kahn's designs was Center City. Framed by the Delaware
and Schuylkill Rivers on the east and west respectively, this
was the area mapped in Thomas Holme's original 1682 plan
for Philadelphia. Much of Kahn's extraordinary body of
work in the city was created without contracts or
remuneration, but he did not work in isolation. His designs
were executed in an era of political reform that began with
the reestablishment and invigoration of the City Planning
Commission in 1943, and he was an active member of
numerous advisory committees whose members encouraged
him and shared ideas as he contended for commissions
and further official involvement in the city. Kahn met with
little success, and after the mid-1950s his designs became
increasingly theoretical and visionary, responding to critical
issues facing cities worldwide. Yet it was the city of
Philadelphia that remained Kahn's drawing board.

The Triangle Plan
The first major redevelopment study undertaken by the City
Planning Commission was for the "Triangle," a 200-acre
parcel of land bordered by the Benjamin Franklin Parkway,
the Schuylkill River, and Market Street, with one apex at
City Hall. The commission considered the Triangle, with its
many dilapidated buildings and vacant lots, to be a blighted
area. The linchpin in the area's long dreamt of renewal was
the removal of the "Chinese Wall," the elevated railroad
viaduct that cut a swath westward from Broad Street Station
to the Schuylkill River. Although agreements to remove the
nineteenth-century viaduct had been made in the 1920s
between the city and the Pennsylvania Railroad, which
owned the land, plans for the area were thwarted by the
Depression and World War II.

Kahn first became involved with the Triangle on October 14,
1946, as a member of the Associated City Planners, who
were commissioned by the City Planning Commission to
prepare a redevelopment study.[2] This team, joined together
only for this study, comprised five members: Oscar
Stonorov and Louis Kahn, architects; Robert Wheelwright
and Markley Stevenson, landscape architects; and C. Harry
Johnson, realtor. The architectural imagery and planning
they developed for the Triangle reflected the conventions of
modernism and embodied a positive, bright future for their
gloomy city. The Associated City Planners suggested that
their Triangle plan proved that the city had overcome its
"reputation of smugness and complacency."[3]

Kahn's chief responsibility on the team was to furnish the
graphic material for their final report of January 19, 1948.
As specified in the contract, this included a redevelopment
plan and ten perspectives.[4] Kahn's picture of a modern,
renovated Triangle was also translated into three dimensions
in the gigantic Center City model for the city-sponsored
Better Philadelphia Exhibition that opened in October 1947
at Gimbels department store. He prepared numerous
drawings of the Triangle (many dated July 7, 1947) to guide
the modelmakers. The Triangle drawings he made for the
Associated City Planners in 1947 and early 1948 reveal a
remarkably consistent vision, with only minor changes from
the earliest sketches to the renderings accompanying the
final report.

The guiding force behind the Triangle plan was land use.[5] In
contrast to the existing variety of buildings, described by the
planners as "the ingredients of Hungarian goulash," their
project presented a clear demarcation and separation of
functions, which they considered economic, efficient, and
modern.[6] In an undated bird's-eye perspective of the
Triangle from the southeast (probably predating the July
1947 drawings for the model) Kahn illustrated the crisp
separation of proposed land-use functions (fig. 408). Four
main areas were identified: Philadelphia's New Business
Address, Civic Center, Amusement Center, and New In
Town Living Center. Also labeled were such highlights of
modern street planning as sunken and raised pedestrian
concourses and subsurface service streets.

Kahn's perspectives for the Associated City Planners' final
report revealed the details of the gleaming new development.
In one such rendering Kahn portrayed the new business
district west of City Hall, an area developed later (in the
1950s) as Penn Center (fig. 409). Its centerpiece was a
sunken pedestrian concourse and plaza, which led to the
underground tracks serving the existing Suburban Station.
As seen in this view, looking north from Market Street to the
station, the plaza was embellished with pools, a fountain,

Philadelphia Urban Design

Philadelphia, Pennsylvania, 1947–62

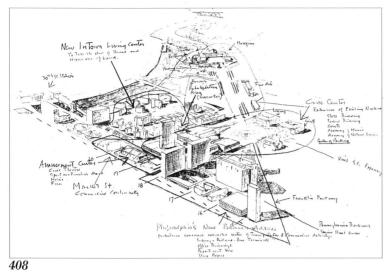

408

409

410

408. *Triangle Area Redevelopment, 1946–48. Bird's-eye perspective, ca. 1947.*
409. *Triangle Area Redevelopment, 1946–48. Perspective of concourse, looking north toward Suburban Station. Inscribed Louis I. Kahn '48.*

410. *Triangle Area Redevelopment, 1946–48. Bird's-eye perspective of Pennsylvania Boulevard and residential area, looking northeast from Thirtieth Street Station. Inscribed Louis I. Kahn '48.*

and sculpture, and flanked by two seven-story office buildings. The distinct modernism of these buildings, with their *pilotis*, ribbon windows, and glass curtain walls, was a deliberate contrast to the moderne station of 1930.

The new civic center, an arrangement of state and city office buildings bordering Logan Circle, was designed as a superblock, a hallmark of modern planning (see fig. 52). A series of pedestrian spaces, neither entirely closed nor open, complemented the asymmetrical building masses to create constantly shifting points of view rather than a precise hierarchical arrangement. From Twentieth Street the main east-west plaza of the superblock unfolded to the east and was framed by tall vertical slabs and broad low-rise buildings of varying heights. Kahn's organic sculpture provided an appealing contrast to the rational geometry of the modern buildings.

Kahn's final perspective in the report was a view from Thirtieth Street Station that depicted several modes of transportation converging on the banks of the Schuylkill River on multiple levels (fig. 410). A new boulevard bridge paralleled the old one, where a train crossed the river after emerging from beneath a proposed parking garage. A landscaped platform covered the Baltimore & Ohio Railroad tracks on the eastern shore of the river. In the distance high-rise towers, set in the midst of superblocks, bordered the river, and Y-shaped low-rise buildings filled out the remainder of the residential district.

After the Associated City Planners completed their report in January 1948, the future of the Triangle lay in the hands of the city and the Pennsylvania Railroad, owners of Broad Street Station and the Chinese Wall. The unified scheme put forth by the report was ultimately broken up into several separate projects, and little of the 1948 Triangle plan was carried out.

When it became evident that the Triangle was to be developed in a piecemeal fashion, the Philadelphia Chapter of the American Institute of Architects established the Triangle Committee in November 1949 to offer the city their support and guidance and to ensure a design consistency in the development.[7] Kahn was appointed chairman,[8] and the small group met for the first time on March 30, 1950.[9] In the next two months they produced guiding principles for the Triangle's development, which are recorded in their final report of June 6, 1950, drafted largely by Kahn's fellow committee members Edmund Krimmel and W. Pope Barney.[10] This was a slightly revised and much condensed version of the richer and more interesting preliminary report of May 1, 1950.[11] The most substantial and significant part of the earlier document identified traffic and street design as primary concerns in urban design. Indeed, the architects claimed that the overwhelming and chaotic problem of traffic would result in the disintegration of cities if a remedy was not found. In the place of old-fashioned existing streets, which were ill-suited to the motor age, the group advocated a hierarchy of road types based on functional segregation: arterial and service roads, superblocks, sunken and elevated streets to aid the separation of cars and pedestrians, and a coordinated parking plan.[12]

Although the Associated City Planners had demonstrated a strong familiarity with these concepts, their guiding principle had been land use. And while the emphasis on traffic in the Triangle Committee was not new to Kahn, this was the first time in his work that these elements of urban design were codified and their primacy clearly stated.[13] In this way, the document anticipated Kahn's later designs and essays.

On July 11, 1950, a month after the Triangle Committee completed its report, Kahn presented a new Triangle model to illustrate its points.[14] The model no longer exists, but it is known from a photograph and a plan (fig. 411). While the apparent land use and building types generally followed the Associated City Planners' scheme, the model, presumably an overall massing study, exhibited several new and noteworthy design developments. It departed from the earlier proposal in its uniform alignment of office buildings along Market Street and Pennsylvania Boulevard, oriented north-south. A sunken concourse ran under the entire stretch of office slabs—a major modification and enlargement of the Associated City Planners' sunken plaza. And appearing for the first time in Kahn's work was a cylindrical building (apparently a hotel), located just west of Suburban Station. Juxtaposed with the series of rectangular slabs, its form provided "variety within unity," one of the Triangle Committee's general and often repeated guidelines.[15] As a form, the circle had rarely appeared in Kahn's work, and its use here anticipated his adoption of a new design vocabulary of simple geometric forms after his European odyssey in 1950–51. Two days before beginning that trip, in a letter of November 28, 1950, Kahn summarized the activities and accomplishments of the Triangle Committee.[16] While he was in Europe, Edmund Krimmel became acting chairman. It appears that the committee disbanded in February 1951; there is no further record.[17]

411. Triangle Area
Redevelopment, 1949–50.
Plan, before July 1950.
412. Civic Center on the
Schuylkill River, 1951–53.
Bird's-eye perspective, ca.
1951–52.
413. Traffic Studies, 1951–53.
Bird's-eye perspective, looking
west.

Movement Studies and Civic Center on the Schuylkill

When Kahn returned from Europe in March 1951, he once again became involved with Philadelphia planning. For the next two years he was devoted to two critical problems facing Philadelphia: traffic congestion and the need for a new city hall. This body of work was summarized in "Toward a Plan for Midtown Philadelphia," Kahn's first publication in almost a decade. It appeared in the summer of 1953 in *Perspecta*, the journal of the Yale University School of Fine Arts, where he taught.[18] Many of the published drawings are undated, and while *Perspecta* provides a *terminus ante quem*, the development of Kahn's thinking can be more fully traced through the record of earlier presentations from 1951 to 1953.

The first milestone in that progression is November 15, 1951, the date of Kahn's initial presentation of his movement plans to the public.[19] The occasion was a slide lecture for the Philadelphia Planners Group, a gathering of young architects and planners. The talk was titled "Where and When to Stop—A New Pattern for Streets and Houses," and the invitation to the lecture explained that "Mr. Kahn will present new ideas for unscrambling traffic and creating liveable neighborhoods."[20]

Kahn found another enthusiastic audience among fellow members of the Committee on Municipal Improvements of the Philadelphia AIA. The committee was transformed in September 1951 by the appointment of Edmund Krimmel as its chairman, and he in turn selected new members, including Kahn, W. Pope Barney, Oscar Stonorov, and Edmund Bacon, the executive director of the Philadelphia City Planning Commission.[21] On November 7, 1951, Krimmel circulated a memo to his committee in which he strongly advocated a citywide study of all the major highways, transportation, and parking garages, with special attention given to the Center City district.[22] Noting that no thought had been given to an overall plan for the district, Krimmel set the challenging agenda for much of the subsequent committee work.[23] It is possible that Kahn was already well advanced in work on his own plan.

Between December 1951 and March 1952, at several meetings of the Committee on Municipal Improvements, Kahn presented the plans that he had made of Center City traffic and street patterns. On December 20, 1951, Bacon referred to this work as "Kahn's recent suggestion for separating slow- and fast-moving traffic on alternating existing streets through the Center City."[24] This concept of reordering the existing street system, based on the

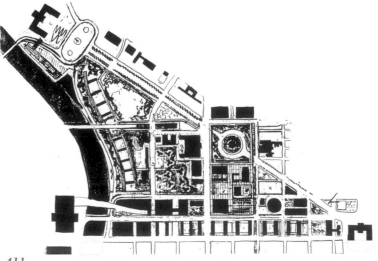

411

separation of traffic, underlay all the movement plans for Center City that Kahn published two years later in *Perspecta*.

Shortly after the new year Kahn presented more schemes for traffic and parking to Krimmel's committee. On January 4, 1952, he displayed a plan for the west half of the city that was also applicable to the east half.[25] Krimmel noted in the minutes, "I am sure Kahn will agree that the plan still has some kinks to iron out. I have asked Kahn to prepare prints and a brief of his plans for distribution among the Committee members."[26]

Before the end of the month Kahn had expanded his system to cover all of Center City and had reproduced the plans for the committee, as Krimmel had requested. Krimmel had also recommended that Kahn devise a system of symbols for his plans in order to facilitate their reproduction. This suggests that up to this point Kahn had relied on verbal description to explain his system, or had used other means not easily reproduced in black and white, such as the color codes published in *Perspecta*.[27]

Kahn seems to have developed Krimmel's recommended symbols for a second series of black-and-white drawings, which were articulated with arrows, dots, and spirals (see fig. 65). In this movement plan, an abstract notation system marked the various tempos of movement and the resting places in the city; Kahn redefined the existing street grid based on types of street traffic or, as he described it, "the activities they [the streets] serve."[28] Expressways were indicated by arrows, and streets zoned for the stop-and-go movement of buses and trolleys were indicated by dots. Parking was symbolized by curved arrows, while acute angles and spirals reflected "wound-up" streets.[29] The hierarchy in these street plans drew on Kahn's earlier Triangle work, but his new "order of movement"[30] integrated the different functions into a unified system, expressed in centralized but highly articulated designs.

In the winter of 1952 Kahn continued to develop his traffic plans and present them to Krimmel's committee. Although his plans were to be submitted to the City Planning Commission once they were endorsed by his colleagues, he never received the committee's full support. Following his last recorded presentation to the group on March 20, 1952, he expressed his frustration with the committee's inability to appreciate the "conceptual" or theoretical nature of his plans, blinded as they were by some of the specific shortcomings.[31] Indeed, they seemed to object less to the

movement scheme than to the details of Kahn's design for a new city hall on the Schuylkill River, which he had begun to sketch into his plans that winter.[32] In a revealing letter Kahn explained his position to his old friend W. Pope Barney, who had departed early from the committee meeting on March 20:

I find difficulty conveying the idea without having it immediately torn apart by specific considerations. Actually this latest development is only an extension of our deliberations on "What is Architectural Unity in Urban Design" which we struggled with on the Triangle Committee a few years ago. If the one controversial recommendation of my plan—City Hall along the river—were excluded I believe that the Municipal Improvements Committee could submit it to the Commission as their contribution to— Towards a solution of the traffic problem of Center City.[33]

Kahn's proposed city hall was only the latest chapter in a long story. Since the 1920s the city had considered abandoning John McArthur's Second Empire City Hall at Center Square and building a new structure elsewhere, and it was this debate that Kahn now joined. In a spare rendering that may date from 1951 or 1952, his proposal for a new civic center consisted of three buildings within a superblock: a cylinder, a prism, and a cube—perfect geometric solids of varying height (fig. 412). In the distance, across the river, lay Thirtieth Street Station, whose railyards were reconfigured as a transportation gateway with a heliport and connections to several major highways. In 1953 Kahn prepared more highly developed schemes for the superblock in which the prism-shaped building had evolved into the first version of the space-frame City Tower he later designed in association with Anne Griswold Tyng.

In his poetic 1953 essay for *Perspecta*, "Toward a Plan for Midtown Philadelphia," Kahn suggested that cities without gateways and expressways to channel traffic around their centers were as ludicrous as "cities without entrances" or "Carcassonne without walls."[34] His analogy between the city and a defensive fortress was brilliantly portrayed in an aerial perspective from a vantage above the Delaware River (fig. 413). Philadelphia was reduced to its principal "walls" and "towers"—the expressways and parking garages that surrounded the city core and its civic buildings and public spaces. Kahn argued that despite their abstract guise and modern function, the cylindrical parking towers and the wall of expressways surrounding the city center were analogous to the defenses of Carcassonne. The modern city's walls acted as a symbolic defense against the forces of decentralization, and the parking towers prevented a flood of incoming cars from overcrowding the pedestrian core.

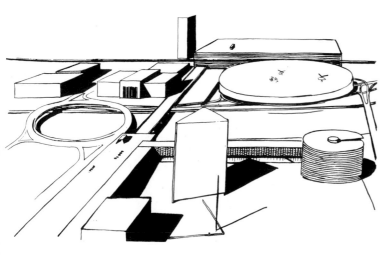

412

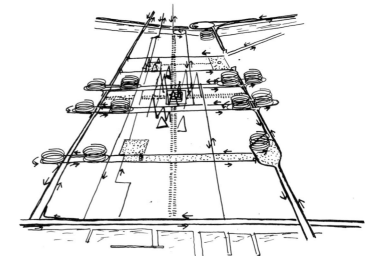

413

Seen in this light, the city bore a striking resemblance to the aerial photographs of English castles in *Castles from the Air*, a book Kahn had borrowed from the Yale Art Library in 1950.[35]

Penn Center

Amid all the talk of traffic plans and a new city hall in Philadelphia, real developments were also taking place. On September 10, 1952, demolition of the Chinese Wall began.[36] The path was now clear for Penn Center, the first major development in Center City since before the Depression. The work was guided by the spectacular proposal the Planning Commission had unveiled on February 21, 1952, reshaping the same three and a half blocks west of City Hall that the Associated City Planners had identified as the business center in their 1947 Triangle plan and using many of the features already established in that earlier work.[37] At the center of the design lay the replacement of the old station and elevated tracks by a group of modern office buildings linked by a sunken, open-air concourse.

Although these general features were carried out, the merits of the earlier plan were compromised to suit economic realities. Like many of his colleagues, Kahn detested the developer's eminently buildable and economical adjustments to the Penn Center plan, and, speaking as a teacher, he suggested that "an architectural student presenting such a plan could expect to be marked 'zero.'"[38]

Anxious for work and dissatisfied with the developer's plans, Kahn, a member of several advisory committees to watch the Penn Center development (including a mayoral appointment to the new Citizens' Advisory Committee on the Penn Center Plan),[39] proposed numerous alternatives in 1953 and 1954.[40] His chief aim was to reduce the number of buildings per block while maintaining a central esplanade whose large, sunken courtyards would provide ample light, air, and access to the concourse below. This had been the central theme of the City Planning Commission's Penn Center plan.

Kahn was dedicated to going beyond the developer's utilitarian program, for he saw Penn Center as more than a collection of office buildings. He intended the huge urban project to be a civic monument—a viewpoint that colored all his Philadelphia plans. To this end, he envisioned a park between Eighteenth and Twentieth Streets, which he somewhat misleadingly described as a "fun center" at the first recorded presentation of his plans on April 8, 1953.[41] He dreamed of a park with fountains, gardens, cafés, and pavilions for music and other entertainment amidst the series of landscaped circles that suggested the pedestrian's irregular, meandering path, in contrast to the strict linear grid of streets for motorized traffic (fig. 414). Favoring a livelier, offset arrangement of tall office buildings, Kahn also proposed a cylindrical glass building, 270 feet in diameter, east of the park between Seventeenth and Eighteenth Streets.[42] The cylinder was to put to rest the "dynamic asymmetry" of the towers.[43] Probably a further development of the anonymous round building in his 1950 Triangle plan, the circular structure was here designed as a hotel wrapped around a department store with a bus station underneath. In plan the building was essentially an equilateral triangle inscribed in a circle, with three entrances on the perimeter that corresponded to the points of the triangle. This was the first of his "buildings within a building."

On September 15, 1953, the Penn Center developer (Uris Brothers of New York) unveiled Emery Roth and Sons' design for 2 and 3 Penn Center, the first buildings to be constructed in the development.[44] This marked a turning point in Kahn's designs; thereafter, he acknowledged Roth's plans in his own drawings, but he consistently urged that the Penn Center plan be enlarged beyond them. On September 16, at a meeting of the Citizens' Advisory Committee on the Penn Center Plan, Kahn cast his vision to the east and west, suggesting that the larger area from Independence Hall to the Schuylkill River be taken into consideration.[45]

Several months later, on June 14, 1954, Kahn presented a model of this much larger area, from Eighth Street to Nineteenth Street, to his colleagues on the Penn Center Committee of the Citizens' Council on City Planning. It included a new development east of City Hall that Kahn called "Penn Center East."[46] While recognizing the principally retail nature of Market Street, which he transformed into a pleasant pedestrian shopping street with minimal traffic, he also planned a variety of cultural amenities, which he had found so desperately lacking in Center City's new development. Two years later the Philadelphia City Planning Commission itself began initial Market Street East studies for a new shopping, transportation, and parking facility in this location.[47]

Penn Center continued to develop in a fragmented fashion that compromised its unity, and after June 1954 Kahn's involvement was less frequent and aggressive. His attendance at meetings of the Citizens' Advisory Committee on the Penn Center Plan became irregular, and the committee finally disbanded on February 7, 1958.[48]

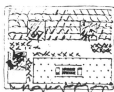

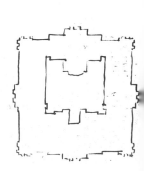

414

414. Penn Center, 1951–58. Plan, ca. 1953.
415. Civic Center, 1956–57. Cutaway perspective of parking tower, ca. 1957.
416. Market Street East Studies, 1956–57. Bird's-eye perspective of Civic Center, looking west, ca. 1957.

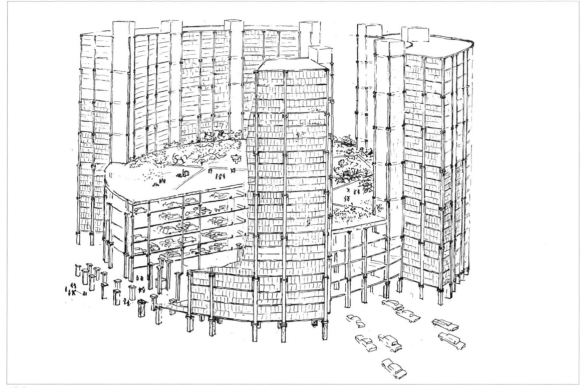

415

416

Civic Center—Forum

In 1956 Kahn again turned his attention to the area east of City Hall, which by this time was also being studied by the Planning Commission. Kahn continued to explore independently the two great themes of his urban designs—the "order of movement" and the idea of the civic center. While he had lectured occasionally on his urban schemes in 1955 and 1956, he did not begin work on drawings for this new project until around May 1956.[49] Over the next year Kahn produced work of an increasingly visionary nature, and he published several of his new drawings in *Perspecta*, accompanied by a text that expressed his profound regard for the symbolism of the civic center.[50]

The majority of Kahn's drawings of the new city center, located between the two most symbolic structures, Independence Hall and City Hall, were aerial perspectives. One group depicted Philadelphia's many institutions surrounded by a wall of parking towers as seen from the south (see fig. 83). In these drawings Kahn clearly emphasized the role of parking towers in defending the city center, which he now called the "forum," from automobiles. He reiterated more boldly the analogy he had used in 1953, which equated the modern city with Carcassonne: the "architecture of stopping" had the same function as the great walls that surrounded medieval cities. Carcassonne was designed from an order of defense. Similarly, a modern city must reconfigure itself, based on a new concept of the order of movement to defend itself against destruction by the automobile.[51] Matching the historicism in his verbal descriptions, Kahn's visual language now also recalled ancient Roman monuments and medieval castles. Taken together, the parking towers formed a meandering fortification wall around the forum, and individually they resembled the Roman Coliseum. Rendered with gaps in the outer walls, the garages suggested varying states of decay.

Like the cylindrical hotel wrapped around a department store in his earlier Penn Center plans, the parking towers were designed to satisfy several functions: the lower floors and inner core contained the garage and storage facilities, while living and office spaces occupied the surrounding outer ring of upper floors (fig. 415). The roof of the garage was transformed into an open-air pedestrian plaza, in itself a miniature forum surrounded by outer walls—a microcosm of the city itself.

A second group of aerial perspectives depicted the forum's pedestrian axis along Market Street, as seen from the east looking toward City Hall (fig. 416). On a platform elevated

above the existing street (visible through a large square opening in the foreground) pedestrians strolled through a variety of spaces that were designed like a sequence of outdoor rooms framed by the walls of the surrounding buildings. Kahn described the city center as "essentially a labyrinth of pedestrian ways threading in the environment of great buildings and varied activities."[52] Only the moving sidewalk, indicated by hatched lines, described a linear movement. The old City Hall, situated in the middle of Market Street, terminated the perspective. To its right Kahn depicted five imposing new structures: his relocated City Tower (the triangular space-frame structure designed with Tyng), a cylindrical parking tower, an office tower with a flared base, the "arena" (an oval-roofed stadium), and a cubic building. Amidst these monuments the forum was filled with square tentlike pavilions, ephemeral structures that sheltered cafés, art exhibits, and other functions. With its multifarious public institutions—"cultural academic, commercial, athletic, health and civic"—the forum was Kahn's "cathedral of the city," a phrase that invoked the increasing reverence with which Kahn spoke of the city center.[53]

Viaduct Architecture

Kahn's last designs for Center City Philadelphia evolved from 1959 to 1962 and represented a further development of his earlier ideas. He now envisioned the city surrounded by an arcuated, multilevel viaduct that served and protected the center. The viaduct established a new urban pattern, pragmatically accommodating modern vehicular transportation in a multilevel structure that segregated different modes of traffic, as well as providing shaftways for the pipes normally buried under city streets. Kahn's modern transformation of the ancient aqueduct made reference to Rome, and it also expressed the symbolic beginnings of the city: water was necessary for the establishment of urban life, and the viaduct was to carry water throughout Philadelphia from a large circular reservoir-cum-traffic interchange.

One of the chief characteristics of viaduct architecture was its hierarchical division of functions. Kahn spoke publicly about this concept for the first time at the Team X meeting held in Otterlo on September 7–15, 1959, where he had been invited by Peter and Alison Smithson.[54] While he did not then refer to his "architecture of movement" as viaduct architecture, nor illustrate his talk, he was soon comparing his street-as-a-building to the aqueducts and bridges of ancient Rome. On June 28, 1960, Kahn referred to Rome in a letter to Justin Herman, executive director of the Redevelopment Agency of San Francisco: "This architecture

417. Market Street East Studies, 1960–63. Bird's-eye perspective of inner viaduct, looking north, ca. 1961–62.

of movement may be compared to the Viaduct architecture of Rome which was of a scale and consistency different from the architectures of other useful buildings."[55] From then on Kahn called his concept "viaduct architecture." Several months later he concluded a Voice of America speech with an anecdote about the symbolic importance of water and its expression in such architecture.[56] He related the story of an Indian architect (presumably B. V. Doshi) who gave a talk at the University of Pennsylvania. When asked to comment on the lecture, Kahn went to the blackboard and in the center drew what he thought would be an appropriate beginning for a town in India: aqueducts radiating from a central tower. For Kahn, the water tower and aqueducts were now seen as the beginnings of a city. His modern viaduct architecture, with its integrated service spaces for water pipes, was similarly designed to express the real presence and symbolic importance of water for urban design.

Although Kahn had talked about viaduct architecture, he had not yet made any drawings. In the winter of 1960–61 he was given two opportunities to explore the visual form of the subject. On February 27, 1961, he won a one-year study grant of $7,500 from the Graham Foundation for Advanced Studies in the Fine Arts.[57] In his letter of application he described the project: "Studies I have made for the central area of Philadelphia are statements in form applicable to any city. . . . I am anxious to make new drawings and models which would develope [sic] in detail the Viaduct Architecture and its relation to the core and its architecture."[58]

Shortly thereafter, on March 10, 1961, Kahn signed a contract with the Philadelphia City Planning Commission engaging him as an architectural consultant on the now officially adopted Market East project, a commercial center and a multidimensional transportation facility located on precisely the site of his earlier forum studies.[59] Kahn met with the Planning Commission on only three occasions, for which he was paid a total of $300.[60] At the first two evening sessions the discussion centered primarily on Market Street East. But the third and final session, which took place about a month after the conclusion of Kahn's studies for the Graham Foundation, was devoted exclusively to his viaduct architecture. The Planning Commission's plan for Market East was never mentioned, and it appears that by this time Kahn had lost interest in the real project.

In March 1962, when his grant from the Graham Foundation came to a conclusion, Kahn exhibited six of his recent designs for viaduct architecture at the foundation in

Chicago, accompanied by four studies from the 1950s illustrating his ideas on urban design.[61] Included in the exhibition was a photograph of a large plaster model of Center City Philadelphia (see fig. 114).[62] In relief, the model clearly depicted a raised viaduct encircling the city and connecting the circular and triangular interchanges that harbored other functions and acted as gateways to the center. A reservoir bordering the Delaware River was circumscribed by a large traffic roundabout. A heliport in the southeast corner was represented in the model by three circular landing pads within a triangle.[63] And the proposed parking garage at Broad and South Streets also housed a convention center. The most compelling forms in the plan— the triangular and circular interchanges—offered a dynamic counterpoint to the existing grid of the colonial city. Functionally, they permitted changes in direction without interrupting the flow of traffic, which would have been impossible with conventional right-angle intersections. The multipurpose interchanges were also the joints in the viaduct, connecting one segment of the road to another wherever it changed direction. Kahn described them as the "knuckles" of the plan.[64] Demonstrating his belief that the "joint is the beginning of ornament,"[65] the triangular and circular intersections were the viaduct's functional embellishments.

An inner viaduct framed the Market East area, then under study by the Planning Commission. Kahn's proposal for Market Street, never fully developed, was dominated by four exedra-shaped buildings sheltering public plazas strung along the north side of the street. They marked a new transportation center that was planned to house garages and commercial space. Just north of here lay Kahn's new "city place," which included a large oval stadium.[66]

One of Kahn's most spectacular perspectives depicted the porous, arcaded wall of the inner viaduct as it encircled the city's tall buildings, rendered only as faint, ghostly outlines (fig. 417). Kahn maintained that only by concentrating buildings into such a center could the city inspire powerful feelings, which could not be achieved in a decentralized city. The juxtaposition of the horizontal viaduct and the soaring towers made tangible the distinction that Kahn desired between viaduct architecture and the buildings it served. Like the aqueducts that had supplied ancient Rome with water, the architecture of movement served the needs of the modern city.

Peter S. Reed

Notes

1. Kahn, "I Love Beginnings" (lecture, International Design Conference, "The Invisible City," Aspen, Colorado, June 19, 1972), excerpted in *What Will Be Has Always Been: The Words of Louis I. Kahn*, ed. Richard Saul Wurman (New York: Access Press and Rizzoli, 1986), 151.

2. Reference is made to the first of two contracts in the Associated City Planners' proposal, March 24, 1947, "Wheelwright & Stevenson ACP," Box LIK 31, Louis I. Kahn Collection, University of Pennsylvania and Pennsylvania Historical and Museum Commission, Philadelphia (hereafter cited as Kahn Collection).

3. *Report on the Redevelopment of "The Triangle,"* Associated City Planners, January 19, 1948, 27. A copy of the report is in the Philadelphia City Planning Commission Library.

4. Contract no. 625, Philadelphia City Planning Commission, May 26, 1947, "Wheelwright & Stevenson ACP," Box LIK 31, Kahn Collection.

5. *Report on the Redevelopment of "The Triangle,"* cover letter, 1.

6. Ibid., 4.

7. Letter, Louis E. McAllister (president, Philadelphia Chapter, AIA) to Edward Hopkinson, Jr. (chairman, Philadelphia City Planning Commission), with a copy to Kahn, November 29, 1949, "PSA A.I.A. Director 1948 1949 1950," Box LIK 60, Kahn Collection.

8. Ibid.

9. Notes, AIA Triangle Committee, March 30, 1950, "AIA Triangle Committee," Box LIK 60, Kahn Collection.

10. "Summary of the Annual Report," AIA Triangle Committee, June 6, 1950, "Triangle Committee," Box LIK 61, Kahn Collection.

11. "Basic Considerations Underlying the Future Architectural Unity of Philadelphia," AIA Triangle Committee, May 1, 1950, "AIA Triangle Committee," Box LIK 60, Kahn Collection.

12. Ibid.

13. See, for example, Kahn's 1939 "Housing in the Rational City Plan"; Peter S. Reed, "Toward Form: Louis I. Kahn's Urban Designs for Philadelphia, 1939–1962" (Ph.D. diss., University of Pennsylvania, 1989), 13–35; Heinz Ronner and Sharad Jhaveri, *Louis I. Kahn: Complete Work, 1935–1974*, 2d ed. (Basel and Boston: Birkhäuser, 1987), 19, RCP.1.

14. Letter, Kahn to Triangle Committee, July 3, 1950, "Triangle Committee," Box LIK 61, Kahn Collection.

15. "The Future Architectural Unity of Philadelphia."

16. Letter, Kahn to Alfred Bendiner (president, Philadelphia Chapter, AIA), November 28, 1950, "PSA AIA—Director 1948 1949 1950," Box LIK 60, Kahn Collection.

17. The latest document on record is a letter, Krimmel to Triangle Committee, February 16, 1951, "AIA Triangle Committee," Box LIK 60, Kahn Collection.

18. Kahn, "Toward a Plan for Midtown Philadelphia," *Perspecta*, no. 2 (1953): 11–27.

19. A copy of the invitation can be found in "Louis I. Kahn (Personal) No. 4 (1951) + 1952," Box LIK 60, Kahn Collection.

20. Ibid.

21. Letter, Krimmel to Kahn, September 19, 1951, "AIA Municipal Improvements Committee," Box LIK 63, Kahn Collection.

22. Memo, Krimmel to AIA Municipal Improvements Committee, November 7, 1951, ibid.

23. Ibid.

24. Notes, AIA Municipal Improvements Committee, December 27, 1951, "AIA Municipal Improvements Committee," Box LIK 63, Kahn Collection.

25. Notes, AIA Municipal Improvements Committee, January 10, 1952, ibid.

26. Ibid.

27. Kahn, "Midtown Philadelphia," 12.

28. Ibid., 11.

29. Ibid., 17.

30. Ibid., 11.

31. Letter, Kahn to Barney, March 21, 1952, "AIA Municipal Improvements Committee," Box LIK 63, Kahn Collection.

32. Kahn's new city hall was discussed as early as December 20, 1951, at the same meeting where Kahn's movement plans were reviewed; notes, AIA Municipal Improvements Committee, December 27, 1951, ibid.

33. Letter, Kahn to Barney, March 21, 1952, ibid. See also letter, Barney to Kahn, March 20, 1952, ibid.

34. Kahn, "Midtown Philadelphia," 11.

35. William Douglas Simpson, *Castles From the Air* (London: Country Life; New York: Charles Scribner's Sons, 1949). In June 1950 Kahn received an overdue notice for this book; "Yale—Professor 1950," Box LIK 61, Kahn Collection.

36. *Philadelphia Evening Bulletin*, January 29, 1953.

37. Philadelphia City Planning Commission, *Penn Center Redevelopment Area Plan* (Philadelphia, 1952).

38. "Citizen Advisors Criticize Slab Design for Penn Center," *Architectural Forum* 99 (October 1953): 37.

39. Letter, Mayor Joseph S. Clark, Jr., to Kahn, August 21, 1953, "Citizens' Advisory Committee on the Penn Center Plan '53 '54 '55," Box LIK 65, Kahn Collection.

40. With one exception, none of Kahn's Penn Center designs is dated (Kahn Collection drawing 395.5 is dated April 13, 1954). According to the written record, he had begun making plans by February 24, 1953; letter, Krimmel to committee members, March 11, 1953, "AIA Municipal Improvements Committee," Box LIK 63, Kahn Collection. He probably ceased making Penn Center plans by June 14, 1954, the last recorded presentation of his schemes; minutes, Citizens' Council on City Planning, Penn Center Committee, June 14, 1954, Citizens' Council on City Planning Papers, Acc. 124 Box 1, Penn Center Committee, Temple University Libraries, Philadelphia.

41. Minutes, Citizens' Council on City Planning, Penn Center Committee, April 8, 1953, Citizens' Council on City Planning Papers, ibid.

42. Kahn, "Midtown Philadelphia," 22.

43. This was inscribed on a drawing in the Kahn Collection (395.14).

44. Minutes, Citizens' Advisory Committee on the Penn Center Plan, October 9, 1953, "Citizens' Advisory Committee on the Penn Center Plan '53 '54 '55," Box LIK 65, Kahn Collection.

45. Minutes, Citizens' Advisory Committee on the Penn Center Plan and the Penn Center Advisory Board of Design, September 16, 1953, ibid.

46. A pair of surviving, undated photographs match the description of his plan; Kahn Collection photographs K12/4P.1.N and K12/4P.2.N.

47. The Philadelphia City Planning Commission had targeted this area for redevelopment as early as December 1956. See Philadelphia City Planning Commission, *Pilot Plan* (Philadelphia, 1957), fig. 18.

48. Letter, Arthur C. Kaufmann (chairman) to Citizens' Advisory Committee on the Penn Center Plan, February 7, 1958, "Citizens' Advisory Committee on the Penn Center Plan 1956," Box LIK 65, Kahn Collection.

49. Letter, Kahn to Johnson E. Fairchild (director of adult education, Cooper Union), May 29, 1956, "LIK lecture 1946–56," Box LIK 64, Kahn Collection.

50. Kahn, "Order in Architecture," *Perspecta*, no. 4 (1957): 58–65.

51. Ibid., 61.

52. Letter, Kahn to E. G. Faludi (town planning consultant), February 9, 1956, "LIK—Miscellaneous 1954–56," Box LIK 65, Kahn Collection. This description recalled the City Planning Commission's contemporary "greenway" concept, which had been developed with Kahn's input and was used in the design of his Mill Creek housing project, begun in 1951.

53. Kahn, "Order in Architecture," 61.

54. Letter, Alison Smithson to Kahn, January 6, 1959, "Alison and Peter Smithson," Box LIK 58, Kahn Collection. Kahn's talk was published: Kahn, "Talk at the Conclusion of the Otterlo Congress," in *New Frontiers in Architecture: CIAM '59 in Otterlo*, ed. Oscar Newman (New York: Universe Books, 1961), 205–16.

55. Letter, Kahn to Herman, June 28, 1960, "Evaluation of the Golden Gate Redevelopment Project 1960," Box LIK 62, Kahn Collection.

56. Kahn, "Voice of America—Louis I. Kahn Recorded November 19, 1960," Box LIK 55, Kahn Collection.

57. Telegram, John Entenza (director, Graham Foundation) to Kahn, February 27, 1961, "Graham Foundation—Mr. John D. Entenza," Box LIK 68, Kahn Collection.

58. Letter, Kahn to Entenza, February 16, 1961, ibid.

59. Contract no. MP95, March 10, 1961, "Philadelphia City Planning Commission," Box LIK 83, Kahn Collection.

60. Invoice, Kahn to City Planning Commission, September 12, 1963, ibid. Copies of all three tape-recorded sessions, which took place on June 7 and August 1, 1961, and April 10, 1962, are in the Kahn Collection.

61. Undated drawing list, "Graham Foundation—Mr. John D. Entenza," Box LIK 68, Kahn Collection. Santo Lipari, a close friend of Kahn's who was also a member of the Planning Commission, recalled the assistance he and Tyng gave Kahn with the viaduct model and other sketches; Lipari, interview with Peter S. Reed, July 19, 1988. Indeed, Kahn acknowledged their help during the tape-recorded sessions with the Planning Commission; tape recordings, Kahn and Philadelphia City Planning Commission, August 1, 1961, and April 10, 1962, Kahn Collection.

62. The model was cast from the surviving negative mold and photographed in February 1962.

63. An annotated drawing (whereabouts unknown) provides a key to Kahn's model. See Ronner and Jhaveri, *Complete Work*, 36, MDM.2.

64. Lipari, interview with Reed.

65. Kahn, "Midtown Philadelphia," 23.

66. See annotated drawing in Ronner and Jhaveri, *Complete Work*, 36, MDM.2.

Louis Kahn received the commission for an addition to the Yale University Art Gallery in January 1951 while he was in residence at the American Academy in Rome. He was selected after a conference called by Charles H. Sawyer, director of Yale's division of fine arts, with George Howe, new chairman of the architecture department, and architect Eero Saarinen, who was then at work on an addition to the Yale physics laboratory. Saarinen himself turned down the commission, and Sawyer wrote to Kahn in Rome, offering him "primary responsibility for the design" and an arrangement with resident associate architect Douglas Orr, who would work with Yale on the program and on the preparation of the final working drawings.[1] For Kahn, the gallery was the first opportunity to design a building that would receive wide attention; for Yale, it was to be the first significant building in the modern style at a university known for its collegiate Gothic and Beaux-Arts architecture (fig. 418; see figs. 262–68).[2]

The Yale collections, which were the oldest of those in university art museums in the United States, had steadily grown in size, most dramatically with Katherine S. Dreier's gift in October 1941 of her Société Anonyme collection: more than 600 twentieth-century paintings and sculptures she had acquired since 1920 with Marcel Duchamp. The collection is still considered one of the best and most comprehensive collections of twentieth-century art in any university museum.[3] By December 1941 new acquisitions had already stimulated a projected extension of the gallery, designed by Philip Goodwin, the architect (with Edward Durell Stone) of the landmark 1938 Museum of Modern Art in New York. World War II precluded its realization, but in 1950 Goodwin brought forward a second version.[4]

The new structure was to occupy a site beside the 1928 gallery by Edgerton Swartwout, and would front Chapel Street on the south, the boundary with the city, and extend to the corner of York Street on the west, a strip then occupied by small shops.[5] On the north a courtyard separated this plot from Weir Hall (a classroom building), a college clubhouse, and a dormitory. Goodwin determined that the height of the addition should conform to the existing gallery, although its style was to be straightforwardly modern in contrast. The university administration, however, found Goodwin's project too costly.

Goodwin's withdrawal from the commission at the end of 1950 because of an impending eye operation opened the door to the selection of Kahn, who had been teaching in the architecture department at Yale since the fall of 1947. Kahn inherited Goodwin's design decisions regarding site and style but was not otherwise bound. In fact, he was expected to find new solutions to accommodate the requirements, for even before Goodwin's resignation Charles Sawyer, acting as Yale's client for the gallery, had expressed reservations about the design.[6] The university's new president, A. Whitney Griswold, had made educational needs the first priority, and for those in the arts at Yale, the new building was to be more than merely functional; it was to be symbolic of Yale's engagement with contemporary art and design. Its importance was far greater than the word "addition" might imply, for the old gallery would actually become its appendage.

In the first few months after Kahn's appointment in January 1951, a new program for a smaller building with specific educational uses and maximum flexibility for future change was devised by a university committee chaired by Sawyer.[7] Kahn himself remained in residence at the American Academy in Rome, but Douglas Orr, whose office was in New Haven, was represented on the committee.[8] The program was written primarily by George Howe, Kahn's friend and colleague and one of the foremost American-born modern architects.[9] As well as adding gallery space, the building was to provide classrooms, studios, and offices for the design and architecture departments. Only at some future, unspecified date was it to be given entirely to the museum. The other major requirement in the minds of the Yale authorities was that maximum useful space be provided within a budget of $1.5 million.

Because Kahn was in Rome until mid-March, he had little opportunity to contribute to the program, but from the start he recognized the importance of his opportunity. Anne Tyng, who worked on the gallery with him, has remarked, "It was his first big prestigious commission and he was very nervous about it."[10] His early perspective sketch of the Chapel Street facade demonstrates the bulk and power he envisioned, qualities more akin to the virtues of traditional architecture than to the near weightlessness of the facades the modern movement valued at the time (fig. 419). Kahn decided on a rectangular plan for a loft building linked to the old gallery, following program suggestions. Using his experience in planning economical and efficient public housing, he grouped the service area and stairway as a core in the center of the main body of the building (see fig. 59).

In early April 1951 Kahn presented the building committee with alternative means of linking old and new galleries.[11]

Yale University Art Gallery

New Haven, Connecticut, 1951–53

The first embodied a suggestion from Howe, explained by Sawyer to Kahn before his return from Rome. In this scheme, the upper floors of the new building formed a "bridge" to the old, a design that would "open Weir Hall court to the street."[12] The other proposal (Kahn's own) was to enclose the ground floor and relate the building to the site with north and west terraces that provided a transition between varying ground levels. The latter scheme was chosen. The committee's decision to follow Kahn's lead demonstrated the respect his colleagues had for his abilities. Quick approval of the preliminary design by the appropriate Yale University Corporation committee came in early June 1951, reflecting both an eagerness to move toward construction and the fact that Kahn's proposal was simple and schematic.[13] In late summer 1951 the plan was changed to accommodate an enlargement of the basement and first floor that would house the service entrance and work areas. Sawyer approved, since he thought this would be advantageous both for the anticipated mixed use of the building and for its future as a gallery.[14]

Kahn searched for an effective yet visually expressive means of spanning the loft space asked for in the program. He first thought of using a series of shallow, nonstructural vaults,[15] but he wanted to avoid a hung ceiling. He arrived at a solution when he realized the potential of applying the geometry of Buckminster Fuller's tetrahedron-octahedron system—which Anne Tyng was using in her own design for an elementary school that summer[16]—to the structure of the gallery. As he worked with the design he found that triangular hollows of the structural slab could provide a continuous space for utilities while meeting the requirements for unsupported spans.[17] A model of Kahn's concept, possibly built in September 1951, was described by structural consultant Henry A. Pfisterer as a "multiplanar truss system (space-frame) of equilateral triangles with the entire top surface filled in to provide the floor and with alternate inclined triangles in each of the three dimensions also made solid."[18]

Kahn's enthusiasm for using an innovative structural concept was readily communicated to Sawyer, Howe, and others on the building committee, although the scheme was briefly abandoned in March 1952 "to go back to the original beam and slab system" when it seemed that a shortage of steel and its cost would prohibit the earlier design.[19] When the New Haven building inspector informed Pfisterer in June that the structure did not meet city requirements, Kahn and Pfisterer worked out a modified system that would satisfy the building code.[20] Pfisterer described what was

eventually constructed as "concrete T-beams with deep inclined stems spanning 40 feet between centers of supporting girders, combined with triangular inclined bridging elements arranged to simulate the original concept" (fig. 420).[21] While thus more conventional than a space frame, it appeared to have that structure, with triangular openings that Kahn used to contain light fixtures, air-conditioning ducts, and conduits.

Orr and Kahn recommended the George B. H. Macomber Company to Yale as builders because of their proven reliability, their quality control, and a favorable cost estimate, as well as their interest in Kahn's design.[22] Steel was rationed by the government in 1952 because of the Korean conflict, but the Macomber Company had supplies on hand that could be used and later replenished by Yale's allotment. Construction proceeded almost immediately, and in June 1952 excavation began. The company developed metal formwork for the tetrahedrons and cast a sample slab for strength tests conducted that August. Interest was keen; a *Progressive Architecture* editor learned of the tests and asked to witness them.[23]

Although exposed architectural concrete had long been the favorite material of European modernists, its use for other than utilitarian buildings had been limited in the United States. The Macomber Company was one of the few builders to have perfected the casting techniques that Kahn considered essential to the building's appearance. A letter from Kahn and Orr to possible contractors emphasized the careful treatment of concrete, specifying the formwork to be used ("narrow vertical boarding rather than plyform") and cautioning that much care in execution would be necessary. "The manner of pouring each floor with particular reference to the exposed concrete will be a matter of extreme interest and will require the utmost cooperation from the contractor to produce 'Architectural' concrete."[24] The Macomber firm had the expertise to do the work, and also conscientiously fulfilled its contractual obligations in managing and budgeting the project. The president of the company believed Kahn's "forward-looking and experimental theories" were nonetheless "practical" and "as economical as standard construction."[25]

Work on the gallery continued through late September 1953, when, some fifteen months after the preparatory foundation work, the classrooms and workshops were occupied by students and faculty for the new academic year.[26] The dedication ceremony and formal opening of the Art Gallery and Design Center took place on November 6, 1953.[27]

418. Entrance, 1953.

418

In its simplicity and lack of ornamentation, its open-plan design, its use of window walls on the north and west facades and at the indented entrance, and its emphasis on contemporary materials, the new building was a clear representation of mid-century modernism. The plane of gray-brown brick facing Chapel Street, broken only by stone drip moldings that marked floor levels and a glass slit at the joint with the old gallery, contrasted with the original structure's richly carved facade. The building exterior carefully introduced the new style into the university and the city. Inside, where the same approach held, Kahn's contribution was most vivid: strong sculptural elements—the tetrahedronal ceiling and the cylinder of the stairwell, all in unadorned concrete that showed the imprint of forms—defined the character of the gallery. Open loft interiors offered flexibility to the early occupants, and in the exhibition areas, where the ceiling defined the space, paintings were hung on movable panels on legs with springs ("pogo panels," suggested by George Howe).

In the summer of 1954, following the gallery's first year of use, Kahn undertook his final work on the building: alterations to the York Street security gate, a second-floor door onto that terrace that resembled the first-floor door to the sculpture court, and handrails for the stairs at the public entrance. At the request of the gallery director, he also proposed a scheme to complete the sculpture court.[28] Remodeling in the late 1950s and early 1960s—which included covering the concrete-block walls and columns and fixing partitions to make separate galleries with more wall space—was done without consulting Kahn, a fact that he bitterly resented. There were few structural changes, however, and in 1988 restoration of the gallery was begun by revealing the circular stairwell, which had been hidden. The intention is eventually to return the museum more completely to its 1953 appearance.

The building has long been recognized for its special qualities as an art gallery, for its contribution to architecture at Yale University, and for its role in establishing Kahn's international reputation. Among the tributes paid to the gallery was the 1979 presentation by the American Institute of Architects of its annual twenty-five-year building award for "enduring significance."[29]

Patricia Cummings Loud

419. *Perspective, March–April 1951.*
420. *Details of ceiling plan. Inscribed April 18, 1952.*

Notes
1. Letter, Sawyer to A. Whitney Griswold (president, Yale University), January 8, 1951, File 247, Box 27, Griswold (YRG Z-A-16), Presidential Records, Yale University Archives; letter, Sawyer to Kahn, January 8, 1951, "Correspondence with Yale University. Yale Art Gallery," Box LIK 107, Louis I. Kahn Collection, University of Pennsylvania and Pennsylvania Historical and Museum Commission, Philadelphia (hereafter cited as Kahn Collection). Kahn's answer is not preserved in the Kahn Collection, but Sawyer's response to it is; letter, Sawyer to Kahn, February 14, 1951, ibid. On the Yale University Art Gallery, see Patricia Cummings Loud, *The Art Museums of Louis I. Kahn* (Durham, N.C., and London: Duke University Press, 1989), 52–98.
2. Loud, *The Art Museums*, 54–55, 89.
3. Alan Shestack, Foreword to *The Société Anonyme and the Dreier Bequest at Yale University: A Catalogue Raisonné*, ed. Robert L. Herbert, Eleanor S. Apter, and Elise K. Kenny (New Haven and London: Yale University Press, 1984), vii.
4. On the Goodwin designs, see "The Art Gallery Extension," *Bulletin of the Associates in Fine Arts at Yale University* 10 (December 1941): 1–3; and "Yale University Gallery to Add to Its Building," *Museum News* 28 (May 1, 1950): 1.
5. These shops were described in a program addendum as "the slums," and building "up to York Street [was] to get rid" of them; "Design Laboratories and Exhibition Space for Yale University," with accompanying letter, Dillingham Palmer (Douglas Orr's office) to Kahn, April 2, 1951, "Correspondence with Douglas Orr, 1951–52," Box LIK 107, Kahn Collection.
6. Kahn credited Goodwin for the commitment to modernism; George A. Sanderson, "Extension: University Art Gallery and Design Center," *Progressive Architecture* 35 (May 1954): 90. Sawyer wrote, however, that he knew Kahn had "not been particularly in sympathy with the existing plans" and that he and others believed that Kahn would find a fresh approach; letter, Sawyer to Kahn, January 8, 1951, "Correspondence with Yale University. Yale Art Gallery," Box LIK 107, Kahn Collection.
7. Sawyer first convened the building committee (John M. Phillips, director of the gallery; Lamont Moore, assistant director; professor Sumner McKnight Crosby; and architect George Howe) on January 6, 1951; "Art Gallery Wing," January 6, 1951, "Correspondence with Yale University. Yale Art Gallery," Box LIK 107, Kahn Collection.
8. Dillingham Palmer was assigned to the building committee and was project architect for Orr thereafter.
9. See Loud, *The Art Museums*, 59–63.
10. Tyng, interview with Alessandra Latour, in *Louis I. Kahn: L'uomo, il maestro*, ed. Latour (Rome: Edizioni Kappa, 1986), 49; see also Tyng, "Louis I. Kahn's 'Order' in the Creative Process," ibid., 285.
11. For illustrations, see Loud, *The Art Museums*, 65, fig. 2.16, and 67, fig. 2.18.
12. Letter, Sawyer to Kahn, February 14, 1951, "Correspondence with Yale University. Yale Art Gallery," Box LIK 107, Kahn Collection.
13. Sawyer asked for designs of the gallery and physics additions for him to present, along with programs, to the Corporation Committee on Architectural Plans; letter, Sawyer to Orr, May 3, 1951, with copies to Kahn and Saarinen, "Correspondence with Yale University. Yale Art Gallery," Box LIK 107, Kahn Collection. After approval by the committee in their meeting on June 8, the architectural contract was drawn up, and an agreement between Orr and Kahn, required by Yale, was executed on June 22, 1951; "Yale Art Gallery," Box LIK 84, Kahn Collection.
14. Letter, Sawyer to Palmer, August 27, 1951, "Correspondence with Yale University. Yale Art Gallery," Box LIK 107, Kahn Collection.
15. See Loud, *The Art Museums*, 67, fig. 2.18.

16. Tyng, "Kahn's 'Order,'" 285. For a model of a wing of the school and a house for Tyng's parents using tetrahedron-octahedron geometry and begun in 1952, see Loud, *The Art Museums*, 69, figs. 2.22 and 2.23.

17. In Philadelphia Kahn talked with an engineer he respected, Major William H. Gavell, who encouraged him in developing the scheme; Nick Gianopulos, interview with Richard Saul Wurman, in *What Will Be Has Always Been: The Words of Louis I. Kahn*, ed. Wurman (New York: Access Press and Rizzoli, 1986), 274. Kahn later told Peter Plagens that he had consulted a friend who had built concrete boats during the Second World War; Plagens, "Louis Kahn's New Museum in Fort Worth," *Artforum* 6 (February 1968): 20.

18. "Design Laboratory—Yale University, Description of Structural System, February 1954," "Correspondence with Yale University. Yale Art Gallery," Box LIK 107, Kahn Collection. A model was supplied to Kahn by Panoramic Studios, Philadelphia; invoice, September 25, 1951, "Yale Art Gallery," Box LIK 107, Kahn Collection.

19. Memorandum of meeting, March 11, 1952, "Correspondence with Yale University. Yale Art Gallery," Box LIK 107, Kahn Collection. Within a month Sawyer described why he thought the "revised ceiling construction was worth the additional cost and the structural complications"; letter, Sawyer to Kahn, April 17, 1952, ibid.

20. Letter, Henry G. Falsey (New Haven building inspector) to Pfisterer, June 18, 1952, "Correspondence with Douglas Orr, 1951–52," Box LIK 107, Kahn Collection.

21. Pfisterer called the early scheme "fireproofed metal rather than reinforced concrete"; Pfisterer, memorandum on floor system, April 8, 1952, "Correspondence with Yale University. Yale Art Gallery," Box LIK 107, Kahn Collection. He explained modifications in "Design Laboratory—Yale University, Description of Structural System, February 1954," ibid.

22. Letter, Orr and Kahn to Sawyer, May 8, 1952, "Correspondence with Douglas Orr, 1951–52," Box LIK 107, Kahn Collection. Estimates for construction were based on drawings dated August 14 and revised September 21, 1951, and April 18, 1952; letter, Palmer to Charles Solomon (Macomber Company), April 25, 1952, ibid. Anne Tyng recalls the interest of the contractor in the concept and the steel he had ready as being of great importance; Tyng, conversation with Patricia Cummings Loud, October 2, 1984.

23. Letter, Pfisterer to Thompson and Lichtner Company, Inc., attention: Miles Claire, July 1, 1952, "Correspondence with Douglas Orr, 1951–52," Box LIK 107, Kahn Collection. Burton Holmes, technical editor of *Progressive Architecture*, asked about the August 28 tests and for permission to publish; letters, Holmes to Orr, August 7, 1952, and Orr to Holmes, August 12, 1952, ibid.

24. Letter for bids, Orr and Kahn to possible contractors, March 21, 1952, ibid.

25. Letter, C. Clark Macomber to the editor, "P/A Views," *Progressive Architecture* 35 (May 1954): 22, 24.

26. The contractor completed a "punch list" on October 5, 1953; letter, Macomber to Orr's office, attention: Palmer, October 7, 1953, "Correspondence with Douglas Orr, 1952–53," Box LIK 107, Kahn Collection. Sawyer forwarded the bill for architectural services dated October 14, 1953, to the comptroller; letter, Sawyer to Orr, October 22, 1953, ibid.

27. Sawyer first anticipated opening on October 9, 1953; letter, Sawyer to Sanderson, August 21, 1953, "Correspondence with Yale University. Yale Art Gallery," Box LIK 107, Kahn Collection. Preparations for the gallery opening are illustrated in "A New Building for the Arts," *Yale Alumni Magazine* 18 (December 1953): 8–13. For critical receptions, see "P/A Views," *Progressive Architecture* 35 (May 1954): 15–16, 22, 24; Sanderson, "Extension," 88–101, 130–31; Maude K. Riley, "Yale: A Tent in Concrete," *Art Digest* 28 (March 1, 1954): 13, 25; Boris Pushkarev, "Order and Form: Yale Art Gallery and Design Center Designed by Louis I. Kahn," *Perspecta*, no. 3 (1955): 47–56; and Vincent J. Scully, "Le Musée des beaux-arts de l'Université Yale, New Haven," *Museum* (UNESCO) 9 (1956): 101–13.

28. Letters, Sawyer to Kahn, June 30 and August 6, 1954; Kahn to Sawyer, August 23, 1954; and Sawyer to Kahn, September 3, 1954; "Correspondence with Yale University. Yale Art Gallery," Box LIK 107, Kahn Collection.

29. "Kahn's Gallery at Yale Wins 25-Year Award," *AIA Journal* 68 (May 1979): 11. For evaluations, see Loud, *The Art Museums*, 79–92.

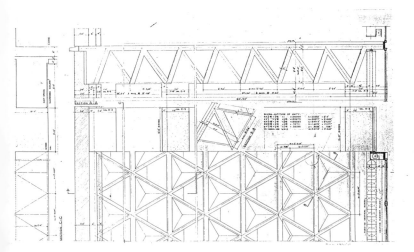

Early in 1955 Louis Kahn was commissioned to design a new Trenton Jewish Community Center planned for Ewing Township, New Jersey.[1] Founded in 1910, the Trenton Jewish Community Center had been known first as the Young Men's Hebrew Association (YMHA), part of a nationwide organization originally established to provide educational services, including "Americanization" classes, for the largely immigrant Jewish population of America's cities.[2] A traditional urban institution, the YMHA had evolved with its membership. As the newcomer population became more adapted to this country, the YMHA usually expanded its role as an athletic, cultural, and social hub for the Jewish populace. The YMHA often became the secular heart of the Jewish community. The Trenton YMHA, for example, had no sanctuary and no connection to a synagogue.

The expansion and relocation of the Trenton YMHA had been contemplated since the 1940s, although the suburban Ewing site, comprising 10.58 owned acres and 37 leased acres, was not acquired until 1954.[3] Removal of the YMHA from the urban center and from a building it had occupied since 1917 reflected demographic changes in an America that had embraced suburban life after World War II. It also heralded the emergence in the 1950s of the multipurpose, campus-oriented community building as an innovative, peculiarly American building type. As early as 1949, the Trenton YMHA had changed its name to the Trenton Jewish Community Center in order to signify its intended role as a nucleus for increasingly diversified Jewish lives.[4]

Kahn probably began work on the community center commission as soon as he was awarded the project.[5] The main community building would have been Kahn's first major work not attached to a preexisting structure. Unfortunately, only two small subsidiary components of the complex were ever built: the building now known as the Trenton Bathhouse (fig. 421), which is actually the locker and shower facility for the outdoor pool, and the nearby day camp (see fig. 94). In spite of the frustration connected with a largely unrealized scheme, Kahn's continuing fascination with the project exceeded any architect's paternalistic view of his first major work. Several times he discussed his work for the Ewing site as a personal triumph; he felt strongly that his designs, particularly for the bathhouse, were a major turning point that influenced his approach to all future work.[6]

Between 1955 and 1958 Kahn produced four major design schemes. During the first phase, from February through October 1955, he provided rudimentary designs for the main community building and concentrated on plans for the bathhouse. The extreme summer heat of 1955, with the hottest July on record, may explain why the bathhouse and pool were put into use on July 31, before the bathhouse roof had been completed.[7] After October 1955, Kahn focused his attention on the main community building. This second phase, which lasted through March 1956, saw the development of several plans composed of octagons and squares. The third phase, marked by publication of a startlingly new plan in early 1957, lasted through the fall. During that period Kahn resolved design problems inherent in the earlier work and provided his most detailed drawings and personal assessment of the project. The program was also expanded that year to include a children's day camp, which was designed and executed within a few months. The final phase, which began in December 1957 and continued through the last extant correspondence in 1960, witnessed budgetary and programmatic changes that had significant aesthetic ramifications. The resulting work of 1958 lacked verve, and although Kahn's letters indicate that he made changes in the design after 1958, no drawings survive to suggest how the plans had been altered by the time the project was abandoned.[8] During this phase there was increased hostility between Kahn and the construction committee, and the correspondence between opposing parties was often channeled through lawyers.

Three drafted drawings, all dated February 7, 1955, are the first evidence of Kahn's involvement with the Trenton Jewish Community Center. These drawings, a plot plan (fig. 422) as well as separate investigations of the community building (fig. 423) and of the bathhouse (fig. 424), indicate that Kahn thought of this project, even at its inception, as a unified, interdependent whole. At all times attention was paid to property lines so that buildings would be constructed only on land owned, not leased, by the community center. The February plans also show that the bathhouse was first proposed as a shallow rectangle open to the sky, with a central roofed checkroom dividing the men's half from the women's half. Subsequent drawings show that by April 14, 1955, the bathhouse had evolved into its final centralized plan of four equal square pavilions grouped around a central, unroofed atrium (fig. 425). Each corner of the pavilions is anchored by a hollow functional column. Kahn had previously pushed the financially pressed construction committee toward accepting his revised concept at the same time that he appeared to give them a choice between the linear and central schemes. On February 15, 1955, he had shown them a comparison between the linear plan, which

Jewish Community Center

Ewing Township (near Trenton), New Jersey, 1954–59

421. Bathhouse, ca. 1959.
422. Site plan. Inscribed February 7, 1955.
423. Plan of community center building. Inscribed February 7, 1955.
424. Plan of bathhouse and swimming pools. Inscribed February 7, 1955.
425. Roof plan of bathhouse. Published in Perspecta in 1957.

allowed for future expansion, and the central plan, which could be executed for less money, calling the comparative drawing the "outdoor pool $ plot plans."[9]

These first dated drawings show that early schemes for the community building were based on an organizing principle of functionally distinct rectangular wings emerging from a long central circulation core. Kahn envisioned the community building with different geometric roof shapes, usually variations on pyramids within squares over the largest spaces, and with a number of small interior courtyards opening up the enclosed spaces. Neither element was ever eliminated from subsequent proposals. The drawings also evidenced confusion about the program, indicating that the construction committee may have been unclear about the exact needs of a suburban community center or unsure of the projected financing. At this stage, for instance, an auditorium was shown as an important feature; but while in the plot plan it appeared as a future addition, in the floor plan it appeared as an integral part of the design.[10] Subsequent plans suggest further confusion.

A note Kahn wrote on a drawing in March 1955 to H. Harvey Saaz, chairman of the construction committee, indicates a warm working relationship and hints at the dynamics that may have brought Kahn to the Trenton project. Saaz, a Trenton lawyer and a graduate of Yale Law School, seems to have been the person who initially suggested Kahn for this commission.[11] He might have seen the *Yale Alumni Magazine* (December 1953) whose cover story detailed Kahn's completion of the Yale Art Gallery.[12] The magazine could have familiarized Saaz with Kahn, whose Philadelphia office was less than thirty-five miles from Ewing. Saaz's role became even more critical after Kahn was selected to design the community center: he was the one person on the construction committee who trusted Kahn's ideas and who tried to persuade his colleagues to accept them.[13] As the major interpreter of Kahn's vision, Saaz continually tried to convince the committee of Kahn's skill and subtlety.

The contract that Kahn signed in May 1955 to design the main community building did not mention the bathhouse, which had gone out for bids at the end of April and was soon to begin construction.[14] Yet it was the bathhouse, with its elemental geometric shapes, clearly defined functions, and fully developed notions of "servant" and "served" spaces, that influenced the first detailed plans for the community building. This is seen in a plan dated November 3 (see fig. 77), a modular, additive scheme, which inaugurated the project's second design phase. Its series of skewed

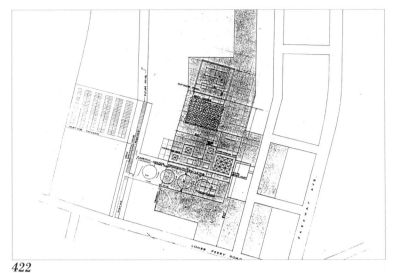

422

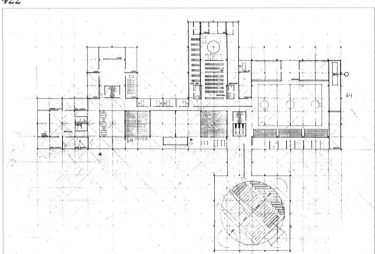

423

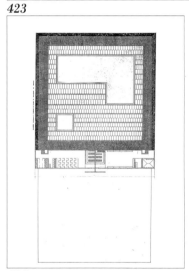

424

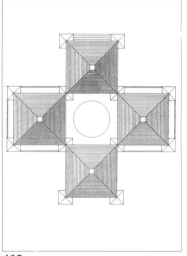

425

421

squares with hollow squares at each corner reproduced and multiplied the key structural element of the bathhouse design, while shifting to an oblique arrangement of the parts. Penned-in insertions of small hollow squares that resemble Greek crosses near the building entrance further the tie to the bathhouse. The second-phase plan was not functionally useful because the proliferation of service squares worked against any rational circulation pattern, but Kahn was more successful in the integration of circulation and structure in several schemes that followed in March 1956. In these, octagons and squares were typically opened up along diagonal axes to provide clear movement to most areas of the building (fig. 426). Small servant squares were employed as bathrooms, storage rooms, and passageways between the larger served areas. Noticeably absent from any of these plans was the indication of an auditorium.[15]

By March 19, 1956, plans indicate that the community building was removed from a position parallel to the major access highway and placed perpendicular to that road. In most previous plans the community building shielded the bathhouse from the street; in the new arrangement, which was to remain basically unchanged, the community building and bathhouse were placed close together, separated only by a paved dining area. The two structures were now simultaneously visible from the main street, with the bathhouse located at the end of a broad axis that would have directed traffic into the complex. Kahn later talked about the generative power of the bathhouse design on his subsequent work, but here he showed by the more dominant siting of the bathhouse that he may have already been aware of its creative potential.[16]

The Jewish Community Center board of trustees and the construction committee held a luncheon December 27, 1956, to "review final plans" with Kahn and to offer suggestions to him.[17] It is unclear what the "final" 1956 plan consisted of, but it was evidently evolving toward the plans and model published by *Architectural Review* in May 1957 (fig. 427; see fig. 86). Those plans showed a long, low rectangular structure that, on first glance, appears far less complex than earlier arrangements of squares or octagons joined in an additive manner. In fact, this plan, based on a building module of a twenty-two-square-foot bay separated by hollow columns eleven feet square, was extremely intricate.[18] Hollow columns were either reserved for corridors, thereby establishing a good circulation pattern, or were used for bathrooms. In both cases the hollow column provided a viable servant space. In contrast to the equality of served spaces expressed internally and externally at the bathhouse,

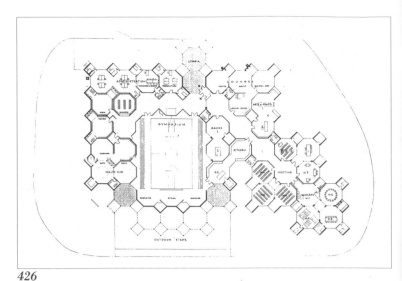

426

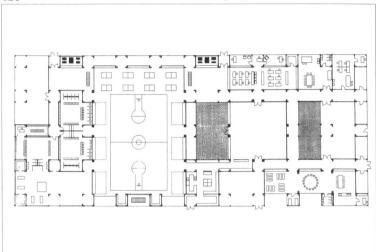

427

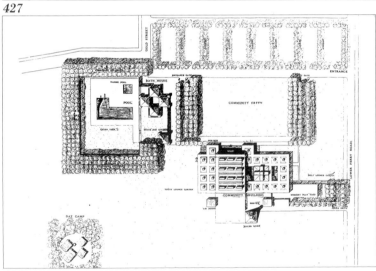

428

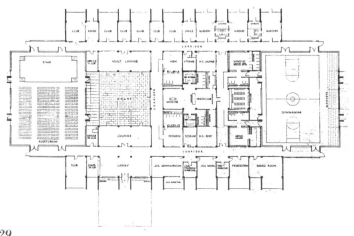

429

the 1957 proposal revealed internal and external spatial hierarchies among the served areas: a high twelve-bay gym roof towered over the entire structure; a lower, intermediate-height four-bay social hall roof defined the second-largest internal space; the remainder of the building's space was expressed by a series of one-story-high pavilions connected by narrower servant spaces with flat roofs. At the same time the roof plan further revealed the bathhouse influence: each served area was topped by a pyramid with an oculus, and each pyramid was anchored at its corners by a hollow column.

Later alterations included two projecting entrance porticoes added for the two lobbies and a variant oculus for the roof of the gymnasium, as presented in drawings published four months later by *Architectural Forum*.[19] The altered version and its accompanying site plan were also published by the Jewish Community Center in its elaborate fund-raising brochure, which proclaimed that the "new Center will be our new spirit, dedicated, united and secure" (fig. 428).[20] Kahn noted pragmatically that the unity of the plan was divided between an active gym area and a quieter social hall area. The result was a symmetrical division of the whole into two spatially distinct entities that could be seen as independent structures unified by both a single roof and an underlying modular system.[21]

The publication of the two plans in *Architectural Review* and *Architectural Forum*, as well as the appearance of the bathhouse in the 1957 *Perspecta*, contributed to the high visibility of this project within the architectural world.[22] It may be telling, however, that when *Casabella* published an extensive article on Kahn in 1963, the Jewish Community Center was represented by the plan first published in *Architectural Review*.[23] For Kahn, who most likely supplied the photographs, the earlier published 1957 plan may have come closest to fulfilling his hopes for this project because it so clearly and simply expressed the integration of space and structure.

The 1957 site plans also reveal the presence of the day camp.[24] Its plan was drafted in 1957 and Kahn submitted his bill in August, thereby indicating that the design was complete.[25] The structures, two of them rectangular and two square, all have flat roofs. The roofs of the rectangular buildings are supported by square columns placed along the perimeter of the roof; the square buildings, which were intended for offices and bathrooms, are largely enclosed by brick walls. The arrangement of the four buildings on the site appears to have been random, perhaps to convey a sense

of disorder intended to invite children's creative play. The drafted circle Kahn placed around the day camp plan recalls his earlier interest in using geometries to contain disparate parts, like the circle he placed around the pool and bathhouse in a grading scheme proposed in October 1955.

Kahn reworked the drawings for the community building in late 1957 and early 1958. His bill for the period November 1957 to March 28, 1958, described the work as preliminary planning for yet another new scheme.[26] Drawings dated late spring and summer 1958 indicate the beginning of this fourth phase, in which a more elaborate program was contained in an increasingly prosaic structure. The auditorium, now an enormous independent space, was located on one side of the main building, while a gymnasium was symmetrically positioned on the other side (fig. 429). The vitality of the exterior had been compromised with a monotonous line of linked pavilions uniting the auditorium and gymnasium wings (fig. 430). Two intimate interior courts, a hallmark of previous proposals, were now united into a single large one. Most significantly, there was no longer a clear delineation between servant and served areas. Although certain hollow areas that had previously worked as servant spaces continued to exist as coatrooms or closets, others became scaled-down served spaces in the form of very small clubrooms and tiny administrative offices. The concept of servant and served space was jettisoned in favor of simplified juxtapositions: high, compact auditorium and gymnasium versus low, sprawling pavilions; small enclosed areas versus one large, open internal space.

This plan should be considered in the context of Harvey Saaz's death on June 25, 1958, following a debilitating illness of more than six months.[27] His illness had forced him to withdraw from public life after November 1957, leaving the construction committee without a strong voice committed to Kahn's aesthetic. Perhaps sensing this directional void, the construction committee consulted an architectural representative of the New Jersey Federation of YMHAs. Their meetings, on December 19 and 26, 1957, produced several memos about classroom and lounge sizes and general layouts, and suggested solutions arrived at by other community centers, including the notions that the main building should have only one lobby and that the optimum size for a clubroom was fourteen by twenty feet.[28] Construction committee minutes show that the purpose of these meetings was to aid in "incorporating some of the recent thinking [about a Jewish Community Center] into Mr. Kahn's present design,"[29] thereby making it apparent that Kahn was being asked at this late date to synthesize into

426. Plan of community center building. Inscribed March 19, 1956.
427. Plan of community center building, before May 1957.
428. Site plan. Inscribed 7/1/57 8/13/57.
429. Plan of community center building. Inscribed 11 August 1958.

his plans formulas that had been used in community centers nationwide. It seems clear, however, that the Trenton construction committee was unaware that they had inadvertently subjugated the art of architecture to the pragmatism of construction and space planning.

Although bids were let for the 1958 plans in August, Kahn had already been placed in a difficult situation.[30] In June the construction committee told him that if the bids did not come within the $500,000 budget, he would have to redraw the plans to meet fiscal restraints. To complicate things, Kahn was also told that he could not cut the building below its presently proposed 40,760 square feet, presumably in order to satisfy all programmatic needs.[31] The August bids exceeded $811,000, and on December 12, 1958, Kahn reported to Arthur Teich, the new chairman of the construction committee, that he had already succeeded in redrawing the building while maintaining the same "area and function and character" of the more expensive plan. Kahn estimated the newer version at $666,698.[32]

No record survives showing the committee's response. In early 1959, however, Kahn advised two previous bidders on the project that there were administrative problems at the community center and that the cost was still too great for them to cover.[33] As late as September 1959, Kahn wrote to another contractor saying that he had not yet received directions from the construction committee to proceed.[34] While it does not appear that Kahn was actually dismissed, it must have become increasingly clear to client and architect that financial and philosophical differences could never be resolved. By early 1960 the construction committee had hired the local architectural firm of Kelly & Gruzen to design the main building, and in 1961 ground was broken for that structure in the same part of the site and in the same position that Kahn had designated for it.[35]

Susan G. Solomon

Notes

1. For a discussion of Kahn's designs for the Trenton Jewish Community Center (JCC), see Heinz Ronner and Sharad Jhaveri, *Louis I. Kahn: Complete Work, 1935–1974*, 2d ed. (Basel and Boston: Birkhäuser, 1987), 82–91; Ian McCallum, ed., "Genetrix: Personal Contributions to American Architecture," *Architectural Review* 121 (May 1957): 344–45; Walter McQuade, "Architect Louis Kahn and His Strong-boned Structures," *Architectural Forum* 107 (October 1957): 134–43; Vincent J. Scully, *Louis I. Kahn* (New York: George Braziller, 1962), 24–26; and Susan G. Solomon, "Beginnings," *Progressive Architecture* 65 (December 1984): 68–73.

2. For a discussion of the origins and development of the YMHA-JCC, see James Yaffee, *The American Jews* (New York: Random House, 1968), 207–10; and Stanley Feldstein, *The Land That I Show You: Three Centuries of Jewish Life in America* (Garden City: Anchor Press/ Doubleday, 1978), 63, 241. A brief history of the Trenton YMHA-JCC, compiled by the history committee of the JCC (Evelyn Edelman, chair), is found in the anniversary booklet *75 and Alive*, published by the Jewish Community Centers of the Delaware Valley, 1985. Information on early Trenton YMHA programs is also found in the unpublished *Report of the Program Committee, New Jewish Community Center*, August 31, 1950. One copy is on file at the JCC.

3. Information on the size of the owned land is found at the Ewing Township Office of the Tax Assessor. Reference to the total size of the plot is contained in a letter, H. Harvey Saaz (chairman, JCC construction committee) to Commissioner McLean (New Jersey Department of Conservation and Economic Development), June 30, 1954, JCC Files.

4. Undated memo, JCC Files.

5. The lack of correspondence prior to Kahn's first studies supports the possibility that his work commenced soon after receiving the commission. It also seems likely that Kahn proceeded with plans before any formal contract had been negotiated.

6. For Kahn's own remarks on the importance of the Trenton complex to his work, see his statements in John W. Cook and Heinrich Klotz, eds., *Conversations With Architects* (London: Lund Humphries, 1973), 178–217; Patricia McLaughlin, "'How'm I Doing, Corbusier?' An Interview With Louis Kahn," *Pennsylvania Gazette* 71 (December 1972): 18–26; Kahn, "Order in Architecture," *Perspecta*, no. 4 (1957): 58–65; and Kahn, Introduction to 2d ed. of *The Notebooks and Drawings of Louis I. Kahn*, ed. Richard Saul Wurman and Eugene Feldman (Cambridge, Mass., and London: MIT Press, 1973).

7. The *Trenton Evening News*, August 1, 1955, 1, reported that July was the hottest on record. The *Trenton Evening Times*, July 29, 1955, 5, reported that the JCC pool would open on July 31, a Sunday. Two things point to the roof being completed in the fall of 1955: a photograph of the bathhouse at the time of its opening (JCC Files) shows no roof; and Kahn sent a fee to Hirsch & Dube, the local, associated architects, in the fall, following the completion of the roof by William Ehret; letter, Kahn to Hirsch & Dube, October 14, 1955, "JCC," Box LIK 35, Louis I. Kahn Collection, University of Pennsylvania and Pennsylvania Historical and Museum Commission, Philadelphia (hereafter cited as Kahn Collection).

8. Letter, Kahn to Alexander Stein (executive director, JCC), August 21, 1959, "JCC," Box LIK 9, Kahn Collection.

9. Office drawing, February 14, 1955, and unsigned, undated job meeting memo, "JCC," Box LIK 108, Kahn Collection.

10. This is a curious inconsistency, since the 1950 *Report of the Program Committee* had urged the erection of an auditorium large enough for 1,000 people.

11. George Warren, interview with Susan G. Solomon, December 5, 1983. Warren was an active member of the construction committee

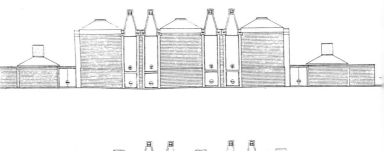

throughout most of its existence and was president of the JCC board of trustees, 1951–53. Similar views were expressed by Evelyn Edelman in an interview with Solomon, July 8, 1984. Edelman was active in JCC affairs throughout the period and her husband had also been an active participant in the construction process.

12. "A New Building for the Arts," *Yale Alumni Magazine* 18 (December 1953): 8–13.

13. Warren and Edelman, interviews with Solomon.

14. Building specifications for bathhouse, April 28, 1955, "JCC," Box LIK 108, Kahn Collection; contract for community building, May 1955, "JCC," Box LIK 35, Kahn Collection.

15. Typed sheets of comparative costs between August 11, 1955, and January 3, 1956, "JCC," Box LIK 35, Kahn Collection. The second sheet compares August 1954 to January 1955, but this date was most likely incorrect due to confusion after the new year; the second sheet did not duplicate information from the top sheet. The January 1956 memo called for 31,660 square feet, whereas the November 3 plan had been calculated at 34,600 square feet.

16. "The hollow columns which I invented for it [the bathhouse] which were containers, became the servant areas and all other spaces became open, served by these hollow columns. From this came a generative force which is recognizable in every building which I've done since"; Kahn, quoted in conversation with Peter Blake, July 20, 1971, in *What Will Be Has Always Been: The Words of Louis I. Kahn*, ed. Richard Saul Wurman (New York: Access Press and Rizzoli, 1986), 130.

17. Postcard, JCC construction committee members to other members and board of trustees, December 21, 1956, "JCC," Box LIK 35, Kahn Collection.

18. McCallum, "Genetrix," 344–45.

19. McQuade, "Strong-boned," 142.

20. "This Is Our. . . Trenton Jewish Community Center" (JCC, 1957), n.p. The back cover carried the message "From nursery to golden age." A sepia reproduction is in the JCC Files.

21. Memorandum, Kahn to construction committee, "Description of the Spaces and Functions of the Community Building," May 21, 1957, "JCC," Box LIK 108, Kahn Collection. Inexplicably, the square footage jumped to 42,870 at this time, even though an auditorium continued to remain absent from the program.

22. Kahn, "Order in Architecture," 58–60.

23. Francesco Tentori, "Il passato come un amico," *Casabella*, no. 275 (May 1963): 29.

24. Here, too, there seems to have been confusion between what the *Report of the Program Committee* had recommended in 1950 and what was developed within the architectural program. The report recommended that the day camp be separate from the community building unless a site chosen for the new complex would have substantial acreage (pp. 5–18). In August 1954, after the Ewing site was acquired, a *Supplementary Report of the JCC Program Committee* recommended a day camp in Ewing for children under seven years of age, and maintenance of the present camp seventeen miles away for older children (p. 5). It is unclear why a day camp did not enter the architectural program prior to 1957.

25. Bill, Kahn to JCC, attention: Harvey Saaz, August 2, 1957, "JCC," Box LIK 35, Kahn Collection.

26. Bill (covering work since November 1, 1957), Kahn to JCC, March 28, 1958, "JCC," Box LIK 9, Kahn Collection.

27. Obituary, *Trenton Evening News*, June 26, 1958; Dorothy (Mrs. H. Harvey) Saaz, interview with Susan G. Solomon, December 19, 1989.

28. Minutes of meetings, December 19 and 26, 1957, JCC Files. Sigmund Taft (field secretary, New Jersey Federation of YMHAs) wrote to

Alexander Stein to recapitulate suggestions expressed to the construction committee, including a small "junior high" size gym and two large meeting rooms to hold 100 and 150 people; letter, January 6, 1958, JCC files.

29. Minutes of meeting, JCC construction committee and representatives of New Jersey Federation of YMHAs and YWHAs, December 19, 1957, JCC files. Ironically, the construction committee used this meeting to set a tentative ground-breaking date of May 1, 1958.

30. Letter, Robert Watkins (treasurer, JCC) to Kahn, with a copy to David Zoob (Kahn's attorney), August 4, 1958, "JCC," Box LIK 9, Kahn Collection. Enclosed was a check for Kahn's fees following the letting of bids.

31. Letter, Arthur Teich to Zoob, with a copy to Kahn, June 27, 1958, ibid. This was in effect an amended contract.

32. Letter, John MacAllister (for Kahn) to Teich, December 12, 1958, ibid.

33. Letters, Kahn to W. Anderson Co., February 3, 1959, and Kahn to Trenton Engineering, March 16, 1959, ibid.

34. Letter, Kahn to William Ehret, September 3, 1959, ibid.

35. Invitations to annual meetings of the JCC for June 21, 1957, and June 6, 1960, and studies for the erected community building, JCC Files.

430. Elevations of community center building (details of sheet). Inscribed 11 August 1958.

In early 1956 the University of Pennsylvania School of Medicine began work on "establishing the requirements for a new facility" for research and teaching.[1] Four years later the Alfred Newton Richards Medical Research Building was formally dedicated (fig. 431; see figs. 269–77). In the intervening years the building's design went through three major stages, in which control of the project was exercised by the medical school, then by Louis Kahn, and finally by the university's trustees. Each made important contributions to the final appearance of the building.

The Richards Building began as a relatively modest project in a decade that saw widespread expansion in medical schools. Enrollments and staff had grown rapidly in medical schools in the years following World War II; at the same time, the social status of a career in medicine was high, many promising young scientists were coming of age, and funding for medical research and construction flowed freely. By the early 1950s space problems at the University of Pennsylvania were extreme.[2] The medical school leadership believed that current problems could be solved and the school's future secured by an ambitious program of expansion; by 1957 nearly $10 million had been earmarked for new facilities for surgery, medicine, radiology, and scientific research.[3] The medical research building was only one of these building projects in the late 1950s, and it was given low priority: it was seen as a mundane, multipurpose building that had neither a powerful departmental patron nor the symbolic power that would be commanded by the more glamorous research and treatment centers, like the Isidor Ravdin Institute for surgical research (named after the chairman of the research surgery department).[4] However, the building was needed, and a medical school committee outlined its program in the summer of 1956.

Five departments—physiology, microbiology, research surgery, public health, and the Johnson Foundation—would be given facilities,[5] and they varied considerably in their size, research needs, and interest in the building. Surgery, with a staff of 150, was more occupied with the design of the new hospital wing (the Ravdin Institute), while the Johnson Foundation, whose 25 biophysicists were being evicted from their old quarters, followed all developments keenly.[6] The building would be located between the main medical school building and the Leidy biology building, and across a walkway from the undergraduate quadrangle (all designed around the turn of the century by Cope and Stewardson); it would be eight stories tall, and measure 48 by 200 feet. Little was said about the internal layout of the building; however,

one member of the committee argued that other medical facilities had shown that "bay type construction with space shaft risers for utility lines . . . offers many advantages."[7] The committee probably intended the building to have modular bays and vertical shafts, since nearly all postwar academic laboratories used this formula of flexible laboratory space and service areas.[8] A university-level planning committee, chaired by Vice President Norman Topping, approved the program in October 1956, and an application for construction funds was sent to the Public Health Service (where Topping had been an administrator).[9] In January the PHS agreed to contribute $1.6 million, but with a caveat: they stipulated that the building have facilities for animal housing separate from the laboratories.[10]

The planning committee asked G. Holmes Perkins, dean of fine arts, and trustee Sidney Martin to recommend an architect for the project in January 1957. Perkins was unhappy with the quality of recent medical school buildings, and he and Martin were both interested in securing commissions for university buildings by major architects. The two had discussed Kahn and Eero Saarinen as prospective designers for future commissions; by chance, a request to recommend an architect for the first building in a proposed "women's quadrangle" arrived on Perkins's desk the same day the planning committee sent its request. Martin chose Saarinen to design the women's dormitory, leaving Perkins to recommend Louis Kahn.[11]

Kahn's acceptance of the commission in February 1957 marks the second phase of the design, in which control moved from the medical community to the architect's office. August Komendant and Ian McHarg were hired as structural architect and landscape architect, respectively. According to Komendant, the three were anxious to make "a big statement."[12] Kahn met the heads of the five departments in May, and he was in communication with them throughout the summer.[13] It was probably clear early on that this was a complicated project: not only would the building house a variety of labs, equipment, and research groups, but it was to be a sign of commitment to scientific research.

In June 1957 Kahn revealed his basic plan to medical school and university leaders. As the building's future users and the Public Health Service had stipulated, the structure was eight stories tall, contained about 75,000 square feet of floor space, and had separate facilities for animals. Interior space was divided into open bays, with utilities run through vertical service towers and spaces in the ceiling. Kahn broke up the traditional horizontal academic lab and reassembled

Alfred Newton Richards Medical Research Building, University of Pennsylvania

Philadelphia, Pennsylvania, 1957–65

it into four large towers, three for research and one for animals. The animal tower would connect with the old School of Medicine building; the research towers would each have separate air-exhaust and stair towers. The laboratory bays were apparently designed to be used as open spaces, despite the scientists' intention to divide them into smaller labs and offices.[14] Kahn's plan emphasized the distinction between what he called "served" and "servant" space. Laboratories had been divided between modular, flexible work spaces and service spaces for decades, and Kahn's earlier work at the Yale Art Gallery had pointed to a similar division; now, however, the difference between served and servant space was elevated into an organizing principle of the design, variations of which Kahn would use throughout the rest of his career.

The plan "progressed considerably" through the summer.[15] A July 1957 drawing shows rectangular exhaust towers clad in brick and concrete; the following month Kahn articulated their function by designing them as a set of pipes.[16] He also experimented with different window designs, settling in September on arcuated windows (fig. 432), then, in October, making them rectangular.[17] During the summer Kahn also began work on a second, adjoining building at the request of biology chairman David Goddard. Initially it consisted of two four-story research towers, a taller service tower, and an eight-floor research tower connected to the old biology building.[18] Komendant suggested using Vierendeel trusses for the cantilevered spans in both buildings: loads would be concentrated near the center, the windows could be shaped as Kahn wanted, and the trusses would provide space for horizontal service ducts. Kahn accepted Komendant's idea.[19] Drawings produced in October 1957 show that both the Richards Building and the Biology Building had taken shape: the animal tower was moved to the rear of the building, the exhaust towers were cantilevered, the stair towers were gently tapered, and the arcuated windows were replaced with rectangles (see fig. 89).[20]

By the fall, however, problems had arisen in the School of Medicine. Throughout the summer department heads had been fighting with higher-level administrators to protect their space allocations.[21] At the same time, a few faculty members had begun wondering aloud about Kahn's credentials and his past work.[22] More faculty grew apprehensive after seeing the building plans for the first time during two meetings with Kahn in September.[23] By early October, Norman Topping, chairman of the planning committee, was besieged with complaints about the layout of

the animal tower and the laboratory bays, the cost of heating and cooling, and the overall appearance of the building.[24] Vice Dean Thomas Whayne, the project's coordinator, was too unpopular with the faculty and too suspicious of Kahn to negotiate a solution.[25] Under the circumstances, a confrontation was inevitable. Faculty members met with Kahn on October 29, 1957; a heated debate ensued, with Kahn, Goddard, and Johnson Foundation director Britton Chance defending the building. Goddard's and Chance's backing, and the advanced development of the design, decided the issue. President Gaylord Harnwell and Topping asked Kahn to draw up final plans.[26]

Kahn did revise his plans, but not to satisfy the building's users: he did so to cut hundreds of thousands of dollars from the building's projected cost because the university now found itself short of funds. In this third phase of the design process, lasting from late 1957 through 1958, economic pressures drove the design. On December 26, 1957, Kahn warned his staff that major revisions would be needed; this was confirmed at a January 1958 meeting with the planning committee.[27] Projected building costs had risen from $2.4 million to $3 million during the fall, while available funds had slipped from $3.1 million to $2.8 million.[28] Kahn and his office worked through April on revisions. Round stair towers, reminiscent of the Yale Art Gallery stairwell, appeared briefly in January, then disappeared (fig. 434).[29] Instead, both the stair towers and the cantilevered air-exhaust towers were redesigned as rectangular towers built out of poured concrete with a brick veneer. The animal tower was reduced from twelve to ten stories.[30] Thermopane windows were replaced with regular glass, blinds were eliminated, and insulation was removed. In April the Vierendeel truss system was reconfigured: half of the secondary truss units were omitted, which cut costs and simplified and enlarged the windows, but also destroyed the carefully designed floor plans. New plans were hurriedly drawn up "with no input from the scientists and no serious planning effort." In the process, "the labs began to find themselves at the corners," where they were overexposed to heat and light, while offices were squeezed into the center of the bays.[31]

Kahn had hoped to finish the design by April 1; one month later, on May 1, members of the planning committee and Kahn's office met to approve "final architectural plans."[32] The specifications were completed on May 19, 1958, and construction bids were invited a week later. The first checks were sent to the winning bidders in August. The basement and foundations were poured later that month, followed by

431. Richards Building, 1961.

432

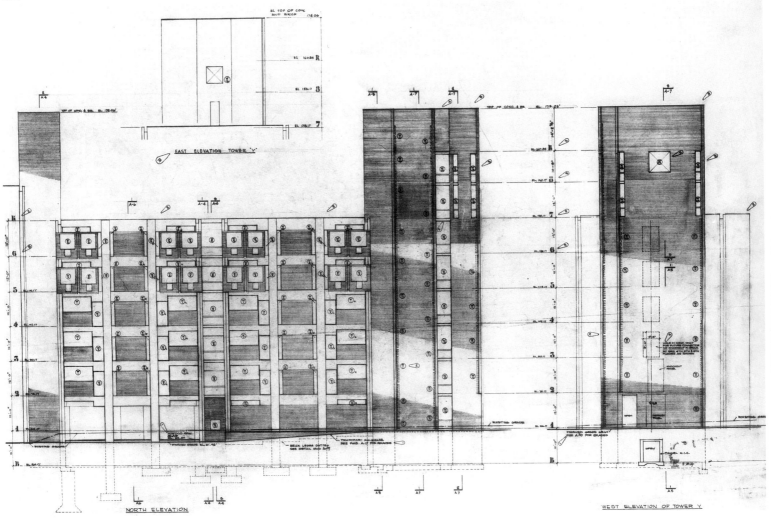

433

432. North elevation of
Richards Building and Biology
Building, ca. September 1957.
433. Biology Building, north
and west elevations. Inscribed
30 Aug 1961 revised 19 Nov 62.
434. Richards Building, plan.
Inscribed January 6, 1958.

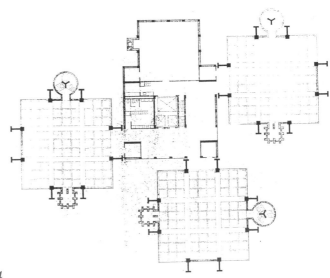

434

the animal tower. In June 1959 the first precast Vierendeel trusses were erected; after working out some scheduling problems, the crew was able to erect three floors a week. The stair towers were completed by the year's end. In the spring of 1960 window glazing, the heating system, and ductwork were installed, and Kahn's office turned its attention to furnishing and painting.[33]

The building was dedicated on May 19, 1960. The decision to name the building after University of Pennsylvania professor Alfred Newton Richards, a noted researcher and director of the World War II–era Committee on Medical Research, had been made the previous year. Richards had initially resisted the honor; in the end, he graciously accepted, writing that "I cherish the thought that through an inscription in stone I may be an unseen participant in future biological and medical advances . . . and the excitement which accompanies discovery."[34] Kahn missed the dedication ceremonies because he was at a conference in Japan, but he soon heard his building praised by critics: Vincent Scully called it "one of the greatest buildings of modern times."[35]

Public acclaim for Kahn was offset by a more private fall from grace within the university over the second stage of the project, the new Biology Building. Kahn had been working on its design since the summer of 1957. By the time the Richards Building was opened, the proposed Biology Building consisted of two five-story research towers, served by stair and exhaust-flue towers, a service tower, a seven-story research tower, and a two-story lounge.[36] Soon after Richards opened, financial problems arose, and Kahn was asked to cut $800,000 from the Biology Building costs. Independent air towers and half of the windows were eliminated, and the service and stair towers were redesigned using an inexpensive concrete framing system.[37] The lounge and the tallest tower also disappeared during the fall. Kahn and Komendant met with the university's financial vice president, Henry Pemberton, and the physical plant planning director, George Turner, in March 1961 to consider cutting another tower, an idea that was rejected.[38]

Kahn's position in the School of Medicine eroded further in April. Problems with the air-conditioning, masonry, windows, and services of the Richards Building had perhaps tarnished Kahn's reputation among the scientists.[39] Despite his revisions, the Biology Building was still over budget, and time was running out on one of the grants secured for construction. On April 14, 1961, the trustees engaged United Engineers, a construction management firm, to finish the

design and oversee construction.[40] Kahn was upset by the trustees' decision, and he protested to Pemberton and Goddard. "It is essential that full responsibility of design and supervision . . . rest with the architect," he wrote. "The limited budget of the Richards Medical Research Building did not interfere with the idealistic demands of architecture."[41] This time, however, budgetary problems overpowered Kahn. The remaining revisions of the Biology Building design, including the addition in late 1962 of a sixth floor on the research towers and an eighth floor and additional windows on the service tower, were made by United Engineers (fig. 433).[42]

Alex Soojung-Kim Pang with Preston Thayer

Notes

1. Letter, Norman Topping (vice president for medical affairs, University of Pennsylvania) to Jonathan Rhoads (professor of surgery), October 16, 1956, "Medical Science Building—Miscellaneous," I. S. Ravdin Collection, University of Pennsylvania Archives, Philadelphia (hereafter cited as Ravdin Collection).

2. Letters, Stuart Mudd (professor of medical microbiology) to John Mitchell (dean), October 6, 1954, and Mudd to Mitchell, November 12, 1954; Bulletin 12, Office of the Business Manager, October 15, 1954; "Mitchell, Dean and Office Communications, 1954–55," Box 25, Medical Microbiology Collection, University of Pennsylvania Archives, Philadelphia (hereafter cited as Microbiology Collection).

3. Letter, Gaylord Harnwell (president) to Mitchell and George Piersol (dean, graduate medical school), June 11, 1956, "Mitchell, Dean," Box 27, Microbiology Collection; memo from Francis Wood (professor of medicine), December 4, 1958, "Mitchell, Dean and Office Communications, 1958–59," Box 29, Microbiology Collection; letter, Henry R. Pemberton (financial vice president) to Harnwell, January 4, 1957, "Medical Division 1955–60: RMRB," Box 11227.77, Gaylord Harnwell Collection, University of Pennsylvania Archives, Philadelphia (hereafter cited as Harnwell Collection).

4. The medical research building is not even mentioned in a 1957 brochure sent to attract grants and donors; "The Next Stop Toward a Greater Medical Center of the University of Pennsylvania," 1957 Ravdin Collection.

5. Letter, William Fitts (department of surgery) to John Brobeck (professor of anatomy), March 15, 1956 (Brobeck Collection, in possession of Dr. Brobeck).

6. On the surgery department, see letter, William Blakemore (professor of surgery) to Louis Flexner (professor of physiology), October 1, 1954, "Medical Science Building—Miscellaneous," Ravdin Collection. On the Johnson Foundation, see correspondence, "Johnson Foundation, 1955–60," Box 11234.94, Harnwell Collection; letter, Britton Chance (director of the foundation) to Alex Pang, November 3, 1986; and University of Pennsylvania School of Medicine course catalogues, 1955–60.

7. Memo, "Planning Committee Tentative Layout," September 26, 1956, "Medical Science Building—Planning Committee," Ravdin Collection; letter, Thomas Whayne (vice dean, medical school) to Fitts, September 24, 1956, "W 1956–57," Box 27, Microbiology Collection; Rhoads, interview with Alex Pang, December 11, 1986.

8. See, for example, "MIT Laboratory," *Progressive Architecture* 34 (October 1953): 79–91; and R. R. Palmer, *Modern Physics Buildings: Design and Function* (New York: Reinhold, 1961).

9. Memo from Harnwell, September 21, 1956; letters, David Drabkin (professor of biochemistry) to Harnwell, September 24, 1956, and Ned Williams (professor of medical microbiology) to Harnwell, September 25, 1956; "Medical Division 1955–60: RMRB," Box 11227.77, Harnwell Collection.

10. Memo from Harnwell, September 21, 1956, "Medical Division 1955–60: RMRB," Box 11227.77, Harnwell Collection. The committee consisted of many of the same people who had drafted the medical school plan; see letters, Drabkin to Harnwell, September 24, 1956, and Williams to Harnwell, September 25, 1956, ibid.

11. Letter, Harnwell to John Moore (business vice president), February 8, 1957, ibid.; letter, Topping to Rhoads, October 16, 1956, "Medical Science Building—Miscellaneous," Ravdin Collection; Holmes Perkins, interview with Alex Pang, December 9, 1986. Signed contract, February 15, 1957, Box LIK 82, Louis I. Kahn Collection, University of Pennsylvania and Pennsylvania Historical and Museum Commission, Philadelphia (hereafter cited as Kahn Collection).

12. Komendant, interview with Preston Thayer, October 19, 1986.

13. Memo, Mitchell to planning committee and chairmen of departments, May 8, 1957, Brobeck Collection; notes of meetings between Kahn and Chance, May 10 and August 27, 1957, "Johnson Foundation," Box LIK 25, Kahn Collection; memos from Ravdin, undated, May 24, and May 29, 1957, "Medical Science Building—Planning Committee," Ravdin Collection; letters, Harry Morton (professor of microbiology) to Mitchell, May 22, 1957, and Mudd to Mitchell, May 22, 1957, "Mitchell, Dean and Office Communications, 1956–57," Box 29, Microbiology Collection; notes of meeting with Harrison Surgical, August 2, 1957, "Harrison Surgical," Box LIK 25, Kahn Collection.

14. Memo, Mitchell to planning committee and chairmen of departments, May 8, 1957, and letter, Russell Squires (professor of physiology) to Topping, June 26, 1957, Brobeck Collection; letter, Topping to Rhoads, October 16, 1956, "Medical Science Building—Miscellaneous," Ravdin Collection.

15. Memo, Mitchell to planning committee, August 27, 1957, "Medical Science Building—Planning Committee," Ravdin Collection.

16. See drawings 490.DD122, section dated July 22, 1957; and 490.DD21, elevation study dated August 5, 1957; Kahn Collection.

17. Drawings 490.DD14, north elevation, ca. September 1957; 490.DD118–21, undated window sketches; and 490.DD51, elevation dated October 10, 1957; Kahn Collection.

18. Goddard presided over the "rehabilitation" of the biology department in the 1950s; letter, Goddard to Harnwell, September 21, 1953, "Harnwell, G. P.—President," Box 7, David Goddard Collection, University of Pennsylvania Archives, Philadelphia (hereafter cited as Goddard Collection); letter, Goddard to Detlev Bronk (director, Rockefeller Institute), April 11, 1957, "The Rockefeller Institute," Box 7, Goddard Collection.

19. Komendant, interview with Thayer.

20. Drawing 490.DD51, elevation dated October 10, 1957, Kahn Collection.

21. Letters, Mudd to Mitchell, May 22, 1957, and Mitchell to Mudd, May 24, 1957, "Mitchell, Dean...1956–57," Box 27, Microbiology Collection; letter, Mudd to Anna Kinnermand (post-doctorate, medical microbiology), May 26, 1959, "K 1958–1959," MMB-29, Microbiology Collection; memo from Ravdin, September 16, 1957, "Medical Science Building—Planning Committee," Ravdin Collection.

22. Letter, Morton to Mitchell, May 22, 1957, "Mitchell, Dean...1956–57," Box 27, Microbiology Collection. See also August E. Komendant, *18 Years with Architect Louis I. Kahn* (Englewood, N.J.: Aloray, 1975), 7–8.

23. Memo, Mitchell to planning committee, August 27, 1957, "Medical Science Building—Planning Committee," Ravdin Collection; memo, Whayne to planning committee, September 9, 1957, Brobeck Collection; memo from Mitchell, September 19, 1957, "U of P Memo of Meetings," Box LIK 25, Kahn Collection; drawing 490.DD47, site plan dated September 5, 1957, Kahn Collection.

24. Letters, Rhoads to Topping, October 7, 1957, and Ravdin to Rhoads, October 8, 1957, "Medical School Building—Miscellaneous," Ravdin Collection; Harry Morton, interview with Alex Pang, November 2, 1986. On the design of the animal tower, see drawing 490.DD89, eastern section of animal tower and laboratory tower dated October 1957, Kahn Collection.

25. Memo from Mitchell, September 8, 1958, "Mitchell, Dean and Office Communication, 1958–59," MMB-29, Microbiology Collection. Inverviewees who expressed this opinion asked not to be directly cited.

26. Letter, Topping to Rhoads, October 16, 1957, "Medical Science Building—Miscellaneous," Ravdin Collection; letter, Topping to Rhoads and Harnwell, October 25, 1957, and memo from Topping, November 4,

1957, Box 9490, Provost's Office Collection, University of Pennsylvania Archives, Philadelphia (hereafter cited as Provost's Collection); letter, Harnwell to Topping, October 15, 1957, Provost's Collection; memo of telephone call from Whayne to Ravdin, October 25, 1957, "Medical Science Building—Planning Committee," Ravdin Collection; letter, Topping to Rhoads, November 4, 1957, Provost's Collection. On Goddard's and Chance's positions, see letter, Goddard to Bronk, August 6, 1959, "The Rockefeller Institute," Box 7, Goddard Collection; Britton Chance, interview with Alex Pang, December 11, 1986; and Rhoads and Perkins, interviews with Pang.

27. Memo from Kahn, December 26, 1957, "UPMRL—Miscellaneous," Box LIK 25, Kahn Collection; George Turner (director, physical plant planning), "Minutes of Meetings in Dr. Topping's Office, 9 a.m.," February 5, 1958, "U of P Memo of Meetings," Box LIK 25, Kahn Collection.

28. Letter, Whayne to Mitchell, n.d. (between January 17 and 21, 1958), "Funds for Medical Research Building," Ravdin Collection; letter, Mitchell to Topping, November 15, 1957, "Medical Division 1955–60: RMRB," Box 11227.77, Harnwell Collection.

29. See drawings 490.DD97, plan dated December 30, 1957; 490.DD66, plan dated January 6, 1958; and 490.DD63, plan dated January 10, 1958; Kahn Collection; Marshall Meyers, interview with Alex Pang, December 12, 1986.

30. Letter, Whayne to Mitchell, n.d. (between January 17 and 21, 1958), "Funds for Medical Research Building," Ravdin Collection; Meyers, interview with Pang.

31. See drawings 490.DD29, east elevation dated April 8, 1958; and A-16, east elevation dated May 21, 1958; Kahn Collection. Quotes are from Meyers, interview with Pang.

32. Memo from Kahn, April 9, 1958, "Master File, October 16, 1957–September 1, 1958," Box LIK 9, Kahn Collection; memo from Whayne, May 1, 1958, "U of P Memo of Meetings," Box LIK 25, Kahn Collection.

33. Reinforced Concrete Daily Report No. 1, October 10, 1958, "UPMRL Daily Reports," Box LIK 25, Kahn Collection. On problems with the trusses, see letters, Joseph R. Farrell (Farrell Construction Company) to Atlantic Prestressed Concrete Co., June 16, 1959, "Joseph R. Farrell 5/1/59–8/31/59," Box LIK 25, Kahn Collection; Kahn to Farrell, March 21, 1960, "Master File, March 1–31, 1960," Box LIK 9, Kahn Collection; Meyers to Farrell, April 22, 1960, "Master File, April 1–May 31, 1960," Box LIK 9, Kahn Collection; and David Wisdom (Kahn's office) to Whayne, May 9, 1960, ibid.

34. Letters, Richards to Harnwell, November 5, 1959; Ravdin to Chester Tucker (vice president for development), February 10, 1959; Mitchell to Harnwell, June 2, 1959; Harnwell to Tucker, June 16, 1960; Tucker to Harnwell, June 19, 1959; and Harnwell to Richards, October 30, 1959; "Medical Division 1955–60: RMRB," Box 11227.77, Harnwell Collection.

35. Vincent J. Scully, *Louis I. Kahn* (New York: George Braziller, 1962), 27.

36. Drawing A-4, north elevation dated May 25, 1960, Kahn Collection.

37. Letter, Tim Vreeland (Kahn's office) to Goddard, July 22, 1960, "Master File, June 1–July 31, 1960," Box LIK 9, Kahn Collection.

38. Letter, Wisdom to Keast & Hood, Dubin, Komendant, March 14, 1961, "Master Files, March 1–May 31, 1961," Box LIK 9, Kahn Collection.

39. Meeting notes, November 18, 1959, "Staff Meeting, July 1959–1960," MMB-29, Microbiology Collection; form letter from Brobeck, July 5, 1961, and memo from Whayne, December 7, 1961, Brobeck Collection; letter, Rhoads to Mitchell, October 23, 1961, acc. UPJ7.6, Box 25, University of Pennsylvania Archives, Philadelphia.

40. Minutes of executive board, board of trustees, University of Pennsylvania, Philadelphia, v. 27, April 14, 1961; letter, Kahn to Turner, October 19, 1961, "Master File, October 2–December 3, 1961," Box LIK 9, Kahn Collection.

41. Letters, Kahn to Pemberton, October 20, 1961, and Kahn to Goddard, October 21, 1961, "Master File, October 2–December 31, 1961," Box LIK 9, Kahn Collection.

42. Drawing A-3, revision 3, dated November 12, 1962, Kahn Collection.

The work of Louis Kahn was brought to Jonas Salk's attention in the fall of 1959 by a friend who heard Kahn speak in Pittsburgh.[1] Kahn and eight other panelists had been invited by the Carnegie Institute of Technology to consider "the relation of art to what is real."[2] Kahn delivered a talk on October 10 entitled "Order in Science and Art,"[3] during which he discussed the design of the Richards Medical Research Building at the University of Pennsylvania, then under construction. Two months after the symposium Salk stopped by the architect's Philadelphia office on his way to New York. He had undertaken a new project, an institute for biological research in California, and had intended to ask Kahn how one selected an architect. The question never came up (fig. 435; see figs. 278–92).[4]

During their first meeting Kahn led Salk through the new laboratory building at Penn. They talked agreeably, and although Salk confessed he was less impressed by Richards than he was by Kahn, the project gave the two men a basis with which to begin their discussion of Salk's plans in California.[5] Salk told Kahn he needed 10,000 square feet for each of ten research scientists, requiring a building nearly the same size as Richards.[6] Salk then added an additional requirement: he said he would like to be able to invite Picasso to the laboratory.[7]

Salk and Kahn quickly discovered they were of like mind—indeed, each grew to regard the other as a collaborator.[8] Their working relationship was characterized by a dialogue that sometimes drifted into abstract and philosophical terrain. To Salk, work at the frontiers of biological science necessarily raised broad questions about the future of humanity—about the meaning of life, values, and the nature of man.[9] Kahn warmly welcomed these themes. Salk recalls that "it was not uncommon for other people to watch us and listen and be utterly confused," although they understood each other perfectly.[10] Indeed, for the first version of the design the architect was given no written program: "Whatever emerged came out of conversations." Any notions Kahn and Salk may have had when work first started on the project did not take the form of strict formal or spatial requirements; "we just began to play," Salk recalls.

This play of minds was not without historical references. In their early discussions about buildings, Salk alluded frequently to the monastery at Assisi, which he had visited in 1954. He later suggested that the physical setting of the monastic cloister—its arcades, columns, and courtyard—provided him with architectural imagery for the new

Salk Institute for Biological Studies

La Jolla, California, 1959–65

institute that suited his concept of its social and intellectual organization.[11] Kahn was familiar with these images, having made several sketches of the church buildings and arcades at Assisi during his travels in 1929.[12]

In the fall of 1959 San Diego city officials learned that Salk wanted to establish a major research institute in their area and proposed several locations for the new facility.[13] Out of these Salk wisely chose a site on the Torrey Pines mesa—"not just any land or merely fine land, but the most beautiful coastal cliff property left in La Jolla."[14] Salk and Kahn visited the site together for the first time early in 1960.[15] Salk credited Kahn for defining the shape of the site, which wrapped around a coastal canyon whose vivid geomorphic peculiarities Salk likened to "cerebral convolutions."[16] The City Council deeded the property to him by resolution on April 26, 1960.

Kahn's initial impressions of the site were recorded in a series of undated sketches that appear to have been executed during his first visit in 1960.[17] At that time he adumbrated three distinct building groups that would define the general layout of the design, and soon after the trip to La Jolla he particularized these groupings. He outlined functions and requirements for two primary "forums," placing a meeting hall by the sea, on the western edge of the site, and the laboratories by the public road, on the eastern edge (the third component was residences).[18]

Office documents indicate that Kahn presented the first version in San Diego on the occasion of Salk's formal public announcement of the project, on March 15, 1960.[19] The laboratory component of this boldly rational composition clearly borrowed its differentiated vertical structure and articulated stacks from the towers of the Richards Building in Philadelphia (fig. 436). Each laboratory ensemble rose from a giant circular platform situated along the public road. Two service buildings of lower profile occupied smaller circular platforms to the west. The four components of the laboratory group were connected by tangential service drives set crosswise between the two smaller buildings, which gave the plan the appearance of belted pulleys. The rectangular meeting house was positioned on the opposite end of the site, at the end of a long service drive, overlooking the Pacific. Along the service drive, between the laboratories and the meeting house, Kahn situated a large cluster of buildings for recreation; to the south, across the gorge from these, a similarly disposed but smaller cluster of buildings constituted the residential complex.

435. Laboratories, seen from west.
436. Model of master plan, ca. March 1960.
437. Master plan, ca. April 1961.

According to Salk, Kahn's first version of the institute was "an early fantasy."[20] Kahn acknowledged this in a letter to Basil O'Connor, president of the National Foundation and principal sponsor of the project, in September 1960: "I assure you," Kahn stated somewhat apologetically, "that [the work] will become more realistic as I develop the architectural interpretation of space requirements."[21] Over the course of the next twelve months, agreements about space requirements, services, and facilities for each of the three program components were sharpened in frequent meetings between the architect, the client, and consulting builders and engineers. The clarification of architectural objectives and quantitative limits did not discourage Kahn from his meditation on the image of Assisi: in August 1960, in a letter to historian William H. Jordy, he indicated his desire to go to Europe, especially to northern Italy, "to see again the wonderful monasteries which have a bearing on what I am doing for Dr. Salk in San Diego."[22]

In April 1961, after nearly a year of development, a second version of the design was published in *Progressive Architecture* in a long article about Kahn's work; that same month Kahn offered the new master plan as a case study for a conference on urban design at Harvard University (fig. 437).[23] In June 1961 Kahn drafted and finalized a formal, typewritten program.[24] It described spatial and functional requirements for the laboratory group and the meeting house group, into which sports and recreational facilities had been incorporated; the third component, houses for fellows, was mentioned but not described. Between August 1961 and April 1962 Kahn refined and developed this second design, but his adjustments did not alter the general scheme and arrangement of the plan. On April 1, 1962, a contract for the construction of the laboratories was signed; it was to the second version that it referred.

In this second design of 1961 to 1962, Kahn placed four identical two-story laboratories at the head of the ravine. The laboratory buildings in this ensemble were set out in reflexive pairs, each with a central garden. Ancillary elements were developed to support the primary work of the laboratory—these included studies, a service area and animal quarters, and an administrative wing, which housed offices, the technical library, and dining facilities. Kahn located the animal quarters and laboratory service drive on the east end of the buildings, and administrative offices and library on the west, overlooking the canyon. On the northwest corner he placed a small entrance room and a plaza connected to parking, which stretched along a 600-foot tree-lined promenade leading to the meeting house complex.

436

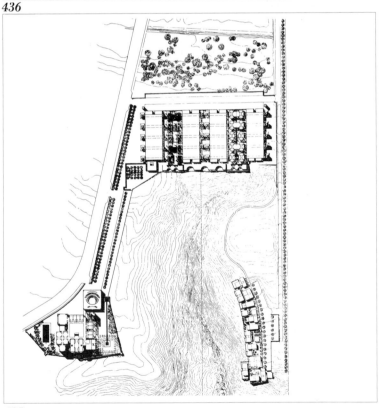

437

435

Between each pair of laboratories Kahn proposed an "architecture of water," a system of pools and channels, inspired by the fountains of the Alhambra, that was designed to spill over and irrigate the gardens.[25] Lining the two central garden spaces were thirty-two studies, eight for each laboratory building—Kahn called them an "architecture of the oak table and the rug" to distinguish them from the setting of scientific equipment.[26] The studies were paired into suites, each connected to the laboratory proper by its own stairway. Kahn supported the upper-level studies with what he called an "arcade," although he used no arches—its "colonnade" consisted of rectangular concrete walls. The studies enjoyed views of gardens, which opened onto roof terraces atop the administrative wing.

The laboratories of this 1961–62 version were conceived as an "architecture of air cleanliness and adjustability"—large, flexible, virtually column-free loft spaces that measured 619 by 380 feet.[27] The structural system, developed by Kahn with the assistance of August Komendant, expressed Kahn's concept of "servant" and "served" space. Giant folded plates spanned between five transverse box girders placed at forty-foot intervals (fig. 440). The folded plates were arranged in pairs that created interlocking hollows; pipes and ducts were to be housed in the longitudinal "folds" of the ceiling structure and then fed transversely through the five girders into vertical service towers placed along the outer wall of each lab. When Kahn explained the integration of the structural and mechanical systems, he enlisted a metaphor conceived by his client: "It all comes from what Dr. Salk called the *mesenchyme space*," Kahn said. "One serves the body, and one is the body itself."[28]

In April 1962, almost immediately after Salk signed the agreement with contractors to build this version of the laboratories, he called for major changes in their design. Two aspects of the four-building version troubled him. First was the possibility that two garden courts might foster unproductive competition—Salk had grown wary of the potential for disunity between "'A'-court people and 'B'-court people."[29] Second was the inflexibility of the structural system, which restricted laboratory partitions to a ten-foot module. Salk and Kahn reviewed these concerns with the project team, and on May 3, 1962, the architect was instructed to revise the design of the laboratories.[30]

In June 1962 Kahn presented Salk with the third and final version of the laboratory complex. The basic design concepts and programmatic organization of the second version were

438

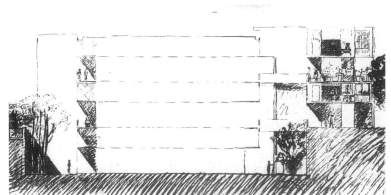

439

transposed directly into the third: the separation of studies and laboratories, the interrelation of servant and served space, the idea of a central "arcaded" garden, east-facing service spaces, and west-facing administrative offices and library (fig. 438). But Kahn had reduced the number of buildings from four to two. He created a subgrade story so that each of the two buildings of the revised design had three laboratory levels, each measuring 65 by 245 feet. He replaced the folded-plate beams and giant box girders of the second version with poured-in-place concrete Vierendeel trusses. The transverse Vierendeels were borne by columns at each end and spanned sixty feet. Thirteen of these nine-foot-high trusses were required to support each of the six laboratories, seventy-eight trusses altogether. The full-story spaces created by the giant Vierendeels, which housed the requisite network of pipes and ducts, became service levels for the laboratories located immediately below.

In each of the twin buildings, the laboratories proper comprised six floor levels (three laboratories plus three service levels); the semidetached study towers that lined the court-facing side of each building comprised four floor levels (fig. 439). Kahn's decision to locate the lowest laboratory level and its service floor below grade generated the design of sunken courts on the north and south side of each building, which provided the labs with natural light; for each building there were eight of these, four on the north side and four on the south. Kahn spaced them evenly between five stair towers. The stair towers facilitated circulation between the three laboratory floors, the central court, and the two levels of studies.

Salk had likened the studies to cells in a monastery and asked Kahn to isolate them from the laboratories, and by pulling the studies away from the laboratories, the architect created a space for such separation—between the realm of oak and rug and the realm of stainless steel.[31] The stair towers defined this space and provided a bridge between the laboratories and studies, but only at the ground and upper laboratory levels. Kahn intensified the separation between the labs and the studies with a change in level: he situated the studies so that they were aligned not with the laboratory floors but with the service floors above them.

At the level of the central court the space beneath the study towers acted as an open arcade, providing shelter and shade. At the level of the uppermost lab, between the two levels of studies, Kahn interposed open-air porticoes that overlooked the central court from the towers. Each portico served as an informal outdoor meeting place, a middle

ground convenient to both labs and studies. In keeping with the spirit of Salk's vision of peripatetic scholarship and the monastic cloister, Kahn appropriately equipped the porticoes with wall-mounted slate blackboards.

There were ten study towers in this final evolution of the design, five on each side of the court. Together they housed thirty-six studies (four for each fifty-foot laboratory division); each tower comprised four offices, except the easternmost, which had only two. The configuration of the towers resolved problems of light, view, structure, and function (see fig. 161). In plan, these powerful elements extended from the laboratory blocks like fingers, although in section they stood like giant hollow columns, lining and defining the space of the central court with basilican authority. Two 45-degree diagonal walls in each tower created triangular, full-height bays with views to the ocean, one for each study.[32]

Throughout the entire building, but especially in the design of the ten study towers, Kahn stipulated exposed structure to articulate the limits of opening and enclosure. He expressed the edges of walls and floors and, through their thickness, revealed the governing lines of his composition. Kahn's gathering of raw bearing walls at the base of the study towers constituted a kind of colonnade that defined the side aisles of the central court. Above, at the levels of the studies, openings between walls were filled with teak window panels. Each panel contained a pocket that received three sliding window components—glazing, screen, and louvered shade.

In the design of the formwork for the laboratories, each joint and seam was assiduously detailed to celebrate the logic of construction and the properties of concrete.[33] Color for Kahn was no less essential a factor. Several types of California concrete were blended with pozzolan and other admixtures to impart a warmer hue.[34] Plywood forms were coated with polyurethane to ensure the consistency of color and finish on the surface of the poured wall; likewise, wood panels were left untreated to allow the teak to weather naturally. Kahn had considered paving the central court with Mexican stone and then decided on Italian slate. But travertine proved considerably less expensive to import than the slate; his decision to use this less costly, light-colored material led him to discover the harmonious marriage of travertine and concrete, which he later stated gave the building its ancient, weathered cast.[35]

Although the construction of the laboratories, which began

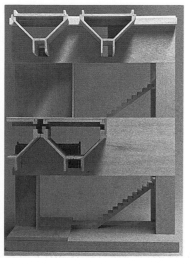

438. Site plan of laboratories, 1962.
439. Section through laboratory showing sunken courts and studies, 1962.
440. Model of laboratory structural system, 1962.

440

in June 1962, was substantially complete by August 1965, the design of the central garden had not yet been resolved. Kahn agreed with Salk that one court had greater power of place than two, but two gardens had proved less vexing for Kahn to design than one. His conception of the central court as a functional amenity began to fade, and it acquired increasingly symbolic, transcendent value. Initially, he carried over the garden configuration from the four-building version—the court was bisected by a narrow, longitudinal canal along which Kahn stationed twin files of columnar Italian cypress planted on a grid (see fig. 160). As the construction of the labs progressed, however, he grew increasingly doubtful about the suitability of his solutions.

In 1966, seeking to refresh his thinking, Kahn invited Luis Barragan, the celebrated Mexican architect, to consult on the problem of the central space. He had written Barragan for the first time in January 1965, as the laboratories neared completion. He made laudatory reference to a recent exhibit of Barragan's work at the Museum of Modern Art in New York and mentioned the possibility of his collaboration on the garden at La Jolla.[36] A full year passed before Kahn contacted Barragan again; but this time he sent him a round-trip ticket to San Diego.[37] Barragan arrived in La Jolla on February 23, 1966; the next day he was joined by Kahn and went to meet Salk and John E. MacAllister, Kahn's project architect, in the central space, which at that time was a field of mud between the two new laboratories.[38]

Prior to his meeting with Barragan, it had been Kahn's intention to embellish the central space with trees. "I told him at first sight, . . . *not one leaf* . . . ," Barragan later recalled: *"Don't put one leaf, nor plant, nor one flower, nor dirt. Absolutely nothing. And I told him, A plaza . . . will unite the two buildings and at the end, you will see the line of the sea."*[39] Salk arrived ten minutes later, Barragan recalled. He and Kahn then put the idea to Salk, who accepted it. "Lou was thinking," Barragan continued, "and stated a very important thing—that the surface is a facade that rises to the sky and unites the two as if everything else had been hollowed out." To some it seemed that at this meeting the matter of the central court was resolved once and for all.[40] But "to those not present at the time of Barragan's realization," Kahn later recalled, "a totally paved Plaza seemed to be a harsh solution."[41]

To mitigate the severity of an empty court, Kahn and Salk asked San Francisco landscape architect Lawrence Halprin to develop alternative plans. Halprin employed orange trees and other species in two alternative designs, which he

submitted in late October and November 1966. The following month, in a three-page letter to Salk, Kahn enumerated his objections to Halprin's plan and forcefully endorsed the spirit of Barragan's approach.[42] He proposed to pave the entire plaza in stone, laid tight without mortar. From earlier versions, he carried forth the idea of a single central canal with continuously running water. The canal would connect a small square pool at the entrance to the court with a wide rectangular pool at its west end, which would then spill through a wall into a small pool in the lower garden. Although over the next several months Kahn considered several other schemes with tree-shaded fountains, drawings for the design of the central court as it exists today emerged ready for construction at the start of the summer in 1967.[43]

The laboratory was only one part of Kahn's image of the institute as an ensemble of buildings, and he proposed a separate meeting place for collegial retreats, integrative studies, and social interaction—seminars, concerts, lectures, informal discussion, dining, and personal research and study. To supplement this component, he also proposed houses for fellows and facilities for physical fitness. In the first version of the master plan (presented in San Diego on March 15, 1960) Kahn positioned the place for meeting as far from the laboratories as the site would permit, on an outlying ridge close to the edge of the bluff (see fig. 436). A long, straight service drive led from the public road to the entry of the facility, which was separated from the rest of the site by a deep ravine and spanned with a bridge. Kahn proposed a large, low, rectangular building with an expressed structural frame, within which modules of varying size and height suggested the differentiation of complex interior functions.

During the year following Kahn's first presentation, the size and configuration of the site was modified by Salk's negotiations with the city. Consequently, the meeting house complex in the second version (with four low-slung laboratory buildings) was set further inland, at the end of the site's northern arm, where the narrow extension of land flared into the shape of a bell (see fig. 437). In the second version, the conference and athletic facilities were combined, presenting Kahn with a formidable puzzle of parts—auditorium, director's residence, library, meeting and banquet hall, seminar and dining rooms, guest suites, exercise facilities, swimming pool, and gardens. As he worked on the new scheme into the summer and fall of 1960, Kahn tried to order these disparate requirements within strong square and rectangular grids, as if to counterpoise

441. *Plan of meeting house and site with partial plan of Hadrian's Villa, 1960.*
442. *Wall diagrams for meeting house, as published in* Progressive Architecture *in April 1961.*
443. *Plan of meeting house. Inscribed 17 Jan '62; rev. 4 April '62.*

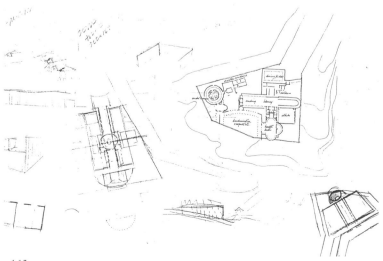

441

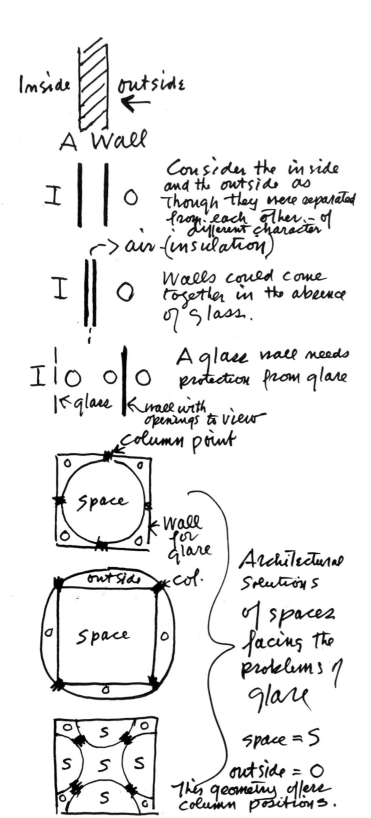

Inside | outside ←

A Wall

I || O — Consider the inside and the outside as though they were separated from each other. — of different character

→ air (insulation)

I || O — Walls could come together in the absence of glass.

I|O O|O — A glass wall needs protection from glare

← glass ← wall with openings to view

column point

space — Wall for glare col.

outside — col.
space

} Architectural solutions of spaces facing the problems of glare

space = S
outside = O

S S S S S — This geometry offers column positions.

442

the irregularity of the site with academic symmetry. Each successive effort, however, seemed only to strengthen the resistance of the site to purely orthogonal intrusions.

The solution to this planning puzzle was arrived at in circumstances recounted by historian Vincent Scully in 1962. According to Scully, "An early sketch had been traced by a draftsman, partly as a joke, from a plan of one of the units of Hadrian's Villa itself. 'That's it,' said Kahn."[44] The draftsman in question was architect Thomas Vreeland, then a young designer assigned by Kahn to work on the schematic design for the meeting house, and he confirms the tale.[45] According to Vreeland, Kahn had often mused upon Hadrian's Villa in his attempt to conjure the essence of a "place of the unmeasurable." After several of his efforts to come up with a satisfactory scheme yielded only withering grimaces from Kahn, Vreeland took a plan of Hadrian's Villa out of a book in the office library and traced a portion of it onto the troublesome site (fig. 441). Kahn did not immediately recognize the graft and responded to Vreeland's drawing with great enthusiasm.

Soon after this incident, the design for the meeting house came alive. Kahn broke down key program elements into discrete parts and then used them to enclose a large, square central hall. In the program developed for the second version, he emphasized the important multiple functions of this space, calling it "the hall of exhibition, the hall of reception and the hall of dining, and . . . the fitting interior entrance place for the place of meeting."[46] Guest suites, the library, dining rooms, the gymnasium, and the residence of the director were situated along the corridor that surrounded the central hall. The auditorium was developed as an independent structure that Kahn placed at the southeast corner of the site, beside the entrance to the meeting house compound (see fig. 437).

The geometry of the dining and reading room plans was composed of circles set in squares and squares set in circles. These simple forms derived in part from Kahn's determination to produce an enclosure that eliminated glare without compromising either material integrity or view. He generated diagrams to demonstrate the plain good sense of an ancient metaphor: by wrapping the building in "ruins," as he had done for the design of the United States consulate buildings in Luanda, Angola (1959–62), he obviated the need for additive, nonstructural shades (fig. 442). In each three-story ensemble, exterior concrete walls surrounded small, glass-clad seminar and reading rooms; the space between them was open to the elements. "This is my answer

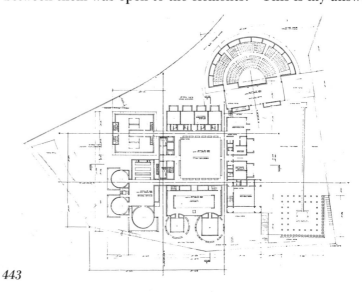

443

to Edward Stone's grille, which just makes little pinpoints of glare and shuts off all else," Kahn said, referring to the architect of the United States Embassy in New Delhi (1957–59). "I have given you an iris to the eye."[47]

Between the fall of 1961 and the spring of 1962, Kahn refined the design of the meeting house, although he did not dramatically revise its plan (fig. 443). The third version was more adjectival than the second, more concerned with hierarchical distinctions and the small spaces of connection between primary geometric elements. Kahn further differentiated the plans of the library and the dining room, limiting circular and square elements to five adjunctive towers that evoked the seminal geometry of the Renaissance *homo ad quadratum*. Giant keyhole windows migrated from earlier projects into the physiognomy of the "walls for glare" and gave the west elevation of the meeting house a striking anthropomorphic character (see fig. 156). To achieve greater spatial clarity and tautness, Kahn inflected the central axis of the complex southward, toward the canyon, so that it was no longer parallel to the central axis of the laboratories.

To accentuate this gesture, Kahn skewed the central axis of the third version's auditorium an additional 5.5 degrees. The square auditorium of the second version was superseded by an overtly classical, semicircular amphitheater. Kahn placed the main entrance to the meeting house compound between the powerful, ribbed enclosure of the auditorium and the ravine, strengthening the wrist of the long promenade that connected the laboratory complex to the meeting house and its gardens. Kahn then marked this space of passage with a "noisy" fountain, out of which he drew a long watercourse that bisected the meeting house garden longitudinally, terminating in a "quiet" fountain surrounded by large, square piers left open to the elements. He called this open-air ambulatory "the religious place."[48]

Across the ravine from the meeting house, at the west end of the wide, rectangular arm that made up the southern portion of the site, Kahn located the houses for fellows. In the June 1961 program Kahn created a building component comprising single rooms and studio apartments designed to accommodate the temporary residence of visiting researchers and scientists.[49] Residential facilities had been represented in the first version by small, randomly clustered courtyard structures located on the south side of the canyon (see fig. 436). In the second and third versions many of the architectural details used in the design of the laboratories and meeting house were carried into the design of the

housing—anti-glare walls, gardens, flat roofs, concrete construction with expressed floor levels, and keyhole windows. In the second version these elements were expressed in a gently curved string of small apartments that lined a pedestrian walk, which was situated between the buildings and a parallel parking lot served by a tree-lined drive along the southern border of the site (see fig. 437). In a description of the second version of the houses for fellows, Kahn compared the forty-eight apartments to a "Pompeian Village . . . a labyrinth of gardens and walkways and fountains, with houses connected by gardens. . . . Every bedroom has a porch that overlooks the canyon or the sea."[50]

In the third version of the houses for fellows, revised for the last time during the early months of 1962, seven different types of two-story buildings equipped with ample porches and balconies lined both sides of a narrow pedestrian street (fig. 444). Together they could accommodate more than fifty residents and guests. At either end, two-bedroom houses shared small plazas with adjacent guest quarters—the larger and more spacious of these was located at the western edge overlooking the ocean (fig. 445). The pedestrian street descended forty feet in elevation, following a gentle arc that inverted the topographical curve of the ridge. Roughly in the middle of the complex, directly across from a central community building, the narrow street opened and stepped down to a canyon-side swimming pool. The pool was surrounded by a row of piers that echoed its counterpart in the garden of the meeting house across the gorge.

The Salk Institute is an incomplete project. An amendment to the contract between Kahn and Salk, signed on August 29, 1963, halted the architect's work on the meeting house and residences "pending further investigation of the design premises."[51] Although financial limitations were not explicitly mentioned as a reason for this postponement, the absence of funds for further construction was plainly a factor. In July 1965 the south laboratory building was still an unoccupied shell. By that time the Salk Institute had spent nearly $14.5 million on the construction of the laboratories, not including nearly $1.5 million in architect's fees. According to Jonas Salk, the meeting house and housing for fellows were suspended in the state of becoming, "neither denied nor dismissed."[52]

Over the course of the following years, as funds became available, the south laboratory was slowly equipped with mechanical and electrical services. One of the three

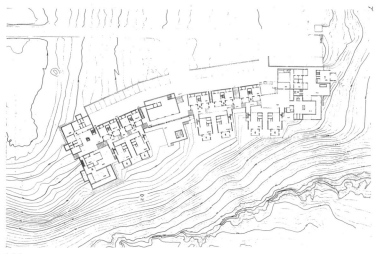

444

445

444. *Ground-floor plan of
residences. Inscribed January
10, 1962.*
445. *Perspective of meeting
house from residences, ca.
1962.*

laboratory floors in the south building is currently occupied by administrative offices and seminar rooms. Space for a third laboratory will become available upon the completion of a new administrative building, plans for which are under way. The new building will occupy a site in the eucalyptus grove on the east side of the building, the same area Kahn had blocked out for an entrance court and service building in a drawing dated May 4, 1964.[53]

Daniel S. Friedman

Notes

1. Salk, interview with David B. Brownlee et al., April 18, 1983, tape recording transcribed by Daniel S. Friedman, Louis I. Kahn Collection, University of Pennsylvania and Pennsylvania Historical and Museum Commission, Philadelphia (hereafter cited as Kahn Collection).
2. Letter, Norman L. Rice (dean, College of Fine Arts, Carnegie Institute of Technology) to Kahn, August 4, 1959, "Carnegie Institute of Technology," Box LIK 65, Kahn Collection.
3. Letter, Kahn to Rice, August 14, 1959, ibid.
4. Salk, interview with Brownlee et al. Salk reiterated this story a year later in the Louis I. Kahn Memorial Lecture, American Institute of Architects, Philadelphia, April 5, 1984, reprinted in part as "Architecture of Reality," *Rassegna* 21 (March 1985): 28–29 (from English translation provided in end pages, n.p.).
5. Salk, interview with Brownlee et al.
6. Kahn, hand-corrected typescript, "Voice of America—Louis I. Kahn Recorded November 19, 1960," Box LIK 55, Kahn Collection.
7. Kahn, "Louis I. Kahn: Talks with Students," *Architecture at Rice*, no. 26 (1969): 12.
8. Salk, "Architecture of Reality," n.p.
9. Salk, "Life: Organization and Processes," loose-leaf typewritten note with autograph comments, n.d., "Jonas Salk," Box LIK 107, Kahn Collection.
10. Salk, interview with Brownlee et al.
11. Ibid.
12. Pennsylvania Academy of the Fine Arts, *The Travel Sketches of Louis I. Kahn* (Philadelphia: Pennsylvania Academy of the Fine Arts, 1978), 27, pl. 15. References to this region of Italy can be found in the margins of two early drawings (540.4 and 540.10, Kahn Collection) that Kahn executed while developing the first version of his design for Salk. On one Kahn wrote the word "Assisi" under a roster of laboratory rooms; on another he has clearly sketched the ancient Roman viaduct at Spoleto, which is located twenty-five miles south of Assisi.
13. Salk, "Statement on a New Institute: Prepared on Occasion of Proposal of Gift of Land by San Diego, California," March 15, 1960, photocopy of typescript, Box LIK 107, Kahn Collection.
14. Mary Huntington Hall, "Gift from the Sea," *San Diego*, February 1962, 41.
15. "I look forward to seeing you on your next visit which I understand will be during the first week of February. You may recall that it was just about three years ago then that we first visited La Jolla together"; letter, Salk to Kahn, January 29, 1963, Box LIK 107, "Salk Projects—Dr. Jonas E. Salk—Correspondence April 1960–June 1963," Kahn Collection.
16. Esther McCoy, "Dr. Salk Talks About His Institute," *Architectural Forum* 127 (December 1967): 29.
17. Seventeen small sketches drawn in black ink and crayon on sixteen loose-leaf sheets (Kahn Collection, 540.1.1–.17) indicate that Kahn surveyed the shape and lie of the site, its knolls and ravines, its color ("pinkish ochre"), and the contents of views in the cardinal directions.
18. Drawing 540.7, Kahn Collection.
19. Letter, Kahn to Sibyl Moholy-Nagy, March 7, 1960, "Master File 1960 March 1 through 31, 1960," Box LIK 9, Kahn Collection. March 15, 1960, was the day Salk announced plans for the new institute in San Diego. Salk later noted that the first version was developed by Kahn before the city voted to allocate the property, since it located buildings on land that was retained by the city after negotiations between the Salk Institute, San Diego, and the University of California; Salk, interview with Brownlee et al.
20. Salk, interview with Brownlee et al.
21. Letter, Kahn to O'Connor, with a copy to Salk, September 16, 1960,

"Salk—O'Connor & Garber, Attys—Hoffman," Box LIK 107, Kahn Collection. The National Foundation, sponsor of the March of Dimes, was established to support research for the treatment and cure of polio.

22. Letter, Kahn to Jordy, August 1, 1960, Box LIK 9, Kahn Collection.

23. Jan C. Rowan, "Wanting to Be: The Philadelphia School," *Progressive Architecture* 42 (April 1961): 140–50; "The Institute as Generator of Urban Form," Harvard Graduate School of Design Alumni Association, Fifth Urban Design Conference, April 1961, Box LIK 60, Kahn Collection.

24. "Abstract of the Program for the Institute of Biology at Torrey Pines, La Jolla, San Diego," n.d., "Salk Program Notes June 19," Box LIK 27, Kahn Collection (hereafter cited as "Program Abstract"). Accompanying this document is an undated draft in Kahn's hand, presumably the first, and an undated typewritten draft with handwritten corrections by Kahn, presumably the second. The contract between Kahn and the Salk Institute, which was dated July 26, 1961, makes reference to "an abstract of the program for the Owner attached hereto as Exhibit A and made part of . . ."; letter, Kahn to Salk, August 14, 1961, "Salk–Kahn Architectural Agreement," Box LIK 89, Kahn Collection.

25. Kahn, quoted in Hall, "Gift from the Sea," 44.

26. Kahn, "Form and Design," *Architectural Design* 31 (April 1961): 151.

27. Ibid.

28. Kahn, quoted in a conversation with Peter Blake, July 20, 1971, in *What Will Be Has Always Been: The Words of Louis I. Kahn*, ed. Richard Saul Wurman (New York: Access Press and Rizzoli, 1986), 130.

29. John E. MacAllister, Kahn's project architect at Salk and now senior principal in the firm of Anshen & Allen, Beverly Hills, telephone interview with Daniel S. Friedman, December 18, 1989.

30. Letter, George S. Conn (assistant to the director, Salk Institute), to H. E. White (assistant treasurer and comptroller, National Foundation), May 16, 1963, "Salk–George Conn Correspondence," Box LIK 89, Kahn Collection. Shortly after the excavation contract had been awarded, the construction report notes that a hold was placed on all work on May 25, and that "a complete redesign of the laboratories followed"; two weeks later, at a meeting in Salk's office on June 9, 1962, preliminary schematic designs for a two-building complex with a single garden courtyard were approved; monthly report no. 1, George A. Fuller Co. (job no. 1994), January 31, 1963, Box LIK 27, Kahn Collection.

31. Salk, "Design Program for the Studies," n.d. (received by Kahn's office on August 9, 1962), "Salk Project—Dr. Jonas E. Salk Correspondence, April 1960–June 1963," Box LIK 107, Kahn Collection.

32. The landward diagonal was slightly larger than its seaward twin; this difference permitted Kahn to stagger the opening of the landward bay, as though in a compensatory gesture designed to provide it with an extra foot of view.

33. Fred Langford, Kahn's project architect for concrete production, wrote an impassioned memo to the general contractor that outlined the importance of the character of each of the several types of joints and seams: "We must make the concrete in this building say 'I am expressive of the hands and forms that hold me in place until I could grasp the inner steel and gain the strength and power that . . . I must possess to . . . span the laboratories in a single leap, to lift the studies to the grand view of the sea, and still be friendly enough to touch with human hands'"; letter, Langford to Greer Ferver (Ferver & Dorland & Associates, Engineers), "Re: Design of form work for concrete," April 15, 1963, "Salk—Dr. August Komendant," Box LIK 89, Kahn Collection.

34. "Laboratory 1: Procession of Massive Forms," *Architectural Forum* 122 (May 1965): 44.

35. Marshall D. Meyers, "The Wonder of the Natural Thing" (interview with Kahn, August 11, 1972), typewritten transcript, 4–5, "Articles and Speeches," Kahn Collection.

36. Letter, Kahn to Barragan, January 20, 1965, "Salk Project—Barragan, Luis, Landscape Architect," Box LIK 108, Kahn Collection.

37. Letter, Kahn to Barragan, February 8, 1966, ibid.

38. Ibid.; see also telegram, Kahn's office to Barragan, confirming reservations at Hotel del Charro in La Jolla on February 23 and 24, 1966, "Salk Project—Barragan, Luis, Landscape Architect," Box LIK 108, Kahn Collection.

39. Barragan, interview (interviewer and date unknown), in Wurman, *What Will Be Has Always Been*, 268–69.

40. MacAllister, interview with Friedman.

41. Letter, Kahn to Salk, December 19, 1966, "Salk Gardens—Exedra," Box LIK 26, Kahn Collection.

42. Ibid.

43. The Theodore Gildred Court was named in honor of the trustee of the Salk Institute who donated the funds for its construction.

44. Vincent J. Scully, *Louis I. Kahn* (New York: George Braziller, 1962), 39.

45. Vreeland, telephone interview with Daniel S. Friedman, March 27, 1990.

46. "Program Abstract," under "The Meeting House Group."

47. Hall, "Gift from the Sea," 41.

48. On a sketch of the auditorium (drawing 540.188, Kahn Collection) Kahn wrote, "revolve the entire house with the auditorium to give more room at site entrance and make the religious place out of parallel with the house"; the sketch was made to indicate that the central axes of the auditorium, the meeting house proper, and the water channel of the fountain should not be parallel with one another.

49. "Program Abstract," under "Rooms for Temporary Residence."

50. Hall, "Gift from the Sea," 41.

51. "Agreement Amending Architect's Agreement Between the Salk Institute for Biological Studies, San Diego, Formerly the Institute for Biology at San Diego, and Louis I. Kahn," August 29, 1963, "Salk–George Conn Correspondence," Box LIK 89, Kahn Collection.

52. Salk, telephone interview with Daniel S. Friedman, December 18, 1989.

53. Drawing 540.22, Kahn Collection. The commission for the new addition has been awarded to Anshen & Allen, Beverly Hills; it is being designed by John MacAllister.

In April 1959 representatives of the First Unitarian Church of Rochester, New York, first contacted Louis Kahn to express interest in retaining him as architect for their new building (fig. 446; see figs. 293–301).[1] The congregation faced inevitable eviction from its church, designed in 1859 by Richard Upjohn, for it stood on land slated for redevelopment. Having occupied the work of a prominent nineteenth-century American architect, the congregation "felt a responsibility of replacing it with one by a leading twentieth-century architect, giving the community a notable example of contemporary architecture."[2] A search committee contacted six nationally known architects, including Kahn.[3] They interviewed the others before visiting Kahn at his Philadelphia office on May 9.[4] After meeting him, the committee members unanimously agreed that he was "the out-of-town architect most ideally suited by training experience, achievement, and outlook to undertake the creative assignment we have in mind."[5] Kahn's appeal stemmed from the high compatibility of his philosophy with Unitarian ideas, as well as the committee's realization, with good foresight, that they were entering "on the ground floor of a new incarnation" of his career.[6]

The evolution of the Unitarian Church was in three distinct phases. The first phase, May and early June 1959, before the architect's first visit to Rochester, involved very simple preliminary sketches of circular and octagonal centralized structures. The second stage, prompted by calls for the submission of a design, saw the development of what Kahn later termed his "first design solution" in December 1959. He persisted with this square shape, despite the misgivings of the building committee, until early March 1960, when his clients' demand for a fresh start initiated the third stage. Responding to their desire for a two-building complex, Kahn compromised his ideal of a centralized plan and developed a loosely elongated scheme. This he tightened into the final design by January 1961. Construction began in June 1961, five months and a few changes later, and was basically complete in time for the church dedication in December 1962. In 1964 the congregation again hired Kahn to design an addition, which was completed in 1969.

On June 2, 1959, Kahn received a copy of the program, entitled "Profile of the New Unitarian Church Building," which outlined the congregation's wishes, culled from a questionnaire.[7] They requested "a church of contemporary—or modern—design, of permanent beauty and real artistic value—rather than the 'exaggerated,' 'bizarre' or 'faddish.'" Their interest in permanence, as well as their preference for brick or stone, proved

First Unitarian Church and School

Rochester, New York, 1959–69

remarkably compatible with the increasing weightiness of Kahn's architecture during the late 1950s. Ironically, given the eventual expansion of the complex, the profile specified that the church "would NOT be built for future enlargement."

Kahn probably began work on the project in early June 1959 in preparation for his presentation in Rochester, scheduled for mid-June, at which the congregation would vote whether to confirm the committee's choice and hire him.[8] From the outset Kahn chose to ignore the standard Unitarian church layout (alluded to in the profile) of separate school and auditorium wings. He preferred a centralized plan, with the school surrounding the auditorium. Kahn later claimed that this arrangement was inspired by a speech about Unitarianism that the minister had given when the architect first met with the congregation.[9] This is doubtful, since he had met no minister in Rochester. He had, however, discussed Unitarianism with a minister in Philadelphia prior to meeting his clients.[10]

Kahn's earliest known sketches show that he was working with a centralized concept from the beginning (see fig. 102). They investigate simple circular or octagonal forms as well as pronounced radiating diagonals, features that contrast with the dominant rectilinearity of the subsequent designs. Beyond his obvious desire to create a single, unified structure appropriate to Unitarianism, Kahn was also calling on other sources of inspiration. Although he later claimed that his conception avoided "a statement that already had many expressions of experience," these studies reveal the influence of past solutions to church planning upon his thinking.[11] One of the most powerful of these influences was Rudolf Wittkower's *Architectural Principles in the Age of Humanism*, which illustrated centrally planned Renaissance churches.[12]

Kahn first visited Rochester to meet the building committee and the congregation on June 17 and 18, 1959.[13] At the congregational meeting he presented his famous "form" drawing, which represented his design concept, and he mesmerized everyone in attendance with a philosophical discussion of his ideas (see fig. 106).[14] The congregation promptly voted in favor of hiring him.[15] His appointment preceded the selection of a site; during this visit he examined possible building locations with Jim Cunningham, who was on the search committee and later described himself as Kahn's "disciple in Rochester," and together they agreed upon the property later purchased, that on South Winton Road.[16]

446. Northeast corner of church, ca. 1969.
447. Plan, December 1959.
448. Model, ca. December 1959.
449. Plan, ca. February 1960.

Kahn next gave attention to the church in late November or early December 1959. The building committee, impatient to get under way, scheduled a meeting for December 13 at which they expected Kahn to submit a tangible proposal.[17] During this second stage he rapidly developed the design, retaining the centralized organization of his preliminary sketches but now setting it within a square plan. At the meeting Kahn presented his "first design solution," both in plan and model (figs. 447, 448).[18] Four-story towers, containing the library, chapel, and offices, defined the corners of this rigorously symmetrical project. Classrooms filled the three-story blocks between the towers. Enclosed beneath a twelve-sided fishbelly truss roof structure, the building's central area comprised a square auditorium ringed by concentric ambulatories and corridors. By creating two circulation areas, Kahn intended to allow for different degrees of faith, a feature that greatly appealed to the building committee.[19]

His clients' support of the design was diminished, however, by the projected cost of $2 million, which they considered exorbitant, given their $400,000 budget for the church.[20] Prompted by complaints about cost, Kahn almost immediately removed one story from the design.[21] But even so revised, the first design again met with an unfavorable response from the building committee in early January 1960. "The members liked your original, basic concept, but none of us care for your subsequent revision," he was told by Helen R. Williams, chairman of the building committee.[22] Their dissatisfaction stemmed from the plan's inflexibility, its lack of classroom space, and its apparent inappropriateness to the site. In the same letter Williams stated, "Under the circumstances we feel that further revision of your present plans would be futile and that a brand new approach to the problem would be preferable."

An undated sketch, probably from February 1960, shows the direction Kahn took at this point (fig. 449). He abandoned the circular and octagonal aspects that had characterized every previous study and instead adopted an exclusively right-angled scheme. Kahn could thereby easily adjust the size of the various spaces, achieving the flexibility his first design lacked. Although he resisted adopting the two-building format outlined in the program, this plan reveals the influence of Frank Lloyd Wright's Unity Temple in Oak Park (1904–05), the archetypal Unitarian church, which separated school from auditorium.[23] Wright's design is reflected in the corner spaces with stairs, the rectangular masses defining the flanks, and, especially, the square sanctuary.

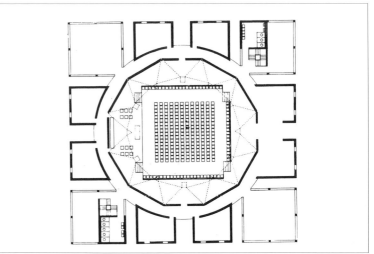

447

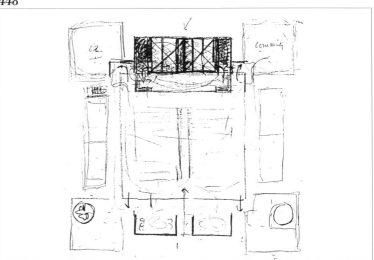

448

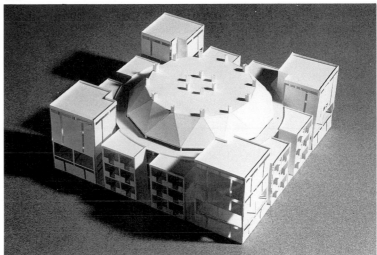

449

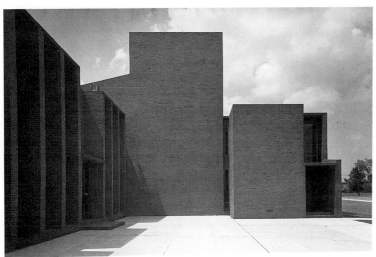

446

The building committee felt that even this new scheme failed to satisfy their needs and budget. In a letter of February 28, 1960, Williams summarized their concerns:

The result of our several meetings this past week is that we are not in any measure happy with the present concept which you have given us. Two sketches dated February 16, 1960 [now lost] represent a modification of your original idea pared down to meet our conflicting space and budget requirements. . . . We feel that we simply cannot enthusiastically recommend this idea to our congregation. In modification most of the charm of the original concept has been lost. . . . Our greatest concern is with the inherent "squareness" of the building.[24]

This last sentence, elevating an aesthetic issue to primary importance, rejected the design's Wrightian geometry and the continued use of a strict symmetrical organization. Within a week Williams's tone became considerably more stern: "We remain steadfast in the conclusion that we must have an entirely new concept, that the first proposal and its modifications are not satisfactory."[25] Shortly thereafter, Williams quit the building committee in frustration, unable to bridge the gap between the needs of the church and Kahn's design.[26] Under the new chairmanship of Maurice Van Horn, the building committee "agonized over saying no [to Kahn] . . . taking the chance that he would say 'Well all right, you want someone else, pay me off,' because that would really cripple our funds. But they finally just decided they had to and were very happy that he accepted it and started designing again."[27]

After the resolution of this potential impasse, in early March 1960, the third stage in the design evolution began. To bring Kahn "back to earth," the building committee suggested he consider designing a two-building complex (akin to the Unity Temple), since it "would be the cheapest [form of] construction."[28] According to Robert Jonas, chairman of the board of trustees, this recommendation "was a device to make him realize that we were aware of our financial limitations."[29] Under such pressure, Kahn evidently yielded to their advice, as seen in a second model, dating from March 1960 (fig. 450).[30] Kahn eliminated the corner towers of the first design, replacing them with two rooms at the east end of the building and another, containing the minister's office, at the west end. By moving spaces that were formerly accommodated by the towers to the two ends, Kahn established a new, more longitudinal emphasis. Although the model did not represent a wholesale adoption of a two-building scheme, it nevertheless shows that Kahn had modified his ideal of a centralized plan to a significant degree. At this stage Kahn also introduced a new roofing

450

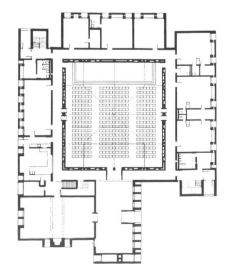

451

452

structure made up of concrete caps, each a shallow pyramid topped by a raised cross shape whose open ends formed four "dormer" windows.

Kahn presented this scheme to the building committee on March 26.[31] In April it was displayed to the congregation.[32] Van Horn expressed doubt about Kahn's proposed roof structure, having calculated that each twenty-two-foot-square concrete "roof dome" would weigh thirty-three tons and present "problems of support, especially in the auditorium."[33] In the next months Kahn proposed supporting the auditorium roof with piers, but the committee rejected this idea.[34]

The roofing controversy, however, did not delay the committee's approval of the plan in mid-June 1960 (fig. 451).[35] Two months later Van Horn reported that "the Committee was unanimous in its reapproval of the overall design submitted in June and [it was] overwhelmingly accepted by the congregation."[36] By this time Kahn had also modified the auditorium roof with the addition of light towers, for which the building committee made the important suggestions of glazing only their inner faces and of using adjustable windowpanes to control brightness in the auditorium.[37] While Kahn worked out these features, August Komendant, who had enhanced his reputation with the Vierendeel truss system he developed for Kahn's Richards Medical Research Building, devised a way to employ the same technology of prestressed reinforced concrete to span the Unitarian church auditorium.[38]

By January 1961 Kahn had arrived at his final design. He had so effectively tightened up the plan that its overall footprint had almost completely returned to a square shape (fig. 452). Kahn achieved this by simplifying the layouts for the rooms surrounding the auditorium. He made the plan even more compact by shortening the length of the foyer's projection out from the auditorium and merging a smaller meeting room opposite the entrance into the south range. He also harmonized the building's exterior by creating elevations with varied but similar patterns of deeply indented windows.

Kahn felt sufficiently proud of the design to send drawings to *Progressive Architecture* and *Architectural Design*; to the latter he also sent his own essay "Form and Design" (see fig. 109).[39] Between January and June little was changed. Despite the building committee's questions about the acoustics of the auditorium, by mid-May nine contractors had been invited to tender bids.[40] The committee's anxiety

over the estimated cost raised doubts that the design would proceed and prompted Kahn to issue a fervent telegram to them on June 15:

I wish to reinforce belief in the building we designed and to encourage that it be built in its present form. Our work and the work of your committee has, I believe, brought together a structure of simplicity and inspiration. Though the bid is higher than our ways of determining cost has indicated we believe that at the present time it is a fair bid. Our experience indicates that the time consumed in modifying a building proves costly[.] I hope that the congregation finds itself prepared to build as specified.[41]

Two days later the building committee awarded the contract to Robert Hyland & Sons, and on June 23 site preparation began in earnest.[42] The church was completed in time for the dedication on December 2, 1962. Kahn was so delighted with it that at the ceremony he delivered a "sermon" to the full congregation in which he discussed the relationship between architecture and religion.[43]

Kahn made his enthusiasm for the First Unitarian Church evident even before it received final approval from the building committee. As early as October 1960, in a lecture in California, he had chosen it to illustrate a pair of terms— "form" and "design"—that were becoming key tenets of his philosophy.[44] He used these words to describe his conception of architecture—and in particular his design procedure—as the translation of the intangible into the real. It was at this time that Kahn mythologized the way the design of the church had evolved, composing an account (accompanied by the now-famous diagram) that, since its publication in April 1961, has been seen as the clearest illustration of his design approach (see fig. 106).[45] Kahn began his description with the famous meeting, where:

from what I heard the minister speak about . . . I realized that the form aspect, the form realization of Unitarian activity was bound around that which is Question. I drew a diagram on the blackboard which I believe served as the Form drawing of the church and, of course, was not meant to be a suggested design. . . . At one stage of discussion some even insisted that the sanctuary be separated entirely from the school. I said fine, let's put it that way, and then put the sanctuary in one place and connected it up with a very neat little connector to the school. Soon everyone realized that . . . the classrooms, when separated, lost their use for religious and intellectual purposes, and, like a stream, they all came back around the sanctuary. . . . So the final design does not correspond to the first design, but the form held.[46]

The account gives the false impression that during a single, intense session—the first meeting with the congregation—

450. *Model, March 1960.*
451. *Plan. Inscribed June 18,*
1960 Louis I. Kahn.
452. *Plan, ca. June 1961.*

Kahn spontaneously conceived the "form" and successfully dissuaded his clients from a two-building scheme. His development of the form actually occurred over several months, and the two-building format influenced his thinking more than halfway through the design procedure. The account also implies that once the plan was set, the architect's design was fully established, when in fact nothing above ground level had been resolved. While one might argue that Kahn's telling of the story merely represents an extreme condensation of the actual sequence of events, such streamlining gave an entirely false view, implying that his form-to-design procedure was carried out with great ease, simplicity, and effectiveness. Most important, his oversimplification belies the rich and complex variety of historical sources influencing his design.[47]

In 1962 Kahn designed tapestries, with a pattern representing the shattering of light into the color spectrum, to adorn the gray cinderblock walls of the auditorium.[48] Following two years' delay due to the difficulty of weaving the intricate design, the tapestries were installed along the side walls of the auditorium.[49] Around this time, less than two years after the dedication, the church trustees realized that they already needed additional space; in September 1964, despite their original plans to the contrary, they decided to expand the complex.[50] The congregation voted in May 1965 to rehire Kahn to design an addition that would preserve the integrity of the earlier building.[51] The addition, extending eastward from the lobby area, provided more space for classrooms, offices, and adult activities. Its unarticulated exterior wall surfaces and rectangular mass act as a foil to the varied and sculptural massing of the original structure. Construction began in the fall of 1967. The addition was dedicated on May 25, 1969, after a longer period of planning and building than the church itself had required.

Robin B. Williams

Notes

1. Letter, James Cunningham (chairman, search committee) to Kahn, April 7, 1959, "Building Committee Correspondence—Rochester, April 1959 through December 1960," Box LIK 15, Louis I. Kahn Collection, University of Pennsylvania and Pennsylvania Historical and Museum Commission, Philadelphia (hereafter cited as Kahn Collection).
2. Jean France, "First Unitarian Church, Rochester, New York," pamphlet (Rochester, 1987). France, an architectural historian at the University of Rochester, has been instrumental in organizing the historical record of the church.
3. "Architectural and Building Committee Reminiscences, First Unitarian Church, Rochester, N.Y.," February 28, 1979, tape 1, side 1 (hereafter cited as "Reminiscences"). These tapes, which were compiled by Jean France and include reminiscences by committee members, are in the possession of the First Unitarian Church; copies are in the Kahn Collection. Besides Kahn, the committee corresponded with Frank Lloyd Wright and met with Paul Rudolph, Carl Koch, Eero Saarinen, and Walter Gropius.
4. Letter, Cunningham to Kahn, May 22, 1959, "Building Committee Correspondence, April 1959 through December 1960," Box LIK 15, Kahn Collection.
5. Letter, William Neuman (chairman, board of directors) to Kahn, June 1, 1959, ibid. The members of the search committee were Jim Cunningham, Beth Mood, and Jack Bennett, who was soon after replaced by Jean France; "Reminiscences," tape 1, side 1.
6. France, "Reminiscences," tape 1, side 1.
7. A copy of the profile, dated March 19, 1959, was enclosed with a letter, Neuman to Kahn, June 1, 1959, "Building Committee Correspondence, April 1959 through December 1960," Box LIK 15, Kahn Collection.
8. The dates for the visit had been set during a telephone conversation between Neuman and Kahn on May 31, 1959; letters, Neuman to Kahn, June 1, 1959, and Kahn to Neuman, June 4, 1959, ibid.
9. Kahn, "Form and Design," *Architectural Design* 31 (April 1961): 148.
10. Cunningham, "Reminiscences," tape 1, side 1.
11. Kahn, quoted in "Kahn" (interview, February 1961), *Perspecta*, no. 7 (1961): 15.
12. In 1956 he had received a copy of the book from Wittkower's distinguished student Colin Rowe; letter, Rowe to Kahn, February 7, 1956, Box LIK 65, Kahn Collection.
13. His visit is confirmed by a letter, France to Kahn, July 1, 1959, "Building Committee Correspondence, April 1959 through December 1960," Box LIK 15, Kahn Collection.
14. Stanwood T. Hyde, interview with Robin B. Williams, May 29, 1990. Tapes are in the Kahn Collection.
15. Hyde, interview with Williams. The contract was not signed until August 8, 1959; "Contract and Contract Corres., First Unitarian Society of Rochester, New York," "Rochester I," Box LIK 81, Kahn Collection.
16. Kahn's involvement in the site selection is documented in "Reminiscences," tape 1, side 1.
17. Letter, Helen R. Williams to Kahn, n.d. (received by Kahn December 7, 1959), "Building Committee Correspondence, April 1959 through December 1960," Box LIK 15, Kahn Collection.
18. This can be inferred from a letter, Kahn to Williams, December 30, 1959, ibid., in which Kahn discussed the features of his "revised plans," implying that he had already made a presentation at the only previous meeting, on December 13. That he presented the "first design" there is confirmed by references in the letter to two-story spaces in the towers, a feature represented in the model by the double-height T-shaped windows.
19. France and Cunningham, "Reminiscences," tape 1, side 2.
20. Robert Jonas "Reminiscences," tape 1, side 2.

21. Letter, Kahn to Williams, December 30, 1959, "Building Committee Correspondence, April 1959 through December 1960," Box LIK 15, Kahn Collection.

22. Letter, Williams to Kahn, January 8, 1960, ibid. Jonas, in interview with Robin B. Williams, May 29, 1990, identified a further problem: that the "first design" lacked a lobby area in which the congregation could meet before entering the sanctuary.

23. Vincent J. Scully, *Louis I. Kahn* (New York: George Braziller, 1962), 34, identifies the influence of Wright's Unity Temple upon the building as constructed.

24. Letter, Williams to Kahn, February 28, 1960, "Building Committee Correspondence, April 1959 through December 1960," Box LIK 15, Kahn Collection.

25. Letter, Williams to Kahn, March 6, 1960, ibid.

26. Jonas, "Reminiscences," tape 1, side 2.

27. Jonas, interview with Williams.

28. Letter, Jonas to Robin B. Williams, May 31, 1990.

29. Ibid.

30. In a letter Helen Williams referred to "the models" of the church, presumably referring to a new model and that of the "first design," as no other models are known to have been made; letter, Williams to Kahn, March 20, 1960, "Building Committee Correspondence, April 1959 through December 1960," Box LIK 15, Kahn Collection. A sketch (now in the Kahn Collection, drawing 525.4) datable to this design phase appears to depict a two-building scheme, offering evidence that Kahn briefly considered such an arrangement.

31. This can be deduced from a pair of letters sent by Maurice Van Horn to Kahn. In one he refers to "concrete roof caps"; letter, Van Horn to Kahn, n.d. (received by Kahn March 29, 1960), "Building Committee Correspondence, April 1959 through December 1960," Box LIK 15, Kahn Collection. In the second, Van Horn mentions Kahn's presentation at the March 26 meeting; letter, Van Horn to Kahn, April 2, 1960, ibid.

32. Letter, Van Horn to Kahn, April 2, 1960, ibid.

33. Letter, Van Horn to Kahn, May 2, 1960, ibid. A sketch of one such "roof dome" on the back of this letter confirms that it was the same type as proposed in the second model.

34. Letters, Van Horn to Kahn, July 7 and August 23, 1960, ibid.

35. Letter, Van Horn to Kahn, June 30, 1960, ibid.

36. Letter, Van Horn to Kahn, August 23, 1960, ibid.

37. Ibid.

38. See Komendant's account of his work at the First Unitarian Church in August E. Komendant, *18 Years with Architect Louis I. Kahn* (Englewood, N.J.: Aloray 1975), 33–40.

39. Letter, Tim Vreeland (Kahn's office) to Monica Pidgeon (editor, *Architectural Design*), January 11, 1961, "Master Files, Jan. 1–Feb 28/61," Box LIK 9, Kahn Collection.

40. Regarding the acoustics, see letter, William Porter (Kahn's Rochester representative) to office of Bolt Beranek and Newman, March 22, 1961, "Master Files, March 1–May 31, 1961," Box LIK 9, Kahn Collection. The nine shortlisted contracting firms are named in a letter, Porter to Rochester Builders Exchange, May 17, 1961, "UCRNY— Correspondence, Miscellaneous," Box LIK 15, Kahn Collection.

41. Telegram, Kahn to Van Horn, June 15, 1961, "Building Committee Correspondence 1961," Box LIK 15, Kahn Collection.

42. Letter, Porter to Sanders, June 21, 1961, "Hyland, Robert F. & Sons—Contractor Correspondence—June 1961 to April 1962," ibid. Information on the progress of site preparation is contained in a report, Hyde to Kahn, n.d. (received by Kahn July 7, 1961), "Rochester Project Inspector's Reports from Beginning to 28 Feb 62," ibid. Problems in obtaining building permits delayed construction of the building proper until at least July 31; letter, Porter to Garratt, July 31, 1961, "UCRNY— Correspondence, Miscellaneous," ibid.

43. Komendant, *18 Years*, 40.

44. See Kahn, "The Difference between Form and Design," speech delivered to Southern California Chapter, American Institute of Architects, Triennial Awards Banquet, October 11, 1960, typescript, "L.I.K. Lectures," Box LIK 15, Kahn Collection. For a Voice of America Forum Lecture, broadcast on November 21, 1960, Kahn read a revised version of the same talk, retitled "Structure and Form," reprinted as "Form and Design," Scully, *Kahn*, 114–21.

45. Kahn's well-known account of the design evolution was first published simultaneously in Kahn, "Form and Design," 148, and Jan C. Rowan, "Wanting to Be: The Philadelphia School," *Progressive Architecture* 42 (April 1961): 134.

46. Kahn, quoted in Rowan, "Wanting to Be," 134.

47. For a more complete analysis of Kahn's mythologization of his design procedure, see Robin B. Williams, "An Architectural Myth: The Design Evolution of Louis Kahn's First Unitarian Church" (M.A. paper, University of Pennsylvania, 1990).

48. France, "Reminiscences," tape 2, side 2.

49. Ibid. In his original plans Kahn had included a pair of hangings for the front wall representing the synthesis of light; but after seeing the first hangings in place, he decided this wall should remain bare.

50. Dave Tuttle (building committee member), "Reminiscences," tape 2, side 2.

51. Ibid.

In 1959, when the Fine Arts Foundation of Fort Wayne, Indiana, first envisioned a complex of buildings for cultural institutions that would provide a focal point for the city's urban renewal program, Fort Wayne was a small midwestern city with a large cultural appetite.[1] Fourteen years after beginning to work with Louis Kahn on plans for this cultural center, the city had built only one theater, dedicated in October 1973 (fig. 453; see figs. 302–4). Kahn died five months after its completion.

The Fort Wayne Fine Arts Foundation was a multifaceted organization and a difficult client. It promoted, raised funds for, and supervised building projects for the historical society, the philharmonic orchestra, the civic theater, the art school and museum, the ballet, community concerts, and their own offices. Each of these institutions was to have used one or more buildings in the complex. The historical society needed a museum of local history. A concert hall, equipped with 2,500 seats, was to serve both the orchestra and the ballet, while a smaller auditorium of 400 seats was to provide a more intimate space for chamber music and lectures.

In the fall of 1959 the Fine Arts Foundation considered several internationally prominent architects for the commission, including Marcel Breuer, Paul Rudolph, Edward Durell Stone, Minoru Yamasaki, Philip Johnson, Eero Saarinen, and Ludwig Mies van der Rohe.[2] Irving Latz, director of the building committee for the foundation, was familiar with the Yale Art Gallery, and on November 3, 1959, he contacted Kahn to ask if he would be interested in the project, which involved not only designing the buildings but also helping to choose a site.[3] Kahn first met with Latz and Richard F. Gibeau, executive director of the foundation, the following June.[4] In October 1960 Latz and the building committee visited Kahn's office in Philadelphia, and the architect gave them a tour of the Richards Medical Research Building; the group also traveled to New Haven to see the Yale gallery.[5] Kahn received confirmation of the commission in January 1961, and Gibeau wrote to him: "We are highly pleased here that we have reached this point in our long journey toward the realization of the Fine Arts Center. We eagerly anticipate working with you and will endeavor to do everything we can to simplify the task ahead to our mutual advantage."[6]

Kahn began work on the project in 1962. His first responsibility was to help the building committee establish an appropriate site for the arts center. In analyzing Fort Wayne's urban plan, Kahn recognized a problem: the peninsula in the northern part of the city—a potentially beneficial park area—was cut off from the city center by the Nickel Plate railway. Kahn made an extensive model that suggested radical changes in the city plan (fig. 454),[7] and it shows how he used the railway to best advantage by including it as part of a citywide "viaduct" system. He hoped that this municipal network, which included a structure running atop the tracks and three immense round parking garages, would link the park on the peninsula, north of the railway, to the rest of the city. In a letter to Latz, Kahn explained: "This link should be a major opening under the present Nickel Plate RR overpass. It should be elegant. It should provide parking, rentable space, an arcaded shopping and resting area and other services. It should be an expression of 'entrance' to both city center and park."[8] In an elevation drawing, probably dating from spring 1962,[9] the arcades of the railway viaduct extend across the page, screening a variety of arts center buildings (fig. 457). The center played an essential role in Kahn's vision of a renewed Fort Wayne, in spite of the fact that in the model it seemed modest compared to the vast viaduct system. The arts center was nestled into the curve of the railway just north of the northeast parking garage, and its elaborate plan offset the city's otherwise even grid pattern.

Once Kahn and the committee agreed on the plot bounded by the railroad on the north, Main Street on the south, Lafayette Street on the east, and Clinton Street on the west, he began to experiment with the placement of buildings.[10] In the early development of the arts center Kahn worked with elemental forms that were not always defined by function; a long rectangular building, for example, was originally designated as the art school and later proposed to house the historical museum and the art alliance,[11] which would contain a reception center and the offices of the Fine Arts Foundation.

Early models indicate that Kahn was at first interested in the relationships between similarly shaped solids and voids and in the repetition of geometric formal patterns. These formal relationships may be seen in a plaster model from 1963 (fig. 455).[12] The philharmonic hall, in the upper left portion of the photograph, occupies the lozenge-shaped building jutting in from the northwest corner of the site (seen from the south in this photograph). Parking garages, parallel to the railway, stretch along the northern edge of the site. The square building, divided diagonally like the philharmonic hall, contained a smaller theater for drama and ballet. Just east of this theater, at the eastern edge of the plot, Kahn placed a dormitory building, which does not seem to have been part of the clients' program. The art alliance building

Fine Arts Center, School, and Performing Arts Theater

Fort Wayne, Indiana, 1959–73

453. *Performing Arts Theater, 1975.*
454. *Model of arts center and downtown Fort Wayne, with viaduct and parking towers, ca. 1963.*
455. *Site model, Summer 1963.*
456. *Site plan. Inscribed LIK 6 Oct 63.*

was set at an angle in the southeast corner. To contrast his angled placement of the reception center, Kahn fixed the historical museum in exact alignment with the southwest corner of the site. Along the southern edge of the site, nearest to downtown Fort Wayne, he delimited the arts center with a long rectangular building for the art school. A more elaborate, and therefore probably later, cardboard model showing these features was presented to the Fort Wayne Fine Arts Foundation in August 1963.[13] Since the plaster model was simpler in design, it may be plausibly dated to the early summer of 1963.

A few months later the Kahn office was busy with newly changed plans for Fort Wayne. In a sketch dated October 6, 1963, Kahn blocked out four structures and a triangular courtyard (fig. 456). Although the philharmonic hall was still oriented on a diagonal, Kahn rounded the inner point of the lozenge to depict an auditorium. The perimeter of the courtyard echoed the triangular structure adjacent to it, and the interior of this building, the civic theater, contained circular voids that mirrored the philharmonic hall. At the southern edge of the site Kahn again separated the complex from the city with a long rectangular building, probably still the art school. Kahn must have intended to combine several functions within these three relatively geometric buildings and the one roughly described structure at right, because he included fewer separate structures than in earlier plans.

A sheet of thumbnail sketches, probably from October 1963,[14] demonstrates how Kahn continued to confront the design of the site plan by sketching a series of elemental forms (see fig. 179). In these seemingly playful drawings, Kahn did not limit himself to a fixed number of buildings. All of the plans do show a large element at the left, however, which must be the philharmonic hall; it never strayed from the northwest corner of the site. Kahn alternated between wedging the structure into the corner of the site and placing it parallel to the site's western edge. The small sketch in the upper left corner of the sheet resembles a subsequent model (see fig. 182). The model shows the large concert hall jutting in at an angle from the northwest corner, and the redefinition of the once rectangular structure along the southern edge of the site into two buildings—the historical museum at the left and the hollowed-out art alliance at the right. Kahn eliminated the parking garages from the northern edge of the site. He intended the modular building at the right to be the art school;[15] the square compartments would have served well as individual studios.

This model was not the only enlarged and elaborated scheme

454

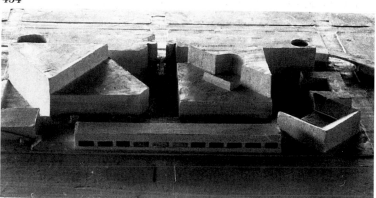

455

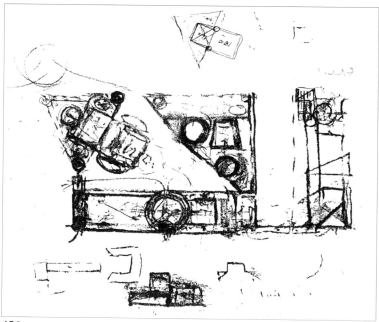

456

453

457

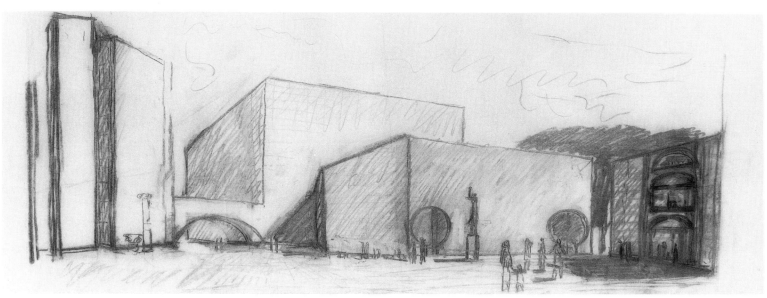

458

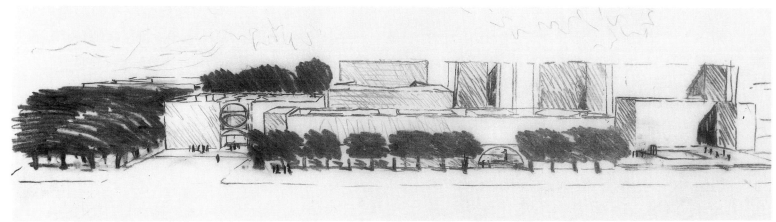

459

457. South elevation of arts
center, showing viaduct
system, ca. April 1962.
458. Perspective of Court of
Entrances. Inscribed Lou K
'66.
459. Bird's-eye perspective, ca.
1966.
460. Plan. Inscribed LIK
30 Oct '63.

based on the thumbnail sketches; one sketch, dated October 30, suggests that by the end of that month Kahn had rejected the diagonal placement of the philharmonic hall and opted instead to place this large building parallel to the western edge of the site (fig. 460). It was also at this time that Kahn arrived at a solution for the plan of the philharmonic hall itself—a rectangle with towerlike attachments on its corners. A lozenge-shaped annex housed the school of music and ballet and linked the philharmonic hall to the smaller theater. The southern edge of the plot was once again delimited by a long rectangular building, but Kahn opened up this building to the city of Fort Wayne with a pedestrian entrance. The entrance led the way to a lozenge-shaped garden; in plan, this garden appeared as a void in the same shape as the solid annex.

Unfortunately, as Kahn continued to refine the site plan in the fall of 1963, the patrons in Fort Wayne determined that they could not afford to build the complex all at once. In December 1963 the Fine Arts Foundation decided to build the 500-seat civic theater and the art museum first, followed by the reception center, a shared facility for welcoming and serving guests of the arts complex.[16] Early in 1964 the historical society pulled out of the project, and Kahn had to rework the site plan.[17] Meanwhile, his clients in Fort Wayne were still attempting to acquire the land, and in September 1964 the commissioners predicted that the site would not be available for building until February or March 1966.[18]

A large sketch by Kahn dated January 2, 1965, closely approximates the eventual plan, after the withdrawal of the historical society but before severe cutbacks made it unlikely that the entire complex would ever be built (see fig. 181). The plan had not changed much since October 1963. Visitors would have entered the arts complex through the garden between the art museum and the reception center, and proceeded past an outdoor amphitheater, on their right. In front of them would be the diverse grouping of the philharmonic hall, the annex, and the theater; these buildings framed what Kahn termed a "court of entrances." This court would be a meeting place for the city and the focal point of the scheme. Kahn placed the art school, no longer a compartmentalized structure but a complicated symmetrical building, away from the central courtyard, in the northeast corner of the site.

One of the few surviving perspective drawings of the complex, dated 1966 (fig. 458), provides a southern view of the court of entrances—the view a visitor would have after passing through the garden in the southernmost structure.

Near the center, an archway connects the lozenge-shaped annex to the civic theater, and a building on the far right, possibly the reception center, has large windows offering an open facade to visitors.[19] In a second, closely related drawing, the entire arts center unfolds before the viewer (fig. 459). Each building fits neatly into the complete "entity," as Kahn called the center.

Kahn may have used these two perspective drawings to prepare for a portentous meeting in June 1966, or perhaps to rouse the committee's enthusiasm after the discouraging encounter. He implored the committee members to consider the public nature of the project and the importance of the arts center in its entirety. Although Kahn and committee members agreed to build the civic theater, the architect hoped to elevate the status of the project beyond that of an ordinary public auditorium. Kahn argued, somewhat obscurely, that the civic theater should be thought of as "a non-flat public square."[20] He hoped that the theater, charged with artistic possibilities, would convince Fort Wayne residents that art could play a more integral part in their lives. In further asserting the worth of the entire plan, he said, "one part is ordinary, [but the] whole thing is exemplary."[21] The meeting adjourned with one of many monetary debates: the committee claimed they could raise funds for the complex only if they broke ground for the first building, and Kahn countered that he could not complete one building until he knew the details of the whole complex.

On October 12, 1966, Richard E. Baker, the director of the Fort Wayne Ballet, baldly stated what may have been the reason for the slow development of the commission in general. Referring to the 500-seat civic theater, he confided; "We have the feeling that the theater is too experimental for Fort Wayne."[22] One week later, on October 19, 1966, the building committee for the foundation resolved that the 2,500-seat philharmonic hall was too large for their needs, and that they would build a simpler version of the civic theater. To compensate for lost seating, they increased the theater's capacity from 500 to 1,000.[23] After 1966 Kahn's effort was directed toward this new Theater of the Performing Arts, which, at least in the short term, would have to serve the needs of dance, orchestra, and ballet. This theater was the one element of Kahn's "entity" that was finally erected (see fig. 453).

Kahn repeatedly used the metaphor of a violin and violin case to describe his design for auditoriums—a metaphor he also used for the Fort Wayne philharmonic hall. In a section drawing of the performing arts theater dated

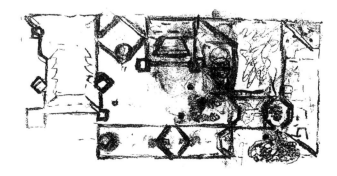

February 1968, Kahn designated the inner structure the "VIOLIN" and the outer wall the "Brick Violin Case" (fig. 461). He noted on a closely related drawing: "The concrete Violin is the structure of the Hall. The exterior of brick is separated from it as is the case of a VIOLIN."[24] Kahn elaborated this idea in a brief statement for the dedication ceremony for the theater: "A whisper on stage must be heard by everyone in the audience. This motivated the thought of the 'Violin' and the 'Violin Case.' The place of the voice is the 'violin'—the stage and the people. The 'Case' is the entrance, the lobby and all other outside services."[25] As explained by Cengiz Yetken, project architect for the theater, Kahn noted that each theatrical performance, like a performance on the violin, happens only once, in a moment that is unique. He also suggested that the range of an actor's voice is as important as the range of notes on the violin—in both instances every nuance deserves close attention. By isolating the actors' precious speech from external noise, he hoped to keep art in a special realm—as a violin is separated from the world by its case.[26] But unlike actors in theaters, violins cannot be heard by anyone so long as they remain in their cases; as his clients in Fort Wayne must have learned, Kahn's metaphoric capabilities were not always flawless. Indeed, Kahn hardly needed the metaphor to justify his design, because the duplicated outer wall that he used in other projects for screening the sun was here desperately needed to eliminate sound from the nearby railroad. More generally, the violin/violin case idea was simply a musical referent for Kahn's longstanding interest in "served" and "servant" spaces.

In the same month that Kahn produced the labeled violin drawing, the board of directors of the Fine Arts Foundation approved the plan for the 1,000-seat multipurpose theater "in principle" but complained that they had no way of knowing what it would look like "to a passer-by."[27] Their complaints were warranted, given Kahn's usual practice of reworking the plan for extended periods of time before developing the elevation. The facade of the theater took shape only in 1968, and, as finally resolved, it strongly resembled a face or mask (see fig. 303). It is unlikely that Kahn planned it as a work of imitative imagery, and if similar keyhole-shaped windows had been carried across the facade of the adjacent art school, its cartoonish effect would have been greatly diminished.

Construction of the theater began in 1970 and was completed in 1973. As the only built part of the complex, the theater stands as an apparent fragment of an unfinished whole. Kahn lamented this situation in a letter to Milford Miller,

461. Section through theater.
Inscribed LIK Feb 12 '68.

executive director of the Fort Wayne Fine Arts Foundation in the early 1970s: "I know you must realize that the Theatre was conceived to be sympathetic and dependent on the buildings framing the 'court of entrances' and without them the theater alone will look lonely and bare."[28] But, lonely or not, the theater was highly regarded. The pianist Rudolf Serkin toured Kahn's not-yet-completed theater with Irving Latz in 1973, and Latz reported to Kahn that "[Serkin] was so excited by the building—your building—that he *volunteered* to come back, if possible, for the dedication, and play—gratis—in tribute to you!"[29] Kahn responded warmly: "Your letter made my day my week my everytime."[30]

Carla Yanni

Notes

1. For a discussion of Kahn's designs for the Fine Arts Center in Fort Wayne, see Heinz Ronner and Sharad Jhaveri, *Louis I. Kahn: Complete Work, 1935–1974*, 2d ed. (Basel and Boston: Birkhäuser, 1987), 198–207; Vincent Scully, "Light, Form, and Power: New Work of Louis Kahn," *Architectural Forum* 121/22 (August–September 1964): 162–70; Jack Perry Brown, *Louis Kahn in the Midwest* (Chicago: Art Institute of Chicago, 1989); and Cengiz Yetken, "Louis Kahn in the Midwest," *Inland Architect* 33 (May/June 1989): 32, 36, 75.

2. Letter, Latz to Kahn, December 9, 1959, "Fort Wayne Fine Arts Foundation Correspondence 11-60 to 6-7-66," Box LIK 17, Louis I. Kahn Collection, University of Pennsylvania and Pennsylvania Historical and Museum Commission, Philadelphia (hereafter cited as Kahn Collection).

3. Letter, Latz to Kahn, November 3, 1959, ibid.

4. Letter, Gibeau to Kahn, June 22, 1960, ibid.

5. Letter, Latz to Kahn, October 13, 1960, ibid.

6. Letter, Gibeau to Kahn, January 27, 1961, ibid.

7. Letter, Kahn to Latz, April 25, 1962, ibid. This letter indicates that in April 1962 Kahn presented a model to the Fine Arts Committee that he used to discuss his preferences for the site selection, but the model presented was not necessarily the one illustrated here. The city-plan model in fig. 454 includes a plan for the arts center in a form that was not established until autumn 1963 (see fig. 182). Either the model from 1962 has been lost, or the model illustrated was altered in 1963.

8. Letter, Kahn to Latz, April 25, 1962, ibid.

9. Ibid.

10. Minutes, April 11, 1963, ibid. Although evidence for the exact date of site selection remains inconclusive, Kahn's recommendations seem to have been accepted by the time of this meeting.

11. Scully, "Light, Form, and Power," 170.

12. Although this model is similar to the small clay massing models in the collection of the Museum of Modern Art, it is large enough for presentation and therefore seems to hold a greater importance in the design development. At any rate, it is the design Kahn chose to enlarge for further study.

13. Minutes, August 22, 1963, "Fort Wayne Fine Arts Foundation Correspondence 11-60 to 6-7-66," Box LIK 17, Kahn Collection. The minutes refer to a cardboard model presented on July 24, 1963. Office drawings dated July 23, 1963, are in the Kahn Collection. The lost model is illustrated in Scully, "Light, Form, and Power," 170, model no. 2.

14. The sheet may be dated to October 1963 because the thumbnail plans resemble two dated sketches, figs. 456 and 460, which are marked, respectively, "6 Oct 63" and "30 Oct."

15. Scully, "Light, Form, and Power," 170.

16. Letter, Russell M. Daane (president, Fort Wayne Fine Arts Foundation), to Kahn, December 5, 1963, "Fort Wayne Fine Arts Foundation Correspondence 11-60 to 6-7-66," Box LIK 17, Kahn Collection.

17. Letter, Roy Vollmer, Jr. (Kahn's office), to George M. Schaefer (executive director, Fort Wayne Fine Arts Foundation), January 16, 1964, ibid.

18. Minutes, September 14, 1964, ibid.

19. There is no surviving dated plan that corresponds exactly to this perspective drawing, but one undated plan clearly shows an archway and is closely related; drawing 605.12, Kahn Collection.

20. Minutes, June 7, 1966, "Fort Wayne Fine Arts Foundation Correspondence 11-60 to 6-7-66," Box LIK 17, Kahn Collection.

21. Ibid.

22. Letter, Baker to Kahn, October 12, 1966, "Fort Wayne Fine Arts Foundation Correspondence 6-7-66 to 1-31-67," LIK Box 17, Kahn Collection.

23. Letter, David Wisdom (Kahn's office) to Edward F. Menerth (executive director, Fort Wayne Fine Arts Foundation), October 19, 1966, ibid.

24. Drawing 605.125, Kahn Collection.

25. Memo for dedication brochure, September 20, 1973, "F.W.F.A.F. '69—Theatre Misc. Correspondence," Box LIK 19, Kahn Collection.

26. Yetken, interview with Carla Yanni, May 17, 1990.

27. Letter, Menerth to Kahn, February 9, 1968, "Fort Wayne Correspondence 2-1-67 thru 12-68," Box LIK 17, Kahn Collection.

28. Letter, Kahn to Miller, n.d., "F.W.F.A.F. '69—Theatre Milford M. Miller Corres," Box LIK 19, Kahn Collection. A duplicate of this undated letter may be found in "Master File 1 January 1971 thru 30 August 71," Box LIK 10, Kahn Collection; it indicates that the letter was mailed on February 16 or 17, 1971.

29. Letter, Latz to Kahn, March 3, 1973, "F.W.F.A.F. '69—Theatre Misc. Correspondence," Box LIK 19, Kahn Collection. This letter also indicates that Serkin was unable to perform at the dedication ceremony because he was in Israel.

30. Letter, Kahn to Latz, March 13, 1973, ibid.

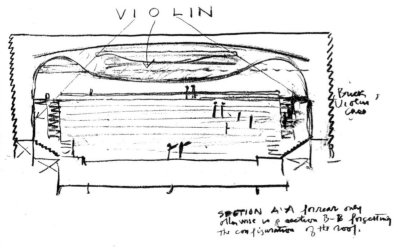

Louis Kahn's Erdman Hall at Bryn Mawr College was among the first of his works to achieve an international reputation (fig. 462; see figs. 305–13). The three diamonds of its plan, the most striking aspect of the design, were the culmination of a decade of experimentation with geometric forms and his musings over an even longer period about the character of private and public space. Erdman was nonetheless atypical. Unlike the more or less linear design histories of Kahn's other buildings, Erdman's development is the story of not one but two parallel schemes, pursued simultaneously but separately, which gradually converged in the built design.

Although Bryn Mawr College was an institutional client, Kahn dealt largely with one individual, Katharine Elizabeth McBride, who had been president of the college since 1942. McBride was a member of the Bryn Mawr class of 1925 and had served as dean of Radcliffe College before her return to Bryn Mawr.[1] She continued the tradition of strong-willed and energetic presidents established by M. Carey Thomas, who presided over the college for a half century after its opening in 1885. During the first seventeen years of McBride's presidency there was little construction at the college, but by the late 1950s it had become clear that a new library and dormitory were needed. McBride was interested in marking her presidency at Bryn Mawr architecturally. For this there was a strong Bryn Mawr precedent: President Thomas had herself been a demanding architectural patron who, together with architects Walter Cope and John Stewardson, had largely created the Gothic campus of gray rubble walls and white limestone trim in which Kahn was to work.[2]

McBride came to Kahn circuitously. In early autumn 1959 she asked her friend Eleanor Marquand Delanoy, a member of the board of trustees, how she should go about finding an architect. Should there be a competition? Or should the college appoint an architect for all of its buildings? Delanoy, who lived in Princeton and had ties to that university, wrote McBride on October 24 to say that it was Princeton's policy to use different architects for different buildings. Her Princeton friends recommended such "world famous names" as Richard Neutra and Marcel Breuer.[3] She thought it might be tactful to use an out-of-town architect, but if a Philadelphian was needed, she recommended Kahn, "who is doing the Penn Science Building [the Richards Medical Research Building]." McBride was inclined toward Neutra at first and made arrangements to meet with him through Delanoy. But Neutra was old and very busy, and when his planned October visit to Princeton was postponed until April 1960, McBride turned elsewhere.[4]

At this critical moment another friend of McBride's seems to have spoken up for Kahn. Phyllis Goodhart Gordan, a trustee of the college and a member of the dormitory building committee, was also familiar with Kahn's work. She was very close to Vanna Venturi, whose son Robert had worked with Kahn.[5] Apparently Venturi recommended Kahn to Goodhart, who in turn spoke with McBride; at any rate, when Kahn was approached by Bryn Mawr in early spring of 1960, he immediately sent a thank-you note to Vanna Venturi.[6]

The approach to Kahn was tentative. Bryn Mawr's endowment was precariously small and there were no certain donors for such a building. McBride was surely counting on her friend Eleanor Donnelley Erdman, a college trustee, who had planned to leave the college over one million dollars. But when Erdman died in early January 1960, her will was not completed.[7] Nonetheless, Kahn indicated his interest and McBride set about preparing a building program. This was completed on May 5, 1960, and sent to Kahn on May 24.[8]

The program specified a dormitory to house 130 students in "a variety of size and shape of rooms." While the building was clearly to be modern, the intention was to retain some of the amenities of Cope and Stewardson's dormitories: the rooms were to have window seats and "concealed moldings for hanging photographs." The "excessive amount of glass" of recent college architecture was also to be avoided. But above all, much attention in the program was paid to the character of dormitory living. Life at Bryn Mawr was strongly colored by its dormitory system, and each of the residences had a dining hall, social rooms, and a staff of live-in maids. The new dormitory was therefore intended to have its own dining hall as well as a "large reception room for teas," several smaller reception rooms, and "one large 'noisy' smoking room with a fireplace."[9]

Kahn attended the World Design Conference in Tokyo in May 1960, but at the end of the month he wrote McBride that he was back and planning to "begin the studies in a week or so."[10] Only a few drawings, none of them dated and some of them preserved only in photographs, record these first probing studies. These are divided into two groups: schematic studies that laid out the required number of rooms graphically (fig. 463), and more resolved sketch plans, which translated the parts of the program into interconnected rectangular figures (fig. 464).[11] In all of these the principal

Eleanor Donnelley Erdman Hall, Bryn Mawr College

Bryn Mawr, Pennsylvania, 1960–65

462. Rear facade.
463. Schematic program diagram, May–November 1960.
464. Plan, May–November 1960.
465. Main-level plan. Inscribed November 25, 1960.

point of interest was the union of several large public spaces with the dormitory rooms themselves.

Bryn Mawr, still without money for the building, did not press Kahn. When Robert M. Cooke, the college's insurance agent, visited Kahn's office on August 26, he found the plans "not developed" and the architect could only assure him that the dormitory would have concrete floors and roofs and be fireproof.[12] Not until November, when McBride invited Kahn to present his proposals to the college, were scale drawings prepared.

Kahn's long-time collaborator Anne Tyng prepared the main scheme for the first meeting (fig. 465). In her choice of forms Tyng reproduced a motif familiar from the studies for the Trenton Jewish Community Center (1954–59). As at Trenton, her plan was based on the repetition of two interlocking polygonal figures: a small square unit and a larger octagon, creating a modular structure that could be extended indefinitely.[13] This geometry suggested a solution for the dormitory rooms, each of which consisted of an octagon, while service facilities filled the adjacent squares. Tyng drew the octagonal rooms together into a six-lobed structure, forming a massive and ambitiously scaled composition. Because of its complex three-dimensional geometry, which was reminiscent of the recent DNA models developed in the research of James Watson and Francis Crick, McBride dubbed the scheme "the molecular plan."[14]

Just in time for the November 25 presentation, Kahn prepared a second project, assisted by the young architect David Polk, a recent University of Pennsylvania graduate who had rejoined the office the week before, after having worked for Kahn in the mid-1950s.[15] This design featured a large rectangular volume into which two light courts were inserted, around which in turn were grouped simple rectangular dorm rooms. The plan was much less finished than Tyng's scheme and much more diagrammatic in character. The blocklike arrangement of courts and rooms was close to the schematic studies (fig. 463). But Kahn seemed less interested in subordinating the parts of the building to a geometric module than in the spatial qualities of the building and its central courts. He rendered Polk's elevations in colored pencil, being careful to show the treetops visible above and through the light courts. The preparation of such an alternative scheme, particularly one so hastily composed, was unusual for Kahn and perhaps suggests his dissatisfaction with Tyng's project. By submitting his own scheme, he left himself an opening in which to work out other ideas.

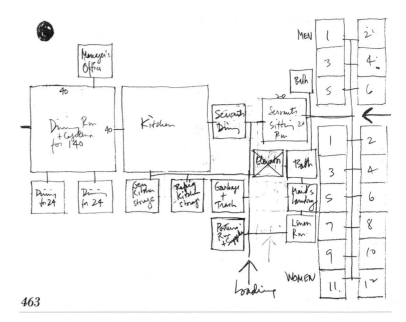

463

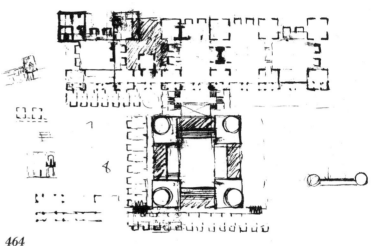

464

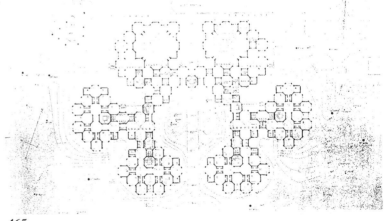

465

462

Kahn was told to study the plans, and he left without a commitment on his part or McBride's toward either design.[16] McBride had been satisfied with neither. The "octangular" or "molecular" scheme was an ingenious solution for the individual dorm rooms, but its small-scale cellular structure made for awkward public spaces of any size. And the composition itself, with its sprawling lobes, suggested growth by accretion rather than formal planning. But if the Tyng project was chaotic in composition, the second project was perhaps too bland, little more than a rectangle into which two symmetrical light courts had been sunk.

The decision not to commit to either scheme but to pursue both was fateful for the course of the Erdman design. Throughout the rest of the design process, well into 1962, the office would work concurrently on both—not the way the office usually handled its work. Tyng would continue to refine her design in a more or less consistent line. Kahn, on the other hand, was much more restless, and his successive projects showed sudden changes and abrupt deviations from preceding plans. He tended to lavish his attention on the large spaces of the building, such as the lobby and dining hall, while Tyng devoted herself to the smaller rooms that established the module for the building. Privately Kahn disparaged the Tyng project, with its additive, cellular structure, calling it "algae."[17] Instead he persisted with his light court idea, shifting to section drawings rather than plans to deal with lighting and the spatial character of the courts.[18]

In early April 1961 the architects presented their revised plans to McBride. Tyng submitted the octangular project, whose composition was now much compressed, with the separated lobes of the earlier version drawn together into an extended rectangular volume (see fig. 162).[19] McBride revealed that she was "more interested" in this scheme and slightly perplexed over Kahn's revised design, which was now "almost completely different."[20] But sensing "more support" among the committee for Kahn's scheme than for Tyng's, she again refused to endorse either.

McBride also declined to commit herself at the next presentation, on May 23, 1961, which was attended by Kahn and two other architects—presumably Tyng and Polk.[21] Kahn was still struggling with the dialogue between the large public spaces and the smaller dormitory rooms, and he now suggested a solution that segregated the public spaces at the front of the building from the private spaces at the rear (fig. 466). To further underscore the difference between these two realms he created two different kinds of geometry. The

dining hall and living room were given monumentally simple forms: a square and a circle, respectively, each inserted within a larger square. For the bedrooms he chose a more intricate geometry: in place of the simple rectangular units of his first submission, he adopted rooms of an irregular L-shape that Polk had suggested.[22]

Tyng for her part continued to discipline the geometry of her composition (fig. 467).[23] She had surrendered the idea of continuing the octangular module throughout the building, and, like Kahn, she now established large, geometrically ordered spaces for the public functions. These formed three large squares, within which were inserted a square, tilted diamond-fashion, for the recreation area, a circle for the lobby, and another tilted square for the dining hall. Almost certainly this reflected the influence of Kahn. But whereas Kahn's design placed these spaces along one flank of his building, Tyng placed them in the middle, wrapping the dorm rooms around the perimeter.

Here was suggested for the first time one of the most characteristic aspects of Erdman's design: the enclosure of monumentally scaled public spaces within a mantle of smaller private spaces. McBride described the plans to Eleanor Delanoy, who had first recommended Kahn. She found the new design "promising," with the "octangular plan . . . reshaped in a long rectangle which is made up of several quadrangles, the inside of each being used for public rooms."[24] Although, she confessed, this design still needed "much more work," she nonetheless preferred it to Kahn's design, which did "not seem as promising . . . to my eye. Mr. Kahn maintains his interest in his set, however, and I think may work on it further."

During the course of the summer and autumn of 1961 the firm worked on the project. Tyng continued to explore variants of the octangular plan.[25] But while she worked consistently within her modular system, in October Kahn made another abrupt turn, discarding most of his May 1961 scheme.[26] From it he retained only Polk's L-shaped rooms, which he assembled into four towerlike blocks grouped around an open courtyard (fig. 468). The effect was close to that created by the detached tower masses of the Richards Building. Kahn clearly had accepted Tyng's idea of wrapping small spaces around large; the question remained how to translate this principle into a unified composition.[27] For this he still had no answer. He confessed his frustrations in a public lecture, titled "Law and Rule in Architecture," which he gave at Bryn Mawr on October 23.[28] Calling the Bryn Mawr dormitory one of the most difficult problems he had

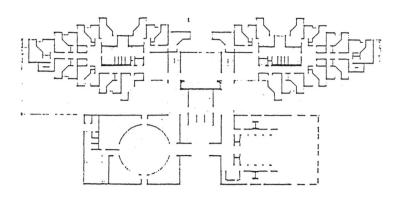

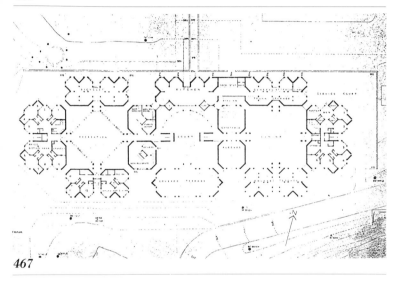

466

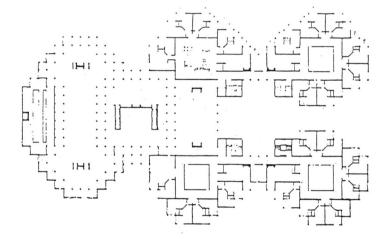

467

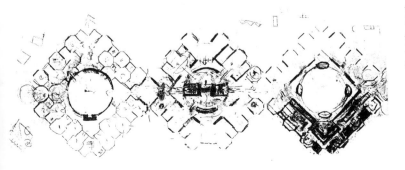

468

faced, Kahn said he was struggling to find "the qualities which make a school great." This, he told the students, was accomplished "through the use of space, architecture itself being a 'thoughtful making of spaces.'" But the peculiar problem at Bryn Mawr was "to distinguish each space, each room as a single entity, not just a series of partitions." Clearly he was still thinking of the design as the union of many discrete entities, the repeated modules of Tyng's octagons or Polk's L-shapes. About the formal unity or monumentality of the building as a whole there was no discussion.

An event then occurred that drastically accelerated the pace of work. The family of Eleanor Donnelley Erdman, who had died before making her promised gift to the college, announced that they would make a bequest in her memory. Since her son Donnelley was studying architecture at Princeton, where Kahn was then giving seminars, a gift to the building fund seemed appropriate. Her husband, C. Pardee Erdman, wrote to Katharine McBride from Santa Barbara: "I am very much interested in the possibility of giving a building to Bryn Mawr in memory of Eleanor. Perhaps you do not need another building, and perhaps there is no room for one . . . but will you please give this a little thought."[29] McBride fairly leapt at the offer. The only condition attached to the gift was that Donnelley might be able to attend the presentation meetings. In December 1961, Erdman made a $1 million bequest.[30]

With the building's finances relatively secure, and with a projected opening date of September 1963, the office struggled to refine the two competing schemes. Kahn, Tyng, and Polk continued to make studies, assisted by David Rothstein, another recent addition to the office. During a frantic three days in mid-December the scheme of the building was finally established. Tyng made another revision to her octangular scheme on December 12 in which she abandoned her ideas of the previous May, where she had treated the building as a series of detached cubical masses, each one housing a principal public space. Now she drew her octangular rooms into a more or less monolithic mass, the rectangular volume relieved by clusters of rooms projecting from the main mass at regular intervals.[31] All along, the trajectory of Tyng's work had been to unify the composition through the continuous geometry of its octangular module. Now, having introduced the theme of the central public spaces, she let the idea fall again. Two days later Kahn picked it up.[32] The result was the first plan with all of the familiar elements of Erdman as built: the three tilted squares (or diamonds) joined at the corners, the large public spaces

466. Main-level plan, before
May 1961.
467. Main-level plan. Inscribed
May 23, 1961.
468. Main-level plan, October
1961.
469. Plan, ca. December 1961.

in the center, and the alternation of interlocking rooms along the perimeter (fig. 469).

Here for the first time was a simple formula that resolved the many program requirements and created both a formal plan and a monumental exterior. When Kahn presented the plans to McBride (no elevations had been prepared) he sketched a quick study of the main elevation to convey the idea of the exterior. The sketch showed the three blocks in strong sunlight, with strong diagonal shadows highlighting the volumes of the three squares in vivid relief. Plan and elevation were unified, each showing the same association of the twin motifs of the square and the diagonal. McBride, finally presented with a design that reconciled the ideas of Kahn and Tyng, gave it her endorsement.

With the basic scheme established, the principal design question remaining was the character of the internal public spaces. These were developed quickly as the project was refined between early January and early May 1962.[33] In the early proposals, which still maintained much of the octangular module of Tyng's work, the bathrooms were housed in the joints between the three large tilted squares. By April 6, when the revised design was submitted to McBride, the bathrooms had been transferred to the corners of the central spaces.

This change in the arrangement of the bathrooms occurred in tandem with the development of the public spaces. At first these were little more than circles inserted within squares. The circles soon gave way to squares at the two ends of the building (January 26) and eventually in the middle (April 6).[34] As these spaces were refined, they took on a more public and monumental character, chiefly through the generous provision of natural light. In the drawings submitted on March 15, the central spaces were raised slightly to form a clerestory, light being admitted through narrow slit windows capped by lunettes.[35] By April 6 the clerestories were raised and a single light tower was also added at one of the corners of each square.[36] This indirect source of light, brought in through a vertical tower, was a theme in other work by Kahn at the time, such as the light towers of the Rochester church or the light hoods of the Esherick house. By the May 2 presentation, the clerestory had vanished and light was now channeled solely through towers at all four corners.[37] The arrangement of light towers was the last major plan issue to be resolved; on May 10, 1962, Kahn wrote to McBride that the design of Erdman was "essentially settled." The working drawings were to be completed by the end of July.[38]

In fact, they did not begin to be completed until March 25, 1963 (see fig. 164).[39] Their preparation went much more slowly than planned and there was resistance to some of Kahn's ideas among members of the college administration. This was particularly true with respect to materials. In a memorandum to McBride dated August 1, 1962, a campus committee criticized some aspects of the design. Above all, the committee wrote, "we oppose exposed concrete anywhere."[40] But McBride supported Kahn stalwartly. Still, compromises were made, especially on the exterior, which was ultimately clad with a revetment of Pennsylvania slate.[41]

Bids for the buildings were opened on March 29, 1963, and the contractors Nason & Cullen were notified of their successful bid on May 7.[42] Excavation began the following July and the reinforced concrete structure was poured in stages throughout the autumn of 1963 and into the spring and summer of 1964. The college accepted the building formally in May 1965. Toward the end, when Erdman was nearing completion, Kahn wrote proudly, "the building committee like my building very much. . . . I had faith in it all the time."[43]

Michael J. Lewis

Notes

1. Cornelia Meigs, *What Makes a College a College* (New York: Macmillan, 1956), 179ff.

2. Ralph Adams Cram, "The Works of Cope and Stewardson," *Architectural Record* 15 (November 1904): 407–31.

3. Letter, Delanoy to McBride, October 24 [1959], Katharine McBride Papers, Bryn Mawr College, Bryn Mawr, Pennsylvania (hereafter cited as McBride Papers).

4. Letter, Delanoy to McBride, September 28 [1959], McBride Papers. Also see letter, Delanoy to McBride, n.d. (probably October 1959), McBride Papers, where Delanoy says that Neutra's trip was rescheduled for the first week of April 1960.

5. Letter, Robert Venturi to Michael J. Lewis, March 21, 1990.

6. Letter, Kahn to Vanna Venturi, April 13, 1960, Box LIK 9, Louis I. Kahn Collection, University of Pennsylvania and Pennsylvania Historical and Museum Commission, Philadelphia (hereafter cited as Kahn Collection).

7. C. Pardee Erdman to McBride, January 15, 1960, McBride Papers.

8. "Plans for New Residence Hall," May 5, 1960, 14A, McBride Papers; copy of cover letter, McBride to Kahn, May 24, 1960, McBride Papers.

9. "Plans for New Residence Hall."

10. Letter, Kahn to McBride, May 31, 1960, "Bryn Mawr Dormitory," Box LIK 9, Kahn Collection.

11. The schematic room studies include drawings 565.2–11, Kahn Collection. The early idea sketches can be only approximately dated by comparing them with the dated drawings beginning in November 1960. The earliest of these probably include drawings 385.67 and 386.67 at the Museum of Modern Art, New York; and three drawings in the collection of Donnelley Erdman (nos. 1, 4, and 5).

12. Letter, Cooke to Horace Smedley (superintendent of buildings, Bryn Mawr), August 29, 1960, 14A, McBride Papers.

13. Several early studies in Kahn's hand for the interlocking octagonal scheme are known. Among these are two drawings in the collection of Donnelley Erdman (nos. 2 and 5) and a now lost drawing reproduced as fig. 3 in Lynn Scholz, "Architecture Alive on Campus: Erdman Hall," *Bryn Mawr Alumnae Bulletin* 47 (Fall 1965): 2–9. Scholz reproduces a number of otherwise unknown studies for Erdman. These early studies do not provide clear indications of Kahn's role in the development of the octagonal plan. They may represent variations on Tyng's already well-defined geometric scheme.

14. Tyng, lecture in the Department of the History of Art, University of Pennsylvania, February 22, 1983; Tyng, interview with Michael J. Lewis, December 12, 1989. Tyng enjoyed a good rapport with McBride, who had been dean of Radcliffe College when Tyng was a student there.

15. Polk, interview with Michael J. Lewis, December 15, 1989. Polk was in Kahn's office in 1960–61, 1962–63 and 1965–68.

16. There is indirect evidence of the meeting in a later letter from McBride to the building committee, May 25, 1961, 14A, McBride Papers. Also see memo to members of the building committee, November 11, 1960.

17. Polk, interview with Lewis.

18. Drawings in the collection of Donnelley Erdman (nos. 11 and 12), dated March 20, 1961.

19. Four undated plans in the Bryn Mawr College Archives are almost certainly the drawings from the April 1961 meeting; they show a composition that is transitional between those presented in the November 25, 1960, drawings and the May 23, 1961, set.

20. Letter, McBride to Delanoy, April 5, 1961, McBride Papers. Kahn's submission at this presentation has not been located.

21. Letter, McBride to Delanoy and Gordan, May 25, 1961, 14A, McBride Papers.

22. Both Polk and Tyng identify the May 23 submission as essentially Polk's project; interviews with Lewis.

23. This scheme has been assigned to Tyng by both Polk and Tyng; ibid.

24. Letter, McBride to Delanoy and Gordan, May 25, 1961, 14A, McBride Papers.

25. Perhaps as a diversion, Tyng revised her long-abandoned plan of November 1960, replacing two of its lobes with three interlocking diamonds to house the public spaces; drawing, June 21, 1961, Bryn Mawr College Archives.

26. Drawing, October 1961, Bryn Mawr College Archives; undated drawing owned by Donnelley Erdman (RP 1287).

27. This plan is reproduced and discussed in Alexandra Tyng, *Beginnings: Louis I. Kahn's Philosophy of Architecture* (New York: John Wiley & Sons, 1984), 44–46.

28. "Kahn Asserts Architect's Duty Is to Make Institutions Great," *The College News* 47 (October 25, 1961): 1.

29. Letter, Erdman to McBride, November 8, 1961, McBride Papers.

30. Letter, McBride to Erdman, December 16, 1961, McBride Papers.

31. Tyng and Polk, interviews with Lewis.

32. Ibid. The earliest drawings for the three-diamond scheme are dated December 14, 1961, and provisionally catalogued as drawings B-61-71 and B-61-72, Bryn Mawr College Archives. The rendering of the foliage and the heavy overlay of explanatory pencil sketches both appear to be in Kahn's hand, suggesting that these are the drawings with which the architect first presented the three-diamond scheme to McBride.

33. Polk, interview with Lewis.

34. Submission sets of drawings (with pencil emendations) dated January 26 and April 6, 1962, Bryn Mawr College Archives. Duplicate submission sets of these (and of the following drawings) are also preserved in the Kahn Collection.

35. Submission set of drawings dated March 15, 1962, Bryn Mawr College Archives.

36. Submission set of drawings dated April 6, 1962, Bryn Mawr College Archives.

37. Submission set of drawings dated May 2, 1962, Bryn Mawr College Archives.

38. Letter, Kahn to McBride, May 10, 1962, McBride Papers.

39. Full sets of floor plans were not completed until May 21, 1963, while the section drawings and many construction details are dated January 10, 1964. Full sets of working drawings survive in the Kahn Collection and in the Bryn Mawr College Archives.

40. Memorandum, Dorothy Marshall (dean), Horace Smedley, and Charlotte Howe (director, halls and wardens) to McBride, August 1, 1962, McBride Papers.

41. Letter, Harlyn E. Thompson (committee member) to McBride, June 11, 1963, "Bryn Mawr Dormitory," Box LIK 28, Kahn Collection.

42. Bid documents, Erdman File, McBride Papers.

43. Letter, Kahn to Gertrude Ely (Bryn Mawr class of 1899), July 3, 1964, "Ely, Miss Gertrude," Box LIK 28, Kahn Collection.

In December 1960 Howard Wolf, the chairman of the board of the Philadelphia Museum College of Art, wrote to Louis Kahn. In his letter Wolf told Kahn that a committee of the college's board had been asked to recommend an architect for a new dormitory.[1] A year later, and again in October 1963, Kahn met with various board members to discuss the college's development program.[2] These discussions must have been fruitful: on March 21, 1964, E. M. Benson, the dean of the college and, as there was not yet a president, its top executive, sent Kahn a booklet detailing the newly completed development plan.[3] A joint meeting of the board and the planning committee, scheduled in order to choose an architect, took place on April 8.[4] Less than two weeks later the college's director of development, Robert Seymour, prepared a press release to announce that Kahn had received the commission.[5] In the release Wolf commented, "These buildings must be inspiring examples of beauty as well as creative utility."[6]

Wolf's statement could have served as a motto for the college, which had been founded in 1876 as an outgrowth of the Centennial Exhibition. In 1893 the school of the Pennsylvania Museum and School of Industrial Art moved to a complex located only a few blocks south of City Hall on Broad Street, one of the city's two major axial boulevards. The campus had been built for the Pennsylvania Institution for the Deaf and Dumb. Its main building, of stone with a Greek Revival–style temple front, built in 1824 by John Haviland, was flanked by slightly recessed five-bay wings added in 1852. In the rear William Strickland's 1838 addition linked the original Haviland building to Furness and Hewitt's characteristically High Victorian parallel brick wings of 1875, which stretched west to Fifteenth Street.[7] The Pennsylvania Museum and School of Industrial Art flourished at this location, and in 1959 it became a college— the Philadelphia Museum College of Art, a title that was changed four years later to the Philadelphia College of Art.[8] The institution became the University of the Arts in 1987.

By 1963 the same growth that had precipitated these changes in the college's name had made its current quarters inadequate. Although moving the college to the suburbs was considered in the early sixties, by April 1963 the decision had been made to expand its existing facilities with the aid of the Philadelphia Redevelopment Authority. The program presented to Kahn called for new dormitories, a library, a design center and exhibition hall, a theater, physical education facilities, and space for classrooms, administrative offices, and parking.[9] The 1824 Haviland building and the Furness and Hewitt wings, but not the 1838

and 1852 additions, were to be preserved. The campus would encompass the entire block bounded on the north, east, south, and west, respectively, by Spruce, Broad, Pine, and Fifteenth Streets (excepting an apartment building on the corner of Fifteenth and Spruce), double the area of the original Institution for the Deaf complex. The trustees envisioned gaining the city's permission to close off Delancey and Rosewood, the two side streets that ran through the site.[10]

Between April and October, when Kahn made a presentation to the faculty's executive council, he worked out his initial scheme for the project in drawings, which served as the basis for the cardboard model he took to the meeting.[11] In the drawings he experimented with various layouts for the site. All of the sketches provided the college with an open area that could become a focus for community life. Kahn initially designed a large courtyard fronting Fifteenth Street, an arrangement that would have required placing tall buildings behind the low Haviland building.[12] By the time of the October meeting he had instead chosen to tuck a smaller court between the original building and the Furness and Hewitt wings (fig. 470). The model he displayed at the October meeting included a dormitory on Pine Street, additional administration offices behind the Haviland building, a theater facing Broad Street, a library behind it, a small design center on Spruce Street, and three long classroom and studio buildings, which stretched from the library and the design center to Fifteenth Street. Two of these structures, and a rough sketch of an elevation or cross section, are already visible in the preparatory drawing. These buildings were the most fully developed part of the design. In each of the three structures, which were connected to each other by raised walkways, south-facing classrooms and north-facing studios with angled skylights were separated by tall light wells, semicircular in plan.

The Broad Street elevations of the buildings, the most important part of the project from the viewpoint of its urban context, were another focus of this early work. Kahn envisioned a tall studio and classroom block and a separate theater between the Haviland building and the Atlantic Building, the tall office tower just across Spruce Street. From the first he intended to leave the corner opposite the Atlantic Building, the part of campus closest to downtown, open as a forecourt. The height of his proposed South Broad Street buildings created a transitional zone between the almost residential scale of the Haviland building and the taller office buildings that lined the blocks of South Broad Street leading to City Hall. The importance of Kahn's

Philadelphia College of Art

Philadelphia, Pennsylvania, 1960–66

470

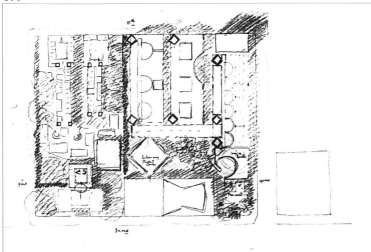

471

472

470. Site plan and elevation of classroom building, April–September 1964.
471. Site plan, October–November 1964.
472. Model from southeast, January–March 1966.

planning was underscored by the presence at the October meeting of Edmund Bacon, the executive director of the Philadelphia City Planning Commission, who also made a presentation to the council.[13]

In a drawing Kahn made in October or November, he began to vary the shape of each of these formerly identical units (fig. 471), and he provided new clues to their interior configurations. Canted skylights let light into the studios, which he separated from the classrooms with towerlike light wells or staircases. These details accompanied a reworking of the entire site plan, in which he moved the dormitory that had once faced Pine Street to a location behind the Haviland building and transformed the library into a diamond-shaped structure.

Ultimately, Kahn found these shifts in the siting and form of the constituent elements unsatisfactory. By December he had decided to unite the library, classrooms, and studios into a single building stretching the length of the site from Broad to Fifteenth Street.[14] To make room for this enormous structure, he moved the theater and design center from Broad to Spruce Street; he also returned the dormitories to their earlier Pine Street location. By eliminating one of the three rows of buildings he had originally planned for the northern half of the site, Kahn gained more light and a livelier profile for the core of campus. Throughout the winter he continued to experiment with the design of the main block and with the siting of the project's other elements (see fig. 186).

In the most important changes he made at this time, Kahn switched the placement of the diamond-shaped library, a corner of which now met Broad Street at the college's main entrance, and of a block of classrooms.[15] He also replaced an above-ground entrance to the parking garage with an inward-facing open-air amphitheater in the middle of the Spruce Street edge of the block. This further increased the light levels within the studios; and, although the main block was screened with trees, its prominence from the street was enhanced.[16] These revisions transformed the area between the main block and the Spruce Street buildings from an oddly shaped corridor into a dynamic sequence of spaces. In many of the drawings through which he worked out details of this scheme, Kahn focused on the circulation spine, lined with lockers, small offices, and studios, that ran from east to west through the main building, and on the highly irregular star-shaped central core of the half of the building closest to Fifteenth Street.[17]

At a May 1965 meeting the college's planning and development committee decided to construct the campus in phases and asked Kahn for more detailed plans.[18] Kahn promised that complete plans and a model would be ready by September 1, when the college would decide whether to proceed with construction.[19] In a letter to Wolf, Kahn's assistant David Wisdom wrote that the plans the office began to draft that June "will be sufficient to come to an agreement between college and architect, but they will not be working drawings." Their cost was set at $25,000.[20]

During the summer of 1965 Kahn's office worked on the project, drawing plans, elevations, and sections.[21] This work centered on the eastern half of the classroom block, which included the library and, above it, the design center. Although semicircular light wells had dominated the early drawings, the library footprint was the purest geometrical form that survived Kahn's autumn 1964 redesign. In the library interior he experimented with the ideal geometries he had purged from the project's floor plans. Here he worked with inscribed triangles and squares within each other, and with the relationship between a generalized communal core and the well-defined uses wrapped around it.

The projected cost of the studio block alone was $12 million to $15 million, despite the fact that the original cost estimates for the entire complex totaled $25 million to $50 million. George Culler, appointed in 1965 as the college's first president, was among those who balked at the enormous expense. Yet when the college asked Kahn for final plans for only the eastern half of the studio block, Culler complained about the inadequacy of any partial solution.[22] Nonetheless, in January 1966 Kahn's office finished a complete set of plans and sections for the first phase of the building, which now carried a $6 million price tag.[23]

In this, his final scheme for the project, Kahn strengthened the massing of the south elevation of the main block and reorganized the center of its western half, refinements that enhanced the building's facades (fig. 472). He shifted the placement of the offices and classrooms to the south of the circulation spine to create a balanced composition of two projecting main blocks, flanked and separated by smaller pavilions. By substituting a partially open rectangular court capped by a circular light well for the star-shaped central space, from which the separate parts of the western half of the studio block radiated in his 1965 design, Kahn was also able to bring a new coherence to the northern facade of this part of the complex.[24] This court supplemented the fourth-floor terrace garden on the southern end of the building, a

feature of the detailed 1965 drawings.[25] Elevation studies for the south facade from the first half of 1965 showed simple grids; now Kahn broke down its mass with projecting shading devices and cantilevered balconies.[26] The battered north facade, where he retained only a hint of the raking clerestories seen in 1964 drawings to supplement the new circular light well, was more austere, and even though it was recessed from Spruce Street itself, it formed a strong boundary wall for the inward-facing campus. Beneath a cluster of trees that maintained the street line on this side street Kahn buried three levels of parking, which he intended to be accessible from the interstate highway then being planned for South Street.[27]

On March 28 the college held a press conference to make public Kahn's design. Their announcement was timed to precede the April 11 opening of the Museum of Modern Art's exhibition of the architect's work, which included a wooden model of his scheme for the entire campus (see fig. 180).[28] Work on the details of drawings for the project continued until May. That month the city Redevelopment Authority's Advisory Board of Design approved Kahn's plans,[29] and in June Kahn wrote to President Culler about a proposed contract.[30] He wrote again in August to discuss the choice of engineers and other collaborators he would need if the work were to go ahead.[31] This is the last letter in the file his office kept on the project, which came to a halt because the college lacked the money to build it. A quarter century later the site still lies vacant.

Kathleen James

Notes

1. Letter, Wolf to Kahn, December 27, 1960, "Phila. Museum College of Art Correspondence—1963," Box LIK 35, Louis I. Kahn Collection, University of Pennsylvania and Pennsylvania Historical and Museum Commission, Philadelphia (hereafter cited as Kahn Collection).

2. Letters, E. M. Benson to Kahn, December 30, 1961, and October 23, 1963, ibid.

3. Letter, Benson to Kahn, March 21, 1964, "Philadelphia College of Art Correspondence 1964–65–67," Box LIK 35, Kahn Collection; Philadelphia Museum College of Art, *Physical Plan for the 10 Year Development Program of the Philadelphia Museum College of Art* (Philadelphia, 1963), ibid.

4. Memo, Philip A. Bregy and Samuel R. Rosenbaum (board members) to members of the executive committee, ibid.

5. Draft press release by Seymour, April 21, 1964, ibid.

6. Press release, Philadelphia College of Art, April 26, 1964, ibid.

7. Richard Webster, *Philadelphia Preserved* (Philadelphia: Temple University Press, 1976), 137; James F. O'Gorman, *The Architecture of Frank Furness* (Philadelphia: Philadelphia Museum of Art, 1973), 97.

8. Press kit, Philadelphia College of Art, March 28, 1966, "Philadelphia College of Art Correspondence 1964–65–67," Box LIK 35, Kahn Collection.

9. *Physical Plan.*

10. Press kit, Philadelphia College of Art, March 28, 1966, "Philadelphia College of Art Correspondence 1964–65–67," Box LIK 35, Kahn Collection; letter, David Wisdom (Kahn's office) to Richard H. Reinhardt (director, Dimensional Art Department), June 18, 1965, "Master file—June 1965 and July–August 1965, September–October," Box LIK 10, Kahn Collection.

11. Memos, Benson to Kahn, October 20 and 27, 1964, "Philadelphia College of Art Correspondence 1964–65–67," Box LIK 35, Kahn Collection. See contact sheets by George Pohl, September 27, 1964, Kahn Collection, for photographs of the models published in Heinz Ronner and Sharad Jhaveri, *Louis I. Kahn: Complete Work, 1935–1974*, 2d ed. (Basel and Boston: Birkhäuser, 1987), 277, PCA.7–9.

12. See Ronner and Jhaveri, *Complete Work*, 276, PCA.1, for an illustration of this drawing, the earliest for the project, which is now lost.

13. Memo, Benson to Kahn, October 20, 1964, "Philadelphia College of Art Correspondence 1964–65–67," Box LIK 35, Kahn Collection.

14. See contact sheets by George Pohl, December 2, 1964, Kahn Collection, for the photograph of the model published in Ronner and Jhaveri, *Complete Work*, 278, PCA.12.

15. Richard Reinhardt, "Description of the New PCA Campus," undated typescript, "Philadelphia College of Art Correspondence 1964–65–67," Box LIK 35, Kahn Collection.

16. See contact sheets by George Pohl, March 12, 1965, Kahn Collection, for the photograph of the model published in Ronner and Jhaveri, *Complete Work*, 278, PCA.13. A transmittal sheet, March 10, 1965, "Philadelphia College of Art Correspondence 1964–65–67," Box LIK 35, Kahn Collection, indicates that this model had already been seen by college authorities when it was photographed.

17. Autograph drawings 580.19–26, Kahn Collection.

18. Letter, Wolf to Kahn, May 24, 1965, "Philadelphia College of Art Correspondence 1964–65–67," Box LIK 35, Kahn Collection.

19. Letters, Wisdom to Wolf, June 4, 1965, and Reinhardt to Kahn, September 22, 1965, ibid.

20. Letter, Wisdom to Wolf, June 4, 1965, "March and April–May Master File 1965," LIK Box 10, Kahn Collection. Wisdom also agreed in this letter to consult with Richard Reinhardt, whom the college had placed in charge of the distribution and assignment of space in the new buildings.

21. Drawings dated to June, August, and September 1965, office drawings 0580, Kahn Collection.

22. Letter, Reinhardt to Kathleen James, May 10, 1990, Kahn Collection; press kit biography sheet for Culler, March 28, 1966, "Philadelphia College of Art Correspondence 1964–65–67," Box LIK 35, Kahn Collection.

23. Letters, Wisdom to Culler, January 19 and 25, 1966, "Philadelphia College of Art Correspondence 1964–65–67," Box LIK 35, Kahn Collection.

24. Only minor revisions and elaborations are to be found in the February 16, May 24, and May 27, 1966, office drawings 580, Kahn Collection.

25. Fourth-floor plans, August 18, 1965, office drawings 580, Kahn Collection.

26. Undated south facade elevation studies, office drawings 580, Kahn Collection.

27. May 24 and 27, 1966, office drawings 580, Kahn Collection.

28. Planning outline, formal press announcement of PCA development plans, February 14, 1966, "Philadelphia College of Art Correspondence 1964–65–67," Box LIK 35, Kahn Collection.

29. Letter, Walter D'Alessio (Advisory Board of Design, Philadelphia Redevelopment Authority) to Culler, May 13, 1966, ibid.

30. Letter, Kahn to Culler, June 22, 1966, ibid.

31. Letter, Kahn to Culler, August 5, 1966, ibid.

In May 1961 the congregation of Mikveh Israel hired Louis Kahn to design a new synagogue in the historic district of Philadelphia.[1] The congregation's roots dated back to 1740, when it was founded by Sephardic Jews from Spain and Portugal. In 1822 they commissioned William Strickland to build a synagogue on Sterling Alley, north of Cherry Street, between Third and Fourth Streets. They moved from that address to 117 North Seventh Street in 1859, and again to another building at Broad and York Streets in 1909.[2] When the congregation decided to return to their original neighborhood in 1961, their aim was to regain their rightful place among the other historic churches still standing in old Philadelphia. It was hoped that such a return would underscore the congregation's historic significance and make it a national symbol for American Jewry, stimulating a successful fund-raising campaign.[3]

Kahn became involved with the Mikveh Israel project at its very beginning, before a specific site had been chosen.[4] Most likely this early association with the congregation was a result of his friendship with Dr. Bernard Alpers, a neurosurgeon who served as chairman of the building committee.[5] Alpers, described by Esther Kahn as a "great scientist," an intellectual, and a "deeply religious man," shared "a common vision" with the architect.[6] During the early years of the project Alpers and Kahn met for regular Friday breakfasts.[7] Due to Alpers's enthusiastic appreciation, the building committee was generally receptive to Kahn's initial architectural conceptions.[8] Kahn was free to pursue artistic considerations without interfering constraints imposed by his patrons.

Kahn's work on the Mikveh Israel project was in three major phases. During the first phase, which lasted from May 1961 until October 1963, Kahn helped with site selection and developed his design of the synagogue based on the concept that it was to be a house of worship. During the second stage, from the end of 1963 through December 1971, he made only minor changes in his design. The final period, 1972, was characterized by Kahn's deteriorating relationship with the building committee and his reluctance to produce the type of design they requested.

Although three sites were initially considered for the new Mikveh Israel, Kahn persuaded the building committee to choose a three-quarter-acre location next to Christ Church Walkway, between Fourth and Fifth Streets.[9] He was excited by the historical context of the site, which adjoined the Christ Church Burial Ground on the north, the Friends Meeting House on the east, and Independence Mall on the

Mikveh Israel Synagogue

Philadelphia, Pennsylvania, 1961–72

west.[10] Christ Church Walkway would provide the pedestrian connection with Christ Church.

After helping to select the site Kahn began to consider the congregation's programmatic requirements and the arrangement of the synagogue and subsidiary buildings on the plot.[11] The initial program had been outlined in general terms by David Arons, president of the congregation, in an interview with the *Philadelphia Inquirer* in 1961.[12] Arons had explained that Mikveh Israel would build a synagogue designed in the Spanish Orthodox tradition, with the bema (the raised platform for the reading of the scriptures) at the opposite end of the room from the ark, and with separate seating for men and women. Next to the synagogue a building would be erected to store and display the congregation's archives. In creating the design Kahn had to consider three diverse activities, for a synagogue was a house of study during the interpretation of the scripture, a house of community during social gatherings, and a house of worship during the performance of ritual.[13] Furthermore, a synagogue had to be able to accommodate large crowds attending services during the high holidays without dwarfing the fraction of the congregation using the sanctuary for daily worship.

Kahn's response to these specific needs was to develop specialized spaces for study, social functions, and, above all, prayer. In an interview published on March 30, 1962, he explained that he was trying to avoid the error made by synagogue designers who were "too concerned with structural ingenuity, decoration, flexibility, confusing the sanctuary with the auditorium."[14] At Mikveh Israel Kahn's solution was not to create a multipurpose building but to contain secular and sacred activities in their own separate architectural spaces. The sanctuary, the spiritual core of the site, would establish the theme for the overall design.

In Kahn's earliest model (probably from late 1961) the synagogue occupied the eastern half of the plot (fig. 473). Its sanctuary was square, with the roof divided into four bays covered by groin vaults. A single-bay entrance hall, also vaulted, was connected to the sanctuary. An enclosed courtyard at the back of the sanctuary was arranged like a medieval cloister, with a covered ambulatory and a garden in the center. Although its intended function is not completely clear, it was probably to house some of the social and pedagogical activities of the congregation. Kahn wanted his sanctuary to be near a garden, "a place apart," and he provided a garden in almost every subsequent plan for Mikveh Israel.[15] In this early model he placed the museum at

473. Model, before February 1962.
474. Site plan and partial section. Inscribed Feb 5 1962.
475. Plan, before April 1962.
476. Plan. Inscribed 22 June 1962.

473

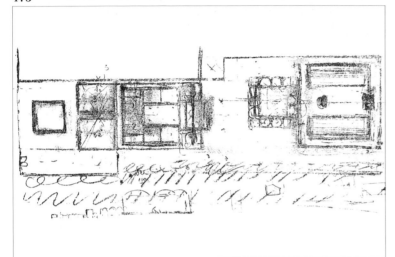

474

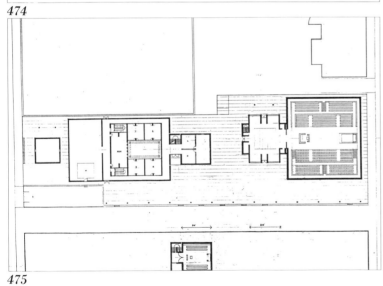

475

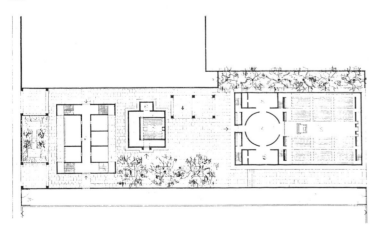

476

the western edge of the plot. A simple square with a flat roof, the structure was much smaller than the sanctuary complex. Kahn inserted a permanent sukkah (usually a temporary structure with a roof of leafy boughs, built for Sukkoth to commemorate the tabernacles of the Exodus) between the two structures.

Drawings show that by February 5, 1962, Kahn had eliminated the cloister and added a school. It was now a separate structure between the museum and the temple (fig. 474). The activities of worship and study were each defined by their own architectural space. In an office plan dated by an unknown hand as "before April 1962," Kahn attached a small square chapel for daily use to the east side of the school (fig. 475). It faced the sanctuary, which would accommodate a much larger crowd for the high holidays. With both a large sanctuary and a chapel on the site, the synagogue builder's perennial problem of fluctuating congregation size was resolved.[16]

In a drawing dated June 22, 1962, Kahn separated the chapel from the school (fig. 476). The interior of the former was subdivided by partitions that defined a little sanctuary (number 3 on the drawing) and an encircling corridor. It accommodated sixty people. The kiddush room, a smaller room on the north side of the chapel (number 6 on the drawing), would house social gatherings after services. The June 22 plan included a small enclosed garden at the western end of the plot. This replaced the museum, which had been reduced to a "historical room" (number 7 on the drawing) on the south side of the entrance hall to the sanctuary.[17] The school, a rectangular box with windows opening up to the east and west, stood next to the garden. Kahn placed the temple at the opposite end of the site, across the courtyard from the school and chapel and on the other side of the sukkah. It had its own kiddush room on the north side of the entrance hall (number 6 on the drawing) and a sanctuary with seating for 528 people to either side of a central aisle defined at each end by the bema and the ark.

The separation of the school, the chapel, and the synagogue provided the secular and spiritual activities of the community with distinct architectural spaces. To further distinguish these activities, Kahn avoided placing the entrances and exits of the three buildings on a simple straight axis. One entered the sanctuary from the west, the chapel from the south, and the school either from the north or around some trees from the south, a circuitous arrangement that forced the congregant to walk around the buildings.

Having defined the identities of the three buildings, Kahn turned to perfecting the design of the sanctuary, a task he began in the summer of 1962. Since no obvious architectural tradition existed in America for synagogue architecture, Kahn, like any other synagogue architect, was free to develop his own architectural conception.[18] In discussing Mikveh Israel in 1962 he explained: "I must be in tune with the spirit that created the first synagogue. I must rediscover that sense of beginnings through beliefs."[19]

The frame of mind with which Kahn approached the design of Mikveh Israel was shaped by his desire to approximate intuitively the spiritual experience that had moved Jews to build the first temple. As an architect, he hoped to convey this experience by using "space and forms to enhance the rituals."[20] In his design for the sanctuary, as in many other projects he was working on at the time, he sought to enhance the spiritual dimension of the sanctuary space by manipulating the illumination of the room, creating a dramatic backdrop for the liturgy. For Kahn, this meant the control of natural light. According to Alan Levy, who was working on the project with Kahn at this time, daylight "compelled the design."[21] Kahn wanted its effects to be "subtle, deep, and emotional."

A drawing dated August 14, 1962, reflects a new conception Kahn had developed for the sanctuary, in which he was able to contain and control its lighting (fig. 477). In this plan, seven huge circular towers punctuated the perimeter of the sanctuary, and four more were to confront congregants as they faced the entrance facade. The chapel was also given four towers. Although these massive structures had the appearance of solid masonry, they were in fact hollow, serving as "window rooms" to contain and direct light into the sanctuary. Kahn wrote:

The spaces are enclosed by window rooms twenty feet in diameter connected by walled passages. These window room elements have glazed openings on one exterior side and larger unglazed arched openings facing the interior. These rooms of light surrounding the synagogue chamber serve as an ambulatory and the high places for women. These window rooms prevail in the composition of the entrance chamber and the chapel across the way. . . . The windows on the outside do not support the building; what supports the building, as you can see on the plan, are the spaces between the windows.[22]

Late in the summer of 1962 Kahn had models made of his towered design; in Fairmount Park he studied the effects of lighting on the interior (fig. 478).[23] He explained:

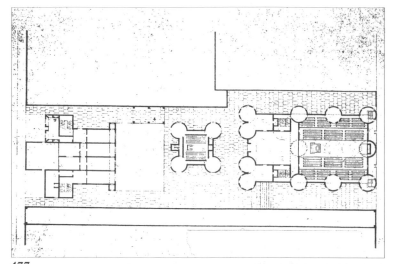

477

478

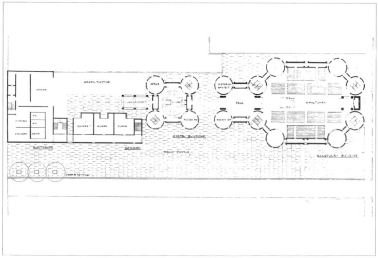

479

477. Plan. Inscribed 14 August 1962.
478. Model looking east, showing interior of sanctuary, ca. August 1962.
479. Plan. Inscribed 23 October 1962.

In the model, the open spaces which made the window rooms independent of the structure are made too wide, but they are important to give light to the round shapes. The light from the exterior captured in the interior room of the window is seen from the synagogue chambers as free of glare. The whole idea comes from realizing that contrasts of walls in darkness against openings in light renders interior shapes illegible and turns the eye away.[24]

From his study of the models Kahn realized that his August 14 plan would not sufficiently illuminate the ark, for the tower behind it did not have windows and the other towers were too far away. Furthermore, the window rooms in the middle of the north and south walls would partially obstruct the view of the ark for people sitting in the two back rows.[25]

These problems were resolved by an octagonal plan, dated October 23, 1962 (fig. 479). In this drawing the ark was now dramatically framed by light towers. The light, filtered through the window rooms, was "free of glare." The view for people sitting along the north and south walls was no longer obstructed, and an ambulatory linked the window rooms, facilitating circulation.[26] In this plan Kahn placed the historical room in the northwest tower of the synagogue entrance hall and the kiddush room in the southwest tower. The chapel, facing the synagogue, was approximately the same size as the entrance hall, retaining its four window rooms from the plan of August 14. The interior of the chapel was to be outfitted with furniture from Strickland's 1819 synagogue.[27] The school had been rearranged and now had an L-shaped plan.

On October 31, 1962, the board of trustees met with Alan Levy and Moshe Safdie, Kahn's assistants, who showed slides of Kahn's plans. The drawings were received enthusiastically; however, two members expressed reservations about the estimated cost of $2.25 million for the project.[28] On November 4, 1962, in a final vote by the congregation, twenty-six members approved the design and eleven rejected it.[29] The treasurer reported that the building fund had a total of $231,000, as well as $100,000 in unwritten pledges.[30]

Kahn did not make any major changes to his basic conception after October 13, 1962, although in an office drawing dated October 29, 1963, he did slightly modify the plan of the school (see fig. 123). Its L-shaped plan was now wrapped around a rectangular multipurpose hall. The ell was illuminated by three light wells, echoing the window room motif in the sanctuary. The entrance to this building was through another light well, facing the sukkah and the

chapel. From the outside the structures did not appear connected, but an underground passage joined the basements of the sanctuary, the chapel, and the school, an element the congregation had requested.[31]

Although an approved design was in hand, sufficient funds for building failed to materialize. During the mid-1960s there was little activity on the synagogue. In drawings made for the Philadelphia Redevelopment Authority dated April 29, 1966, there is evidence of only minor changes in decorative details; the windows have small panes of leaded glass and are surmounted by brick segmental caps that take the place of pediments.[32] In 1968 the congregation of Mikveh Israel finally bought the property from the Redevelopment Authority, but construction still did not begin.[33]

In 1972 William S. Fishman, president of ARA Services and a pioneer in automated food systems, took over the chairmanship of the fund-raising campaign. Fishman was a talented fund-raiser, and hope for the project was rekindled.[34] A new committee within the congregation was formed, the Independence Mall Project Action Committee, chaired by Ruth (Mrs. Joseph B.) Sarner.[35] After ten years of failure, the new group was determined to get the job accomplished. Unlike Bernard Alpers, who had supported Kahn's spiritual and architectural goals, the new leaders believed that in order to get Mikveh Israel back to Independence Mall they would have to emphasize the building of a Jewish museum rather than a synagogue. Only this would attract sufficient national attention for effective fund-raising.[36] They therefore redefined the program for Mikveh Israel in a letter to Kahn: "The amended Mall Project . . . shall consist of two units, a synagogue reminiscent of the Synagogue of the American Revolution and a Museum of American Jewish history."[37]

The fundamental conception of Kahn's 1962 design was scrapped. Sketchy minutes from a meeting with the building committee on January 13, 1972, indicate that Kahn had difficulty with the new directives. He was told: "You are asking for a building which will mean the synagogue will not be built. It is a completely new building design . . . not enough dollars for the dream of before."[38] The leaders of the building committee wanted to eliminate or cut back Kahn's costly light towers and, most important, to do away with what they felt to be the unnecessarily strict separation and containment of the variously functioning spaces.[39] For budgetary reasons, they sought to join the houses of study, community, and prayer. The committee also requested additional offices near the sanctuary and, below it, a kitchen and a community room with movable partitions to create classrooms.[40] The new building committee conceived of the temple as an auditorium, exactly the approach Kahn had criticized in 1962. Unable to revise the thinking that had produced his 1962 conception of a sacred space carefully separated from areas containing secular activities, the architect balked at the new requests.[41] In an impatient memo from Ruth Sarner he was urged to keep in mind that "the Museum–Synagogue–School Complex MUST be integrated. . . . There can be no division of 'sacred' and 'profane.'"[42]

Kahn's office halfheartedly developed three plans in response to the building committee's goals.[43] In one of these, by Vince Rivera, the museum and the synagogue were joined by a common foyer, a scheme that had been strongly requested by the building committee in order to reduce the number of costly towers.[44] Kahn, however, did not like the plan and refused to compromise. Sarner warned Kahn's associates: "Matter of a common foyer for Museum and Synagogue is still unresolved. It is a philosophic matter to Mr. Kahn, rather than aesthetic. The unity of Mikveh Israel's historic past and its spiritual present must be demonstrated effectively to the Architect. . . . There is no separation of past and present—of history and worship—of sacred and lay use."[45]

To Kahn the committee's new approach to the project represented the profane taking precedence over the sacred. The differences between the architect and the committee were profound, and no common ground for progress could be reached between them; negotiations broke down sometime late in December 1972.[46] In response to Kahn's resulting dismissal, his old friend Bernard Alpers protested to the president of the congregation:

It is not difficult to understand the wish to build a museum, but combining the museum and Synagogue in a single structure is . . . undignified and in a sense sacrilegious. . . . I have seen and studied the plans which Mr. Kahn has been forced to develop. If we are to have a museum, what is the objection to separate museum and synagogue buildings? This concept is one which Mr. Kahn prefers . . . our primary purpose is to build a house of worship.[47]

Michele Taillon Taylor

Notes

1. Information on the history of Mikveh Israel can be found in Edwin Wolf and Maxwell Whiteman, *The History of the Jews in Philadelphia from Colonial Times to the Age of Jackson* (Philadelphia: Jewish Publication Society of America, 1956), 117–21, 360–71. For discussion of Kahn's designs for Mikveh Israel, see Heinz Ronner and Sharad Jhaveri, *Louis I. Kahn: Complete Work, 1935–1974*, 2d ed. (Basel and Boston: Birkhäuser, 1987), 188–197; Robert Coombs, "Light and Silence. The Religious Architecture of Louis Kahn," *Architectural Association Quarterly* 13 (October 1981): 26–36; Joseph Burton, "Notes from Volume Zero: Louis Kahn and the Language of God," *Perspecta*, no. 20 (1983): 69–90; Eugene Johnson, "A Drawing of the Cathedral of Albi by Louis I. Kahn," *Gesta* 25 (1986): 159–65; and Michele T. Taylor, "The Evolution of Mikveh Israel and Louis Kahn's Vision of Sacred Space," *Faith and Forum* 22 (Winter 1988–89): 25–28.
2. Wolf and Whiteman, *History of the Jews*, 360–71.
3. "Any building on the Mall must be a symbol for all American Jewry"; job meeting memo by Moshe Safdie (Kahn's office), October 31, 1962, "Mikveh Israel," Box LIK 38, Louis I. Kahn Collection, University of Pennsylvania and Pennsylvania Historical and Museum Commission, Philadelphia (hereafter cited as Kahn Collection).
4. Alan Levy, interview with Michele T. Taylor, November 24, 1986. Levy worked in Kahn's office on this project during its initial stage, presenting the November 4, 1962, plans to the congregation for general approval. Kahn was formally hired on May 25, 1961; letter, Alpers to Kahn, May 25, 1961, "Mikveh Israel," Box LIK 38, Kahn Collection.
5. Luis Vincent Rivera, interview with Michele T. Taylor, December 4, 1986. Rivera worked on this project in 1963–64 and again in 1972.
6. Esther Kahn, interview with Michele T. Taylor, November 4, 1986. Mrs. Kahn said that Alpers was an observant Jew who went to services daily. The shared point of view on architectural matters between Kahn and Alpers was corroborated by Vince Rivera; interview with Taylor. An insight into their relationship can also be seen in an undated, handwritten letter from Alpers to Kahn that referred to a conversation they had had on the nature of Plato's definition of the word "art"; letter, Alpers to Kahn, n.d., "Mikveh Israel," Box LIK 38, Kahn Collection.
7. E. Kahn, interview with Taylor.
8. See office memos dated 1962, "Mikveh Israel," Box LIK 38, Kahn Collection.
9. Levy, interview with Taylor. The other two options were Willing's Alley and Fourth Street, and a lot between Eighth and Ninth Streets near Mikveh Israel's original cemetery on Spruce Street; "Description of Potential Sites," David Arons and Irving Wasserman, June 26, 1961, "Mikveh Israel," Box LIK 38, Kahn Collection.
10. Levy, interview with Taylor.
11. Job meeting memo by R. S. Wurman (Kahn's office), February 6, 1962, "Mikveh Israel," Box LIK 38, Kahn Collection.
12. "Oldest Synagogue to Return to Colonial Site in Center City," *Philadelphia Inquirer*, November 10, 1961, 31.
13. Richard Meier, Introduction to *Recent American Synagogue Architecture* (New York: Jewish Museum, 1963), 8.
14. Kahn, as quoted in Gertrude Benson, "The Man Behind Mikveh Israel's New Building," *The Jewish Exponent*, March 30, 1962.
15. Ibid.
16. A chapel had been under consideration since early May 1961, when it was suggested at a meeting that a chapel be built to replicate the interior of Strickland's synagogue; summary of meeting, May 3, 1961, "Mikveh Israel," Box LIK 38, Kahn Collection.
17. The collection of documents dating to the early years of American Jewry was quite small, though at one job meeting a board member

questioned the adequacy of the size of the historical room; job meeting memo for meeting of September 4, 1962, September 10, 1962, ibid. Alpers had written a memo to Kahn in 1961 explaining the committee's skepticism about a museum: "In regard to the problem of separate units for the synagogue and archives, much skepticism was expressed whether the collection would be big enough—even with addition of outside sources— to require a separate building. It was the general belief that the archives could be embodied in a separate room in the synagogue building itself"; memorandum, Alpers to Kahn, June 6, 1961. Unfortunately, the building committee reversed itself completely on this issue in 1972. Kahn agreed with Alpers's position. See below.

18. Myron Schoen, "Fine Exhibit of Synagogue Architecture," *National Jewish Post and Opinion*, November 1, 1963, 10.

19. Kahn, quoted in Benson, "The Man Behind Mikveh Israel."

20. Ibid.

21. Levy, interview with Taylor.

22. Kahn, quoted in Alexandra Tyng, *Beginnings: Louis I. Kahn's Philosophy of Architecture* (New York: John Wiley & Sons, 1984), 167.

23. Levy, interview with Taylor.

24. Kahn, quoted in Tyng, *Beginnings*, 167.

25. Levy, interview with Taylor.

26. Evidence for the resolution of these design problems was provided by Levy; interview with Taylor.

27. The committee's desire to replicate Strickland's work had been expressed on November 1, 1961, in a meeting between the building committee and the architect: "Mr. Kline discussed the value of designing (the) synagogue as replica of Strickland synagogue for fund raising purposes. Discussion followed on meaning of history and tradition and possibility of achieving such a copy. Mr. Kline also suggested doing interior to resemble the historic synagogue. Mr. Kahn said he would consider the question but not as a directive"; job meeting minutes by Alan Levy, November 1, 1961, "Mikveh Israel," Box LIK 38, Kahn Collection.

28. Joseph El-Maleh, an officer of the congregation, argued that such a sum of money would be extremely difficult to raise and said that although the design was "magnificent," he would vote against it; job meeting memo by Safdie, October 31, 1962, ibid.

29. Meeting minutes by Safdie, November 4, 1962, ibid.

30. Ibid. The materials that Kahn wanted for the synagogue compound were walls in reinforced brick with concrete trim; structural supports made of concrete columns, beams, and slabs; sanctuary and chapel floors covered in marble, seats and rails of solid oak, chandeliers for lighting; stairs with marble treads and concrete structures, exterior walls in brick, and windows in clear glass with stainless steel sashes; letter, John W. Furlow (engineer) to Kahn, October 29, 1962, "Mikveh Israel," Box LIK 38, Kahn Collection.

31. Job meeting memo by Safdie, September 4, 1962, ibid.

32. Office drawing 615, F1, Kahn Collection; Rivera, interview with Taylor.

33. "Mikveh Israel Changes Location; Fishman Chairs National Campaign," *Philadelphia Jewish Times*, April 13, 1972.

34. Ibid.

35. The congregation also had a new rabbi, Ezekiel N. Musleah, a new president, Meyer Klein, and several new members on the building committee.

36. Ruth Sarner wrote Kahn: "Let me reiterate the cruel reality of ten years of inaction ... necessitated such drastic modification of your original artistic concept"; letter, Sarner to Kahn, with copies to Alpers and Klein, January 13, 1972, "Mikveh Israel," Box LIK 38, Kahn Collection.

37. Letter, Sarner to Kahn, with a copy to Klein, February 17, 1972, ibid.

38. Job meeting memo, January 13, 1972, ibid.

39. Letter, Sarner to Kahn, March 3, 1972, ibid.

40. Ibid. The kitchen beneath the sanctuary was particularly distasteful to Kahn; Rivera, interview with Taylor.

41. Rivera, interview with Taylor.

42. Memo, Sarner to Kahn, September 13, 1972, "Mikveh Israel," Box LIK 38, Kahn Collection.

43. Letter, Sarner to Anthony Pellecchia and Rivera, September 13, 1972, ibid.; Rivera, interview with Taylor.

44. Rivera, interview with Taylor.

45. Letter, Sarner to Pellecchia, Rivera, and Kahn's office, September 6, 1972, "Mikveh Israel," Box LIK 38, Kahn Collection.

46. Rivera, interview with Taylor. According to Rivera, Kahn continually referred to the joint foyer plan as "Vince's plan."

47. Letter, Alpers to Klein, February 5, 1973, "Mikveh Israel," Box LIK 38, Kahn Collection.

The Indian Institute of Management was organized in 1962 as a business school run by the government of India and the western Indian state of Gujarat (fig. 480; see figs. 314–36). Modeled on the Harvard Business School, it was established in Ahmedabad, a regional center for industry and commerce.[1] In 1962 the school's founders, who included members of the Sarabhai family, local industrialists with a distinguished tradition of architectural patronage, offered the commission to design its buildings to Balkrishna Doshi, one of the city's few foreign-trained architects. Doshi, who had come to Ahmedabad as the project manager for Le Corbusier's city museum (1951–56), instead suggested that they hire Kahn, whom he had visited most recently in the fall of 1960 at the University of Pennsylvania.[2] He believed that bringing Kahn to India would give his students at the National Institute of Design an important opportunity to work with a major architect.[3] The Sarabhais concurred, and on June 6, 1962, Kahn received an invitation from Gautam Sarabhai to participate in the design of the new institute.[4] During the summer Kahn negotiated the terms of the project with Doshi, who acted as an intermediary, and in September 1962 Kahn accepted the offer.

The commission was for an entire campus: a school building; housing for students, faculty, and servants; a mechanical services tower; and a market (plans for which were later dropped). The program for the school building alone included six auditorium-style classrooms, faculty offices, a library, a kitchen, and dining facilities. By April 1969 a building for the Executive Development Program had been added to the original requirements. All of this was to be built on a flat and dusty sixty-five-acre site at the edge of the city, a location lacking any urban context.[5]

Kahn was not at first the architect of record. That position was assumed by the Institute of Design, where the project initially served as the subject of studios taught by Doshi and Kahn. The first publication of the Institute of Management in the Indian magazine *Marg* in 1967 listed Kahn as the "consulting architect" and Doshi as the "assistant architect."[6] During his many trips to Ahmedabad, Kahn made sketches that the students at the Institute of Design converted into working drawings. The drawings were then sent to Philadelphia for Kahn to correct. As a rule, no one in Kahn's office worked on the Institute of Management, except for a succession of Indians dispatched to Philadelphia by the Institute of Design.[7] They occupied themselves there making working drawings and models. At least three of these men— M. K. Thackeray, Anant Raje, and M. S. Satsangi—went on

Indian Institute of Management

Ahmedabad, India, 1962–74

to hold important positions on the Ahmedabad end of the job. The process was complicated by unreliable mail, confiscation by customs officials, and confusion about changes in the program. Occasional shortages of construction funds and more frequent shortages of foreign exchange, needed to pay for Kahn's airfare or to support the Indians in Philadelphia, also contributed to the problems.[8]

The first preliminary autograph drawings for the project date to November 1962, during Kahn's first visit to the site.[9] An early drawing of the entire site suggests a culmination of his initial thinking about the commission (fig. 481). In one corner of the site he placed the school building, a collection of rectangular blocks assembled around two courtyards. Six large dormitories projected diagonally from two external sides of these courtyards. Each was composed of a square nestled against the school building, a second square facing a lake, and a long diagonal, possibly a hallway, connecting the two. The lake isolated the students from the faculty housing, which consisted of single-family dwellings grouped into L-shaped clusters that opened away from the lake. The market sat east of the last of these clusters; on the southern edge of the site a winding road separated the servants' housing from the rest of the complex. Although he quickly changed most details of the design, Kahn never altered the fundamental relationship between school building, dormitories, and faculty housing illustrated in this drawing.

During his second visit to the site, in March 1963, Kahn completely rearranged his original conception of the school building and brought a new level of detail to his ideas about the housing.[10] These changes are documented in the earliest office drawings for the project and in a model (fig. 482). The school building now consisted of a taller central rectangular structure like a mastaba, with battered sides and four lower surrounding trapezoids, each separated from the others by narrow passageways. In this scheme the complicated plans of the six student dormitories were composed mostly of repetitive right triangles. On the other side of the lake the grouping of faculty houses within the larger L-shaped units, whose orientation Kahn now flipped, became more complex, as each house was turned 45 degrees away from the dominant axes of the composition. Smaller units of married-student housing were added to the program at this point and were sited northwest of the faculty housing. At the same time Kahn eliminated the road separating the irregularly grouped servants' housing from the rest of the campus.

In a 1963 talk at Yale University, Kahn explained the

480. *Courtyard of classroom building, seen from corridor.*
481. *Site plan, ca. March 1963.*
482. *Site model, ca. March 1963.*
483. *Plan of classroom building and dormitories, ca. December 1963.*

preponderance of diagonals in his designs for the institute: "If you have a square in which everything is normally answerable to a square, you find two sides are oriented improperly. By taking the diagonal, you form odd conditions, but you do answer, you can conquer this geometry if you want to. And you must relentlessly look at orientation as something that you give to people because it is desperately needed. That's the basis of these shapes."[11]

In July Doshi experimented with reorienting the individual elements of Kahn's March 1963 plan in relation to the prevailing breezes.[12] Between July and December Kahn reorganized Doshi's revisions into what was nearly a mirror image of the original plan (see fig. 167). He also added new details to the plans of the school building and the dormitories.[13]

This version was radically modified as Kahn rethought the project. Once again, he transformed his conception of the school building. A memo from the summer of 1963 written in an unrecognized hand states, "Remove library from central space and substitute an open court."[14] Following this directive, Kahn placed faculty offices with keyhole light wells along the northern edge of the new courtyard; the library and two classrooms opposite the dining facilities to the east and west respectively; and more classrooms along the southern edge (fig. 483). He covered part of the courtyard with a tentlike canopy. Two staircases, both square in plan, also projected into the courtyard. The inward-facing design enhanced Kahn's stated conception of the campus as a monastery.[15] The switch from a mastaba model to the more flexible courtyard eased but did not completely eliminate the tensions between a variety of functions that needed to be brought together in a single structure. Over the next three years Kahn would repeatedly experiment with the exact placement and form of each of the parts, swaying between formal unity and functional individuality.

Until his December 1963 trip to Ahmedabad, Kahn's designs seemed largely confined to planning, and the models that survive give few hints of his thinking about the building's elevations. But during this visit he prepared drawings for the dormitories that include the complex's first detailed elevations. The building committee approved them later that month.[16] As finalized, Kahn divided the student residences into eighteen units, with small variations on the first two of their four stories (fig. 484). In each, he grouped ranges of five balconied rooms along two sides of an isosceles triangle containing a half-circular stair and identified the spaces surrounding the stairs as lounges, places for the casual

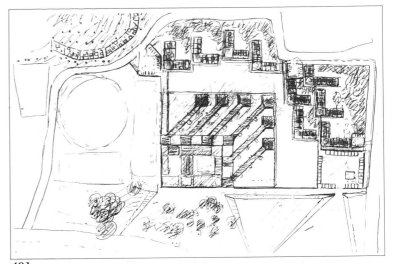

481

482

483

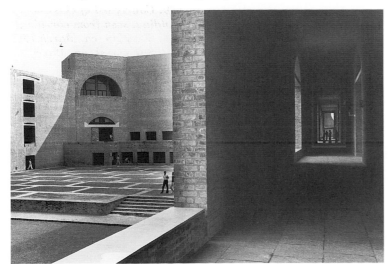

480

484

485

meetings that he believed were a key ingredient of education. On the other side of the stair he placed a square projection containing bathrooms and a tearoom.[17] In December 1964 he revised the design of three final dormitories (see fig. 318). On the eastern edge of the dormitory zone, he changed the prototype, enlarging the main block of each building to incorporate the functions of the separate bathroom/tearoom wing. Uninterrupted by projecting cubes, these units thus formed a definitive boundary for this part of the complex.[18]

A combination of function and climate determined the dormitory plans, and a similar balance between climate and material influenced their elevations. These specifically Indian conditions demanded ventilation of the interiors and protection from the harsh Gujarati light. Throughout the housing and the school building, interior rooms were protected from direct light by balconies, hallways, and lounges. The outer screen walls were often punctuated by giant arched and circular openings.

Like climate, local construction methods played a decisive role in shaping the appearance of all of Kahn's work at the institute. His patrons believed that they could limit costs by insisting that locally made brick be used for everything but the floor slabs and tie-beams. These could be built out of reinforced concrete, a material that was very popular for large-scale construction in India but was also more expensive than brick. The building committee wished to maximize the use of labor-intensive materials and methods in a country where labor was cheap and the steel needed in reinforced concrete was a costly import.[19] In the resulting facades Kahn juxtaposed taut planar surfaces, cut by enormous circular voids that opened onto lounges and corridors, with the more sculptural ground-story buttresses and upper-floor balconies of the bedroom sides of the buildings. He later commented on the forms he chose: "I had to learn to lay brickwork from scratch. . . . Why hide the beauty of open brickwork? I asked the brick what it wanted and it said I want to be an arch, so I gave it an arch."[20]

Having established the design for the dormitories late in 1963, Kahn tinkered with the details of the classroom building over the next several years. Its first elevations date to July 1964. In these drawings and the model built from them, Kahn combined the repetition of the enormous circular openings he had used in the dormitories with the more nuanced scale and texture of a "composite order," which, he claimed, combined the order of his two materials, brick and concrete (fig. 485).[21] The plan that accompanied these elevations resulted from a refinement of his decision in

April 1964 to place a diamond-shaped library in the central court. Later that month he introduced two diamond-shaped dining halls at the other end of the building.[22]

That October the construction of the first dormitory units began.[23] The following year, in 1965, Kahn completed his design of the faculty housing, and its construction proceeded soon thereafter. Like the lounge facades of the dormitories, the faculty housing elevations were entirely two-dimensional, but they were distinguished from their monumental neighbors by their smaller scale and more nuanced detail.

In September 1965 the building committee rejected two further Kahn proposals for the school building, both variants of the July 1964 design and both much larger than the 80,000 square feet required by the program.[24] In this decision the committee was influenced by the shape taken by the dormitories, in which less than half the total area responded to the committee's program. Their program had included neither the upstairs lounges nor Kahn's complicated system of connecting passageways and extra rooms threaded through their first and sometimes second stories, all of which added to the cost and time of construction.

In April 1966 the first units of the dormitories and faculty housing were completed.[25] The same month Kahn began to design the mechanical services tower.[26] That year he also drew the first plans for a row and a half of austere servants' housing, located across a small road south of the faculty housing.[27] Meanwhile, he continued work on the school building. During and after his visit to Ahmedabad in June 1966 he devoted his attention principally to its entrance and the library, for which he drew detailed plans for the first time (fig. 486). In order to save space, he now brought the library back into the main bulk of the building. At the same time, in a more cursory reexamination of the opposite end of the building, he reduced the heights of the dining hall and kitchen and eliminated the redundant walls in which he had originally wrapped them. He also trimmed off a seventh classroom he had added in 1964. The changes in interior spaces and exterior elevations gave this version a rectilinear coherence that, in the last phases of the building's design, began to replace the more articulated character of the earlier phases.

The latest plan resembled quite closely what was actually built, but the work of completing construction documents sometimes seemed interminable. As he fine-tuned the school building design between 1967 and 1969, Kahn altered its

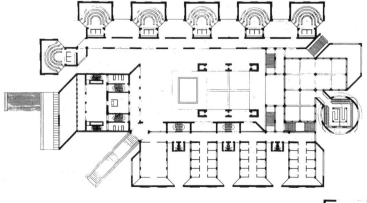

486

facades, substituting flat surfaces with rectangular openings for some of the more delicate combinations of "composite orders" and openings found in the 1965 model (see figs. 326, 328). Work on the foundations of the school building began in November 1968, although Kahn had still not supplied adequate drawings.[28] By the following April the institute was anxious to build and impatient with him. They wrote that he would either have to fly to India immediately to salvage the project or allow it to be turned over to an Indian, preferably Doshi. Kahn went to India.[29]

In the shake-up that followed, the Institute of Design lost its role in the project. The job was officially executed by Doshi's office, but it was Anant Raje, associated with the commission from the beginning, who established an office on the site and supervised construction of its final components.[30] Kahn and Raje continued to consult one another, but Kahn's interest had waned. Raje traveled to Philadelphia and borrowed sets of blueprints for other Kahn buildings in order to ensure that the school building details would be in keeping with Kahn's other work.[31] Still, he was forced to make decisions relatively quickly about the building's construction and design, and they were not always in harmony with Kahn's philosophy. For example, Kahn acquiesced to Raje's decision to reinforce the exterior walls of the building with hidden steel, but he expressed his discomfort with such a departure from the truth-to-materials philosophy that had originally shaped his design.[32]

Raje added new blocks of servants' housing, following the example established by Kahn's prototype, and supervised the construction of the final three dormitories, for which he slightly revised Kahn's design.[33] Completing the school building was, however, his principal task. As built, the library and faculty office block elevations were slightly plainer than those Kahn had drawn in 1968, and were different in character from the southern classroom facade, facing the dormitories, which retained the southern elevation shown in the 1964 model (see fig. 485). The plan of the completed building, attuned to the now more rectilinear facades, lacked the tension between the rectangular court and the diagonal axes feeding into it that was found in early versions. In a final revision of Kahn's original conception of the complex, the west end of the large central court was left open, and the dining facilities were placed in a separate building (see fig. 480).

During his final visit to the institute, in March 1974, Kahn found the complex largely complete, except for the lake, which institute officials feared would provide a breeding ground for malaria-carrying mosquitoes.[34] His initial enthusiasm for the project was gone, and the defense of it he now offered was at times nostalgic, at times cynical. Facing complaints from those who used the buildings daily that they were overscaled, he responded with gentle sarcasm: "How big is big? You are looking at an interpretation of a building within a building. This is a porch you are looking at. There is a building for communing with nature, and another building inside. Everyone is crazy in his own way."[35]

Since 1974 the Indian Institute of Management has continued to grow. Raje's dining facilities, management center, and married-student housing, added to the periphery of the site after Kahn's death, are respectful additions that fulfill the expanding needs of a successful institution.[36]

Kathleen James

Notes

1. The importance of the Harvard Business School as a model is highlighted in a 1964 brochure announcing the first session of the school's Program for Management Development, "National Institute of Design," LIK 113, Louis I. Kahn Collection, University of Pennsylvania and Pennsylvania Historical and Museum Commission, Philadelphia (hereafter cited as Kahn Collection). Other Harvard references are contained in "A Base in Cambridge—An Institute in India," *Harvard Today*, Spring 1963, 27–30; and Kahn, "Remarks" (lecture, Yale University, October 30, 1963), *Perspecta*, no. 9/10 (1965): 322.

2. Letter, Doshi to G. Holmes Perkins (dean, Graduate School of Fine Arts, University of Pennsylvania), February 25, 1961, "National Institute of Design," Box LIK 113, Kahn Collection.

3. Doshi, interview with Kathleen James, December 20, 1986.

4. Anant, Suhrid, and Manorama Sarabhai, interview with David B. Brownlee and David G. De Long, January 10, 1990; letter, Gautam Sarabhai to Kahn, April 4, 1962, "National Institute of Design," Box LIK 113, Kahn Collection.

5. Program, December 28, 1962, included with office drawings, Kahn Collection. First blueprints, dated April 1969, for Executive Management Center, and site plan, dated February 18, 1961, office drawings, Kahn Collection.

6. "Indian Institute of Management, Ahmedabad," *Marg* 20 (June 1967): 32.

7. Anant Raje, interview with Kathleen James, December 17, 1986.

8. Letters, Satsangi to Bhagwat (National Institute of Design), October 1967 to April 1968, Master Files, Box LIK 10, Kahn Collection, provide the most detailed evidence of the bureaucratic problems that hampered work on the project and of the relationship between the Philadelphia office and the National Institute of Design in Ahmedabad.

9. Heinz Ronner and Sharad Jhaveri, *Louis I. Kahn: Complete Work, 1935–1974*, 2d ed. (Basel and Boston: Birkhäuser, 1987), 208–9, dates some of the preliminary drawings, illustrated as figs. IIM.1–4 and IIM.6, to November 14 and 15, 1962.

10. Letter, Doshi to Kahn, February 26, 1963, "National Institute of Design," Box LIK 113, Kahn Collection, details plans for this visit.

11. Kahn, "Remarks," 324.

12. Office drawings are dated July 14, 1963, and model 0645-M2 was completed according to Doshi's designs. Both are in the Kahn Collection. They are published in Ronner and Jhaveri, *Complete Work*, 212, IIM.28–36. This version's relationship to the prevailing breezes is described by Kahn, "Remarks," 322.

13. This version is known from undated office drawings and has been published in Ronner and Jhaveri, *Complete Work*, 214, IIM.37–38.

14. Memo, n.d. (Summer 1963), "National Institute of Design," Box LIK 113, Kahn Collection. The memo contains a reference in Raje's hand that September 1963 is the latest date bricks could be ordered for construction to begin in July 1964.

15. Kahn, "Remarks," 322.

16. Letter, Doshi to Kahn, December 23, 1963, "National Institute of Design," Box LIK 113, Kahn Collection.

17. Kahn, "Remarks," 322.

18. Elevations dated December 15, 1964, office drawings, Kahn Collection.

19. Raje, interview with James.

20. Kahn, quoted in a May 31, 1974 [sic; Kahn died on March 17, 1974], interview conducted in Ahmedabad and supplied by Doshi, in *What Will Be Has Always Been: The Words of Louis I. Kahn*, ed. Richard Saul Wurman (New York: Access Press and Rizzoli, 1986), 252.

21. Ronner and Jhaveri, *Complete Work*, 230.

22. Autograph drawings 645.11, 645.52, and 645.119, Kahn Collection.

23. Letter, Kapadia (Philadelphia office) to Thackeray, October 26, 1964, "National Institute of Design," Box LIK 113, Kahn Collection.

24. Letter, Lalbhai (Ahmedabad office) to Kahn, September 3, 1965, ibid.

25. Letter, Doshi to Kahn, April 26, 1966, ibid.

26. Office drawings, April 2, 4, 8, 9, and 11, 1966, Kahn Collection.

27. Office drawing, April 5, 1966, Kahn Collection.

28. Letter, Kapadia to Kahn, November 19, 1968, "IIM 1 January '66 to date," Box LIK 113, Kahn Collection.

29. Letters, Lalbhai to Kahn, April 18 and 29, 1969, ibid.

30. Letter, Sarabhai to Kahn, May 29, 1969, ibid.; Raje, interview with James.

31. Letter, Raje to Kahn, April 19, 1970, "IIM 1 January '66 to date," Box LIK 113, Kahn Collection, documents Raje's upcoming six-week trip to Philadelphia. Raje, interview with James, said that he worked in part from his experience of other Kahn buildings, and had in his office sets of plans for Erdman Hall at Bryn Mawr College and the library at Phillips Exeter Academy. Both were sent to him by the Philadelphia office; letter, Henry Wilcots (Kahn's office) to Raje, December 2, 1969, "IIM 1 January '66 to date," Box LIK 113, Kahn Collection.

32. Letter, Kahn to Raje, August 13, 1969, "Indian Institute of Management," Box LIK 113, Kahn Collection.

33. Raje, interview with James.

34. Building committee notes, August 2, 1963, "National Institute of Design," Box LIK 113, Kahn Collection.

35. Kahn, quoted in Ahmedabad interview, 252.

36. James Bailey, "Louis I. Kahn in India: An Old Order at a New Scale," *Architectural Forum* 125 (July–August 1966): 63–67, was the first important article devoted to IIM; Yukio Futagawa and Romaldo Giurgola, "Louis I. Kahn: Indian Institute of Management; Exeter Library," *Global Architecture*, no. 35 (1975), is one of the most thorough treatments of the subject.

One of the twentieth century's great architectural monuments, the capital complex in Dhaka, Bangladesh, was the most ambitious work of Louis Kahn's career (fig. 487; see figs. 337–59).[1] The commission gave Kahn a rare opportunity: a tabula rasa on which to erect a nation's most important and symbolic buildings, in essence a small city. Although such a project is every architect's dream, it proved to be daunting. Begun in 1962 to provide the second capital of divided Pakistan, the project was interrupted by civil war and remained unfinished at the time of Kahn's death in 1974. The difficulty of building in a developing nation on the other side of the world was compounded by constant program changes, shifting political pressures, and the architect's notorious inability to meet deadlines. Nevertheless, Kahn's monumental vision of the new capital was ultimately realized in one of the world's poorest nations.

On August 27, 1962, three years after the government of Field Marshall Ayub Khan decided to build new capital cities in East and West Pakistan, Kahn received the first of hundreds of telegrams from the Pakistani Department of Public Works.[2] The message was terse: Was he interested in designing the new National Assembly Building in Dhaka, East Pakistan? Kahn readily responded that he was.[3] He had not been the government's first choice, however. On the advice of the Bengali architect Mazharul Islam, the senior architect for the government of East Pakistan, the commission had been offered to Le Corbusier, but he was too busy to take on such a demanding job.[4] Alvar Aalto was ill at the time and was also unable to accept. Kahn, who had met Islam at Yale in 1960–61, was quick to accept such an important commission, although he delayed his initial visit for several months.

At the end of January 1963 Kahn flew for the first time to Karachi and on to Dhaka, where he met his principal liaison, Kafiluddin Ahmad, then deputy chief engineer of the Pakistan Public Works Department.[5] During his six-day visit Kahn received the straightforward program and toured the unremarkable site: 1,000 acres of flat, open farmland adjacent to the airport on the northern outskirts of town. The most important buildings were approved for immediate construction on the 200-acre parcel already acquired by the government: the National Assembly Building; offices and residences for Assembly members and secretaries, government ministers, and their staff; and individual residences for the president, the speakers, and the secretary of the Assembly.[6] The National Assembly Building was the first priority. Its program was extensive and

included a 200-seat assembly chamber—increased to 300 almost immediately after Kahn's visit[7]—with gallery seating for press and visitors, a prayer hall, a mosque,[8] a dining hall, numerous offices, and a spacious lawn for large ceremonial gatherings.

In anticipation of future development on the remaining 800 acres, Kahn was also asked to devise a master plan for the entire site, which included a supreme court, a hospital, a library, a mosque, a museum, schools, clubs, markets, offices, recreation areas, a special diplomatic enclave, and low- and high-income residential areas.[9]

While no agreement was signed during this first trip, Kahn managed to negotiate nearly full control of the site. The government urged him to collaborate with one of the British architectural firms with experience in Pakistan (indeed, some were already familiar with the site of the new capital), but Kahn insisted that he be the sole architect for the buildings slated for construction and requested that all planning for the larger site also be done under his guidance.[10] Kahn's capital was to be a unified composition uncompromised by political expediency.

Early Designs

During discussions on his first trip, Kahn scribbled notes in the margins of the program. One sheet may record his earliest ideas, anticipating some of the essential characteristics of the site plan and the assembly building (fig. 488).[11] This quick sketch shows the rectangular site divided into two parcels: on the smaller, 200-acre sector the assembly building was located on a central axis at the site's southern boundary. The dark shading surrounding the isolated building suggested either lakes or lawns. Two diagonal lines (avenues?) flanking the site led to a crescent-shaped residential area. Beyond, and on axis with the assembly building, was a large oval stadium surrounded by other buildings. Kahn also delineated his nascent thoughts for the assembly building. Several sketches revealed a round chamber at the center of a larger square with four corner towers. Other sketches explored square and diamond patterns, the basic geometry of the complex.

Kahn had little more than a month to develop the scheme before his next trip to Dhaka in mid-March 1963. Accompanied by Carles Vallhonrat, his assistant, and August Komendant, his structural engineer, Kahn returned with drawings and photographs of his first schematic site model, dated March 12, 1963 (see fig. 126). In this initial presentation of the master plan, Kahn divided the program

Sher-e-Bangla Nagar, Capital of Bangladesh

Dhaka, Bangladesh, 1962–83

487. National Assembly Building and east hostels.
488. Site plan, ca. February 1963.
489. Site plan. Inscribed May 3, 1963.

into two distinct realms: the Citadel of Assembly (located in the acquired, 200-acre parcel) and the Citadel of Institutions (to be located in the area slated for future development). The two citadels were separated by a large park and aligned on a common axis. The master plan was a balanced but not symmetrical composition.

In the assembly group the three most important buildings were sited on the central axis. The monumental diamond-shaped assembly building was set in a lake whose southern border formed a graceful crescent. The mosque with four minarets abutted the assembly building, and the supreme court was sited across a courtyard. Two low wings of hostels formed symmetrical walls flanking the citadel and the lake. Kahn intended all buildings to be concrete with marble embellishments, although both materials would have to be imported.

The Citadel of Institutions across the park was never built, but throughout the decade it appeared with minor revisions in all subsequent site plans. Its three most important constituents bordered the park facing the assembly complex—the sports complex on the central axis, flanked by the school of arts and the school of sciences. Kahn later explained this highly symbolic arrangement, which he considered unprecedented:

The area opposite the Assembly is for the School of Arts and the School of Science reflecting in spirit and in harmony with the buildings of the National Assembly. . . . The idea stems from the realization that the House of Legislation sanctions the INSTITUTIONS OF MAN. Arts and Science being fundamental—Art is immeasurable Science is measurable.

In conjunction with the School of the Arts and of the Sciences is the INSTITUTION OF WELL BEING [the sports center] expressed as the center of the regard for the gifts of nature—sound body and mind. . . . This conception of relationships in the mind of the Architect has no counterpart to any buildings in the world.[12]

The symbolic importance of each building in the plan was critical to Kahn's design. The hospital, initially depicted as a composition of four stellate structures, was placed on Mirpur Road along the western border. Although it was slated for immediate construction, philosophically Kahn could not reconcile its location within the assembly sector and close to the other first-phase buildings.[13]

Two months after his first presentation, on May 16, 1963, Kahn sent photographs of a second site model and drawings to Dhaka with an accompanying narrative (fig. 489).[14] A

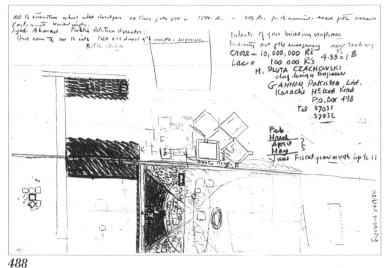

488

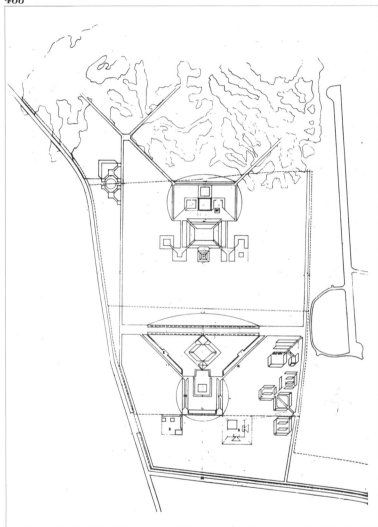

489

487

significant change had occurred in the orientation of the
assembly group and the flanking hostels. Rotated 180
degrees, they now faced north, opening toward the Citadel
of Institutions across the park. The two citadels were also
brought closer together, reducing the site to 600 acres,
an area the government might more easily procure. The
mosque, previously a separate structure, was now eliminated
(several government officials objected to its placement), and
the prayer hall was given greater architectural emphasis
and symbolic importance in the diamond-shaped assembly
building. Kahn described the new design:

The first design submitted on our last visit showed a Mosque as a
separate building adjoining the Assembly Building. In this new
second scheme, the Prayer Hall of the program is made a part of
the spaces of the Assembly block and woven into the architecture
as one. In this way, its meaning is equally emphatic as a mosque
and gives equal spiritual significance without inviting controversy.
The consolidation of all the space requirements of the building into
one articulated block gives a strong, single image.[15]

Indeed, the assembly building was an imposing structure,
towering fortresslike above the surrounding hostels, its
"strong, single image" reinforced by its isolated position in
the lake. A southern forecourt with a pedestrian bridge
spanning the water led directly to the prayer hall. On the
north a bi-level road and pedestrian walkway perpendicular
to the building traversed the site.

Several important aspects of Kahn's design were a response
to the harsh subtropical climate, with its scorching sun and
seasonal monsoons. The man-made lake surrounding the
assembly building and hostels was intended to fulfill
practical, symbolic, and aesthetic functions. Low areas on
the site were to be filled with earth excavated from the lake,
which was conceived as a giant basin to control periodic
flooding. For Kahn, water was an important symbol of the
beginnings of urban life, a belief that had recently found
expression in his visionary Philadelphia city plans. He
admitted that celebrating the troublesome monsoons so
prominently in Dhaka was also largely an aesthetic choice.[16]
Like the great Mughal monuments, the "citadel" was
surrounded by a pool of water, which would dissolve the
concrete and marble edifice into endless shimmering
reflections. Moreover, the lake and park formed a
boundary around the assembly complex, thus guarding
its spectacular vistas.

The buildings Kahn envisioned also responded to the heat
and strong sun of South Asia. Recalling his earlier projects
for the U.S. Consulate in Luanda and the Salk Institute

490. Perspective of secretaries'
hostels with elevations and
section, Spring 1963.
491. Plan and elevation studies
of National Assembly Building
roof, ca. 1963–64.
492. Kahn and assistants with
model of assembly complex,
Spring 1964.

490

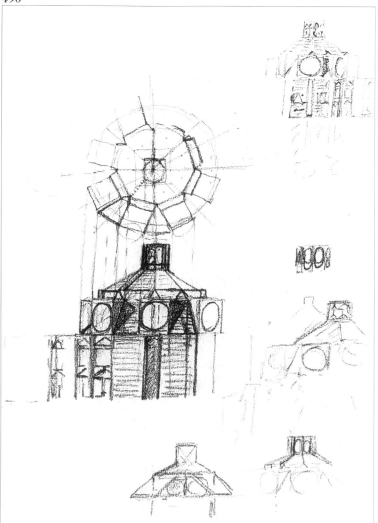

491

meeting house, the Dhaka design included elaborate screen walls perforated with large openings that sheltered interior spaces from the elements. He described the concept: "The architectural approach to the Assembly Building as for all the buildings is to find a design which protects both enclosed and outdoor spaces from sun, heat, rain and glare by the use of overhangs, deep verandas and protecting walls to accompany the directly usable spaces."[17] Designed to soften the light while welcoming precious breezes, perforated screen walls and deep verandas appeared in all the buildings. An early sketch from spring 1963 depicted the secretaries' hostels with trapezoidal openings (viewed from within a porch screened by arches) (fig. 490). On the same sheet Kahn explored various alternatives—round, arched, and trapezoidal apertures—and his annotations explained the function of the elaborate brise-soleils.

A similar treatment was given to the roof of the assembly building. In an early undated study of the assembly chamber Kahn explored the shape of the crowning roof—a ring of eight dormers with large circular openings topped by a cupola that channeled light and air into the space below (fig. 491). While the giant dormers were similar in the final design, the design of the roof itself proved the most demanding engineering challenge at Dhaka and would not be resolved for nearly a decade.

While experimenting with geometric forms in elevation, Kahn continued to express his great ambitions for a profound philosophical relationship between the buildings. He made a fundamental distinction between the monumental public realm of the assembly building and the smaller hostels containing individual apartments. The secretaries' hostels were not merely housing:

The hostels are designed as studies and their gardens. This idea stems from the realization that a man leaving his home to participate in the acts of Assembly is given privacy, a place of honor and a place for reflection in relation to his duties as a member of the Assembly. This approach to a place of stay distinguishes such a place from a mere hotel which is fitting to ordinary business rather than extraordinary business of assembly.[18]

On several occasions the government had suggested that the hostels might double as hotels during the six months when the parliament was not in session.[19] Perhaps a sound economic idea, it nevertheless violated Kahn's distinction between man's private and public spaces and the sanctity of both in a nation's capital.

During the remainder of 1963 Kahn continued to modify the site plan, gather program information, and discuss the terms of a contract. Fearful that the government would compromise his designs in its zeal to commence building, he made it clear that one of his principal concerns was to maintain almost complete control over the project. One safeguard for this control that he suggested was a field office in Dhaka staffed with representatives from Philadelphia. Kahn's single-mindedness derived in part from what he saw as the great importance of the work. As he wrote to his assistant Duncan Buell while in the throes of hammering out a contract in Dhaka, "Since this is new capital new country . . . must strive to establish climate that brings forth total concept recognized by world as great value given for ages by Pakistan. We must aspire to nothing less."[20] After much negotiation Kahn signed an agreement on January 9, 1964.[21] The government granted his request for a field office so that architects from Philadelphia, assisted by local draftsmen, could supervise the project and assure proper construction standards.

Under great pressure from the government to produce physical results, the Public Works Department was extremely anxious to begin construction. But every time the government requested changes in the master plan, such as the additions of the central secretariat building[22] and the combined meteorological observatory[23] in late summer of 1963, Kahn felt compelled to restudy the plan. Furthermore, he began to complain about the fact that only 200 acres were immediately available. This complicated the precise siting of the structures, especially the assembly building—the keystone of the plan. In January 1964 he explained the delays in finalizing the master plan: "Location (of Assembly Building) not settled because of limited acreage. Doing site studies of 200, 400, 600, 1000 acres. Buildings must be like a good position on a chess board. For its symbolic value no building must be in the wrong place. If I had 1000 acres now I could proceed without delay."[24]

Taking Shape
In the spring and summer of 1964 Kahn and his assistants pored over a new site model as though the buildings were pieces on a chess board (figs. 492, 496). Armed with new drawings, models, a master plan, and preliminary plans for the contracted buildings, Kahn made his sixth trip to Pakistan in May 1964. The design of the Citadel of Assembly had matured and was close to its final form, although changes occurred even after construction had commenced.

The massive assembly building dominated the site by its

492

493

494

495

493. Model of north side of
National Assembly Building
with Presidential Square, ca.
1964.
494. Presidential Square,
substructure under
construction, ca. 1965.
495. National Assembly
Building under construction,
ca. October 1968.
496. Site plan. Inscribed May
10, 1964, revised July 6, 1964.
497. Model of prayer hall, ca.
1964–65.

height and its central location. The circular apertures of
the crowning light wells were repeated at different scales
throughout the assembly building and the surrounding
hostels, providing a formal unity to the entire complex.
The assembly building was set back from the ceremonial
approach road on the north, a move the client praised.
Between that road and the now more isolated assembly
building, Kahn designed elaborate gardens and a ceremonial
plaza known as Presidential Square. With its elevated
platform that afforded commanding views over the gardens,
the plaza was both an impressive entrance and an assembly
area designed to hold large crowds.[25] This plaza was
balanced on the other side of the building by the South Plaza
entrance, where the supreme court and central secretariat
buildings were to frame the open space (neither was built).
The South Plaza also sheltered beneath it an automobile
entrance, a garage, and a central mechanical plant that were
intended to service the hostels and other buildings that
would surround the plaza. Like umbilical cords, pipes and
conduits emanated from this central plant, threading
through overhead chases in the covered sidewalks that led to
the hostels flanking the assembly building. This concept,
recalling ideas in Kahn's multilevel "viaduct architecture"
for Philadelphia, was only partially realized, for its cost
was prohibitive.

The plan of the assembly building had evolved into an
extraordinarily complex centralized form by the summer
of 1964 (see fig. 129). The assembly chamber, oriented to the
west, occupied the inner core. Protected from the outside
world, the chamber received light and ventilation from the
surrounding tier of dormers and shafts. Mediating between
the inner assembly core and the exterior ring of buildings
was an ambulatory—an inner street open to the ceiling seven
stories above. Eight structurally distinct units formed the
octagonal outer sector: those in the four cardinal directions
were each given a unique shape and function and were
separated by four identical office buildings. The unit
containing the northern entrance off Presidential Square
was essentially square in plan, and it housed an impressive
double staircase. Great circular openings in the walls
framing the stairs afforded views across the landscape (fig.
493). The orthogonal geometry of this entrance contrasted
with the exuberant curvilinear plan of the southern entrance
block, which contained the prayer hall and the court of
ablutions. Essentially square in plan, the four corners of the
prayer hall were embedded in cylinders—enormous "hollow
columns," open at the top for light and ventilation.[26] Skewed
slightly off axis to achieve the proper orientation toward
Mecca, the prayer hall was hinged to the main building by

496

the oval court of ablutions, which also contained the stairs to the upper level. The complexity of the spatial forms created by the cylinders and the canted prayer hall necessitated a separate study model (fig. 497).

The two lateral units on the east and west sides of the assembly building contained lounge and dining facilities. The rectangular east wing, with interior curving walls, was designated for members of the Assembly, who were thus placed in proximity to their entrances into the chamber and given outward views of their hostels. The oval west wing, designed as two half-circles separated by an open court, contained lounges for the ministers and secretaries. They, too, enjoyed views of their hostels lying west of the assembly building and were placed close to their chamber entrances.

The three groups of hostels began to assume their final layout in the plan of May 1964, and they shared several features. All were two stories tall with roof terraces hidden behind high parapet walls. In plan, the hostels ranged from one to three rooms, with the larger apartments reserved for high-ranking officials. Apartments were grouped around large central staircases, porches, vestibules, and common rooms. On the east flank, the 300 members of the Assembly were housed in dormitory-like buildings arranged in staggered blocks and grouped around common dining and lounge facilities. West of the assembly building stood a block of more prestigious houses for the ministers, and beyond, the secretaries' hostels echoed the staggered arrangement seen on the eastern side. Several private residences, for the speakers and the president, were also planned in this area. They were never built.

In May 1964 the plans were received favorably by the Public Works Department in Dhaka and the ministers in Rawalpindi (West Pakistan), save for one notable objection. The ministers criticized what looked like "air vents" on top of the building. Some said Kahn's huge monitors looked like smokestacks. They suggested that perhaps by connecting them the appearance of a dome would be achieved, and hence a greater "Islamicness."[27] With regard to housing, they advised a greater simplification and a slight reduction in square footage. Shortly thereafter, the client made the important economic decision to build the hostels in brick—the only material that could be produced locally.[28]

By the fall of 1964 public criticism of the government for hiring a slow-paced, Western architect was mounting. It was an election year. During President Ayub's August visit to Dhaka, he had complained bitterly that there was nothing to show for two years of work, and in a crass comparison he observed that the Intercontinental Hotel had been planned and built in only eighteen months.[29] But the Public Works Department defended their architect, emphasizing his sensitivity to the Muslim tradition. Ahmad quickly summarized Kahn's accomplishments:

The fact is that the architect took full two years to develop the Master Plans and the plans for various buildings in Second Capital. He had sufficient time to study the physical and climatic conditions in East Pakistan as well as the architectural heritage of our country. For instance, provision of lakes, public parks and gardens around the buildings is in the best of tradition established by the Muslim planners of the past. Huge concrete and brick arches provided in all the buildings and deep porch treatment given to them is also in accordance with the old designs of buildings during the Muslim rule in India. . . . On our part we feel sure that architectural character of the Second Capital will be a landmark in the architectural history of Pakistan reflecting a happy blend of the rich Muslim cultural heritage and the dynamic spirit of a progressive Pakistan.[30]

Ahmad's praise for Kahn was indicative of his department's enormous respect for the architect (whom they addressed as "Professor"), but the politicians were pacified only when the walls began to rise above ground.

Construction Begins

On October 6, 1964, young Roy Vollmer from Kahn's office arrived in Dhaka to establish the field office. He was soon joined by his colleague Gus Langford.[31] Traveling with Vollmer was Nick Gianopulos, the structural engineer with Keast & Hood in Philadelphia; Komendant was no longer working on the project.[32] The road layout was being developed and the positions of the major buildings were fixed; pile driving commenced under Gianopulos's supervision, even though a full set of construction drawings was not ready.

Construction began with Presidential Square, the large ceremonial plaza entrance on the north side of the assembly building (fig. 494). The plaza, sheathed in marble, was supported by brick arches—a vast space which Kahn compared to that under the mosque at Cordoba.[33] While the cavernous space was not intended to serve any particular purpose, it became the training ground for the native work force who learned to lay brick according to Kahn's high standards. Indeed, these arches were the model for all future brickwork at Dhaka. Kahn inspected the site in January 1965, and Vollmer enthusiastically reported to the Philadelphia office:

497

Lou looked at the brickwork and was pleased. Care is being exercised and special tools employed to keep all the joints uniform. The work looks very impressive appearing as some great ancient structure being unearthed. Politically it saved the moment for most of the MNA's [Members of the National Assembly] thought and were told it was the National Assembly Building under construction, thus being pleased by the rapid progress of the work.[34]

Presidential Square was largely finished in October 1965, months before any concrete was poured for the assembly building. By this time construction had also commenced on the hostels, which proceeded rapidly.

Several important changes had occurred in the residences since the summer of 1964. The switch from concrete to brick seems to have stimulated modifications of the unglazed openings. By September 1965 the "glare wall" apertures had increased to no fewer than fifty different shapes and sizes, ranging from circles to flat arches, and some designed with concrete ties for structural stability—what Kahn called his "composite arch."[35] Kahn later recollected, "Though I first resisted this change (from concrete to brick), I have now discovered, in the development of the design, some beautiful shapes that are true to the order of brickwork."[36] The differentiation between the large common areas and the smaller private apartments was expressed in the elevations by openings of varying shapes and sizes, designed to take advantage of welcome breezes.

A major change had also occurred in the design of the members' lounge and dining facilities in the spring of 1965. For every three hostel blocks, there was to be a grouping of three giant cylinders containing these facilities and bordering the lake. Their curving walls complemented the rectilinear geometry of the apartments and mitigated the staggered layout of the east flank. The outer wall of each cylinder wrapped around an outdoor courtyard and was perforated by giant arches. In the corner cylinder of each group a narrow staircase threaded through the outer wall, its ascent to the second floor reflected in the inclined base of the arched opening (see figs. 351–53). The field office constructed a special model to study this structure, a tour de force in brick construction.[37] All three hostel groups were largely completed in 1967, and that summer the site was renamed Ayub Nagar after the president.[38]

While the pile foundations for the assembly building were being driven in 1965, the design of the enormous edifice underwent further refinement in the Philadelphia office.

The most significant change was made in the elevations of the office wings, resulting in greater monumentality. In August 1965 Kahn wrote to Vollmer, "We are really grinding out the drawings and I only require of you just a little more patience so that we do not fall into the same trap of giving bits and pieces which maybe we will have to retract. I am determined to see that the whole structure of the Hostels and the Assembly Building is completed."[39] The interior elevations of the four office wings facing the ambulatory were now finalized, whereas before they had been merely a series of identical arches and circles, "subject to arbitrary decisions."[40] The seven-story facade was a monumental composition that combined a variety of simple shapes: large lunettes, sharply acute pediments, and small portholes (fig. 499).[41] The exterior elevations were also revised; gone were the two large superimposed circles, replaced by a vertically oriented rectangle (forty feet high) surmounted by a slightly taller, slender triangle (fig. 498).[42] The new design, with its greater height and vertical thrust, was impressive. The side walls retained their enormous circular openings. Thus the facade of the assembly building exhibited three primary shapes: triangle, rectangle, and circle.

In January 1966 a set of drawings was issued for construction, and in the following month Fred Langford, who had recently completed overseeing the concrete work at Salk, arrived in Dhaka for sixteen weeks to supervise the beginning of the concrete pouring for the assembly building.[43] Langford's first task was to teach the work force to build the wooden formwork and pour the concrete. In March 1966 pouring began, but the desired standards were not always achieved. The work force swarmed around the site; hand labor was cheap, and at the peak of construction activity more than two thousand laborers were employed.[44] Like a human conveyor belt, the stream of workers (each with a basket on his head) dumped their loads into the forms (fig. 495). The concrete was poured in five-foot-high sections, the maximum feasible daily total. This established a module that was reflected in the walls, with ribbons of marble marking each day's pour. The result was a delicate network of white marble lines that contrasted with the sober concrete; this Kahn described as the "male" strength and stability of concrete, and the "female" beauty of marble.[45]

With the hostels largely finished and the assembly building continuing to rise, construction began on the hospital in September 1967. The program for Ayub Central Hospital had undergone frequent revisions, and when Kahn signed a separate contract for this complex on January 31, 1965, it had been expanded to include a school of tropical medicine

498

and public health, an outpatient department, and staff quarters.[46] Only the latter two components were built. The most distinctive aspect of the outpatient department was its western facade—a long, eight-bay arcaded entrance veranda and open-air waiting room (see figs. 356, 358). The outer arcade was composed of twenty-five-foot circular openings. Parallel inner arcades consisted of circles and arches, and the veranda lying between the inner and outer walls was an extraordinary space, defined by arching buttresses. The outpatient department was finished in 1969.

The most perplexing problem at Dhaka remained the roof of the assembly building. When construction had commenced in the spring of 1966, the crown spanning the octagonal assembly chamber was designed with Vierendeel trusses supported on concrete fins. In keeping with the earlier design, a ring of dormers with circular windows and "mansard" roof slabs surrounded the chamber.[47] Apparently, under pressure to begin construction, Kahn had underestimated the structure's weight in the preliminary designs. Final engineering calculations proved this design untenable.[48] Moreover, lifting the trusses into place would pose a vast problem.

In November 1968, more than two years after construction had commenced on the assembly building, M. G. Siddiqui (who had replaced Ahmad as chief engineer in Dhaka) came to Philadelphia, frustrated by Kahn's slow pace and anxious to complete drawings for the assembly building and other unfinished work. This was the first visit to Philadelphia by any representative of the Public Works Department. During his two-week visit Siddiqui reviewed all drawings for Dhaka and took stock of the remaining work, hoping to coerce the architect and his staff into finishing. However, the roof design remained unresolved, and Siddiqui returned to Dhaka pessimistic about meeting any deadline. Six months later Abdul Wazid (the superintendent engineer) arrived from Dhaka and also attempted to extract a design from the Philadelphia office, but still no solution was found. In the summer of 1969 this impasse was temporarily broken when a steel-cable suspension structure, designed with the structural engineer Harry Palmbaum, was approved by the client. But the Japanese contractor's cost estimate proved too high, and this plan was also scrapped. A solution was not found for nearly two more years.

The design of the prayer hall roof was also problematic. When construction began in 1966 its roof was conceived as a pyramid. But members of parliament were dissatisfied with the form, preferring a dome.[49] The issue was debated, and

Kahn finally relented. Henry Wilcots, Kahn's assistant, informed the field office: "We sought to find something historical that would reaffirm our thoughts. . . . In summary the pyramidal form was an architectural offering and was not fulfilling the spiritual needs of the space."[50]

In August 1970, four and a half years after construction had begun, the walls reached their finished height of 135 feet. The installation of the marble strips began. Wilcots inspected the site and reported that "the exterior marble samples are in place and the concrete changes completely. . . . The first sign of the PWD [Public Works Department] appreciating our work outwardly. The total is a fine piece of work."[51] But the assembly building remained roofless for several years, unusable and open to the elements. In February 1971 the architects and engineers finally cut through this Gordian knot. The solution to the vexing problem of roofing the assembly building and the prayer hall was seen to lie in vaulted structures. But before the designs could be finalized, the entire project was thrown into turmoil by civil war.

A New Nation

On March 26, 1971, war broke out in Pakistan when Bangladesh (East Pakistan) claimed independence from West Pakistan. Kahn's contract was immediately terminated and his architects closed the field office and evacuated Dhaka. Kahn nevertheless decided to finish the design of the assembly building roof so that construction could resume when peace was restored. The new design was a parabolic reinforced-concrete "umbrella" engineered by Palmbaum and rising an additional twenty-five feet over the octagonal drum that was already built. A groined vault was designed for the prayer hall. In August 1972 Kahn resumed negotiations with the new republic when he and Wilcots toured the three projects he had under construction on the subcontinent (the others being in Ahmedabad and Kathmandu). The unfinished capital, renamed Sher-e-Bangla Nagar (the city of the Bengal tiger), had suffered little damage from the war. A contract was discussed, and the new nation requested designs for a desperately needed secretariat building.

Several months later, in January 1973, Kahn returned to Dhaka and unveiled a new master plan (see fig. 133). Across the park from the assembly building, the Citadel of Institutions was now replaced by an imposing secretariat, an enormous office building of 2.5 million square feet.[52] The highly detailed program established by the new nation demanded a building too large to be located adjacent to

498. Model of National Assembly Building from north, 1966.
499. National Assembly Building ambulatory.

499

the assembly building's South Plaza, where the central secretariat had originally been planned a decade earlier.[53] In its new location, the massive, nine-story-high rectangular building formed a 2,100-foot-long brick wall interlaced with concrete supports and ties. This home for bureaucracy, with its relatively dull, repetitive facade, was designed as a backdrop for the much more sculptural and prominent assembly building; it would not compete with the Citadel of Assembly.[54]

A year later, on January 14, 1974, during his last trip to Dhaka, Kahn signed two new agreements: one for the design of the secretariat and another for a new master plan for a 2,600-acre site that included the original capital complex and an additional 2,000 acres.[55] The master plan was intended to guide the government in placing all new buildings and in developing the future use of the considerably expanded area. But Kahn declined to reopen a field office; it was too costly to maintain. The Public Works Department would have to oversee the execution of the designs. During his last visit to Dhaka the assembly building roof was finally under construction.

When Kahn died in March 1974, the preliminary design for the secretariat was nearly finished, but the structure was never built. The remaining unfinished work, including the completion of the assembly building, was overseen by David Wisdom & Associates, comprising Kahn's long-time colleagues Wisdom, Henry Wilcots, and Reyhan T. Larimer. Their work was largely complete in July 1983. Six years later, on October 15, 1989, Kahn was posthumously presented the Aga Khan Award for Architecture for the Sher-e-Bangla Nagar National Assembly Building.

Peter S. Reed

Notes

1. The most complete study of the new capital is Florindo Fusaro, *Il Parlamento e la nuova capitale a Dacca di Louis I. Kahn 1962/1974* (Rome: Officina Edizioni, 1985).
2. Telegram, CapDap to Kahn, received in Philadelphia August 27, 1962, "Second Capital—Pakistan Cablegrams To/From Kafiluddin Ahmad August 27, 1962 through Nov. 26, 1963," Box LIK 117, Louis I. Kahn Collection, University of Pennsylvania and Pennsylvania Historical and Museum Commission, Philadelphia (hereafter cited as Kahn Collection).
3. Telegram, Kahn to William O. Hall (Minister Councillor, Pakistan), copy received in Philadelphia September 6, 1962, ibid.
4. Mazharul Islam, conversation with David B. Brownlee and David G. De Long, January 17, 1990.
5. Kahn arrived in Karachi on January 28, 1963, before going on to Dhaka; letter, Pakistan International Airlines to Kahn, January 22, 1963, "Second Capital—Pakistan Travel Only," Box LIK 119, Kahn Collection.
6. Programs, "Second Capital—Pakistan 62–63 Pakistan Public Works Department, (Ahmad, Farqui, Qureshim, Hasan, etc.)," Box LIK 117, Kahn Collection.
7. Letter, J. Huq (Pakistan Public Works Department) to Kahn, February 11, 1963, ibid.
8. A mosque and a prayer hall were both included in the detailed requirements of the National Assembly Secretariat [sic] presented to Kahn on his first trip. It seems that Kahn suggested the mosque be a separate adjoining structure, and he received written approval for this immediately after his visit; ibid. Compare this with Kahn's account of his first visit to Dhaka in Keller Smith and Reyhan Tansal, eds., "The Development by Louis I. Kahn of the Design for the Second Capital of Pakistan at Dacca," *Student Publication of the School of Design, North Carolina State College, Raleigh* 14 (May 1964): n.p.
9. "Requirements for Second Capital at Dacca," "Second Capital—Pakistan 62–63 Pakistan Public Works Department, (Ahmad, Farqui, Qureshim, Hasan, etc.)," Box LIK 117, Kahn Collection.
10. Letter, Ahmad to Kahn, February 6, 1963, ibid.
11. This drawing has not been published previously. For Kahn's account of his early designs for Dhaka, see Smith and Tansal, "The Development of the Design for Dacca."
12. Letter, Kahn to M. G. Siddiqui (Pakistan Public Works Department), September 23, 1969, "PAK PWD Correspondence 1969," Box LIK 117, Kahn Collection.
13. Letter, Kahn to Ahmad, May 16, 1963, "Pakistan Correspondence—Miscellaneous," Box LIK 120, Kahn Collection.
14. Ibid.
15. Ibid.
16. Notes, May 20, 1964, "Lou's Notes 5-20-64," Box LIK 122, Kahn Collection.
17. Letter, Kahn to Ahmad, May 16, 1963, "Pakistan Correspondence—Miscellaneous," Box LIK 120, Kahn Collection.
18. Ibid.
19. See, for example, letter, A. R. Qureshi (Pakistan Rehabilitation and Works Division) to A. K. Khattak (Pakistan Public Works Department), November 13, 1963, "Second Capital—Pakistan 62–63 Pakistan Public Works Department, (Ahmad, Farqui, Qureshim, Hasan, etc.)," Box LIK 117, Kahn Collection.
20. Telegram, Kahn to Buell, November 18, 1963, "Second Capital—Pakistan Cablegrams to/from Kafiluddin Ahmad August 27, 1962 through Nov. 26, 1963," Box LIK 117, Kahn Collection.
21. Agreement, January 9, 1964, "PAK CAP Contract," Box LIK 116, Kahn Collection. Kahn's fee for work specified in the agreement was $840,000. After Kahn experienced enormous cost overruns, a new

agreement was signed on March 28, 1968. This agreement accounted for the increased program, including Presidential Square, South Plaza, and the entrance gate (not built).

22. Letter, Ahmad to Kahn, August 18, 1963, "Second Capital—Pakistan 62–63 Pakistan Public Works Department, (Ahmad, Farqui, Qureshim, Hasan, etc.)," Box LIK 117, Kahn Collection.

23. Letter, Ahmad to Kahn, September 7, 1963, ibid.

24. Telegram, Kahn to Ahmad, January 22, 1964, "PAC—Cablegrams to/from ADDLCHIEF 1964," Box LIK 117, Kahn Collection.

25. "Description of Presidential Square and Gardens," October 8, 1964, "PAKCAP—Correspondence to/from ROYGUS October 8, 1964 thru June 30, 1965," Box LIK 117, Kahn Collection.

26. The open cylinders proved unsatisfactory. They were later covered and the room was air-conditioned.

27. Letter, Ahmad to Kahn, May 26, 1964, "Second Capital—Pakistan Pakistan Public Works Department Correspondence—1964," Box LIK 117, Kahn Collection. This was reiterated in April 1965; letter, Pakistan Public Works Department to AddlChief (Ahmad), with a copy to Kahn, April 4, 1965, ibid.

28. Telegram, Kahn to AddlChief (Ahmad), August 7, 1964, "PAC—Cablegrams to/from ADDLCHIEF 1964," Box LIK 117, Kahn Collection.

29. Letter, Ahmad to Kahn, September 2, 1964, "Second Capital—Pakistan Pakistan Public Works Department Correspondence—1964," Box LIK 117, Kahn Collection.

30. Statement by Ahmad, November 28, 1964, ibid.

31. Telegram, Vollmer to Kahn, October 6, 1964, "PAC—Cablegrams to/from ROYGUS 10/6/64 thru 12/31/65," Box LIK 120, Kahn Collection.

32. For Komendant's account of the events that led up to his dissociation from the project, see August E. Komendant, *18 Years with Architect Louis I. Kahn* (Englewood, N.J.: Aloray, 1975), 75–90.

33. See Kahn's note on the back of a telegram, Kahn to Ahmad, September 9, 1964, "PAC—Cablegrams to/from ADDLCHIEF 1964," Box LIK 117, Kahn Collection.

34. Report, Vollmer to Philadelphia office, received in Philadelphia February 9, 1965, "PAKCAP—Correspondence to/from ROYGUS October 8, 1964 thru June 30, 1965," Box LIK 117, Kahn Collection.

35. Office drawings, Arch Types Schedule, September 7, 1965, Kahn Collection.

36. Printed statement sent to Vollmer, May 24, 1965, "PAKCAP—Correspondence to/from ROYGUS October 8, 1964 thru June 30, 1965," Box LIK 117, Kahn Collection.

37. Letter, Gus Langford to Henry Wilcots (Philadelphia office), December 5, 1966, "PAC—Correspondence—ROYGUS July 1966 thru December 1966," Box LIK 117, Kahn Collection.

38. Letter, F. Donald Barbaree (Kahn's Dhaka representative) to Wilcots, July 28, 1967, "PAC—Correspondence—to/from GUS June 1967 thru December 1967," Box LIK 117, Kahn Collection.

39. Letter, Kahn to Vollmer, August 25, 1965, "PAKCAP—Correspondence to/from ROYGUS June 30, 1965 thru December 31, 1965," Box LIK 117, Kahn Collection.

40. Ibid.

41. Office drawing NA A44, June 14, 1965, Kahn Collection.

42. The change is apparent in the assembly building model constructed in March 1966, and it was recorded on office drawing NA A44, Kahn Collection, as a revision on July 19, 1966.

43. In June 1966 Fred Langford wrote a report of his experience, later published as "Concrete in Dacca," *Mimar*, no. 6 (1982): 50–55.

44. Telegram, Gus Langford to Wilcots, February 27, 1967, "PAC—Correspondence—ROYGUS January 1967 thru May 1967," Box LIK 117, Kahn Collection.

45. Kahn, quoted in M. G. Siddiqui, "Philosophy of Ayub Nagar," ca. 1967, "PAC—Entrance Gate—Ayub Nagar All Correspondence," Box LIK 120, Kahn Collection.

46. Hospital agreement, "Ayub Hospital—Contract," Box LIK 122, Kahn Collection. The contract was terminated on May 1, 1970, after completion of the outpatient department; letter, Kahn to Y. A. Khan (Joint Secretary, Ministry of Agriculture and Works, Rehabilitation and Works Division, Islamabad), May 21, 1970, "Hospital PAK PWD Correspondence 11/63–11/70," Box LIK 123, Kahn Collection.

47. See office drawings dated April 7 and April 29, 1966, Kahn Collection.

48. Letter, Kahn to Siddiqui, December 19, 1966, "PAKCAP—Correspondence PAK PWD 1966–1967," Box LIK 117, Kahn Collection.

49. Letter, Wazid to Wilcots, July 27, 1969, "PAK PWD—Correspondence 1969," Box LIK 117, Kahn Collection.

50. Letter, Wilcots to Don Barbaree, Richard Garfield, and Subodh K. Das (structural engineer), September 15, 1970, "Master File," Box LIK 10, Kahn Collection.

51. Letter, Wilcots to David Wisdom (Kahn's office), August 4, 1970, "PAK CAP Invoices—July '63–Feb '71," Box LIK 122, Kahn Collection.

52. Letter, Wilcots to Gabriele Aggugini (Marelli Aerotecnica), December 29, 1972, "Master File," Box 10, Kahn Collection.

53. "Bangladesh Secretariat Program," June 14, 1973, "Original Secretariat Program 14 June 1973 Received from Dacca," Box LIK 119, Kahn Collection. The extensive program is 132 pages long.

54. Reyhan Tansal Larimer (former Kahn associate), interview with Peter S. Reed, September 19, 1990.

55. Both agreements are in "Dacca Secretariat Agreement LIK 1974," Box LIK 119, Kahn Collection.

The project for the Dominican Motherhouse in Media, Pennsylvania, is an odd episode in the work of Louis Kahn. Although unbuilt, it is a superb case study of some of Kahn's most cherished notions about architecture: the role of formal geometry, the dialogue between public and private spaces, the interaction between light and ritual. In this, his only fully developed project for the Catholic Church and for a monastic community as well, Kahn found a client whose sense of ritual and historical community closely paralleled the concerns of his own mature work. At the Salk Institute Kahn had imagined that the scientists formed a kind of medieval monastery; at Media he dealt with the real thing.

In the early 1960s the Dominican Motherhouse of St. Catherine de Ricci had moved from upstate New York to Upper Providence township, near Media. Originally located in an old farmhouse complex, the order was soon pressed for space by the growing number of new entrants, or vocations. Under the leadership of the new Mother General, Mary Emmanuel, the decision was made in 1965 to build a new motherhouse, including dormitories, a chapel, and dining facilities. The choice of architect fell to Mother Emmanuel.[1]

Kahn, although Jewish, was not an illogical choice as an architect for the convent. He had served as a member of the Art and Architecture panel at the Catholic Liturgical Conference held in Philadelphia in August 1963 and had spoken at the Twentieth Liturgical Conference on Church Architecture, held in Chicago in 1965. He had recently been commissioned to design a Catholic monastery in Valyermo, California.

Mother Emmanuel had heard about Kahn from her friend the Reverend Thomas Phelan. Phelan was chaplain at the Rensselaer Polytechnic Institute in Troy and was intensely interested in liturgical art, serving as a consultant for church-building projects throughout the Albany diocese.[2] He had recommended Kahn's First Unitarian Church in Rochester to Mother Emmanuel as a model of modern religious architecture. On March 26, 1965, Mother Emmanuel wrote to ask if Kahn would be willing to work on the Media project.[3]

Kahn did not meet with the nuns for over a year, as they were woefully underfunded and presumably needed time to assess their resources.[4] Finally, on April 26, 1966, the architect and his assistant Galen Schlosser met with Mother Emmanuel and the building committee in Media.[5] As the sisters explained their program Kahn listened and

commented while Schlosser took notes. The convent was to be an intricate complex of interrelated and interconnecting buildings: a chapel, dormitories, a refectory, classrooms with an attached library, and an administrative block. Kahn spontaneously proposed that the administration be placed near the entrance to serve as a kind of ceremonial gate. The sisters approved enthusiastically; this was exactly the sort of advice for which they had sought out Kahn.[6]

From the beginning Kahn was predisposed by temperament toward certain aspects of the program. Intrigued by communal or contemplative architecture, he relished the tradition of the "double life" as he imagined it at the convent, devoted to silence but also to communication and conversation. Kahn was also fascinated by the hierarchy of the sisters. Four grades of sisters would live in the convent: the newly arrived postulants, the novices who had taken their first vows, the younger sisters who had entered the order, and, finally, the older professed sisters. Kahn immediately suggested that this hierarchy could be expressed through geometry, with the older sisters in large rectangular rooms and the novices in ten-by-eight-foot cells. The "more square" cells would serve to "measure the servitude." About the character and construction of the buildings themselves there was no doubt. They would be of concrete and stone, their structure articulated with arches.[7]

Kahn's first tentative sketches were scarcely architectural, consisting only of rows of rectangles labeled according to the rooms needed and the classes of sisters who would use them: the program itself transferred to paper geometry (fig. 500).[8] It was as if he needed to see the program graphically, in terms of volumes and square footages, before he could begin to manipulate its spaces. On the basis of this graphic program, with its linear character, Kahn prepared sketches, including one that arranged the principal spaces to either side of a long formal axis (fig. 501).[9]

Kahn was in India in June and was not able to oversee the submission of the preliminary studies. Instead, his assistant David Polk was assigned to translate his sketches into scale drawings.[10] Discarding Kahn's linear studies, Polk tried to express the complex and variegated social organism of the convent, which the sisters had discussed with Kahn at the April meeting. Before leaving, Kahn examined Polk's studies and approved them for further development.[11]

The controlling idea of the scheme Polk worked out during June was the dual public-private nature of the convent, which he resolved as a building with two distinct components

The Dominican Motherhouse of St. Catherine de Ricci

Media, Pennsylvania, 1965–69

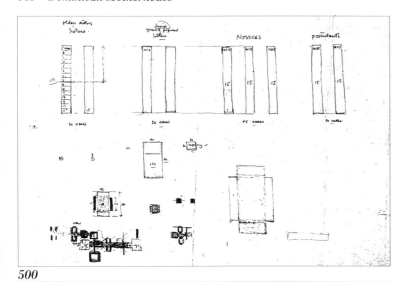

500

501

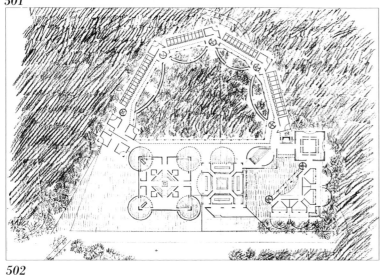

502

*500. Schematic program
diagrams, ca. April–May 1966.
501. Plan. Inscribed LIK '66.
502. Plan, June–July 1966.*

(fig. 502).[12] Along the north flank were the "public" spaces of the building: a refectory, a school, a chapel, and an entrance pavilion marked by a tower. To the south was the private realm, consisting of four blocks of dormitory rooms, each devoted to one of the classes of sisters, spread out in a loose arc facing south. The two precincts ringed a wooded garden, defining between them a private and intimate cloister. To reinforce the cloister theme a covered arcade was to run along the perimeter of the garden.

If the orientation of the residences to the woods was determined by topography and by the sun, no such constraints affected the public half of the building. Here there was much more experimentation, in which Kahn himself joined.[13] At issue was the joining of three cubic volumes—chapel, school, and refectory; how they should be connected, how the parts could be unified. On June 22 the finalized scheme was submitted in Kahn's absence, accompanied by a brief statement by Kahn's office manager, David Wisdom.[14] He described the orientation of the dormitories in their south-facing arc, "placed so that each room has its own private relationship with the woods." And the serried arrangement of chapel, refectory, and school to the north, connected by a continuous gallery, was "a community of buildings." Surely these words reflected Kahn's own thinking.

Upon Kahn's return, he and Polk were presented with a detailed critique of the scheme in a meeting with Mother Emmanuel and the building committee on July 22.[15] For the overall conception there was praise, and the arrangement of the cells and the orientation of the dormitory blocks on the site was approved. In fact, these dormitory rooms remained the stable anchor of the plan until the end. And the sisters liked the tower motif of the entrance, agreeing with Kahn that it formed "a special space." But they also proved determined clients with well-developed architectural preferences. When it came to their personal living spaces, they were most particular. The window seats he proposed for the individual cells were dismissed out of hand. And the great dining tables he suggested for the refectory were rejected in favor of smaller, more intimate tables. Kahn protested that the smaller tables would "make the place feel like a restaurant." But the nuns were adamant.

The meeting ended on an upbeat note as Kahn waxed poetic about his plans, speaking of "the presence of the chapel, the sense of ritual, not convenience, a feeling of exultation."[16] Polk recorded that "the sisters do not seem overawed by the size of their project." They should have been.

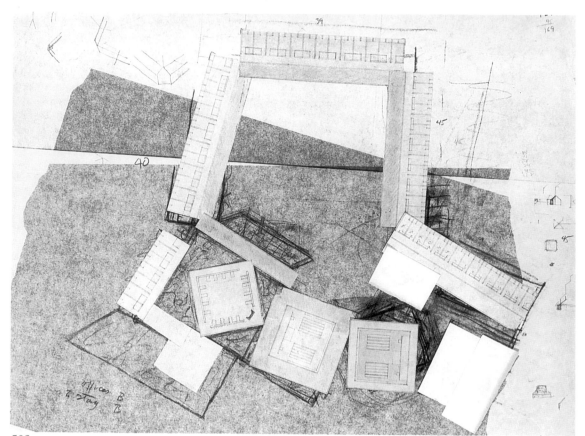

503

504

The sisters had warned Kahn about their limited budget, and he began to reassess the submitted scheme during August and September of 1966. Perhaps the most glaring problem was the quantity of public space: the entire inner face of the cloister was rimmed with a continuous ambulatory that expanded to the width of a generous public hall along the refectory and chapel flank. Now Kahn began to wonder if the public spaces might be integrated in such a way that there would be no need to devote any spaces to corridors. It was to this end that the next bold round of revisions was made.[17]

Since the pressing issue was the interrelationship of several self-contained blocks—and not so much their inner particulars—Kahn settled upon a work method that for him was atypical. Rather than endlessly redrafting the same identical four blocks of refectory, school, chapel, and entrance in order to experiment with different arrangements, he simply cut them out of a drawing at one-quarter-inch scale. With these he could experiment, easily rearranging them by hand, taping them in place when needed (fig. 503).[18] This simple drafting expedient, which he seems to have used first on October 9, soon had unexpected consequences. Previously, all of the building parts had been assembled in more or less conventional axial fashion, either along straight lines and perpendiculars or along 45-degree diagonals. The cutouts now inspired an alternative work method, with its own logic and geometry. It was suddenly easy to move the blocks of the building into infinitely shifting oblique and acute angles, echoing the haphazard axiality of archaeology and ancient foundation plans, not the rectilinearity of Western architectural tradition.

On October 10, 1966, Kahn and Polk presented their third submission, complete with the long-promised elevations and sections and a scale model of the complex (see fig. 177).[19] The change from the July submission was dramatic; the three dormitory wings of the earlier design remained, but the square blocks of the public rooms had broken out of their axial positions. Rather than following any larger monumental geometry, they ambled more loosely across the site, touching at their corners. The nuns liked the new approach and praised "the easy but strong relationships between the major elements themselves and between those elements and the cells."[20]

Kahn also submitted his long-deferred estimate. His building measured nearly 140,000 square feet and would cost roughly $3,587,030—well over twice the $1.5 million budget with which Mother Emmanuel was working.[21] Surprised, she now

discussed building the convent in several phases. Kahn was agreeable to the notion in principle but had reservations. He spoke of "the need for that which is built to invite construction of the whole. The promise of the beauty of the whole must be in the part. Thus the inclusion of the tower and possibly the auditorium which might also be used temporarily as [a] Chapel . . . should be considered."[22] Clearly Kahn feared that the project, once begun, would never be completed, leaving only disjointed fragments. He suggested that the location of future buildings be indicated in the form of garden plantings—a reminder that more was to come. Apparently reconciled to a complex built in stages, the committee adjourned.

On December 16 Mother Emmanuel formally asked Kahn to plan a first phase that would house fifty sisters for $1 million.[23] In the same letter she gently chastised the architect, who persisted in measuring the convent against the architecture of medieval monasticism, particularly the Cistercian architecture of the twelfth and thirteenth centuries.[24] This fantasy of a medieval monastery did not tally with Mother Emmanuel's vision. Her Dominican order, unlike the Carmelites or Trappists, did not seek solitude for its own sake; instead they were devoted to the precept of "action flowing from contemplation."[25]

On February 16, 1967, Kahn and Polk met in Media to present a drastically reduced scheme to Mother Emmanuel and five sisters.[26] The project had evolved remarkably since the previous October (fig. 504). The separate blocks of the public buildings, having once been cut loose from rectilinear geometry and allowed to shift across the drafting board as movable stencils, no longer rambled across the northern half of the complex; instead they were drawn tightly together into the cusp of the dormitory wings. What had been an open cloister was now filled with five unequal squares and rectangles, all tilted with respect to one another and leaving sharp-edged shards of open spaces between them. But while the angles of the building ranged from the most acute to the most oblique, the composition was anything but loose. Here in the procession of axes, cross-axes, and spatial sequences was a geometry as formal as anything in the classical tradition. It was as if Kahn had deliberately set out to re-create the monumental Beaux-Arts system that his mentor Paul Cret had taught him forty years before—but without the constraint of the right angle.

But Kahn and the Media sisters were now on different trajectories. The pattern of convent life that had so fascinated the architect was changing swiftly. Already there were signs of the relaxed discipline that was coming to characterize convent life in the late 1960s. The sisters were asking about swimming and tennis, and such modern amenities as intercoms and air-conditioning. And Kahn's refectory, for example, was to be less mystic and communal and have more "family room atmosphere"; it was even meant to permit "cafeteria-style serving"![27]

With the plan settled in its broad outlines, Kahn turned his attention to the elevations, with their brick arches and circular windows, and the details of the individual buildings (see fig. 176).[28] The most challenging of these, and the one on which Kahn lavished special attention, was the chapel.[29] Here he directly confronted the liturgical issues of Catholic architecture—something he had not done in any of his buildings to date. Because of these concerns Father Phelan, who had recommended Kahn to Mother Emmanuel, was invited to confer with the architect on August 7, 1967. Phelan's modernist sympathies were close in many respects to Kahn's, and he encouraged the architect to develop spatial solutions outside of Catholic tradition. Instead of the standard confessional booth, usually a large item of built-in furniture, they agreed on a separate confessional room. This would be "an agreeable room for two persons to converse, convenient to the sacristy."[30] He also reminded Kahn, as had Mother Emmanuel, that the Dominicans practiced an "action religion" and worried that the constraint of pews might "limit the possibility of action." Kahn agreed, and suggested using movable chairs in the chapel. These changes to the program were formalized in a memo at the end of the meeting; at the same time, the architect formally entered into a contract with the sisters for the design of the building.[31]

The first set of working drawings was completed by April 22, 1968.[32] But it seemed that the drawings could never be put out for bid: each time they neared completion, another round of budget reductions pared them still further.[33] The elevations were simplified drastically. Originally the buildings were to be picturesquely walled, with brick relicving arches and circular windows, as in Kahn's contemporary work in Dhaka; the final elevations, however, were sober and austere, the proposed arches and cutout windows casualties of Mother Emmanuel's budget reductions.

The project was lumbering to an end. Even the reduced version of the building, pared to the bone, was beyond the sisters' means (see fig. 175). New vocations had been dropping rapidly, and the demand for new quarters was not as critical as it had been in 1965. The blunt truth was that

Kahn could not reduce his drawings in size as fast as the number of new postulants to the order was shrinking. Rather than begin anew at a much reduced level, Kahn chose to terminate the relationship, leaving the order to choose another architect. On March 18, 1969, Kahn and the sisters formally severed their ties, sadly but amicably. Sister Irene, assistant to Mother Emmanuel and a member of the building committee, recalls, "We parted friends."[34]

Michael J. Lewis

Notes

1. Sister Irene (building committee member), interview with Michael J. Lewis, May 1, 1990.
2. Ibid.
3. When Mother Emmanuel's letter arrived, Kahn was in Pakistan, but office manager David Wisdom responded; letter, Wisdom to Mother Emmanuel, April 2, 1965, "Dominican Sisters Mother House," Box LIK 10, Louis I. Kahn Collection, University of Pennsylvania and Pennsylvania Historical and Museum Commission, Philadelphia (hereafter cited as Kahn Collection).
4. Memo by Wisdom, June 5, 1968, "Dominican Sisters Mother House," Box LIK 32, Kahn Collection. This memo lists most of the meetings, transmittals, and other communications between the sisters at Media and Kahn.
5. Job meeting minutes, unsigned (but in Kahn's handwriting), April 26, 1966, ibid.
6. Ibid.
7. Ibid.
8. Drawing 700.1, Kahn Collection. Like most of the drawings for this project, this one is undated, but it must have closely followed the April 26 meeting. The design development chronology established in Heinz Ronner and Sharad Jhaveri, *Louis I. Kahn: Complete Work, 1935–1974*, 2d ed. (Basel and Boston: Birkhäuser, 1987), 302–11, although based partly on conjecture, is plausible.
9. Among these are drawings 700.2–4, Kahn Collection. David Polk (Kahn's assistant) confirms that these drawings are among Kahn's earliest studies, made before the younger architect began preparing sketches in June; Polk, interview with Michael J. Lewis, May 8, 1990.
10. Polk, interview with Lewis, April 30, 1990.
11. Virtually no studies in Kahn's hand survive to document this early stage of the project. The sole exception consists of a group of ink studies, hastily jotted on the back of a letter from Europe dated March 28, 1966; drawing 700.5, Kahn Collection. These appear to be later variants of Polk's initial scheme.
12. Several versions of this scheme, apparently dating from June and July 1966, are reproduced in Ronner and Jhaveri, *Complete Work*, 302–3, DCM.2–7.
13. Among the drawings in the Kahn papers are a series of undated and unsigned variants of this scheme, including 700.5.1 and 700.6, Kahn Collection.
14. Letter, Wisdom to Mother Emmanuel, June 22, 1966, "Dominican Sisters Mother House," Box LIK 32, Kahn Collection.
15. Minutes by Polk, building committee meeting of July 22, 1966, transcribed August 3, 1966, ibid.
16. Ibid.
17. Polk, interview with Lewis, May 8, 1990.
18. See drawings 700.10–13, Kahn Collection. Related studies include 700.7 (signed and dated October 1966), 700.8, and 700.9.
19. Minutes by Polk, October 10, 1966, "Dominican Sisters Mother House," Box LIK 32, Kahn Collection. Also see Ronner and Jhaveri, *Complete Work*, 306, DCM.21 and DCM.22.
20. Minutes by Polk, October 10, 1966, "Dominican Sisters Mother House," Box LIK 32, Kahn Collection.
21. Estimates, Kahn [?], October 10, 1966, ibid.
22. Ibid.
23. Letter, Mother Emmanuel to Kahn, December 16, 1966, "Mother Mary Emmanuel, Motherhouse," Box LIK 32, Kahn Collection.
24. Sister Irene, interview with Lewis. Kahn had been praising Cistercian architecture since his lecture at the Twentieth Liturgical Conference on Church Architecture in 1965, where he saluted the French complex at La Thornet. I am indebted to Keevan Hawkins for this reference.
25. Letter, Mother Emmanuel to Kahn, December 16, 1966, "Mother Mary Emmanuel, Motherhouse," Box LIK 32, Kahn Collection.
26. Minutes by Polk, February 16, 1967 (mistakenly dated 1966), "Dominican Sisters Mother House," Box LIK 32, Kahn Collection.
27. Letter, Sister Irene to Kahn, December 23, 1966, ibid.
28. Meetings were held in Media on March 13, April 4, May 2, and May 28, 1967. The estimate discussed at these meetings—a total projected cost of $1,593,060—was provided in a letter, Polk to Mother Emmanuel, March 2, 1967, ibid.
29. Ronner and Jhaveri, *Complete Work*, 309, DCM.32–34.
30. Minutes, August 7, 1967, "Dominican Sisters Mother House," Box LIK 32, Kahn Collection.
31. "Changes in Convent Program" (verso of minutes), August 7, 1967, ibid. The space- and money-saving changes were accomplished chiefly by combining functions. The school was to be moved over the auditorium, the library over the tower, the living quarters over the sacristy. It was not remarkable that Kahn had not signed a formal contract with the sisters earlier. During the construction of Erdman Hall, for example, he never had a formal contractual relationship with Bryn Mawr College.
32. Kahn took a leading role in refining the design of the individual buildings. Among the dated studies in Kahn's hand are 700.26 (for the library, August 23, 1967), 700.27 (for the chapel, August 24, 1967), and 700.22–24 (overall plan studies, March 7, 1968), Kahn Collection.
33. In a letter, Kahn to Mother Emmanuel, August 24, 1967, "Dominican Sisters Mother House," Box LIK 32, Kahn Collection, the architect recommended possible contractors. Several of them had worked for Kahn: Joseph Farrell, on the Richards Medical Research Building; and Nason & Cullen, on Erdman Hall at Bryn Mawr.
34. Sister Irene, interview with Lewis.

With its exterior of tapering brick piers and jack arches embracing timber carrels and its majestic, light-filled central hall, the Phillips Exeter Academy Library has long been recognized as one of Louis Kahn's most successful designs (fig. 505; see figs. 360–68). However, this remarkable building was constructed only after a lengthy and difficult design process.[1] Since 1950 the academy had been formulating a program and organizing the design for a new library.[2] In the mid-1960s a new principal, Richard Day, rejected a proposed neo-Georgian building and sent the building committee on a search for a new architect capable of designing a significant contemporary building.

Committee members traveled widely to visit existing buildings and several architects' offices, including those of Paul Rudolph, Philip Johnson, I. M. Pei, Edward Larrabee Barnes, and Kahn. Visiting Kahn in July 1965, they were impressed by the human warmth of his somewhat cluttered office and the energetic young staff working close at hand.[3] The committee was also attracted by Kahn's sympathetic response to their aspirations for the new library as a vital cultural institution, forcefully described in the subsequent program of March 1966 but surely already in the minds of the committee members at this stage: "No longer a mere depository of books and periodicals, the modern library becomes a laboratory for research and experimentation, a quiet retreat for study, reading and reflection, the intellectual center of the community."[4] The building Kahn designed and constructed over the next six years, however, was even more ambitious than the academy's vision of a modern library in the complexity of activities it could accommodate.

The library committee, with the Exeter librarian Rodney Armstrong as chairman, recommended Kahn to the trustees' buildings and grounds committee.[5] They in turn convinced the trustees of the academy at their November 13, 1965, meeting to commission Kahn.[6] He was given a budget of $2 million and sent information on the site, a central location on campus. An existing white clapboard building was to be demolished.[7]

The final version of the program, written by the library committee and the educational consulting firm of Engelhardt, Engelhardt and Legget, was sent to the architect in March 1966.[8] The concepts of the nature and function of a library articulated there were closely akin to Kahn's own ideas, and clearly helped guide his design. In the library, "emphasis should not be on housing books but housing

readers using books." The building must "encourage and insure the pleasure of reading and study," which could be achieved through the creation of "a green garden or, on another level, a shaded terrace." Individual carrels, sufficient to accommodate half the number of readers, "should be placed near windows for enjoyment of natural light and pleasant view." Kahn's sensitive manipulation of light in his earlier buildings was entirely in keeping with the committee's desire that "daylight should be intelligently used whenever possible since . . . artificial light lacks the color range of natural light." The program also specified that the building's spatial relations must be intelligible, such that "a reader as he enters [should] be able to sense at once the building's plan."[9]

In early 1966 design work began in earnest, as Kahn was to present an initial scheme at Exeter on May 19.[10] The drawings and model produced for this meeting show a brick building with a clear three-part division: a grand central hall rising through three stories to a pyramidal roof; an inner zone, with mezzanines for book stacks, framed by servant spaces at the corners; and an outer zone, containing desks and carrels for reading (figs. 506, 507). The arches that shape the reading unit form an arcade on the ground level and also appear on the roof as an arcade surrounding a roof garden. The emphatic statement of three vertically continuous elements was central to Kahn's conception of the library; despite major transformations, including choice of materials, this concept was ultimately expressed in the actual building. The scheme was also characterized by two prominent towers flanking the entrance front. These contained balconies and the stairs that led the student to the main hall.

Kahn's design for the main hall and reading area can be explicated by his own statements. In his view, the ideal activity of a librarian established the program for the architect: "I see the library as a place where the librarian can lay out the books, open especially to selected pages to seduce the readers. There should be a place with great tables on which the librarian can put the books, and the readers should be able to take the book and go to the light."[11] The architect's design would transform this horizontal table containing the books into vertical layers of bookshelves viewed through openings in the walls of a grand central hall. Although the program never mentioned such a space, this hall came to stand at the center of Kahn's concept of a library. He commented appreciatively on the "great imperialistic room" of Étienne-Louis Boullée's Royal Library of 1785, which conveyed "a feeling for what

Library and Dining Hall, Phillips Exeter Academy

Exeter, New Hampshire, 1965–72

a library should be—you come into the chamber and there are all the books."[12]

The library also required private spaces for reading. Kahn had already achieved poetic insight into the nature of such spaces ten years earlier, when he designed a scheme for the Washington University Library in St. Louis. At that time, guided by his interest in the origins of institutions, he was particularly influenced by an account of the medieval library at Durham, England, where the reading carrels were placed beside the cloister and close to the light.[13] Inspired by such history, he noted that while designing, "thoughts were centered around the desire to find a construction system in which the carrels were inherent in the support which harbored them. Reading within a cloistered space with natural light in nearness to the building surfaces seemed good."[14] Although a reinforced concrete structure was then envisioned, his sympathies lay with a different constructional system: "Wall-bearing masonry with its niches and vaults has the appealing structural order to provide naturally . . . spaces [for reading]."[15] Kahn's mature understanding of the library thus embraced both a grand public hall surrounded by books and an intimate reading space.

Following the May meeting, Armstrong wrote to Kahn enthusiastically: "You have caught the spirit of the kind of building we seek for the school . . . [and] a concept that we tried to describe . . . in the Program of Requirements. You have designed a beautiful building which assures its being the intellectual center of the school."[16] Over the next five months Kahn and the client worked harmoniously, refining the design. (During this period the academy also commissioned Kahn to design a dining center adjacent to the library.[17]) At Armstrong's suggestion, the disposition of library functions throughout the building was clarified. Most important, the rare-book room and two seminar rooms were relocated on the roof level.[18] The roof garden, although now smaller than first conceived, held great significance for the overall design; at one point, Armstrong wrote of the merits of the dark green tone of local evergreen planting, as opposed to the more brilliant foliage of wisteria.[19]

One change was not welcomed by Kahn. Head-height brick balustrades replaced open railings on the terraces and the balconies to allay the committee's fear of falls.[20] However, the exterior was enriched by Kahn's concept of the timber carrels set within the structural frame of brick piers and arches (fig. 508). The two small windows in each bay seen on the elevation identify two carrels, while the single window

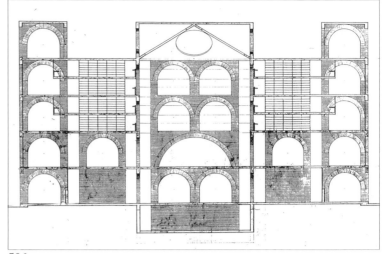

506

507

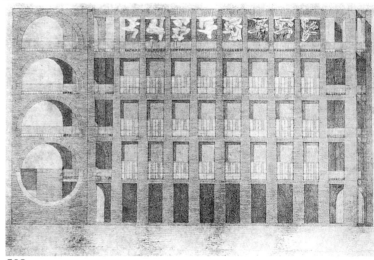

508

505

above lights larger desks located between the carrels and the stacks.

The walls of the central hall, originally connected to the stacks, were disengaged and their elevations transformed, the upper two levels of arches being replaced by grand circles. Now a discrete room capped with a double-shelled pyramid roof, the hall became a container of diffused, ever-changing natural light (fig. 510). Symbolic geometry and textured light, along with the presence of the surrounding books, charged the space with meaning appropriate to a building celebrating knowledge and learning. As an imaginative response to functional, social, and spiritual values, this second scheme, conceived in the months following the May 19 meeting, was highly valued by both client and architect.

Yet problems soon shattered this idyllic situation, and a third phase began, characterized by hurried design decisions. Tensions were first felt in a meeting of the buildings and grounds committee on October 3, 1966, when the terraces, outdoor staircases, and roof garden were criticized as unsuited to the severe New England climate.[21] On November 7 Kahn's drawings were scrutinized by Stanton Legget of the educational consulting firm involved in the initial program. He recommended to Richard Day that approval of the scheme be deferred at the forthcoming meeting of the trustees' buildings and grounds committee on November 11.[22] The problems highlighted by Legget included the difficult access to the building through outdoor stairs, the lack of flexibility of the space, and the location of wooden carrels at the periphery, directly below large expanses of glass, with the attendant possibility of cold drafts. Armstrong, who had heard Kahn's own responses to these objections, wrote a letter to Day countering the criticisms, pointing out, for instance, that proper heating would ensure that the carrels were habitable in winter. He urged that the project be allowed to move swiftly ahead.[23]

Not far beneath the surface of many of the questions being raised at this time was the issue of the budget, which Armstrong had explained on October 28 could not exceed $2.5 million.[24] At the end of October, George Macomber and Co., a contractor employed by Kahn, delivered an estimate of $3,441,000.[25] With just a few days left before the key meeting of November 11, Kahn had to redesign. In his estimate, Macomber listed a number of possible economies, including such distasteful measures as the use of brick as a veneer over a concrete structure. A few days later, Macomber made more palatable suggestions: the

substitution of concrete for masonry in the interior and a reduction of the dimensions in plan.[26] In response, Kahn's office omitted the ground-floor mezzanine and the smaller towers and replaced some interior brick with concrete. The estimate was reduced. At the November 11 meeting a large wooden model demonstrating these changes impressed the trustees, and Kahn was authorized to proceed with working drawings.[27]

The loss of the ground-floor mezzanine in this third scheme disrupted the even exterior proportions based on full-floor height divisions. The height of the ground-level arcade was reduced by half, and it became the squat element found in the completed building. The substitution of concrete for brick in the central hall was readily acceptable to Kahn, as it was sanctioned by his theory that activity, materials, and type of lighting had to be conceived together. Public activities were contained by the top-lit, grand concrete volume, while private reading was defined by the human scale and warmer texture and color of brick, pierced by windows. Although the great circles set within the square walls of the central hall survived the change of materials, the lower semicircular arch, a form generated by the nature of load-bearing masonry, was removed. The walls were now suspended, supported only by the corner piers. Further modifications were made later. The piers were turned diagonally, and in the built scheme they support the deep cross beams that diffuse clerestory light.

In a lecture at Exeter on February 15, 1970, and in a publication of 1972, Kahn explained the principles informing the three-part organization of brick reading spaces, concrete hall, and stacks:

Exeter began with the periphery, where light is. I felt the reading room would be where a person is alone near a window, and I felt that would be a private carrel, a kind of discovered place in the folds of the construction. I made the outer depth of the building like a brick doughnut, independent of the books. I made the inner depth of the building like a concrete doughnut, where the books are stored away from the light. The center area is a result of these two contiguous doughnuts; it's just the entrance where books are visible all around you through the big circular openings. So you feel the invitation of the books.[28]

Yet, even after the acceptance of this strong scheme, problems continued to emerge; many more months of designing would be necessary before completion of the fourth and final design and the working drawings. On December 6, 1966, Kahn was informed of a new town zoning code banning buildings over three stories.[29] The academy, hoping to avoid

509

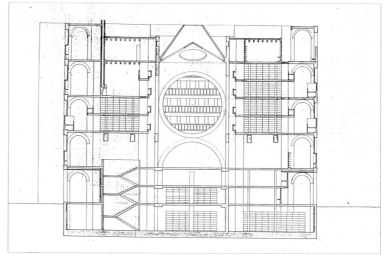

510

511

509. Model, ca. November
1966, revised before May 1967.
510. Section, facing east.
Inscribed Nov 10, 1966.
511. Perspective, ca. May
1967. Inscribed Lou K '67.

seeking a variance, asked him to reconsider the design. Although he could not comply completely, in drawings submitted to the academy around January 26, 1967, he sloped the roofs of the top floor toward the edge of the building, thereby placing the school in a stronger position to receive the variance, which was subsequently granted on April 21, 1967.[30]

The entrance of the building was also reconsidered at the beginning of 1967. The stairs were removed from the flanking towers and located within the building, connecting directly to the central hall. Many alternative schemes for this stairway were considered. Even as late as July and August 1968, when working drawings were well under way, its final state was still being discussed in meetings with the client. Kahn finally decided upon a circular form just prior to the completion of working drawings.[31] The towers, having lost their primary function, were again reduced in size; on February 7, 1967, Armstrong wrote, "The disappearance of the towers and elimination of all exterior arches has been especially regretted."[32] The resolution of the corners was achieved with a diagonal cut, thereby revealing the full depth of the brick reading doughnut. Revisions were made to the large model constructed for the November 11 presentation and the new scheme was displayed at a meeting on May 27, 1967 (fig. 509).[33]

The following week Kahn was informed that the academy, which was having budget problems with other projects, had employed the firm of Wood and Tower, of Princeton, as cost control consultants.[34] They were asked to make a pre-bid estimate based on drawings and outline specifications from Kahn's office. Their estimate of $4,522,961, submitted at the beginning of 1968, far exceeded the budget, and they suggested eliminating the central hall.[35] Kahn could not countenance the loss of the "invitation of the books," but an entrance court that had figured prominently in previous schemes as another public "place of invitation," and one of almost equal significance to the library, had to be omitted.[36]

In February 1968, in a moment of desperation, Kahn designed a "Scheme E," removing the second-floor mezzanine and shifting its functions, which included a staff room and work spaces, to the top floor. As a result, the building was reduced in height by 8'9".[37] On March 4 the academy increased the budget to $3.8 million and instructed Kahn to complete the working drawings incorporating the proposed changes.[38] Yet the new design was clearly an unhappy compromise; as Armstrong wrote to Kahn, the library committee "cannot help feeling a sense of real loss."[39]

In April 1968, following a month of frustrating work, Kahn sent a moving and powerfully argued letter to the academy in which he outlined the dire consequences of his hastily conceived "Scheme E" for the functional, spatial, and surface organization of the building:

I will do anything necessary to convince the Buildings and Grounds Committee that the only right way to build is to the height and proportions we so painstakingly worked out over so many months. One important aspect of the height is that it was the result, in a very fortuitous way, [of] the requirements. . . .

The building was originally conceived and finally worked out to be very delicately simple with each part of the structure, space and material so interdependent that one aspect or part cannot be removed without affecting all the others. The more I worked on it, the more I found that the slightest change affected the building drastically. . . .

The building from the exterior is intended to present a rhythmic development of the order of brick wall-bearing construction. The regularly spaced brick piers diminish in size as they rise in a slow rhythm of double-story units. The loss of one story broke this rhythm and the grace and simplicity was lost. My fullest consideration has convinced me that my hopeful proposal of saving a story would have presented an intolerable condition that I now firmly say I cannot accept.[40]

Ultimately, the academy allowed Kahn to reinstate the mezzanine, and he completed all documentation for the opening of bids, on February 7, 1969.[41] Construction was carried out with no subsequent major design changes. The builder was H. P. Cummings Construction, of Ware, Massachusetts. The library was ready for occupancy on November 9, 1971.[42]

The finished building fulfills the academy's ideal of a cultural and social center for the campus (fig. 511). Kahn's design was shaped around the idea that learning necessarily involved two complementary activities: on the one hand, the quiet introspective act of reading, and on the other, the interpersonal exchange of ideas.[43] The intimately scaled spaces for private contemplation thus encircle the grand hall for debate and communication, creating a spatial representation of this two-level process.

Peter Kohane

Notes

1. The most complete and accurate study of the evolution of the design, and the most thorough study of the construction, is Jay Wickersham, "The Making of Exeter Library," *Harvard Architecture Review*, no. 7 (1989): 138–49.

2. Rodney Armstrong (Exeter librarian), tape-recorded interview with David Carris, April 1982, Louis I. Kahn Collection, University of Pennsylvania and Pennsylvania Historical and Museum Commission, Philadelphia (hereafter cited as Kahn Collection). See also Annette Le Cuyer, "Kahn's Powerful Presence at Exeter," *Architecture: The AIA Journal* 74 (February 1985): 74.

3. Armstrong, interview with Carris; letters, Armstrong to Kahn, July 14 and September 3, 1965, "The Phillips Exeter Academy. July 1965 through December 1966. All correspondence," Box LIK 6, Kahn Collection.

4. "The Phillips Exeter Academy, Exeter, New Hampshire, Program Requirements for the New Library Recommended by the Library Committee of the Faculty," Rodney Armstrong, Elliot Fish, and Albert Ganley, n.d., 1, ibid.

5. Letter, Armstrong to Kahn, October 28, 1965, ibid.

6. Letter, Day to Kahn, November 16, 1965, ibid.

7. Letters, Armstrong to Kahn, January 31 and May 2, 1966, ibid.

8. Letter, Armstrong to Kahn, March 15, 1966, ibid.

9. "Exeter Program," 6, 7, 19, 22.

10. Letters, Armstrong to Louise Badgley (Kahn's secretary), May 2, 1966, and Badgley to Armstrong, May 6, 1966, "The Phillips Exeter Academy. July 1965 through December 1966. All correspondence," Box LIK 6, Kahn Collection.

11. Kahn, quoted in John Lobell, *Between Silence and Light: Spirit in the Architecture of Louis I. Kahn* (Boulder, Colo.: Shambhala, 1979), 100. For an analysis of Kahn's insights into the meaning of the library and a fuller exposition of his sketches for Exeter, see Peter Kohane, "Louis I. Kahn and the Library: Genesis and Expression of 'Form,'" *Via*, no. 10 (1990): 98–131.

12. Kahn, "Comments on the Library, Phillips Exeter Academy, Exeter, New Hampshire, 1972," in *What Will Be Has Always Been: The Words of Louis I. Kahn*, ed. Richard Saul Wurman (New York: Access Press and Rizzoli, 1986), 182.

13. See Kahn, "Space Form Use: A Library," *Pennsylvania Triangle* 43 (December 1956): 43–47. In this essay Kahn quoted a section on the Durham library from Russell Sturgis, *A Dictionary of Architecture and Building*, 3 vols. (New York: Macmillan, 1901), 2:750.

14. Kahn, "Space Form Use," 43.

15. Ibid.

16. Letter, Armstrong to Kahn, May 27, 1966, "The Phillips Exeter Academy. July 1965 through December 1966. All correspondence," Box LIK 6, Kahn Collection.

17. Letter, Armstrong to Kahn, June 3, 1966, ibid.

18. Ibid.

19. Letter, Armstrong to Kahn, September 20, 1966, ibid.

20. Letter, Armstrong to Kahn, September 21, 1966, ibid.

21. Minutes of meeting, buildings and grounds committee, October 3, 1966, ibid.

22. Letter, Legget to Day, November 7, 1966, ibid.

23. Letter, Armstrong to Day, November 8, 1966, ibid.

24. Letter, Armstrong to Kahn, October 28, 1966, ibid.

25. Letter, George Macomber to Kahn, November 9, 1966, ibid.

26. Letter, Macomber to Kahn, November 10, 1966, ibid.

27. Letter, Day to Kahn, November 14, 1966, ibid.

28. Kahn, lecture in the Lamont Gallery, Phillips Exeter Academy, February 15, 1970, tape recording, Kahn Collection; quoted in "The Mind of Louis Kahn," *Architectural Forum* 137 (July–August 1972): 77.

29. Letters, Colin Irving (assistant principal and treasurer, Exeter) to Armstrong, December 5, 1966, and Armstrong to Kahn, December 6, 1966, "The Phillips Exeter Academy. July 1965 through December 1966. All correspondence," Box LIK 6, Kahn Collection.

30. Letters, Armstrong to Kahn, January 26 and April 21, 1967, "The Phillips Exeter Academy, January 13, 1967 through August 1967. All correspondence," Box LIK 6, Kahn Collection.

31. Job meeting notes, meetings of July 17 and August 16, 1968, "Job Meeting Notes. Exeter Dining Hall and Library," Box LIK 6, Kahn Collection. See Kahn's personal sketches, for example, drawings 710.1 and 710.112, Kahn Collection; and Wickersham, "The Making of Exeter Library," 143.

32. Letter, Armstrong to Kahn, February 7, 1967, "The Phillips Exeter Academy. January 13, 1967 through August 1967. All correspondence," Box LIK 6, Kahn Collection.

33. Letter, Armstrong to Kahn, April 21, 1967, ibid.

34. Letter, Armstrong to David Wisdom (Kahn's office), June 1, 1967, ibid.

35. Letter, Wisdom to Irving, February 6, 1968, "Phillips Exeter Academy. All Correspondence 1/19/68 through current date," Box LIK 6, Kahn Collection; "Progress Estimate for the New Library," Wood and Tower, January 2, 1968, "Estimate Library," Box LIK 4, Kahn Collection.

36. Letter, Wisdom to Irving, February 6, 1968, "Phillips Exeter Academy—Library. All Correspondence 1/19/68 through current date," Box LIK 6, Kahn Collection.

37. Ibid.

38. Letter, Irving to Wilton Scott, Jr. (Kahn's office), March 4, 1968, ibid.

39. Letter, Armstrong to Kahn, March 16, 1968, ibid.

40. Letter, Kahn to Armstrong, April 17, 1968, ibid.

41. Letter, Irving to Wisdom, January 8, 1969, ibid.

42. For a discussion of the construction of the building, see Wickersham, "The Making of Exeter Library," 144–48.

43. These issues are further explored in Kohane, "Kahn and the Library."

In October 1966 Louis Kahn was asked to design the Kimbell Art Museum in Fort Worth, Texas (fig. 512; see figs. 369–91).[1] In contrast to his 1952 art gallery for Yale, the oldest college art museum in the country, the Kimbell was a completely new institution: it was to be developed from Mr. and Mrs. Kay Kimbell's private collection and housed in a building financed by the art foundation they established in 1936. Richard F. Brown was selected as director of the museum in 1965 by the Kimbell Art Foundation and was asked to oversee development of the collection, to recommend an architect, and to act as client for the building. The collection, which for decades had been exhibited on a rotating basis at the Fort Worth Public Library, was now expected to grow rapidly. This lack of certainty about the shape of the collection created some ambiguity in the beginning, but Kahn accepted it as an opportunity for creating an ideal setting for works of art.

The Kimbell site, selected by the trustees and approved by the city council in November 1964, was a nine-and-a-half-acre trapezoid bisected by a tree-shaded street whose paving was to be removed. It lay within a park shared with three existing museums—the Amon Carter Museum (then the Amon Carter Museum of Western Art), the Modern Art Museum of Fort Worth (then the Art Center), and the Museum of Science and History (then the Children's Museum)—and with a city coliseum, an auditorium, and exposition buildings.[2] The land falls gently eastward toward the Clear Fork of the Trinity River and another, riverside park a mile away. The Carter Museum, designed by Philip Johnson in 1959, is on the higher ground to the west. Since its entrance, porch, and terrace focused on the distant tall buildings downtown, it was agreed by the Kimbell trustees that their museum would rise no higher than forty feet in order not to obstruct this view.[3]

Brown's "Policy Statement" and detailed "Pre-Architectural Program," both dated June 1, 1966, incorporated everything he thought essential and desirable for the future museum.[4] In response to this program, Kahn came to define the building as a "friendly home" with a diversity of experiences for visitors: "There'll be a canteen to provide rest away from what one sees. When I enter a museum, I want a cup of tea. That seems to punctuate that I'm in the presence of things particular. . . . There'll also be interior gardens with access to natural conditions such as fresh air and the sound of water."[5] Brown required flexible, open-plan exhibition space similar to that in the Yale University Art Gallery, but Kahn felt now that individual galleries should be more strongly defined, even though he liked some

Kimbell Art Museum

Fort Worth, Texas, 1966–72

spatial flexibility and was to provide the Kimbell with movable partitions for changeable arrangements.[6] The two men agreed completely, however, on the need to introduce natural light where art would be seen, using electric lamps only for auxiliary illumination. In the end, light was the definitive consideration for the museum.[7]

Kahn rapidly devised his first scheme for the museum during the winter of 1966–67, and it was well developed by May 1967. Plans, together with study models made in March and May 1967, depict this proposal as very large—a 450-foot square with reflecting pools surrounded by porches and arcades, covered with skylit angular vaults, and containing variously sized courtyards (fig. 513). The single-story museum nearly filled the site, although existing trees that had lined the former roadway were incorporated in the two main courtyards. The fourteen vaults were thirty feet high and, beneath their skylights, had sculptural, three-dimensional reflectors that were intended to contain ducts and conduits (fig. 514).

After the scheme was presented to Brown and the board members, reactions were conveyed to Kahn in a letter from Brown: "The basic principle of design and conception of the building, as presented so far, is wholly and completely liked. More than that, it is found exciting and in absolute harmony with what we are envisioning and how we expect to function in it."[8] But Brown raised questions about the building's scale and its size—he thought that the square was too big and that upkeep would be too expensive. The paintings in the collection would continue to be easel-sized, and he did not want the interiors to overwhelm them; nor did he want the scale of the museum to dwarf the average visitor, personified by Brown as "a little old lady from Abilene." He suggested making the enclosed courtyards smaller, moving the service areas to a sub-floor level beneath the public galleries (as he had specified in his program), and reducing the width of the central axial circulation corridor, which ran perpendicular to the long vaults and connected the temporary-exhibition galleries with those housing the permanent collection.

In early July 1967 Kahn left a conceptual sketch to be developed by his staff when he went to Bangladesh (then East Pakistan) in connection with his commission for the capitol buildings in Dhaka.[9] By late September the second design was ready for a presentation, amplified by several sketches prepared by Kahn: a schematic site plan, perspective views of the front from the northwest and southwest, and an interior section, all dated September 22, 1967 (fig. 516). A model was then constructed to show how

512. West facade, 1989.
513. Site model, also showing Amon Carter Museum, May 1967.
514. Section through vaults and diffusers, January–March 1967.
515. Model, September–November 1967.

the first version had been reduced by removing the north and south arcades and the porches beside the large courtyards and by decreasing the length and number of vaults (fig. 515). The central connector was narrowed, the whole building was moved westward toward the center of the site, and support services were shifted to a lower floor.

These changes transformed the earlier square into a rectangle with sculpture gardens cut deeply into its north and south flanks, in effect creating two linked pavilions (the same distance apart as before). On the west, the smaller unit with the main entrance contained an auditorium to the north and a gallery for temporary exhibitions to the south. The larger east pavilion contained galleries for the permanent collection and had interior courtyards and light wells, some reaching down through the public level to the ground floor, where museum offices, shops, the library, and the conservation studio were placed, as Brown had suggested. The bookstore was located in the central connector between pavilions.

Instead of the thirty-foot-high vaults of the first design, Kahn now introduced low, Mediterranean vaults, as prefigured in some of his earlier sketches, split by skylights overhead (see fig. 223). The curvature of these vaults was defined as a cycloid in October 1967.[10] Reflectors in this second design were thin, appropriate to the height of the vaults, and shaped to echo their curve. They were to be of one-way glass. Services previously located within the reflectors were now moved to void spaces between the vaults. Kahn described this design in a talk in Boston in November 1967:

Here I felt that the light in the rooms structured in concrete will have the luminosity of silver. I know that rooms for paintings and objects that fade should only most modestly be given natural light. The scheme of enclosure of the museum is a succession of cycloid vaults each of a single span 150 feet long and 20 feet wide, each forming the rooms with a narrow slit to the sky, with a mirrored glass shaped to spread natural light on the sides of the vault. This light will give a touch of silver to the room without touching the objects directly, yet give the comforting feeling of knowing the time of day.[11]

The schematic design was accepted by Brown and the Kimbell trustees after a presentation at the end of November 1967, with the understanding that some adjustments would be made.[12] Over the next two months cost estimates were prepared, and during the following five months changes, first in materials and then in vault modules, were made to reduce expenses while retaining the basic design and desired

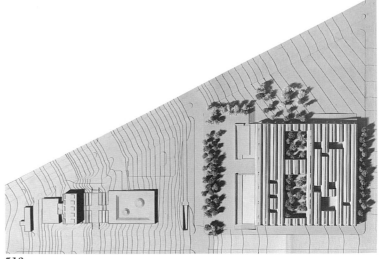

513

514

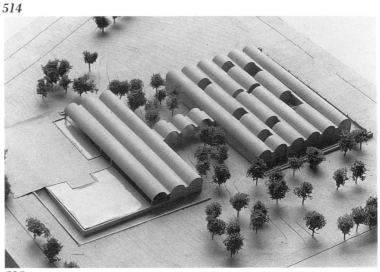

515

512

features.[13] In late August 1968 Kahn grew dissatisfied with these piecemeal modifications, and he seized the opportunity offered by Brown's request to relocate the temporary-exhibition gallery away from the main entrance to initiate yet another design.

This third phase had a different plan. A model made in September 1968 shows a single, consolidated building instead of two pavilions joined by a narrow connector (see fig. 225). Two wings of seven vaults were now aligned on either side of a central unit whose four vaults, recessed behind a forecourt and pool, covered the west-facing lobby, the bookshop (with a children's gallery on the mezzanine floor above), and the upper floor of the staff library. The north wing, to be occupied by the permanent collection, had four courtyards, one of which penetrated to the floor below to light the conservator's studio. The south wing contained galleries for temporary exhibitions, a reception hall, a "canteen," and a kitchen, all arranged around a large open-air garden. A lower floor beneath the north wing and central block was dedicated to staff facilities: offices, shops, storage, conservation and photography studios, a truck dock, the library, and a mechanical room. Except for the inclined auditorium floor, which sank below the galleries, the south wing was largely unexcavated at the lower level. Each vault was 22 by 154 feet, separated by flat-ceilinged interstitial spaces. The building, placed behind the trees on the site, measured 468 feet in length and 202 feet in depth.

Over the remaining months of 1968 and in early 1969, revisions, adjustments, and refinements took place. The north and south wings were reversed in their functions and the number of their courtyards; two courtyards were eliminated and the remaining ones were reduced, as were the size and number of vaults. The lower floor was enlarged to provide work space and a public entrance from the parking lot; an even deeper basement level was also added. Working drawings were initiated and information was gathered for estimates during this time.[14] After extensive research, Kahn decided in March 1969 to make the reflectors not of glass or plastic but of pierced aluminum, a material already manufactured for lamps. Further study that year refined the extended bird's-wing shape of the reflectors, designed to spread light on the underside of the vaults and down the walls (see fig. 382).[15] Beginning March 19, 1969, additional revisions to decrease costs were undertaken and estimates were reworked.[16] Plans were sufficiently advanced for the construction agreement to be let on May 9, 1969, and for work to begin in July.[17] As typical of Kahn's method, the start of construction did not end the work of design, which

went on continuously as he sought improvement, listening attentively and considering suggestions and requests from Brown and others.[18]

The Kimbell Art Museum, completed in 1972, is a final distillation of this process: six low-vaulted wings north and south of the central four (fig. 517). The westernmost vaults create three sheltering porticoes that open onto the forecourt and its flanking pools. "Green rooms"—groves of small trees, courtyards, and open, grassy spaces—unite building and park. The public level, completely vaulted and naturally lighted, rests serenely on a podium that contains the museum services. The 20-foot-high vaults (100 feet long and 23 feet wide) are roofed by lead and pierced by skylights. They seem to contain light—so significant in Kahn's concept from the beginning—a quality that shapes a viewer's experience in the galleries. The eight-foot channels that link the vaults contain ducts above their aluminum soffits. The building's structural elements are concrete, while travertine and white oak form screen walls, paneling, and floors. There is a unity and a consistency in the forms, materials, and detailing. Kahn considered every detail. When, for example, Brown responded favorably to Kahn's suggestion that they use large flowerpots like those at the American Academy in Rome, but noted that finding a source for them was difficult, the architect sketched models a potter might follow.[19]

Light and space in Kahn's museum rooms confer a "luminosity of silver" and a "comforting feeling of knowing the time of day," as he foresaw. Relatively small and remote from renowned art centers, the Kimbell Art Museum nevertheless has had significant impact upon the architecture of museums, as an example of both masterly natural lighting and the logical organization of functional requirements.[20] As an institution, it has been enhanced by the reciprocal nature of collection and building. Each contributes to and reinforces the total experience, as Brown had hoped.[21] The fusion of traditional architectural features—vaults, skylights, courtyards, and a park setting recalling earlier museums—combined with the spare aesthetic, the absence of ornament, and the technical prowess typical of modernism is hardly unique to Kahn's work. But this fusion is achieved with uncommon elegance by Kahn at Fort Worth.

Patricia Cummings Loud

Notes

1. Contract, October 5, 1966, Kimbell Art Museum Files, Fort Worth, Texas (hereafter cited as Kimbell Files). Preston M. Geren Associates was resident associate architect. On the Kimbell Art Museum, see *In Pursuit of Quality: The Kimbell Art Museum, An Illustrated History of the Art and Architecture* (Fort Worth: Kimbell Art Museum, 1987), with essay by Patricia Cummings Loud, "History of the Kimbell Art Museum," 9–95; and Patricia Cummings Loud, *The Art Museums of Louis I. Kahn* (Durham, N.C., and London: Duke University Press, 1989), 100–169.
2. Minutes of joint meeting of executors of the estate of Kay Kimbell and board of directors, Kimbell Art Foundation, September 15, 1964, Kimbell Art Foundation Archives, Fort Worth.
3. With the view from his building in mind, Johnson proposed a forty-foot height limitation for the new museum when asked by the president of the Amon Carter board of trustees; correspondence file, Kimbell Files.
4. See Brown's "Policy Statement" and "Pre-Architectural Program," June 1, 1966, in *In Pursuit of Quality*, 317–18, 319–27.
5. Latryl L. Ohendalski, "Kimbell Museum To Be Friendly Home, Says Kahn," *Fort Worth Press*, May 4, 1969.
6. After alteration of the interiors of the Yale University Art Gallery addition, Kahn changed his mind about the complete flexibility he created there; Kahn, "Talk at the Conclusion of the Otterlo Congress," in *New Frontiers in Architecture: CIAM '59 in Otterlo*, ed. Jürgen Joedicke and Oscar Newman (London: Alec Tiranti, 1961), 213. Yet he respected Brown's wish for flexible space; Kahn, conversation with Brown, October 1966, quoted in *Light Is the Theme: Louis I. Kahn and the Kimbell Art Museum*, comp. Nell E. Johnson (Fort Worth: Kimbell Art Museum, 1975, 3rd printing 1988), 47.
7. Kahn, interview with Patsy Swank for KERA-TV, Dallas, October 27, 1973, transcript, Box 2, Kimbell Files.
8. Letter, Brown to Kahn, July 12, 1967, "Correspondence with Dr. Richard F. Brown 1, 3.66–12.70," Box LIK 37, Kahn Collection, University of Pennsylvania and Pennsylvania Historical and Museum Commission, Philadelphia (hereafter cited as Kahn Collection).
9. Letter, David Polk (Kahn's office) to Brown, July 13, 1967, ibid.
10. In October 1967 Marshall D. Meyers showed Kahn a book by Fred Angerer, *Surface Structures in Building* (New York: Reinhold, 1961), which had illustrations of vaults (p. 43), and the selection was made; letters, Meyers to Nell Johnson (assistant curator, Kimbell), August 8 and 18, 1972, "Cycloid," Box 2, Kimbell Files.
11. Kahn, "Space and the Inspirations" (lecture, New England Conservatory of Music, Boston, November 14, 1967), *L'architecture d'aujourd'hui* 40 (February–March 1969): 15–16.
12. Letter, Brown to Kahn, December 4, 1967, "Correspondence with Dr. Richard F. Brown 1, 3.66–12.70," Box LIK 37, Kahn Collection.
13. These are documented in letters, Meyers and Richard Garfield (Kahn's office) to Brown, and Brown to Meyers, April 5–August 15, 1968, ibid.
14. Letters between the Geren firm and Meyers, October 23–March 4, 1969, "Correspondence with Preston M. Geren 1, 11.11.66–7.21.69 (1.14.70)," Box LIK 37, Kahn Collection; letters between Meyers and Brown and Bowen King (business manager, Kimbell), January 7–April 9, 1969, "Correspondence with Dr. Richard F. Brown 1, 3.66–12.70," Box LIK 37, Kahn Collection.
15. Letter, Meyers to T. H. Harden, Jr. (Geren office), March 4, 1969, "Correspondence with Preston M. Geren 1, 11.11.66–7.21.69 (1.14.70)," Box LIK 37, Kahn Collection. See "Lighting Starts with Daylight, Lighting Design: Richard Kelly," *Progressive Architecture* 54 (September 1973): 82–85; and M. D. Meyers, "Masters of Light: Louis I. Kahn," *AIA Journal* 68 (September 1979): 60–62.

16. Letters, A. T. Seymour III (Thos. S. Byrne, Inc., Contractors) to Meyers, February 25, March 9, and March 24, 1969; Brown to Seymour, March 25, 1969; Seymour to Brown, March 28, 1969; Meyers to Seymour, April 18 and 23, 1969; "Correspondence with Preston M. Geren 1, 11.11.66–7.21.69 (1.14.70)," Box LIK 37, Kahn Collection. On specific changes and their chronology, see Loud, "History of the Kimbell Art Museum," 50–61.
17. Letter, Seymour to Brown, May 9, 1969, "Thos. S. Byrne Inc., 2.27.69–11.70," Box LIK 37, Kahn Collection.
18. "Kahn's Museum: An Interview with Richard F. Brown," *Art in America* 60 (September–October 1972): 46.
19. Letter, Meyers to Brown, July 10, 1972, "Correspondence with Dr. Richard F. Brown 2, 1.71–," Box LIK 37, Kahn Collection. See also various correspondence, July 5–September 5, 1972, "Terra-cotta Pots," Box LIK 37, Kahn Collection.
20. For evaluations, see William Jordy, "The Span of Kahn," *Architectural Review* 155 (June 1974): 318–42; Lawrence W. Speck, "Evaluation: The Kimbell Art Museum," *AIA Journal* 71 (August 1982): 36–43; "After Architecture: The Kimbell Art Museum," *Design Book Review*, no. 11 (Winter 1987): 35–55; and Loud, *The Art Museums*, 150–60.
21. Brown, "Pre-Architectural Program," 319.

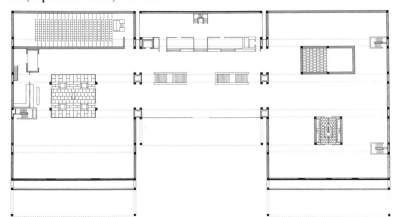

516. *Perspective from northwest. Inscribed LIK 9-22-67.*
517. *Main floor plan.*

When Louis Kahn accepted a commission in 1967 to design a Holocaust memorial in New York City, he embarked on a project that already had a complex twenty-year history.[1] In 1947, New York, home of the largest Jewish population in America, had set aside a site in Riverside Park, in upper Manhattan, for a monument to be known as the Memorial to the Six Million Jewish Martyrs.[2] Designs for this site were subsequently provided by sculptor Jo Davidson in the late 1940s;[3] by architect Eric Mendelsohn in the early 1950s;[4] and by sculptor Nathan Rapoport in 1965.[5] Each of these schemes raised either aesthetic concerns or doubts about the propriety of a Holocaust memorial within a public park, and none was executed.

In 1965 thirty major American Jewish organizations formed an umbrella group known as the Committee to Commemorate the Six Million Jewish Martyrs (the Committee for Six Million) to facilitate erection of the public monument. The group also expanded the architectural program to include a meeting house.[6] Aiming for the support of the largest possible cross section of the Jewish community, the committee included immense national organizations, such as B'nai Brith, which had 500,000 members in the United States, as well as smaller, more specialized groups that had been formed after World War II, such as the Jewish Nazi Victims in America and the Bergen Belsen Association. Because of the committee's inclusive nature, its structural hierarchy was inherently vague and its ability to control its member organizations was weak.

Resuming the quest for a suitable memorial, the Committee for Six Million began to formulate plans for a monument on a new site, never pursuing their initial idea of erecting a building. In late 1965 the committee commissioned Neil Estern to design a statue for tiny Lincoln Square Park across from Lincoln Center.[7] Estern's proposal was subsequently accepted by the New York City Art Commission, which had quasi-judicial authority over objects placed within the park system, but it was, ironically, rejected by its own sponsor. The Committee for Six Million heatedly debated the design, a thirty-foot-high marble slab with a bronze depiction of Cain slaying Abel, before a majority voted that the generality of Estern's biblical theme was inappropriate to the specificity of the Nazi horror.[8] The early history of the New York City Holocaust memorial was characterized by this serious division, a disagreement between those who felt that monuments should express general themes concerning humanity and those who felt that the monument had to make explicit reference to Holocaust crimes.

Memorial to the Six Million Jewish Martyrs

New York, New York, 1966–72

In 1966 the American Jewish Committee (AJC), a large nationwide human rights organization that had been among the original organizers of the Committee for Six Million, began to assume an aggressive role within the umbrella organization. The AJC, acting at the behest of the Committee for Six Million, enlisted the leadership of David Lloyd Kreeger, a Washington philanthropist and art collector. He became chairperson of a newly conceived art advisory committee with the understanding that he would have no fund-raising responsibilities.[9] Kreeger brought a keenly sensitive eye and a receptivity to new artistic ideas to the beleaguered project. He quickly assembled the Art Committee (Kreeger Committee), which would select an artist for the monument.[10] Among the members of Kreeger's committee were architect Philip Johnson; René d'Harnoncourt, director of the Museum of Modern Art; Sherman Lee, director of the Cleveland Museum of Art; and H. H. Arnason, vice president of the Solomon R. Guggenheim Foundation. In November 1966 Kreeger invited Kahn to join his committee and Kahn accepted immediately.[11] Kahn was not, however, part of the subcommittee—comprising Arnason, Johnson, and architect Percival Goodman as chairman—that in February 1967 accepted Johnson's suggestion that Kahn be appointed project architect.[12]

A new site for the monument, in Battery Park, at the southern tip of Manhattan adjacent to Castle Clinton, had been offered by the city in 1966, and this had been accepted by the Committee for Six Million before Kahn had had any connection with the project.[13] The spectacular site looked out to the nearby Statue of Liberty and to Ellis Island, the reception center where many Jews had first landed in America. Castle Clinton, a fortress that had been known as "Castle Garden," had also served as the major immigrant processing area between 1855 and the opening of Ellis Island in the early 1890s; this evoked further memories of immigration history.[14] The proposed site for the monument was roughly trapezoidal and outlined by a low stone wall on which was mounted a bronze plaque in memory of Emma Lazarus (1849–1887).[15] Lazarus's poem "The New Colossus" (1883), emblazoned on the pedestal of the Statue of Liberty, was also inscribed on this plaque, providing another reminder of the immigrant experience.

Kahn's design work on the Holocaust memorial can be broken down into three periods. The first extended from the commission, in April 1967, through November 1967, during which time he began to explore different geometries and several mathematical permutations. These culminated in the

presentation of a monument composed of nine glass piers arranged on a grid. The second phase began in December 1967, when Kahn substituted seven piers for the original nine. Between that time and the end of December 1971, Kahn held steadfastly to a scheme based on six similar piers, representing the six million dead, and a seventh, somewhat different pier. By early 1968 this seventh pier had evolved into a small chapel. A final design phase began in December 1971 and continued until January 1973. The last design studies, done in spring 1972, before the project was abandoned due to lack of funds, only vaguely recalled the shapes and materials of the earlier schemes.

Glass was the first and only material Kahn considered using for the project, a fact that instantly divorced his work from previous Holocaust memorials, which had been designed for execution in stone, metal, or concrete. A transparent as well as reflective medium, glass would serve to unite the nearby immigration monuments with this act of Holocaust remembrance.[16] Kahn hoped to make the piers of solid cast glass. In September 1967, shortly after executing his earliest tentative schemes, he and his assistant Marshall D. Meyers traveled to the Corning glass factory in upstate New York to investigate whether the company, then considered the leader in scientific and artistic glass production, could supply the material Kahn wanted. There were several technical difficulties. Kahn and Meyers looked at the range of glass colors available and found ordinary glass too green and fused silica too expensive. Only a custom manufactured glass would contain some of the "warm straw color" of optical glass.[17] They learned, too, that the actual process of casting glass would pose a great problem: the amount of time needed for annealing—heating and properly cooling—cast glass monoliths of such thickness would be enormous. With these considerations in mind, Kahn began to design piers of cast glass bricks. Not only would this method avoid the problem of excessive annealing time, but the bricks could also be arranged in various coursing patterns.

When Kahn first presented his ideas to Kreeger's committee on November 5, 1967, he had already begun to concentrate his energies on drawings and a model of nine identical glass piers, each twelve feet square and fifteen feet high, arranged on a base platform approximately sixty feet square (see figs. 234, 237).[18] Having earlier developed gridded designs based on nine or sixteen circular piers,[19] or designs of nine or thirteen square piers, Kahn appears to have settled on the nine-pier plan as a compelling architectural solution. He apparently did not realize that the choice of the number nine would elicit a severely negative reaction from segments of the

Committee for Six Million. Some members of the general committee present at the Kreeger Committee briefing were observant, theologically knowledgeable Jews who recognized that Jewish numerology equated the number nine with the months of human gestation. They felt that a number associated with the joy of childbirth was inappropriate to a memorial so charged with sadness. Several people urged Kahn to substitute the number six, since it was immediately identifiable with the six million Jewish victims of the Holocaust.[20] The Committee for Six Million, which in 1965 had demanded a more explicit representation of the Holocaust, was now inclined to accept an abstracted evocation of the universality of human experience,[21] as long as it contained a recognizable numerical reference to the Nazi tragedy. A vocal minority, however, remained uncomfortable with a monument that was neither figurative nor overtly narrative.[22]

Kahn accepted the criticism, and by December 19 he had adopted a six-pier scheme that included an additional, noticeably different seventh pier, an idea first seen in a perspective dated December 3 (see fig. 236).[23] The Kreeger Committee unanimously recommended that this plan be accepted.[24] Their recommendation and Kahn's latest proposal, in which the piers were now ten-foot cubes rather than the tall towers of early sketches, were presented to the entire Committee for Six Million on December 27, 1967 (fig. 518).[25] The full committee rejected Kahn's proposal. One member explained to Kahn: "As you undoubtedly noted from the reaction of those who suffered most (from the Holocaust), not all present felt that your model totally fulfilled their longings, represented their thoughts or relieved their tragic memories."[26] The tension between abstract and literal interpretations had apparently exploded at that meeting, possibly aggravated by Kahn's own depiction of his work as a nonaccusatory symbol of hope and forgiveness.[27]

Following this setback, Kahn reworked the seventh pier, having been instructed that an infusion of specificity in that element might mollify the dissatisfied members of the committee. He subsequently presented several new schemes to a special meeting of six members from the Committee for Six Million brought together by Kreeger on January 20, 1968, at his home. That meeting, called not only to discuss the seventh pier but also to set an appropriate timetable for completion of the project, highlighted Kreeger's ability to mediate disagreements. An informal contract was written and signed by all present.[28] They agreed that Kahn would produce, within three weeks, a scheme based on six piers

518. Model, before January 1968.
519. Perspective of central pier. Inscribed LIK 68.

along with a seventh pier, "in the form of a shrine with passages in it. The shrine is to be of the same material as the six pillars, but with some lilac in its color. The walls of the shrine are to have several suitable inscriptions in Yiddish, Hebrew and English, both on the outside and on the inside. The ceiling of the shrine is to bear some artistic Jewish symbol."[29] The seventh pier had thus become a kind of chapel (fig. 519).

Kahn continued to modify his plans in March and early April 1968. He concentrated on three problems: the interior shape of the seventh pier, public access to the memorial, and the final disposition of the existing Emma Lazarus plaque. By March 1 he had incorporated the plaque into a low platform for the monument, situated close to where it had been originally.[30] After experimenting with a sixty-six-foot-square, two-tier platform, Kahn had refined the design by April 4 to a single low socle (fig. 521). The platform was accessible from steps on the north and south sides, and the chapel was now a circular space within the central square pier.

Plans dated March 28, 1968, were approved unanimously and enthusiastically by the New York City Art Commission on April 8.[31] Their approval, however, was contingent on the outcome of a conference on siting and scale to be held between Kahn and a small subcommittee of the commission. It was understood by all participants that these would be minor adjustments. After meeting with the commission's subcommittee on April 19,[32] Kahn agreed to move the memorial slightly to the north, and to retain the Lazarus plaque at its original site, separate from the Holocaust memorial.[33] Although Kahn spoke to the Committee for Six Million about preparing additional site models in order to gain final approval from the Art Commission, little work was done and few subsequent meetings were held. Kreeger later recalled that the project collapsed after 1968.[34] No adequate funding apparatus had been put into place, and Kahn, aware of this situation, let his plans rest.

The most significant detriment to fund-raising was inherent in the structure of the Committee for Six Million. It was a loose, informal confederation of separate organizations, each with its own constituency and often its own faltering budget. Since the committee remained an amalgam of people representing groups rather than individuals representing personal views, it was never able to go beyond organizational parochialism. Several times in late 1968 Kreeger tried to steer the Committee for Six Million out of this structural morass, urging its leaders to hire a professional fund-raiser or to get the help of strong fund-raising leaders.[35] Neither action was taken, and, as a result, no large-scale fund-raising was attempted. Even the display of a large model for the project in the lobby of New York's Museum of Modern Art in the fall of 1968, and the subsequent positive reception from the press, failed to galvanize the Committee for Six Million into aggressive financial action (see fig. 235).[36]

In February 1971 Kreeger mused to Jerry Goodman, the secretary of Kreeger's committee, that perhaps "someday . . . you and I can help bring Louis Kahn's brilliant conception to fruition."[37] But other supporters of the project sought to modify the conception so that it would be easier to realize. To this end, the Committee for Six Million sent a small delegation to Philadelphia to see Kahn in December 1971. They paid his fee (which had been billed in June 1968)[38] and invited him to resume work, using readily available materials. The resulting plans, dated May 28 and 29, 1972, were new and far less ambitious (fig. 520). Still employing seven elements arranged in a 2-3-2 pattern, the new concept replaced the piers with small open buildings. Each consisted of four uprights supporting a gabled roof. The central element was closed while the other six opened toward it, creating a new, inward-focused emphasis.

Although this proposal seemed quite modest, there had apparently been no change in the fund-raising possibilities. In January 1973 Kreeger wrote to Percival Goodman that unless there were some way "to spark a fund-raising drive the prognosis for the Memorial is not favorable."[39] Kahn's design was never realized.

Susan G. Solomon

520. Plan and elevations.
Inscribed May 29, 1972.
521. Model, after April 1968.

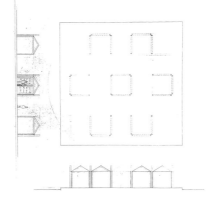

Notes

1. For a discussion of Kahn's designs for the Memorial to the Six Million Jewish Martyrs, see Heinz Ronner and Sharad Jhaveri, *Louis I. Kahn: Complete Work, 1935–1974*, 2d ed. (Basel and Boston: Birkhäuser, 1987), 336–39. The commission was conveyed to Kahn in a letter, David Lloyd Kreeger to Kahn, April 12, 1967, "Six Million," Box LIK 36, Louis I. Kahn Collection, University of Pennsylvania and Pennsylvania Historical and Museum Commission, Philadelphia (hereafter cited as Kahn Collection).

2. Letter, Jerry Goodman (American Jewish Committee) to Kahn, July 5, 1967, "Six Million," Box LIK 36, Kahn Collection.

3. "Memorial to 6 Million Planned," *New York Times*, June 19, 1947, 23.

4. Wolf von Eckardt, *Eric Mendelsohn* (New York: George Braziller, 1960), 30–31.

5. "City Rejects Park Memorials to Slain Jews," *New York Times*, February 11, 1965, 1; "Jewish Memorial At 65th St. Approved by Art Commission," *New York Times*, December 18, 1965, 31.

6. "Monument to Jews Scored at Meeting," *New York Times*, December 31, 1965, 22. Information on the formation of the Committee to Commemorate the Six Million Jewish Martyrs is found in a July 1969 proposal for the funding of the memorial, submitted to the Federation of Jewish Philanthropies; American Jewish Committee archives, office of Executive Vice President Bertram H. Gold, New York City (hereafter cited as AJC Archives). It is unclear, however, whether the original number of organizing groups was twenty-seven, twenty-eight, or thirty.

7. "Jewish Memorial at 65th St.," 31.

8. "Monument to Jews Scored at Meeting," 22.

9. Letter, Kreeger to David Altshuler (director, Museum of Jewish Heritage), January 14, 1988, David Lloyd Kreeger personal files, Washington, D.C. (hereafter cited as Kreeger Files); and memo, Kreeger to Jerry Goodman, June 2, 1967, Kreeger Files.

10. Kreeger, interview with Susan G. Solomon, March 20, 1990. Kreeger stated that he agreed to chair the committee only if he was not responsible for fund-raising, since he was already heavily committed to aiding several Washington cultural organizations, and if he was assured that the "blue ribbon" committee he would assemble would be given full power to select an artist for the monument.

11. Letters, Kreeger to Kahn, November 1, 1966, and Kahn to Kreeger, November 2, 1966, "Six Million," Box LIK 36, Kahn Collection. The first meeting of the Art Committee (Kreeger Committee) was on December 5, 1966, at the AJC–Institute of Human Relations; letter, Kreeger to Kahn, November 18, 1966, ibid. See list of Kreeger Committee members, n.d., ibid.

12. Letter, Kreeger to Percival Goodman, February 9, 1967, Kreeger Files. Von Eckardt, *Mendelsohn*, 30–31, reports that Goodman had also submitted a Holocaust design for Riverside Park before Mendelsohn. Kreeger, interview with Solomon, reported that Johnson had been the first to suggest Kahn for this commission. Kreeger, in the same interview, and Marshall D. Meyers, interview with Solomon, March 5, 1990, both reported that Johnson played a supportive role throughout the project.

13. Letter, Kreeger to Kahn, November 1, 1966, "Six Million," Box LIK 36, Kahn Collection.

14. For a short discussion of Jewish immigration, see Moses Rischin, "The Great Migration," in *The American Jewish Experience* (Philadelphia: National Museum of American Jewish History, 1989), 29–31.

15. The plaque was a gift of the Federation of Jewish Women's Organizations Inc. in 1954, on the occasion of the 300th anniversary of the arrival of the first Jews in America.

16. Press release, May 3, 1968, "Six Million," Box LIK 36, Kahn

Collection. It is unclear whether an article on an ancient glass slab sent to Kahn by Moshe Davidowitz, a member of the general committee, had any bearing on the choice of material; letter, Davidowitz to Kahn, n.d., ibid.

17. Memo, Meyers to Kahn, September 5, 1966, ibid.; Meyers, interview with Solomon.

18. A technical drawing hand-dated November 5, 1967, Kahn Collection, for an alternate coursing shows fifteen-foot columns.

19. The earliest dated drawings are 576.81, 577.81, and ASC/68.1–8, Museum of Modern Art, New York.

20. Letter, Abram Duker (director of libraries, Yeshiva University) to Kahn, November 13, 1967, "Six Million," Box LIK 36, Kahn Collection. Another letter, Kreeger to Art Committee, October 24, 1967, ibid., indicates that at the November 5 meeting Kahn primarily discussed concepts of nine piers rather than specific details.

21. Kahn did write in a press release, May 3, 1968, ibid., that "before the architect was chosen, the Committee of Art decided that the Artist of the Memorial should express its meaning without pictorial representation." No such dictum was ever put into writing, although the choice of Kahn as architect was an implicit vote for abstraction.

22. Kreeger and Meyers, interviews with Solomon, indicated that some members of the organizing committee expressed continuing unhappiness.

23. Memo, Meyers to Kahn, December 19, 1967, "Six Million," Box LIK 36, Kahn Collection.

24. Ibid.

25. Ibid.; memo from Kahn, January 11, 1968, "Six Million," Box LIK 36, Kahn Collection.

26. Letter, Joseph L. Lichten (Anti-Defamation League) to Kahn, January 8, 1968, ibid.

27. Kreeger, interview with Solomon.

28. Informal contract between Kahn and Kreeger, Benjamin Gebiner, Vladka Meed, Julius Borenstein, Julius Schatz, and Joseph Tekulsky, January 20, 1968, "Six Million," Box LIK 36, Kahn Collection.

29. Ibid.

30. Memo, Meyers to Kahn, March 1, 1968, "Six Million," Box LIK 36, Kahn Collection.

31. Certificate no. 11410, Archives of the New York City Art Commission. The land was formally offered to the committee by the Department of Parks in a letter from August Heckscher (commissioner), March 22, 1968, "Six Million," Box LIK 36, Kahn Collection.

32. Letter, Elliot Willensky (design director, Department of Parks) to Kahn, April 19, 1968, "Six Million," Box LIK 36, Kahn Collection.

33. Memo, Meyers to Kahn, July 3, 1968, ibid. No photos of a revised model exist.

34. Letter, Kreeger to Altshuler, January 14, 1988, Kreeger Files.

35. Letter, Kreeger to Jerry Goodman, December 3, 1968, AJC Archives.

36. The model was displayed October 17–November 14, 1968. See Ada Louise Huxtable, "Plan for Jewish Martyrs' Monument Here Unveiled," *New York Times*, October 17, 1968, 47.

37. Letter, Kreeger to Jerry Goodman, February 18, 1971, Kreeger Files.

38. Letter, David Geller to Kahn, December 17, 1971, "Six Million," Box LIK 36, Kahn Collection. Kreeger was not a member of the delegation, nor was Jerry Goodman.

39. Letter, Kreeger to Percival Goodman, January 3, 1973, Kreeger Files.

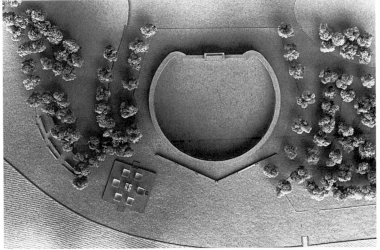

In March 1968 Louis Kahn was invited by the mayor of Venice to participate in the Biennale, the international biannual art exhibition.[1] A month later, in late April, Kahn was visited in Philadelphia by Giuseppe Mazzariol, a well-known Venetian professor and art historian.[2] Mazzariol came as a representative of the Azienda Autonoma di Soggiorno e Turismo, the Venetian tourist agency, to offer a commission for a conference center for Venice. Mazzariol had been entrusted by the Azienda to choose an architect, and Kahn was his first and immediate choice: "On the name of the architect," he later wrote, "I must confess that I didn't have even a moment of uncertainty."[3] The program was straightforward: to create a meeting hall—a Palazzo dei Congressi—that would accommodate 2,500 to 3,000 people.[4] The Azienda had already considered and rejected the possibility of reusing any of the existing Venetian palaces for the conference center, determining that none was suitable.[5] Mazzariol remained in Philadelphia for several days, during which time he and Kahn pored over slides of Venice's Giardini Pubblici, the proposed location for the center, and began to discuss the parameters of a major new building for the ancient city.

The Giardini Pubblici, where the Biennale is held, are located in the once-impoverished Castello quarter, and the Palazzo was viewed as a tool to revitalize the area—and to benefit all of Venice—both economically and socially.[6] The Giardini were designed in 1807 by G. Antonio Selva on land that had been reclaimed from the Adriatic during the Napoleonic occupation.[7] With their open feeling and their allées of trees facing the canal, the gardens are among the few green areas of Venice. The gardens have been the site of the Biennale since the art exhibition was established in 1895; they contain the international pavilions, which are erected by each participating country in a "vivid array of national self-images" and sometimes characterized by a "bold architectural experimentation."[8]

Exactly when Kahn formally accepted the commission is unknown, but on May 4, 1968, Azienda president Vito Chiarelli wrote Kahn to express thanks for accepting the commission and to say that "we applied to you through the kindest professor Mazzariol, since we are acquainted with the exceptional importance of your work." He also reminded Kahn that building in Venice would place him in the company of "the greatest masters of architecture of all the times."[9]

At the request of the Venetian authorities, Kahn stopped in

Palazzo dei Congressi

Venice, Italy, 1968–74

Venice to inspect the Giardini site from May 21 to 23, on his way to Pakistan.[10] On May 29 Chiarelli wrote Kahn to thank him for the visit and to candidly warn him of the frustrations Kahn might encounter in Venice, including a notoriously entrenched bureaucracy and a conservative attitude toward modern architecture.[11] Kahn replied on July 22, expressing his "complete sense of dedication to your problem" and to "the challenge to create that which can stand amongst the masterpieces of Venice."[12]

Work began in earnest after July 25, when Carles Enrique Vallhonrat, an architect then in Kahn's office, arrived in Venice to gather information about the site and its relationship to the rest of the historic city.[13] Meeting notes indicate that Kahn requested exhaustive site information: "LIK wants: aerial view of all Venice towards several models, survey every lamp post, position of stationary trees, kinds etc., optimum site lines . . ."[14] Presumably Vallhonrat was back in Philadelphia by August 5, when Mazzariol wrote Kahn to commend Vallhonrat's work and to report that "the public opinion of the Venetian politic [sic] and cultural environments begins to move with a great sense of wait [sic] and sympathy to the Venetian-Kahnian initiative." And he told Kahn that the project would be formally unveiled in January 1969 at a presentation at Venice's Ducal Palace.[15]

On September 6 Vallhonrat wrote Mazzariol to report that "we are now putting together papers and thoughts for the work of the Palazzo dei Congressi."[16] Even at this early stage, Kahn apparently conceptualized the Palazzo as a long, narrow suspension structure supported only by a massive pier with an underlying caisson at either end, no doubt partly in response to the periodic flooding and poor soil conditions in Venice (fig. 523).[17] Early sketches show that Kahn considered alternatives for the building's entrances, stair configurations, triangular shapes for the piers, and roof plans with as many as five domes. Kahn also sketched a pair of winged lions to flank the entrances to the Palazzo.

Mazzariol returned to Philadelphia on October 29 and spent the next four days reviewing Kahn's progress.[18] He was shown sketches; an enormous clay model—to be cast in plaster in Venice—depicting much of the city and illustrating the project in relation to the monuments of Venice; and a rough paper model of the Palazzo itself, to be replaced by a detailed wooden model.[19]

On December 2 Kahn reported to Chiarelli about Mazzariol's visit: "We presented to him ideas of the major

522. Site plan of Giardini Pubblici, April 1968–January 1969.
523. Plan and sectional study of suspension system.

522

architectural elements, their form, shape and structure, and their relation to and composition on the site."[20] Kahn's use of the word "elements" at this stage seems to imply an expanded commission. And by the time of the January 1969 presentation, the commission had indeed been substantially enlarged as a result of discussions between Kahn and the Venetians.[21] Two additional buildings were added: a new pavilion for the Italian Biennale and a small entrance structure on the banks of the Canale di San Marco (fig. 522). With his letter Kahn included an invoice for expenses incurred for preliminary studies for the Palazzo and noted that he would bill the Azienda only for expenses through the completion of the presentation; his personal fee was waived for that period.[22]

Kahn and Vallhonrat went to Venice on December 26, 1968, and spent the next four days finalizing plans for the presentation that would unveil Kahn's project to the public.[23] Vallhonrat returned to Venice on January 24, 1969; Kahn followed on January 27.[24] The presentation was made on January 30 at Venice's Ducal Palace and was attended by about 500 architects, students, critics, journalists, and officials.[25] Chiarelli assured the assemblage that the project "does not touch a single one of the 820 trees which form Selva's public gardens,"[26] and he introduced Kahn, who spoke poetically, detailing the project, its forms, and its inspirations.

"I can see the Congress hall as if it were a theatre in the round—where people look at people," Kahn said.[27] The 2,500-seat auditorium, he continued, had a ring of concentric circles at its nucleus, with radial aisles. The central section could be isolated as a theater in the round for 500. "The curve of the meeting hall is slight in order to retain the sense that it is really a street-like piazza gently sloping. . . . One could be reminded of the Palio Square in Siena" (which Kahn had painted during a 1951 visit) (see fig. 247). On either side of the main hall were two fifteen-foot-wide corridors—Kahn referred to them as "streets"—and along the walls were a series of bracing elements, running perpendicular to the walls and ceiling, which formed a series of niches for more intimate gatherings (see fig. 151). The second floor was to contain a reception hall, crowned by three vaults, each seventy feet in diameter and made of rings of stainless metal and glass. The vaults also implied that the hall could be divided into three meeting rooms. As on the auditorium level, the supporting beams created a series of private spaces.

Kahn conceived of the outdoor spaces as an integral part of

523

the Palazzo. The third floor, Kahn told the gathering, "is the roof where the sky is the ceiling." The three enormous domes were covered with lead "just as those of St. Mark." The roof parapet was cut with three large crescent-shaped openings on each side that opened to views of Venice and the lagoon. The ground floor he described as "a piazza covered by the underside of the auditorium where you can sense the sweep of the structure" (fig. 524). The entire building was to be of reinforced concrete with marble details, he said, and was "conceived like a hanging bridge supported on the two ends by two columns . . . where also the stairs and elevators reach for various levels [and] there are other rooms for different purposes." The Palazzo was to be 460 feet long, 78 feet high, and 100 feet wide. Kahn described the separate Biennale Building as a pair of 200-foot-long structures facing each other across an 80-foot-wide square. Each side was to contain workshops, galleries, and artists' studios. A movable roof, framed in glass and metal, and moving doors could enclose the square (fig. 525). "These buildings should actively be used throughout the year as a free self-supervised academy, as a free community of involvement and exchange," Kahn said at the presentation. The third component of the expanded commission, the entrance building, was to be a fifty-foot cube, located by the lagoon and intended, according to Kahn, "as a signature building which will personify the meaning of the Congress Hall. It will act as an information centre and [be] used for other services, such as [a] restaurant, etc."

Following Kahn's presentation, the Palazzo dei Congressi received warm reviews and extensive coverage in the international architectural press.[28] Typical of the times, there were student objections: "The students at the unveiling clearly felt that what the city of Venice ought to be doing is to save the city from drowning—rather than to add to the load by building additional tourist attractions."[29] But public interest was strong. On February 28, 1969, Mazzariol wrote Kahn that an exhibition of the models and drawings for the Palazzo at the Ducal Palace following the unveiling had been extremely well attended. He also reported that the Azienda was working to get the necessary approvals to begin construction.[30] The Azienda was unable, however, to meet its financial obligations to Kahn, and throughout 1969 there were no fewer than seventeen cables and letters between Kahn's office and the Azienda about money. Kahn had received a $20,000 payment in January 1969, but the Azienda accumulated an unpaid balance of over $44,000, which was never settled.[31]

On May 16, 1969, Kahn wrote to Mazzariol to report that he had been thinking along "richer lines" for the Biennale Building. He inquired "how far we can go about the redesign of the garden and its relation to other buildings of the Biennale fully realizing that this might be a project more in the distant future." Kahn also mentioned the possibility of developing a square on the north side of the Palazzo to be a "wonderful site for a new kind of civic place with buildings complementary to the purposes of the Palazzo dei Congressi and the establishment of a new focci [sic]. A school of the natural talents would be timely."[32]

In September 1969 the Azienda's request for permission to build the Palazzo in the Giardini went before the Venice City Council. Opposed by the councillor who headed the committee on urban affairs, the proposal fell victim to complicated political machinations and was never brought to a vote.[33] Nevertheless, Kahn continued to work actively on the design. Dated drawings of 1970 reveal a major change. Earlier drawings and models show the parapet with three large crescent-shaped arches. Structural engineer August E. Komendant claims that he advised Kahn that they were structurally wrong and would collapse: "I explained that the openings are located in the compression line of the frame and will crash due to relatively high shear and compressive stresses."[34] In his final scheme, Kahn lowered the parapet wall, eliminated the arches, and replaced them with a simple railing and square marble balusters. The balustrade made reference to one at the canal landing at the Giardini site and, with its classical connotations, complicated the Palazzo's profile.

With that change, it appears that Kahn and his office did no further work on the Palazzo dei Congressi until 1972, when, in January, Kahn visited Venice for two weeks to lecture at the Università Internazionale dell'Arte at Mazzariol's invitation.[35] On April 29 of that year Kahn was once again invited to participate in the Biennale as part of a special exhibit about Venice.[36] On the same day, a Venetian associate urged him to accept: "I think it is important that you should be present with some material . . . because it would certainly help towards a decision about your project of the Palazzo dei Congressi."[37] By May 1972 drawings and correspondence show that Kahn's office was actively at work redesigning the Palazzo for a new site at the nearby Venice Arsenale (fig. 526). The Azienda had shifted the site because the Giardini were overcrowded and there was concern about endangering any of the trees so precious to Venice.[38] Located adjacent to the Giardini, the Arsenale was an industrial district that had been economically depressed by the closing of its shipyards following World War II.[39] The Arsenale may

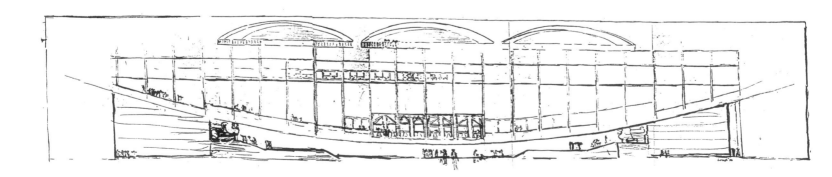

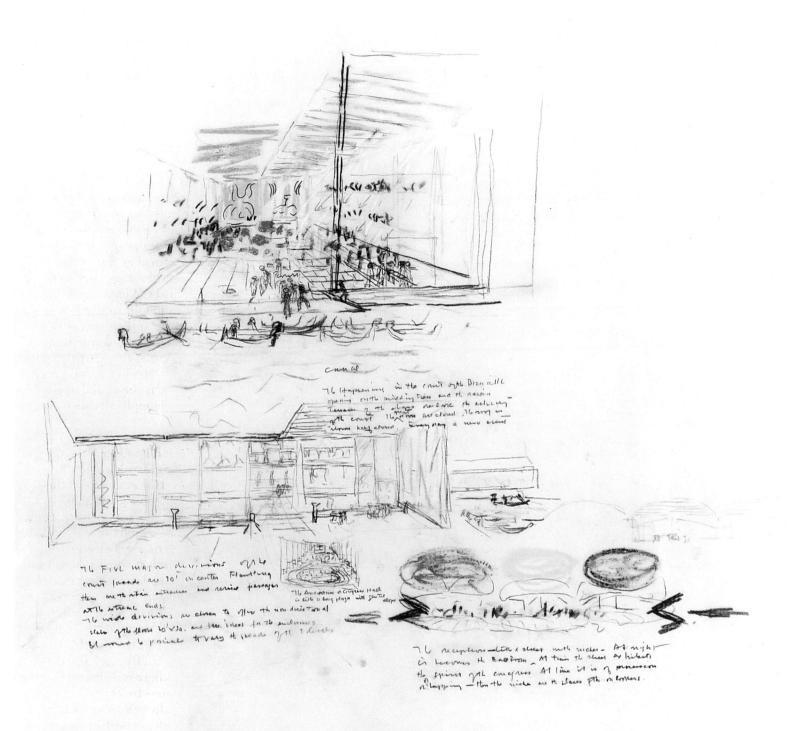

525

have been selected because, as city property, it was readily available.[40] The transformed arsenal was to include the Palazzo, surrounded by open meeting places, arcades, and shops, and a cooperative settlement for industry and crafts with an associated vocational school.[41] Kahn clearly saw and pondered these uses: the last page of a sheaf of handwritten notes from his office includes his sketch labeled "vital change," in which the arsenal basin is labeled "Harbor of the crafts" and the arsenal entrance is a "second San Marco."[42]

At the Arsenale, the Palazzo had a more logical siting—the suspension structure became a true bridge, straddling the Canale delle Galeazze (fig. 527). The building was almost exactly the same size, and only minor modifications were made to adapt the first design to the new site. The piazza at the entrance level was by necessity eliminated; instead, entry was to be from either bank of the canal into the huge piers, which, with their underlying caissons, supported the structure. Kahn reconfigured the seating plan of the auditorium. Gone were the concentric circles, replaced by slightly curved rows of seats both parallel and perpendicular to the central stage.[43] At the next level were three small reception rooms and ballrooms. The roof parapet was the 1970 balustrade version. The Biennale and entrance buildings were abandoned.

Kahn sent three 1972 drawings of the Palazzo, along with several views of Venice drawn during his 1951 visit, to the 1972 Biennale.[44] The Palazzo was shown as part of the Biennale's exhibit called "Quattro Progetti per Venezia," which also included works by Frank Lloyd Wright, Le Corbusier, and Isamu Noguchi.[45]

Kahn's staff built a model of the Arsenale site that was photographed on May 6, 1973.[46] Later that month sketches and the model were exhibited in New York as part of ceremonies honoring Kahn at the National Institute of Arts and Letters.[47] But work on the project was effectively over. Based on the absence of archival evidence, it appears that in the last year of his life, Kahn gave little attention to the Palazzo. Politics, bureaucracy, and changes in the Italian government doomed the plan, according to an associate of Kahn's. "Venice was waiting for money from Rome and the money never came," he said. "It was part of a gamble."[48]

Elise Vider

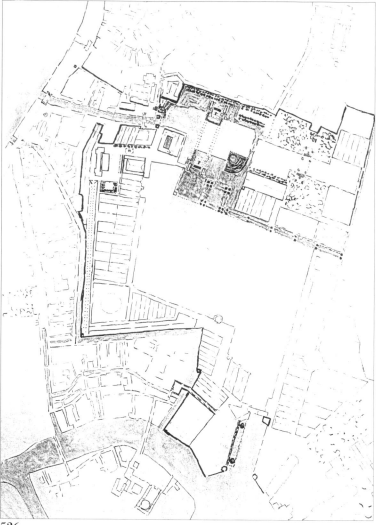

526

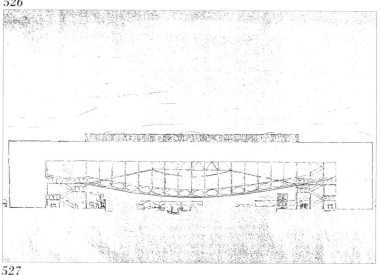

527

526. *Site plan of Arsenale, ca. 1972.*
527. *Elevation. Inscribed Lou K '72.*

Notes

1. Letter, Mayor G. F. Fisca to Kahn, March 13, 1968, "Venice Biennale 1972," Box LIK 46, Louis I. Kahn Collection, University of Pennsylvania and Pennsylvania Historical and Museum Commission, Philadelphia (hereafter cited as Kahn Collection).

2. Cable, Kahn to Fisca, April 18, 1968, ibid.

3. Giuseppe Mazzariol, "Un Progetto per Venezia," *Lotus*, no. 6 (1969): 17.

4. Ibid., 16.

5. Vito Chiarelli, speech at the Ducal Palace, Venice, January 30, 1969, transcript, "Palazzo dei Congressi," Box LIK 36, Kahn Collection.

6. Ibid.

7. Lawrence Alloway, *The Venice Biennale 1895–1969: From Salon to Goldfish Bowl* (Greenwich, Conn.: New York Graphic Society, 1968), 32.

8. Ibid., 17; Deborah Howard, *The Architectural History of Venice* (New York: Holmes & Meier, 1981), 228.

9. Letter, Chiarelli to Kahn, May 4, 1968, "Palazzo dei Congressi," Box LIK 36, Kahn Collection.

10. "LIK Calendar, 1968," Box LIK 121, Kahn Collection.

11. Letter, Chiarelli to Kahn, May 29, 1968, "Venezia," Box LIK 55, Kahn Collection. Venice had not been successful in integrating the abstract forms of modern architecture into its complex and ancient urban fabric. The greatest modern architects had been thwarted in their efforts to design for Venice. In 1953 Frank Lloyd Wright's Masieri Memorial building, which was to be a center for foreign architectural students on the Grand Canal, was rejected. In 1964 Le Corbusier designed a vast civic hospital for the site of a nineteenth-century slaughterhouse. In 1968 the project was still under discussion, but ultimately it was not built.

12. Letter, Kahn to Chiarelli, July 22, 1968, "Master File, Apr. 1968–July 1968," Box LIK 10, Kahn Collection.

13. Cable, Kahn to Mazzariol, July 22, 1968, "Venice Biennale 1972," Box LIK 46, Kahn Collection.

14. Meeting notes, July 20, 1968, "Venezia," Box LIK 55, Kahn Collection.

15. Letter, Mazzariol to Kahn, August 5, 1968, "Palazzo dei Congressi," Box LIK 36, Kahn Collection.

16. Letter, Vallhonrat to Mazzariol, September 6, 1968, "Master File, Aug. 1968–Apr. 30, 1969," Box LIK 10, Kahn Collection.

17. August E. Komendant, *18 Years with Architect Louis I. Kahn* (Englewood, N.J.: Aloray, 1975), 108.

18. Letter, Mazzariol to Vallhonrat, October 22, 1968, "Venezia," Box LIK 55, Kahn Collection.

19. Letter, Kahn to Chiarelli, December 2, 1968, "Palazzo dei Congressi," Box LIK 36, Kahn Collection.

20. Ibid.

21. Kahn associate, telephone conversation with Elise Vider, April 3, 1990. The associate was closely connected with the work but wishes to remain anonymous.

22. Invoice, December 2, 1968, "Palazzo dei Congressi," Box LIK 36, Kahn Collection.

23. Travel itinerary, ibid.

24. Cable, Kahn to Chiarelli, January 17, 1969, ibid.

25. "Kahn in Venice," *Architectural Forum* 130 (March 1969): 64.

26. Chiarelli, speech at the Ducal Palace.

27. Kahn, "Louis I. Kahn Talks About His Project," speech at the Ducal Palace, Venice, January 30, 1969, transcript, "Palazzo dei Congressi," Box LIK 36, Kahn Collection.

28. For example, in *Le Monde* and *Architectural Forum*.

29. "Kahn in Venice," 66.

30. Letter, Mazzariol to Kahn, February 28, 1969, "Palazzo dei Congressi," Box LIK 36, Kahn Collection.

31. Invoice, February 24, 1969, "Venezia," LIK 55, Kahn Collection; Esther Kahn, telephone conversation with Elise Vider, November 8, 1989.

32. Letter, Kahn to Mazzariol, May 16, 1969, "Venezia," Box LIK 55, Kahn Collection.

33. Luisa Querci della Rovere, "Il Palazzo dei Congressi di Louis Kahn ai Giardini," in *Le Venezie possibili: Da Palladio a Le Corbusier* (Venice: Museo Correr, 1985), 286.

34. Komendant, *18 Years*, 113.

35. Letter, Mazzariol to Kahn, December 17, 1971, "Venice IUA, G. Mazzariol, 1972," Box LIK 46, Kahn Collection.

36. Letter, Mario Penelope (Biennale official) to Kahn, April 29, 1972, "Venice Biennale 1972," Box LIK 46, Kahn Collection.

37. Letter, Renzo Salvadori to Kahn, April 29, 1972, ibid.

38. Kahn associate who requested anonymity, telephone conversation with Vider, November 28, 1989.

39. Press release, Azienda Autonoma di Soggiorno e Turismo, January 30, 1969, "Palazzo dei Congressi," Box LIK 36, Kahn Collection.

40. Notes, "Venice Arsenal Fall '72—Documents of Existing Conditions," Box LIK 46, Kahn Collection.

41. Ibid.

42. Ibid.

43. *Architectural Forum* 137 (July–August 1972): 72–73.

44. Insurance certificate, August 9, 1972, "Venice Biennale 1972," Box LIK 46, Kahn Collection.

45. Poster, "Quattro Progetti per Venezia," 1972, ibid.

46. Journal, George Pohl (photographer), Kahn Collection.

47. Letter, Kathleen Condé (Kahn's secretary) to Felicia Geffen (exhibition director, National Institute), May 4, 1973, "Master File," Box LIK 10, Kahn Collection.

48. Kahn associate who requested anonymity, conversation with Vider (1989).

In February 1969 Louis Kahn was approached by Jules D. Prown, director of the Paul Mellon Center for British Art and British Studies at Yale University in New Haven, about designing a building (fig. 528; see figs. 392–407).[1] Paul Mellon had announced in 1966 that he intended to give Yale his collection of British art from the early seventeenth to the mid-nineteenth century, along with funds to construct and endow a building and to support fellowships for the study of British culture. Yale president Kingman Brewster, Jr., had then appointed interdisciplinary committees to consider how best to utilize the Mellon gift. In early 1968 they proposed an integrated center including an art gallery, rare book and research libraries, and supportive study areas in order to stimulate new approaches and enhance research.[2]

While the committees were at work, President Brewster asked Edward Larrabee Barnes, his advisor and consulting architect for the university, to oversee the selection of a location. (Barnes later suggested Kahn as architect to Prown, who already had him in mind, and acted as intermediary in contacting him.[3]) His firm recommended a site directly across Chapel Street from the Yale Art Gallery, which would keep Yale's art-related activities close together. The buildings in the block between High and York Streets were gradually purchased over the course of the next two years. A former church at the corner of Chapel and York Streets, used by the Yale Repertory Theater, was expected to become the site of a unified art library. Kahn was to be asked to prepare schematics for the library as part of the Mellon program.[4] Future development on the far south side of the block ("possibly for drama facilities") was projected, according to the 1970 program.[5]

Although the center was welcomed by Mayor Richard C. Lee when the city and Yale jointly announced it in 1966, hostility toward university expansion soon became an issue. A compromise was sought by including tax-revenue-producing shops as a part of the Mellon Center. Rather than finding this unusual requirement for a museum burdensome, Kahn, already the architect for the twenty-acre Hill Central redevelopment project in New Haven, welcomed the idea.[6] To him it was an opportunity to enliven and respond to the street.

Prown, who was appointed by Brewster as director in July 1968 with the charge to implement the committees' proposals, to recommend an architect, and to act as client for Yale, presented his preliminary thoughts on the building to the president in January 1969.[7] He wanted it to be

Yale Center for British Art

New Haven, Connecticut, 1969–74

"humanistic," appropriate to the collection and to the people who would use it. Its relationship to the university and to the city was of crucial importance, he thought, characterizing the university neighbors of the new building as representatives of the visual and performing arts and of academic creativity and pointing out the presence of commercial "pleasurable establishments" nearby. Prown asked that the scale be appropriate to the characteristically small paintings, prints and drawings, and illustrated books, although he asked too that some rooms be designed to accommodate large oils and sculpture. Daylight was requested for galleries, offices, and conservation studios and filtered or artificial light for the display of works on paper. A variety of spaces to counter fatigue; a clarity of plan; and special places for contemplation, conversation, and refreshment would make visitors comfortable, he believed.

After devoting much of the 1968–69 academic year to studying museums and architects, Prown chose Kahn as designer, a choice confirmed in June 1969 by the Yale Corporation and later announced to the public.[8] The cost of the projected building—a matter that was to affect program and design—had earlier been set between $5 million and $9 million, but it was now set at $6 million.[9] In September 1969 Prown and Kahn visited the Mellons at their homes in Upperville, Virginia, and Georgetown. They also went to the National Gallery and the Phillips Collection in Washington, D.C.[10] The Mellons' houses and the Phillips Collection, a house transformed into a museum, suggested the ambience that both architect and client sought for the Mellon Center. Kahn associated the collection with a domestic setting, and he particularly responded to Paul Mellon's library; he spoke of "the idea of intimacy between book, painting, drawing— this is in the room-like quality of the collections."[11] Prown cherished the hope that the complex institution would be like the Phillips Collection, appropriate in his mind to British art, which he described as "an art of places, and human activities."[12]

Kahn's initial proposal for the Mellon Center was presented in plan sketches in February, based on the program, issued in January 1970, which enumerated nearly 150,000 gross square feet. The first floor had commercial space, entrances from both Chapel and High Streets into a courtyard with the main stairwell, an auditorium, and museum workshops (fig. 529). Galleries and libraries—the institution proper— began on the second floor. A second courtyard, fulfilling a traditional museum *parti*, was placed above the large reading room, which in turn occupied the space above the auditorium. A section of February 4, 1970, shows the

528. View from northeast.
529. First-floor plan. Inscribed Louis I. Kahn Feb 4 '70.
530. Longitudinal section, looking south. Inscribed Louis I. Kahn Feb 4, 1970.
531. Model of first version, May–June 1970.

significance of the courts for bringing in natural light and
organizing the interiors, features that were requested in the
program (fig. 530). Prown found these plans, described
by him as domino shapes of rectangles and squares,
disappointing; they seemed rudimentary compared to his
expectation of interpenetrating spaces and varied levels.[13]
Indeed, the very complexity of the program inspired Kahn to
seek simple solutions. This characteristic concentration
on planning, and the simplicity of the plans themselves,
remained constant during design development. It was the
way Kahn worked. As Prown observed, the facade, although
never an afterthought, came later.

Painting galleries with natural lighting were fundamental to
the Yale Center and remained so throughout its design. Kahn
placed these on the top floor under double longitudinal
arches with clerestory windows that stretched the length of
the building on the north and the south (see fig. 229).
Expansive openings were made possible by the use of
Vierendeel trusses on the upper and lower floors. (Parking
was to be under the building.) The shape of the arches was
pervasive, echoed in lower-floor windows and even in
exterior paneling on a model dating from early June 1970
(fig. 531). While Prown liked the early design, he had doubts
about the top-floor galleries, fearing that such strong
architectural spaces would overpower small works of art.

Kahn was persuaded to use another approach in a scheme
developed between the summer of 1970 and the winter of
1970–71. A new (January 1971) north elevation of the
center, including a schematic fine arts library replacing the
church/theater at right, shows a large building regularly
articulated by structural bays and expressing the dual
functions of exhibition and study (or museum and library)
through a two-part division (fig. 532). Kahn said of this:
"Another characteristic is the expansion joint between the
two buildings. I emphasized and dramatized the expansion
joint, causing it to have two entrances at this point instead of
the usual one. I felt that this was in itself an aesthetic
emergence, rather than what was just necessary."[14]

The 1971 design was the culmination of work based on the
first program: four floors, two mezzanines (first and second
floors), and two basements (one for parking), totaling
103,653 net square feet.[15] It was considerably larger than
the 88,000 net square feet requested, but as plans were
developed, the program allowances often seemed
inadequate. Those at Yale were pleased by what they saw:
an enclosed east court with a spectacular glass-enclosed
stairwell surrounded by shops; the specialized library lit by

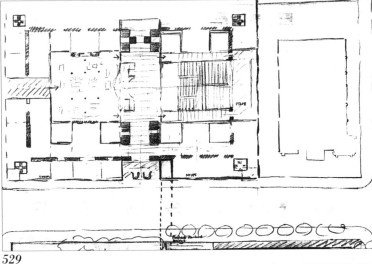

529

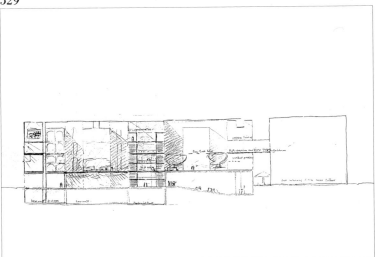

530

531

528

overhead glass pyramids and with gardens and terraces; an open court above that would be seen from the upper floor; skylit, barrel-vaulted galleries—still strong architectural spaces—at the summit; and four metal-clad towers housing service utilities at the corners. According to Prown:

It just simply developed and developed and developed to a point where people were happy with it. . . . The gardens were fantastic. The office space was looking out over the library gardens. Even now, I feel that that first building [for the first program] would have been a better building architecturally, but I do feel that it would have been less successful for the exhibition of English paintings.[16]

Kahn wrote Paul Mellon in March 1971: "The building has developed to a maturity that I believe in, and I hope it can be realized."[17] Estimates now mounted to $14-16 million, however, at a time when the donor was also concerned with increasing costs for the east wing of the National Gallery, for which he and his sister were the principal contributors. A Yale study indicated that the project would have to be reduced by one third.[18]

A second, revised program for 63,570 net square feet, or 106,200 gross, was issued by Yale on May 6, 1971.[19] Without apparent disappointment at beginning anew, Kahn sketched plans for a third and smaller design. As early as May 20 he showed drawings to Prown and his assistant Henry Berg.[20] Retaining a double-court scheme, he discarded the openness that required Vierendeel trusses in favor of smaller structural bays throughout. Skylights on the top floor reflected the twenty-foot-square module established by the bays (see fig. 233). The structure would be concrete, with infill panels of steel and glass. To welcome both students and public, Prown suggested opening the corner at High and Chapel Streets,[21] and Kahn did so, using that as the main entrance and making it an urban forecourt for the Mellon Center. He also lowered the ground level on the west to create an outdoor terrace and a separate auditorium entrance. Prown and Berg worked closely with Kahn and his office on the interior arrangements, offering lengthy, detailed comments on plans.[22]

In November 1971 the design was presented to the donor and the Yale Corporation.[23] Its size had been reduced to 61,411 net square feet, or 114,332 gross including the shops,[24] and plans were close to final, although the central stairwell in the library court was an oblique square rather than the round silo eventually built (see fig. 232). As before, the first floor provided stores, the entrance to the center, and the auditorium and nonpublic museum areas. On the second

floor the library court had double-height reading rooms lit by large windows on three sides; exhibition space surrounded the entrance court. The third floor, similar to the second, continued library stacks around the west court and galleries around the east. The top floor with the primary picture exhibition galleries and the study collection also had offices for curators and administrators.

Problematic components, such as the skylights and light diffusers, and the design as a whole continued to be studied after design approval by Mellon and the Yale Corporation. The stair tower in the library took its final, freestanding, columnar shape—reminiscent of the stairway in Kahn's Yale Art Gallery—during design development between November 1971 and May 1972 (see fig. 400). A curatorial and spatial separation of rare books from prints and drawings was made at Yale's request. Excavation started in November 1972, but revised working drawings were not issued until August 1973.[25] At the time of Kahn's sudden death on March 17, 1974, precast roof beams for the skylights were in New Haven, ready to be placed.[26] Yale assigned completion to Pellecchia and Meyers, Architects. Both had worked with Kahn: Marshall D. Meyers had been the Kimbell Art Museum project architect, and Anthony Pellecchia was project architect for the Theater of Performing Arts, Fort Wayne, Indiana; and in the fall of 1973 Meyers had become field representative for both Kahn and Yale on the Mellon project. He and Pellecchia saw the building to completion in 1977, undertaking to design only details that were not complete at the time of Kahn's death.[27]

The Yale Center for British Art has changed little since its completion; wooden shutters (as Kahn originally wanted) have been installed on windows to the exterior, and one of the High Street shops has been refitted as the museum bookstore. Assessments have been highly favorable, although some critics find it Kahn's most conservative building and see it as a return to modernist preoccupations,[28] and criticisms have been made of specific operational features. Jules Prown has perhaps best summed up the building in saying that it is the center's architectural poetry—light, scale, mood, and embodied values—rather than its prose that is most successful.[29]

Patricia Cummings Loud

532. *North elevation, January 1971.*

Notes

1. Letter, Prown to Kahn, February 19, 1969, "Correspondence with Yale Mellon Office, J. Prown and H. Berg," Box LIK 109, Louis I. Kahn Collection, University of Pennsylvania and Pennsylvania Historical and Museum Commission, Philadelphia (hereafter cited as Kahn Collection). The change of name to the Yale Center for British Art was made at the request of Paul Mellon and took effect after Kahn's death. On the Yale Center, see Patricia Cummings Loud, *The Art Museums of Louis I. Kahn* (Durham, N.C., and London: Duke University Press, 1989), 172–243.

2. Committee reports were sent to Kahn by Prown with his letter of February 19, 1969, "Correspondence with Yale Mellon Office, J. Prown and H. Berg," Box LIK 109, Kahn Collection.

3. Letter, Prown to Kahn, February 19, 1969, ibid. Prown has mentioned that Barnes suggested he talk with Kahn; "Louis I. Kahn, Yale Center for British Art, Yale University, New Haven, Connecticut," in *Processes in Architecture: A Documentation of Six Examples*, Hayden Gallery, Massachusetts Institute of Technology, published as a special issue of *Plan*, no. 10 (Spring 1979): 31; Prown, interview with Alessandra Latour, June 23, 1982, in *Louis I. Kahn: L'uomo, il maestro*, ed. Latour (Rome: Edizioni Kappa, 1986), 133.

4. Yale Office of Buildings and Grounds Planning, "Building Design Program, Preliminary, The Paul Mellon Center for British Art and British Art Studies," January 21, 1970, "Mellon I Program Void," Box 112, Kahn Collection.

5. Ibid.

6. "The Paul Mellon Center: A Classic Accommodation Between Town and Gown," *Yale Alumni Magazine* 35 (April 1972): 30. Prown has said that professor George Kubler, his colleague in art history, wrote Mellon as early as 1967 to suggest including stores in the new building; symposium, "The Art Museums of Louis I. Kahn: Personal Viewpoints," March 3, 1990, Yale University.

7. Prown, *The Architecture of the Yale Center for British Art*, 2d ed. (New Haven: Yale University, 1982), 12–14. See Loud, *The Art Museums*, 174. Prown deals with his role as client, as well as Yale's as owner and Mellon's as donor, in "On Being a Client," *Society of Architectural Historians Journal* 42 (March 1983): 11–14.

8. Statement by Prown, June 5, 1969, "Correspondence with Yale Mellon Office, J. Prown and H. Berg," Box LIK 109, Kahn Collection; Robert Kilpatrick, "Louis Kahn May Design Arts Center," *New Haven Register*, June 4, 1969, photocopy of clipping received in Kahn's office June 9, 1969, ibid. In July Yale's director of buildings and grounds planning referred to the approval of the Corporation Committee; letter, E. W. Y. Dunn, Jr., to Kahn, July 22, 1969, "Correspondence with University of Yale Offices, Buildings and Grounds," Box LIK 110, Kahn Collection. Clipping of the announcement of the appointment in *New Haven Journal-Courier*, October 27, 1969, in "Mellon Art Gallery (Yale)," Box LIK 111, Kahn Collection.

9. Kilpatrick gave the range in "Louis Kahn May Design Arts Center." Kahn noted that press announcements set the cost at $6 million; letter, Kahn to Dunn, February 19, 1970, "Master Files, 1969–73," Box LIK 10, Kahn Collection.

10. Letter, Prown to Kahn, September 11, 1969, "Correspondence with Yale Mellon Office, J. Prown and H. Berg," Box LIK 109, Kahn Collection. Prown describes their visit to the Phillips Collection in *The Architecture*, 16.

11. "The Mind of Louis Kahn," *Architectural Forum* 137 (July–August 1972): 83.

12. Prown, *The Architecture*, 12.

13. Prown, interview with Latour, 137–39.

14. Heinz Ronner and Sharad Jhaveri, *Louis I. Kahn: Complete Work,* 1935–1974, 2d ed. (Basel and Boston: Birkhäuser, 1987), 381.

15. Drawings dated March 15, 1971, "Mellon, Net Areas, 3-15-71 to 8-16-71," Box LIK 112, Kahn Collection.

16. Prown, *Processes in Architecture*, 35–36.

17. Letter, Kahn to Mellon, March 31, 1971, "Master Files, 1969–73," Box LIK 10, Kahn Collection.

18. Prown, *The Architecture*, 32.

19. "Revised Building Design Program, Preliminary," May 6, 1971, "Correspondence with University of Yale Offices, Buildings and Grounds," Box LIK 110, Kahn Collection; "Revised 6 May 71 Mellon Yale Program," Box LIK 111, Kahn Collection.

20. Memorandum, Berg to David Wisdom (Kahn's office), May 21, 1971, "Correspondence with Yale Mellon Office, J. Prown and H. Berg," Box LIK 109, Kahn Collection.

21. Letter, Prown to Kahn, June 16, 1971, ibid.

22. For example, letter, Berg to Kahn, September 9, 1971, and memorandums, Berg to Kahn's office, September 30 and October 11, 1971, ibid.

23. The dates for presentations were November 3, 1971, for Mellon in New York, and November 5 and 6, 1971, for the Yale Corporation in New Haven; letter, Berg to Kahn, October 1, 1971, ibid.

24. Drawings for programmed net areas in square feet, and gross area in square feet, dated October 29, 1971, "Mellon, Net Areas, 3-15-71 to 8-16-71, Gross 6-8-71," Box LIK 112, Kahn Collection.

25. On changes and chronology, see Loud, *The Art Museums*, 196–221.

26. Letter, Theodore R. Burghart (Macomber Co.) to V. Peter Basserman (Office of Buildings and Grounds, Yale), March 13, 1974, "Macomber Correspondence IV, 12-20-73 to 3-25-74," Box LIK 110, Kahn Collection.

27. On their contributions, see Loud, *The Art Museums*, 227; and accounts by Meyers and Pellecchia in *Processes in Architecture*, 39–54.

28. Vincent J. Scully, "The Yale Center for British Art," *Architectural Record* 161 (June 1977): 95–104; William Jordy, "Kahn at Yale," *Architectural Review* 162 (July 1977): 37–44; Martin Filler, "Opus Posthumous," *Progressive Architecture* 59 (May 1978): 76–81; Michael J. Crosbie, "Evaluation: Monument Before Its Time. Yale Center for British Art, Louis Kahn," *Architecture* 75 (January 1986): 64–67. See Loud, *The Art Museums*, 227–32.

29. Prown, symposium, "The Art Museums of Louis I. Kahn," March 3, 1990.

In the early 1970s Louis Kahn designed several projects in connection with the celebration of the Bicentennial of the Declaration of Independence in Philadelphia.[1] The first design called for a huge tentlike pavilion for an international exposition at Penn's Landing on the Delaware River. After this site was rejected, Kahn proposed an ambitious project for an exposition in southwest Philadelphia, near the International Airport. It never came to fruition due to the federal government's lack of support. The third and last project called for a more modest national exposition on Independence Mall, but it, too, was not realized.

As early as 1966 Kahn, as a member of the Bicentennial Committee of the Philadelphia Chapter of the American Institute of Architects, had expressed his view that the bicentennial should not be commemorated in the traditional manner—with a world's fair celebrating cultural and scientific achievements—but rather with a celebration of the new institutions that would answer America's needs as it entered its third century.[2] In an unpublished essay, written in February 1969 for *Avant Garde*, a radical New York art journal, Kahn reiterated his call for a bicentennial that would highlight future institutions, especially those promoting fraternity and cooperation among all people.[3]

On January 22, 1971, the Bureau of International Expositions in Paris approved preliminary proposals for an international exposition in Philadelphia, submitted by the Philadelphia 1976 Bicentennial Corporation, an alliance of civic and political leaders representing the city's interests.[4] (John Bunting, president of First Pennsylvania Bank, was chairman of the corporation, William H. Rafsky its president, and John Andrew Gallery its executive director.) Any bicentennial project also had to win approval from both the United States Department of Commerce and the American Revolution Bicentennial Commission, the latter authorized by Congress in 1966 to oversee plans for federal participation in the bicentennial.[5] Support from these federal agencies was a prerequisite before Congress could appropriate the $250 million requested by the Philadelphia 1976 Bicentennial Corporation.[6] Kahn soon became active in the city's campaign for that support.

In the wake of approval from the Bureau of International Expositions, Kahn let it be known that he did not favor "fresh ground and new buildings . . . to feel the spirit of the creators of American Independence."[7] Instead, he advocated the use of part of Center City, between Sixth Street and the Delaware River, closing off streets and using

churches and Quaker meetinghouses for the planned international assemblies.[8] Kahn's insistence that the bicentennial be a forum for discussion and meeting would prevail in all his subsequent proposals.

Kahn formally presented his ideas in an exhibition entitled "City/2" (City over Two), held at the Philadelphia Museum of Art between June 10, 1971, and January 2, 1972. The exhibition, organized by Philadelphia architect Richard Saul Wurman, a former student of Kahn's, sought to demonstrate ways to improve the public environment.[9] Kahn submitted four drawings, one of which, entitled "The American Anonymous Building" (fig. 533), referred to the upcoming exposition. Kahn intended to utilize Penn's Landing on the Delaware River as his site. A large pavilion would shelter the exhibitions of all invited countries along "an enclosed street, several thousand feet long." As Kahn noted on the drawing, the building would be defined not by its "anonymous" and simple crystal-like appearance but by the beehive of human activity and interaction occurring around the exhibition areas under the hall's long roof. Such a scheme marked a departure from past world's fair architecture where individual nations constructed separate pavilions, richly decorated with the allegorical symbols and motifs of the nation in question.

Shortly after the exhibition closed, Kahn set to work officially for the Philadelphia 1976 Bicentennial Corporation, making a design for presentation to federal agencies for approval.[10] Although at this time he envisioned the celebration as occurring primarily at Penn's Landing, Kahn also projected a complementary site on the east bank of the Schuylkill River, as outlined in a letter to Stephen S. Gardner, president of Girard Bank and chairman of Mayor Frank Rizzo's Bicentennial Site Committee, which was charged with finding a suitable location for the celebration.[11] The riverbank sites, or "strategic docks," as Kahn called them, were composed of hotels and shopping and parking facilities as well as exhibition halls, and were to be linked by an overhead pedestrian bridge some thirty city blocks in length, "a major structure of engineering."[12] The Schuylkill River site, landscaped with spray fountains, would be occupied by buildings dedicated to what Kahn called the three major human inspirations: "learning," "meeting," and "well-being."[13] He believed that these three inspirations encompassed all national and civic concerns.

The 1976 Bicentennial Corporation and the mayor's site committee did not seriously review Kahn's site suggestions. After considering several other locations for the exposition,

Bicentennial Exposition

Philadelphia, Pennsylvania, 1971–73

The Bicentennial on the Delaware

The American Building is an enclosed Street several thousand feet long offered to all Nations for their expressions. It is the place of the inspired addenda coming from children and adults invited to formulate plans to bring new availabilities to all people. This crystal like building of Invitation would present a simple image, inside of which would be the place of happening and a variety of structures tied to ordered services.

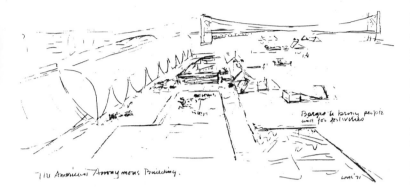

The American Anonymous Building.

533

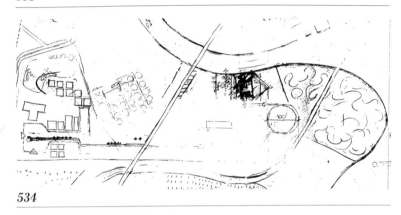

534

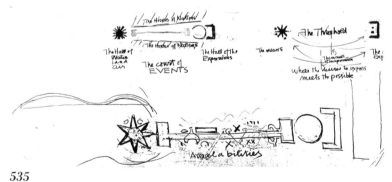

535

533. *Bird's-eye perspective of Penn's Landing site. Inscribed Lou K '71.*
534. *Plan of Eastwick site, 1971.*
535. *Plan of Eastwick site, 1972.*

including the Penn Central railroad yards adjacent to Thirtieth Street Station and a site in the Byberry area of North Philadelphia, they decided on an 1,100-acre site in the Eastwick section of southwest Philadelphia. This large site, away from residential areas and hence free of the neighborhood opposition that had doomed some earlier proposals, was at the center of a great transportation hub—adjacent to the future Delaware Expressway (now Interstate 95), the Delaware and Schuylkill Rivers, and Philadelphia International Airport.[14]

With the selection of Eastwick finalized in February 1972, Kahn abandoned his concept of a trans-city celebration and focused on the new site, proposing auditoriums, communications buildings, and a "happening" building for live celebrations and events (fig. 534). Kahn then gave names to the various buildings and exhibition areas and refined their relationships (fig. 535). The Hall of Water, Land, and Air and the Hall of the Expressions were connected by a long rectangular Court of Events lined by the Houses of Nations. The Hall of Water, Land, and Air was to be dedicated to scientific achievements, which would be highlighted in multimedia presentations.[15] It would house exhibitions concerning natural and urban resources.[16] The Hall of the Expressions would be an area where festivals, theatrical performances, films, and art exhibitions would illustrate the cultural character of participating nations.[17] Connecting the halls was the Court of Events, a major thoroughfare with a canal running parallel to it. The importance of such a canal was suggested to Kahn by the Canadian architect Edouard Fiset, who had been the chief architect for Expo '67 in Montreal.[18] The use of water linked Kahn's design to those of past expositions, where fountains and canals played a major role. This exposition was to be one giant thoroughfare featuring movement and intercommunications between the larger installations and the smaller, flanking Houses of Nations, or national exhibition pavilions, which were intimate in scale, unlike the usual monuments characteristic of world's fair architecture.[19]

Kahn's most complete drawing of the Eastwick site (see fig. 211) was included in the March 1972 master plan of the Philadelphia 1976 Bicentennial Corporation.[20] Following the advice of Henry Putsch, director of theme and program development for the corporation, Kahn renamed the Hall of Water, Land, and Air the Courts of the Physical Resources, while the Hall of Expressions became the Courts of the Expressions. The entire scheme was entitled the Forum of the Availabilities.[21] The designation of exhibition halls and auditoriums as "courts" and "forums" underlined Kahn's belief in the celebration as an opportunity for discussing the institutions of the future. The plan—a large "street" flanked by pavilions—encouraged active participation by visitors, and it was well suited to the exhibition's theme: "to gather the peoples of the world into an exploration of their historic and cultural achievements, their concerns and goals, and their continuing search for greater mutual understanding."[22]

Kahn's design for the Eastwick site failed to win the support of either the Department of Commerce or the American Revolution Bicentennial Commission. Even before official notification, William Rafsky, sensing rejection, asked Kahn to cease work on the design.[23] And four days later, on May 16, 1972, when Rafsky and John Andrew Gallery presented Kahn's master plan and a new model of the site (see fig. 212) to the Federal Bicentennial Commission, the commission voted overwhelmingly against it.[24] Competition from other cities, notably Boston, Washington, and Miami, was the chief reason for the rejection of Philadelphia's bid.[25] Instead of making the city the centerpiece of America's bicentennial celebration, the federal government chose instead to disperse funds to all fifty states and many major cities. On May 18 Rafsky asked Kahn to make a final report and submit a bill, and on June 8 John Bunting dissolved the Philadelphia 1976 Bicentennial Corporation.[26]

Following the rejection of the Bicentennial Corporation's project for the Eastwick site, Mayor Rizzo created an interim organization under Rafsky, the Bicentennial Planning Group, to determine what type of celebration might be held in Philadelphia.[27] A more modest exposition was proposed on Independence Mall and Kahn was asked to make "explorations" of that site.[28] He had always spoken fondly of Independence Hall, "a lovely little building," and often reminisced about sketching it as a young boy.[29] Although as a youth Kahn had also explored the old shops that then lined the north side of Chestnut Street, demolished to create the mall, he had not objected to their demise, for it gave Independence Hall "a more glorious position."[30]

Kahn was not asked to design a complete rebuilding of the mall. Existing facilities would be used as much as possible, and only special shelter roofs, temporary walkways, and exhibition spaces were to be built.[31] Kahn first envisioned a central court between Market and Arch Streets as a gathering place, or Village Green as he called it, in the tradition of New England. Arch Street between Fifth and Sixth Streets would be the location of a series of "community houses" or centers, while at the site's northern end, on Vine Street, a monumental exhibition building would

dramatically close the axis and screen the Vine Street Expressway.[32] Preliminary construction costs were estimated at $61,355,000.[33]

On February 3, 1973, the Bicentennial Planning Group and city leaders met with federal officials to discuss their plans for Philadelphia's scaled-down bicentennial.[34] Approval was granted for $100 million in federal funds for the celebration.[35] During the week of February 19 Rafsky, Gallery, and Kahn went ahead with their work, and Kahn now elaborated on his earlier plans (fig. 536). A large T-shaped hall at the northern end of the mall, covered by two simple interlocking barrel vaults, was to be utilized for meetings and special exhibitions, and would serve as a museum after the bicentennial.[36] Two domical-vaulted square buildings in the center of the mall, just north of Arch Street, were to serve as information centers and additional exhibition areas, illustrating the growth of American institutions over the last 200 years. To the south, between Arch and Market Streets, a horseshoe-shaped staircase would lead to a sunken outdoor theater, meant to be a lunching area or a place for popular music, theater, and dance (fig. 537).

Kahn analyzed the theme of his design in a report entitled "The Bicentennial of the Signing of the Declaration of Independence in Philadelphia—A Proposal for Independence Mall as the Seat of the Congress of the Institutions."[37] A group of simple yet bold buildings, again free of traditional world's fair symbolism and iconography and characterized only by their barrel and domical vaults, would house the Congress of the Institutions. The exhibition buildings would record the history of the American institutions that had sustained the nation in the past and also suggest new institutions for the future. Kahn hoped for an international congress or gathering at the fair, where "the desire to learn, the desire to meet, the desire to provide the means toward well-being" would be the central focus.

On August 6, 1973, Kahn presented these proposals for the mall to the executive committee of the Bicentennial Planning Group, which had formally incorporated as Philadelphia '76 earlier in March.[38] Nothing decisive resulted from that or subsequent meetings. Municipal funds were in short supply and the $100 million in federal funds were still not forthcoming. Plans for the bicentennial celebration were still being discussed when Kahn died in March 1974. In the end, none of Kahn's plans was adopted by the city.

Marc Philippe Vincent

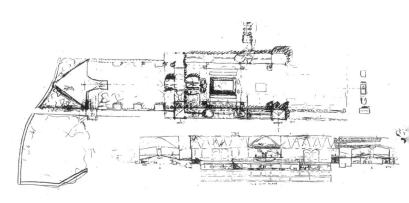

536

Notes

1. Kahn had also participated in the planning and design for the Sesquicentennial Exposition in 1926 in Philadelphia, his first major work after having graduated from the University of Pennsylvania in June 1924.

2. "Report on the Bicentennial," July 3, 1967, "Philadelphia Bicentennial Committee," Box LIK 58, Louis I. Kahn Collection, University of Pennsylvania and Pennsylvania Historical and Museum Commission, Philadelphia (hereafter cited as Kahn Collection). The other members of the Bicentennial Committee of the Philadelphia Chapter of the American Institute of Architects were Edmund Bacon, Roy Carroll, Jr., Vincent Kling, Roy Larson, George Qualls, Oscar Stonorov, David Wallace, Richard Saul Wurman, and C. Clark Zantzinger, Jr., the chairman of the committee.

3. Essay for *Avant Garde*, stamped "Received, LIK, February 20, 1969," "Avant Garde," Box LIK 69, Kahn Collection. Kahn's essay was prepared for, but not published in, the article entitled "Towards a New Spirit of 1976," in the February 1969 issue of *Avant Garde*. Among the short essays that were published were those of architects Charles W. Moore, Louis J. Bakanowsky, Percival Goodman, and Roger Katan; New York City planner Robert Moses; and Philadelphia mayor James H. J. Tate.

4. "A Report to the United States Department of Commerce and to the American Revolution Bicentennial Commission," March 1972, i, "The United States Bicentennial International Exposition," Box LIK 1, Kahn Collection.

5. Brian Feldman, "Another War for 1776 Bicentennial," *The Baltimore Sun*, clipping in "Bicentennial Miscellaneous Correspondence," Box LIK 50, Kahn Collection.

6. Ibid.

7. Kahn, quoted in "In the Hall of the Mountain King: A Block Party," *Thursday's Drummer* (Philadelphia), February 25, 1971, 4.

8. Ibid.

9. John Corr, "Half of Philadelphia Belongs to You," *Philadelphia Inquirer Sunday Magazine*, June 13, 1971, 2.

10. Letter, Kahn to Philadelphia 1976 Bicentennial Corporation, January 13, 1972, "1972 Bicentennial Corporation Correspondence," Box LIK 50, Kahn Collection.

11. Letter, Kahn to Gardner, January 16, 1972, ibid.

12. Ibid.

13. Ibid.

14. "A Report to the Department of Commerce," ii.

15. Kahn, "City Environment," proposal no. 10, "Summary of Proposals for an Independence Celebration Received by the Philadelphia 1976 Bicentennial Corporation," "Philadelphia 1976 Bicentennial," Box LIK 44, Kahn Collection.

16. Report, stamped "Received LIK, May 11, 1972," "1972 Bicentennial Corporation Bulletins," Box LIK 50, Kahn Collection. The report was prepared by Kahn, Stanhope S. Browne, Bowen C. Dees, Ewen C. Dingwall, Graeme Ferguson, Anthony Garvan, Thomas Hoving, Herman Kahn, Roman Kroiter, Martin Meyerson, John McHale, Rodney Napier, Terry Rankine, Herbert Rosenthal, Denise and Robert Venturi, Novella Williams, Edwin Wolf III, Robert Wussler, and Henry E. Putsch (director of theme and program development for the Philadelphia 1976 Bicentennial Corporation).

17. Kahn, "City Environment."

18. Letter, Fiset to John Andrew Gallery, May 3, 1972, "1972 Bicentennial Corporation Correspondence," Box LIK 50, Kahn Collection. Fiset had traveled to Philadelphia to meet with the Bicentennial Corporation.

19. Report, stamped "Received LIK, May 11, 1972."

20. *Master Plan Concept, Forum '76*, "Bicentennial—Forum '76 Brochures," Box LIK 50, Kahn Collection.

21. Memo, Putsch to Kahn, n.d., "1972 Bicentennial Corporation Correspondence," Box LIK 50, Kahn Collection.

22. "A Report to the Department of Commerce," 3–5.

23. Report, stamped "Received LIK, May 11, 1972."

24. Memorandum, "Bicentennial Meeting Notes," Kathleen Condé (Kahn's secretary) to Kahn, May 17, 1972, "Bicentennial 1972," Box LIK 50, Kahn Collection. The vote was 23 negative, 4 affirmative, and 2 abstentions.

25. Constance M. Greiff, *Independence, The Creation of a National Park* (Philadelphia: University of Pennsylvania Press, 1987), 234.

26. Letter, Rafsky to Kahn, May 18, 1972, "1972 Bicentennial Corporation Bulletins," Box LIK 50, Kahn Collection; letter, Bunting to members of the board of directors and executive committee, June 8, 1972, "1972 Bicentennial Corporation Correspondence," Box LIK 50, Kahn Collection.

27. Caye Christian, *Final Report, Philadelphia '76* (Philadelphia: Philadelphia '76, ca. 1977), 41.

28. Memorandum of telephone conversation, Gallery to Marshall Meyers, September 21, 1972, "Philadelphia 1976 Bicentennial," Box LIK 44, Kahn Collection. For a complete history of Independence Mall, consult Greiff, *Independence*.

29. Kahn, quoted in "At Independence Mall; May 19, 1971," *What Will Be Has Always Been: The Words of Louis I. Kahn*, ed. Richard Saul Wurman (New York: Access Press and Rizzoli, 1986), 122.

30. Ibid., 123.

31. Letter, Gallery to Kahn, with attachments, September 25, 1972, "Philadelphia 1976 Bicentennial," Box LIK 44, Kahn Collection.

32. Letter, Paul C. Harbeson to Kahn, with copies to Roy Larson and partners, November 8, 1972, ibid. In 1954, H2L2 (Hough, Harbeson, Livingston, and Larson) had been given the commission by the National Park Service to design Independence Mall.

33. Memorandum, estimate summary by International Consultants, Inc., November 9–10, 1972, ibid.

34. *Final Report, Philadelphia '76*, 41.

35. Memorandum, Gallery to Bicentennial Consultants, February 15, 1973, "Philadelphia 1976 Bicentennial," Box LIK 44, Kahn Collection. In the same memo Gallery announced his resignation from the Bicentennial Planning Group, "now that some agreements had been reached with the Federal people."

36. Memorandum, Gallery to Meyers, with copy to Rafsky, February 27, 1973, ibid.

37. "The Bicentennial of the Signing of the Declaration of Independence in Philadelphia—A Proposal for Independence Mall as the Seat of the Congress of the Institutions," June 29, 1973, ibid.

38. Letter, Peter C. Luquer (director of programming, Philadelphia '76) to Kahn, August 16, 1973, ibid.

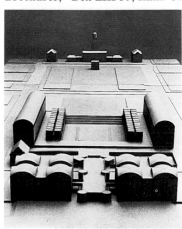

536. Plan and section of Independence Mall site, 1973.
537. Model of Independence Mall site, 1973.

The Louis I. Kahn Collection records the lifework of an architect whose significance is yet to be fully realized. It has been the center of scholarly activity in the preparation of this exhibition and the book that accompanies it. The very existence of Kahn's archives is a testimony to the dedication and vision of Kahn's friends and associates, who saved the collection from dispersal following his death.

Kahn died unexpectedly on March 17, 1974, in New York's Pennsylvania Station. He was returning to Philadelphia from Ahmedabad, India, the site of his recently completed Indian Institute of Management. Still under construction at the time of his death were two of his greatest masterpieces: the Yale Center for British Art, and the national capital of Bangladesh at Dhaka. After his death, Kahn's office was closed, but his former associates vowed to complete, when possible, the projects still under construction.

It was soon ascertained that substantial financial obligations, primarily wages and professional fees owed to employees and consultants, were left outstanding. The estate was, in fact, several hundred thousand dollars in debt. David Zoob, Kahn's lawyer, and Esther Kahn, his widow and executor of the estate, were forced to make an agonizing decision: the assets of the firm would have to be liquidated, and Kahn's papers, project records, sketches, drawings, and models would be sold to settle the estate. In July 1974 a group of Kahn's supporters, fearful that the archives would be dispersed among diverse collections, formed a nonprofit corporation dedicated to preserving the archives in their entirety. The foundation was led by a distinguished board of directors and a group of sponsors that included Edward Larrabee Barnes, Lewis B. Davis, Balkrishna Doshi, Buckminster Fuller, Romaldo Giurgola, Bruce Graham, Ada Louise Huxtable, Philip Johnson, Esther Kahn, the Honorable Teddy Kollek, August Komendant, Robert Le Ricolais, Martin Meyerson, I. M. Pei, Norman Rice, Lessing J. Rosenwald, Jonas Salk, Vincent Scully, Kenzo Tange, and Thomas R. Vreeland. An executive committee, comprising Samuel Maitin, Theodore T. Newbold, David Scully, and the chairman, Carles Enrique Vallhonrat, approached a number of foundations in Philadelphia to solicit funding for the acquisition of the archives. Finding insufficient support in the private sector, the committee enlisted the help of Pennsylvania Secretary of Commerce Walter G. Arader to guide a bill through the state legislature proposing that the state purchase the Kahn papers on behalf of the Pennsylvania Historical and Museum Commission.

Grass-roots movements, organized by architects William Huff in Pittsburgh and Luis Vincent Rivera in Philadelphia, and by Anthony P. Nolfi, president of the Delaware Valley Masonry Institute, helped raise the general awareness among Pennsylvania residents of the importance of preserving the Kahn papers within the Commonwealth. Petitions signed by thousands of state residents were delivered to the capitol in Harrisburg during the summer of 1975. Eventually, with the support of Governor Milton Shapp of Pennsylvania, who had enthusiastically promoted Kahn's design for the unrealized Pocono Arts Center (1972–74), a bill proposing the state's purchase of the collection was introduced in the state House of Representatives. A heated debate on the floor of the House was followed by a negative vote. Then, as now, funds for the support of such activities were scarce, and competition for the allocation of state funds was keen. When the bill was reintroduced, majority leader K. Leroy Irvis, who represented a constituency of inner-city residents from Pittsburgh, delivered an impassioned speech urging support of the measure. Following his dramatic speech on October 2, 1975, the bill passed by a single vote, and the preservation of the Kahn Collection was at last assured.

The purchase of the Kahn papers was finalized on April 30, 1976. The following year the Pennsylvania Historical and Museum Commission agreed to place the Louis I. Kahn Collection on permanent loan to the University of Pennsylvania, Kahn's alma mater. The trustees of the university assumed responsibility for the maintenance, supervision, and exhibition of the vast collection. The loan agreement noted that during his life Kahn had expressed the wish that the records of his work be made available to "students of all ages and degrees." The university was considered the appropriate repository for this collection not only because Kahn, as the Paul Philippe Cret Professor of Architecture, had inspired a generation of architects, but also because he had designed for the university campus one of his most significant works, the Alfred Newton Richards Medical Research Building and Biology Building (1957–65).

The extent of the Kahn Collection's resources was staggering, including nearly 6,500 sketches by Kahn, 40,000 office drawings, Kahn's notebooks and sketchbooks, more than 15,000 photographs, 100 models, and 150 boxes of correspondence and project files, as well as his personal library, awards, and memorabilia. The first curator of the Kahn Collection was G. Holmes Perkins. As the legendary dean of the Graduate School of Fine Arts of the University of

The Louis I. Kahn Collection

Julia Moore Converse

Pennsylvania from 1951 to 1971, Perkins had hired Kahn as a professor of architecture in 1955. In 1979 Perkins oversaw the installation of the Kahn Collection in the university's historic Furness Building, where it was housed in its own quarters near the other collections of the Architectural Archives. The organization and cataloguing of Kahn's drawings, initiated immediately after his death by Luis Vincent Rivera and members of the Kahn office, was continued under Perkins's direction by graduate students in the master's and doctoral programs of the university. Major responsibilities were undertaken by Neslihan Dostoglu, with Enrique Vivoni, Peter S. Reed, and Peter Kohane. They were assisted by former Kahn associates who helped identify the drawings and clarify the design development within a given project. Contributors to this effort included Balkrishna Doshi, David Karp, Reyhan Tansal Larimer, Alan Levy, John MacAllister, Marshall Meyers, Harriet Pattison, David Polk, Luis Vincent Rivera, Galen Schlosser, Anne Griswold Tyng, Carles Vallhonrat, Henry Wilcots, David Wisdom, Cengiz Yetken, and many others.

Support for the microfilming, cataloguing, and archival housing of the collection was received from the National Endowment for the Arts, the Graham Foundation for Advanced Studies in the Fine Arts, and the International Union of Bricklayers and Allied Craftsmen. The Kahn Associates, a group of friends of the collection, contributed generously to the installation of the archives at the university, as did the many other individuals who responded wholeheartedly to the preservation needs of the collection. A special exhibition gallery for the collection was made possible through the generosity of Harvey and Irwin Kroiz.

The collection's six-year cataloguing project came to a successful completion with the publication in 1987 of Kahn's personal drawings. Although special exhibitions had been organized by the Kahn Collection and by other institutions, the first major retrospective of Kahn's life and work was still awaited. In 1983 professors David B. Brownlee and David G. De Long of the University of Pennsylvania initiated an intense period of scholarly research, with a view toward the eventual mounting of the long hoped for Kahn retrospective. A series of graduate seminars, directed by Brownlee and De Long, included the exhaustive review of all documents in the archives, a five-year process that involved more than fifty researchers. This unprecedented research from primary source materials produced a precisely documented list of Kahn's buildings and projects as well as a complete description of the sequence of design phases in Kahn's works, which frequently corrects previously published sources.

Peter Reed was selected as the director of research for the Kahn Collection retrospective project. Reed's long association with the collection had culminated in 1989 with the completion of his doctoral dissertation, *Toward Form: Louis I. Kahn's Urban Designs for Philadelphia, 1939–1962*, a landmark in Kahn scholarship. Working in close collaboration with Brownlee and De Long, Reed applied his knowledge of and familiarity with the records of Kahn's work to the supervision of research in the archives and the development of a timeline for the Kahn Collection's database. This database proved to be an extraordinary tool for research, providing access to detailed information on the day-to-day activities, travels, and project development at any given time in the Kahn office.

Since the establishment of the Kahn Collection at the university, published materials about Kahn have been collected by bibliographer Jean Bullitt Reeves. In 1990 Shilpa Mehta undertook the detailed documentation of Kahn's own words, including his published articles, unpublished manuscripts, and lectures. Culled from primary sources available only in the Kahn Collection, Mehta's annotated bibliography, published here with additions by David Brownlee and Peter Reed, is an important contribution to Kahn scholarship.

The Kahn Collection has continued to grow, enriched by the addition of drawings, photographs, and models. Most significant is Richard Saul Wurman's donation of an exceptional collection of original drawings, which has greatly strengthened the archival holdings of Kahn's travel sketches. Taped interviews with former Kahn associates, clients, and family members have also been added to the permanent collection, along with related research materials.

The Kahn Collection, whose very survival was once uncertain, is today visited by scholars, architects, and students from all over the world. It serves as the basis for true scholarly explorations into Kahn's life and work. The present book and exhibition seem a most fitting way to honor Kahn and to share with the world the riches of the Louis I. Kahn Collection.

Sesquicentennial International Exposition
Packer Avenue, 10th Street, Pattison Avenue, 11th Street, Government
Avenue, and 12th Street, Philadelphia, Pennsylvania
Chief of design for all buildings for the Exhibition Association
1925–26; built, demolished

Model Slum Rehabilitation Project
South Philadelphia, Pennsylvania
Architectural Research Group (Kahn, organizer and designer)
1933; unbuilt

Northeast Philadelphia Housing Corporation Housing Project
Algon Avenue, Faunce Street, Elgin Avenue, Frontenac Street, and
Cottman Avenue, Philadelphia, Pennsylvania
Architectural Research Group (Kahn, organizer and designer), associated
with Louis Magaziner and Victor Eberhard
1933; unbuilt

M. Buten Paint Store (alterations)
6711 Germantown Avenue, Philadelphia, Pennsylvania
Kahn and Hyman Cunin
1934; built, demolished

St. Katherine's Village Housing Project
Between Frankford Avenue and Pennsylvania Railroad right-of-way at
Liddonfield Station, Philadelphia, Pennsylvania
Magaziner and Eberhard, and Kahn
1935; unbuilt

Ahavath Israel Synagogue (now Grace Temple)
6735 North 16th Street, Philadelphia, Pennsylvania
1935–37; built

Jersey Homesteads (now Roosevelt Borough; housing, factory, school,
stores, pumping station, and sewage plant)
Near Hightstown, New Jersey
Kahn, assistant principal architect and co-designer with Alfred Kastner,
as employees of the Resettlement Administration
1935–37 (Kahn's employment); houses and factory built; sewage plant and
school built to Kastner's designs

Unidentified Housing Project
Magaziner and Eberhard, and Kahn
1936; unbuilt

Unidentified House
Magaziner and Eberhard, and Kahn
ca. 1936; unbuilt

Dr. David K. Waldman Dental Office (alterations)
5203 Chester Avenue, Philadelphia, Pennsylvania
1937; built

Prefabricated House Studies (sponsored by Samuel Fels)
Magaziner, Kahn, and Henry Klumb
1937–38; unbuilt

Horace Berk Memorial Hospital (now Philadelphia Psychiatric Hospital;
alterations)
1218–48 North 54th Street, Philadelphia, Pennsylvania
1937–38; unbuilt

Old Swedes' (or Southwark) Housing Project (housing and community
building)
Catherine Street, Swanson Street, Washington Avenue, 2nd Street,
Christian Street, and Front Street, Philadelphia, Pennsylvania
Kahn and Kenneth Day
1938–40; unbuilt

Pennsylvania Hospital (or Kirkbride's) Housing Project (housing and
community building)
Site bordered by Haverford Avenue, 42nd Street, Market Street, and
46th Street, Philadelphia, Pennsylvania
1939–40; unbuilt

Illustrations for United States Housing Authority Booklets: *Housing
Subsidies: How Much and Why?; Tax Exemption of Public Housing; The
Housing Shortage; Public Housing and the Negro; Housing and Juvenile
Delinquency*
1939; published

"Housing in the Rational City Plan" (panels for "Houses and Housing"
exhibition, organized by the United States Housing Authority)
Museum of Modern Art, New York
1939; executed

Philadelphia Psychiatric Hospital
Ford Road and Monument Avenue, Philadelphia, Pennsylvania
1939; unbuilt; commission reassigned to Thalheimer and Weitz

A. Abraham Apartment and Dental Office (alterations)
5105 Wayne Avenue, Philadelphia, Pennsylvania
1940; built

Van Pelt Court Apartments (for E. T. Pontz; alterations)
231 South Van Pelt Street, Philadelphia, Pennsylvania
1940; unbuilt

Battery Workers Union, Local 113 (now Commandment Keepers of the
House of God; alterations)
1903 West Allegheny Avenue, Philadelphia, Pennsylvania
1940; built

Mr. and Mrs. Jesse Oser House
628 Stetson Road, Elkins Park, Pennsylvania
1940–42; built

Pine Ford Acres (housing, community building, and maintenance
building)
Middletown, Pennsylvania
Howe and Kahn
1941–43; built, housing demolished

Pennypack Woods (housing, community building, and stores)
Philadelphia, Pennsylvania
Howe, Stonorov, and Kahn
1941–43; built

Buildings and Projects, 1925–74

Mr. and Mrs. Louis Broudo House
Juniper Park Development, Elkins Park, Pennsylvania
1941–42; unbuilt

Carver Court (or Foundry Street Housing; housing and community building)
Caln Township (near Coatesville), Pennsylvania
Howe, Stonorov, and Kahn
1941–43; built

M. Shapiro and Sons Prefabricated Houses
Newport News, Virginia
Stonorov and Kahn (Stonorov in charge)
1941–42; unbuilt

Stanton Road Dwellings (housing and community building)
Bruce Place, Stanton Road, Alabama Avenue, and 15th Street, S.E.,
Washington, D.C.
Howe and Kahn
1942–47; unbuilt

Willow Run (or Bomber City), **Neighborhood III** (housing and school)
Washtenaw County (near Ypsilanti), Michigan
Stonorov and Kahn
1942–43; unbuilt

Lincoln Highway Defense Housing (housing and community building)
Caln Road and Lincoln Highway, Caln Township (near Coatesville),
Pennsylvania
Stonorov, Howe, and Kahn
1942–44; built

House for 194X (sponsored by *Architectural Forum*)
Stonorov and Kahn
1942; not submitted, unbuilt

Lily Ponds Houses (housing and community building)
Anacostia, Eastern, and Kenilworth Avenues, N.E., Washington, D.C.
Stonorov and Kahn
1942–43; built, housing demolished

Hotel for 194X (sponsored by *Architectural Forum*)
Stonorov and Kahn
1943; published, unbuilt

International Ladies Garment Workers Union Health Center (now law offices; alterations)
2136 South 22nd Street, Philadelphia, Pennsylvania
Stonorov and Kahn
1943–45; built

Model Neighborhood Rehabilitation Project for *Why City Planning is Your Responsibility* (New York: Revere Copper and Brass, 1943)
Morris, 20th, McKean, and 22nd Streets, Philadelphia, Pennsylvania
Stonorov and Kahn (Stonorov in charge)
1943; published, unbuilt

"Design for Postwar Living" House (competition sponsored by *California Arts and Architecture*)
Stonorov and Kahn
1943; submitted, unbuilt

Model Neighborhood Rehabilitation Project (sponsored by Architects' Workshop on City Planning, Philadelphia Housing Association, and Citizens' Council on City Planning)
Moore Street, Howard Street, Water Street, Snyder Avenue, and Moyamensing Avenue, Philadelphia, Pennsylvania
Stonorov and Kahn
1943; model built and published in *You and Your Neighborhood: A Primer for Neighborhood Planning* (New York: Revere Copper and Brass, 1944)

Industrial Union of Marine and Shipbuilding Workers of America, Local 1 (alterations)
2332–34 Broadway, Camden, New Jersey
Stonorov and Kahn (Stonorov in charge)
1943–45; built

Phoenix Corporation Houses
Bridge Street, Phoenixville, Pennsylvania
Stonorov and Kahn (Stonorov in charge)
1943–44; unbuilt

Philadelphia Moving Picture Operators' Union
Vine and 13th Streets, Philadelphia, Pennsylvania
Stonorov and Kahn
1944; unbuilt

Parasol Houses (for Knoll Associates Planning Unit)
Stonorov and Kahn
1944; unbuilt

Model Men's Shoe Store and Furniture Store (for Pittsburgh Plate Glass)
Stonorov and Kahn
1944; published, unbuilt

Dimitri Petrov House (alterations and addition)
713 North 25th Street, Philadelphia, Pennsylvania
Stonorov and Kahn
1944–48; unbuilt

National Jewish Welfare Board (clubhouse furnishings)
Washington, D.C.
Stonorov and Kahn (Stonorov in charge)
1944; built

Paul W. Darrow House (adaptation of old power plant)
Vare Estate, Fort Washington, Pennsylvania
Stonorov and Kahn
1944–46; unbuilt

Philadelphia Psychiatric Hospital (new wing)
Philadelphia, Pennsylvania
Stonorov and Kahn; Isadore Rosenfield, hospital consultant
1944–46; unbuilt

Borough Hall (alterations)
Phoenixville, Pennsylvania
Stonorov and Kahn (Stonorov in charge)
1944; unbuilt

Dr. and Mrs. Alexander Moskalik House (alterations)
2018 Spruce Street, Philadelphia, Pennsylvania
Stonorov and Kahn
1944–45; built

Radbill Oil Company (renovation of offices)
1722–24 Chestnut Street (second floor), Philadelphia, Pennsylvania
Stonorov and Kahn
1944–47; built

Westminster Play Lot
Markoe Street, Westminster Avenue, and June Street, Philadelphia, Pennsylvania
Stonorov and Kahn
ca. 1945; unbuilt

Unidentified House
Stonorov and Kahn
ca. 1945; unbuilt

Mr. and Mrs. Edward Gallob House (alterations)
2035 Rittenhouse Square Street, Philadelphia, Pennsylvania
1945–47; unbuilt

Gimbels Department Store (interior alterations)
8th and Market Streets, Philadelphia, Pennsylvania
Stonorov and Kahn (Stonorov in charge)
1945–46; built, demolished

"House for Cheerful Living" (competition sponsored by Pittsburgh Plate Glass and *Pencil Points*)
Stonorov and Kahn
1945; submitted, unbuilt

Business Neighborhood in 194X (advertisement for Barrett Division, Allied Chemical and Dye Corporation)
Stonorov and Kahn
1945; published, unbuilt

B. A. Bernard House (addition)
195 Hare's Hill Road at Camp Council Road, Kimberton, Pennsylvania
Stonorov and Kahn
1945; built

Department of Neurology, Jefferson Medical College (alterations)
1025 Walnut Street, Philadelphia, Pennsylvania
Stonorov and Kahn
1945–46; built

Mr. and Mrs. Samuel Radbill Residence (alterations)
224 Bowman Avenue, Merion, Pennsylvania
Stonorov and Kahn
1945–46; partially built

William H. Harman Corporation Prefabricated Houses
420 Pickering Road, Charlestown, Chester County, Pennsylvania; Rosedale Avenue and New Street, West Chester, Pennsylvania
Stonorov and Kahn (Stonorov in charge)
1945–47; built, some demolition

Drs. Lea and Arthur Finkelstein House (addition)
645 Overhill Road, Ardmore, Pennsylvania
Stonorov and Kahn
1945–48; unbuilt

Pennsylvania Solar House (for Libbey-Owens-Ford Glass Company)
Stonorov and Kahn
1945–47; published, unbuilt

"Action for Cities" (panel for "American Housing" exhibition)
France
1945–46; executed

Thom McAn Shoe Store (alterations)
72 South 69th Street, Upper Darby, Pennsylvania
Stonorov and Kahn
1945–46; unbuilt

Two Dormitories, Camp Hofnung
Pipersville, Bucks County, Pennsylvania
Stonorov and Kahn
1945–47; built

Philadelphia Building, International Ladies Garment Workers Union
Unity House, Forest Park, Pike County, Pennsylvania
Stonorov and Kahn
1945–47; built

Mr. and Mrs. Arthur V. Hooper House (addition)
5820 Pimlico Road, Baltimore, Maryland
Stonorov and Kahn
1946; unbuilt

Container Corporation of America (cafeteria, offices, and depot)
Nixon and Fountain Streets, Manayunk, Philadelphia, Pennsylvania
Stonorov and Kahn
1946; unbuilt

Memorial Playground, Western Home for Children
715 Christian Street, Philadelphia, Pennsylvania
Stonorov and Kahn
1946–47; built, demolished

Triangle Redevelopment Project
Benjamin Franklin Parkway, Market Street, and Schuylkill River, Philadelphia, Pennsylvania
Associated City Planners (Kahn, Oscar Stonorov, Robert Wheelwright, Markley Stevenson, and C. Harry Johnson)
1946–48; unbuilt

Tana Hoban Studio (alterations)
2018 Rittenhouse Square Street, Philadelphia, Pennsylvania
Stonorov and Kahn
1947; unbuilt

Coward Shoe Store (now Lerner Woman)
1118 Chestnut Street, Philadelphia, Pennsylvania
Stonorov and Kahn (Stonorov in charge)
1947–49; built, altered

Dr. and Mrs. Philip Q. Roche House
2101 Harts Lane, Conshohocken, Pennsylvania
Stonorov and Kahn
1947–49; built

X-ray Department, Graduate Hospital, University of Pennsylvania
(alteration)
Lombard and 19th Streets, Philadelphia, Pennsylvania
1947–48; built

Mr. and Mrs. Harry A. Ehle House
Mulberry Lane, Haverford, Pennsylvania
Kahn and Abel Sorensen
1947–48; unbuilt

Jefferson National Expansion Memorial (competition, first stage)
St. Louis, Missouri
1947; submitted, unbuilt

Mr. and Mrs. Morton Weiss House
2935 Whitehall Road, East Norriton Township, Pennsylvania
1947–50; built

Dr. and Mrs. Winslow T. Tompkins House
Lot 18, Apologen Road, Philadelphia, Pennsylvania
1947–49; unbuilt

M. Buten Paint Store (alterations)
Kaighns and Haddon Avenues, Camden, New Jersey
Kahn and George Von Uffel, Jr.
1947–48; built, demolished

Mr. and Mrs. Harry Kitnick House
2935 Whitehall Road, East Norriton Township, Pennsylvania
1948–49; unbuilt

Mr. and Mrs. Joseph Rossman House (alteration)
1714 Rittenhouse Square Street, Philadelphia, Pennsylvania
1948–49; unbuilt

Jewish Community Center
1186 Chapel Street, New Haven, Connecticut
Kahn, consultant architect; associated with Jacob Weinstein and
Charles Abramowitz, Architects
1948–54; built, altered

**Bernard S. Pincus Building and Samuel Radbill Building, Philadelphia
Psychiatric Hospital**
Kahn; Isadore Rosenfield, hospital consultant
1948–54; built, altered

Mr. and Mrs. Samuel Genel House
201 Indian Creek Road, Wynnewood, Pennsylvania
1948–51; built

Jewish Agency for Palestine Emergency Housing
Israel
1949; unbuilt

Dr. and Mrs. Jacob Sherman House (alterations)
414 Sycamore Avenue, Merion, Pennsylvania
1949–51; unbuilt

Mr. and Mrs. Nelson J. Leidner House (addition to former Oser House)
626 Stetson Road, Elkins Park, Pennsylvania
1950–51; built, addition demolished

Ashton Best Corporation Garden Apartments
200 Montgomery Avenue, Ardmore, Pennsylvania
1950; unbuilt

American Federation of Labor Health Center, St. Luke's Hospital
(now Girard Medical Center; alterations)
Franklin and Thompson Streets, Philadelphia, Pennsylvania
1950–51; built, demolished

Southwest Temple Public Housing
Philadelphia, Pennsylvania
Kahn, consultant architect; Architects Associated (1951–52): Kenneth
Day, Louis E. McAllister, Sr., George Braik, Anne Tyng
1950–52; unbuilt

East Poplar Public Housing
Philadelphia, Pennsylvania
Architects Associated: Kahn, Day, McAllister, Braik
1950–52; unbuilt

University of Pennsylvania Study (for Philadelphia City Planning
Commission)
Philadelphia, Pennsylvania
Architects Associated: Kahn, Day, McAllister, Braik, Tyng
1951; unbuilt

Row House Studies (for Philadelphia City Planning Commission)
Philadelphia, Pennsylvania
Architects Associated: Kahn, Day, McAllister, Braik, Tyng
1951–53; unbuilt

Traffic Studies
Philadelphia, Pennsylvania
1951–53; unbuilt

Yale University Art Gallery
1111 Chapel Street, New Haven, Connecticut
Kahn and Douglas Orr, associated architects
1951–53; built

Mr. and Mrs. H. Leonard Fruchter House
51st Street and City Line Avenue, Philadelphia, Pennsylvania
1951–54; unbuilt

Penn Center Studies
Philadelphia, Pennsylvania
1951–58; unbuilt

Mill Creek Project (first-phase housing)
46th and Aspen Streets, Philadelphia, Pennsylvania
Kahn, Day, Braik, McAllister
1951–56; built

Cinberg House (alterations)
5112 North Broad Street, Philadelphia, Pennsylvania
1952; unbuilt

Zoob and Matz Offices (alterations)
1600 Western Saving Fund Building, Philadelphia, Pennsylvania
1952; built

Apartment Redevelopment Project
New Haven, Connecticut
Published in *Perspecta*, 1953

Riverview Competition
State Road at Rhawn Street, Philadelphia, Pennsylvania
Kahn and Tyng, associated architects
1953; unbuilt

City Tower Project
Philadelphia, Pennsylvania
Kahn and Tyng, associated architects
1952–57; unbuilt

Ralph Roberts House
Schoolhouse Lane, Germantown, Philadelphia, Pennsylvania
1953; unbuilt

Adath Jeshurun Synagogue and School Building
6730 Old York Road, Philadelphia, Pennsylvania
1954–55; unbuilt

Dr. and Mrs. Francis H. Adler House
Davidson Road, Philadelphia, Pennsylvania
1954–55; unbuilt

Mr. and Mrs. Weber DeVore House
Montgomery Avenue, Springfield Township, Pennsylvania
1954–ca. 1955; unbuilt

American Federation of Labor Medical Services Building
1326–34 Vine Street, Philadelphia, Pennsylvania
1954–57; built, demolished

Jewish Community Center (bathhouse, day camp, and community building)
999 Lower Ferry Road, Ewing Township (near Trenton), New Jersey
Kahn, architect; John M. Hirsh and Stanley R. Dube, supervising architects; Louis Kaplan, associated architect
1954–59; bathhouse and day camp built

Dr. and Mrs. Francis H. Adler House (kitchen remodeling)
7630 Huron Avenue, Philadelphia, Pennsylvania
1955; built

Wharton Esherick Workshop (addition)
Horseshoe Trail, Paoli, Pennsylvania
1955–56; built

Mr. and Mrs. Lawrence Morris House
Mt. Kisco, New York
1955–58; unbuilt

Washington University Library Competition
St. Louis, Missouri
1956; submitted, unbuilt

Enrico Fermi Memorial
Fort Dearborn, Chicago, Illinois
1956–57; unbuilt

Civic Center Studies
Philadelphia, Pennsylvania
1956–57; unbuilt

Research Institute for Advanced Science
Near Baltimore, Maryland
1956–58; unbuilt

Mill Creek Project (second-phase housing and community center)
46th Street and Fairmount Avenue, Philadelphia, Pennsylvania
1956–63; built

Mr. and Mrs. Irving L. Shaw House (additions and alterations)
2129 Cypress Street, Philadelphia, Pennsylvania
1956–59; built

Dr. and Mrs. Bernard Shapiro House
417 Hidden River Road, Narberth, Pennsylvania
1956–62; built (addition by Kahn and Tyng, associated architects; completed by Tyng, 1975)

Mr. and Mrs. Eugene Lewis House
2018 Rittenhouse Square Street, Philadelphia, Pennsylvania
1957; unbuilt

American Federation of Labor Medical Center (Red Cross Building; remodeling of hospital and office building)
253 North Broad Street, Philadelphia, Pennsylvania
1957–59; unbuilt

Fred E. and Elaine Cox Clever House
417 Sherry Way, Cherry Hill, New Jersey
1957–62; built

Alfred Newton Richards Medical Research Building and Biology Building (now David Goddard Laboratories), **University of Pennsylvania**
3700 Hamilton Walk, Philadelphia, Pennsylvania
1957–65; built

Mount St. Joseph Academy and Chestnut Hill College
Chestnut Hill, Philadelphia, Pennsylvania
1958; unbuilt

Zoob and Matz Offices (alterations)
Western Saving Fund Building (14th floor), Philadelphia, Pennsylvania
1958; built

Tribune Review Publishing Company Building
Cabin Hill Drive, Greensburg, Pennsylvania
1958–62; built

Mr. and Mrs. M. Morton Goldenberg House
Frazier Road, Rydal, Pennsylvania
1959; unbuilt

Robert H. Fleisher House
8363 Fisher Road, Elkins Park, Pennsylvania
1959; unbuilt

Space Environment Studies (for General Electric Co., Missile and Space
Vehicle Department)
Philadelphia, Pennsylvania
Kahn, consultant architect
1959; unexecuted

Awbury Arboretum Housing Development (for International Ladies
Garment Workers Union)
Walnut Lane, Ardleigh Street, and Tulpehocken Street, Philadelphia,
Pennsylvania
1959–60; unbuilt

Margaret Esherick House
204 Sunrise Lane, Chestnut Hill, Philadelphia, Pennsylvania
1959–61; built

U.S. Consulate and Residence
Luanda, Angola
1959–62; unbuilt

Salk Institute for Biological Studies (laboratory, meeting house, and
housing)
10010 North Torrey Pines Road, La Jolla, California
1959–65; laboratory built

First Unitarian Church and School
220 South Winton Road, Rochester, New York
1959–69; built

Fine Arts Center, School, and Performing Arts Theater (now
Performing Arts Center)
303 East Main Street, Fort Wayne, Indiana
Kahn, architect; T. Richard Shoaff, supervising architect
1959–73; theater and offices built

Bristol Township Municipal Building
2501 Oxford Valley Road, Levittown, Pennsylvania
1960–61; unbuilt

General Motors Exhibit, 1964 World's Fair
Grand Central Parkway and Long Island Expressway, New York,
New York
1960–61; unbuilt

Barge for the American Wind Symphony Orchestra
River Thames, England
1960–61; built

Market Street East Studies
Philadelphia, Pennsylvania
1960–63; unbuilt

University of Virginia Chemistry Building
Charlottesville, Virginia
Kahn, architect for design; Stainback and Scribner, architects
1960–63; unbuilt

Eleanor Donnelley Erdman Hall, Bryn Mawr College
Morris and Gulph Roads, Bryn Mawr, Pennsylvania
1960–65; built

Philadelphia College of Art (now University of the Arts)
Broad and Pine Streets, Philadelphia, Pennsylvania
1960–66; unbuilt

Franklin Delano Roosevelt Memorial Competition
West Potomac Park, Washington, D.C.
1960; unbuilt

Dr. and Mrs. Norman Fisher House
197 East Mill Road, Hatboro, Pennsylvania
1960–67; built

Carborundum Company Warehouses and Offices
Chicago, Illinois; Mountain View, California; and Niagara Falls,
New York
1961; built

Plymouth Swim Club
Gallagher Road, Montgomery County, Pennsylvania
1961; unbuilt

Shapero Hall of Pharmacy, Wayne State University
Detroit, Michigan
1961–62; unbuilt

Carborundum Company Warehouses and Offices
Atlanta, Georgia
1961–62; unbuilt

Gandhinagar, Capital of Gujarat State, India
1961–66; unbuilt

Levy Memorial Playground
Between 102nd and 105th Streets in Riverside Park,
New York, New York
Isamu Noguchi, sculptor; Louis I. Kahn, architect
1961–66; unbuilt

Mikveh Israel Synagogue
Commerce Street between 4th and 5th Streets, Philadelphia,
Pennsylvania
1961–72; unbuilt

Lawrence Memorial Hall of Science, University of California Competition
Berkeley, California
1962; unbuilt

Mrs. C. Parker House (addition to former Esherick House)
204 Sunrise Lane, Chestnut Hill, Philadelphia, Pennsylvania
1962–64; unbuilt

Delaware Valley Mental Health Foundation, Family and Patient Dwelling
833 Butler Avenue, Doylestown, Pennsylvania
1962–71; unbuilt

Indian Institute of Management
Vikram Sarabhai Road, Ahmedabad, India
1962–74; built

Sher-e-Bangla Nagar, Capital of Bangladesh
Dhaka, Bangladesh
1962–83; built (design and construction completed after Kahn's death by David Wisdom and Associates)

Peabody Museum, Hall of Ocean Life, Yale University
New Haven, Connecticut
1963–65; unbuilt

President's Estate, First Capital of Pakistan
Islamabad, Pakistan
1963–66; unbuilt

Barge for the American Wind Symphony Orchestra
Pittsburgh, Pennsylvania
1964–67; built

Interama Community B
Miami, Florida
Kahn, architect; Watson, Deutschman & Kruse, associate architects
1963–69; unbuilt

St. Andrew's Priory
Hidden Valley Road, Valyermo, California
1961–67; unbuilt

Maryland Institute College of Art
Site bordered by Park Avenue, Howard Street, and Dolphin Street, Baltimore, Maryland
1965–69; unbuilt

The Dominican Motherhouse of St. Catherine de Ricci
Providence Road, Media, Pennsylvania
1965–69; unbuilt

Library and Dining Hall, Phillips Exeter Academy
Exeter, New Hampshire
1965–72; built

Broadway United Church of Christ and Office Building
Broadway and Seventh Avenue between 56th and 57th Streets, New York, New York
1966–68; unbuilt

Mr. and Mrs. Max L. Raab House
Waverly, Addison, and 21st Streets, Philadelphia, Pennsylvania
1966–68; unbuilt

Olivetti-Underwood Factory
Valley View Road and Township Line, Harrisburg, Pennsylvania
1966–70; built

Mr. and Mrs. Philip M. Stern House
2710 Chain Bridge Road, Washington, D.C.
1966–70; unbuilt

Kimbell Art Museum
3333 Camp Bowie Boulevard, Fort Worth, Texas
Kahn, architect; Preston Geren, associate architect
1966–72; built

Memorial to the Six Million Jewish Martyrs
Battery Park, New York, New York
1966–72; unbuilt

Temple Beth-El Synagogue
220 South Bedford Road, Chappaqua, New York
1966–72; built

Kansas City Office Building
Walnut, 11th, and Grand Streets (site 1); Main, Baltimore, 11th, and 12th Streets (site 2); Kansas City, Missouri
1966–73; unbuilt

Rittenhouse Square Housing
Philadelphia, Pennsylvania
1967; unbuilt

Hurva Synagogue
Jerusalem, Israel
1967–74; unbuilt

Hill Renewal and Redevelopment Project (housing and school)
New Haven, Connecticut
1967–74; unbuilt

Albie Booth Boys Club
1968; unbuilt

Palazzo dei Congressi
Giardini Pubblici (site 1); Arsenale (site 2); Venice, Italy
1968–74; unbuilt

Wolfson Center for Mechanical and Transportation Engineering (mechanical and electrical buildings)
Tel Aviv, Israel
Kahn, architect; J. Mochly-I. Eldar, Ltd., resident architect
1968–74; mechanical building built, 1976–77, after Kahn's design, by J. Mochly-I. Eldar, Ltd.

Raab Dual Movie Theater
2021–23 Sansom Street, Philadelphia, Pennsylvania
1969–70; unbuilt

Rice University Art Center
Houston, Texas
1969–70; unbuilt

Inner Harbor
Pratt and Light Streets, Baltimore, Maryland
Kahn, architect; Ballinger Company, associate architects
1969–73; unbuilt

Yale Center for British Art
1080 Chapel Street, New Haven, Connecticut
1969–74; built (design and construction completed after Kahn's death by
Pellecchia and Meyers, Architects)

John F. Kennedy Hospital (addition)
Philadelphia, Pennsylvania
1970–71; unbuilt

President's House, University of Pennsylvania (alterations and
additions)
2216 Spruce Street, Philadelphia, Pennsylvania
1970–71; built

Family Planning Center and Maternal Health Center
Ram Sam Path, Kathmandu, Nepal
1970–75; partially built

Treehouse, Eagleville Hospital and Rehabilitation Center
Eagleville, Pennsylvania
1971; unbuilt

Washington Square East Unit 2 Redevelopment
Philadelphia, Pennsylvania
ca. 1971; unbuilt

Bicentennial Exposition
Eastwick, Southwest Philadelphia, Pennsylvania
Kahn with a team of architects
1971–73; unbuilt

Mr. and Mrs. Steven Korman House
6019 Sheaf Lane, Fort Washington, Pennsylvania
1971–73; built

Mr. and Mrs. Harold A. Honickman House
Sheaf Lane, Fort Washington, Pennsylvania
1971–74; unbuilt

Government House Hill Development
Jerusalem, Israel
1971–73; unbuilt

Graduate Theological Union Library
Ridge Road and Scenic Avenue, Berkeley, California
Schematic design by Kahn
1971–74; designed and built after Kahn's death by Esherick Homsey
Dodge and Davis, and Peters Clayberg & Caulfield

De Menil Foundation (now Menil Collection)
Yupon, Sul Ross, Mulberry, and Branard Streets, Houston, Texas
1972–74; unbuilt

Independence Mall Area Redevelopment (in conjunction with
Bicentennial)
Philadelphia, Pennsylvania
1972–74; unbuilt

Pocono Arts Center
Luzerne County, Pennsylvania
1972–74; unbuilt

Rabat Project (cultural and commercial complex)
Bou-Regreg zone on the River Oued, Rabat, Morocco
1973–74; unbuilt

Franklin Delano Roosevelt Memorial
Roosevelt Island, New York
1973–74; unbuilt

Abbasabad Development (financial, commercial, and residential areas)
Tehran, Iran
Kahn and Kenzo Tange
1973–74; unbuilt

Bishop Field Estate
Lenox, Massachusetts
1973–74; designed and built after Kahn's death based on Kahn's site plan

1875
Leopold Kahn born, Estonia
1878
Bertha Mendelsohn (Kahn) born, Latvia
1901
February 20, Louis Isadore Kahn born, Kingisepp, Saaremaa, Estonia
1904
Leopold Kahn immigrates to Philadelphia
1906
Bertha Kahn and three children (Louis, Sarah, and Oscar) immigrate to Philadelphia
1908–12
Louis Kahn attends elementary school (Landberger School), 4th and George Streets, Philadelphia
1912–16
Attends grammar school (General Philip Kearny School), Sixth and Fairmount Streets, Philadelphia. Also attends Public Industrial Art School, 13th and Master Streets, Philadelphia
1913
First prize in City Art Contest, sponsored by John Wanamaker, Philadelphia
1915
May 4, becomes naturalized citizen, along with parents, brother, and sister
1916–20
Attends Central High School, Broad and Green Streets, Philadelphia. Also attends Graphic Sketch Club (Fleisher Art Memorial), 719 Catherine Street, and Pennsylvania Academy of the Fine Arts, Philadelphia
1919
First prize for best drawing by high school student, Pennsylvania Academy of the Fine Arts, Philadelphia
1920–24
Attends School of Fine Arts, University of Pennsylvania, Philadelphia
1921
July–September, draftsman, Hoffman and Henon, Philadelphia
1922
June–September, draftsman, Hewitt and Ash, Philadelphia
1924
Society of Beaux-Arts Architects, two Second Medals
Arthur Spayd Brooke Memorial Prize, University of Pennsylvania
June, Bachelor of Architecture, University of Pennsylvania
1924–25
July 1924–June 1925, senior draftsman, office of John Molitor, City Architect, Philadelphia
1925–26
July 1925–October 1926, chief of design, Sesquicentennial Exposition, Philadelphia
1926–27
November 1926–March 1927, senior draftsman, office of John Molitor, City Architect, Philadelphia
1927–28
April 1927–March 1928, designer, office of William H. Lee, Philadelphia
1928–29
April 1928–April 1929. European tour. Travels through England, the Netherlands, Germany, Denmark, Sweden, Finland, Estonia, Latvia, Lithuania, Czechoslovakia, Hungary, Austria, Italy, Switzerland, France. Returns to Philadelphia via England
1929
November–December, exhibition of travel sketches, Pennsylvania Academy of the Fine Arts

1929–30
May 1929–September 1930, designer, office of Paul P. Cret, Philadelphia
1930
August 14, marries Esther Virginia Israeli (born 1905, Philadelphia)
Moves into Israeli family residence, 5243 Chester Avenue, Philadelphia
1930–32
December 1930–February 1932, designer, Zantzinger, Borie, and Medary, Architects, Philadelphia
1932–34
March 1932–May 1934, organizer and director, Architectural Research Group, Philadelphia
1933–35
December 1933–December 1935, squad head in charge of housing studies, City Planning Commission, Philadelphia
1935
Registered architect. Establishes independent practice
1935–37
December 1935–March 1937, assistant principal architect, Resettlement Administration, Washington, D.C. (principal architect, Alfred Kastner)
1937
Opens office at 1701 Walnut Street; shares space with Magaziner and Eberhard
1939
January–May, technical advisor, Informational Service Division, United States Housing Authority
1941
April, becomes associate of George Howe, moves office to Bulletin Building, Philadelphia
1942
February, termination of Howe's association with Kahn. Stonorov and Kahn continue practice
1946
Vice president, American Society of Planners and Architects
1947
March, Kahn and Stonorov terminate association
Moves office to 1728 Spruce Street, Philadelphia
President, American Society of Planners and Architects
May, first serves on thesis juries at Princeton University
Fall, visiting critic in advanced design, Yale University. Subsequently named chief critic in architectural design, Yale University
1949
April, travels to Israel and Paris
1950–51
December 1950–February 1951, resident architect, American Academy in Rome. January 5–February 2, 1951, travels to Egypt and Greece. Returns to Philadelphia via Paris
1951
Moves office to 138 South 20th Street, Philadelphia
1952
Medal of achievement, New York Chapter, American Institute of Architects
1953
Fellow, American Institute of Architects
1955–74
Professor of architecture, University of Pennsylvania, Philadelphia
1956
Albert F. Bemis Professor of Architecture and Planning, Massachusetts Institute of Technology

Chronology

1959
September, CIAM Conference (Team X), Otterlo, Holland. Travels to Albi, Carcassonne, and Ronchamp
1960
May, participant, World Design Conference, Tokyo, Japan
May, Arnold W. Brunner Memorial Prize, National Institute of Arts and Letters
1961
February, grant from the Graham Foundation for Advanced Studies in the Visual Arts for the study of city planning
June–July, single-building exhibition of Richards Medical Research Building, Museum of Modern Art, New York
1961–67
Class of 1913 Visiting Lecturer, Princeton University
1962
March, moves office to 1501 Walnut Street, Philadelphia
March, Philadelphia Art Alliance Medal for Achievement in Architecture
March, exhibition of drawings at Graham Foundation, Chicago
June, Philadelphia Arts Festival Award
1964
Member, National Institute of Arts and Letters
Gold Medal of Achievement, Directors Club of Philadelphia
Honorary Doctor, Politecnico di Milano
Honorary Doctor of Humanities, School of Design, University of North Carolina
Frank P. Brown Medal, Franklin Institute, Philadelphia
1965
May–June, USIA "Architecture USA" tour of Russia
June, Honorary Doctor of Fine Arts, Yale University
Month? Exhibition, La Jolla Museum of Art
Medal of Honor, Danish Architectural Association
1966
April–May, retrospective exhibition, Museum of Modern Art, New York
Appointed Paul Philippe Cret Professor of Architecture, University of Pennsylvania
Annual Award, Philadelphia Sketch Club
Member, Royal Swedish Academy of Fine Arts
1967
Moves into residence at 921 Clinton Street, Philadelphia
Honorary Doctor of Laws, LaSalle College, Philadelphia
Honorary Member, College of Architects, Peru
1968
Fellow, American Academy of Arts and Sciences
Honorary Doctor of Fine Arts, Maryland Institute, Baltimore
Member, City of Philadelphia Art Commission
1969
January, single-building exhibition of Palazzo dei Congressi, Biennale, Venice
February, exhibition, Eidgenössische Technische Hochschule, Zurich
Centennial Gold Medal, Philadelphia Chapter, American Institute of Architects
1970
Honorary Doctor of Arts, Bard College
Gold Medal of Honor, New York Chapter, American Institute of Architects
Fellow, Royal Society of Arts, London
1971
Gold Medal, American Institute of Architects
Philadelphia Bok Award
Golden Plate Award, American Academy of Achievement

Doctor of Fine Arts, University of Pennsylvania
Fellow, Franklin Institute, Philadelphia
Member, Academy of Arts and Letters
1972
Honorary Doctor of Laws, Tulane University
Creative Arts Award in Architecture, Brandeis University
Gold Medal, Royal Institute of British Architects
Member, Royal Institute of Architects, Ireland
1973
Gold Medal for Architecture, National Institute of Arts and Letters
1974
March 17, dies of heart attack at Pennsylvania Station, New York, on return from Ahmedabad, India. Buried at Montefiore Cemetery, Fox Chase, Pennsylvania
June, Doctor of Humane Letters, Columbia University (posthumous award)
1977
Furness Prize, Pennsylvania Academy of the Fine Arts (posthumous award)
1979
American Institute of Architects Twenty-five Year Award for the Yale University Art Gallery
1989
Aga Khan Award for Architecture for the National Assembly Building, Sher-e-Bangla Nagar, Dhaka, Bangladesh

Brown, Jack Perry. *Louis Kahn in the Midwest*. Chicago: Art Institute of Chicago, 1989.

————, comp. *Louis I. Kahn: A Bibliography*. Garland Reference Library of the Humanities, vol. 678. New York: Garland Publishing, 1987.

Burton, Joseph Arnold. "The Architectural Hieroglyphics of Louis I. Kahn, Architecture as Logos." Ph.D. diss., University of Pennsylvania, Philadelphia, 1982.

Büttiker, Urs. *Entwerfen mit Licht: Lernen von Louis I. Kahn*. Basel: Birkhäuser, in press.

Chang, Ching-Yu, ed. "Louis I. Kahn: Silence and Light," *Architecture and Urbanism* 3, no. 1, special issue (January 1973).

Fusaro, Florindo. *Il Parlamento e la nuova capital a Dacca di Louis I. Kahn, 1962/1974*. Rome: Officina Edizioni, 1985.

Giurgola, Romaldo, and Jaimini Mehta. *Louis I. Kahn*. Boulder, Colo.: Westview Press, 1975.

Hochstim, Jan. *The Paintings and Sketches of Louis I. Kahn*. New York: Rizzoli International Publications, 1991.

Hubert, Bruno J. *Le Yale Center for British Art (Louis I. Kahn)*. Marseilles: Editions Parenthèses, 1991.

Kimbell Art Museum. *Light Is the Theme: Louis I. Kahn and the Kimbell Art Museum*. Fort Worth, Tex.: Kimbell Art Foundation, 1975.

————. *Louis I. Kahn: Sketches for the Kimbell Art Museum*. Essay by Marshall D. Meyers. Fort Worth, Tex.: Kimbell Art Foundation, 1978.

Komendant, August E. *18 Years with Architect Louis I. Kahn*. Englewood, N.J.: Aloray Publishers, 1975.

La Jolla Museum of Art. *The Works of Louis I. Kahn*. Introduction by Vincent J. Scully. La Jolla, Calif.: La Jolla Museum of Art, 1965.

Latour, Alessandra. *Louis I. Kahn: Writings, Lectures, Interviews*. New York: Rizzoli International Publications, 1991.

————, ed. *Louis I. Kahn: L'uomo, il maestro*. Rome: Edizioni Kappa, 1986.

Lobell, John. *Between Silence and Light: Spirit in the Architecture of Louis I. Kahn*. Boulder, Colo.: Shambhala, 1979.

Loud, Patricia Cummings. *The Art Museums of Louis I. Kahn*. Durham, N.C., and London: Duke University Press in association with Duke University Museum of Art, 1989.

"Louis I. Kahn," *Architecture + Urbanism*, special issue (1975).

The Louis I. Kahn Archive: Personal Drawings. 7 vols. New York: Garland Publishing, 1987.

"Louis I. Kahn: Oeuvres 1963–1969," *L'architecture d'aujourd'hui* 40, no. 142, special issue (February–March 1969): 1–100.

"Louis Kahn," *L'architecture d'aujourd'hui* 33, no. 105 (December 1962–January 1963): [1]–39.

Max Protetch Gallery, *Louis I. Kahn: Drawings*. Los Angeles: Access Press, 1981.

"The Mind of Louis I. Kahn," *Architectural Forum* 137, no. 1 (July–August 1972): 42–89.

Nakamura, Toshio, ed. "Louis I. Kahn: Conception and Meaning," *Architecture + Urbanism*, special issue (November 1983).

Norberg-Schulz, Christian. *Louis I. Kahn: Idea e immagine*. Rome: Officina Edizioni, 1980.

Pennsylvania Academy of the Fine Arts. *The Travel Sketches of Louis I. Kahn*. Introduction by Vincent J. Scully, catalogue by William G. Holman. Philadelphia: Pennsylvania Academy of the Fine Arts, 1978.

Prown, Jules David. *The Architecture of the Yale Center for British Art*. New Haven, Conn.: Yale University, 1977.

Reed, Peter Shedd. "Toward Form: Louis I. Kahn's Urban Designs for Philadelphia, 1939–1962." Ph.D. diss., University of Pennsylvania, Philadelphia, 1989.

Roca, Miguel Angel. *Louis Kahn: Arquetipos y Modernidad*. Buenos Aires: Ediciones Summa, 1984.

Ronner, Heinz, and Sharad Jhaveri, *Louis I. Kahn: Complete Work, 1935–1974*. 2d ed. Basel and Boston: Birkhäuser, 1987.

Sabini, Maurizio, ed. "Louis I. Kahn 1901/1974." *Rassegna* 21, no. 1, special issue (March 1985).

Scully, Vincent J. *Louis I. Kahn*. New York: George Braziller, 1962.

Tyng, Alexandra. *Beginnings: Louis I. Kahn's Philosophy of Architecture*. New York: John Wiley & Sons, 1984.

Vivoni-Farage, Enrique. "A Measure of Silence: A Theory of the Transformation of the Wall." Ph.D. diss., University of Pennsylvania, Philadelphia, 1985.

Wurman, Richard Saul, ed. *What Will Be Has Always Been: The Words of Louis I. Kahn*. New York: Access Press and Rizzoli International Publications, 1986.

Wurman, Richard Saul, and Eugene Feldman, eds. *The Notebooks and Drawings of Louis I. Kahn*. 2d ed. Cambridge, Mass., and London: MIT Press, 1973.

Selected Bibliography

This is a chronological list of Kahn's principal published and unpublished lectures, interviews, and articles. The initial entry of a title usually coincides with its earliest publication date. Below this are then listed manuscripts and transcripts, in most cases from the holdings in the Kahn Collection. These are followed by subsequent reprints, translations, and substantial excerpts, in chronological order. Titles that were first published long after Kahn's death are placed at the time they were first written or spoken. Only precisely documented material has been included, and there has been no attempt to integrate the many quotations and short excerpts that pepper publications about Kahn. Not included in this list are Kahn's notebooks (there are six in the Kahn Collection), untranscribed tape recordings, and films. Researchers should also consult *Louis I. Kahn: A Bibliography*, by Jack Perry Brown, and *Louis I. Kahn: Writings, Lectures, Interviews*, edited by Alessandra Latour. They are invited to bring additional material to the attention of the Kahn Collection, Architectural Archives of the University of Pennsylvania, Philadelphia, Pennsylvania 19104-6311.

"The Value and Aim in Sketching." *T-Square Club Journal* (Philadelphia) 1, no. 6 (May 1931): 4, 18–21.
• Translated in *Rassegna* 21, no. 1 (March 1985): 24–25.

Howe, George, Oscar Stonorov, and Louis I. Kahn. "Standards Versus Essential Space: Comments on Unit Plans for War Housing." *Architectural Forum* 76, no. 5 (May 1942): 308–11.

Stonorov, Oscar, and Louis I. Kahn. *Why City Planning Is Your Responsibility*. New York: Revere Copper and Brass, 1943.

Stonorov, Oscar, and Louis I. Kahn. *You and Your Neighborhood: A Primer for Neighborhood Planning*. New York: Revere Copper and Brass, 1944.

"Can Neighborhoods Exist?" [1944] MS for screenplay version of the 1944 Revere Copper booklet. Stonorov Papers, Box 22, American Heritage Center, University of Wyoming, Laramie.

"Monumentality." In *New Architecture and City Planning, A Symposium*, edited by Paul Zucker, 577–88. New York: Philosophical Library, 1944.
• Excerpt in Alexandra Tyng, *Beginnings: Louis I. Kahn's Philosophy of Architecture*, 59. New York: John Wiley & Sons, 1984 (hereafter cited as Tyng, *Beginnings*).
• Reprinted and translated in *Louis I. Kahn: L'uomo, il maestro*, edited by Alessandra Latour, 433–41. Rome: Edizioni Kappa, 1986.

"A Dairy Farm: The Whitney Warren Prize." *Bulletin of the Beaux-Arts Institute of Design* 25, no. 3 (May 1949): 36–37. Warren Prize competition program.
• "A Dairy Farm." [1948] MS. "Programs 1948–49, Beaux-Arts Institute of Design," Box LIK 61, Kahn Collection.

"Toward a Plan for Midtown Philadelphia." *Perspecta*, no. 2 (August 1953): 10–27.
• "Toward a Plan for Midtown Philadelphia." [1953] MSS. "Perspecta 2," Box LIK 62, and "Misc.," Box LIK 64, Kahn Collection.
• Excerpt in Tyng, *Beginnings*, 59–60, 103–7.

"On the Responsibility of the Architect." *Perspecta*, no. 2 (August 1953): 44–47. Studio discussion at Yale School of Architecture with Philip Johnson, Louis Kahn, Vincent Scully, Pietro Belluschi, and Paul Weiss.

Architecture and the University: Proceedings of a Conference Held at Princeton University, December Eleventh and Twelfth Nineteen Hundred and Fifty Three, 27, 29–30, 46, 67–68. Princeton: Princeton University, 1954.

Louis I. Kahn on Architecture: An Annotated Bibliography

Compiled by David B. Brownlee, Shilpa Mehta, and Peter S. Reed

• "Architecture and the University Conference." [December 1953] Transcript with handwritten notes. "Princeton University—correspondence, December, 1953–February, 1958," Box LIK 55, Kahn Collection.

"How to Develop New Methods of Construction." *Architectural Forum* 101, no. 5 (November 1954): 157. Excerpt from lecture at Conference on Architectural Illumination, North Carolina State College, Raleigh, February 27–28, 1953.
• "The Relation of Light to Form." [July 1953] Annotated partial transcript of lecture. "North Carolina State College—LIK," Box LIK 56, Kahn Collection.

"A Lecture by Louis I. Kahn." *Student Publication of the School of Architecture, Tulane University* 1 (1955): n.p. Excerpts from lecture at Tulane University, New Orleans, December 1954.

"Order Is." *Perspecta*, no. 3 (1955): 59.
• Reprinted in "Louis Kahn," *Zodiac*, no. 8 (1961): 20.
• Reprinted in Vincent J. Scully, *Louis I. Kahn*, 113–14. New York: George Braziller, 1962.
• Reprinted and translated in *L'architecture d'aujourd'hui* 33, no. 105 (December 1962–January 1963): n.p.
• Translated in Marta Rabinovich and Jorge Piatigorsky, *Louis Isadore Kahn 1901– : Forma y Diseño*, 62–63. Buenos Aires: Ediciones Nueva Vision, 1965.
• Reprinted in "An Architect's Music of the Spheres—Conversation with Louis Kahn," *34th Street Magazine, Daily Pennsylvanian* (Philadelphia), April 22, 1971, 5.
• Excerpt in Charles Jencks, *Modern Movements in Architecture*, 43. Garden City, N.Y.: Anchor Press/Doubleday, 1973.
• Reprinted in Romaldo Giurgola and Jaimini Mehta, *Louis I. Kahn*, 9–10. Boulder, Colo.: Westview Press, 1975.
• Translated in Christian Norberg-Schulz, *Louis I. Kahn: Idea e immagine*, 6. Rome: Officina Edizioni, 1980 (hereafter cited as Norberg-Schulz, *Kahn*).
• Reprinted in *America Builds*, edited by Leland Roth, 572–73. New York: Harper and Row, 1983.
• Reprinted in Tyng, *Beginnings*, 66–67.
• Reprinted in *What Will Be Has Always Been: The Words of Louis I. Kahn*, edited by Richard Saul Wurman, 305. New York: Access Press and Rizzoli International Publications, 1986 (hereafter cited as Wurman, *What Will Be Has Always Been*).

"Two Houses." *Perspecta*, no. 3 (1955): 60–61.

"A Synagogue." *Perspecta*, no. 3 (1955): 62–63.

"An Approach to Architectural Education." *Pennsylvania Triangle* (Philadelphia) 42, no. 3 (January 1956): 28–32.

Review of *Synagogue Architecture in the U.S.*, by Rachael Wischnitzer. *Jewish Voice* (Los Angeles), January 6, 1956.
• [Review of *Synagogue Architecture in the U.S.*, November 1955.] MSS. "LIK—Miscellaneous 1954–56," Box LIK 65, and "Descriptions of Buildings," Box LIK 54, Kahn Collection.
• Reprinted as "Places of Worship," *Jewish Review and Observer* (Cleveland), February 17, 1956.

"Space Form Use—A Library." *Pennsylvania Triangle* (Philadelphia) 43, no. 2 (December 1956): 43–44.

Kahn, Louis I., and Anne Griswold Tyng. " A City Tower: A Concept of Natural Growth." Universal Atlas Cement Company, United States Steel Corporation Publication 110, no. ADUAC-707-57 (5-BM-WP), [1957].
• Excerpt in "L. I. Kahn, Form & Design, and Other Writings," *America Builds*, edited by Leland Roth, 580. New York: Harper and Row, 1983.

"Architecture is the Thoughtful Making of Spaces." *Perspecta*, no. 4 (1957): 2–3.
• "Architecture is the Thoughtful Making of Places." [1957] MSS. "LIK Lectures 1969," Box LIK 53, and "Perspecta 4," Box LIK 62, Kahn Collection.
• Reprinted in "Spaces Order and Architecture," *Royal Architectural Institute of Canada Journal* 34, no. 10 (October 1957): 375, 377.
• Translated in Norberg-Schulz, *Kahn*, 66–67.

"The Continual Renewal of Architecture Comes from Changing Concepts of Space." *Perspecta*, no. 4 (1957): 3.
• "The Continual Renewal of Architecture Comes from Changing Concepts of Space." [1957] MSS. "LIK Lectures 1969," Box LIK 53, and "Perspecta 4," Box LIK 62, Kahn Collection.
• Reprinted in "Spaces Order and Architecture," *Royal Architectural Institute of Canada Journal* 34, no. 10 (October 1957): 375–76.
• Translated in Norberg-Schulz, *Kahn*, 67–68.

"Order in Architecture." *Perspecta*, no. 4 (1957): 58–65.
• "Order in Architecture." [1957] MS. "Perspecta 4," Box LIK 62, Kahn Collection.
• Excerpt in "Spaces Order and Architecture," *Royal Architectural Institute of Canada Journal* 34, no. 10 (October 1957): 376–77.
• Translated in Marta Rabinovich and Jorge Piatigorsky, *Louis Isadore Kahn 1901– : Forma y Diseño*, 55–61. Buenos Aires: Ediciones Nueva Vision, 1965.
• Excerpt in Tyng, *Beginnings*, 107–8.

"The Entrance to a Theater." *National Institute for Architectural Education Bulletin* 33 (January 1957): 10–11. Emerson Prize competition program.

"Statements by Architects on Frank Lloyd Wright." *Architectural Forum* 110, no. 5 (May 1959): 114.
• [Statement on Frank Lloyd Wright, April 1959.] MS. "Architectural Forum—Louis I. Kahn," Box LIK 61, Kahn Collection.

"Reflections on a Theatre." [November 22, 1959] MS. "The Theatre, Ford Foundation," Box LIK 65, Kahn Collection.

"A Symposium Revisited." *Carnegie Tech. Quarterly*, no. 1 (1960): n.p. Excerpts from "The Arts, the Artist and Society," Bicentennial Symposium, Pittsburgh, October 9–10, 1959.

"Space Order in Architecture." [March 1960] Annotated transcript of lecture in "Directions in Architecture" series at Pratt Institute, New York, October 13–November 10, 1959. "LIK Lectures 1959," Box LIK 54, Kahn Collection.

"On Philosophical Horizons." *AIA Journal* 33, no. 6 (June 1960): 99–100. Transcribed excerpts from "Philosophical Horizons," panel at American Institute of Architects Convention, San Francisco, April 27, 1960.
• Excerpt in Tyng, *Beginnings*, 109–11.

"Louis Kahn: Order for Concrete." *Kokusai Kentiku* 27 (June 1960): 49. Translated excerpt from World Design Conference panel discussion, Tokyo, May 11–16, 1960.
• Original English excerpt published in "World Design Conference: East and West Discuss Their Common Problems in Tokyo," *Industrial Design* 7, no. 7 (July 1960): 49.

"Minutes of 46th Annual Meeting: Resolutions." *Journal of Architectural Education* 15, no. 3 (Fall 1960): 62–65. "Form and Design" lecture, American Collegiate Schools of Architecture meeting, University of California, Berkeley, April 22, 1960.

"10th Anniversary Letters." *Landscape* (Santa Fe) 10, no. 1 (Fall 1960): 4.
• [Statement concerning landscape, July 27, 1960.] MS. "Miscellaneous Correspondence, 1 April through July 1960," Box LIK 64, Kahn Collection.

"Marine City Redevelopment." *Progressive Architecture* 41, no. 11 (November 1960): 149–53. Excerpts from P/A Design Awards Seminar at Architectural League, New York, 1960.

"Talk at the Conclusion of the Otterlo Congress." In *New Frontiers in Architecture: CIAM '59 in Otterlo*, edited by Oscar Newman, 205, 209–17. New York: Universe Books, 1961. Lecture at CIAM Conference, Otterlo, Netherlands, September 7–15, 1959.

"Acceptance by Louis I. Kahn." *Proceedings of the American Academy of Arts and Letters and the National Institute of Arts and Letters*, 2nd series, no. 11, 37. New York: National Institute of Arts and Letters, 1961. Revised acceptance speech for Brunner Award from National Institute of Arts and Letters, May 25, 1960.
• "Acceptance by Louis I. Kahn." [July 1960] Annotated transcript. "National Institute of Arts and Letters, 1960," Box LIK 56, Kahn Collection.

"Kahn." *Perspecta*, no. 7 (1961): 9–28. Transcribed discussion in Kahn's office, Philadelphia, February 1961.
• Translated in Marta Rabinovich and Jorge Piatigorsky, *Louis Isadore Kahn 1901– : Forma y Diseño*, 27–54. Buenos Aires: Ediciones Nueva Vision, 1965.
• Excerpt translated in Norberg-Schultz, *Kahn*, 79–94.
• Excerpt in Tyng, *Beginnings*, 163.

Structure and Form, Voice of America Forum Lectures, Architecture Series, no. 6. Washington, D.C.: Voice of America, [1961]. Transcribed broadcast from Washington, D.C., November 21, 1960.
• "Structure and Form." [April 1960] MSS. "Voice of America—Louis I. Kahn. Recorded November 19, 1960," Box LIK 55, Kahn Collection.
• "Form and Design." [December 1960] Annotated transcripts. "Voice of America—Louis I. Kahn Recorded Nov. 19th 1960," Box LIK 55, Kahn Collection.
• Reprinted as "A Statement by Louis I. Kahn," *Arts and Architecture* 78, no. 2 (February 1961): 14–15, 28–30.
• Reprinted as "Form and Design," *Architectural Design* 31, no. 4 (April 1961): 145–54.
• Reprinted as "Form and Design," in Vincent J. Scully, *Louis I. Kahn*, 114–21. New York: George Braziller, 1962.
• Translated as "Forma y Diseño," *Punto* (Caracas), no. 14 (September 1963): 29–33.

• Excerpt in "Planning Nursery School Facilities and Premises: Some Thoughts of a Foremost Architect," *Journal of Nursery Education* 19, no. 3 (April 1964): 144–45.
• Translated in Marta J. Rabinovich and Jorge Piatigorsky, *Louis Isadore Kahn 1901– : Forma y Diseño*, 7–26. Buenos Aires: Ediciones Nueva Vision, 1965.
• Reprinted as "Structure and Form," *Royal Architectural Institute of Canada Journal* 42, no. 11 (November 1965): 26–28, 32.
• Translated in Norberg-Schulz, *Kahn*, 69–75.
• Excerpt in *America Builds*, edited by Leland Roth, 574–79. New York: Harper and Row, 1983.
• Excerpts in Tyng, *Beginnings*, 68–73, 108–9.
• Excerpt in Wurman, *What Will Be Has Always Been*, 8–9.

The Institution as a Generator of Urban Form. Harvard Graduate School of Design Alumni Association Fifth Urban Design Conference, 47. Cambridge, Mass.: Harvard University, 1961. Transcribed excerpts from panel discussion, Harvard University, April 14, 1961.

"The Sixties, a P/A Symposium on the State of Architecture: Part 1," edited by Thomas H. Creighton. *Progressive Architecture* 42, no. 3 (March 1961): 122–33.

Jan C. Rowan, "Wanting to Be: The Philadelphia School." *Progressive Architecture* 42 (April 1961): 131–63. Based on interview by Rowan.
• Excerpt in Wurman, *What Will Be Has Always Been*, 89–92.

[Statement for the Museum of Modern Art, May 7, 1961.] MSS. "Museum of Modern Art," Box LIK 57, Kahn Collection.

"Lou Kahn: The Baths of Caracalla, Rome," in "What Is Your Favorite Building?" *New York Times Magazine*, May 21, 1961, 34.

"The New Art of Urban Design: Are We Equipped?" in "Architecture—Fitting and Befitting," *Architectural Forum* 114, no. 6 (June 1961): 88. Excerpt from "The New Forces in Architecture," panel discussion, Architectural League and *Architectural Forum*, New York, October 1960.
• "The New Art of Urban Design: Are We Equipped?" [December 1960] Transcript. "Louis I. Kahn, Architectural League," Box LIK 61, Kahn Collection.
• Translated in Norberg-Schulz, *Kahn*, 86.

"The Nature of Nature," in "Need and Responsibility." *Journal of Architectural Education* 16, no. 3 (Autumn 1961): 95–97. Lecture and discussion at "Education for Urban Design," AIA-ACSA Seminar, Cranbrook Academy of Art, Bloomfield Hills, Michigan, June 14, 1961.
• "Catalyst of Thinking, Evangelist of Architecture." [December 1962] Annotated transcript of lecture. "Cranbrook Speech—1961 to be edited," Box LIK 54, Kahn Collection.

[Theater architecture.] Annotated transcript of lecture for the Board of Standards and Planning for the "Living Theatre," New York, November 14, 1961. "Board of Standards and Planning, N.Y. Chapter—ANTA," Box LIK 57, Kahn Collection.

"A Talk with Louis I. Kahn." Notes by Paul Otto Heyer. Philadelphia, November 24, 1961. Unmarked file, Box LIK 66, Kahn Collection.

"Law and Rule in Architecture." Transcript of lecture at Princeton University, November 29, 1961. "LIK Lectures 1969," Box LIK 53, Kahn Collection.

The Notebooks and Drawings of Louis I. Kahn, 1st ed., edited by Richard Saul Wurman and Eugene Feldman. Philadelphia: Falcon Press, 1962. Foreword and excerpts from miscellaneous sources by Kahn.
• Foreword reprinted in "Notebooks and Drawings," *Arts & Architecture* 80, no. 4 (April 1963).
• Excerpt in "Not for the Faint-Hearted," *AIA Journal* 55, no. 6 (June 1971): 26–7, 29–31.
• [Not for the Faint-Hearted, March 1971.] MS. for *AIA Journal* 55, no. 6. "AIA Gold Medal National 1971–Jun. 24th," Box LIK 52, Kahn Collection.
• Full text reprinted with a new introductory letter (June 15, 1973) by Kahn in *The Notebooks and Drawings of Louis I. Kahn*, 2d ed., edited by Richard Saul Wurman and Eugene Feldman. Cambridge, Mass., and London: MIT Press, 1973.
• Foreword translated in Norberg-Schulz, *Kahn*, 87–90.
• Foreword reprinted in Max Protetch Gallery, *Louis I. Kahn Drawings*, n.p. New York: Access Press, 1981.
• Excerpts translated in "Arquetipos y Modernidad II: Louis I. Kahn," *Summarios* nos. 74/75 (1984): 51–52. *Summarios* excerpts reprinted in *Louis Kahn: Arquetipos y Modernidad*, edited by Miguel Angel Roca, 95–96. Buenos Aires: Ediciones Summa, 1984.
• New introductory letter (June 15, 1973) reprinted in Tyng, *Beginnings*, 179–80.
• Excerpts reprinted in Wurman, *What Will Be Has Always Been*, 124–27, 256–63.

"Coffee Break with Louis I. Kahn." *Philadelphia Sunday Bulletin Magazine*, January 28, 1962, 12. Interview by Ros Dixon.

"Design with the Automobile: The Animal World." *Canadian Art* 19, no. 1 (January–February 1962): 50–51. Excerpt from interview by H. P. Daniel van Ginkel in Cambridge, Mass., Spring 1961.
• Reprinted in Tyng, *Beginnings*, 111–14.
• Reprinted in Wurman, *What Will Be Has Always Been*, 5–8.

"Law and Rule in Architecture." Transcript of lecture at Royal Institute of British Architects, London, March 14, 1962. "LIK Lectures 1969," Box LIK 53, Kahn Collection.

"Thoroughly an Architect." *The Guardian* (London), March 16, 1962, 7. Interview by Diana Rowntree.

"The Architect and the Building." *Bryn Mawr Alumnae Bulletin* 43, no. 4 (Summer 1962): 2–5. Excerpts from a discussion with Kahn.
• Reprinted in Wurman, *What Will Be Has Always Been*, 3–5.

"A Visit to Louis Kahn's Office." Notes by Denise Scott Brown, March 4, 1963. "Brown, Mrs. Denise Scott, Correspondence," Box LIK 57, and unmarked file, Box LIK 122, Kahn Collection.

"Medical Research Laboratories, Philadelphia." In *World Architecture*, no. 1, 35–36. London: Studio Books, 1964.

"The Development by Louis I. Kahn of the Design for the Second Capital of Pakistan at Dacca." In *Student Publication of the School of Design, North Carolina State College, Raleigh* 14, no. 3 (May 1964): n.p. Lecture at Yale School of Architecture, October 30, 1963, edited for publication by Keller Smith and Reyhan Tansal.
• "North Carolina Revisions." [May 28, 1964] Annotated transcripts. "North Carolina State—Raleigh, North Carolina," Box LIK 56, Kahn Collection.

"A Statement by Louis I. Kahn." *Arts and Architecture* 81, no. 5 (May 1964): 18–19, 33. Lecture at International Design Conference, Aspen, Colorado, June 27, 1962.
• "Container Corp. . ." [January 1963] Edited transcript. "Aspen Conference—June 1962," Box LIK 59, Kahn Collection.
• Excerpt translated in *L'architettura: cronache e storia* 10, no. 7 (November 1964): 480–81.
• Excerpts in Tyng, *Beginnings*, 73–74, 114–115, 163–65.

"Our Changing Environment." In *The First World Congress of Craftsmen*, 120–21. New York: American Craftsmen's Council, [1965]. Transcribed from panel discussion at Columbia University, June 8–19, 1964.

[Lecture on institutions.] In *Report of Proceedings, Sixth Annual Conference on Graduate Medical Education: Medicine in the Year 2000*, 148–60. Philadelphia: University of Pennsylvania, 1965. Lecture and discussion at Sixth Annual Conference on Graduate Medical Education at School of Medicine, University of Pennsylvania, Philadelphia, December 3–4, 1964.
• [Sixth Annual Conference on Graduate Medical Education, Philadelphia, December 1964.] Transcript. "Report of Proceedings," Box LIK 54, Kahn Collection.

"Board Meeting, Fort Wayne Fine Arts Foundation, Fort Wayne, Indiana, 1965." In Wurman, *What Will Be Has Always Been*, 9–10.

"Comments on Fort Wayne Fine Arts Center, Fort Wayne, Indiana, 1961–1965." In Wurman, *What Will Be Has Always Been*, 10–12.

"Remarks: Louis I. Kahn." *Perspecta*, no. 9/10 (1965): 303–35. Edited and revised lecture at Yale School of Architecture, October 30, 1963.
• [*Perspecta*, June 1964.] Revised transcript. "Yale—Perspecta 9," Box LIK 54, Kahn Collection.
• [*Perspecta*, August 13, 1964.] Revised transcript. "Perspecta 9 (R. Stern—editor)," Box LIK 56, Kahn Collection.
• Excerpt in "Louis I. Kahn—Oeuvres 1963–1969," *L'architecture d'aujourd'hui* 40, no. 142, special issue (February–March 1969): 1.
• Excerpt in "Louis I. Kahn 1901–1974," *Architecture, mouvement, continuité*, no. 34 (July 1974): 111–14.
• Excerpt translated in Norberg-Schulz, *Kahn*, 96–108.
• Excerpts in Tyng, *Beginnings*, 74, 115–19, 166–68.
• Excerpt in Wurman, *What Will Be Has Always Been*, 12–13.

"Architecture Faces the Struggle for Truth & Justice." Transcript of address at 26th National Conference on Church Architecture, Chicago, April 27–29, 1965. "National Council of Churches of Christ," Box LIK 68, Kahn Collection.

"Conversation: Louis I. Kahn and Karl Linn—May 14, 1965." Transcript of interview. "Linn, Karl," Box LIK 58, Kahn Collection.

"On the Death of Le Corbusier, 28 August 1965." In Wurman, *What Will Be Has Always Been*, 10.

"Panelists Can't Agree Upon U.S. Art Image in Europe." *Evening Bulletin* (Philadelphia), November 19, 1965, 23E. Excerpt from Philadelphia Chapter Artists Equity Association symposium, Philadelphia, November 18, 1965.

[*Time* magazine interview, February 20–21, 1966.] MSS. of prepared answers. "Time Article—Answers by LIK," Box LIK 58, Kahn Collection.

"Top Sketch Club Honor Goes to Kahn." *The Advertiser* (Philadelphia), May 18, 1966, 12. Excerpts from lecture at Philadelphia Sketch Club Second Annual Award Reception, Philadelphia, May 13, 1966.

"Address by Louis I. Kahn." *Boston Society of Architects Journal*, no. 1 (1967): 5–20. Address to Boston Society of Architects, Boston, April 5, 1966.
• "Louis Kahn—Illustrated Impressions." [1967] Edited transcript. "Boston Society of Arch. Earl Flansburgh," Box LIK 57, Kahn Collection.

"Louis I. Kahn: Statements on Architecture." *Zodiac*, no. 17 (1967): 55–57. Excerpt from lecture at Politecnico di Milano, January 1967.
• Excerpts in Tyng, *Beginnings*, 120–22.

"Twelve Lines." In University of St. Thomas, *Visionary Architects: Boullée, Ledoux, Lequeu*, 9. Houston: Gulf Printing, 1967.
• "Twelve Lines." MS. "University of St. Thomas," Box LIK 58, Kahn Collection.
• Reprinted in "Revolutionary Champions," *AIA Journal* 49, no. 1 (January 1968): 80.
• Reprinted in "Hommage à Louis I. Kahn (1901–1974)," *Werk* 61, no. 7 (July 1974): 807.
• Reprinted in *Architecture in Australia* 63, no. 6 (December 1974): 54.

Foreword. In *Pioneer Texas Buildings—A Geometry Lesson*, by Clovis Heimsath, n.p. Austin: University of Texas Press, 1968.
• [Foreword, 1968.] MSS. "Heimsath Clovis," Box LIK 54, Kahn Collection.

"Silence." *Via* 1 (1968): 88–89.
• Excerpt in "Louis I. Kahn—Oeuvres 1963–1969," *L'architecture d'aujourd'hui*, 40, no. 142, special issue (February–March 1969): 7.

["The brain and the mind," 1968.] Annotated transcript of lecture at Computer Graphics Conference, Yale University. "LIK Lectures 1969," Box LIK 53, Kahn Collection.

"The White Light and the Black Shadow, Lecture at Princeton University, Princeton, New Jersey, 6 March 1968." In Wurman, *What Will Be Has Always Been*, 14–21. Lecture and discussion.

"The Institutions of Man, Lecture at Princeton University, Princeton, New Jersey, 13 March, 1968." In Wurman, *What Will Be Has Always Been*, 21–27. Lecture and discussion.

"Distinguished Artists, Critics Stimulate Institute Climate." *Contact: The Maryland Institute College of Art Journal* 5, no. 4 (Summer 1968): n.p. Excerpt from commencement address at Maryland Institute College of Art, Baltimore, June 5, 1968.

"Lecture at Drexel (University) Architectural Society, Philadelphia, PA, 5 November, 1968." In Wurman, *What Will Be Has Always Been*, 27–32.

"Lecture to Towne School of Civil and Mechanical Engineering, University of Pennsylvania, 19 November, 1968." In Wurman, *What Will Be Has Always Been*, 33–36.

Foreword. In *Villages in the Sun: Mediterranean Community Architecture*, by Myron Goldfinger, 7. New York: Praeger Publishers, 1969, 1975.

"Louis I. Kahn: Talks With Students." *Architecture at Rice*, no. 26 (1969): 1–53. Excerpts from lecture and discussion at Rice University, Houston, [1969].
• Excerpt translated as "Kahn: dialoghi di architettura; conversazioni con gli studenti della Rice University," *Casabella* 34, nos. 350–51 (July–August 1970): 18–23.
• Excerpt translated as "Kahn: Gespräche mit Studenten," *Bauwelt* 62, nos. 1/2 (January 1971): 13–17.
• Excerpt in Wurman, *What Will Be Has Always Been*, 102–11. [Misidentified as part of interview with Arnold J. Aho.]

["Bicentennial Exposition," January 1969.] Annotated transcript. "LIK Lectures 1969," Box LIK 53, Kahn Collection.

"An interview, *VIA* magazine, Philadelphia, Pennsylvania, 11 January 69." In Wurman, *What Will Be Has Always Been*, 36–52.

"Silence and Light—Louis I. Kahn at ETH." In *Louis I. Kahn: Complete Work, 1935–1974*, 1st ed., edited by Heinz Ronner, Sharad Jhaveri, and Alessandro Vasella, 447–49. Boulder, Colo.: Westview Press, 1977. Lecture at Eidgenössische Technische Hochschule, Zurich, Switzerland, February 12, 1969.
• Translated in Norberg-Schulz, *Kahn*, 115–127.
• Excerpt in Tyng, *Beginnings*, 172–74.
• Translated as "Conferencia en le ETH de Zurich," in "Arquetipos y Modernidad II: Louis I. Kahn," *Summarios*, nos. 74/75 (1984): 43–50. *Summarios* text reprinted in *Louis Kahn: Arquetipos y Modernidad*, edited by Miguel Angel Roca, 87–94. Buenos Aires: Ediciones Summa, 1984.
• Reprinted in Wurman, *What Will Be Has Always Been*, 54–63.
• Reprinted in *Louis I. Kahn: Complete Work, 1935–1974*, 2d ed., edited by Heinz Ronner and Sharad Jhaveri, 6–9. Basel and Boston: Birkhäuser, 1987.

"Louis I. Kahn as a Teacher." In "Louis I. Kahn—Oeuvres 1963–1969," *L'architecture d'aujourd'hui* 40, no. 142, special issue (February–March 1969): 88–91. Notes from studio discussions with Kahn, Robert Le Ricolais, and Norman Rice, University of Pennsylvania, 1964.
• Reprinted in Wurman, *What Will Be Has Always Been*, 101.

"Space and the Inspirations." In "Louis I. Kahn—Oeuvres 1963–1969," *L'architecture d'aujourd'hui* 40, no. 142, special issue (February–March 1969): 13–16. Lecture at "The Conservatory Redefined," New England Conservatory of Music Centennial Symposium, November 14, 1967.

• "Space and the Inspirations." Annotated transcript. "LIK Lectures 1969," Box LIK 53, Kahn Collection.
• Translated in Norberg-Schulz, *Kahn*, 109–14.

"Palais des Congrès, Venise." In "Louis I. Kahn—Oeuvres 1963–1969," *L'architecture d'aujourd'hui* 40, no. 142, special issue (February–March 1969): 33–34. Translated excerpts from lecture at Ducal Palace, Venice, January 30, 1969.
• "Louis I. Kahn Talks About His Project." [January 1969] Transcript. "Venezia," Box LIK 55, Kahn Collection.
• English text published as "Kahn Talks about His Project," *Domus*, no. 472 (March 1969): 6.
• *Domus* text reprinted in Wurman, *What Will Be Has Always Been*, 53–54.

"Monument commemoratif aux six millions de martyrs juifs, Battery–New York." In "Louis I. Kahn—Oeuvres 1963–1969," *L'architecture d'aujourd'hui* 40, no. 142, special issue (February–March 1969): 74.

"This is how the Program Starts." In "Louis I. Kahn—Oeuvres 1963–1969," *L'architecture d'aujourd'hui* 40, no. 142, special issue (February–March 1969): 82. Excerpt from unidentified conference in Boston.
• Translated in Norberg-Schulz, *Kahn*, 128–29.

"Interview, *VIA* magazine, Philadelphia, Pennsylvania, 16 March 1969." In Wurman, *What Will Be Has Always Been*, 64–71.

"From a lecture, University of Cincinnati, Cincinnati, Ohio, 3 May 1969." In Wurman, *What Will Be Has Always Been*, 72–75.

"In the L.I.K. Studios, University of Pennsylvania, 29 September 1969." In Wurman, *What Will Be Has Always Been*, 77–88.

"Speaking with Louis I. Kahn." *Space Design: Journal of Art and Architecture*, no. 60 (November 1969): 5. Translated discussion with Ichiro Hariu and Yukihisa Isobe, Philadelphia, October 21, 1967.

"Architecture: Silence and Light." In Solomon R. Guggenheim Museum, *On the Future of Art*, 20–35. New York: Viking Press, 1970. Lecture at Guggenheim Museum, New York, December 3, 1968.
• "Architecture—Silence and Light." [1969] Annotated transcript. "LIK Lectures 1969," Box LIK 53, Kahn Collection.
• Reprinted in "Architecture: Silence and Light," *Design* (Bombay) 15 (October 1971): 26–30.
• Excerpt translated in "Recent Works by Louis I. Kahn," *Kenchiku Bunka* 24, no. 267 (January 1969): 145–67.

"The Profession and Education Address to the International Congress of Architects, Isfahan, Iran, September 1970." In Wurman, *What Will Be Has Always Been*, 92–100. Address and panel discussion at the First International Congress of Architects.

[Introduction.] In *An Exhibition of the Work of the Architect Oskar Stonorov*, n.p. Philadelphia: Moore College of Art Gallery, 1971.
• ["Oscar Stonorov," May 10, 1971.] MS. "Oscar Stonorov—LIK Writing," Box LIK 53, Kahn Collection.
• Excerpt in "His Thoughts on Oscar Stonorov," *L'architettura: cronache e storia* 18, no. 2 (June 1972): 108.

"In the Hall of the Mountain King: A Block Party." *Thursday's Drummer* (Philadelphia), February 25, 1971, 1, 4.
• Reprinted in Wurman, *What Will Be Has Always Been*, 111–12.

"On the Roof of the Ducal Palace, Venice, Italy, 26 February, 1971." In Wurman, *What Will Be Has Always Been*, 112.

"Louis I. Kahn: Master Architect." *Pennsylvania Triangle* (Philadelphia) 58, no. 5 (March 1971): 22–23, 35. Interview by Evelyn M. Karson.

["Louis Kahn—Speech at the Third World Congress of Engineers and Architects."] *Aleph-Aleph: Monthly Review of the Israel Institute of Architects, Association of Engineers and Architects in Israel*, no. 5 (June 1974): 8–14. Translated lecture at the Third World Congress of Engineers and Architects, Israel, April 1971.

[Philadelphia Award, April 1971.] Transcript of acceptance speech for Bok Award, Philadelphia, April 21, 1971. "Dr. Salk & LIK Acceptance Speech," Box LIK 53, Kahn Collection.

"From a Conversation with Robert Wemischner, 17 April 1971." In Wurman, *What Will Be Has Always Been*, 113–22.

"An Architect's Music of the Spheres—Conversation with Louis Kahn." *34th Street Magazine, Daily Pennsylvanian* (Philadelphia), April 22, 1971, 3–5, 11. Interview by Robert Wemischner.

"At Independence Hall, 19 May 1971." In Wurman, *What Will Be Has Always Been*, 112–24.

"Architect Kahn Is Avid Reader of Fairy Tales." *Evening Bulletin* (Philadelphia), June 24, 1971, 3. Conversation with Hans Knight.

"From a Conversation with Peter Blake, 20 July 1971." In Wurman, *What Will Be Has Always Been*, 127–33.

"The Room, the Street and Human Agreement," *AIA Journal* 56, no. 3 (September 1971): 33–34. Text of AIA Gold Medal acceptance speech, Detroit, June 24, 1971.
• ["The Room, the Street and Human Agreement," June 1971.] Handwritten notes and annotated MS. "Draft—AIA National Gold Medal Lecture—1971," Box LIK 52, Kahn Collection.
• ["The Room, The Street and Human Agreement," July–August 1971.] Annotated MSS. and transcript of speech for AIA Journal. "Draft—AIA National Gold Medal Lecture—1971," Box LIK 52, Kahn Collection.
• Reprinted in *Arts in Society* 9, no. 1 (1972): 110–18.
• Reprinted and translated in "Louis I. Kahn: Silence and Light," *Architecture and Urbanism* 3, no. 1, special issue (January 1973): 7–22.
• Excerpt in "The Spirit of Architecture," *Man Is the Measure: The Human Element in Design*, n.p. New York: American Iron and Steel Institute, n.d. Summary of talks at Design Seminar, Cincinnati, March 29, 1973.
• Reprinted in "Room, Window and Sun," *Canadian Architect* 18, no. 6 (June 1973): 52–55.
• Reprinted in "Credo: Louis I. Kahn 1901–74," *Architectural Design* 44, no. 5 (May 1974): 280–81.
• Reprinted in *Architecture in Australia* 63, no. 6 (December 1974): 54–57.
• Translated in Norberg-Schulz, *Kahn*, 130–36.
• Excerpt in Tyng, *Beginnings*, 122–27.

[Address to new United States citizens, Philadelphia, October 6, 1971.] Transcript. "Judge Edward R. Becker (Lecture 6th October 1971)," LIK Box 52, Kahn Collection.

[Statement regarding tapestries by Charles Madden, December 27, 1971.] MS. "Misc. M," Box LIK 53, Kahn Collection.

"Comments on the Library, Phillips Exeter Academy, Exeter, New Hampshire, 1972." In Wurman, *What Will Be Has Always Been*, 178–83.

Architecture: The John William Lawrence Memorial Lectures. New Orleans: Tulane University School of Architecture, 1972. Lecture at the Tulane University School of Architecture, New Orleans, June 1972.

"Architecture and Human Agreement." *Modulus* (University of Virginia School of Architecture), no. 11 (1975): n.p. Lecture at School of Architecture, University of Virginia, Charlottesville, April 18, 1972.
• Excerpt in Wurman, *What Will Be Has Always Been*, 133–39.

"Louis Kahn on Learning," in "The Invisible City." *Design Quarterly* nos. 86/87 (1972): 41–44. Excerpts from "I Love Beginnings," lecture at "The Invisible City," International Design Conference, Aspen, Colorado, June 19, 1972.
• Excerpt in "A Report on the 22nd International Design Conference at Aspen," *Mountain Gazette* (Denver) 2 (October 1972): 17.
• Excerpts from conference in "I Love Beginnings," in "Louis I. Kahn." *Architecture + Urbanism*, special issue (1975): 279–86.
• Excerpt translated in Norberg-Schulz, *Kahn*, 137–46.
• Excerpt in Tyng, *Beginnings*, 177–78.
• Excerpts and subsequent discussion in Wurman, *What Will Be Has Always Been*, 150–63, 165–73.

"Dedication, Temple Beth-El, Chappaqua, New York, 5 May 1972." In Wurman, *What Will Be Has Always Been*, 142.
• Excerpt published in *Louis I. Kahn: Complete Work, 1935–1974*, 2d ed., edited by Heinz Ronner and Sharad Jhaveri, 355. Basel and Boston: Birkhäuser, 1987.

"Conversation with Jonas Salk, San Diego, California, 20 May 1972." In Wurman, *What Will Be Has Always Been*, 143–49.

"From a Conversation with Richard Saul Wurman, Aspen, Colorado, June 1972." In Wurman, *What Will Be Has Always Been*, 163–64, 174.

"His Thoughts on Oscar Stonorov." *L'architettura: cronache e storia* 18, no. 2 (June 1972): 109, 128–29. Translated excerpts from interviews by Frederick Gutheim.

[Interview by William Marlin, Philadelphia, June 24, 1972.] Transcript, Kimbell Art Museum Files, Fort Worth.

"Louis I. Kahn: Royal Gold Medalist." *Royal Institute of British Architects Journal* 79, no. 8 (August 1972): 324–26. Royal Gold Medal acceptance speech, London, June 13, 1972.

"The Wonder of the Natural Thing." In *Louis I. Kahn: L'uomo, il maestro*, edited by Alessandra Latour, 399–404. Rome: Edizioni Kappa, 1986. Original English and translated interview by Marshall D. Meyers, Philadelphia, August 11, 1972.

• "The Wonder of the Natural Thing." [August 11, 1972] MS. "Articles and Speeches," clippings file, Kahn Collection.

"Kimbell Museum Dedication, Fort Worth, Texas, Autumn 1972." Excerpt in Wurman, *What Will Be Has Always Been*, 177.

"An Architect Speaks His Mind: Louis Kahn Talks about Color, Light, the Ideal House, the Street, and other Inspirations for Living." *House & Garden* 142, no. 4 (October 1972): 124–25, 219. Interview by Beverly Russell.
• Excerpt in Wurman, *What Will Be Has Always Been*, 174–75.

"Architect Kahn's Idea of a Street." *Evening Bulletin* (Philadelphia), October 10, 1972, 22. Excerpt from remarks to Pennsylvania Convention of American Institute of Architects, Philadelphia, October 1972.

"Ein Gesprach mit Louis I. Kahn" and "Entretien avec Louis I. Kahn," in "Hommage à Louis I. Kahn (1901–1974)." *Werk* 61, no. 7 (July 1974): 800–801, 802–3. Translated interview by Paul R. Kramer, Philadelphia, October 11, 1972.

"How'm I Doing, Corbusier? An Interview with Louis Kahn" *Pennsylvania Gazette* (Philadelphia) 71, no. 3 (December 1972): 18–26. Interview by Patricia McLaughlin.
• Excerpts in Tyng, *Beginnings*, 76, 175–76.
• Excerpt in Wurman, *What Will Be Has Always Been*, 175–76.

"The Variety of Things Yet Unsaid: Interviews with Louis Kahn." Transcript of interviews with Rolf Sauer and James Bryan, January–March 1973, Kahn Collection.

"Clearing: Interviews with Louis I. Kahn." *Via* 2 (1973): 158–61. Remarks from Kahn's master's studio, Philadelphia, 1969–70, and excerpts from lecture at Princeton University, Spring 1968.
• Reprinted in Wurman, *What Will Be Has Always Been*, 139–41.

"Louis I. Kahn." In *Conversations with Architects*, edited by John Wesley Cook and Heinrich Klotz, 178–217. New York: Praeger Publishers, 1973. Interview by Cook and Klotz.
• Excerpt in "Louis Kahn: Only a Fascist Plans the 'Sociological' City," *Philadelphia Inquirer*, August 27, 1973, 9A.
• Excerpt in Wurman, *What Will Be Has Always Been*, 184–210.

"Comments on the Kansas City Tower, Kansas City, Kansas, 1973." In Wurman, *What Will Be Has Always Been*, 211–12.

"Kahn on Beaux-Arts Training." *Architectural Review* 155 (June 1974): 332. From an interview with William Jordy, [1973].

"From a Conversation with William Jordy." In Wurman, *What Will Be Has Always Been*, 236–42. From an interview with William Jordy, [1973].

"L'Accord de l'homme et de l'architecture." *La Construction Moderne* 4 (July–August 1973): 11–21. Translated lecture from conference, Paris, May 11, 1973.
• Original English text published as "Harmony Between Man and Architecture," *Design* (Bombay) 18, no. 3 (March 1974): 23–28.

["I have taught self rewarded . . ."] In "Context of Man: Louis I. Kahn, FAIA," *Utah Architect*, no. 53 (Summer 1973): 11.

• Reprinted as "Poetics" in *Journal of Architectural Education* 27, no. 1 (February 1974): 10.

[Interview by Dennis Farney, *Wall Street Journal*, August or September 1973.] Rough transcript, Kahn Collection.

"From a Conversations [sic] with Richard Saul Wurman, Flight to San Francisco, California, October 1973." In Wurman, *What Will Be Has Always Been*, 231–36.

"Architecture and Human Agreement." In *The Art of Design Management: Design in American Business*, 17–30. New York: Tiffany and Co., 1975. Tiffany-Wharton lecture at Wharton School, University of Pennsylvania, Philadelphia, October 10, 1973.
• Excerpt in Tyng, *Beginnings*, 176.
• Reprinted in Wurman, *What Will Be Has Always Been*, 212–17.

"From a Conversation with Jaimini Mehta, 22 October 1973" and "A Verbal Autobiography, From a Conversation with Jaimini Mehta, 22 October 1973." In Wurman, *What Will Be Has Always Been*, 218–31.

"From a Conversation with David Rothstein and Jim Hatch, Autumn 1973." In Wurman, *What Will Be Has Always Been*, 242.

"1973: Brooklyn, New York." *Perspecta*, no. 19 (1982): 89–100. Lecture at Pratt Institute, New York, Fall 1973. [This is re-edited and used for most of Lobell's *Between Silence and Light*.]

"Writings to Karel Mikolas, November 1973." In Wurman, *What Will Be Has Always Been*, 243.
• "To Karel Mikolas." November 1973. MS. "Master File 1 November 1973 to 29 March 1974," Box LIK 10, Kahn Collection.

"Key Lecture, Symposium on the Education and Training of Architects, Tel Aviv, Israel, 20 December 1973." In Wurman, *What Will Be Has Always Been*, 244–50.

"From Lecture and Walking Tour, Fort Wayne Art Center Dedication, Fort Wayne, Indiana, 1974." In Wurman, *What Will Be Has Always Been*, 250–51.

Foreword. In *Carlo Scarpa architetto poeta*, n.p. London: Royal Institute of British Architects, 1974.
• Manuscript reproduced in Wurman, *What Will Be Has Always Been*, n.p.

"Louis I. Kahn Defends—Interview, Indian Institute of Management, Ahmedabad, India, 31 May 1974 [sic; March 1974]." In Wurman, *What Will Be Has Always Been*, 251–54.

"The Samuel S. Fleisher Art Memorial." *Philadelphia Museum of Art Bulletin* 68, no. 309 (Spring 1974): 56–57.
• Excerpts in Tyng, *Beginnings*, 127–28, 174–75.
• Excerpt in Wurman, *What Will Be Has Always Been*, 243–44.

"In His Own Words." *Interior Design* 45, no. 11 (November 1974): 134.
• Reprinted in Wurman, *What Will Be Has Always Been*, 255.

"Le Ricolais, Robert." In *Unbuilt America*, edited by Alison Sky and Michelle Stone, 165. New York: McGraw-Hill, 1976.

Index

The following list is organized by figure number and acknowledges published sources as well as the individuals, institutions, and photographers who have generously provided illustrations. The Louis I. Kahn Collection, University of Pennsylvania and Pennsylvania Historical and Museum Commission, Philadelphia, has been abbreviated as Kahn Collection.

1–2. Collection of Mrs. Louis I. Kahn. **3.** From *American Architect* 126 (September 24, 1924): 297. **4.** Collection of the Pennsylvania Academy of the Fine Arts, Philadelphia. Gift of Mrs. Louis I. Kahn. **5.** From *American Architect* 130 (November 5, 1926): pl. 378. **6.** Collection of the late Norman N. Rice. **7.** Collection of Mrs. Louis I. Kahn. **8.** Collection of Sue Ann Kahn. **9.** Photo: Bachrach Studio. **10.** From "The Carl Mackley Houses in Philadelphia—Juniata Park Housing Development," *Architectural Record* 78 (November 1935): 292. Photo: F. S. Lincoln. **11.** From Bernard J. Newman, *Housing in Philadelphia, 1933* (Philadelphia: Philadelphia Housing Association, 1934), fig. 9. **12.** Photograph by Lange for Resettlement Administration. Kastner Papers, American Heritage Center, University of Wyoming, Laramie. **13–16.** Kahn Collection. **17.** Kahn Collection. Photo: Gottscho-Schleisner. **18.** Kahn Collection. **19.** Kahn Collection. Photo: Gottscho-Schleisner. **20.** Kahn Collection. **21.** Kahn Collection. Photo: Thomas Scott. **22–23.** Kahn Collection. **24.** From *You and Your Neighborhood: A Primer for Neighborhood Planning* (New York: Revere Copper and Brass, 1944), [47]. **25.** From *You and Your Neighborhood: A Primer for Neighborhood Planning* (New York: Revere Copper and Brass, 1944), [91]. **26–32.** Kahn Collection. **33.** From Maron J. Simon, *Your Solar House* (New York: Simon and Schuster, 1947), 42. **34.** From James Ford and Katherine Morrow Ford, *The Modern House in America* (New York: Architectural Book Publishing, 1940), 50. Photo: Richard T. Dooner. **35.** Photo: Grant Mudford. **36–37.** Kahn Collection. **38.** Photo: John Ebstel. **39.** Kahn Collection. **40–43.** Paul Clark, delineator. **44.** Kahn Collection. **45.** Photo: John Ebstel. **46.** Kahn Collection. **47.** From *Progressive Architecture* 27 (November 1946): 86–87. **48.** Photo: John Ebstel. **49.** Photo: Cortlandt V. D. Hubbard. **50.** From Paul Zucker, ed., *New Architecture and City Planning* (New York: Philosophical Library, 1944), 588. **51.** From *L'architettura: cronache e storia* 18 (June 1972): 106. **52.** Kahn Collection. **53.** Collection of Sue Ann Kahn. **54.** Kahn Collection. **55.** From Auguste Choisy, *Histoire de l'Architecture*, vol. 1 (Paris: Librairie G. Baranger Fils, 1899), 572. **56.** Collection of the Art Institute of Chicago. Gift of Centennial Fund and Three Oaks Wrecking Company by exchange. 1986.1055. **57.** Kahn Collection. **58.** Photo: Lionel Freedman. **59.** Kahn Collection. **60.** Collection of Anne Griswold Tyng. Photo: Kenneth Welch. **61.** Photo: Lionel Freedman. **62.** Kahn Collection. Photo: John Ebstel. **63.** Photo: John Ebstel. **64.** Collection, The Museum of Modern Art, New York. Gift of the architect. 388.64. **65.** Collection, The Museum of Modern Art, New York. Gift of the architect. 389.64. **66–67.** Kahn Collection. **68.** From "Toward a Plan for Midtown Philadelphia," *Perspecta*, no. 2 (1953): 22. **69.** Kahn Collection. **70.** From Emil Kaufmann, "Three Revolutionary Architects: Boullée, Ledoux and Lequeu," *Transactions of the American Philosophical Society* 42 (October 1952): 510, fig. 135. **71.** Collection, The Museum of Modern Art, New York. Gift of the architect. 359.67. **72.** Photo: John Ebstel. **73–78.** Kahn Collection. **79.** From D'Arcy Wentworth Thompson, *On Growth and Form*, vol. 2 (Cambridge: Cambridge University Press, 1968; reprint of 1942 edition), 551, fig. 213. **80.** Kahn Collection. Photo: Robert Damora. **81.** Kahn Collection. **82.** Kahn Collection. Photo: Bernie Cliff. **83.** Collection, The Museum of Modern Art, New York. Gift of the architect. 413.64. **84–86.** Kahn Collection. **87.** Photo: Eileen Christelow. **88.** Photo: John Ebstel. **89.** Collection, The Museum of Modern Art, New York. Gift of the architect. 367.67. **90.** Kahn Collection. **91.** Kahn Collection. Photo: Mildred F. Schmertz. **92.** Kahn Collection. Photo: Marshall D. Meyers. **93.** From Henry-Russell Hitchcock, *In the Nature of Materials* (New York: Duell, Sloan and Pearce, 1942), fig. 299. **94.** Kahn Collection. **95.** Kahn Collection. Photo: James Cook. **96.** Kahn Collection. Photo: Marshall D. Meyers. **97–99.** Kahn Collection. **100.** Kahn Collection. Photo: Marshall D. Meyers. **101.** Kahn Collection. **102.** Collection, The Museum of Modern Art, New York. Gift of the architect. 406.64.3. **103.** From Rudolf Wittkower, *Architectural Principles in the Age of Humanism*, 2d ed. (London: A. Tiranti, 1952), pl. 5a. **104.** From Richard Krautheimer, "Mensa-Coemeterium-Martyrium," *Cahiers Archéologiques*, no. 11 (1960): 21, fig. 5. **105.** Kahn Collection. **106.** From Jan C. Rowan, "Wanting to Be: The Philadelphia School," *Progressive Architecture* 42 (April 1961): 134. **107.** Paul Clark, delineator. **108.** From David MacGibbon and Thomas Ross, *The Castellated and Domestic Architecture of Scotland*, 5 vols. (Edinburgh, 1887), vol. 1, 238; as published in Vincent J. Scully, *Louis I. Kahn* (New York: George Braziller, 1962), pl. 116. **109.** Collection, The Museum of Modern Art, New York. Gift of the architect. 407.64. **110.** Photo: John Ebstel. **111.** Kahn Collection. Photo: John Condax. **112–13.** Kahn Collection. **114.** Kahn Collection. Photo: George Pohl. **115.** From *The Institution as a Generator of Urban Form. Harvard Graduate School of Design Alumni Association Fifth Urban Design Conference* (Cambridge, Mass.: Harvard University, 1961), n.p. **116.** From Thomas S. Hines, *Richard Neutra and the Search for Modern Architecture* (New York and Oxford: Oxford University Press, 1982), 212, fig. 251. **117.** From Joseph Burton, "Notes from Volume Zero: Louis I. Kahn and the Language of God," *Perspecta*, no. 20 (1983): 82, fig. 23. **118.** Photo: © Shahidul Alam/Drik Picture Library Ltd., Bangladesh. **119.** Kahn Collection. **120.** Collection, The Museum of Modern Art, New York. Gift of the architect. 404.64. **121.** From Ludwig H. Heydenreich and Wolfgang Lotz, *Architecture in Italy 1400 to 1600* (Harmondsworth, Eng., and Baltimore: Penguin Books, 1974), 135, fig. 43. **122.** Collection, The Museum of Modern Art, New York. Gift of the architect. MC 41. **123.** Kahn Collection. **124.** From Giuseppe Lugli, *La Tecnica Edilizia Romana*, vol. 2 (Rome: Presso Giovanni Bardi, 1957), pl. 181, no. 2. **125.** Collection, The Museum of Modern Art, New York. Gift of the architect. 400.64. **126.** Kahn Collection. **127.** From Emil Kaufman, "Three Revolutionary Architects: Boullée, Ledoux and Lequeu," *Transactions of the American Philosophical Society* 42 (1952): 510, fig. 136. **128.** Photo: © Shahidul Alam/Drik Picture Library Ltd., Bangladesh. **129–30.** Kahn Collection. **131–32.** Kahn Collection. Photos: Will Brown. **133.** Kahn Collection. Photo: George Pohl. **134.** From Warren J. Cox, "The Observatories of the Maharajah Sawai Jai Singh II," *Perspecta*, no. 6 (1960): 72, fig. 5. Photo: Isamu Noguchi. **135.** Kahn Collection. Photo: Fred Langford. **136.** Kahn Collection. **137–38.** Kahn Collection. Photos: George Pohl. **139.** Kahn Collection. **140.** From Julian A. Kulski, "Toward a Better Environment," *AIA Journal* 55 (March 1971): 32. **141–42.** Kahn Collection. **143.** Kahn Collection. Photo: George Pohl. **144–47.** Kahn Collection. **148.** From James Fergusson, *A History of Architecture*, 2 vols. (New York: Dodd, Mead, and Company, 1883), vol. 1, 214, fig. 107. **149.** Photo: George Pohl. **150.** Kahn Collection. Photo: George Pohl. **151.** Kahn Collection. **152.** Collection of Mrs. Louis I. Kahn. Photo: Vipool Shah. **153–54.** Kahn Collection. **155.** From *The Institution as a Generator of Urban Form. Harvard Graduate School of Design Alumni Association Fifth Urban Design Conference* (Cambridge, Mass.: Harvard University, 1961), n.p. Photo: George Pohl. **156.** Collection, The Museum of Modern Art, New York. Gift of the architect. 381.67. **157.** Kahn Collection. Photo: George Pohl. **158.** Model: Collection of the Salk Institute. Photo: George Pohl. **159.** Kahn Collection. **160.** Kahn Collection, Architectural Archives of the University of Pennsylvania. Gift of Mrs. Louis I. Kahn. **161.** Kahn Collection. Photo: Will Brown. **162.** Collection of Anne Griswold Tyng. **163–65.** Kahn Collection. **166.** Photo: Marshall D. Meyers. **167.** Kahn Collection. Photo: George C. Alikakos. **168.** Kahn Collection. Photo: George Pohl. **169–70.** Photos: B. V. Doshi. **171.** Kahn Collection. **172.** Photo: B. V. Doshi. **173.** Kahn Collection. Photo: Dalwadi. **174.** Model: Collection of Saint Andrew's Priory, Valyermo, Calif. Photo: George Pohl. **175–76.** Kahn Collection. **177.** Kahn Collection. Photo: George Pohl. **178.** Kahn Collection. **179.** Collection, The Museum of Modern Art, New York. Gift of the architect. 399.64. **180–81.** Kahn Collection. **182.** Kahn Collection. Photo: George Pohl. **183–84.** Courtesy of the Isamu Noguchi Foundation, Inc. Photos: Shigeo Anzai. **185–88.** Kahn Collection. **189.** From Le Corbusier and Pierre Jeanneret, *Oeuvre complète, 1910–1929*, 7th ed. (Zurich: Girsberger, 1960), 163. **190.** From Henry-Russell Hitchcock, *In the Nature of Materials* (New York: Duell, Sloan and Pearce, 1942), fig. 406. **191.** Kahn Collection. **192.** From Hugh Ferriss, *The Metropolis of Tomorrow* (New York: Ives Washburn, 1929), 75. **193–94.** Kahn Collection. **195.** From Vincent Scully, *American Architecture and Urbanism* (New York and Washington: Frederick A. Praeger, 1969), 200, fig. 426. **196.** Kahn Collection. **197.** Collection of Arnold Garfinkel. **198.** Kahn Collection. **199–200.** Collection of Arnold Garfinkel. **201–2.** Kahn Collection. **203.** Kahn Collection. Photo: George Pohl. **204.** From Romaldo Giurgola and Jaimini Mehta, *Louis I. Kahn* (Boulder, Colo.: Westview Press, 1975), 243. **205.** Paul

Illustration Credits

Clark, delineator. **206–7.** Kahn Collection. Photos: George Pohl. **208–9.** Kahn Collection. **210.** From Alex Boethius and J. B. Ward-Perkins, *Etruscan and Roman Architecture* (Harmondsworth, Eng., and Baltimore: Penguin Books, 1970), 142, fig. 78. **211.** Kahn Collection. **212.** Kahn Collection. Photo: George Pohl. **213–14.** Kahn Collection. **215.** Collection of the Philadelphia Museum of Art. Gift of the architect. 72.32.4. **216–18.** Kahn Collection. **219.** Photo: Grant Mudford. **220.** Kahn Collection. **221.** From William Jordy, "Span of Kahn," *Architectural Review* 155 (June 1974): 336. **222.** Courtesy of the Library, Phillips Exeter Academy, Exeter, N.H. Photo: Joseph W. Molitor. **223.** Kahn Collection. **224.** Kahn Collection. Harriet Pattison, delineator. **225.** Collection of the Kimbell Art Museum, Fort Worth, Tex. **226.** Photo: Grant Mudford. **227–29.** Kahn Collection. **230.** Kahn Collection. Photo: George Pohl. **231–33.** Kahn Collection. **234–35.** Kahn Collection. Photos: George Pohl. **236.** Kahn Collection. **237.** Kahn Collection. Photo: George Pohl. **238–41.** Kahn Collection. **242–45.** Collection of Sue Ann Kahn. **246–47.** Collection of Nathaniel Kahn. **248.** Collection of Sue Ann Kahn. **249.** From *Perspecta*, no. 2 (1953): 16. **250–301.** Photos: Grant Mudford. **302.** Kahn Collection. Photo: Craig Kuhner. **303–4.** Kahn Collection. **305–13.** Photos: Grant Mudford. **314.** Photo: Kathleen James. **315.** Photo: David B. Brownlee. **316–18.** Photos: Kathleen James. **319–20.** Photos: David B. Brownlee. **321–22.** Photos: Kathleen James. **323–25.** Photos: David B. Brownlee. **326.** Photo: Kathleen James. **327.** Photo: David B. Brownlee. **328–34.** Photos: Kathleen James. **335–37.** Photos: David B. Brownlee. **338.** Photo: © Shahidul Alam/Drik Picture Library Ltd., Bangladesh. **339.** Photo: Kazi Khaleed Ashraf. **340.** Courtesy of the Aga Khan Award for Architecture, Geneva. **341.** Photo: © Shahidul Alam/Drik Picture Library Ltd., Bangladesh. **342.** Photo: David B. Brownlee. **343–44.** Photos: David B. Brownlee. **345–47.** Photos: Kazi Khaleed Ashraf. **348–49.** Photos: © Shahidul Alam/Drik Picture Library Ltd., Bangladesh. **350.** Courtesy of the Aga Khan Award for Architecture, Geneva. Photo: Gunay Reha. **351.** Photo: Akhtar Badshah. **352–53.** Photos: David B. Brownlee. **354.** Courtesy of the Aga Khan Award for Architecture, Geneva. Photo: Gunay Reha. **355.** Photo: David G. De Long. **356–58.** Photos: David B. Brownlee. **359.** Photo: Kazi Khaleed Ashraf. **360.** Photo: Caroline Maniaque. **361–63.** Photos: Grant Mudford. **364.** Photo: David B. Brownlee. **365–407.** Photos: Grant Mudford. **408–12.** Kahn Collection. **413.** Kahn Collection, Architectural Archives of the University of Pennsylvania. Gift of Richard Saul Wurman. **414.** Kahn Collection. **415–16.** Kahn Collection, Architectural Archives of the University of Pennsylvania. Gift of Richard Saul Wurman. **417.** Kahn Collection. **418.** Photo: Lionel Freedman. **419–20.** Kahn Collection. **421.** Photo: John Ebstel. **422–24.** Kahn Collection. **425.** From *Perspecta*, no. 4 (1957): 58. **426–28.** Kahn Collection. **429–30.** Kahn Collection. David N. Rothstein, delineator. **431.** Kahn Collection. Photo: Malcolm Smith. **432–34.** Kahn Collection. **435.** Photo: Grant Mudford. **436.** Kahn Collection. **437.** From *The Institution as a Generator of Urban Form. Harvard Graduate School of Design Alumni Association Fifth Urban Design Conference* (Cambridge, Mass.: Harvard University, 1961), n.p. **438.** Kahn Collection. Harriet Pattison, delineator. **439.** Kahn Collection. **440.** Kahn Collection. Photo: George Pohl. **441.** Kahn Collection. Thomas R. Vreeland, delineator. **442.** From Jan C. Rowan, "Wanting to Be: The Philadelphia School," *Progressive Architecture* 42 (April 1961): 141. **443–45.** Kahn Collection. **446.** Photo: John Ebstel. **447.** Kahn Collection. **448.** Kahn Collection. Photo: William L. Porter. **449.** Kahn Collection. **450.** Kahn Collection. Photo: William L. Porter. **451–52.** Kahn Collection. **453.** Kahn Collection. Photo: Craig Kuhner. **454–55.** Kahn Collection. Photos: George Pohl. **456–61.** Kahn Collection. **462.** Photo: Grant Mudford. **463.** Kahn Collection. **464.** From Lynn Scholz, "Architecture Alive on Campus," *Bryn Mawr College Alumnae Bulletin* 47 (Fall 1965): fig. 2. **465.** Collection of Bryn Mawr College Archives, Bryn Mawr, Pa. A-60-24. Anne Griswold Tyng, delineator. **466.** Collection of Donnelley Erdman. Photo: Jeffrey L. Riggenbach. **467.** Collection of Bryn Mawr College Archives, Bryn Mawr, Pa. A-61-31. Anne Griswold Tyng, delineator. **468.** Collection of Donnelley Erdman. Photo: Jeffrey L. Riggenbach. **469.** Collection of Donnelley Erdman. **470.** Collection, The Museum of Modern Art, New York. Gift of the architect. 428.67. **471.** Kahn Collection. **472.** Model: Kahn Collection, on permanent loan from the University of the Arts, Philadelphia. Photo: George Pohl. **473.** Kahn Collection. Photo: George Pohl. **474.** Kahn Collection, Architectural Archives of the University of Pennsylvania. Gift of Richard Saul Wurman. 615.1. **475–79.** Kahn Collection. **480.** Photo: B. V. Doshi. **481.** Kahn Collection. **482.** Kahn Collection. Photo: George Pohl. **483–84.** Collection of Sue Ann Kahn. **485.** Kahn Collection. Photo: George Pohl. **486.** Kahn Collection. **487.** Photo: © Shahidul Alam/Drik Picture Library Ltd., Bangladesh. **488–89.** Kahn Collection. **490.** Collection, The Museum of Modern Art, New York. Gift of the architect. 417.67. **491.** Kahn Collection. **492.** Kahn Collection. Photo: George C. Alikakos. **493.** Kahn Collection. Photo: Will Brown. **494–96.** Kahn Collection. **497.** Kahn Collection. Photo: George Pohl. **498.** Kahn Collection. Photo: George Pohl. **499.** Photo: © Shahidul Alam/Drik Picture Library Ltd., Bangladesh. **500–504.** Kahn Collection. **505.** Collection of the Library, Phillips Exeter Academy, Exeter, N.H. Photo: Willard Traub. Courtesy LEA Architects, Boston. **506–7.** Kahn Collection. **508–9.** Collection of the Library, Phillips Exeter Academy, Exeter, N.H. **510–11.** Kahn Collection. **512.** Photo: Michael Bodycomb. **513.** Collection of the Kimbell Art Museum, Fort Worth, Tex. **514.** Kahn Collection. **515.** Collection of the Kimbell Art Museum, Fort Worth, Tex. **516.** Kahn Collection. **517.** From Patricia Cummings Loud, *In Pursuit of Quality: The Kimbell Art Museum, An Illustrated History of the Art and Architecture* (Fort Worth: Kimbell Art Museum, 1987), 58, fig. 53. **518.** Kahn Collection. Photo: George Pohl. **519.** Collection of Sue Ann Kahn. **520.** Kahn Collection. **521.** Kahn Collection. Photo: George Pohl. **522.** Collection of the Centre Canadien d'Architecture/Canadian Centre for Architecture, Montreal. **523–24.** Kahn Collection. **525.** Collection of the Centre Canadien d'Architecture/Canadian Centre for Architecture, Montreal. **526.** Kahn Collection. **527.** Collection of the Centre Canadien d'Architecture/Canadian Centre for Architecture, Montreal. **528.** Photo: Grant Mudford. **529–30.** Kahn Collection. **531.** Kahn Collection. Photo: George Pohl. **532.** Kahn Collection. **533.** Collection of the Philadelphia Museum of Art. Gift of the architect. 72.32.1. **534–36.** Kahn Collection. **537.** Kahn Collection. Photo: George Pohl.

Published on the occasion of the exhibition "Louis I. Kahn: In the Realm of Architecture," organized by The Museum of Contemporary Art, Los Angeles. The exhibition and this book have been made possible by Ford Motor Company. Significant additional support has been provided by Leslie H. Wexner and The Pew Charitable Trusts. The Graham Foundation for Advanced Studies in the Fine Arts, Maguire Thomas Partners, and the National Endowment for the Arts, a federal agency, have also provided funding for the exhibition.

Exhibition Itinerary
Philadelphia Museum of Art
October 20, 1991–January 5, 1992

Centre Georges Pompidou, Centre de Création Industrielle, Paris
March 5–May 4, 1992

The Museum of Modern Art, New York
June 14–August 18, 1992

The Museum of Modern Art, Gunma, Japan
September 26–November 3, 1992

The Museum of Contemporary Art, Los Angeles
March 7–May 30, 1993

Kimbell Art Museum, Fort Worth, Texas
July 3–October 10, 1993

Wexner Center for the Arts, The Ohio State University, Columbus, Ohio
November 17, 1993–February 1, 1994

First published in the United States of America in 1991 by
RIZZOLI INTERNATIONAL PUBLICATIONS, INC.
300 Park Avenue South, New York, N.Y. 10010

Library of Congress Cataloging-in-Publication Data
Brownlee, David Bruce.
Louis I. Kahn, In the realm of architecture/by David B. Brownlee and David G. De Long; preface by Vincent Scully.
p. cm.
Includes bibliographical references and index
ISBN 0-8478-1323-1 (HC)
ISBN 0-8478-1330-4 (PBK)
1. Kahn, Louis I., 1901–1974—Criticism and interpretation.
2. Architecture, Modern–20th century—United States. I. De Long, David Gilson, 1939–   . II. Title.
NA737.K32876   1991   91-9760
720′ . 92—dc20   CIP

MOCA Editor: Catherine Gudis
Rizzoli Editor: Kate Norment
Designer: Massimo Vignelli with Abigail Sturges

Printed and bound in Hong Kong.

Reprinted in 1997

Louis I. Kahn:
In the Realm of Architecture

David B. Brownlee / David G. De Long
Introduction by Vincent Scully
New Photography by Grant Mudford

Kahn